ASP.NET at Work:
Building 10 Enterprise Projects

Eric Smith

Wiley Computer Publishing

John Wiley & Sons, Inc.

Publisher: Robert Ipsen
Editor: Theresa Hudson
Managing Editor: Angela Smith
New Media Editor: Brian Snapp
Text Design & Composition: John Wiley Composition Services

Designations used by companies to distinguish their products are often claimed as trademarks. In all instances where John Wiley & Sons, Inc., is aware of a claim, the product names appear in initial capital or ALL CAPITAL LETTERS. Readers, however, should contact the appropriate companies for more complete information regarding trademarks and registration.

This book is printed on acid-free paper. ♾

Published by John Wiley & Sons, Inc., New York

Published simultaneously in Canada.

This publication is designed to provide accurate and authoritative information in regard to the subject matter covered. It is sold with the understanding that the publisher is not engaged in professional services. If professional advice or other expert assistance is required, the services of a competent professional person should be sought.

Library of Congress Cataloging-in-Publication Data:

ISBN: 0471-08512-X

Printed in the United States of America.

10 9 8 7 6 5 4 3 2 1

To my daughter, Lauren

Contents

Acknowledgments

First of all, I give God the glory for giving me the strength to get this book done. In Psalm 29:11, David writes, "The Lord gives strength to his people; the Lord blesses his people with peace." (NIV) Through the stress and world events, God gives strength to anyone who calls on his name. The events of September 11th, 2001 help put the normal daily stresses in perspective for many people, including me. Trusting in God makes all the difference.

My family, including my daughter born around Chapter 4, helped keep me on track. My wife kept wondering when I was going to get done, and my daughter kept me entertained with dirty diapers and her beautiful smiles. My dog, Max, played with me when I got done with chapters.

Kathryn Malm showed extraordinary patience with me through a cross-country move from Virginia to Indiana, constant delays in beta products from Microsoft, a new baby, and at least a cold or two. Thanks for helping me get this book to press, Kathryn.

Shawn Dillon and Jason Beres took care of some of the projects in this book that a newborn baby prevented me from doing. Thanks for your help, guys!

Thanks to my .NET students down in Sydney, Australia who helped me come up with the projects for this book. As business developers already using .NET, they helped make sure that the projects would be useful for fellow developers like you.

Studio B Productions did a great job making sure that I was getting the job done and making sure that I got paid.

And to you, my readers, I appreciate your input and feedback about my books. While no book is ever perfect, knowing that you all are out there watching my every word makes me work twice as hard to make sure all the words are correct. Your questions turn into my chapters and books, so keep them up!

About the Author

Eric A. Smith is an author, consultant, and trainer specializing in Active Server Pages, Visual Basic, and SQL Server. He is a Microsoft Certified Trainer, Microsoft Certified Solution Developer, and Microsoft Certified Systems Engineer. He has written, edited, or contributed to ten books covering Microsoft technologies and products.

Eric is president of Northstar Computer Systems, a company providing web development, hosting, and consulting to companies both locally in the Indianapolis area and across the country. He also maintains sites for several of the books he's written, including the ones for this book: 10projectswithasp.net and teamworknetwork.com.

Eric is also an Emergency Medical Technician (EMT-B) and volunteers with the Westfield Fire Department. If you have comments, questions, or suggestions about this book, you can reach him via e-mail at info@10projectswithasp.net.

Getting Started

Microsoft's .NET initiative has created quite a buzz among developers. Visual Basic developers are finally getting many of the features they have been asking Microsoft to create, such as true object-oriented programming and greater compatibility with other languages like C++. For Active Server Page developers, the new ASP.NET promises to deliver better stability and performance and gives users the ability to write code using the same languages as everyone else. No longer will Web development be subjected to the horrors of VBScript. For developers who liked the coding structure of languages like Java, C# offers a similar structure with similar performance.

However, there are still questions. The .NET Framework is so large that people are still exploring its features and how to apply them. There is a lot of existing code out there that Microsoft has admitted won't easily convert to the new .NET languages. In addition, corporations are nervous about adding new software the day it comes out; for proof, look at how slowly Windows 2000 has been adopted in the corporate community. What all this means is that developers who learn .NET are: 1) getting a jump on everyone else and 2) going to be working with multiple technologies at the same time. ASP.NET applications will be built side-by-side with traditional ASP applications. VB developers may be using VB.NET components, and vice versa.

The point is that by learning how these new technologies work today, you'll be ready to build applications when your company decides it's time to start using .NET in the future.

What This Book Is About

We have all read books about new technology that go on for pages and pages about something or other, slipping you little code fragments as they go. You're always waiting for that big example, the payoff for having waded through explanations and theory. Suddenly, you come to the end of the book, having seen only a few trivial examples of the technology's use; no more information than that provided in documentation in the Microsoft Developer Network.

This book is designed to help solve this problem. The assumption is that you've worked with Visual Studio.NET and ASP.NET and understand the basics. The hard part is trying to figure out how to connect all these new technologies and build useful applications from them. That's what this book focuses on. You'll be building 10 projects in this book, some of which are grouped together into larger applications. These applications are complete programs that you can adapt and modify for use in your own company. While the projects aren't using every single part of the .NET Framework or all the features of ASP.NET, they do try to cover the features that you'll be using most often. Once you've got more understanding on how to put all the pieces together, you'll be able to add new features as you discover them.

Organization

The projects in the book are all organized the same way. Each starts with a statement of the problem that will be solved by the project, as well as a description of our solution. It will detail the supplies you need to build the project and the technologies that will be used. Usually, an informative section follows the introduction that teaches what you need to know about the technology used in the project, explaining key concepts and some of the important details. The rest of the section is all about the project. You'll learn more about the technology by doing. At the end of each project is a list of suggestions for enhancing the project. The enhancements could be simple upgrades or completely new features. Whatever the case, they will give you something else to build on your own.

Take a look at the projects you'll be building in this book:

Project 1: Building an Address Book. This application takes you through the basics of building an ASP.NET application connected to Microsoft SQL Server. The feature set of the application is simple so that you can see a method of building ASP.NET applications that is familiar to current ASP developers.

Project 2: Contact Manager Application. This project builds on Project 1 and shows you how to use the new object-oriented approach in ASP.NET to build reusable business objects to handle the business logic and validation necessary for most applications. You'll add a feature to the address book so you can track your contacts with the people you have stored in your database.

Project 3: Building the Calendar Application. ASP.NET includes many new controls, including a Calendar control. Showing a calendar is only half the battle, however. In this project, you'll learn to use many of the date and time functions included in .NET to handle all sorts of calendar events, both one-time and recurring. You'll also build more business objects in this project for use with your application.

Project 4: Building the Web Log Analyzer. In this project, you will create several new types of applications for analyzing and reporting Web traffic to a number of Web sites. You'll build a Windows Service (also known as an NT Service) to periodically gather logs and import them into SQL Server. You'll also build an ASP.NET application to view the analysis performed on the Web log data.

Project 5: Building the ASP.NET Error Manager. This project will teach you to use the built-in Event Log objects so that you can collect errors from your ASP.NET applications in a central location, provide your users and administrators with information on what happened and when, and help provide a solution.

Project 6: Building the Online Store. In this project, you'll build the "classic" online store, from start to finish. You'll be building both the front-end of the store, where your customers can browse your merchandise, add items to a shopping cart, and check out, as well as the back-end of the store, where the store administrator can maintain the information in the database.

Projects 7-10: Teamwork Network. In the last four projects in the book, you'll be building an online collaboration system that includes project tracking, file sharing, and discussion forums. This system also includes an internal messaging system, as well as all the administration utilities necessary for users to get accounts and to maintain a basic security level over the data in the system. This application uses many of the features that you'll learn in earlier projects and puts them all together into a robust application that some of you may end up using in your own companies.

All of these projects will be running live at the book's Web site: www. 10projectswithasp.net. Additionally, the Teamwork Network site has its own Web site: www.teamworknetwork.com. Feel free to use these online resources to see how the applications are designed to run in the real world.

Setting Up Your Workbench

You will need some background knowledge and a small pile of software tools to complete the projects in this book. This section will detail exactly what those are.

Prerequisites

This book assumes that you can already create programs with Active Server Pages and are familiar with ASP.NET. We are not going to teach you how to use the environment or do basic things with the language. We will be building components in Visual Studio.NET and getting into the more-complex system programming when we build a Windows Service application in Project 4.

All of the projects use SQL Server and ADO.NET. If you don't know SQL Server but are familiar with other databases, like Oracle or Access, the projects will instruct you on how to use other databases instead of SQL Server.

On Your Computer

Visual Studio.NET and ASP.NET are heavy-duty applications, and you'll need some serious hardware to build the projects. Even after Microsoft fine-tunes Visual Studio.NET for performance, it will still require a reasonably good computer to run well. As a developer, you'll have lots of windows and applications open, so be sure your computer is up to the challenge.

Hardware

The projects in this book were built using a Pentium III, 300-MHz Dell laptop with an 8.4-GB hard drive and 320 MB of RAM, but a faster computer would have been better. I also used a Pentium III, 866-MHz desktop with 768 MB of RAM when I wasn't on the road. I personally recommend getting as much hardware as you can possibly afford.

Operating System

You will need Microsoft Windows 2000 to build these projects. You can also use Windows XP Professional. We used Windows 2000 for the entire process, and it worked beautifully.

Software Tools

There are quite a few software tools required if you want to complete all the projects. Fortunately, you will already have most of them, and the others are free.

Microsoft Visual Studio.NET Professional Edition. This version or later of the development environment is required. We used the Enterprise Edition, and enjoyed having all those extra features around.

Microsoft SQL Server. This database is used for all the projects. You could use another database engine as well, such as Microsoft Access or Oracle. You'll just have to modify the code a little to do so (connection strings and the ADO.NET DB objects created). It will be easier to just use SQL Server if you have it available so you don't have to change the code at all. You can use either SQL Server 7.0 or 2000 without any code changes.

Internet Information Server. All the projects include ASP.NET applications, so IIS is a must. Be sure that you keep it updated with the security patches available through the Windows Update site, as IIS is notoriously full of security holes.

What's on the CD-ROM?

The companion CD-ROM contains all the source code for every project in the book. It also includes any supporting files that might be needed, such as sample databases, diagrams, or graphics files. Anything you need for a project should be there, which makes it easier to import the data into SQL Server.

The CD-ROM is organized by project. There is a directory at the root called Projects. Underneath that is a folder for each project in the book, containing all the files for each project. For example, all the source material for Project 2 is located at: \Projects\Project2.

Time to Embark

With your computers ready and your fingers ready to type, it's time to get started. The projects generally increase in complexity from the start of the book to the end, and there is a lot of code to read and understand. Take it a little bit at a time and don't rush through the code, or you'll miss the good stuff. I enjoyed building these projects, and I hope you will also.

Building an Address Book

How many separate places do you have available to you to store other peoples' information? A while back, I determined that I had far too many: my cellular phone, my speed dialer on my desk phone, my copy of Lotus Organizer; my copy of Eudora Pro had e-mail addresses, as did my PDA. The problem was that none of them had the same information and when I needed to change a name, address, or phone number, I had to make changes to at least five different locations. My solution was to build a Web-based address book that I could access anywhere and use it as the sole source of information. I've been using my online PDA in this capacity for almost a year now, and it has greatly simplified my life.

THE PROBLEM

We have too many places to keep information about other people with no easy way to synchronize them.

THE SOLUTION

Build a Web-based address book that can be accessed via the Web from virtually anywhere.

Project Background

In this project, you will design and build an address book application using ASP.NET, which will provide the required user interface and business rules. SQL Server 2000 will be used as the back-end database. SQL Server is far more reliable than Microsoft Access and, in my opinion, is easier to use. This application will also serve as a framework for other applications in this book. Because the application does not have a complex structure, it can be used as a guide for building your own applications.

The address book application will also be built using a text editor instead of the Visual Studio .NET environment so that you can see the key objects and code required to make the page work. In other projects, you'll be using Visual Studio .NET to build the applications.

This project consists of a single data entity and four logical functions to manipulate the data. Here are the steps to build this application:

1. Create the database table that will be used to hold the data.

2. Create a page to retrieve all the entries in the table.

3. Create a page to add a new record.

4. Create a page to modify an existing record.

5. Create a page to delete a record.

 ## You Will Need

✔ **Windows 2000**

✔ **Internet Information Server 5.0 with .NET Framework installed**

✔ **A text editor, such as Notepad, TextPad, or HomeSite, preferably one with line-numbering capabilities**

✔ **SQL Server 7.0 or 2000**

Creating the Database Table

We're going to start small with this application. All of the information for each person will be stored in a single record in a single table. You might choose to do a more complicated data structure, such as one that includes separate tables for multiple addresses per person, multiple phone numbers, and so on. Since the primary purpose of this project is to demonstrate some of the new ASP.NET technology and how to use it with a simple application, it makes more sense to keep the database as simple as possible for now. We'll add to this application later, but for now, we want to start out small and focus more on the user interface and the flow of one page to another.

The first thing you need to do is figure out what information you want to store regarding each person in the database. Here's a list of possible entries:

- Name, company name, title, division/department
- Multiple addresses (home, work)
- Multiple phone numbers (home, work, mobile, fax)
- Multiple e-mail addresses (home, work)
- Web page addresses
- Miscellaneous notes area

For some of these entries, you might want to break the single table into multiple tables. For example, instead of having duplicate address fields in a single record, you might want to create an address table that is linked to the primary table with a primary key/foreign key relationship. For this application, we're going to keep things simple and use a single table called tblPeople. Table 1.1 lists the fields we're going to use for the database, as well as their data types.

NOTE

For all text fields (other than the Notes field), we are using variable-length text fields. In SQL Server, the data type is the varchar type. Using this data type prevents the database from adding trailing spaces to your data. SQL Server requires a few extra bytes of storage for the overhead required for this data type, but the benefits outweigh this minor cost.

Table 1.1 Fields for tblPeople

NAME	DATA TYPE	LENGTH
pkPersonID	int	N/A
LastName	varchar	40
FirstName	varchar	40
Title	varchar	80
CompanyName	varchar	80
Address	varchar	240
HomePhone	varchar	40
WorkPhone	varchar	40
Fax	varchar	40
Email	varchar	120
WebPage	varchar	120
Notes	text	N/A

Most of the field names are self-explanatory, but there are a few fields that need a bit more explanation:

pkPersonID. This field should be set up as an IDENTITY column. An IDENTITY column will automatically supply a new, non-repeating number for this record. Once the value is set for a record, it will stay constant as long as the record exists. This key piece of information allows you to link this record to others in the system as it is expanded. If you're using Access, you'll need to use the AutoNumber feature. In Oracle, this feature is known as a sequence.

Title. The person's position or title at their place of employment. Some databases provide the ability to store a salutation, which could be Dr., Mr., Mrs., and so on.

Address. Instead of having individual fields for each part of the address (street, city, state, ZIP, and so on), I prefer to use a larger text field with no character limit. This allows for different address formats, such as those used outside of the United States. This way, you can type the address exactly as it needs to be printed regardless of what format it may need.

Notes. The *text* data type in SQL Server allows for up to 2 gigabytes of text. The text is stored as part of the database and is treated just like any other text type when read in ASP.NET. I prefer to use this data type for unlimited-character text fields. For performance reasons, you might want to use a large *varchar* field (up to 8,000 characters) instead of a text field. Depending on the amount of data you're normally putting into the field, there are some performance considerations to take into account regarding SQL Server and text fields. For more details, refer to the SQL Server documentation on the text data type.

 If you've built databases before, you may be wondering why we didn't mention which fields are required and which aren't. In this particular table, I've chosen not to require any of the fields. This allows for the most flexible data entry method. For example, you might have a record for a company, but not a person at that company. Of course, if you have other requirements, feel free to modify the design as necessary. We'll be doing more validation in other projects in this book.

Once you have created the table, you might want to put some initial data into it. This will make building and testing the address book list page a bit easier. If you have contacts in another database table, you can use SQL Server's Data Transformation Services to copy your data from that other source. If you don't have another table to use as a data source for your initial test data, you can open the table using SQL Server Enterprise Manager and enter data into the table manually. When you are viewing the list of tables in the database, right-click the table you want to open, and select Open Table—>View All Rows from the menu that appears.

Building the Contact Viewer

The first page that you need to build is the page that will show all the contacts in the database. From this page, you can then select a contact to view, modify, or delete. You can also add a new contact.

To build this page, you can use either Visual Basic .NET or C# for the code. Both languages are supported in ASP.NET and, as you'll see, are quite similar. Visual Basic .NET shares some syntax similarities with previous versions of Visual Basic, but there are some major functionality differences. C# is a brand new language and shares features with both Java and C++. Because Visual Basic .NET is easier to read for most developers, we'll be building the applications throughout this book using Visual Basic .NET exclusively.

ASP.NET includes a number of controls that are designed to make life easier for you as an ASP.NET developer. With these controls, you can use data binding, which is an automatic way to put data on the page. For example, this page could be built using the DataGrid server control, which provides additional useful features, such as paging between blocks of records, automatic text styling, and more.

There are some performance issues to consider with data binding, however. Depending on how many server controls you use on the page, you may see up to 30 percent slower code than you would building the HTML code and displaying it, as you'll do in this application. You'll be using server controls in later projects, but it's important to know how to use both bound and unbound controls so that you have the most flexibility when building your own applications.

We're going to build this page by generating the HTML code ourselves and placing the result in an ASP.NET control called a Label control. The Label control shows text on a page, but it gives us a programmable name to which we can assign content. The code to build the list page follows this rough outline:

1. Make a connection to the database for the application using a SqlConnection object.
2. Select the contacts from the database using a SqlCommand object.
3. Retrieve the data from the database using a SqlDataReader object.
4. Loop through the data, add some HTML tags to it, and put the HTML output in the Label control you create.

This is going to be done in a few steps so that you don't get too bogged down in the fancy details. This page will be built in three phases:

- A simple viewer that lists data
- A styled viewer that lists data but adds some styles and colors to the output
- A final version that incorporates links to the other pages that you'll be building in this project

Let's begin!

Phase 1: Simple Viewer
in Visual Basic .NET

The first version of this project's output, shown in Figure 1.1, is somewhat unattractive, since we don't have any extra HTML or style sheet code in the output we're generating. However, the point of this version is to not let the important code get lost in the fancy details. Phase 2 creates a version with more features.

The code for this version of the viewer is shown in Listing 1.1. The page is broken into three parts: the initial declarations and directives, the HTML wrapper, and the ASP.NET code used to fill the page.

```
<% @ Page    Language="VB" Debug="True" %>
<% @ Import Namespace="System" %>
<% @ Import Namespace="System.Data" %>
<% @ Import Namespace="System.Data.SqlClient" %>


<html>
   <head>
      <title>Contact Manager: View All Contacts</title>
   </head>
   <body bgcolor="#FFFFFF">
      <h1>View All Contacts</h1>
      <table cellpadding="4" cellspacing="0" width="100%">
      <tr>
         <th>Name</th>
         <th>Title</th>
         <th>Company Name</th>
         <th>Work Phone</th>
      </tr>

         <asp:label id="lblOutput" runat="server"></asp:Label>

   </table>
   </body>
</html>



<script runat="SERVER">

Sub Page_Load(Src As Object, e As EventArgs)
   Dim sqlConn As New SqlConnection
   Dim sqlCmd  As New SqlCommand
   Dim sdrData As SqlDataReader
   Dim sb As New StringBuilder
```

Listing 1.1   Simple viewer in Visual Basic .NET

```
    sqlConn.ConnectionString = _
        "server=localhost;database=ASPNetProject01;uid=sa;pwd=;"
    sqlConn.Open()
    sqlCmd.CommandText = "SELECT * FROM tblPeople " _
        & "ORDER BY LastName, FirstName"
    sqlCmd.Connection = sqlConn

    sdrData = sqlCmd.ExecuteReader()
    While sdrData.Read()
        sb.Append("<tr>" + vbCrLf)
        sb.AppendFormat("   <td>{0}, {1}</td>" + vbCrLf, _
            sdrData("LastName"), _
            sdrData("FirstName"))
        sb.AppendFormat("   <td>{0}</td>" + vbCrLf, sdrData("Title"))
        sb.AppendFormat("   <td>{0}</td>" + vbCrLf, _
            sdrData("CompanyName"))
        sb.AppendFormat("   <td>{0}</td>" + vbCrLf, sdrData("WorkPhone"))
        sb.Append("</tr>" + vbCrLf)
    End While
    sdrData.Close()
    sqlConn.Close()
    lblOutput.Text = sb.ToString()
End Sub

</script>
```

Listing 1.1 Simple viewer in Visual Basic .NET (continued)

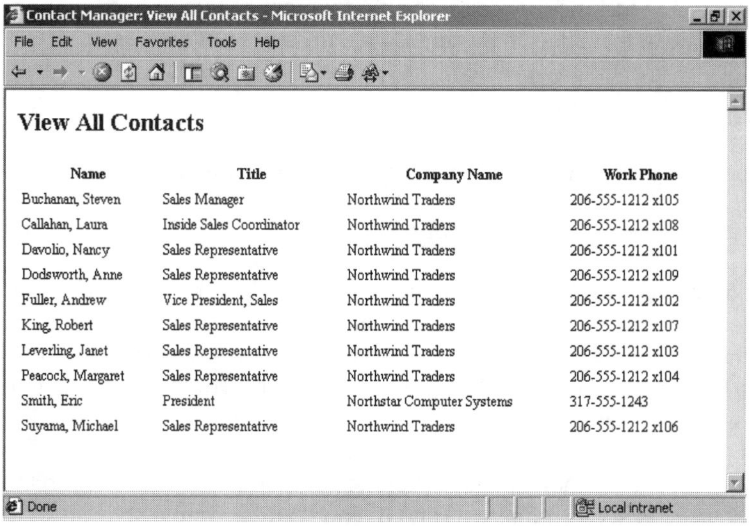

Figure 1.1 The simple contact viewer

Page Declarations and Directives

At the top of the ASP.NET page are four lines:

```
<% @ Page    Language="VB" Debug="True" %>
<% @ Import Namespace="System" %>
<% @ Import Namespace="System.Data" %>
<% @ Import Namespace="System.Data.SqlClient" %>
```

Each of these lines gives us capabilities in our code. The first line is the Page directive, which you can use to control a number of system features for this particular ASP.NET page. The Language parameter specifies that Visual Basic .NET is used as the language for the code on the page. The Debug parameter specifies that detailed debugging information is to be provided when any errors occur. However, you can always change this to *false* before you deploy the page.

The three lines following the Page directive specify various system libraries that need to be referenced. Each of these libraries is analogous to referencing DLLs in other applications, such as Visual Basic. In the .NET world, these are known as *assemblies*, and each one contains different objects that we need for our application. By referencing each of these assemblies here, we gain access to all the objects, but more importantly, we don't have to specify each object's full name. For instance, the SqlConnection object we use later has the following full name:

```
System.Data.SqlClient.SqlConnection
```

Typing all that every single time would soon get old. By importing the System.Data.SqlClient assembly, ASP.NET looks in all the imported assemblies for an object called SqlConnection. In this case, it finds one in the System.Data.SqlClient assembly. If, however, there are two objects named SqlConnection, it will use the one that is more "specific." For instance, if the same object were part of both System.Data and System.Data.SqlClient, the object in System.Data.SqlClient would be used.

The HTML Wrapper

The HTML wrapper is fairly straightforward, except for the addition of this line:

```
<asp:label id="lblOutput" runat="server"></asp:Label>
```

This control is known as an ASP.NET server control because its content can be controlled using server-side code, as you'll do later in the page. The ID property gives us a name with which we can write code against, but the important tag here is the RUNAT property, which should be set to SERVER. If you leave this off, you won't be able to write any server-side code using this control and you'll get an error message stating that the control doesn't exist.

You can put any valid HTML code in this part of the page, and it will show up in the resulting page that the user sees. In Phases 2 and 3, you'll add a simple style sheet to add some color to your output, and that content will go in this section of the page.

The ASP.NET Code

This is the heart of the page. This particular block of code only includes the Page_Load event, which occurs when the user requests this particular page from the server. You can specify more than one language in a page by adding the Language parameter to the SCRIPT tag; however, we'll use the default language of VB in this particular page. You also have to specify that this script is to run at the server. Otherwise, the ASP.NET server will ignore the script as client-side code.

We start with the event handler's definition, which should always be defined as shown in the listing. We then declare the key variables for this code:

SqlConnection. Maintains a connection to a particular SQL Server database on the network. One SqlConnection object is required for each combination of server, database, and user ID. If you are using a database other than SQL Server, you can use the OleDbConnection object instead. The SQLConnection object is roughly equivalent to the ADO Connection object, with the exception that this particular object is specifically built to connect to SQL Server.

SqlCommand. Used to run a query against the database and have the data returned in a variety of ways to a number of different objects. This is roughly equivalent to the ADO Command object, with the exception that this particular object is specifically built to connect to SQL Server. An OleDbCommand exists for use with other databases.

SqlDataReader. Provides access to the data returned from the SqlCommand query. The DataReader class is the fastest and most efficient way to get data from a database in a read-only fashion. This object works in a similar manner to a forward-only ADO Recordset object, but only for SQL Server. There is a more generic OleDbDataReader class available for other databases.

StringBuilder. In the .NET Framework, strings are handled in a different manner than they were in Visual Basic, and the default method of simply concatenating strings together (using a plus sign or an ampersand) is significantly slower. The StringBuilder object (full name is System.Text.StringBuilder) provides a more efficient way to concatenate strings. Because of the way strings work in .NET, Microsoft recommends the use of the StringBuilder for more efficient string building and manipulation. See the StringBuilder documentation for more details on this new class.

The next order of business is to get our result set. Open up a connection to the database, and use the SqlCommand object to run the query. The results are made available through the SqlDataReader by calling the ExecuteReader method on the SqlCommand object. At this point, we're ready to build the HTML output required for this page.

TIP

You can also use a stored procedure here instead of a text SQL query. Put the stored procedure name in the CommandText property, and change the CommandType to CommandType.StoredProcedure.

As long as the SqlDataReader's Read method returns a True value, we keep working through the result set. When the Read method returns a False value, it indicates that we are at the end of the recordset. Each row has five fields of importance: Last-Name, FirstName, Title, CompanyName, and WorkPhone. Each one of these fields will be added to a row in the table, but LastName and FirstName will be concatenated together. The HTML format of the row is as shown:

```
<tr>
   <td>Callahan, Laura</td>
   <td>Inside Sales Coordinator</td>
   <td>Northwind Traders</td>
   <td>206-555-1212 x108</td>
</tr>
```

Use the AppendFormat method of the StringBuilder to build each part of this output. The AppendFormat method takes care of a lot of the concatenation we would have had to do manually by providing a template for how the data is to be formatted. For instance, in the following lines, we concatenate a comma between the first and last names, but we don't have to concatenate them ourselves.

```
sb.AppendFormat("    <td>{0}, {1}</td>" + vbCrLf, _
   sdrData("LastName"), _
   sdrData("FirstName"))
```

The {0} and {1} are used to represent positional parameters that follow the format string. In this case, the LastName field is plugged into where the {0} is, and the First-Name field goes where the {1} is. This is a nice improvement over the endless concatenations that were common in ASP.

As you can see from the code, we can easily retrieve information from the Sql-DataReader object by using the field name. Specify the field you want, and it will return the data. If you are feeding the data into another function, such as the Append-Format, you don't have to call any functions to get the data out. However, if you're printing the data, you will want to use the ToString() method on any non-text data that you retrieve. Otherwise, you may get data conversion errors.

Notice that the code includes spaces in front of each <TD> tag and includes a vbCrLf constant at the end of each line. This gives us a nicer format in the resultant HTML code. Otherwise, it could be impossible to find any HTML errors that you might have in the output. This is a technique that I always use in ASP and find that it's helpful in ASP.NET as well.

Once the loop is complete, close the SqlDataReader and SqlConnection objects, and put the HTML output that we built into the Label control in the HTML wrapper. Call the ToString() method on the StringBuilder object to convert the StringBuilder's content into a usable string value for the Label control. If you're not already familiar with this method, you soon will be as you code more ASP.NET.

At this point, the page is complete and we're done. Like I said at the beginning, the output is not pretty, but there's nothing in the way of the Visual Basic .NET code on this page.

Phase 2: Styled Viewer in Visual Basic .NET

In this phase, we'll take the version of the viewer we built in the first phase and add color to it using style sheets. As you'll quickly see, we're not changing any of the important data-access code, but learning to format data is an important skill to learn. The new version of the viewer is shown in Figure 1.2.

In the new version, all of the text has been styled using a style sheet included in the page. In addition, the table heading has a dark red background, and every other row is shown in gray, making it easier to read. We made a few code modifications to make the last feature work, but the rest of the modifications were restricted to the HTML code. In addition, we made use of a server-side include directive to bring the style sheet into the page. This way, you can use the same style sheet (shown in Listing 1.2) for the Visual Basic .NET examples in this directory, as well as in the third phase of our Contact Viewer page, which will be covered later in this project.

```
<% @ Page   Language="VB" Debug="True" %>
<% @ Import Namespace="System" %>
<% @ Import Namespace="System.Data" %>
<% @ Import Namespace="System.Data.SqlClient" %>

<html>
   <head>
      <title>Contact Manager: View All Contacts</title>
<!--#include file="styles.css" -->
   </head>
   <body bgcolor="#FFFFFF">
      <p class="pageheading">View All Contacts</p>
      <table cellpadding="4" cellspacing="0" width="100%">
      <tr class="tableheading">
         <td>Name</td>
         <td>Title</td>
         <td>Company Name</td>
         <td>Work Phone</td>
      </tr>

      <asp:label id="lblOutput" runat="server"></asp:Label>

   </table>
   </body>
</html>


<script runat="SERVER">

Sub Page_Load(Src As Object, e As EventArgs)
   Dim sqlConn As New SqlConnection
   Dim sqlCmd  As New SqlCommand
```

Listing 1.2   Contact Viewer with styles in Visual Basic .NET

```
    Dim sdrData As SqlDataReader
    Dim sb As New StringBuilder
    Dim strColor As String

    sqlConn.ConnectionString = _
        "server=localhost;database=ASPNetProject01;uid=sa;pwd=;"
    sqlConn.Open()
    sqlCmd.CommandText = "SELECT * FROM tblPeople " _
        & "ORDER BY LastName, FirstName"
    sqlCmd.CommandType = CommandType.Text
    sqlCmd.Connection = sqlConn

    sdrData = sqlCmd.ExecuteReader()
    strColor = "tabletext"
    While sdrData.Read()
       sb.AppendFormat("<tr class=""{0}"">" + vbCrLf, strColor)
       sb.AppendFormat("   <td>{0}, {1}</td>" + vbCrLf, _
          sdrData("LastName"), _
          sdrData("FirstName"))
       sb.AppendFormat("   <td>{0}</td>" + vbCrLf, sdrData("Title"))
       sb.AppendFormat("   <td>{0}</td>" + vbCrLf, _
          sdrData("CompanyName"))
       sb.AppendFormat("   <td>{0}</td>" + vbCrLf, sdrData("WorkPhone"))
       sb.Append("</tr>" + vbCrLf)
       If strColor = "tabletext" Then
          strColor = "tabletext_gray"
       Else
          strColor = "tabletext"
       End If
    End While
    sdrData.Close()
    sqlConn.Close()
    lblOutput.Text = sb.ToString()
End Sub

</script>
```

Listing 1.2   Contact Viewer with styles in Visual Basic .NET (continued)

The simple style sheet used for this application is shown in Listing 1.3. Feel free to use whatever colors, fonts, and font features you want. These are just for demonstration purposes.

```
<style type="text/css" title="Application Style Sheet">
<!--
.pageheading
{
    COLOR: #000000;
    FONT-FAMILY: Tahoma, Arial;
    FONT-SIZE: 16pt;
```

Listing 1.3   Contact style sheet

```
      FONT-WEIGHT: bold;
}
.tableheading
{
   COLOR: #FFFFFF;
   FONT-FAMILY: Tahoma, Arial;
   FONT-WEIGHT: bold;
   FONT-SIZE: 9pt;
   BACKGROUND-COLOR: #AA0000;
   TEXT-ALIGN: center;
}
.tabletext
{
   COLOR: #000000;
   FONT-FAMILY: Tahoma, Arial;
   FONT-SIZE: 9pt;
}
.tabletext_gray
{
   COLOR: #000000;
   FONT-FAMILY: Tahoma, Arial;
   FONT-SIZE: 9pt;
   BACKGROUND-COLOR: #CCCCCC;
}

-->
</style>
```

Listing 1.3   Contact style sheet (continued)

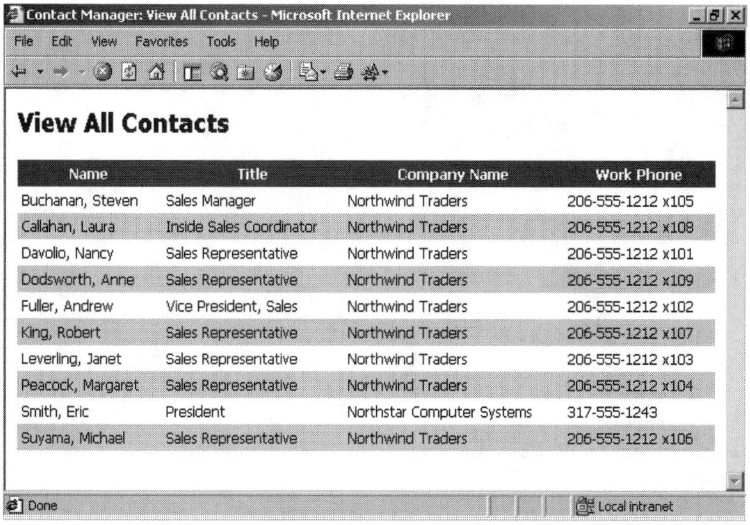

View All Contacts

Name	Title	Company Name	Work Phone
Buchanan, Steven	Sales Manager	Northwind Traders	206-555-1212 x105
Callahan, Laura	Inside Sales Coordinator	Northwind Traders	206-555-1212 x108
Davolio, Nancy	Sales Representative	Northwind Traders	206-555-1212 x101
Dodsworth, Anne	Sales Representative	Northwind Traders	206-555-1212 x109
Fuller, Andrew	Vice President, Sales	Northwind Traders	206-555-1212 x102
King, Robert	Sales Representative	Northwind Traders	206-555-1212 x107
Leverling, Janet	Sales Representative	Northwind Traders	206-555-1212 x103
Peacock, Margaret	Sales Representative	Northwind Traders	206-555-1212 x104
Smith, Eric	President	Northstar Computer Systems	317-555-1243
Suyama, Michael	Sales Representative	Northwind Traders	206-555-1212 x106

Figure 1.2   The Contact Viewer page with style sheets.

The changes that we made were fairly simple. First of all, we added a style to the page heading and changed the H1 tag to a P with a style class added to it. We then added a style to the table heading row and changed the TH tags to just TD tags. The rest of the formatting will come from the TABLEHEADING style in the style sheet.

The rest of the styling code took a bit more work. When I show potentially large lists of data like this, I prefer to show the rows in alternating colors. I find that this makes it easier to find the data you want and prevents your eyes from blurring. We have two defined styles to help us here: TABLETEXT and TABLETEXT_GRAY. We want to alternate between these styles on every other row, and we do that with a couple of lines of code. First of all, we set the starting style into a variable called strColor. Each <TR> tag is given a CLASS attribute, and the current color is substituted for the {0} in the AppendFormat routine. (We had an Append routine there before.) The other change that is required is to flip the color after we've displayed a row. This is handled using a simple If/Then statement at the end of the routine. The result is a more attractive view of the contacts in our database.

Phase 3: Adding Page Links

The last step in building the Contact Viewer page is to add links to the viewer to support the other three functions in the application:

- Adding a new record
- Modifying an existing record
- Deleting a record

Implementing the links is fairly straightforward, and the code for the Visual Basic .NET version is provided for you. We'll cover building the modification pages in the next section of this project. The changes to the code marked in boldface are explained in Listing 1.4.

```
<% @ Page   Language="VB" Debug="True" %>
<% @ Import Namespace="System" %>
<% @ Import Namespace="System.Data" %>
<% @ Import Namespace="System.Data.SqlClient" %>

<html>
   <head>
      <title>Contact Manager: View All Contacts</title>
<!--#include file="styles.css" -->
   </head>
   <body bgcolor="#FFFFFF">
      <p class="pageheading">View All Contacts</p>

      <p class="tabletext">
      <a href="updatecontact_vb.aspx">Add New Contact</a>
      </p>
```

Listing 1.4   Viewer with links in Visual Basic .NET

```
      <table cellpadding="4" cellspacing="0" width="100%">
      <tr class="tableheading">
         <td>Name</td>
         <td>Title</td>
         <td>Company Name</td>
         <td>Work Phone</td>
         <td>Actions</td>
      </tr>

      <asp:label id="lblOutput" runat="server"></asp:Label>

   </table>
   </body>
</html>


<script runat="SERVER">

Sub Page_Load(Src As Object, e As EventArgs)
   Dim sqlConn As New SqlConnection
   Dim sqlCmd  As New SqlCommand
   Dim sdrData As SqlDataReader
   Dim sb As New StringBuilder
   Dim strColor As String

   sqlConn.ConnectionString = _
      "server=localhost;database=ASPNetProject01;uid=sa;pwd=;"
   sqlConn.Open()
   sqlCmd.CommandText = "SELECT * FROM tblPeople " _
      & "ORDER BY LastName, FirstName"
   sqlCmd.CommandType = CommandType.Text
   sqlCmd.Connection = sqlConn

   sdrData = sqlCmd.ExecuteReader()
   strColor = "tabletext"
   While sdrData.Read()
      sb.AppendFormat("<tr class=""{0}"">" + vbCrLf, strColor)
      sb.AppendFormat("   <td>{0}, {1}</td>" + vbCrLf, _
         sdrData("LastName"), _
         sdrData("FirstName"))
      sb.AppendFormat("   <td>{0}</td>" + vbCrLf, sdrData("Title"))
      sb.AppendFormat("   <td>{0}</td>" + vbCrLf, _
         sdrData("CompanyName"))
      sb.AppendFormat("   <td>{0}</td>" + vbCrLf, sdrData("WorkPhone"))

      sb.Append("   <td align=middle>")
      sb.AppendFormat("<a href=""updatecontact_vb.aspx" _
         & "?id={0}"">Update</a>", _
         sdrData("pkPersonID"))
      sb.Append("  ")
```

Listing 1.4   Viewer with links in Visual Basic .NET (continued)

```
        sb.AppendFormat("<a href="""deletecontact_vb.aspx" _
          & "?id={0}"">Delete</a>", _
          sdrData("pkPersonID"))
        sb.Append("    </td>")

      sb.Append("</tr>" + vbCrLf)
      If strColor = "tabletext" Then
        strColor = "tabletext_gray"
      Else
        strColor = "tabletext"
      End If
    End While
    sdrData.Close()
    sqlConn.Close()
    lblOutput.Text = sb.ToString()
  End Sub

</script>
```

Listing 1.4 Viewer with links in Visual Basic .NET (continued)

We are making the following changes:

- Add a static HTML link to a page called addcontact_vb.aspx
- Modify the table to include a new column called "Actions," which will include links to update and delete the selected record
- As we display each record, we generate the following HTML code for the Update and Delete links in both versions of the file:

```
updatecontact_vb.aspx?id=33
deletecontact_vb.aspx?id=33
```

At this point, the viewer is ready to connect to the form pages, where we will create new records and edit existing records. All the links are available for use so that when we're ready to test the page, we have a way to run the pages. Before you go to the next step, be sure that you have some data in your table to test the editing feature.

Adding a New Record

Now that we've got the record viewer working, the next step is to build a page where we can add a new record. The basic form is fairly simple, using text boxes for the stored data for each contact. In addition, since the database does not require any of the fields other than the primary key (which is automatically generated), our validation tasks will be basically nonexistent this time around. Again, this will let us focus on the important code, which is the code required to make the actual database changes. This page will share the input form with the Update Record page. We can take care of this using another server-side Include file. When we get to the point where we are updating a record, we will also need to store the record number that we are updating. This will be done using a hidden-input field that we will set in the Update page. However, we need to put the tag in at this point so that it is available later on.

The Visual Basic .NET version of the code is shown in Listing 1.5.

```
<% @ Page   Language="VB" Debug="True" %>
<% @ Import Namespace="System" %>
<% @ Import Namespace="System.Data" %>
<% @ Import Namespace="System.Data.SqlClient" %>

<html>
   <head>
      <title>Contact Manager: Add New Contact</title>
<!-#include file="styles.css" ->
   </head>
   <body bgcolor="#FFFFFF">
   <p class="pageheading">Add New Contact</p>
<!-#include file="inputform.aspx" ->
   </body>
</html>

<script runat="SERVER">

Sub Page_Load(objSender As Object, objArgs As EventArgs)
   Dim sqlConn As New SqlConnection
   Dim sqlCmd  As New SqlCommand
   Dim sb As New StringBuilder

   If Page.IsPostBack Then
      sqlConn.ConnectionString = _
         "server=localhost;database=ASPNetProject01;uid=sa;pwd=;"
      sqlConn.Open()
      sb.Append("INSERT INTO tblPeople (LastName, FirstName,")
      sb.Append("Title, CompanyName, Address, HomePhone, ")
      sb.Append("WorkPhone, Fax, EMail, WebPage, Notes) VALUES (")

      sb.AppendFormat("'{0}', '{1}', '{2}',", _
         Request.Form("txtLastName"), _
         Request.Form("txtFirstName"), _
         Request.Form("txtTitle"))

      sb.AppendFormat("'{0}', '{1}', '{2}',", _
         Request.Form("txtCompanyName"), _
         Request.Form("txtAddress"), _
         Request.Form("txtHomePhone"))

      sb.AppendFormat("'{0}', '{1}', '{2}',", _
         Request.Form("txtWorkPhone"), _
         Request.Form("txtFax"), _
```

Listing 1.5   Add Contact page—Visual Basic .NET version

```
          Request.Form("txtEMail"))

      sb.AppendFormat("'{0}', '{1}')", _
          Request.Form("txtWebPage"), _
          Request.Form("txtNotes"))

      sqlCmd.CommandText = sb.ToString()
      sqlCmd.CommandType = CommandType.Text
      sqlCmd.Connection = sqlConn
      sqlCmd.ExecuteNonQuery()
      sqlConn.Close()
      Response.Redirect("viewcontacts_vb_linked.aspx")
    End If
End Sub

</script>
```

Listing 1.5 Add Contact page—Visual Basic .NET version (continued)

This is the first page where we've had any interactivity, so let's go through the page a section at a time. When the page is first requested, you see the screen shown in Figure 1.3. There is a control visible for all the fields in the database except for the primary key, which is automatically generated when we save the file. Each one of the controls is a *server-side ASP.NET control*, which gives us the ability to program with it using the same code used to write the various events. This is especially important when we write the Update Contact page, since we need to initially populate the form.

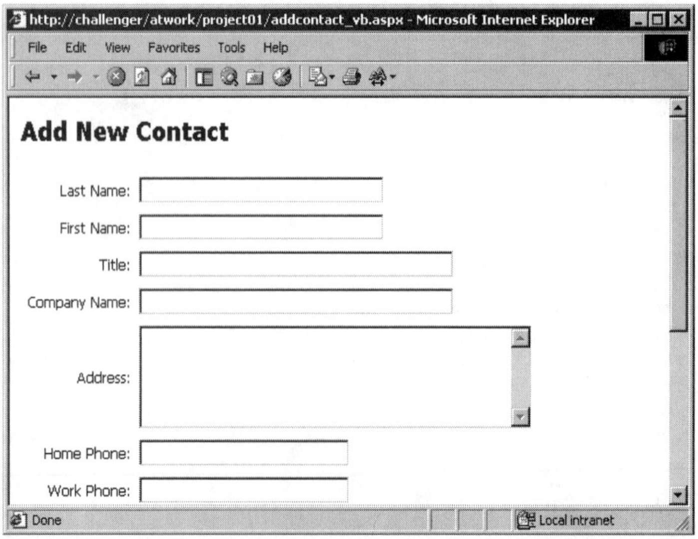

Figure 1.3 Add Contact page in the browser.

Working through the file, the first thing you see is a new Include file called Input-form.aspx. Since the code is provided in both Visual Basic .NET and C#, this Include file gives you the ability to share the form between the two files. In addition, you can use the same Include file when writing the Update Contact page later in the project. The input form itself is shown in Listing 1.6. The code essentially repeats the same block of code over and over again for each field that we want to accept. The ASP:TextBox control represents a server control that holds the text the user enters. Each text box is given a name that we'll be able to use in the code in the ID parameter. The Columns parameter specifies how long the box should appear on the screen, and the Maxlength parameter specifies the maximum length of the data that can be entered by the user. This pattern is repeated for every box except for the Notes field, which has a different set of parameters since the box is a multiple-line text field (a TEXTAREA tag in HTML). This type of field also includes the number of rows and columns that should be shown:

```
<form runat="server">
<input
    type="hidden"
    runat="server"
    id="hiddenPersonID">
<table cellspacing="5">
<tr class="tabletext">
    <td align="right">Last Name:</td>
    <td>
        <asp:textbox
            id="txtLastName"
            columns="30"
            maxlength="40"
            runat="server" /></td>
</tr>
<tr class="tabletext">
    <td align="right">First Name:</td>
    <td>
        <asp:textbox
            id="txtFirstName"
            columns="30"
            maxlength="40"
            runat="server" /></td>
</tr>
<tr class="tabletext">
    <td align="right">Title:</td>
    <td>
        <asp:textbox
            id="txtTitle"
            columns="40"
            maxlength="80"
            runat="server" /></td>
</tr>
<tr class="tabletext">
```

Listing 1.6 Inputform.aspx

```
            <td align="right">Company Name:</td>
            <td>
                <asp:textbox
                    id="txtCompanyName"
                    columns="40"
                    maxlength="80"
                    runat="server" /></td>
        </tr>
        <tr class="tabletext">
            <td valign="middle" align="right">Address:</td>
            <td>
                <asp:textbox
                    id="txtAddress"
                    rows="5"
                    columns="40"
                    maxlength="240"
                    wrap="true"
                    textmode="Multiline"
                    runat="server" /></td>
        </tr>
        <tr class="tabletext">
            <td align="right">Home Phone:</td>
            <td>
                <asp:textbox
                    id="txtHomePhone"
                    columns="25"
                    maxlength="40"
                    runat="server" /></td>
        </tr>
        <tr class="tabletext">
            <td align="right">Work Phone:</td>
            <td>
                <asp:textbox
                    id="txtWorkPhone"
                    columns="25"
                    maxlength="40"
                    runat="server" /></td>
        </tr>
        <tr class="tabletext">
            <td align="right">Fax Number:</td>
            <td>
                <asp:textbox
                    id="txtFaxNumber"
                    columns="25"
                    maxlength="40"
                    runat="server" /></td>
        </tr>
        <tr class="tabletext">
            <td align="right">E-Mail:</td>
            <td>
                <asp:textbox
```

Listing 1.6 Inputform.aspx (continued)

```
            id="txtEMail"
            columns="40"
            maxlength="120"
            runat="server" /></td>
   </tr>
   <tr class="tabletext">
      <td align="right">Web Page:</td>
      <td>
         <asp:textbox
            id="txtWebPage"
            columns="40"
            maxlength="120"
            runat="server" /></td>
   </tr>
   <tr class="tabletext">
      <td valign="middle" align="right">Notes:</td>
      <td>
         <asp:textbox
            id="txtNotes"
            rows="5"
            columns="40"
            wrap="true"
            textmode="Multiline"
            runat="server" /></td>
   </tr>
   <tr class="tabletext">
      <td colspan=2 align=middle>
      <input type="submit"
         name="btnSubmit"
         runat="server"
         value="Save" />
      <input type="reset"
         name="btnReset"
         runat="server"
         value="Clear" />
      </td>
   </tr>
   </table>
   </form>
```

Listing 1.6 Inputform.aspx (continued)

There are a few things you should note about this form that are important to its operation:

■ The form does not have the traditional ACTION or METHOD parameters. All that is required is to specify that the form run on the server. That will make the rest of the code we create work properly.

- All of the input controls are server-side ASP controls so that we can program with them. The exceptions are the Submit and Reset buttons at the end of the page, which can be simple HTML-style controls.

- Each server-side control is given an ID property that matches closely to the database field, as well as a Maxlength property that prevents the user from typing in too much text. This saves you some effort in handling the validation later.

- All of the server-side controls are marked with a Runat property so that we can write code using their properties.

Once the page is assembled from the various files that are brought in, it's shown to the user, and the user is able to enter any or all of the fields before clicking the Save button. Once the Save button is clicked, a connection to the database must occur to store the new record in the tblPeople table. The Visual Basic .NET version of the code we're using is shown here for reference:

```
Sub Page_Load(objSender As Object, objArgs As EventArgs)
    Dim sqlConn As New SqlConnection
    Dim sqlCmd  As New SqlCommand
    Dim sb As New StringBuilder

    If Page.IsPostBack Then
        sqlConn.ConnectionString = _
            "server=localhost;database=ASPNetProject01;uid=sa;pwd=;"
        sqlConn.Open()
        sb.Append("INSERT INTO tblPeople (LastName, FirstName,")
        sb.Append("Title, CompanyName, Address, HomePhone, ")
        sb.Append("WorkPhone, Fax, EMail, WebPage, Notes) VALUES (")

        sb.AppendFormat("'{0}', '{1}', '{2}',", _
            Request.Form("txtLastName"), _
            Request.Form("txtFirstName"), _
            Request.Form("txtTitle"))

        sb.AppendFormat("'{0}', '{1}', '{2}',", _
            Request.Form("txtCompanyName"), _
            Request.Form("txtAddress"), _
            Request.Form("txtHomePhone"))

        sb.AppendFormat("'{0}', '{1}', '{2}',", _
            Request.Form("txtWorkPhone"), _
            Request.Form("txtFax"), _
            Request.Form("txtEMail"))

        sb.AppendFormat("'{0}', '{1}')", _
            Request.Form("txtWebPage"), _
            Request.Form("txtNotes"))

        sqlCmd.CommandText = sb.ToString()
        sqlCmd.CommandType = CommandType.Text
        sqlCmd.Connection = sqlConn
```

```
        sqlCmd.ExecuteNonQuery()
        sqlConn.Close()
        Response.Redirect("viewcontacts_vb_linked.aspx")
    End If
End Sub
```

We only want to add a new record if we know the user has clicked the Save button, so we check the Page.IsPostBack property before doing anything. If we are in "posting" mode, we make a database connection using the SqlConnection object. We have to provide a connection string, which specifies which server and which database we want to use, as well as the user name and password to use for connecting to the database. We then start building the SQL statement using a StringBuilder object. We then run the query using the ExecuteNonQuery method and send the user back to the appropriate list window. This has the effect of refreshing the list window and making the new record visible.

A few things are missing from this code so that we could focus on the more important pieces:

At a minimum, you should require that the LastName and FirstName or the Company fields be filled in. Otherwise, you could potentially add an empty record to the database table.

If you attempt to add a name like O'Brien, the SQL statement will have an error because the single-quote character is a SQL delimiter. The solution is to replace each single quote with two single quotes (not a double quote character). The database will properly interpret the two single quotes as a quote that you want to store in the record.

There is no verification that the record was added successfully. The ExecuteNonQuery method returns the number of records that were affected by the statement. In this case, we will get either one or zero records affected and should create the appropriate error message if we can't save the record.

In the next project, we'll correct a number of these problems and add some additional features to the application. For now, you can add a new record by clicking the *Add New Contact* link on your list window and try out your new code.

Modifying a Record

To modify an existing record, you use the same form as that used for the Add Record page, with a couple of minor changes. First, you have to store the record ID that you're modifying. You do this using a hidden-input field that is populated from the Page_Load event. You also need to populate the rest of the fields with the current field values for the record. This way, the user can make changes and click the Save button to preserve those changes. Thus, we need to create an UPDATE SQL statement instead of an INSERT statement. The code for this page is shown in Visual Basic .NET (Listing 1.7).

```
<% @ Page    Language="VB" Debug="True" %>
<% @ Import Namespace="System" %>
<% @ Import Namespace="System.Data" %>
<% @ Import Namespace="System.Data.SqlClient" %>

<html>
   <head>
      <title>Contact Manager: Update Contact</title>
<!--#include file="styles.css" -->
   </head>
   <body bgcolor="#FFFFFF">
   <p class="pageheading">Update Contact</p>
<!--#include file="inputform.aspx" -->
   </body>
</html>


<script runat="SERVER">

Sub Page_Load(objSender As Object, objArgs As EventArgs)
   Dim sqlConn As New SqlConnection
   Dim sqlCmd  As New SqlCommand
   Dim sdrData As SqlDataReader
   Dim sb As New StringBuilder

   sqlConn.ConnectionString = _
      "server=localhost;database=ASPNetProject01;uid=sa;pwd=;"
   sqlConn.Open()
   If Not Page.IsPostBack Then
      sqlCmd.CommandText = "SELECT * FROM tblPeople " _
         & "WHERE pkPersonID = " _
         & Request.QueryString("ID")
      sqlCmd.CommandType = CommandType.Text
      sqlCmd.Connection = sqlConn
      sdrData = sqlCmd.ExecuteReader()
      sdrData.Read()
      hiddenPersonID.Value = Request.QueryString("ID")
      txtLastName.Text = sdrData("LastName").ToString()
      txtFirstName.Text = sdrData("FirstName").ToString()
      txtTitle.Text = sdrData("Title").ToString()
      txtCompanyName.Text = sdrData("CompanyName").ToString()
      txtAddress.Text = sdrData("Address").ToString()
      txtHomePhone.Text = sdrData("HomePhone").ToString()
      txtWorkPhone.Text = sdrData("WorkPhone").ToString()
      txtFaxNumber.Text = sdrData("Fax").ToString()
      txtEMail.Text = sdrData("EMail").ToString()
      txtWebPage.Text = sdrData("WebPage").ToString()
      txtNotes.Text = sdrData("Notes").ToString()
      sdrData.Close()
      sqlConn.Close()
   Else
      sb.Append("UPDATE tblPeople SET ")
```

Listing 1.7   Update Contact—Visual Basic .NET version

```
            sb.AppendFormat("LastName = '{0}',", _
                txtLastName.Text)
            sb.AppendFormat("FirstName = '{0}',", _
                txtFirstName.Text)
            sb.AppendFormat("Title = '{0}',", _
                txtTitle.Text)
            sb.AppendFormat("CompanyName = '{0}',", _
                txtCompanyName.Text)
            sb.AppendFormat("Address = '{0}',", _
                txtAddress.Text)
            sb.AppendFormat("HomePhone = '{0}',", _
                txtHomePhone.Text)
            sb.AppendFormat("WorkPhone = '{0}',", _
                txtWorkPhone.Text)
            sb.AppendFormat("Fax = '{0}',", _
                txtFaxNumber.Text)
            sb.AppendFormat("EMail = '{0}',", _
                txtEMail.Text)
            sb.AppendFormat("WebPage = '{0}',", _
                txtWebPage.Text)
            sb.AppendFormat("Notes = '{0}' ", _
                txtNotes.Text)
            sb.AppendFormat("WHERE pkPersonID = {0}", _
                hiddenPersonID.Value)

        sqlCmd.CommandText = sb.ToString()
        sqlCmd.CommandType = CommandType.Text
        sqlCmd.Connection = sqlConn
        sqlCmd.ExecuteNonQuery()
        sqlConn.Close()
        Response.Redirect("viewcontacts_vb_linked.aspx")
    End If
End Sub

</script>
```

Listing 1.7   Update Contact—Visual Basic .NET version (continued)

The code performs the following steps to save the changes to the record:

- The Request.QueryString collection holds the ID value of the record that the user of the page chose to edit. That value is used to create a Person object with that record's data.

- The form is populated from the database by reading each field from the DataReader into the form.

- When the user clicks the Save button, a SQL UPDATE statement is built that makes the changes and reads the data out of the form into the statement.

- The user is returned to the list window.

When the form is being populated, note that the ToString() method is being used to retrieve data from each field. This is because some of the fields can be NULL, which will return an error message if you try to put a null value in the field. The ToString() counters this by returning an empty string. The end result of this code is a page that shows the current data for a record and allows you to edit and save the changes.

Deleting a Record

Deleting a record is the simplest of all the available actions in our application. The files delete the record in the database and return to the list window. You could add functionality to the page by adding JavaScript to the list window to confirm the deletion. You will add this code in the next project. The code for the Delete Record function is shown in Listing 1.8.

```
<% @ Page    Language="VB" Debug="True" %>
<% @ Import Namespace="System" %>
<% @ Import Namespace="System.Data" %>
<% @ Import Namespace="System.Data.SqlClient" %>


<script runat="SERVER">

Sub Page_Load(objSender As Object, objArgs As EventArgs)
   Dim sqlConn As New SqlConnection
   Dim sqlCmd  As New SqlCommand

   sqlConn.ConnectionString = _
      "server=localhost;database=ASPNetProject01;uid=sa;pwd=;"
   sqlConn.Open()
   sqlCmd.CommandText = "DELETE FROM tblPeople " _
      & "WHERE pkPersonID = " _
      & Request.QueryString("ID")
   sqlCmd.CommandType = CommandType.Text
   sqlCmd.Connection = sqlConn
   sqlCmd.ExecuteNonQuery()
   Response.Redirect("viewcontacts_vb_linked.aspx")
End Sub

</script>
```

Listing 1.8   Delete Contact—Visual Basic .NET version

As before, a connection is first made to the application database in SQL Server. We then build up a fairly short SQL statement by concatenating in the ID passed on by the list window. This SQL statement will look something like this when we're done building it:

```
DELETE FROM tblPeople WHERE pkPersonID = 5
```

The "5" in the query is supplied by the Request.QueryString collection, which is populated from the data passed to this page on the URL's query string. The query is then sent to the database, and the user is returned to the list window.

Wrap Up

In this project, you learned how to retrieve data from a database and display it in a variety of formats, include style sheets and other files to minimize the amount of duplicated code, and add, modify, and delete records from a selected table.

In Project 2, you'll expand this application to include the ability to save individual calls and other correspondence to each contact in the system. You'll also add some validation code and code that handles the SQL single-quote issue discussed earlier.

Contact Manager Application

In the previous project, you built a simple address book application using no other tools than a text editor. In this project, you'll rebuild some of that application using a more object-oriented and structured approach. You'll add several new features to the application so that users can keep track of contacts you make with individuals in the tblPeople table, as well as any notes they may need to make about a person. You'll also add some fairly rigorous data validation to the application. This validation will be part of the business objects you build to help manage the data the user is entering. Keeping the validation logic in the business objects helps to consolidate it all in one place. While most of the application will be ASP.NET pages, you'll also be creating several assemblies for the application.

THE PROBLEM

The address book created in Project 1 does not do validation and uses a fair amount of duplicate code. The address book needs to be enhanced with a contact manager, as well as with the ability to store notes about a particular entry.

THE SOLUTION

Build a series of business objects to encapsulate the database activity required to view, add, modify, and delete records.

Project Background

We're going to be building several *assemblies* in this project. Assemblies are a new concept in .NET that represent logical blocks of code that can be used in an application. Assemblies are stored in DLL files, which can be confusing, since dynamic link libraries in traditional Windows programming are also stored in DLL files. DLLs in traditional Windows programming are compiled once for a particular platform (32-bit Windows, for instance) and are loaded into the memory of the application. They are not released until the application shuts down. Assemblies, on the other hand, are compiled initially in Intermediate Language (IL) code. When they are required by the application, they are compiled on demand for the platform where the application is running. Microsoft is working with Corel to build a version of the .NET runtime for Linux, so you'll be able to build a single assembly, compile it to IL code, and then deploy it to both Windows and Linux. When the application requests the DLL, it will be compiled on-the-fly for that operating system. With assemblies, you can also easily recompile and change the contents of the assembly without having to shut down the Web services or reboot. When you change an assembly, the .NET runtime detects the change and loads the new version of the assembly. This is an improvement over the traditional Windows DLL programming since you can rapidly build, compile, test, and recompile as needed. In this project, you'll build seven classes:

Database. In the previous project, you probably noticed that we used a lot of the same code to handle opening the database, retrieving and writing data, and so on. In this project, we'll be building a Database class that encapsulates all our database operations. Each of the main objects (Person, Contact, Note, and so on) will be aware of how this object operates and will be able to create their own connections when necessary. This limits the amount of direct database code in your ASP.NET pages. For the most part, all you'll be doing is populating objects and detecting any errors.

Person. This class encapsulates the validation and database logic needed to maintain the tblPeople table. All the validation rules will be built into this object, and, if an error is detected, it will generate a PersonException error. The PersonException error can then be trapped in the ASP.NET page and processed.

Contact. This class manages the data in the tblContacts table, which you'll be creating in this project. Any detected errors will generate a ContactException error.

Note. This class handles the tblNotes table, which you'll also be creating in this project. Any errors cause a NoteException error to be raised to the calling code.

PersonException, ContactException, and NoteException. One of the nicest things about .NET Framework programming is the highly structured error handling process. In this project, we'll create four of our own errors. Prior to this, we would have had to pick a number to indicate a particular error occurred. Now, we just give our error a name and look for it.

Besides the classes, you will also build a number of new pages to deal with the new types of data. You'll link these pages into the main address book viewer, since the other two entities are "child" entities; that is, a contact can't exist by itself without a related person record. The steps for this project are:

1. Set up the development environment.

2. Build the Database class and test it.

3. Build the BaseServices class and test it.

4. Build the Person and PersonException classes and test them.

5. Modify the existing pages to use the Person class for all data storage and retrieval activities.

6. Build the Note Manager portion of the application, including the Note and NoteException classes and the Web pages needed to use these objects.

7. Build the Contact Manager portion of the application, including the Contact and ContactException classes and the Web pages needed to use these objects.

You Will Need

✔ **Windows 2000**

✔ **Internet Information Server 5.0 with .NET Framework installed**

✔ **Visual Studio .NET**

✔ **SQL Server 7.0 or 2000**

✔ **Your code from Project 1**

Set Up the Development Environment

There are a few things we need to do before we can get started in this project. First of all, we need to have a database. If you like, you can use the database from the previous project. However, I'll be creating a new database called ASPNetProject02, located on the companion CD-ROM. This way, I have a point of reference as to how the old project worked.

We also want to make a copy of the files that we created in Project 1 since we'll be making substantial changes to some of them. We'll still be using one file for each logical function: list, add, update, and delete. For this project, I have created a new directory on my Web server called project02.

The last change we need to make is to create a new application. This is because we are going to build and use our own assemblies. Assemblies for a project need to be located in a *bin* (stands for binary) directory at the root of the application. Internet Information Server (IIS) allows you to define an application anywhere on the server, but you have to use the IIS Console to set it up. Follow these steps to create a new application:

1. Create a new directory on your computer for your Project 2 files. On my computer, all my projects are located in the atwork directory, and each project is named project01, project02, and so on.

2. Start the Internet Service Manager.

3. Right-click the Default Web Site, and select New —>Virtual Directory.

4. From the introductory screen of the wizard, click the Next button.

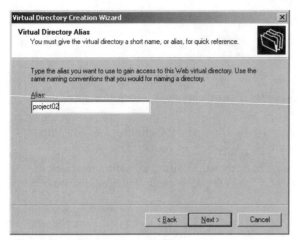

Figure 2.1   Virtual directory alias screen.

5. The second page of the wizard (shown in Figure 2.1) asks you for an alias for your virtual directory. I would suggest a name of *project02*. Type the alias, and click the Next button.

6. In the next step of the wizard (shown in Figure 2.2), specify the physical directory of your new directory. Browse to the directory for your Project 2 files, if necessary, and then click the Next button.

7. On the last screen of the wizard, verify that the Read and Run Scripts permissions are selected, and then click the Next button to create the virtual directory.

8. You should now see your new virtual directory listed in the navigation pane on the left side of the Internet Services Manager window. If you don't, click the Refresh button on the toolbar. Right-click the virtual directory you created, and select Properties from the menu. The dialog box shown in Figure 2.3 appears.

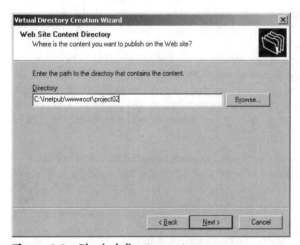

Figure 2.2   Physical directory entry screen.

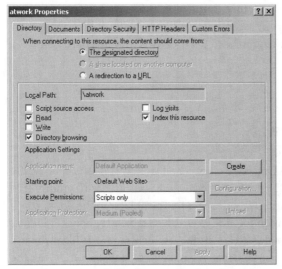

Figure 2.3 Virtual directory properties dialog box.

9. To create a new application, click the Create button, and then click the OK button at the bottom of the window. When you look at your virtual directory in the Internet Service Manager, you'll notice that the icon has changed from a plain folder icon into the icon shown in Figure 2.4. Close Internet Services Manager.

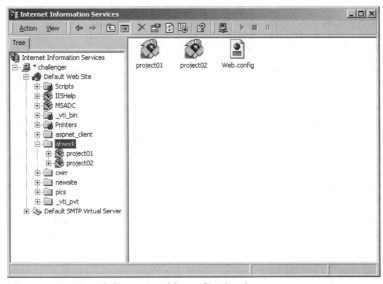

Figure 2.4 Virtual directory with application icon.

At this point, you can create a *bin* directory in the virtual directory that you made. This is where ASP.NET will look for your assemblies. You can create applications wherever you like, but typically, they are going to be in the root directory of a particular Web site.

Build the Database Class

The first class that we'll build is the Database class. The Database class is specifically designed to communicate with a SQL Server database, but you can easily modify it to use your favorite type of database. Since we will reuse this class later in the book, you'll see that it has a little bit of flexibility with regards to which database it opens. This class can run queries that either return or don't return data, which makes it ideal for use with the other classes we will build. For instance, we have to be able to retrieve all the people in the database to display them on the Web page. The Database class will need to support the following functions:

- Use a SqlConnection object to make the connection, but allow the user to either pass a connection string through a method call or through the Web.config file.
- Make the live connection available as a property of the class.
- Run queries that return data sets. Return the data in the form of a SqlDataReader or DataSet object.
- Run queries that do not return data sets, but instead return the number of rows that were affected, as is typical with Insert, Update, and Delete queries.
- Close the database connection. We could let the connection simply time out, but I prefer to explicitly close the connection when all operations are done.
- Raise any errors that might have occurred during the connection process.

As mentioned, this class will be created as an assembly. We want this assembly to be separate from the one we'll build later in this project since we will use the Database class in later projects. The easiest way to set this up is to use Visual Studio .NET to create a new Visual Basic .NET Class Library project. In this project, I have called the class library AtWorkUtilities, but feel free to use whatever name you want.

Add Assembly Information

The first thing I do when I start a new class library is to fill in the appropriate information in the Assembly Information file, called AssemblyInfo.vb. The file is automatically created by Visual Studio .NET when you create a new class library project. The information you provide here is available to users when they use Windows Explorer to view the properties of your DLL, as shown in Figure 2.5.

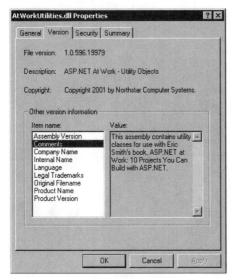

Figure 2.5   Version properties for an assembly.

This is helpful information and should always be provided since it can help you as a programmer (and often support person) determine if the problem a user is having is due to a version mismatch. The code in the empty AssemblyInfo.vb file is shown in Listing 2.1.

```
Imports System.Reflection
Imports System.Runtime.InteropServices


' General Information about an assembly is controlled through the
following
' set of attributes. Change these attribute values to modify the
information
' associated with an assembly.

' Review the values of the assembly attributes

<Assembly: AssemblyTitle("")>
<Assembly: AssemblyDescription("")>
<Assembly: AssemblyCompany("")>
<Assembly: AssemblyProduct("")>
<Assembly: AssemblyCopyright("")>
<Assembly: AssemblyTrademark("")>
<Assembly: CLSCompliant(True)>


'The following GUID is for the ID of the typelib if this project is
exposed to COM
<Assembly: Guid("158D682E-8BAC-423D-B17C-21991330CC79")>
```

Listing 2.1   Assembly Information file

```
' Version information for an assembly consists of the following four
values:
'
'       Major Version
'       Minor Version
'       Build Number
'       Revision
'
' You can specify all the values or you can default the Build and
Revision Numbers
' by using the '*' as shown below:

<Assembly: AssemblyVersion("1.0.*")>
```

Listing 2.1 Assembly Information file (continued)

You don't have to provide all the information requested, but if you don't, the entry will be empty when a user views it in the Properties dialog box from Windows Explorer. Some of the information, such as the creator of the assembly and the version number, is important for debugging purposes so I would suggest you always supply it. For this assembly, I've provided the following information, as shown in Listing 2.2.

```
Imports System.Reflection
Imports System.Runtime.InteropServices

' General Information about an assembly is controlled through the
following
' set of attributes. Change these attribute values to modify the
information
' associated with an assembly.

' Review the values of the assembly attributes

<Assembly: AssemblyTitle("ASP.NET At Work - Utility Objects")>
<Assembly: AssemblyDescription("This assembly contains utility " _
    & "classes for use with Eric Smith's book, ASP.NET " _
    & "at Work: 10 Projects You Can Build with ASP.NET.")>
<Assembly: AssemblyCompany("Northstar Computer Systems")>
<Assembly: AssemblyProduct("ASP.NET At Work")>
<Assembly: AssemblyCopyright("Copyright 2001 by Northstar " _
    & "Computer Systems. All Rights Reserved.")>
<Assembly: AssemblyTrademark("Copyright 2001 by Northstar " _
    & "Computer Systems. All Rights Reserved.")>
<Assembly: CLSCompliant(True)>

'The following GUID is for the ID of the typelib if this project is
'exposed to COM
```

Listing 2.2 Populated version of AssemblyInfo.vb

```
<Assembly: Guid("91DB34F3-5F71-41FC-85E1-4E22A12501B2")>

' Version information for an assembly consists of the following four
values:
'
'       Major Version
'       Minor Version
'       Build Number
'       Revision
'
' You can specify all the values or you can default the Build and
' Revision Numbers by using the '*' as shown below:

<Assembly: AssemblyVersion("2.0.*")>
```

Listing 2.2   Populated version of AssemblyInfo.vb (continued)

In the longer text fields, such as AssemblyDescription, you can use the concatenation operator to break the description on to more than one line. You don't have to do this, but it can make the description easier to read.

The other information you should provide is the version number of your assembly. By default, the first two portions of the version number (major and minor) are 1.0. The other two parts, build number and revision, can either be automatically generated or supplied manually. If you choose to have them automatically generated, the build number is the number of days after January 1st, 2000. The revision number is the number of seconds that have elapsed since midnight, local time, modulo 2. On most development projects, the standard for version, build, and revision numbers is normally established, so you can use this property to make your work in VS.NET comply with those standards. For this application, the version number has been changed to 2.0 since we're in Project 2.

Design the Database Class

The Database class is designed to communicate with the SQL Server database and handle the multiple database tasks. It is also designed to save us from having to type the repetitive code required by most database operations: create a connection, create a command, run the command, and possibly build a DataReader or other object. The Database object will encapsulate much of that functionality and the features we want for this class, which in turn reduces the amount of code we have to write elsewhere. Listing 2.3 lists all the code for this class.

```
Imports System.Data.SqlClient
Imports System.Configuration


Public Class Database
```

Listing 2.3   Code for Database.vb class

```
Private m_cnDB As SqlConnection


'
' This constructor reads the application configuration
' file (Web.config for web applications) for a string
' called ConnectionString. If it's not there, an exception
' is thrown. Otherwise, the connection is made.
'
Public Sub New()
   Dim objCnf As ConfigurationSettings
   If objCnf.AppSettings("ConnectionString") = "" Then
      Throw New Exception("Connection string not found " _
         & "in application configuration file.")
   Else
      m_cnDB = New _
         SqlConnection(objCnf.AppSettings("ConnectionString").ToString)
      m_cnDB.Open()
   End If
End Sub


'
' This constructor accepts a connection string as input
' and makes a connection to that SQL Server.
'
Public Sub New(ByVal ConnectionString As String)
   m_cnDB = New SqlConnection(ConnectionString)
   m_cnDB.Open()
End Sub


'
' In case there are other objects that need the live
' connection, make it available through a read-only
' property.
'
Public ReadOnly Property Connection() As SqlConnection
Get
   Return m_cnDB
End Get
End Property


'
' Run a query that does not return records.
'
Public Function Execute(ByVal SQL As String) As Integer
   Dim lngRecords As Integer
   Dim cmdQuery As New SqlCommand()
   cmdQuery.Connection = m_cnDB
   cmdQuery.CommandText = SQL
   cmdQuery.CommandType = CommandType.Text
   lngRecords = cmdQuery.ExecuteNonQuery()
```

Listing 2.3 Code for Database.vb class (continued)

```vb
    End Function


    '
    ' Run a stored procedure that does not return records.
    '
    Public Function ExecuteStoredProc(ByVal SQL As String) As Integer
        Dim lngRecords As Integer
        Dim cmdQuery As New SqlCommand()
        cmdQuery.Connection = m_cnDB
        cmdQuery.CommandText = SQL
        cmdQuery.CommandType = CommandType.StoredProcedure
        lngRecords = cmdQuery.ExecuteNonQuery()
    End Function


    '
    ' Run a query that returns records in the form
    ' of a SqlDataReader.
    '
    Public Function GetDataReader(ByVal SQL As String) As SqlDataReader
        Dim cmdQuery As New SqlCommand()
        Dim dr As SqlDataReader
        cmdQuery.Connection = m_cnDB
        cmdQuery.CommandText = SQL
        cmdQuery.CommandType = CommandType.Text
        dr = cmdQuery.ExecuteReader
        dr.Read()
        Return dr
    End Function


    '
    ' Run a query that returns records in the form
    ' of a DataSet.
    '
    Public Function GetDataSet(ByVal SQL As String) As DataSet
        Dim da As New SqlDataAdapter(SQL, m_cnDB)
        Dim ds As New DataSet("Results")
        da.Fill(ds)
        Return ds
    End Function


    '
    ' Close the database connection.
    '
    Public Sub Close()
        m_cnDB.Close()
    End Sub
End Class
```

Listing 2.3   Code for Database.vb class (continued)

Let's walk through the listing. First, we reference two system assemblies:

System.Configuration. Provides access to the application-configuration information from the configuration file.

System.Data.SqlClient. Provides the various SQL Server objects.

We have a shared, private variable that will hold the SQL connection once it's been created. Since we are providing various access points to get to the connection, we make it a private variable. If you plan to build other classes that inherit from this one, make this variable a protected one instead of private. However, since we're not planning that for this book, a private variable will do just fine.

There are two overloaded constructors for this class: one that takes a connection string, and one that doesn't. The second constructor is the easiest to understand: Accept a connection string and open a SqlConnection object for it. The first constructor uses the ConfigurationSettings type (System.Configuration.ConfigurationSettings is the full name) to access the data in the application's configuration file. Since this is a Web application, the Web.config file will be used. Since it's easier to change that configuration file than it is to recompile the whole assembly, this method provides a way to store information in the Web.config file that will be read at runtime. The new code for the Web.config file is shown in bold in Listing 2.4.

```xml
<?xml version="1.0" encoding="utf-8" ?>
<configuration>

  <system.web>

    .
    .
    other settings go here
    .
    .
  </system.web>
  <appSettings>
      <add key="ConnectionString"
           value="server=localhost;database=ASPNetProject02;uid=sa;pwd=;"
  />
  </appSettings>
</configuration>
```

Listing 2.4 Web.config file listing

In the appSettings section in the Web.config file, add the settings that your application can read at runtime. In this case, we've chosen the name ConnectionString to be read by the Database class. If the string is there, it will be read and the connection string used to make a database connection. If the string is not there, we trigger, or *throw*, an exception. This error can be trapped by the calling code and displayed to the user in an error message.

Between these two constructors, we can easily open the database. We're going to build a number of methods to simplify the amount of code required to retrieve data from the database, but there are probably going to be cases in which you need a Sql-Connection object. For that reason, I've created a read-only property that makes the connection available directly:

```
'
' In case there are other objects that need the live
' connection, make it available through a read-only
' property.
'
Public ReadOnly Property Connection() As SqlConnection
Get
    Return m_cnDB
End Get
End Property
```

This property has been added strictly for flexibility in case we need it later. The Execute method is designed for SQL statements that don't return data, as shown in the following:

```
'
' Run a query that does not return records.
'
Public Function Execute(ByVal SQL As String) As Integer
    Dim lngRecords As Integer
    Dim cmdQuery As New SqlCommand()
    cmdQuery.Connection = m_cnDB
    cmdQuery.CommandText = SQL
    cmdQuery.CommandType = CommandType.Text
    lngRecords = cmdQuery.ExecuteNonQuery()
End Function
```

This statement is designed for handling raw, non-stored procedure queries that don't return data. If we need to use a stored procedure that doesn't return any records, there is a separate method used:

```
'
' Run a stored procedure that does not return records.
'
Public Function ExecuteStoredProc(ByVal SQL As String) As Integer
    Dim lngRecords As Integer
    Dim cmdQuery As New SqlCommand()
    cmdQuery.Connection = m_cnDB
    cmdQuery.CommandText = SQL
    cmdQuery.CommandType = CommandType.StoredProcedure
    lngRecords = cmdQuery.ExecuteNonQuery()
End Function
```

Adding another input parameter to the Execute method indicating which type of query should be run would have accomplished the same goal. However, this method is just as easy and makes it obvious to the caller which type of SQL statement (stored procedure versus statement) is running.

For queries that need to return data, we have two options: Return the data in a Sql-DataReader, or return it in a DataSet. In some of the code that you'll build throughout this book, you'll need to read all the records in a recordset quickly without making any changes to those records. In that case, a SqlDataReader is the most efficient way to retrieve and read the data. In other cases, you'll need to be able to read, modify, add, and delete rows to a table. The DataSet object is the recommended way to make those changes in .NET. We'll be using both of these methods in various places throughout the other projects in this book. The two methods that implement these return types are shown here for reference:

```
'
' Run a query that returns records in the form
' of a SqlDataReader.
'
Public Function GetDataReader(ByVal SQL As String) As SqlDataReader
    Dim cmdQuery As New SqlCommand()
    Dim dr As SqlDataReader
    cmdQuery.Connection = m_cnDB
    cmdQuery.CommandText = SQL
    cmdQuery.CommandType = CommandType.Text
    dr = cmdQuery.ExecuteReader
    dr.Read()
    Return dr
End Function


'
' Run a query that returns records in the form
' of a DataSet.
'
Public Function GetDataSet(ByVal SQL As String) As DataSet
    Dim DA As New SqlDataAdapter(SQL, m_cnDB)
    Dim DS As New DataSet("Results")
    DA.Fill(DS)
    Return DS
End Function
```

The final method needed is the Close method, which closes the database connection. Since we don't know when the garbage collection routine will run, we want to make sure that our object has completed its cleanup before we let it go out of scope. The Close method takes care of releasing the database connection so that when the garbage collector does run, we don't have a stray connection.

This object is designed for typical functionality. However, there is enough flexibility in it that you can use the database in a variety of different ways. In the next step of this project, you'll create a SqlCommand object and read the connection from this object.

The main idea behind the Database object is to give you a base on which you can build more functionality. For instance, you could add a feature to your Database object that automatically checks an application's security level when performing a particular change. The database itself can provide information about security to you, and your Database object could interpret that information and return it to the caller. Your Database object could also be used to retrieve the structure of the database using the system-stored procedures available in databases such as SQL Server and Oracle. Calling code could look at an array or collection of tables, and your Database object would be responsible for populating those collections. As you work with the object, you'll come up with other uses for it and may come up with features specific to your enterprise. You can then reuse this code in other applications in your company.

Build and Test the Assembly

The last step in writing the Database class is to build the assembly file. If you're using Visual Studio .NET, right-click the project and select Build from the menu. Once you've got the assembly built, you can test it. The easiest way to test the DLL is to take one of your .aspx files from the previous project and make the changes to it using the new assembly. To do this, follow these steps:

1. Copy the assembly to the *bin* directory in the virtual directory you created for this project. You can also copy the PDB file, which contains debugging information. These files will be located in a *bin* directory beneath your Visual Studio project directory on your computer.

2. Make a copy of the viewcontacts_vb.aspx file from the previous project, and put it into the root of your virtual directory.

3. Change the code in the Page_Load event handler to use the new object, as shown here:

```
Sub Page_Load(Src As Object, e As EventArgs)
    Dim sdrData As SqlDataReader
    Dim sb As New StringBuilder
    Dim strColor As String
    Dim db as new AtWorkUtilities.Database("server=localhost;" _
        & "database=ASPNetProject01;uid=sa;pwd=;")
    sdrData = db.GetDataReader("SELECT * FROM tblPeople " _
        & "ORDER BY LastName, FirstName")
    strColor = "tabletext"
    While sdrData.Read()
        sb.AppendFormat("<tr class=""{0}"">" + vbCrLf, strColor)
        sb.AppendFormat("    <td>{0}, {1}</td>" + vbCrLf, _
            sdrData("LastName"), _
            sdrData("FirstName"))
        sb.AppendFormat("    <td>{0}</td>" + vbCrLf, sdrData("Title"))
        sb.AppendFormat("    <td>{0}</td>" + vbCrLf, _
            sdrData("CompanyName"))
        sb.AppendFormat("    <td>{0}</td>" + vbCrLf, _
            sdrData("WorkPhone"))

        sb.Append("    <td align=middle>")
```

```
                sb.AppendFormat("<a href=""updatecontact_vb.aspx" _
                   & "?id={0}"">Update</a>", _
                   sdrData("pkPersonID"))
                sb.Append("  ")
                sb.AppendFormat("<a href=""deletecontact_vb.aspx" _
                   & "?id={0}"">Delete</a>", _
                   sdrData("pkPersonID"))
                sb.Append("    </td>")

                sb.Append("</tr>" + vbCrLf)
                If strColor = "tabletext" Then
                    strColor = "tabletext_gray"
                Else
                    strColor = "tabletext"
                End If
            End While
            sdrData.Close()
            db.Close()
            lblOutput.Text = sb.ToString()
        End Sub
```

When you run this page, you should see no difference between it and the previous version. All you see is that there is less code in this page since you've moved all the database code into the new Database class. If you repeat this throughout your application, you'll be pleasantly surprised at how much less code you'll be writing over and over again.

Build the BaseServices Class

The next step in our project is to build a number of classes that can communicate with the database. Each one of these classes needs some common services; we're going to build a base class that each of the data classes will inherit. This base class won't be one that can actually be created, since, by itself, it won't be able to do anything. However, it will provide some common services, such as error management and validation, which will be used in the other classes. The class code is shown in Listing 2.5, and the file is called BaseServices.vb on the companion CD-ROM.

```
Imports System.Text
Imports System.Data
Imports System.Data.SqlClient
Imports AtWorkUtilities

Public MustInherit Class BaseServices
    Private m_arrErrors As ArrayList
    Protected m_DB As Database
    Protected m_DA As SqlDataAdapter
    Protected m_CB As SqlCommandBuilder
```

Listing 2.5 BaseServices.vb

```
Protected m_DS As DataSet


'
' This constructor should be overloaded and called
' by each derived class. It sets up the protected
' objects available to all derived classes for handling
' database activities.
'
Protected Sub New(ByVal DB As Database, ByVal strSQL As String)
    m_DB = DB
    m_DA = New SqlDataAdapter(strSQL, m_DB.Connection)
    m_CB = New SqlCommandBuilder(m_DA)
    m_DS = New DataSet()
    m_DA.Fill(m_DS)
End Sub


'
' The DataSet will have either zero rows or one row
' so we simply return the current row in the dataset.
' This code makes it easier to get at the data instead
' of having to duplicate the full hierarchy in the
' calling code. For empty DataSets, we return an empty
' row that can be populated.
'
Public Function GetRow() As DataRow
    If m_DS.Tables(0).Rows.Count > 0 Then
        Return m_DS.Tables(0).Rows(0)
    Else
        Return m_DS.Tables(0).NewRow()
    End If
End Function


'
' This routine accepts a data row as input and stores
' the data into the dataset. In cases where the row
' is new, we add the new row to the DataSet. If the
' DataSet has data in it, we read the data row and
' replace each field in the DataSet one column at a
' time.
'
Protected Sub SaveRow(ByVal dr As DataRow)
    Dim val As DataColumn
    '
    ' Handle new row
    '
    If m_DS.Tables(0).Rows.Count = 0 Then
        m_DS.Tables(0).Rows.Add(dr)
        Exit Sub
    End If
```

Listing 2.5   BaseServices.vb (continued)

```
        `
        ` Handle existing row
        `
    m_DS.Tables(0).Rows(0).BeginEdit()
    For Each val In m_DS.Tables(0).Columns
        m_DS.Tables(0).Rows(0).Item(val) = dr.Item(val)
    Next
    m_DS.Tables(0).Rows(0).EndEdit()
End Sub


`
` Adds another validation error to the array list
` object. This saves some work for the calling/inheriting
` class.
`
Protected Sub AddError(ByVal strInput As String)
    If m_arrErrors Is Nothing Then
        m_arrErrors = New ArrayList()
    End If
    m_arrErrors.Add(strInput)
End Sub


`
` This method empties the array list of any previous errors
` that had been detected.
`
Protected Sub ClearErrors()
    If m_arrErrors Is Nothing Then
        m_arrErrors = New ArrayList()
    Else
        m_arrErrors.Clear()
    End If
End Sub


`
` This method formats the array into a message that can be
` used in a message box.
`
Public Function ValidationError( _
    Optional ByVal Header As String = _
        "The following errors were detected in your data:" & vbCrLf, _
    Optional ByVal ItemFormat As String = "- {0}" & vbCrLf, _
    Optional ByVal Footer As String = "") As String
    Dim strMessage As New StringBuilder()
    Dim strErr As String

    If m_arrErrors.Count > 0 Then
        strMessage.Append(Header)
        For Each strErr In m_arrErrors
            strMessage.AppendFormat(ItemFormat, strErr)
```

Listing 2.5   BaseServices.vb (continued)

```
        Next
        strMessage.Append(Footer)
        Return strMessage.ToString
    Else
        Return ""
    End If
End Function


'
' Provides access to the list of errors that were detected
' during the validation process. This is used for applications
' that need custom error messages.
'
Public ReadOnly Property ValidationErrors() As ArrayList
Get
    Return m_arrErrors
End Get
End Property


'
' Indicates whether any validation errors were detected
' as the data was stored into the object.
'
Public ReadOnly Property IsValid() As Boolean
Get
    Return (m_arrErrors.Count = 0)
End Get
End Property


End Class
```

Listing 2.5   BaseServices.vb (continued)

Let's go through each part of the BaseServices class so that you understand what each method and property is doing for the derived classes.

Writing the Class Declarations

The BaseServices class itself is defined as shown:

```
Public MustInherit Class BaseServices
```

The MustInherit keyword indicates that this class cannot be created. The only place that we can use this class is as a base class for other classes. Thus, other classes that inherit it can use the services provided by this class.

The next part is an ArrayList variable defined as follows:

```
Private m_arrErrors As ArrayList
```

The variable is declared as Private since we aren't going to access it directly outside of this class or any derived classes; instead, you'll create a property procedure to access it from this class. Private variables are not available in derived classes; instead, you have to access them using properties also located in the base class.

Write the Class Methods and Properties

The BaseServices class provides important functionality to the business object classes you will build later in this project. It knows how to communicate with the database so that we don't have to write the same tedious code repeatedly as we build the various classes. We're using a number of new features included in the .NET Framework to handle database activity, so let's go through each method in more detail now.

New Constructor

The New constructor is designed to be overloaded. In other words, a derived class that inherits BaseServices can use this base method in addition to its own implementation of the constructor. For instance, this constructor expects to receive a Database object and a SQL statement. In cases where there isn't already an existing database connection, the derived class will need to create one. In addition, the derived class will need to have a SQL statement so that we can connect to the proper table. Since this base class will be used for a variety of other classes, we don't want anything specific to one type of data in it.

The first object that we instantiate is the SqlDataAdapter object. The SqlDataAdapter is designed to make it easier to deal with SQL Server databases. In Project 1, you wrote quite a bit of code to make your database activity work properly. You wrote a Select statement, an Insert statement to add new rows, an Update statement to make changes, and a Delete statement to remove records. When you stop to think about it, each one of those statements could have been generated automatically as long as you knew the primary key of the table. The SqlDataAdapter does just that. When you create or instantiate the object, you give it a SQL statement as well as a SqlConnection object. The SQL statement you provide here is known as the SelectCommand and is stored in that property of the object. Since this statement includes the primary key, we can use the next object to do a little magic.

The SqlCommandBuilder object performs many of the tasks that ASP programmers, including myself, had done in previous versions of ASP. It looks at the SqlDataAdapter object, determines the structure of the table being used, and then automatically builds the Insert, Delete, and Update statements necessary to manage the table. In addition, it registers itself to listen for any events generated by the SqlDataAdapter that indicate data changes are taking place. When we call the Update method of the SqlDataAdapter, the SqlDataAdapter looks through the DataSet object (which we'll talk about next) and determines what rows have been added, modified, or deleted since the last save. It then generates events that the SqlCommandBuilder listens for in order to send the appropriate SQL statements. The end result is that you make all your changes in the DataSet and call the Update method of the SqlDataAdapter to make all the changes for you. It saves a lot of work and a lot of tedious code writing in which you populate a long SQL statement or a long list of parameters for a SqlCommand object.

The DataSet object is another new object in .NET and is roughly equivalent to a record set in old Active Data Objects. However, it does have some distinct differences, the key one being that a DataSet object is not tied to any particular type of database. There isn't a SqlDataSet or OleDBDataSet object—just a DataSet object. A DataSet object has the ability to store multiple tables of data. Each of these tables is a DataTable object, containing a Rows collection; each Row is a DataRow object. We'll be manipulating DataRow objects when we want to save the data. These DataRows are stored in the DataTable and DataSet objects. The DataSet object is fed back into the SqlDataAdapter to make the changes permanent. We'll be covering many of the features of the DataSet object in this book, but for more information, refer to the MSDN documentation on this object as well as the rest of the data objects. If you'd like a good book on the new ADO.NET, check out *Programming ADO.NET* by Richard Hundhausen and Steven Borg (John Wiley & Sons, 2002).

GetRow Function

The DataSet object that we'll keep in memory will have either zero rows or one row in it at any time. For cases where we don't instantiate the derived class with a primary key ID, we're going to add a new row, and the GetRow function will return an empty row that we can then fill up. For cases where we did provide a primary key, the constructor selected that row from the database and populated it into the DataSet object. We simply return that single row to the caller so that it can be edited.

SaveRow Function

The derived class will overload this routine, but this base class function does handle some key tasks and has to be called by the derived class. First of all, it accepts a DataRow object containing either a new record or a modified copy of the current record. For new records, the DataRow is simply added to the DataSet. Modified records are a little harder since we can't just store the DataRow into the DataSet. Instead, we take the fields from the copy and put them into the original one in the DataSet using a loop. The derived class will then need to call any other validation or other code that needs to be run once this step is complete.

Data Validation Utilities

All the derived classes will have validation code in them verifying data before we attempt to store it in the database. The DataSet object is useful; however, it doesn't prevent you from putting potentially bad data into it. In addition, there are cases in which we have custom validation that involves more than one field at a time. The derived class is responsible for its own validation, but the BaseServices class provides some utilities to make it easier.

Before validation starts, the derived class can reset the error list by calling the ClearErrors method, which eliminates any past errors. As errors are detected during validation, the derived class can call the AddError method. This method accepts a string as input and stores the string in the private variable called m_arrErrors. This ArrayList accumulates all the collected errors as the validation continues.

Once the validation routine is complete, the derived class has a few options for displaying the error. The ValidationError function allows the errors to be returned in a variety of formats. The ValidationError function accepts a string as input for the header of the error message, a format string for each validation error that was detected, and a string for the footer of the message. The default format for the error message looks something like this:

```
The following errors were detected in your data:
- error message 1
- error message 2
```

You can easily supply other information for the default (and optional) parameters to this function. This routine can also be used to generate HTML lists of various sorts, or even JavaScript, with a little bit of extra work.

The last feature provided here is a simple property called IsValid that returns a True if no errors are in the validation error array. This provides a quick check for any calling code before it attempts to save data permanently.

The point behind these features is to provide services to the base classes. The base class does not force anything to happen, such as throwing an exception if an error is stored, although it could. I prefer to build the object with features that I can use in a logical method elsewhere.

Build the Person Class

The first class we'll build in this project that deals specifically with data is the Person class. It will use the BaseServices class as its base class and build functionality on top of that. The Person class will:

- Allow code to create either a new object of this type or pass in a primary key for a person to load from the database.
- Make the existing data available or allow a new row to be added to the table.
- Validate the data before saving it to the database.
- Provide a list of error messages applicable to the object's data.
- Save the new or updated record to the database.

The complete listing for the Person class is shown in Listing 2.6. Because the class code is quite lengthy, we'll work through each logical chunk one at a time.

```
Imports AtWorkUtilities
Imports System.Data.SqlClient


Public Class Person
    Inherits BaseServices
```

Listing 2.6   Person.vb Class

```
'
' If no arguments are supplied, build a separate
' database connection for this object.
'
Public Sub New()
   MyBase.New(New Database(), "SELECT * FROM tblPeople WHERE 1=0")
End Sub


'
' If database connection is supplied, store it
' in the private connection variable for this
' object.
'
Public Sub New(ByVal db As Database)
   MyBase.New(db, "SELECT * FROM tblPeople WHERE 1=0")
End Sub


'
' If both database and ID are supplied, retrieve
' data into the object from the database.
'
Public Sub New(ByVal db As Database, _
   ByVal ID As Integer)

   MyBase.New(db, "SELECT * FROM tblPeople WHERE pkPersonID = " _
      & ID.ToString)

End Sub


'
' Verify that all data validation rules have been
' met. Any errors get stored into the errors collection
' inherited from the BaseServices class.
'
Public Sub Validate()
   Dim dr As DataRow

   ClearErrors()
   For Each dr In m_DS.Tables(0).Rows
      If dr.RowState = DataRowState.Added _
      Or dr.RowState = DataRowState.Modified Then
         ValidateRow(dr)
      End If
   Next

End Sub


'
' Checks an individual row for validation rule
' compliance. Any errors are added to the errors
```

Listing 2.6 Person.vb Class (continued)

```vb
' collection.
'
Private Sub ValidateRow(ByVal dr As DataRow)

    If IsDBNull(dr("CompanyName")) And _
        IsDBNull(dr("LastName")) And _
        IsDBNull(dr("FirstName")) Then
        AddError("You must provide the company name, " _
            & "the person's first or last name.")
    End If

    If Not IsDBNull(dr("CompanyName")) And _
        Not IsDBNull(dr("LastName")) And _
        Not IsDBNull(dr("FirstName")) Then
        If dr("CompanyName") = "" _
        And dr("LastName") = "" _
        And dr("FirstName") = "" Then
            AddError("You must provide the company name, " _
                & "the person's first or last name.")
        End If
    End If

    If Not IsDBNull(dr("LastName")) Then
        If dr("LastName").Length > 40 Then
            AddError("Last name must be less than 40 characters long.")
        End If
    End If

    If Not IsDBNull(dr("FirstName")) Then
        If dr("FirstName").Length > 40 Then
            AddError("First name must be less than 40 characters long.")
        End If
    End If

    If Not IsDBNull(dr.Item("Title")) Then
        If dr("Title").Length > 80 Then
            AddError("Title must be less than 80 characters long.")
        End If
    End If

    If Not IsDBNull(dr.Item("Title")) Then
        If dr("CompanyName").Length > 80 Then
            AddError("Company name must be less than 80 characters
long.")
        End If
    End If

    If Not IsDBNull(dr.Item("Title")) Then
        If dr("Address").Length > 240 Then
            AddError("Address must be less than 240 characters long.")
```

Listing 2.6 Person.vb Class (continued)

```
            End If
        End If

        If Not IsDBNull(dr.Item("Title")) Then
            If dr("HomePhone").Length > 40 Then
                AddError("Home phone must be less than 40 characters long.")
            End If
        End If

        If Not IsDBNull(dr.Item("Title")) Then
            If dr("WorkPhone").Length > 40 Then
                AddError("Work phone must be less than 40 characters long.")
            End If
        End If

        If Not IsDBNull(dr.Item("Title")) Then
            If dr("Fax").Length > 40 Then
                AddError("Fax number must be less than 40 characters long.")
            End If
        End If

        If Not IsDBNull(dr.Item("Title")) Then
            If dr("EMail").Length > 120 Then
                AddError("Email address must be less than " _
                    & "120 characters long.")
            End If
        End If

        If Not IsDBNull(dr.Item("Title")) Then
            If dr("WebPage").Length > 120 Then
                AddError("Web page address must be less than " _
                    & "120 characters long.")
            End If
        End If

End Sub


' The base SaveRow method stores the DataRow into the
' DataSet, whether it's a new or existing row. The
' rest of this routine handles specific validation
' for this type of data.

Public Overloads Sub SaveRow(ByVal dr As DataRow)
    MyBase.SaveRow(dr)
    Validate()

End Sub


' We separate the SaveRow method from the Save method
' to give us a chance to handle any validation. We have
```

Listing 2.6   Person.vb Class (continued)

```
' a verification here that the data is good before we
' continue, however.
'
Public Sub Save()

    If Not Me.IsValid Then
        Throw New PersonException(Me.ValidationError)

        Exit Sub
    End If

    m_DA.Update(m_DS)
End Sub


'
' Since we only have a single row in our DataSet,
' delete it and then update the database with the
' change.
'
Public Sub Delete()
    If m_DS.Tables(0).Rows.Count > 0 Then
        m_DS.Tables(0).Rows(0).Delete()
        m_DA.Update(m_DS)
    End If
End Sub

End Class
```

Listing 2.6   Person.vb Class (continued)

Set Up the Class Structure

The first part of the class sets up the inheritance between this class and the BaseServices class. It also makes the SQL Server objects and the utility objects available by way of an Imports statement. We can always access our Database object as AtWorkUtilities.Database, but the Imports statement eliminates the need to type the namespace every time. In some cases, you may have to type the namespace to properly select the class. For example, if you have two assemblies, each of which has a class called Account, specifying the namespace will select the right one. In this case, we only have one Database class, so the Imports statement saves us from typing and makes the code a bit shorter. It doesn't translate into more or less efficient code, since the compiler will figure out which object we need and use the correct one with or without the namespace prefix.

```
Imports AtWorkUtilities
Imports System.Data.SqlClient
```

```
Public Class Person
   Inherits BaseServices
```

The next step is to define any variables that need to be used at the class level. However, for this particular class, all the important variables are already defined in the BaseServices class.

Write the Class Constructors

The Person class has three constructors. The first takes no parameters and is used to create a new object of this type. The SQL statement is used to format the structure of the tblPeople table so that the SqlDataAdapter object and the SqlCommandBuilder objects will work properly. The statement is written to never return any records—just the structure of the table.

```
'
' If no arguments are supplied, build a separate
' database connection for this object.
'
Public Sub New()
   MyBase.New(New Database(), "SELECT * FROM tblPeople WHERE 1=0")
End Sub
```

The second constructor accepts a Database object, but is also used for a new record. This handles cases in which the database connection has already been established.

```
'
' If database connection is supplied, store it
' in the private connection variable for this
' object.
'
Public Sub New(ByVal db As Database)
   MyBase.New(db, "SELECT * FROM tblPeople WHERE 1=0")
End Sub
```

The final constructor accepts both a database connection and the unique ID of the person to load. This case is used to edit the record.

```
'
' If both database and ID are supplied, retrieve
' data into the object from the database.
'
Public Sub New(ByVal db As Database, _
   ByVal ID As Integer)

   MyBase.New(db, "SELECT * FROM tblPeople WHERE pkPersonID = " _
      & ID.ToString)

End Sub
```

Note that each constructor calls MyBase.New. The MyBase object refers to the base class from which this class derived; in this case, the base class is BaseServices.

Create the Validation Routine

The next step is to build the validation routine that validates the data in the object. Having the validation in the Person class keeps it consolidated in one place. The validation routine verifies that all the fields are less than the maximum length defined by the database table. It also makes sure that either the person's first and last name are supplied or that the company name is supplied. You could also write code verifying that the email address and Web page are properly formatted.

The first part of the routine is the public method, called Validate. This checks the data currently in the object's DataSet to verify that it meets the data validation rules that you have created in your object. Although we are only storing a single row, we use a loop here to go through all the rows anyway, thus supporting future expansion of the class to handle multiple additions at the same time. Building the loop here this way saves you from having to recode it later.Before validation, we check the row's Row-State property. This property gives us an indication as to what has been done to the row. A row can be unmodified, added, modified, deleted, or detached. We don't need to validate deleted rows, and we're not using the DataSet feature to detach rows, so we only check the new or modified rows. Detached rows are DataRow objects that have either not been added to a DataSet or ones that were removed from a DataSet. Since the rows we are checking are always part of a DataSet, we don't have to worry about detached rows here.

```
'
' Verify that all data validation rules have been
' met. Any errors get stored into the errors collection
' inherited from the BaseServices class.
'
Public Sub Validate()
   Dim dr As DataRow

   ClearErrors()
   For Each dr In m_DS.Tables(0).Rows
      If dr.RowState = DataRowState.Added _
      Or dr.RowState = DataRowState.Modified Then
         ValidateRow(dr)
      End If
   Next

End Sub
```

The private ValidateRow routine checks each row of data against the various rules we've already described. Note that we have to verify that a field is non-null before we attempt to check the data. If we don't do that, we get errors. We use the IsDBNull function to check for null in an object like this. Each field's length is verified. We also check the first fields to verify that at least a company name, first, or last name is provided.

```
'
' Checks an individual row for validation rule
' compliance. Any errors are added to the errors
' collection.
'
Private Sub ValidateRow(ByVal dr As DataRow)

    If IsDBNull(dr("CompanyName")) And _
        IsDBNull(dr("LastName")) And _
        IsDBNull(dr("FirstName")) Then
        AddError("You must provide the company name, " _
            & "the person's first or last name.")
    End If

    If Not IsDBNull(dr("CompanyName")) And _
        Not IsDBNull(dr("LastName")) And _
        Not IsDBNull(dr("FirstName")) Then
        If dr("CompanyName") = "" _
        And dr("LastName") = "" _
        And dr("FirstName") = "" Then
            AddError("You must provide the company name, " _
                & "the person's first or last name.")
        End If
    End If

    If Not IsDBNull(dr("LastName")) Then
        If dr("LastName").Length > 40 Then
            AddError("Last name must be less than 40 characters long.")
        End If
    End If

    If Not IsDBNull(dr("FirstName")) Then
        If dr("FirstName").Length > 40 Then
            AddError("First name must be less than 40 characters long.")
        End If
    End If

    If Not IsDBNull(dr.Item("Title")) Then
        If dr("Title").Length > 80 Then
            AddError("Title must be less than 80 characters long.")
        End If
    End If

    If Not IsDBNull(dr.Item("Title")) Then
        If dr("CompanyName").Length > 80 Then
            AddError("Company name must be less than 80 characters long.")
        End If
    End If

    If Not IsDBNull(dr.Item("Title")) Then
        If dr("Address").Length > 240 Then
            AddError("Address must be less than 240 characters long.")
```

```
          End If
     End If

     If Not IsDBNull(dr.Item("Title")) Then
         If dr("HomePhone").Length > 40 Then
             AddError("Home phone must be less than 40 characters long.")
         End If
     End If

     If Not IsDBNull(dr.Item("Title")) Then
         If dr("WorkPhone").Length > 40 Then
             AddError("Work phone must be less than 40 characters long.")
         End If
     End If

     If Not IsDBNull(dr.Item("Title")) Then
         If dr("Fax").Length > 40 Then
             AddError("Fax number must be less than 40 characters long.")
         End If
     End If

     If Not IsDBNull(dr.Item("Title")) Then
         If dr("EMail").Length > 120 Then
             AddError("Email address must be less than 120 characters
 long.")
         End If
     End If

     If Not IsDBNull(dr.Item("Title")) Then
         If dr("WebPage").Length > 120 Then
             AddError("Web page address must be less than 120 " _
                 & "characters long.")
         End If
     End If

 End Sub
```

Build the Save Routine

Most of the work in the save routine is handled automatically by the SqlCommand-Builder and SqlDataAdapter objects in the BaseServices class. We need two methods in the derived class to make this code work. The first, SaveRow, takes either a new or modified row and puts it back into the DataSet object by calling the SaveRow method of the base class. Once the data is saved to the DataSet object, the validation routine is called.

```
 '
 ' The base Save method stores the DataRow into the
 ' DataSet, whether it's a new or existing row. The
```

```
' rest of this routine handles specific validation
' for this type of data.
'
Public Overloads Sub SaveRow(ByVal dr As DataRow)
   MyBase.SaveRow(dr)
   Validate()

End Sub
```

The second part of the save routine is called to store the changes to the database. This routine has a safety check that won't let the data be saved if any validation errors are still present. The Save method is meant to be called separately once the calling code has cleared any validation errors. The IsValid property, as well as the other validation features provided by BaseServices, are meant for these tasks.

```
'
' We separate the SaveRow method from the Save method
' to give us a chance to handle any validation. We have
' a verification here that the data is good before we
' continue, however.
'
Public Sub Save()

   If Not Me.IsValid Then
      Throw New PersonException(Me.ValidationError)
      Exit Sub
   End If

   m_DA.Update(m_DS)
End Sub
```

At this point, the data has been saved and the calling application would continue. In the Web portion of the application, when the data is saved, the Web browser is returned to the list of available records, which reflects any changes you made using the object.

Build the Delete Routine

The one feature we haven't handled yet is the deletion of records. We'll use a separate Delete method for this function. We can delete rows from the DataSet object, and when the DataSet is updated, the row will be removed from the database. You need to be careful with this method, however; certain types of records should never actually be deleted. For instance, if you have a table that has a reference to a customer table, you can't simply delete the customer without taking care of the reference first. In some databases, like Access and SQL Server, you can instruct the database to delete any related records. In this example, any records related to the customer you delete would also be deleted. However, this has the unfortunate side effect of eliminating any history of that customer as ever having existed. The implementation you choose may simply mark a row as deleted but not really delete it. Any lists of records can then look at the record to see if the "Deleted" flag that you marked is set; if so, the record would not show up in reports. Most larger systems implement a system like this to prevent important data from being lost, while at the same time allowing the database to be trimmed to active records only.

In this portion of the project, we'll actually be removing the records from the database since we are not dealing with critical data. You'll also be updating any related tables in the project. The code to handle deletions is shown here:

```
'
' Since we only have a single row in our DataSet,
' delete it and then update the database with the
' change.
'
Public Sub Delete()
    If m_DS.Tables(0).Rows.Count > 0 Then
        m_DS.Tables(0).Rows(0).Delete()
        m_DA.Update(m_DS)
    End If
End Sub
```

For this task, we remove the row from the DataSet object and call Update directly from here. There's no need to do validation since we don't have to validate data we're removing.

Creating the PersonException Class

One of the best new features of .NET is the ability to do structured exception handling. In traditional VB and ASP programming, you had to look for particular error numbers to detect when certain errors occurred. This led to conflicts if you picked an error number that was already used.

In .NET programming, you can use the built-in Exception class for your errors. As you saw in the code listing for this class, we want to generate an error if the caller of the code attempts to save the data in the object before all the validation errors have been cleared. While we could simply raise an error of type Exception, the code where the exception is handled would not know where the error originated. Instead, we will inherit from the base Exception class and create our own class called PersonException. The best thing about inheritance is that we don't have to reinvent the wheel for error handling. We simply call the methods of the base class for each of the constructors supported by the Exception class. Microsoft recommends implementing all the constructors for maximum flexibility in custom Exception classes.

The code for the PersonException class is shown here:

```
Public Class PersonException
    Inherits Exception

    Public Sub New()
        MyBase.New()
    End Sub
```

```
Public Sub New(ByVal Message As String)
    MyBase.New(Message)
End Sub

Public Sub New(ByVal Message As String, ByVal baseError As Exception)
    MyBase.New(Message, baseError)
End Sub

End Class
```

There are three ways to create a PersonException object: no parameters, a message only, or a message and another Exception object. The third method is used so that you can build a "chain" of errors. If your object failed because of another exception, you can pass that Exception object as part of your new exception. This provides the debugging information on the Web page for the developer.

For each of these constructors, we use the MyBase object to refer to the class from which we are inheriting. The base Exception class has these three constructors, so we pass the data on from the PersonException's constructors to the Exception constructors. Our PersonException class will work just like the base Exception class wherever we want to use it.

We'll be building custom Exception classes throughout the rest of the book whenever we create business objects in the way we did in this section. While we should never see this exception occur because of the way we handle errors, we are taking steps to safeguard the data from possible problems caused by other applications using these objects.

Build and Test the Assembly

Now that you've got all the code written for your Database, BaseServices, and Person classes, it's time to build the assembly and a test application where you can exercise the features of your classes. If you haven't done so already, you'll need to include some references between the projects:

AtWorkUtilities Assembly. No project references required.

BusinessObjects Assembly. Reference to AtWorkUtilities project required.

If you don't have these references, you'll probably be seeing a lot of blue squiggly lines under all the objects from each assembly. To add a reference to a project, right-click the References item in the Solution Explorer window. You'll be able to add the project references in the dialog box that appears.

When the references are in place, you can build the solution by selecting the Build Solution choice from the Build menu, or by using the appropriate toolbar button. Once you've debugged any typos that you may have made, you're ready to test the functions of your assemblies. In the following sections, you'll test each piece of functionality:

- Adding a record
- Editing an existing record
- Deleting a record

To make it easier to test these functions, you'll be building a simple Windows application in which you will write code to populate and call methods on your Person object to test it. Testing the object individually is a good idea to make sure that it works by itself before you wrap Web pages around it, thus creating other places for errors to occur.

Adding a Record

Once the assemblies are built, you can create a test project to try out the various objects. You can choose any type of application you want, but I've created a simple Windows application that I can use for testing. You'll first want to reference both the AtWorkUtilities and BusinessObjects projects in the References section of the project you choose. In the Form_Load event of my Windows application, I wrote the following code to test the addition of a new record:

```
Private Sub Form1_Load(ByVal sender As System.Object, _
    ByVal e As System.EventArgs) Handles MyBase.Load

    Dim db As New AtWorkUtilities.Database("server=localhost;" _
        & "database=ASPNetProject02;uid=sa;pwd=;")
    Dim o As New BusinessObjects.Person(db)
    Dim dr As DataRow

    dr = o.GetRow()
    dr("FirstName") = "Joe"
    dr("LastName") = "Shmo"
    dr("CompanyName") = "New Company"
    dr("WebPage") = "http://www.shmo.com"
    o.SaveRow(dr)
    If o.IsValid Then
        o.Save()
    Else
        MessageBox.Show(o.ValidationError())
    End If
    db.Close()

End Sub
```

Begin by creating a Database object by passing in the connection string. Don't forget to change the connection string to point to your local computer. Then create a Person object, using the constructor that accepts a database connection. Behind the scenes, the Person object is setting itself up to add a new record, which is done by retrieving an empty row using the GetRow method. We populate a few of the fields and then call the SaveRow method to store the DataRow back into the internal DataSet object. If the data is valid, we call the Save method. Otherwise, an error message generated by the object is displayed. If we were building a real application, we would display the message to the user, have him or her correct the error, and try saving the data again.

Editing an Existing Record

Code for testing the editing feature is basically the same, except for the constructor that we call. You'll need to check your database and find the pkPersonID for a record that you can use in the code shown here:

```
Private Sub Form1_Load(ByVal sender As System.Object, _
   ByVal e As System.EventArgs) Handles MyBase.Load

   Dim db As New AtWorkUtilities.Database("server=localhost;" _
      & "database=ASPNetProject02;uid=sa;pwd=;")
   Dim o As New BusinessObjects.Person(db, 61)
   Dim dr As DataRow

   dr = o.GetRow()
   dr("FirstName") = "Joe"
   dr("LastName") = "Shmo"
   dr("CompanyName") = "New Company #2"
   dr("WebPage") = "http://www.shmo2.com"
   o.SaveRow(dr)
   If o.IsValid Then
      o.Save()
   Else
      MessageBox.Show(o.ValidationError())
   End If
   db.Close()

End Sub
```

In this code, you'll want to replace the "61" with the primary key value of a record you can edit. The object hides the details of how adding records is different from editing them. This makes it easier to use these objects in your other applications.

Deleting a Record

The Delete function is probably the easiest to test since you don't really have to do anything other than create the Person object, as shown here:

```
Private Sub Form1_Load(ByVal sender As System.Object, _
   ByVal e As System.EventArgs) Handles MyBase.Load

   Dim db As New AtWorkUtilities.Database("server=localhost;" _
      & "database=ASPNetProject02;uid=sa;pwd=;")
   Dim o As New BusinessObjects.Person(db, 61)
   o.Delete()
   db.Close()
End Sub
```

This causes the SqlDataAdapter to remove the row by way of the SqlCommand-Builder object. When you check your table, the row in question has been removed.

Deploy the Assemblies

The next step in this project is to take the assemblies we built and use them in the Web application that we created in Project 1. These objects remove a great deal of the manual data-access code that we had to write and makes it faster to add new pages to the site. We have four files to modify:

- View People
- Add Person
- Modify Person
- Delete Person

We're using the term Person here instead of Contact, since we'll now have a Contact object, which is an instance of you corresponding or talking to a Person. We'll be making minor changes to filenames and page titles to make this consistent throughout the application.

Set Up

The first thing that we have to do to make these changes is to take the assemblies we built and put them on our Web server. Unlike the old way, which involved installation and registration, we can simply copy the DLLs that we built into a *bin* directory at the root of the Web application. You'll want to copy both the AtWorkUtilities and BusinessObjects assemblies to your *bin* directory on your Web server. If you don't have one yet, create one at the root directory of your Web site or Web application. The output DLL files are located in the *bin* directory beneath the Visual Studio project directory on your computer. If you see .PDB files, those are debugging symbol files that should be copied as well. You wouldn't do this in a production environment, but for now, you do need them for certain debugging applications.

Rebuild the View People Page

The next step is to make changes to the View People page. This page will be named Viewpeople.aspx, and we'll use a new method of coding Web pages called "Code Behind." The Code Behind method uses a more structured approach to building Web pages, and physically separates the visual design from the code that makes things work. As you'll see, it's easier to follow, especially for larger applications, as this one is slowly becoming.

The first page we need to change is the HTML portion of the code, which will be called Viewpeople.aspx. The code for this file is shown in Listing 2.7.

```
<%@ Page Inherits="Proj02Web.ViewPeople" Src="viewpeople.aspx.vb" %>

<html>
   <head>
      <title>Contact Manager: View All People</title>
<!-#include file="styles.css" ->
   </head>
   <body bgcolor="#FFFFFF">
      <p class="pageheading">View All People</p>
      <p class="tabletext">
      <a href="addperson.aspx">Add New Person</a>
      </p>

      <table cellpadding="4" cellspacing="0" width="100%">
      <tr class="tableheading">
         <td>Name</td>
         <td>Title</td>
         <td>Company Name</td>
         <td>Work Phone</td>
         <td>Actions</td>
      </tr>

      <asp:label id="lblOutput" runat="server"></asp:Label>

   </table>
   </body>
</html>
```

Listing 2.7 Viewpeople.aspx

All the Visual Basic .NET code has been removed from the file. The only clue you have to the code's whereabouts is in the new Page directive at the top of the page:

```
<%@ Page Inherits="Proj02Web.ViewPeople" Src="viewpeople.aspx.vb" %>
```

This directive instructs the ASP.NET engine that the page uses the ViewPeople class in the Proj02Web namespace and that the source for the class is in the viewpeople. aspx.vb file.

The only other changes in this page are the global changes of Contact to Person. The application is still called Contact Manager for our project, but you can rename it as you see fit. We modified the link to add a person so that it points to Addperson.aspx, which we'll modify in the next section.

The code for this page is placed in Viewpeople.aspx.vb, and is basically the code that we had previously, with a few minor changes, shown in bold. The code is shown in Listing 2.8.

```
Imports System
Imports System.Data
Imports System.Data.SqlClient
Imports System.Text
Imports System.Environment
Imports System.Web.UI
Imports System.Web.UI.WebControls


Namespace Proj02Web
    Public Class ViewPeople
        Inherits System.Web.UI.Page

        Protected lblOutput As Label

        Sub Page_Load(Src As Object, e As EventArgs)
            Dim sdrData As SqlDataReader
            Dim sb As New StringBuilder
            Dim strColor As String
            Dim db as New AtWorkUtilities.Database("server=localhost;" _
                & "database=ASPNetProject02;uid=sa;pwd=;")
            sdrData = db.GetDataReader("SELECT * FROM tblPeople " _
                & "ORDER BY LastName, FirstName")
            strColor = "tabletext"
            While sdrData.Read()
                sb.AppendFormat("<tr class=""{0}"">" + NewLine, strColor)
                sb.AppendFormat("   <td>{0}, {1}</td>" + NewLine, _
                    sdrData("LastName"), _
                    sdrData("FirstName"))
                sb.AppendFormat("   <td>{0}</td>" + NewLine,_
                    sdrData("Title"))
                sb.AppendFormat("   <td>{0}</td>" + NewLine, _
                    sdrData("CompanyName"))
                sb.AppendFormat("   <td>{0}</td>" + NewLine, _
                    sdrData("WorkPhone"))

                sb.Append("   <td align=middle>")
                sb.AppendFormat("<a href=""updateperson.aspx" _
                    & "?id={0}"">Update</a>", _
                    sdrData("pkPersonID"))
                sb.Append("  ")
                sb.AppendFormat("<a href=""deleteperson.aspx" _
                    & "?id={0}"">Delete</a>" + NewLine, _
                    sdrData("pkPersonID"))
                sb.Append("   </td>" + NewLine)
                sb.Append("</tr>" + NewLine)
                If strColor = "tabletext" Then
                    strColor = "tabletext_gray"
                Else
                    strColor = "tabletext"
                End If
```

Listing 2.8 Viewpeople.aspx.vb

```
            End While
            sdrData.Close()
            db.Close()
            lblOutput.Text = sb.ToString()
        End Sub
    End Class
End Namespace
```

Listing 2.8 Viewpeople.aspx.vb (continued)

There are a few new libraries referenced at the top of the page in the Imports statements. Note that we don't have to declare them the way we did in Project 1. Since this file is all VB code, we can use the standard Imports statement the same way we did in our other classes.

The new libraries we've added are:

System.Text. Provides a StringBuilder object

System.Environment. Provides a NewLine object replacing the vbCrLf from older versions of ASP

System.Web.UI. Provides the ability to inherit from the Page class and create our own page class

System.Web.UI.WebControls. Provides the ability to use the Label control from within this class

The next batch of changes is in the way we start the code. Instead of starting with a SCRIPT tag, we first create a namespace and class declaration. The namespace and class names don't really matter; however, in larger applications you might want to combine more than one class into a single code-behind file. In this case, the class and namespace hierarchy will become far more important. We also mark the ViewPeople class as inheriting from Page, which is actually System.Web.UI.Page. This Page object is integral to making the Code-Behind class work properly. The Page object itself will provide a link to the operating system and the .NET Framework and allow our page to receive the events any other Page receives.

The final bit of new code here is the declaration of the lblOutput control as a Label. You're probably wondering why we do this, especially since the control is already declared on the page as the destination for our output text. When using a code-behind page, you have to explicitly create class-level variables for each ASP.NET server control on your ASP.NET page. The system will link the controls on the page to your variables automatically, so any changes you make to the local variable will be reflected in the output page. The data flow goes the other way as well. When we create the code-behind page for the add and edit functions, we'll have variables declared for each control and we'll read the contents into our Person object.

Once we finish declaring the class, we have our Page_Load event handler, as in the previous project. Instead of creating the SqlDataReader directly from the SqlConnection object, use the Database object. This gives you the ability to store the connection string in the Web.config file since the Database object will read from that file if not given a connection string of its own.

The last change we had to make was to replace the vbCrLf constant with the New-Line constant available from the System.Environment object. The vbCrLf constant is left in when you're writing consolidated pages, but it is not available by default when you go to the code-behind method. Since we want to be consistent with the new way of doing things in ASP.NET and the .NET Framework, we use the NewLine constant. This provides the ability to use a different NewLine string if you're on a different environment, such as Linux/UNIX, which doesn't use the carriage return/line feed combination to mark a new line. We've replaced all the vbCrLf constants with this NewLine constant, and the page runs as before. Just remember to put the End Class and End Namespace statements at the bottom of the file.

Rebuild the Add Person Page

The next page to convert handles the addition of a new person to the database. The new ASPX file, called Addperson.aspx, is shown in Listing 2.9. It follows the same format as the Viewpeople.aspx file, but it uses the Inputform.inc (formerly known as Inputform.aspx) to provide the same form used in the edit function.

```
<%@ Page Inherits="Proj02Web.AddPerson" Src="addperson.aspx.vb" %>
<html>
   <head>
      <title>Contact Manager: Add New Contact</title>
<!--#include file="styles.css" -->
   </head>
   <body bgcolor="#FFFFFF">
   <p class="pageheading">Add New Contact</p>

   <asp:label id="lblErrorMessage" class="errortext" runat="server" />

<!--#include file="inputform.inc" -->
   </body>
</html>
```

Listing 2.9   Addperson.aspx

The other addition here is a new label control called lblErrorMessage, which stays hidden as long as no errors are generated during validation. If errors are generated, they are displayed in this space. The Class attribute in the label control refers to a Style Sheet class that you can create for this purpose. The style sheet is basically the same as before, with a minor addition highlighted in bold in Listing 2.10.

```
<style type="text/css" title="Application Style Sheet">
<!--
.pageheading
{
    COLOR: #000000;
    FONT-FAMILY: Tahoma, Arial;
```

Listing 2.10   Styles.css

```
      FONT-SIZE: 16pt;
      FONT-WEIGHT: bold;
}
.tableheading
{
   COLOR: #FFFFFF;
   FONT-FAMILY: Tahoma, Arial;
   FONT-WEIGHT: bold;
   FONT-SIZE: 9pt;
   BACKGROUND-COLOR: #AA0000;
   TEXT-ALIGN: center;
}
.errortext
{
   COLOR: #FF0000;
   FONT-FAMILY: Tahoma, Arial;
   FONT-SIZE: 9pt;
}

.tabletext
{
   COLOR: #000000;
   FONT-FAMILY: Tahoma, Arial;
   FONT-SIZE: 9pt;
}
.tabletext_gray
{
   COLOR: #000000;
   FONT-FAMILY: Tahoma, Arial;
   FONT-SIZE: 9pt;
   BACKGROUND-COLOR: #CCCCCC;
}

-->
</style>
```

Listing 2.10   Styles.css (continued)

By using a Style Sheet class here, we eliminate the need to do a lot of manual HTML formatting and can keep our formatting consistent between pages.

The code-behind for this page is shown in Listing 2.11 and uses the new Database and Person objects to handle data storage tasks. As you can see, the code here is easier to follow than the older version that used manually built SQL statements to save information.

```
Imports System
Imports System.Data
Imports System.Data.SqlClient
Imports System.Text
Imports System.Environment
Imports System.Web.UI
Imports System.Web.UI.WebControls

Namespace Proj02Web
    Public Class AddPerson
        Inherits System.Web.UI.Page
        Protected txtLastName As TextBox
        Protected txtFirstName As TextBox
        Protected txtTitle As TextBox
        Protected txtCompanyName As TextBox
        Protected txtAddress As TextBox
        Protected txtHomePhone As TextBox
        Protected txtWorkPhone As TextBox
        Protected txtFaxNumber As TextBox
        Protected txtEMail As TextBox
        Protected txtWebPage As TextBox
        Protected txtNotes As TextBox
        Protected lblErrorMessage As Label

        Sub Page_Load(objSender As Object, objArgs As EventArgs)

            If Page.IsPostBack Then
                Dim DB As New AtWorkUtilities.Database()
                Dim P As New BusinessObjects.Person(DB)
                Dim DR As DataRow = P.GetRow()
                DR("LastName") = txtLastName.Text
                DR("FirstName") = txtFirstName.Text
                DR("Title") = txtTitle.Text
                DR("CompanyName") = txtCompanyName.Text
                DR("Address") = txtAddress.Text
                DR("HomePhone") = txtHomePhone.Text
                DR("WorkPhone") = txtWorkPhone.Text
                DR("Fax") = txtFaxNumber.Text
                DR("EMail") = txtEMail.Text
                DR("WebPage") = txtWebPage.Text
                DR("Notes") = txtNotes.Text
                P.SaveRow(DR)
                If Not P.IsValid Then
                   lblErrorMessage.Text = _
                      P.ValidationError("<b>ERROR:</b> The following " _
                         & "errors were detected in your data:<br>", _
                         "&bull; {0}<br>", "")
                Else
                   P.Save()
                   DB.Close()
```

Listing 2.11   Addperson.aspx.vb

```
                    Response.Redirect("viewpeople.aspx")
              End If
          End If
      End Sub

    End Class
End Namespace
```

Listing 2.11 Addperson.aspx.vb (continued)

Initially, we don't have any work to do, since we want an empty form to be displayed. However, when the user clicks the Save button, the IsPostBack property of the form will be True, and we have some work to do. As in the previous code-behind page, we have to declare class variables for each of the controls on the page. We then instantiate a Database object, which in this case uses the ConnectionString stored in the Web.config file. If you want, you can put the connection string in manually, but that's up to you. We then create a new Person object and pass it the Database object. Since we're creating a new record, we don't have an ID to supply the Person's constructor method. The GetRow method of the Person object returns an empty row that we can populate with data from the form. One interesting thing about reading data from Web pages is that even if the field is empty, it is not considered null and won't be trapped by the IsDBNull. That's why the validation routine checks for both nulls and empty strings. After we store all the form data, we call the SaveRow method to put the row back into the object. The validation routine is called behind the scenes, and we can see the results by using the IsValid property and the ValidationError message, which is shown to the user if necessary. Instead of the default format, we use a small amount of HTML to format the message for Web viewing. If everything is fine, we save the data, close the database connection, and return to the list window.

The Person object has simplified our life here and makes the application more consistent. If we ever need to change the validation rules, we simply change the Business object. If we need to use the object in other applications, we can. We've also eliminated a lot of tedious code when we got rid of the SQL statement builder. The other method works, but this is easier to understand.

Rebuild the Update Person Page

The update feature is basically the same as the add function, with the addition of a hidden input field that lets us update the proper record. We also have to initially fill the form with the current record's data. The page is again broken into an ASPX and ASPX.VB code-behind file. The ASPX file, shown in Listing 2.12, is nearly identical to the Addperson.aspx file you just completed, so you may just want to copy it and make the minor changes highlighted in bold in the listing.

```
<%@ Page Inherits="Proj02Web.UpdatePerson" Src="updateperson.aspx.vb" %>
<html>
    <head>
      <title>Contact Manager: Update Person</title>
<!--#include file="styles.css" -->
    </head>
```

Listing 2.12 Updateperson.aspx

```
<body bgcolor="#FFFFFF">
<p class="pageheading">Update Person</p>

<asp:label id="lblErrorMessage" class="errortext" runat="server" />

<!--#include file="inputform.inc" -->
</body>
</html>
```

Listing 2.12   Updateperson.aspx (continued)

The code-behind page has added more code to the Page_Load event, as well as a new class-level variable to accommodate the hidden-input field that holds the unique ID of the record being edited. This hidden-input field is part of the System.Web. UI.HTMLControls namespace, so it has a slightly different declaration, as shown with the rest of the code in Listing 2.13.

```
Imports System
Imports System.Data
Imports System.Data.SqlClient
Imports System.Text
Imports System.Environment
Imports System.Web.UI
Imports System.Web.UI.WebControls

Namespace Proj02Web
    Public Class UpdatePerson
        Inherits System.Web.UI.Page
        Protected hiddenPersonID As HTMLControls.HtmlInputHidden
        Protected txtLastName As TextBox
        Protected txtFirstName As TextBox
        Protected txtTitle As TextBox
        Protected txtCompanyName As TextBox
        Protected txtAddress As TextBox
        Protected txtHomePhone As TextBox
        Protected txtWorkPhone As TextBox
        Protected txtFaxNumber As TextBox
        Protected txtEMail As TextBox
        Protected txtWebPage As TextBox
        Protected txtNotes As TextBox
        Protected lblErrorMessage As Label

        Sub Page_Load(objSender As Object, objArgs As EventArgs)
            Dim DB As New AtWorkUtilities.Database()

            If Not Page.IsPostBack Then
                Dim P As New BusinessObjects.Person(DB, _
                    Request.QueryString("ID"))
```

Listing 2.13   Updateperson.aspx.vb

```
                        Dim DR As DataRow = P.GetRow()
                        hiddenPersonID.Value = Request.QueryString("ID")
                        txtLastName.Text = DR("LastName").ToString()
                        txtFirstName.Text = DR("FirstName").ToString()
                        txtTitle.Text = DR("Title").ToString()
                        txtCompanyName.Text = DR("CompanyName").ToString()
                        txtAddress.Text = DR("Address").ToString()
                        txtHomePhone.Text = DR("HomePhone").ToString()
                        txtWorkPhone.Text = DR("WorkPhone").ToString()
                        txtFaxNumber.Text = DR("Fax").ToString()
                        txtEMail.Text = DR("EMail").ToString()
                        txtWebPage.Text = DR("WebPage").ToString()
                        txtNotes.Text = DR("Notes").ToString()
                        DB.Close()
                    Else
                        Dim P As New BusinessObjects.Person(DB, _
                            hiddenPersonID.Value)
                        Dim DR As DataRow = P.GetRow()
                        DR("LastName") = txtLastName.Text
                        DR("FirstName") = txtFirstName.Text
                        DR("Title") = txtTitle.Text
                        DR("CompanyName") = txtCompanyName.Text
                        DR("Address") = txtAddress.Text
                        DR("HomePhone") = txtHomePhone.Text
                        DR("WorkPhone") = txtWorkPhone.Text
                        DR("Fax") = txtFaxNumber.Text
                        DR("EMail") = txtEMail.Text
                        DR("WebPage") = txtWebPage.Text
                        DR("Notes") = txtNotes.Text
                        P.SaveRow(DR)
                        If Not P.IsValid Then
                            lblErrorMessage.Text = _
                                P.ValidationError("<b>ERROR:</b> The following " _
                                    & "errors were detected in your data:<br>", _
                                    "&bull; {0}<br>", "")
                        Else
                            P.Save()
                            DB.Close()
                            Response.Redirect("viewpeople.aspx")
                        End If
                    End If
                End Sub

            End Class
        End Namespace
```

Listing 2.13   Updateperson.aspx.vb (continued)

In the Page_Load event handler, we determine if we're in postback view or not. If we're not, it means we're loading the page for the first time and we should load up the current record. The ID is being passed to this page by way of the query string as it was before, and we can read it via the Request.QueryString collection. That ID value is then fed into the Person object's constructor to load that person's data. When we call GetRow, we get the current record and populate it into the form. The GetString here takes care of fields that may be null in the database.

In postback mode, we do the same thing as the add function, but we have to instantiate the Person object with the ID of the record being edited. The ID value is stored in a hidden-input field in the form that is populated, along with the rest of the person's data for editing. We follow the same path as before for handling the validation and saving of data.

Rebuild the Delete Person Page

The Delete Person page started off with no confirmations as to what the user was going to do. In this section, we're going to modify the page a bit so that the user gets a chance to cancel the delete request. This could also be done on the list page with some JavaScript, but this method works well. The key thing we're doing here is passing the ID that we initially passed using the query string so that the code-behind page knows what record to delete, assuming the user gets that far.

The first file to create is the Deleteperson.aspx file, shown in Listing 2.14.

```
<%@ Page Inherits="Proj02Web.DeletePerson" Src="deleteperson.aspx.vb" %>
<html>
    <head>
        <title>Contact Manager: Delete Person</title>
<!--#include file="styles.css" -->
    </head>
    <body bgcolor="#FFFFFF">
    <p class="pageheading">Delete Person</p>
    <p class="tabletext">Are you sure you want to delete this person?</p>
    <form runat="server">
    <input type="hidden" runat="server" id="hiddenPersonID">
    <p class="tabletext">
    <a href="javascript:document.forms[0].submit();">Yes</a>
      
    <a href="javascript:history.go(-1);">No</a>
    </p>
    </form>
    </body>
</html>
```

Listing 2.14 Deleteperson.aspx

Instead of using buttons for the Yes and No choices, we are using links instead. I think I first saw the use of links as buttons on Expedia.com and have used them on the dialog boxes that look like this in my own sites. They look different than the regular buttons, but you could always use a Submit button here instead. The key part of this form is the hidden-input field called hiddenPersonID. Note that the hidden-input field has a runat=server attribute. If this attribute was missing, the control's values would not be available to the code-behind page.

Clicking the Yes link will submit the form, but clicking the No link will back you up a page in your browser's history. You could also change this link to point to Viewpeople.aspx if you wanted to refresh the screen.

The code-behind file for this page is fairly short and is shown in Listing 2.15.

```
Imports System
Imports System.Data
Imports System.Data.SqlClient
Imports System.Text
Imports System.Environment
Imports System.Web.UI
Imports System.Web.UI.WebControls

Namespace Proj02Web
    Public Class DeletePerson
        Inherits System.Web.UI.Page

        Protected hiddenPersonID As HTMLControls.HTMLInputHidden

        Sub Page_Load(objSender As Object, objArgs As EventArgs)
            If Not Page.IsPostBack Then
                hiddenPersonID.Value = Request.QueryString("ID")
            Else
                Dim DB As New AtWorkUtilities.Database()
                Dim P As New BusinessObjects.Person(DB, _
                    hiddenPersonID.Value)
                P.Delete()
                DB.Close()
                Response.Redirect("viewpeople.aspx")
            End If
        End Sub

    End Class
End Namespace
```

Listing 2.15   Deleteperson.aspx.vb

The first time the page loads, we simply have to store the person ID in the hidden-input field. If and when the user clicks the Yes link to confirm the deletion, we create a Database object and a Person object and call the Delete method. We then close the Database object before reloading the View People page. Again, we have to have the hidden-input field declared as a class-level variable in order to access it at runtime.

That's It!

Once you've gotten all the pages done, you'll have a good working model of code-behind development, as well as how to use the assemblies and objects that you built. We'll build on this model for the other two features of our new application: Notes and Contacts. These additional classes will go more quickly since they use the same development techniques that we used here for our assemblies and ASP.NET pages.

Build the Note Manager

The next feature you'll add to this application gives you the ability to add notes to the person records. In this section, you'll build the database table, the objects required to access the data in the database, and the Web pages used to manage them. The nice thing is that you've already got most of the infrastructure built. Building the Note class is fairly simple and just involves writing the validation specific to this object . . . everything else is in the BaseServices class that you already built.

Build the tblNotes Table

The first step to building this portion of the application is to build the new database table. This is a fairly small table, names tblNotes, with just four fields. Use the information in Table 2.1 to build the table in SQL Server:

The fkPersonID field is a foreign key in the tblPeople table and matches the pkPersonID field on that table. Every note must be related to a person in the system; the Note object will verify that the field is filled in. Since the user won't actually be typing in this value, we will fill in this field from the Web interface by forcing the ID into the field.

You may want to pre-populate the table with a few rows of data so that you can test the view notes feature, which will be first on the list of things to do. Be sure that you pick a valid value for fkPersonID; in other words, match the notes up with person records that you already have in the tblPeople table.

Table 2.1 tblNotes Fields

FIELD NAME	SQL DATA TYPE	LENGTH	OTHER
pkNoteID	int	N/A	Identity, Primary Key, Not Null
fkPersonID	int	N/A	Not Null
Title	varchar	80	Not Null
Content	text	N/A	

Build the Note Class

The next step is to build the Note class, which will be part of the BusinessObjects assembly that you built previously. This class is straightforward to build, both because there are only a few fields and because you already have most of the code. The easiest way to proceed is to make a copy of the Person class and make modifications to it. The full listing for the Note class, called Note.vb, is shown in Listing 2.16.

```
Imports AtWorkUtilities
Imports System.Data.SqlClient

Public Class Note
   Inherits BaseServices


   '
   ' If no arguments are supplied, build a separate
   ' database connection for this object.
   '
   Public Sub New()
      MyBase.New(New Database(), "SELECT * FROM tblNotes WHERE 1=0")
   End Sub


   '
   ' If database connection is supplied, store it
   ' in the private connection variable for this
   ' object.
   '
   Public Sub New(ByVal db As Database)
      MyBase.New(db, "SELECT * FROM tblNotes WHERE 1=0")
   End Sub


   '
   ' If both database and ID are supplied, retrieve
   ' data into the object from the database.
   '
   Public Sub New(ByVal db As Database, _
      ByVal ID As Integer)

      MyBase.New(db, "SELECT * FROM tblNotes WHERE pkNoteID = " _
         & ID.ToString)

   End Sub


   '
   ' Verify that all data validation rules have been
   ' met. Any errors get stored into the errors collection
   ' inherited from the BaseServices class.
   '
   Public Sub Validate()
      Dim dr As DataRow
```

Listing 2.16 The Note class

```
      ClearErrors()
      For Each dr In m_DS.Tables(0).Rows
         If dr.RowState = DataRowState.Added _
         Or dr.RowState = DataRowState.Modified Then
            ValidateRow(dr)
         End If
      Next

   End Sub


   '
   ' Checks an individual row for validation rule
   ' compliance. Any errors are added to the errors
   ' collection.
   '
   Private Sub ValidateRow(ByVal dr As DataRow)

      If Not IsDBNull(dr("fkPersonID")) Then
         '
         ' Foreign keys are automatically started at 1
         ' and never are negative or zero.
         '
         If dr("fkPersonID") <= 0 Then
            AddError("This note must be associated with a person.")
         End If
      End If

      If IsDBNull(dr("Title")) Then
         AddError("The note must have a title.")
      End If

      If Not IsDBNull(dr("Title")) Then
         If dr("Title") = "" Then
            AddError("The note must have a title.")
         ElseIf dr("Title").Length > 80 Then
            AddError("The title must be less than 80 characters.")
         End If
      End If

   End Sub


   '
   ' The base Save method stores the DataRow into the
   ' DataSet, whether it's a new or existing row. The
   ' rest of this routine handles specific validation
   ' for this type of data.
   '
   Public Overloads Sub SaveRow(ByVal dr As DataRow)
      MyBase.SaveRow(dr)
      Validate()
```

Listing 2.16   The Note class (continued)

```
    End Sub


    '
    ' We separate the SaveRow method from the Save method
    ' to give us a chance to handle any validation. We have
    ' a verification here that the data is good before we
    ' continue, however.
    '
    Public Sub Save()

        If Not Me.IsValid Then
            Throw New NoteException(Me.ValidationError
            Exit Sub
        End If

        m_DA.Update(m_DS)
    End Sub


    '
    ' Since we only have a single row in our DataSet,
    ' delete it and then update the database with the
    ' change.
    '
    Public Sub Delete()
        If m_DS.Tables(0).Rows.Count > 0 Then
            m_DS.Tables(0).Rows(0).Delete()
            m_DA.Update(m_DS)
        End If
    End Sub

End Class
```

Listing 2.16 The Note class (continued)

The structure of the Note class follows the format of the Person class exactly, with the only difference being the specifics for working with the tblNotes table instead of tblPeople. The constructors use the tblNotes table instead of tblPeople, and the third constructor that takes an ID as input uses pkNoteID instead of pkPersonID.

The ValidateRow subroutine verifies that the title of the note has been supplied and is less than 80 characters. It also verifies that the person ID, which is a foreign key, has been filled into the object before it can be saved.

In the Save routine, we throw a NoteException if a validation error still exists when the user attempts to save it. This gives you a specific exception to trap; however, you can use a plain exception if you like. The code for the NoteException class is shown in the next section of this part of the project, so be sure to create this class before attempting to compile your Note class, or you'll get errors in the compilation process.

As mentioned before, the key to building this class quickly is having a good base class to work with. I built this class in just a few minutes once I had the Person class working. It's just a matter of writing the validation routine . . . everything else stays the same.

Build the NoteException Class

The NoteException class is identical to the PersonException class in every way, except for the name. It inherits from the base Exception class and has all three constructors available, as shown in Listing 2.17.

```
Public Class NoteException
    Inherits Exception

    Public Sub New()
        MyBase.New()
    End Sub

    Public Sub New(ByVal Message As String)
        MyBase.New(Message)
    End Sub

    Public Sub New(ByVal Message As String, ByVal baseError As Exception)
        MyBase.New(Message, baseError)
    End Sub

End Class
```

Listing 2.17   NoteException class

This class is used in a similar way to the PersonException class you already built. It gives you a specific exception that another application using your object can detect. If the calling application receives this error, it can determine that the error occurred in relation to your Note object and not somewhere else.

Rebuild the BusinessObjects Assembly

You'll want to rebuild your BusinessObjects assembly and copy the new DLL files to your Web directory for the next part of this project. When you have all the classes in place, select Rebuild Solution from the Build menu to recompile all the related files in your assemblies. Rebuilding this assembly in Visual Studio will also cause the AtWorkUtilities assembly to be rebuilt. That's perfectly fine and makes it easier, since you'll have a copy of both DLLs in your BusinessObjects *bin* folder. Copy those DLLs over to the *bin* directory in your Web site. If you're building the DLLs manually, be sure that you have updated the BusinessObjects assembly in the Web site from wherever you are building your assembly.

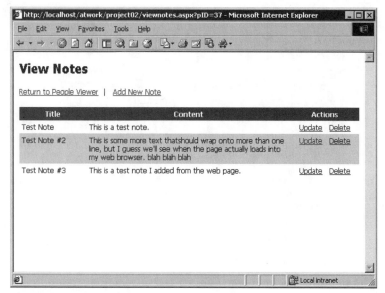

Figure 2.6   View Notes page at runtime.

Create the View Notes Page

The next step, now that you've got the objects built and redeployed to the Web site, is to build the View Notes page. This page follows the same format as the View Person page; however, we're using some new features of .NET to build it. In this page, we'll use a combination of a Repeater control and data binding to show the page. At the time of this writing, I had read mixed reports of whether data binding was faster than simply displaying the data, so it seemed logical to cover both. As you'll see, using the Repeater control makes the ASPX file more complicated, but the code-behind file is relatively simple. With both techniques at your disposal, you'll be able to choose your favorite.

The View Notes page is shown in Figure 2.6 with some sample data already loaded in it. The code for the ASPX file is shown in Listing 2.18.

```
<%@ Page Inherits="Proj02Web.ViewNotes" Src="viewnotes.aspx.vb" %>
<html>
<head>
    <title>Contact Manager: View Notes</title>
<!--#include file="styles.css" -->
</head>
```

Listing 2.18   Viewnotes.aspx

```
<body bgcolor="#FFFFFF">
   <p class="pageheading">View Notes</p>
   <p class="tabletext">
   <a href="viewpeople.aspx">Return to
   People Viewer</a>   |  
   <a href="addnote.aspx?pID=<% = Request.QueryString("pID") %>">Add
   New Note</a>
   </p>
   <asp:Repeater id="rptList" runat="server">
     <HeaderTemplate>
     <table cellpadding="4" cellspacing="0" width="100%">
     <tr class="tableheading">
     <td width="20%">Title</td>
     <td width="60%">Content</td>
     <td width="20%">Actions</td>
     </tr>
     </HeaderTemplate>
     <ItemTemplate>
     <tr class="tabletext">
     <td valign="top"><%# DataBinder.Eval(Container.DataItem, _
        "Title") %></td>
     <td valign="top"><%# DataBinder.Eval(Container.DataItem, _
        "Content") %></td>
     <td valign="top" align="center">
     <a href="updatenote.aspx?id=<%# DataBinder.Eval(Container.DataItem, _
        "pkNoteID") %>">Update</a>  
     <a href="deletenote.aspx?id=<%# DataBinder.Eval(Container.DataItem, _
        "pkNoteID") %>&pID=<%# DataBinder.Eval(Container.DataItem, _
        "fkPersonID") %>">Delete</a>
     </td>
     </tr>
     </ItemTemplate>
     <AlternatingItemTemplate>
     <tr class="tabletext_gray">
     <td valign="top"><%# DataBinder.Eval(Container.DataItem, _
        "Title") %></td>
     <td valign="top"><%# DataBinder.Eval(Container.DataItem, _
        "Content") %></td>
     <td valign="top" align="center">
     <a href="updatenote.aspx?id=<%# DataBinder.Eval(Container.DataItem, _
        "pkNoteID") %>">Update</a>  
     <a href="deletenote.aspx?id=<%# DataBinder.Eval(Container.DataItem, _
        "pkNoteID") %>&pID=<%# DataBinder.Eval(Container.DataItem, _
        "fkPersonID") %>">Delete</a>
     </td>
     </tr>
     </AlternatingItemTemplate>
```

Listing 2.18   Viewnotes.aspx (continued)

```
        <FooterTemplate>
        </table>
        </FooterTemplate>
    </asp:Repeater>
</body>
</html>
```

Listing 2.18   Viewnotes.aspx (continued)

Begin with the normal @Page directive pointing to the code-behind file, which we'll build next. We have the header HTML as well as the Style Sheet Include directive. We then have to build two links: one to point back to the View People page and one to add a new note. The first link is not difficult, but the second one has an extra twist. In order to add a note, it has to be associated with a particular person's record. This means that we have to pass the person ID to the add routine. Do this by reading from the Request.QueryString collection. Put the value into the link using the <% = assignment operator. This is exactly the same as the Active Server Pages method. We're reading the pID parameter, which is what we will supply this page from the View People page, and we pass that variable on to the Addnote.aspx file that we'll also create in this project.

Once we get the header done, we move on to the Repeater control. With the Repeater control, we can control what our data looks like when it is shown on the page. It provides templates to use: a header, footer, and item template. The item template has an "alternating" item template, which gives you the ability to change colors (as we did in Project 1) using the alternate style that shows the row in a different color. The color is already specified in the style sheet, so you just have to use it instead of setting the colors using extra tags. This is a nice way to get the benefits of data binding without all the manual work.

Start by building the HeaderTemplate, which includes the table tags and column headings. We use the same styles as in the View People page, just with fewer headings. We don't need to show the person ID since all the notes we're viewing are associated with the person we selected in the View People page. The only information we need to show is the title and the content of the note. We set up the table headings, and then close the HeaderTemplate tag.

The next tag is the most complicated part: the ItemTemplate tag. Each row will be fed into either the ItemTemplate or the AlternatingItemTemplate. In our page, these two templates will be identical with the exception of the style sheet class referenced: ItemTemplate uses tabletext, and AlternatingItemTemplate uses tabletext_gray.

The next step is to fill in the data fields in each TD tag in the row. We do this using the syntax shown here:

```
<%# DataBinder.Eval(Container.DataItem, "Title") %>
```

This instructs ASP.NET to use the Title field from the bound data source and to put the data at this location. Regardless of the name of your class or any other variables, you always use these object and property names to accomplish this task. The DataBinder object is made available through the data-bound controls, such as the Repeater, the DataGrid, and so on. We use this syntax to pull out the data from the Title, Content, and pkNoteID fields, the latter of which we actually use twice: once for the update link, and once for the delete link.

As mentioned earlier, the AlternatingItemTemplate is exactly the same as the ItemTemplate with one change: using the other class for style sheets. I simply copied and pasted the information between the ItemTemplate and AlternatingItemTemplate to take care of that bit of code.

The final template we build is the FooterTemplate, which is a closing TABLE tag. We then close the Repeater tag, as well as the page. The next step is to build the code-behind file, named Viewnotes.aspx.vb. This code is much shorter and is shown in Listing 2.19.

```vb
Imports System
Imports System.Data
Imports System.Data.SqlClient
Imports System.Web.UI
Imports System.Web.UI.WebControls


Namespace Proj02Web
    Public Class ViewNotes
        Inherits System.Web.UI.Page


        Protected rptList As Repeater


        Sub Page_Load(Src As Object, e As EventArgs)

            Dim DB as New AtWorkUtilities.Database()
            Dim DS As DataSet = DB.GetDataSet("SELECT * FROM tblNotes " _
                & "WHERE fkPersonID = " & Request.QueryString("pID") _
                & " ORDER BY Title")
            rptList.DataSource = DS
            rptList.DataBind()

            db.Close()
        End Sub
    End Class
End Namespace
```

Listing 2.19   Viewnotes.aspx.vb

As promised, the code here is almost trivial. The viewer has no postback mode, so we simply fill the page by retrieving a DataSet from our Database object. We feed it the SQL statement, including the pID that will be passed to this page from the Viewpeople. aspx file. We then assign the DataSet as the DataSource property of the Repeater, and the DataBind method does the rest. Be sure that you've got the Repeater control defined as a variable of the class, however, or you won't get too far in compilation.

The last step to making this page work is to feed it data. You can manually call the page using the following URL:

```
http://yourserver/viewnotes.aspx?pID=37
```

This way, you can test the Viewnotes.aspx file without making the next set of changes. In fact, I'd recommend you test the page by itself before testing with more than one file.

To make the changes to the View People page, edit the Viewpeople.aspx.vb file and make the changes highlighted in bold in Listing 2.20.

```vb
Imports System
Imports System.Data
Imports System.Data.SqlClient
Imports System.Text
Imports System.Environment
Imports System.Web.UI
Imports System.Web.UI.WebControls


Namespace Proj02Web
    Public Class ViewPeople
        Inherits System.Web.UI.Page


        Protected lblOutput As Label


        Sub Page_Load(Src As Object, e As EventArgs)
            Dim sdrData As SqlDataReader
            Dim sb As New StringBuilder
            Dim strColor As String
            Dim db as New AtWorkUtilities.Database("server=localhost;" _
                & "database=ASPNetProject02;uid=sa;pwd=;")
            sdrData = db.GetDataReader("SELECT * FROM tblPeople " _
                & "ORDER BY LastName, FirstName")
            strColor = "tabletext"
            While sdrData.Read()
                sb.AppendFormat("<tr class=""{0}"">" + NewLine, strColor)
                sb.AppendFormat("    <td>{0}, {1}</td>" + NewLine, _
                    sdrData("LastName"), _
                    sdrData("FirstName"))
                sb.AppendFormat("    <td>{0}</td>" + NewLine, sdrData("Title"))
                sb.AppendFormat("    <td>{0}</td>" + NewLine, _
                    sdrData("CompanyName"))
                sb.AppendFormat("    <td>{0}</td>" + NewLine, _
                    sdrData("WorkPhone"))

                sb.Append("    <td align=middle>")
                sb.AppendFormat("<a href=""viewnotes.aspx" _
                    & "?pID={0}"">View Notes</a>", _
                    sdrData("pkPersonID"))
                sb.Append("  ")
```

Listing 2.20 Viewpeople.aspx.vb file with changes

```
            sb.AppendFormat("<a href=""updateperson.aspx" _
                & "?id={0}"">Update</a>", _
                sdrData("pkPersonID"))
            sb.Append("  ")
            sb.AppendFormat("<a href=""deleteperson.aspx" _
                & "?id={0}"">Delete</a>" + NewLine, _
                sdrData("pkPersonID"))
            sb.Append("    </td>" + NewLine)
            sb.Append("</tr>" + NewLine)
            If strColor = "tabletext" Then
                strColor = "tabletext_gray"
            Else
                strColor = "tabletext"
            End If
        End While
        sdrData.Close()
        db.Close()
        lblOutput.Text = sb.ToString()
    End Sub
  End Class
End Namespace
```

Listing 2.20   Viewpeople.aspx.vb file with changes (continued)

Adding this other link will build the URL that feeds the person ID to your Viewnotes.aspx file. We'll repeat this process when we add the contact management feature later in the project. For now, we need to add our other functions: add, modify, and delete.

Create the Add Notes Page

The next page is designed to let you add notes for a particular person in the system. This is a nice short page in both the HTML/ASPX file and the code-behind file. Listing 2.21 shows the ASPX file, called Addnote.aspx.

```
<%@ Page Inherits="Proj02Web.AddNote" Src="addnote.aspx.vb" %>
<html>
    <head>
        <title>Contact Manager: Add New Note</title>
<!--#include file="styles.css" -->
    </head>
    <body bgcolor="#FFFFFF">
    <p class="pageheading">Add New Note</p>

    <asp:label id="lblErrorMessage" class="errortext" runat="server" />
```

Listing 2.21   Addnote.aspx

```
<!--#include file="noteform.inc" -->
    </body>
</html>
```

Listing 2.21   Addnote.aspx (continued)

This page looks like most of the other ASPX files we've built, with the exception of the specific text and the new Noteform.inc file. The code for Noteform.inc is shown in Listing 2.22.

```
<form runat="server">
<input type="hidden" id="pkNoteID" runat="server">
<input type="hidden" id="fkPersonID" runat="server">
<table cellspacing="5">
<tr class="tabletext">
    <td align="right">Title:</td>
    <td>
       <asp:textbox
          id="txtTitle"
          columns="30"
          maxlength="80"
          runat="server" /></td>
</tr>
<tr class="tabletext">
    <td valign="middle" align="right">Content:</td>
    <td>
       <asp:textbox
          id="txtContent"
          rows="15"
          columns="60"
          wrap="true"
          textmode="Multiline"
          runat="server" /></td>
</tr>
<tr class="tabletext">
   <td colspan=2 align=middle>
   <input type="submit" name="btnSubmit" runat="server" value="Save" />
   <input type="reset"  name="btnReset"  runat="server" value="Clear" />
   </td>
</tr>
</table>
</form>
```

Listing 2.22   Noteform.inc

The Note form has one regular text box and one large multiline text box. I've made this box larger than the one used for the address, since we will presumably have more content here. We also have two hidden-input fields: one for the note ID (used for editing), and one for the person ID (used in both adding and editing). We'll be filling these fields in as necessary.

The final part of this file is the code-behind file, called Addnote.aspx.vb, shown in Listing 2.23.

```
Imports System
Imports System.Data
Imports System.Data.SqlClient
Imports System.Web.UI
Imports System.Web.UI.WebControls

Namespace Proj02Web
    Public Class AddNote
        Inherits System.Web.UI.Page
        Protected txtTitle As TextBox
        Protected txtContent As TextBox
        Protected pkNoteID As HTMLControls.HTMLInputHidden
        Protected fkPersonID As HTMLControls.HTMLInputHidden

        Protected lblErrorMessage As Label

        Sub Page_Load(objSender As Object, objArgs As EventArgs)
            Dim DB As New AtWorkUtilities.Database()

        If Not Page.IsPostBack Then
            fkPersonID.Value = Request.QueryString("pID")
        Else
            Dim N As New BusinessObjects.Note(DB)
            Dim DR As DataRow = N.GetRow()
            DR("Title") = txtTitle.Text
            DR("Content") = txtContent.Text
            DR("fkPersonID") = Int32.Parse(fkPersonID.Value)
            N.SaveRow(DR)
            If Not N.IsValid Then
                lblErrorMessage.Text = _
                    N.ValidationError("<b>ERROR:</b> The following " _
                        & "errors were detected in your data:<br>", _
                        "&bull; {0}<br>", "")
            Else
                N.Save()
                DB.Close()
                Response.Redirect("viewnotes.aspx?pID=" _
                    & fkPersonID.Value)
            End If
        End If
        End Sub

    End Class
End Namespace
```

Listing 2.23 Addnote.aspx.vb

To add a record, we initially have to take the person ID (passed via the query string as pID) and put it into the form's fkPersonID hidden-input field. Once the user has clicked the Submit button and we're in postback mode, we create a new Note object and retrieve a new blank row, which will be populated using the GetRow method. The Title and Content fields are easy to read since they are text fields being stored in string fields in the DataRow object, but the fkPersonID field presents a minor challenge. Since the fkPersonID field in the DataRow is a 32-bit integer, we can't just take the string from the hidden-input field and put it in. Instead, I use the Int32.Parse method to convert the string to a 32-bit integer before storing it. There are other ways to do numeric conversions, but this one works fine. Once we have the DataRow filled, we store it back into the Note object and check for validation errors. If any occur, we display the error message; if not, we go back to the View Notes page, using the person ID to go to the correct listing.

Create the Update Note Page

The next step is to build the edit note feature, which feeds directly from the add note feature. We populate the form when it initially loads. The ASPX file, called Updatenote.aspx, is shown in Listing 2.24.

```
<%@ Page Inherits="Proj02Web.UpdateNote" Src="updatenote.aspx.vb" %>
<html>
   <head>
      <title>Contact Manager: Update Note</title>
<!--#include file="styles.css" -->
   </head>
   <body bgcolor="#FFFFFF">
   <p class="pageheading">Update Note</p>

   <asp:label id="lblErrorMessage" class="errortext" runat="server" />

<!--#include file="noteform.inc" -->
   </body>
</html>
```

Listing 2.24   Updatenote.aspx

Nothing new in this listing. Just the new titles and the changes to the @Page directive. The code-behind file does have some new code, however, as shown in Listing 2.25.

```
Imports System
Imports System.Data
Imports System.Data.SqlClient
Imports System.Web.UI
Imports System.Web.UI.WebControls
```

Listing 2.25   Updatenote.aspx.vb

```
Namespace Proj02Web
    Public Class UpdateNote
        Inherits System.Web.UI.Page
        Protected txtTitle As TextBox
        Protected txtContent As TextBox
        Protected pkNoteID As HTMLControls.HTMLInputHidden
        Protected fkPersonID As HTMLControls.HTMLInputHidden
        Protected lblErrorMessage As Label

        Sub Page_Load(objSender As Object, objArgs As EventArgs)

            Dim DB As New AtWorkUtilities.Database()
            If Not Page.IsPostBack Then
                Dim N As New BusinessObjects.Note(DB, _
                    Request.QueryString("ID"))
                Dim DR As DataRow = N.GetRow()
                pkNoteID.Value = DR("pkNoteID").ToString()
                txtTitle.Text = DR("Title").ToString()
                txtContent.Text = DR("Content").ToString()
                fkPersonID.Value = DR("fkPersonID").ToString()
            Else
                Dim N As New BusinessObjects.Note(DB, pkNoteID.Value)
                Dim DR As DataRow = N.GetRow()
                DR("Title") = txtTitle.Text
                DR("Content") = txtContent.Text
                DR("fkPersonID") = Int32.Parse(fkPersonID.Value)
                N.SaveRow(DR)
                If Not N.IsValid Then
                    lblErrorMessage.Text = _
                        N.ValidationError("<b>ERROR:</b> The following " _
                        & "errors were detected in your data:<br>", _
                        "&bull; {0}<br>", "")
                Else
                    N.Save()
                    DB.Close()
                    Response.Redirect("viewnotes.aspx?pID=" _
                        & fkPersonID.Value)
                End If
            End If
        End Sub

    End Class
End Namespace
```

Listing 2.25   Updatenote.aspx.vb (continued)

We start in the non-postback mode by retrieving the note that the user requested. The pID value in the query string tells us where to go, so we use that value to retrieve the appropriate note. We then populate the form and get ready to edit the record.

When the user clicks the Save button, the only difference between this code and the add code is in the creation of the Note object. Here, we have to specify the note that was edited. We pull the value from the hidden pkNoteID field and feed it to the Note object's constructor. The rest of the code is the same as that used for handling the update.

Create the Delete Note Page

The last feature we need to create is the delete note feature. This code is nearly identical to the Delete Person page you wrote in the last section. Listing 2.26 shows the ASPX file.

```
<%@ Page Inherits="Proj02Web.DeleteNote" Src="deletenote.aspx.vb" %>
<html>
   <head>
      <title>Contact Manager: Delete Note</title>
<!--#include file="styles.css" -->
   </head>
   <body bgcolor="#FFFFFF">
   <p class="pageheading">Delete Note</p>
   <p class="tabletext">Are you sure you want to delete this note?</p>
   <form runat="server">
   <input type="hidden" runat="server" id="pkNoteID">
   <input type="hidden" runat="server" id="fkPersonID">
   <p class="tabletext">
   <a href="javascript:document.forms[0].submit();">Yes</a>
     
   <a href="javascript:history.go(-1);">No</a>
   </p>
   </form>
   </body>
</html>
```

Listing 2.26   Deletenote.aspx

Both the note ID and the person ID are stored in this page. This way, we can go back to the correct list when the note is deleted without having to read the data from the Note object itself. You'll see that in action in the code-behind file, shown in Listing 2.27.

```
Imports System
Imports System.Data
Imports System.Data.SqlClient
Imports System.Web.UI
Imports System.Web.UI.WebControls

Namespace Proj02Web
   Public Class DeleteNote
```

Listing 2.27   Deletenote.aspx.vb

```
      Inherits System.Web.UI.Page

      Protected pkNoteID As HTMLControls.HTMLInputHidden
      Protected fkPersonID As HTMLControls.HTMLInputHidden

      Sub Page_Load(objSender As Object, objArgs As EventArgs)
         If Not Page.IsPostBack Then
            pkNoteID.Value = Request.QueryString("ID")
            fkPersonID.Value = Request.QueryString("pID")
         Else
            Dim DB As New AtWorkUtilities.Database()
            Dim N As New BusinessObjects.Note(DB, pkNoteID.Value)
            N.Delete()
            DB.Close()
            Response.Redirect("viewnotes.aspx?pID=" & fkPersonID.Value)
         End If
      End Sub


   End Class
End Namespace
```

Listing 2.27   Deletenote.aspx.vb (continued)

In non-postback mode, we fill up both the note ID and person ID fields from the data passed on from the query string. When the user clicks the Yes button to confirm deletion of the record, we load the record to delete and call the Delete method to remove it. We then use the hidden-input person ID field to redirect the user back to the correct page.

Test the Application

At this point, the note management feature is complete. However, you should go through and ensure that all the validations are working properly. If you've added extra fields beyond what we've done here, such as a field for the name of the person that entered the note or the date or time of the note, be sure that those fields are also validated, if necessary. Now that you have a separate function for managing notes on a person, you might want to go back to the Person object and remove the Notes field.

Build the Contact Manager

The final feature we're adding to the application is a contact manager. In tools like ACT! or Outlook, you have the ability to keep a record of any contact you've had with people in the system. This lets you keep a record that you called someone or emailed them at some point in the past, and allows you to see the history of your conversations with a particular person. The main screen for the contact manager is shown in Figure 2.7.

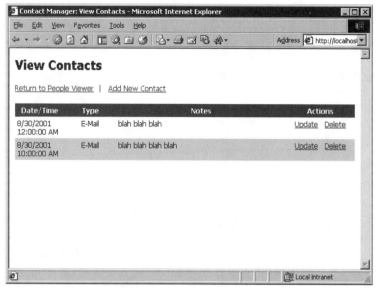

Figure 2.7 Contact Manager.

We'll be adding this feature to our application next, and it will follow the same pattern as the note taker. We'll link to it from the Person window and show a list of the contacts we've had with the person. From that list window, we'll handle adding, modifying, and deleting contacts. Each contact will have the date and time of the contact, the type of contact (phone, email, and so on), a field to enter the length of the call, and a field for notes about the contact. The Notes field will be large enough in the database so that users can actually paste emails sent into the box. If you have more than one person using this contact manager, this feature will prevent you from asking the same thing that another person just asked by letting you copy any emails into the Notes field.

Create the tblContacts Table

The first step is to build the database table, which I'll call tblContacts. The fields that I've chosen for the table are shown in Table 2.2.

Table 2.2 tblContacts Fields

FIELD NAME	SQL DATA TYPE	LENGTH	OTHER
tblContactID	int	N/A	Identity, Primary Key, Not Null
fkPersonID	int	N/A	Not Null
ContactDate	datetime	N/A	Not Null
Type	varchar	15	Not Null
Length	varchar	15	
Notes	text	N/A	

Note that we used the name "ContactDate" here since the word "Date" is a reserved word in SQL Server. While you can use reserved words as field names, the convention is not to do this. The other field names may sound like reserved words, but they are not within SQL Server.

Pre-populate the table with some data. The type of contact will be one of the following:

- Phone Call
- Fax
- Email
- Meeting
- Other

That list covers most types of contacts that you might have with a person, but feel free to add to the list. We'll be using a drop-down list to provide these values in the form. For simplicity, we'll be storing the actual string in the database. We could use a secondary table to hold these contact types, but the list is not going to grow significantly over time, and we would have to join the tables every time to retrieve the data. Thus, we'll store the type directly in the Contacts table.

Create the Contact Class

The next step is to build the Contact class in the BusinessObjects assembly. The validation rules that you need to enforce are:

- fkPersonID, ContactDate, and Type are required fields
- The maximum length of the Type and Length fields is 15 characters
- ContactDate is a valid date/time entry

You might also want to verify that the Length field is in a particular format, but I prefer to leave that up to the user. The code for the Contact class is shown in Listing 2.28.

```
Imports AtWorkUtilities
Imports System.Data.SqlClient

Public Class Contact
   Inherits BaseServices

   '
   ' If no arguments are supplied, build a separate
   ' database connection for this object.
   '
   Public Sub New()
      MyBase.New(New Database(), "SELECT * FROM tblContacts WHERE 1=0")
   End Sub

   '
```

Listing 2.28 Contact class

```
' If database connection is supplied, store it
' in the private connection variable for this
' object.
'
Public Sub New(ByVal db As Database)
   MyBase.New(db, "SELECT * FROM tblContacts WHERE 1=0")
End Sub


'
' If both database and ID are supplied, retrieve
' data into the object from the database.
'
Public Sub New(ByVal db As Database, _
   ByVal ID As Integer)

   MyBase.New(db, "SELECT * FROM tblContacts WHERE pkContactID = " _
      & ID.ToString)

End Sub


'
' Verify that all data validation rules have been
' met. Any errors get stored into the errors collection
' inherited from the BaseServices class.
'
Public Sub Validate()
   Dim dr As DataRow

   ClearErrors()
   For Each dr In m_DS.Tables(0).Rows
      If dr.RowState = DataRowState.Added _
      Or dr.RowState = DataRowState.Modified Then
         ValidateRow(dr)
      End If
   Next

End Sub


'
' Checks an individual row for validation rule
' compliance. Any errors are added to the errors
' collection.
'
Private Sub ValidateRow(ByVal dr As DataRow)

   If IsDBNull(dr("fkPersonID")) Then
      AddError("This contact must be associated with a person.")
   End If

   If Not IsDBNull(dr("fkPersonID")) Then
      '
```

Listing 2.28   Contact class (continued)

```
            ' Foreign keys are automatically started at 1
            ' and never are negative or zero.
            '
            If dr("fkPersonID") <= 0 Then
               AddError("This contact must be associated with a person.")
            End If
        End If

        If IsDBNull(dr("ContactDate")) Then
            AddError("The contact must have a valid date/time.")
        End If

        If Not IsDBNull(dr("Type")) Then
            If dr("Type") = "" Then
               AddError("The contact must have a type.")
            ElseIf dr("Type").Length > 15 Then
               AddError("The type must be less than 15 characters.")
            End If
        End If

        If Not IsDBNull(dr("Length")) Then
            If dr("Length").Length > 15 Then
               AddError("The length must be less than 15 characters.")
            End If
        End If

    End Sub


    '
    ' The base Save method stores the DataRow into the
    ' DataSet, whether it's a new or existing row. The
    ' rest of this routine handles specific validation
    ' for this type of data.
    '
    Public Overloads Sub SaveRow(ByVal dr As DataRow)
        MyBase.SaveRow(dr)
        Validate()

    End Sub


    '
    ' We separate the SaveRow method from the Save method
    ' to give us a chance to handle any validation. We have
    ' a verification here that the data is good before we
    ' continue, however.
    '
    Public Sub Save()

        If Not Me.IsValid Then
            Throw New ContactException(Me.ValidationError)
            Exit Sub
        End If
```

Listing 2.28   Contact class (continued)

```
        m_DA.Update(m_DS)
    End Sub


    '
    ' Since we only have a single row in our DataSet,
    ' delete it and then update the database with the
    ' change.
    '
    Public Sub Delete()
        If m_DS.Tables(0).Rows.Count > 0 Then
            m_DS.Tables(0).Rows(0).Delete()
            m_DA.Update(m_DS)
        End If
    End Sub

End Class
```

Listing 2.28   Contact class (continued)

As in the Note class, there's nothing particularly exciting about this class. The validation is a bit different because we have different fields to check, but for the most part, this is a clone of the Note and Person classes. We use a specific ContactException class that can be used for error trapping, the code for which is shown next.

Build the ContactException Class

The ContactException class follows the same design pattern as the NoteException and PersonException classes and is shown in Listing 2.29.

```
Public Class ContactException
    Inherits Exception

    Public Sub New()
        MyBase.New()
    End Sub

    Public Sub New(ByVal Message As String)
        MyBase.New(Message)
    End Sub

    Public Sub New(ByVal Message As String, ByVal baseError As Exception)
        MyBase.New(Message, baseError)
    End Sub

End Class
```

Listing 2.29   ContactException Class

As with the other specific Exception classes, this class gives you a way to trap errors specific to the Contact object.

Rebuild the BusinessObjects Assembly

You'll want to rebuild your BusinessObjects assembly and copy the new DLL files to your Web directory for the next part of this project. Rebuilding this assembly in Visual Studio also means that the AtWorkUtilities assembly needs to be rebuilt. That's perfectly fine and makes it easier in the long run, since you'll have a copy of both DLLs in your BusinessObjects Bin folder. Copy those DLLs over to the *bin* directory in your Web site. If you're building the DLLs manually, be sure that you have updated the Business-Objects assembly in the Web site from wherever you are building your assembly.

Create the View Contacts Page

Next, we want to show the contacts in the system on the View Contacts page. This page, like the note viewer, accepts a person ID for input on the query string and passes that value to the add, modify, and delete pages when necessary. The ASPX file for this page is shown in Listing 2.30.

```
<%@ Page Inherits="Proj02Web.ViewContacts" Src="viewcontacts.aspx.vb" %>
<html>
<head>
   <title>Contact Manager: View Contacts</title>
<!--#include file="styles.css" -->
</head>
<body bgcolor="#FFFFFF">
   <p class="pageheading">View Contacts</p>
   <p class="tabletext">
   <a href="viewpeople.aspx">Return to
   People Viewer</a>  |  
   <a href="addcontact.aspx?pID=<% = Request.QueryString("pID") %>">Add
   New Contact</a>
   </p>
   <asp:Repeater id="rptList" runat="server">
      <HeaderTemplate>
      <table cellpadding="4" cellspacing="0" width="100%">
      <tr class="tableheading">
      <td width="15%">Date/Time</td>
      <td width="15%">Type</td>
      <td width="50%">Notes</td>
      <td width="20%">Actions</td>
      </tr>
      </HeaderTemplate>
      <ItemTemplate>
```

Listing 2.30   Viewcontacts.aspx

```
            <tr class="tabletext">
            <td valign="top"><%# DataBinder.Eval(Container.DataItem, _
                "ContactDate") %></td>
            <td valign="top" align="middle">
            <%# DataBinder.Eval(Container.DataItem, "Type") %></td>
            <td valign="top"><%# DataBinder.Eval(Container.DataItem, _
                "Notes") %></td>
            <td valign="top" align="center">
        <a href="updatecontact.aspx?id=<%# DataBinder.Eval(Container.DataItem, _
                "pkContactID") %>">Update</a>  
        <a href="deletecontact.aspx?id=<%# DataBinder.Eval(Container.DataItem, _
                "pkContactID") %>&pID=<%# DataBinder.Eval(Container.DataItem, _
                "fkPersonID") %>">Delete</a>
            </td>
            </tr>
            </ItemTemplate>
            <AlternatingItemTemplate>
            <tr class="tabletext_gray">
            <td valign="top"><%# DataBinder.Eval(Container.DataItem, _
                "ContactDate") %></td>
            <td valign="top" align="middle">
            <%# DataBinder.Eval(Container.DataItem, _
                "Type") %></td>
            <td valign="top"><%# DataBinder.Eval(Container.DataItem, _
                "Notes") %></td>
            <td valign="top" align="center">
        <a href="updatecontact.aspx?id=<%# DataBinder.Eval(Container.DataItem, _
            "pkContactID") %>">Update</a>  
        <a href="deletecontact.aspx?id=<%# DataBinder.Eval(Container.DataItem, _
            "pkContactID") %>&pID=<%# DataBinder.Eval(Container.DataItem, _
            "fkPersonID") %>">Delete</a>
            </td>
            </tr>
            </AlternatingItemTemplate>
            <FooterTemplate>
            </table>
            </FooterTemplate>
        </asp:Repeater>
    </body>
    </html>
```

Listing 2.30 Viewcontacts.aspx (continued)

As in the note viewer, we'll use a Repeater control to show our data. We have a few more columns this time than before, but the pattern is the same. The HeaderTemplate sets up the column headers; the ItemTemplate and AlternatingItemTemplate show each of the fields using the DataBinder object; and the FooterTemplate closes out the table. We also format our links to both the previous page (View Person) and to the contact management pages for adding, modifying, and deleting contacts. The code-behind file to make this control work is shown in Listing 2.31.

```
Imports System
Imports System.Data
Imports System.Data.SqlClient
Imports System.Web.UI
Imports System.Web.UI.WebControls

Namespace Proj02Web
    Public Class ViewContacts
        Inherits System.Web.UI.Page

        Protected rptList As Repeater

        Sub Page_Load(Src As Object, e As EventArgs)

            Dim DB as New AtWorkUtilities.Database()
            Dim DS As DataSet =
                DB.GetDataSet("SELECT * FROM tblContacts " _
                & "WHERE fkPersonID = " & Request.QueryString("pID") _
                & " ORDER BY ContactDate")
            rptList.DataSource = DS
            rptList.DataBind()

            db.Close()
        End Sub
    End Class
End Namespace
```

Listing 2.31   Viewcontacts.aspx.vb

Other than the SQL statement and the class name, this file is identical to the Viewnotes.aspx.vb file you created in the previous section. When you put these two files on your Web server, you'll be able to view contacts that are currently available, provided you pre-populated the tables with data. If you want to load the page directly, use the following URL:

```
http://yourserver/viewcontacts.aspx?pID=37
```

The next step is to change the Viewpeople.aspx.vb file to produce the View Contacts link for each person in the system. This link follows the same pattern as the View Notes link you built in the last section, so the code below shows just the new information (shown in bold) and not the entire file.

```
While sdrData.Read()
    sb.AppendFormat("<tr class=""{0}"">" + NewLine, strColor)
    sb.AppendFormat("   <td>{0}, {1}</td>" + NewLine, _
        sdrData("LastName"), _
        sdrData("FirstName"))
```

```
   sb.AppendFormat("    <td>{0}</td>" + NewLine, sdrData("Title"))
   sb.AppendFormat("    <td>{0}</td>" + NewLine, _
      sdrData("CompanyName"))
   sb.AppendFormat("    <td>{0}</td>" + NewLine, sdrData("WorkPhone"))

   sb.Append("    <td align=middle>")
   sb.AppendFormat("<a href=""viewnotes.aspx" _
      & "?pID={0}"">View Notes</a>", _
      sdrData("pkPersonID"))
   sb.Append("  ")
   sb.AppendFormat("<a href=""viewcontacts.aspx" _
      & "?pID={0}"">View Contacts</a>", _
      sdrData("pkPersonID"))
   sb.Append("  ")
   sb.AppendFormat("<a href=""updateperson.aspx" _
      & "?id={0}"">Update</a>", _
      sdrData("pkPersonID"))
   sb.Append("  ")
   sb.AppendFormat("<a href=""deleteperson.aspx" _
      & "?id={0}"">Delete</a>" + NewLine, _
      sdrData("pkPersonID"))
   sb.Append("    </td>" + NewLine)
   sb.Append("</tr>" + NewLine)
   If strColor = "tabletext" Then
      strColor = "tabletext_gray"
   Else
      strColor = "tabletext"
   End If
End While
```

Create the Add Contact Page

Now let's build the Add Contact page. We'll also create the shared Contactform.inc file in this section so that we can reuse it when building the Update Contact page. The ASPX file for the Add Contact page is shown in Listing 2.32.

```
<%@ Page Inherits="Proj02Web.AddContact" Src="addcontact.aspx.vb" %>
<html>
   <head>
      <title>Contact Manager: Add New Contact</title>
<!--#include file="styles.css" -->
   </head>
   <body bgcolor="#FFFFFF">
   <p class="pageheading">Add New Contact</p>

   <asp:label id="lblErrorMessage" class="errortext" runat="server" />

<!--#include file="contactform.inc" -->
   </body>
</html>
```

Listing 2.32 Addcontact.aspx

If you're copying and pasting the note viewer files, be sure to change the @Page directive and the word Note to Contact. Other than that, the file is identical. The form file, Contactform.inc, is shown in Listing 2.33.

```
<form runat="server">
<input type="hidden" id="pkContactID" runat="server">
<input type="hidden" id="fkPersonID" runat="server">
<table cellspacing="5">
<tr class="tabletext">
    <td align="right">Date/Time:</td>
    <td>
        <asp:textbox
            id="txtContactDate"
            columns="30"
            maxlength="30"
            runat="server" /></td>
</tr>
<tr class="tabletext">
    <td align="right">Contact Type:</td>
    <td>
        <asp:DropDownList
            id="lstType"
            width="150px"
            runat="server">
        <asp:ListItem></asp:ListItem>
        <asp:ListItem>Phone Call</asp:ListItem>
        <asp:ListItem>Fax</asp:ListItem>
        <asp:ListItem>Email</asp:ListItem>
        <asp:ListItem>Meeting</asp:ListItem>
        <asp:ListItem>Other</asp:ListItem>
        </asp:DropDownList>
    </td>
</tr>
<tr class="tabletext">
    <td align="right">Length:</td>
    <td>
        <asp:textbox
            id="txtLength"
            columns="15"
            maxlength="15"
            runat="server" /></td>
</tr>

<tr class="tabletext">
    <td valign="middle" align="right">Notes:</td>
    <td>
```

Listing 2.33   Contactform.inc

```
            <asp:textbox
                id="txtNotes"
                rows="15"
                columns="60"
                wrap="true"
                textmode="Multiline"
                runat="server" /></td>
    </tr>
    <tr class="tabletext">
        <td colspan=2 align=middle>
        <input type="submit" name="btnSubmit" runat="server" value="Save" />
        <input type="reset"  name="btnReset"  runat="server" value="Clear" />
        </td>
    </tr>
    </table>
    </form>
```

Listing 2.33   Contactform.inc (continued)

This page is unique from our other forms in that it has a drop-down list box for the type of contact we're entering. When we are populating our Contact class with the information from the Web page, we can read the text from the drop-down item into our object. In the update feature, we'll have to loop through the items to find the one that should be selected.

The code-behind file is shown in Listing 2.34.

```
Imports System
Imports System.Data
Imports System.Data.SqlClient
Imports System.Web.UI
Imports System.Web.UI.WebControls

Namespace Proj02Web
    Public Class AddContact
        Inherits System.Web.UI.Page
        Protected pkContactID As HTMLControls.HTMLInputHidden
        Protected fkPersonID As HTMLControls.HTMLInputHidden
        Protected txtContactDate As TextBox
        Protected lstType As DropDownList
        Protected txtLength As TextBox
        Protected txtNotes As TextBox

        Protected lblErrorMessage As Label

        Sub Page_Load(objSender As Object, objArgs As EventArgs)
            Dim DB As New AtWorkUtilities.Database()
```

Listing 2.34   Addcontact.aspx.vb

```
        If Not Page.IsPostBack Then
            fkPersonID.Value = Request.QueryString("pID")
        Else
            Dim C As New BusinessObjects.Contact(DB)
            Dim DR As DataRow = C.GetRow()
            DR("fkPersonID") = Int32.Parse(fkPersonID.Value)
            Try
                DR("ContactDate") = DateTime.Parse(txtContactDate.Text)
            Catch e As FormatException
                ' Contact object will display error, this prevents
                ' FormatException from appearing.
            End Try

            DR("Type") = lstType.SelectedItem.Text
            DR("Length") = txtLength.Text
            DR("Notes") = txtNotes.Text
            C.SaveRow(DR)
            If Not C.IsValid Then
                lblErrorMessage.Text = _
                    C.ValidationError("<b>ERROR:</b> The following " _
                        & "errors were detected in your data:<br>", _
                        "&bull; {0}<br>", _
                        "")
            Else
                C.Save()
                DB.Close()
                Response.Redirect("viewcontacts.aspx?pID=" _
                    & fkPersonID.Value)
            End If
        End If
    End Sub

    End Class
End Namespace
```

Listing 2.34   Addcontact.aspx.vb (continued)

This file follows the same format as Addnote.aspx.vb, with a minor exception. When we take the date and time of the contact and put it into the DataRow object, the DataRow will attempt to validate that the data we enter is actually a valid date/time value. This unfortunate side effect of our object design means that we'll have to do some minor error trapping in the code-behind file. When we get ready to store the date/time value into the DataRow, we set up a Try block. This will let us handle the FormatException error that might occur. Since the Contact object itself will generate an error message if no data is entered for the date and time of the contact, we don't have to do anything when the error occurs. The validation error message will already state that the contact date/time is invalid and must be entered. Other than that, the rest of the code follows the pattern we've already set up.

Create the Update Contact Page

The next page to be built gives you the ability to edit the contacts in the system. The ASPX page is shown in Listing 2.35.

```
<%@ Page Inherits="Proj02Web.UpdateContact" Src="updatecontact.aspx.vb"
%>
<html>
    <head>
        <title>Contact Manager: Update Contact</title>
<!--#include file="styles.css" -->
    </head>
    <body bgcolor="#FFFFFF">
    <p class="pageheading">Update Contact</p>

    <asp:label id="lblErrorMessage" class="errortext" runat="server" />

<!--#include file="contactform.inc" -->
    </body>
</html>
```

Listing 2.35 Updatecontact.aspx

Again, if you're copying and pasting between the note files, be sure to change all the references of Note to Contact, or you'll get runtime errors. This page provides the basic structure of the Update Contact page and brings in the form shared between this page and the Add Contact page. The code-behind file is shown in Listing 2.36.

```
Imports System
Imports System.Data
Imports System.Data.SqlClient
Imports System.Web.UI
Imports System.Web.UI.WebControls

Namespace Proj02Web
    Public Class UpdateContact
        Inherits System.Web.UI.Page
        Protected pkContactID As HTMLControls.HTMLInputHidden
        Protected fkPersonID As HTMLControls.HTMLInputHidden
        Protected txtContactDate As TextBox
        Protected lstType As DropDownList
        Protected txtLength As TextBox
        Protected txtNotes As TextBox
```

Listing 2.36 Updatecontact.aspx.vb

```
Protected lblErrorMessage As Label

Sub Page_Load(objSender As Object, objArgs As EventArgs)

    Dim DB As New AtWorkUtilities.Database()
    Dim i As Integer

    If Not Page.IsPostBack Then
        Dim C As New BusinessObjects.Contact(DB, _
            Request.QueryString("ID"))
        Dim DR As DataRow = C.GetRow()
        pkContactID.Value = DR("pkContactID").ToString()
        fkPersonID.Value = DR("fkPersonID").ToString()
        txtContactDate.Text = DR("ContactDate").ToString()
        For i = 0 To lstType.Items.Count
            If lstType.Items(i).Text = DR("Type") Then
                lstType.SelectedIndex = i
                Exit For
            End If
        Next i
        txtLength.Text = DR("Length").ToString()
        txtNotes.Text = DR("Notes").ToString()
    Else
        Dim C As New BusinessObjects.Contact(DB, pkContactID.Value)
        Dim DR As DataRow = C.GetRow()
        DR("fkPersonID") = Int32.Parse(fkPersonID.Value)
        Try
            DR("ContactDate") = DateTime.Parse(txtContactDate.Text)
        Catch e As FormatException
            ' Contact object will display error, this prevents
            ' FormatException from appearing.
        End Try

        DR("Type") = lstType.SelectedItem.Text
        DR("Length") = txtLength.Text
        DR("Notes") = txtNotes.Text
        C.SaveRow(DR)
        If Not C.IsValid Then
            lblErrorMessage.Text = _
                C.ValidationError("<b>ERROR:</b> The following " _
                    & "errors were detected in your data:<br>", _
                    "&bull; {0}<br>", _
                    "")
        Else
            C.Save()
            DB.Close()
            Response.Redirect("viewcontacts.aspx?pID=" _
                & fkPersonID.Value)
        End If
    End If
```

Listing 2.36   Updatecontact.aspx.vb (continued)

```
        End If
      End Sub

   End Class
End Namespace
```

Listing 2.36 Updatecontact.aspx.vb (continued)

The new piece of code in this file is a loop that you haven't seen before. It is designed to help select data from a drop-down list on the page. The code is shown here:

```
For i = 0 To lstType.Items.Count
   If lstType.Items(i).Text = DR("Type") Then
      lstType.SelectedIndex = i
      Exit For
   End If
Next i
```

Since we want to reselect the same item in the list, we can loop through the items in the drop-down list to find the one that we have in the database. Once we find it, we set the SelectedIndex property of the drop-down list to be equal to that index value, and then we exit the loop using Exit For. This accomplishes our goal, and the item is reselected when you choose to update a contact.

Create the Delete Contact Page

Deleting a contact is just like deleting a note, so we won't go into it in repetitive detail here. Listing 2.37 shows the ASPX file, and Listing 2.38 shows the code-behind file. Like the notes file, we are passing both the contact ID and the person ID so that we can go back to the proper page after the deletion is complete.

```
<%@ Page Inherits="Proj02Web.DeleteContact" Src="deletecontact.aspx.vb"
%>
<html>
   <head>
      <title>Contact Manager: Delete Contact</title>
<!--#include file="styles.css" -->
   </head>
   <body bgcolor="#FFFFFF">
   <p class="pageheading">Delete Contact</p>
   <p class="tabletext">Are you sure you want to delete this
contact?</p>
   <form runat="server">
   <input type="hidden" runat="server" id="pkContactID">
   <input type="hidden" runat="server" id="fkPersonID">
```

Listing 2.37 Deletecontact.aspx

```
  <p class="tabletext">
  <a href="javascript:document.forms[0].submit();">Yes</a>
    
  <a href="javascript:history.go(-1);">No</a>
  </p>
  </form>
  </body>
</html>
```

Listing 2.37 Deletecontact.aspx (continued)

```
Imports System
Imports System.Data
Imports System.Data.SqlClient
Imports System.Web.UI
Imports System.Web.UI.WebControls

Namespace Proj02Web
   Public Class DeleteContact
      Inherits System.Web.UI.Page


      Protected pkContactID As HTMLControls.HTMLInputHidden
      Protected fkPersonID As HTMLControls.HTMLInputHidden

      Sub Page_Load(objSender As Object, objArgs As EventArgs)
         If Not Page.IsPostBack Then
             pkContactID.Value = Request.QueryString("ID")
             fkPersonID.Value = Request.QueryString("pID")
         Else
             Dim DB As New AtWorkUtilities.Database()
             Dim C As New BusinessObjects.Contact(DB, pkContactID.Value)
             C.Delete()
             DB.Close()
             Response.Redirect("viewcontacts.aspx?pID=" _
                 & fkPersonID.Value)
         End If
      End Sub

   End Class
End Namespace
```

Listing 2.38 Deletecontact.aspx.vb

As before, the links on the first page could be replaced with some JavaScript code on the View Contacts page, but that is left as an option for you.

Wrap Up

In this chapter, you built an entire object hierarchy for your Web site and used a number of features of the ASP.NET platform. You used data binding to show data in Web pages, custom-built objects to manage the database activity needed, and handled a variety of validations in several different ways.

One key thing about the method we used in this project: It's not the only way or even the best way to code. It's simply an option that you have to use. As you use ASP.NET more, you'll probably come up with enhancements that will make this code look like a Model T compared to a Lamborghini. However, this should give you a base to work from for your own applications. You might want to add more information to the Contact Manager to better track what your follow-up requirements are. You might also build a search feature to look in all the types of data (people, contacts, and notes) for particular keywords. We'll be using variations of these objects in the other projects of this book, but the basic structure will remain similar throughout.

In Project 3, you'll build a calendar that supports a wide range of events, including both one-time and recurring events. You'll be building several new classes to support the calendar, as well as both the Display and Maintenance pages for your calendar.

Building the Calendar Application

One of the problems with having lots of people bidding for your time is trying to keep them all posted on your schedule. When I started doing training courses several years ago, I found that it was impossible to maintain static copies of my schedule, so I built a Web-based calendar application. People could now use this to check my availability and schedule appointments. Part of the calendar was still kept hidden, however, since people don't need to know all the details on my engagements.

We'll be building a similar system in this project. The events you put on the calendar can be single-day or multiday events. They can also be recurring events, using several different methods to schedule them. An event can be scheduled for a particular day in the month, such as the first Friday of the month. Events can also be scheduled to repeat every two weeks. Events can even be scheduled for the same day of the month, each month, if you can have an event that occurs on the 15th of every month, for example. We'll be building all this logic into a series of objects so that we can display and edit the data through a series of Web pages. We'll also be creating both a monthly and daily view of the calendar. For the monthly view, we'll be using the built-in Calendar control to save ourselves some tedious formatting work. Then, all we have to do is fill in the boxes with our data. The daily view will require a bit more programming, but it won't require a lot of new logic. We'll also be building a management page for adding and modifying the events that are on the calendar.

THE PROBLEM

You need a calendar that is accessible and modifiable through the Web and that doesn't require the purchase of an expensive server, such as Microsoft Exchange.

THE SOLUTION

An ASP.NET application that provides the ability to do simple and recurring events, as well as the ability to publish the calendar on the Web.

Project Background

You'll need to complete the following steps to build this project:

1. Design the Events table.
2. Build the business objects.
3. Build the administration Web pages to add, modify, and delete events.
4. Build the monthly calendar viewing page.
5. Build the daily calendar viewing page.

You Will Need

✔ **Windows 2000**

✔ **Internet Information Server 5.0 with .NET Framework installed**

✔ **Visual Studio .NET**

✔ **SQL Server 7.0 or 2000**

✔ **A text editor, like HomeSite or TextPad, to edit pages if you don't want to edit them within Visual Studio .NET**

Designing the Events Table

In this section, we'll design the tblEvents table used to hold our events. We first have to determine how we're going to handle each type of event. We can then move on to the actual table design and creation.

Creating the Recurrence Logic

Our calendar is going to support the following types of events:

Simple events that occur only once. These events may span several days; however, they only occur once.

Events that occur at a regular interval, such as every two weeks or once a year. These events can be ongoing or can have specific starting and ending dates.

Events that occur on a particular day in a month. These events can also be ongoing or can have specific starting and ending dates.

Anniversaries. These events occur on the same day of the month, once a year. They may be a birthday, an anniversary, or some other type of yearly event.

You might come up with other types of recurring events you want to add to the system, but this list will keep us busy in this project. Most other recurrences are simply combinations of these basic types. Once you've seen how the system works in handling these events, you'll be able to add your own and expand this system.

The first order of business is to design the table into which we'll store the events shown on the calendar. Part of the table contains basic information common to every type of event, but we also have to make space for storing information about each type of recurring event that we need to store in the system. For simplicity, we'll be storing the information for each type of recurrence in a different field or set of fields and using a flag in one of the fields to indicate the type of event it is. This will make it easier to select the appropriate events when displaying them on the calendar.

The general information we need to store for each event is as follows:

Name. A short description of event that can be shown in small views of the calendar.

Description. A text field for notes about the event.

Event Start and End. The starting and ending dates for this particular event. These dates will be used in events that occur periodically so that you can have an event that is a week long occur every two weeks. The starting and ending dates will be used in calculations to determine when the recurrence should occur.

Public or Private. Event details are shown to everyone on a public calendar. Private events are also shown on the calendar, but no details are provided.

For recurring events, we have to store the following additional information, based on the rules that we established earlier in the project:

Recurrence Type. This is a single-letter code indicating what type of recurrence we're using. N = Non-recurring, P = periodic event, occurring on a regular basis, M = monthly event, A = anniversary.

Recurrence Start, Recurrence End. This indicates when the recurring event should start and end. This is separate from the start and end date we already identified. For an event that doesn't have an ending date, the Recurrence End can be empty or null.

Periodic Code, Periodic Amount. For events that occur at regular intervals, the Periodic Code is the code used by the date functions (DateAdd, DateDiff) to indicate the time period. The Periodic Amount is the number of those units. The codes for the Periodic Code are shown in Table 3.1. We have left out the codes for units smaller than a day.

Monthly Code, Monthly Ordinal, Monthly Day. For events that occur once a month, we have to first indicate whether the event is on a particular day of the month or if the event is on a logical day in the month, like the first Thursday, for example. The Monthly Code value will hold an A for the first case, standing for

Actual, and a L for the second case, standing for Logical. The Monthly Ordinal field will only be used when we are using a logical date and will have a number in it from 1-5, since there can only be five Mondays, for instance, in any month. The Monthly Day field will be used in both actual and logical date events. For actual events, this value will be the day number to use. For logical events, it will be a number from 1-7 indicating the day of the week, with the value 1 indicating Sunday, which is the U.S. standard.

AnniversaryDate. This field will hold the anniversary date for yearly events. Users can store the actual date, such as the date of a wedding or birthday, along with the year. While the year is irrelevant for date calculations, it is easier to store this way than as separate fields.

NOTE   **These codes are also documented in the DateAdd and DateDiff function documentation in your .NET installation.**

It may seem that we're using a lot of separate and even duplicate fields, but each type of recurrence requires slightly different information to be processed correctly. You could combine them, but it makes it more difficult to work with later.

Creating the tblEvents Table

Since this application is separate from the previous two applications you've built, I decided to start a brand new database for it, which I'm naming ASPNetProject03 in my own system. You could easily combine the application built in the last project with this one, at which point you'd probably want to have a single database for both parts. We're going to create a new table called tblEvents to hold both single and recurring events. The table definition is shown in Table 3.2.

Table 3.1 Periodic Code Values

CODE	UNIT
d	Day
m	Month
q	Quarter of year
w	Weekday
ww	Week of year
yyyy	Year

Table 3.2 tblEvents Table Definition

FIELD NAME	SQL DATA TYPE	LENGTH	OTHER
pkEventID	int	N/A	Identity, Primary Key, Not Null
Name	varchar	80	Not Null
Description	text	N/A	Nullable
EventStart	datetime	N/A	Not Null
EventEnd	datetime	N/A	Not Null
IsPublic	bit	N/A	Not Null, Default = 0
RecurrenceType	char	1	Not Null, Default = 'N'
RecurrenceStart	datetime	N/A	Nullable
RecurrenceEnd	datetime	N/A	Nullable
PeriodicCode	varchar	4	Nullable
PeriodicAmount	tinyint	N/A	Nullable
MonthlyCode	char	1	Nullable
MonthlyOrdinal	tinyint	N/A	Nullable
MonthlyDay	tinyint	N/A	Nullable
AnniversaryDate	datetime	N/A	Nullable

If you're using SQL Server, a copy of the script to create this table is available on the CD-ROM. If you're not using SQL Server, you can use the table above to convert to your particular database's data types.

We'll be adding test data along the way to test various conditions and recurrence types of the calendar. For now, I'd hold off adding data until you understand how the table is designed to hold it.

Building the Business Objects

The next step is to build the objects that will help manage our calendar data. We're going to use some of the code we built in the previous project. Specifically, we'll be using the AtWorkUtilities assembly and the BaseServices class. The AtWorkUtilities assembly is already done, so I'm simply making a copy of it for this new project. In real life, you wouldn't need to copy the project, but I'm doing this so that everything is kept together and so you don't have to hunt for the files.

The second assembly we'll be building will contain the logic for the CalendarEvent class and will be built on top of the BaseServices class we built in the previous project. I'll be creating a new assembly project and copying the BaseServices class to be used here. For simplicity, we'll be calling this assembly CalendarObjects, but feel free to name it whatever you want. If you have decided to combine this application with the application you built in the last project, the Event class will become part of the BusinessObjects assembly.

 The class is called CalendarEvent since the word Event is a reserved word in Visual Basic .NET.

NOTE

Preparing the Environment

Since this Web application will use a number of graphical controls, it's easiest to build it from scratch within the Visual Studio environment. Our Solution file will contain all of these projects when we're done:

AtWorkUtilities. Assembly created in Project 2 with the Database class.

CalendarObjects. Assembly you'll build in this project to manipulate your events.

Calendar. ASP.NET application that will be used to show and administer the calendar.

You may also have a test Windows application to work with your CalendarObjects class, but you won't typically need to keep that application.

Since I want to keep all the projects together in a single solution, I use Visual Studio .NET to create a blank solution, into which I can add projects. This makes it easier to get the Solution file in the right place. You don't have to use this method, but it makes for easier organization. To create a blank solution, do the following:

1. Select New from the File menu. Then select New Solution.

2. In the dialog box that appears, select where to put the solution. Note that Visual Studio automatically creates a new folder for your solution.

Once you have the empty solution, you can copy other project directories to the Solution directory and then add each project to the solution. The first project you'll want to add, either as an actual project or as a reference to the assembly DLL, is the AtWorkUtilities assembly. If you're not sure how to build it, you can look at Project 2 for all the details on this assembly and the features and classes it provides. At this time, the only object included in the AtWorkUtilities assembly is the Database class. The code for the class is shown in Listing 3.1.

```
Imports System.Data.SqlClient
Imports System.Configuration


Public Class Database
```

Listing 3.1 Database class in AtWorkUtilities assembly

```
Private m_cnDB As SqlConnection


'
' This constructor reads the application configuration
' file (Web.config for web applications) for a string
' called ConnectionString. If it's not there, an exception
' is thrown. Otherwise, the connection is made.
'
Public Sub New()
    Dim objCnf As ConfigurationSettings
    If objCnf.AppSettings("ConnectionString") = "" Then
        Throw New Exception("Connection string not found " _
            & "in application configuration file.")
    Else
        m_cnDB = New _
        SqlConnection(objCnf.AppSettings("ConnectionString").ToString)
        m_cnDB.Open()
    End If
End Sub


'
' This constructor accepts a connection string as input
' and makes a connection to that SQL Server.
'
Public Sub New(ByVal ConnectionString As String)
    m_cnDB = New SqlConnection(ConnectionString)
    m_cnDB.Open()
End Sub


'
' In case there are other objects that need the live
' connection, make it available through a read-only
' property.
'
Public ReadOnly Property Connection() As SqlConnection
Get
    Return m_cnDB
End Get
End Property


'
' Run a query that does not return records.
'
Public Function Execute(ByVal SQL As String) As Integer
    Dim lngRecords As Integer
    Dim cmdQuery As New SqlCommand()
    cmdQuery.Connection = m_cnDB
    cmdQuery.CommandText = SQL
    cmdQuery.CommandType = CommandType.Text
    lngRecords = cmdQuery.ExecuteNonQuery()
End Function
```

Listing 3.1 Database class in AtWorkUtilities assembly (continued)

```
'
' Run a stored procedure that does not return records.
'
Public Function ExecuteStoredProc(ByVal SQL As String) As Integer
    Dim lngRecords As Integer
    Dim cmdQuery As New SqlCommand()
    cmdQuery.Connection = m_cnDB
    cmdQuery.CommandText = SQL
    cmdQuery.CommandType = CommandType.StoredProcedure
    lngRecords = cmdQuery.ExecuteNonQuery()
End Function


'
' Run a query that returns records in the form
' of a SqlDataReader.
'
Public Function GetDataReader(ByVal SQL As String, _
    Optional ByVal blnSkipRead As Boolean = False) As SqlDataReader

    Dim cmdQuery As New SqlCommand()
    Dim dr As SqlDataReader
    cmdQuery.Connection = m_cnDB
    cmdQuery.CommandText = SQL
    cmdQuery.CommandType = CommandType.Text
    dr = cmdQuery.ExecuteReader
    If Not blnSkipRead Then dr.Read()
    Return dr
End Function


'
' Run a query that returns records in the form
' of a DataSet.
'
Public Function GetDataSet(ByVal SQL As String) As DataSet
    Dim da As New SqlDataAdapter(SQL, m_cnDB)
    Dim ds As New DataSet("Results")
    da.Fill(ds)
    Return ds
End Function


'
' Replaces all single quotes with two single
' quote characters. Useful for building SQL
' statements.
'
Public Function Clean(strInput as string) as string
    Return strInput.Replace("'", "''")
End Function


'
' Close the database connection.
'
```

Listing 3.1   Database class in AtWorkUtilities assembly (continued)

```
      Public Sub Close()
         m_cnDB.Close()
      End Sub
   End Class
End Class
```

Listing 3.1 Database class in AtWorkUtilities assembly (continued)

One change that we've made is to the GetDataReader method, which now accepts a second, optional argument. The SqlDataReader object requires that you do a read call in order to access data. However, if you're looping through the data, you'll use a While loop and read all the records. This new optional argument allows the code to skip the initial read.

Once you've got the AtWorkUtilities assembly or project added to the solution, your next step is to create a new VB Class Library project called CalendarObjects. This is where you should add a copy of the BaseServices class you built in the previous project, provided you're building a new assembly for this project. The BaseServices class is shown in Listing 3.2 and is documented in the previous project.

```
Imports System.Text
Imports System.Data
Imports System.Data.SqlClient
Imports AtWorkUtilities

Public MustInherit Class BaseServices
   Private m_arrErrors As ArrayList
   Protected m_DB As Database
   Protected m_DA As SqlDataAdapter
   Protected m_CB As SqlCommandBuilder
   Protected m_DS As DataSet

   `
   ` This constructor should be overloaded and called
   ` by each derived class. It sets up the protected
   ` objects available to all derived classes for handling
   ` database activities.
   `
   Protected Sub New(ByVal DB As Database, ByVal strSQL As String)
      m_DB = DB
      m_DA = New SqlDataAdapter(strSQL, m_DB.Connection)
      m_CB = New SqlCommandBuilder(m_DA)
      m_DS = New DataSet()
      m_DA.Fill(m_DS)
   End Sub

   `
   ` The DataSet will have either zero rows or one row
   ` so we simply return the current row in the dataset.
   ` This code makes it easier to get at the data instead
```

Listing 3.2 BaseServices class

```
' of having to duplicate the full hierarchy in the
' calling code. For empty DataSets, we return an empty
' row that can be populated.
'
Public Function GetRow() As DataRow
    If m_DS.Tables(0).Rows.Count > 0 Then
        Return m_DS.Tables(0).Rows(0)
    Else
        Return m_DS.Tables(0).NewRow()
    End If
End Function


'
' This routine accepts a data row as input and stores
' the data into the dataset. In cases where the row
' is new, we add the new row to the DataSet. If the
' DataSet has data in it, we read the data row and
' replace each field in the DataSet one column at a
' time.
'
Protected Sub SaveRow(ByVal dr As DataRow)
    Dim val As DataColumn
    '
    ' Handle new row
    '
    If m_DS.Tables(0).Rows.Count = 0 Then
        m_DS.Tables(0).Rows.Add(dr)
        Exit Sub
    End If


    '
    ' Handle existing row
    '
    m_DS.Tables(0).Rows(0).BeginEdit()
    For Each val In m_DS.Tables(0).Columns
        m_DS.Tables(0).Rows(0).Item(val) = dr.Item(val)
    Next
    m_DS.Tables(0).Rows(0).EndEdit()
End Sub


'
' Adds another validation error to the array list
' object. This saves some work for the calling/inheriting
' class.
'
Protected Sub AddError(ByVal strInput As String)
    If m_arrErrors Is Nothing Then
        m_arrErrors = New ArrayList()
    End If
    m_arrErrors.Add(strInput)
End Sub
```

Listing 3.2   BaseServices class (continued)

```
' This method empties the array list of any previous errors
' that had been detected.
'
Protected Sub ClearErrors()
   If m_arrErrors Is Nothing Then
      m_arrErrors = New ArrayList()
   Else
      m_arrErrors.Clear()
   End If
End Sub


' This method formats the array into a message that can be
' used in a message box.
'
Public Function ValidationError( _
   Optional ByVal Header As String = _
      "The following errors were detected in your data:" & vbCrLf, _
   Optional ByVal ItemFormat As String = "- {0}" & vbCrLf, _
   Optional ByVal Footer As String = "") As String
   Dim strMessage As New StringBuilder()
   Dim strErr As String

   If m_arrErrors.Count > 0 Then
      strMessage.Append(Header)
      For Each strErr In m_arrErrors
         strMessage.AppendFormat(ItemFormat, strErr)
      Next
      strMessage.Append(Footer)
      Return strMessage.ToString
   Else
      Return ""
   End If
End Function


' Provides access to the list of errors that were detected
' during the validation process. This is used for applications
' that need custom error messages.
'
Public ReadOnly Property ValidationErrors() As ArrayList
Get
   Return m_arrErrors
End Get
End Property


' Indicates whether any validation errors were detected
' as the data was stored into the object.
```

Listing 3.2 BaseServices class (continued)

```
`
    Public ReadOnly Property IsValid() As Boolean
    Get
        Return (m_arrErrors.Count = 0)
    End Get
    End Property


End Class
```

Listing 3.2   BaseServices class (continued)

For this class to work properly, you have to add a reference from the new Class Library project to the AtWorkUtilities project or to the AtWorkUtilities assembly DLL. Otherwise, the Database object will be unresolved and will have a blue squiggly line under it.

The CalendarObjects project also needs a populated assembly information file, which is shown in Listing 3.3. I made a copy of the BusinessObject assembly information file and made a few minor changes.

```
Imports System.Reflection
Imports System.Runtime.InteropServices

' General Information about an assembly is controlled through the
following
' set of attributes. Change these attribute values to modify the
information
' associated with an assembly.

' Review the values of the assembly attributes

<Assembly: AssemblyTitle("ASP.NET At Work - Project 3")>
<Assembly: AssemblyDescription("This assembly contains business " _
    & "objects for Project 3. ")>
<Assembly: AssemblyCompany("Northstar Computer Systems")>
<Assembly: AssemblyProduct("ASP.NET At Work")>
<Assembly: AssemblyCopyright("Copyright 2001 by Northstar " _
    & "Computer Systems. All Rights Reserved.")>
<Assembly: AssemblyTrademark("Copyright 2001 by Northstar " _
    & "Computer Systems. All Rights Reserved.")>
<Assembly: CLSCompliant(True)>

'The following GUID is for the ID of the typelib if this project
'is exposed to COM
<Assembly: Guid("5AC6EBE3-2690-41F1-B6BA-862C515715C8")>

' Version information for an assembly consists of the following four
values:
```

Listing 3.3   AssemblyInfo.vb file for CalendarObjects project

```
'       Major Version
'       Minor Version
'       Build Number
'       Revision
'
' You can specify all the values or you can default the Build and
Revision Numbers
' by using the '*' as shown below:

<Assembly: AssemblyVersion("3.0.*")>
```

Listing 3.3   AssemblyInfo.vb file for CalendarObjects project (continued)

In this assembly, we've updated the comments to indicate that this is Project 3, and the version of the assembly has been marked as 3.0. The build number and revision will be automatically generated by Visual Studio .NET as we recompile the application. Feel free to fill these values in if you have a development scheme already in place.

Now that the CalendarObjects project is ready, we can add the ASP.NET application to our solution. You don't need to create any code here yet; however, you should reference both the CalendarObjects project and the AtWorkUtilities assembly or project in the References item in the Solution Explorer. This will give the Web application access to all the objects we've built already and to the new ones that we'll be building in this project.

With the configuration done, the next step is to start building the classes in the CalendarObjects project.

Creating the CalendarEvent Class

The next object you need to build is the CalendarEvent class. As mentioned earlier, we have to use a longer name than just Event, since the word Event is a reserved word in Visual Basic .NET. This object follows the same pattern as all the other objects we've built so far, but it does a great deal more validation of the data being stored in it. The validation rules we set up so far in this project provide for five different types of event data to be stored in this single object and single table. This means that we have quite a bit of conditional validation to do, based on the input provided by the user.

The CalendarEvent class is shown in Listing 3.4 and is part of a separate assembly called CalendarObjects.

```
Imports AtWorkUtilities
Imports System.Data.SqlClient

Public Class CalendarEvent
    Inherits BaseServices

    Private Const RECUR_NONE = "N"
```

Listing 3.4   CalendarEvent class

```
      Private Const RECUR_PERIODIC = "P"
      Private Const RECUR_MONTHLY = "M"
      Private Const RECUR_ANNIV = "A"
      Private Const MONTHLY_ACTUAL = "A"
      Private Const MONTHLY_LOGICAL = "L"


      '
      ' If no arguments are supplied, build a separate
      ' database connection for this object.
      '
      Public Sub New()
         MyBase.New(New Database(), "SELECT * FROM tblEvents WHERE 1=0")
      End Sub


      '
      ' If database connection is supplied, store it
      ' in the private connection variable for this
      ' object.
      '
      Public Sub New(ByVal db As Database)
         MyBase.New(db, "SELECT * FROM tblEvents WHERE 1=0")
      End Sub


      '
      ' If both database and ID are supplied, retrieve
      ' data into the object from the database.
      '
      Public Sub New(ByVal db As Database, _
         ByVal ID As Integer)

         MyBase.New(db, "SELECT * FROM tblEvents WHERE pkEventID = " _
            & ID.ToString)

      End Sub


      '
      ' Verify that all data validation rules have been
      ' met. Any errors get stored into the errors collection
      ' inherited from the BaseServices class.
      '
      Public Sub Validate()
         Dim dr As DataRow

         ClearErrors()
         For Each dr In m_DS.Tables(0).Rows
            If dr.RowState = DataRowState.Added _
            Or dr.RowState = DataRowState.Modified Then
               ValidateRow(dr)
            End If
         Next

      End Sub
```

Listing 3.4 CalendarEvent class (continued)

```
'
' Checks an individual row for validation rule
' compliance. Any errors are added to the errors
' collection.
'
Private Sub ValidateRow(ByVal dr As DataRow)

   If IsDBNull(dr("Name")) Then
      AddError("The name of the event is required.")
   Else
      If dr("Name") = "" Then
         AddError("The name of the event is required.")
      ElseIf dr("Name").ToString.Length > 80 Then
         AddError("The event name must be 80 characters or less.")
      End If
   End If

   If IsDBNull(dr("EventStartDate")) Then
      AddError("The start date of the event is required.")
   End If
   If IsDBNull(dr("EventStartTime")) Then
      AddError("The start time of the event is required.")
   End If

   If IsDBNull(dr("EventEndDate")) Then
      AddError("The ending date of the event is required.")
   End If
   If IsDBNull(dr("EventEndTime")) Then
      AddError("The ending time of the event is required.")
   End If

   If IsDBNull(dr("IsPublic")) Then
      AddError("The start date/time of the event is required.")
   End If

   If IsDBNull(dr("RecurrenceType")) Then
      AddError("The type of event is required.")
   Else
      Select Case dr("RecurrenceType")
      Case RECUR_NONE
         '
         ' No additional data is required for a
         ' non-recurring event
      Case RECUR_PERIODIC, RECUR_MONTHLY, RECUR_ANNIV
         If IsDBNull(dr("RecurrenceStart")) Then
            AddError("For a recurring event, the " _
               & "recurrence start date is required.")
         End If
         Select Case dr("RecurrenceType")
            Case RECUR_PERIODIC
               ValidatePeriodicEvent(dr)
```

Listing 3.4   CalendarEvent class (continued)

```
                    Case RECUR_MONTHLY
                        ValidateMonthlyEvent(dr)
                    Case RECUR_ANNIV
                        If IsDBNull(dr("AnniversaryDate")) Then
                            AddError("For an anniversary event, the " _
                                & "anniversary date is required.")
                        End If
                End Select
            Case Else
                AddError("The recurrence type must be N, P, M, or A.")
            End Select
        End If
End Sub

Private Sub ValidatePeriodicEvent(ByVal dr As DataRow)
    If IsDBNull(dr("PeriodicCode")) Then
        AddError("For a periodically recurring event, " _
            & "the period code is required.")
    Else
        If dr("PeriodicCode") = "" Then
            AddError("For a periodically recurring event, " _
                & "the period code is required.")
        End If
    End If
    If IsDBNull(dr("PeriodicAmount")) Then
        AddError("For a periodically recurring event, " _
            & "the period amount is required.")
    End If
End Sub

Private Sub ValidateMonthlyEvent(ByVal dr As DataRow)
    If IsDBNull(dr("MonthlyCode")) Then
        AddError("For a monthly event, the monthly " _
            & "type code is required to be either A or L.")
    Else
        Select Case dr("MonthlyCode")
        Case MONTHLY_ACTUAL
            If IsDBNull(dr("MonthlyDay")) Then
                AddError("For this type of monthly event, " _
                    & "the day of the month must be specified.")
            Else
                If dr("MonthlyDay") < 1 Or dr("MonthlyDay") > 31 Then
                    AddError("The day of the month is out of range.")
                End If
            End If
        Case MONTHLY_LOGICAL
            If IsDBNull(dr("MonthlyOrdinal")) Then
                AddError("For this type of monthly event, " _
                    & "the day ordinal is required.")
            Else
                If dr("MonthlyOrdinal") < 1 Or dr("MonthlyOrdinal") > 5
Then
```

Listing 3.4 CalendarEvent class (continued)

```
                    AddError("The day ordinal must be between 1 and 5.")
                End If

            End If
            If IsDBNull(dr("MonthlyDay")) Then
                AddError("The day number is required.")
            Else
                If dr("MonthlyDay") < 1 Or dr("MonthlyDay") > 7 Then
                    AddError("The day number must be between 1 and 7.")
                End If
            End If
        Case Else
            AddError("The monthly event type must be either A or L.")
        End Select
    End If

End Sub
'
' The base Save method stores the DataRow into the
' DataSet, whether it's a new or existing row. The
' rest of this routine handles specific validation
' for this type of data.
'
Public Overloads Sub SaveRow(ByVal dr As DataRow)
    MyBase.SaveRow(dr)
    Validate()

End Sub


'
' We separate the SaveRow method from the Save method
' to give us a chance to handle any validation. We have
' a verification here that the data is good before we
' continue, however.
'
Public Sub Save()

    If Not Me.IsValid Then
        Throw New CalendarException(Me.ValidationError)
        Exit Sub
    End If


    m_DA.Update(m_DS)
End Sub


'
' Since we only have a single row in our DataSet,
' delete it and then update the database with the
' change.
'
```

Listing 3.4 CalendarEvent class (continued)

```
    Public Sub Delete()
        If m_DS.Tables(0).Rows.Count > 0 Then
            m_DS.Tables(0).Rows(0).Delete()
            m_DA.Update(m_DS)
        End If
    End Sub


End Class
```

Listing 3.4   CalendarEvent class (continued)

Because the validation is fairly complex, it is broken down into a series of subroutines that are used for each type of event that we have identified. Let's work through the validation code first, since it is the most important and unique part of this class.

As part of this class, we define a series of constants to use in each of the flag values. These constants are defined as Private to the class, but if we wanted to, we could make them Public and make them usable outside of the class. This is not necessary, but feel free to do so if you want.

The first thing we do is make sure that the standard data required for all events is provided. This routine verifies that the name of the event is provided and that the data is not more characters than is allowed by the field. We have to do this in several steps and check for both null values and empty values, as they are not the same thing. A null value means that no value has ever been stored in the field. This is common in databases and when you retrieve data from a database. An empty value means that the value is of zero length. These two conditions sound similar but they have to be checked individually. The length check is done after verifying that something is in the field. We then verify that the Starting and Ending Date and Time fields are provided. We're not doing data-type validation here since that will be done when the data is parsed and stored in the DataRow object.

The next part of the code begins working with the various recurrence types and verifies that one of the event types has been selected and stored in the object. Because our Web form automatically selects an option when the form is initially started, it is nearly impossible to cause this error to occur. However, we have to be sure to prevent invalid data from entering the database.

Once we've determined what type of event we have, we call the specific method in this class to verify that the data is supplied for each type of event we support. For all recurring events, the recurrence start date is required. Anniversary events only require that the anniversary date be entered. The complex recurring events have subroutines for each type. The code for periodic events is in the ValidatePeriodicEvent subroutine, shown here:

```
Private Sub ValidatePeriodicEvent(ByVal dr As DataRow)
    If IsDBNull(dr("PeriodicCode")) Then
        AddError("For a periodically recurring event, " _
            & "the period code is required.")
```

```
      Else
         If dr("PeriodicCode") = "" Then
            AddError("For a periodically recurring event, " _
               & "the period code is required.")
         End If
      End If
      If IsDBNull(dr("PeriodicAmount")) Then
         AddError("For a periodically recurring event, " _
            & "the period amount is required.")
      End If
   End Sub
```

We pass the DataRow object into this object and then check the fields specific for periodic-type events. Again, we are just verifying that the data is in the fields. When we fill the DataRow, data-type errors will be detected and trapped. Some errors will already be trapped, such as if the user enters a negative number of time units as the periodic amount. Since we're storing this field in a Tinyint field, we can only handle positive numbers from 0 to 255. Any numbers that don't fit this range will be trapped by our other code.

The monthly event validation routine is shown here:

```
Private Sub ValidateMonthlyEvent(ByVal dr As DataRow)
   If IsDBNull(dr("MonthlyCode")) Then
      AddError("For a monthly event, the monthly " _
         & "type code is required to be either A or L.")
   Else
      Select Case dr("MonthlyCode")
      Case MONTHLY_ACTUAL
         If IsDBNull(dr("MonthlyDay")) Then
            AddError("For this type of monthly event, " _
               & "the day of the month must be specified.")
         Else
            If dr("MonthlyDay") < 1 Or dr("MonthlyDay") > 31 Then
               AddError("The day of the month is out of range.")
            End If
         End If
      Case MONTHLY_LOGICAL
         If IsDBNull(dr("MonthlyOrdinal")) Then
            AddError("For this type of monthly event, " _
               & "the day ordinal is required.")
         Else
            If dr("MonthlyOrdinal") < 1 Or dr("MonthlyOrdinal") > 5 Then
               AddError("The day ordinal must be between 1 and 5.")
            End If

         End If
         If IsDBNull(dr("MonthlyDay")) Then
            AddError("The day number is required.")
         Else
            If dr("MonthlyDay") < 1 Or dr("MonthlyDay") > 7 Then
               AddError("The day number must be between 1 and 7.")
            End If
```

```
            End If
        Case Else
            AddError("The monthly event type must be either A or L.")
        End Select
    End If

End Sub
```

We first verify that a particular type of monthly event has been specified in the Month-lyCode field. For actual monthly events, we are dealing with an event that occurs, for example, on the 15th of every month. For these events, only the day number is required. For logical monthly events that occur, on the third Tuesday of the month, for example, we have to specify both the day of the week and the ordinal number during the month. Again, data-type errors will be detected when we store the data into the DataRow object.

As in the other classes, we generate a CalendarException if an error is detected. The code for this class is shown in Listing 3.5. You need to build this class and add it to the project before you attempt to compile the CalendarEvent class you built in the last section. If you don't, you'll get errors when the compiler sees references to this class that doesn't exist yet.

```
Public Class CalendarException
    Inherits Exception

    Public Sub New()
        MyBase.New()
    End Sub

    Public Sub New(ByVal Message As String)
        MyBase.New(Message)
    End Sub

    Public Sub New(ByVal Message As String, ByVal baseError As Exception)
        MyBase.New(Message, baseError)
    End Sub

End Class
```

Listing 3.5 CalendarException class

This class works just like the other exception classes that we've used, so we'll move on to the Web portion of the administration application next.

Building the Administration Application

The next feature to build is the Web administration application. You can use this to view, add, modify, and delete events on the calendar. This view is simply a list of all the events in the system . . . we'll be building the actual calendar next. The View Events window is shown in Figure 3.1 and shows the event name, description, start and end date, as well as a flag indicating if the event is a recurring event or not.

We'll start with the list window and then go on to the editing window, shown in Figure 3.2. It provides a lengthy but complete interface for entering all the required data for events, especially the recurring events, which are the most complex.

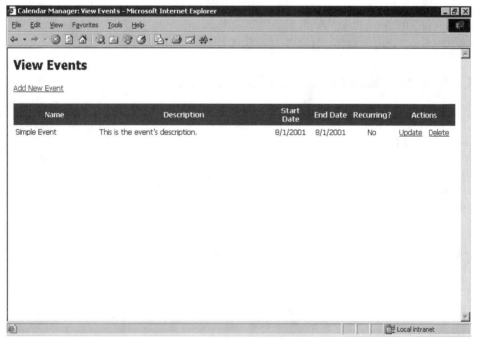

Figure 3.1 View Events window.

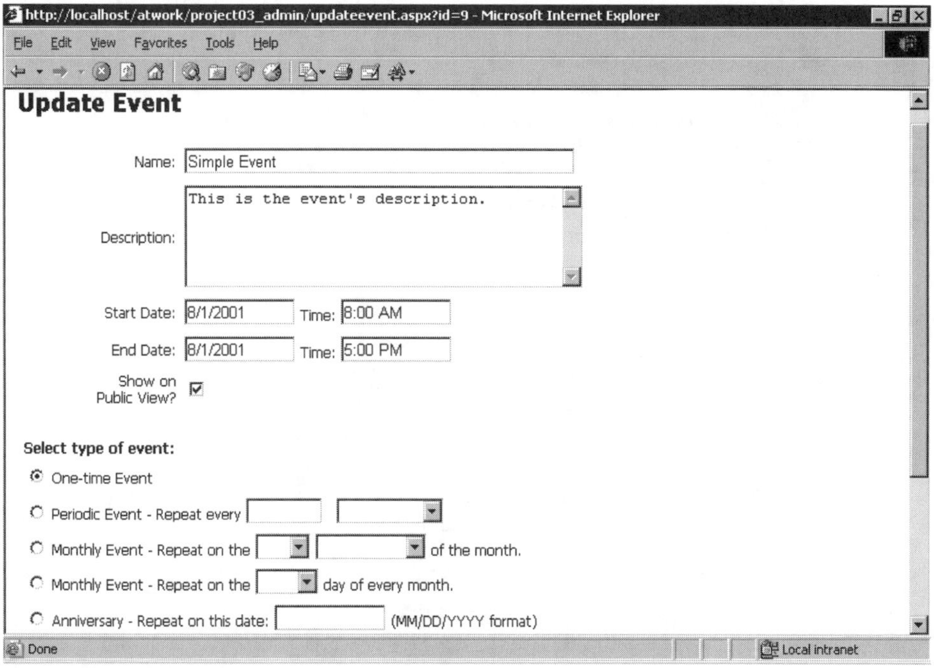

Figure 3.2 Add and Update Event window.

The editing window uses a new technique to combine the code for both adding and editing records so that we don't have to duplicate our efforts. The code for handling deletions works in the same way as the other applications in prior projects.

Coding the View Events Window

The first window to build is the View Events window. This window displays a list of all the events on the calendar and provides links for adding, updating, and deleting them. The ASPX file for this portion of the application is shown in Listing 3.6. We're using the data-binding method here to show each column. In addition, we are linking to the style sheet instead of using a server-side include. A server-side include works just as well, but at one point would not work properly in Netscape. Be sure to test the page and the related styles in your target browser first.

```
<%@ Page Inherits="Proj03Web.ViewEvents" Src="viewevents.aspx.vb" %>
<html>
<head>
    <title>Calendar Manager: View Events</title>
    <link href="styles.css" rel="stylesheet" type="text/css">
</head>
<body bgcolor="#FFFFFF">
    <p class="pageheading">View Events</p>
    <p class="tabletext">
    <a href="addevent.aspx">Add New Event</a>
    </p>
    <asp:Repeater id="rptList" runat="server">
        <HeaderTemplate>
        <table cellpadding="4" cellspacing="0" width="100%">
        <tr class="tableheading">
        <td width="20%">Name</td>
        <td width="40%">Description</td>
        <td width="10%">Start Date</td>
        <td width="10%">End Date</td>
        <td width="5%">Recurring?</td>
        <td width="15%">Actions</td>
        </tr>
        </HeaderTemplate>
        <ItemTemplate>
        <tr class="tabletext">
        <td valign="top"><%# DataBinder.Eval(Container.DataItem, _
            "Name") %></td>
        <td valign="top"><%# DataBinder.Eval(Container.DataItem, _
            "Description") %></td>
        <td valign="top" align="center">
        <%# DataBinder.Eval(Container.DataItem, _
            "EventStartDate").ToShortDateString %>
        </td>
        <td valign="top" align="center">
```

Listing 3.6   Viewevents.aspx

```
         <%# DataBinder.Eval(Container.DataItem, _
            "EventEndDate").ToShortDateString %>
         </td>
         <td valign="top" align="center">
         <%# DataBinder.Eval(Container.DataItem, _
            "IsRecurrence") %></td>
         <td valign="top" align="center">
         <a href="updateevent.aspx?id=<%#
DataBinder.Eval(Container.DataItem, _
            "pkEventID") %>">Update</a>  
         <a href="deleteevent.aspx?id=<%#
DataBinder.Eval(Container.DataItem, _
            "pkEventID") %>">Delete</a>
         </td>
         </tr>
         </ItemTemplate>
         <AlternatingItemTemplate>
         <tr class="tabletext_gray">
         <td valign="top">
         <%# DataBinder.Eval(Container.DataItem, _
            "Name") %></td>
         <td valign="top">
         <%# DataBinder.Eval(Container.DataItem, _
            "Description") %></td>
         <td valign="top" align="center">
         <%# DataBinder.Eval(Container.DataItem, _
            "EventStartDate").ToShortDateString %>
         </td>
         <td valign="top" align="center">
         <%# DataBinder.Eval(Container.DataItem, _
            "EventEndDate").ToShortDateString %>
         </td>
         <td valign="top" align="center">
         <%# DataBinder.Eval(Container.DataItem, _
            "IsRecurrence") %></td>
         <td valign="top" align="center">
         <a href="updateevent.aspx?id=<%# DataBinder.Eval(Container.DataItem, _
            "pkEventID") %>">Update</a>  
         <a href="deleteevent.aspx?id=<%# DataBinder.Eval(Container.DataItem, _
            "pkEventID") %>">Delete</a>
         </td>
         </tr>
         </AlternatingItemTemplate>
         <FooterTemplate>
         </table>
         </FooterTemplate>
      </asp:Repeater>
</body>
</html>
```

Listing 3.6   Viewevents.aspx (continued)

We use the same syntax as in the last project to show each data field in the ItemTemplate and AlternatingItemTemplate sections. The code-behind file is shown in Listing 3.7 and binds the class to this page so that the data is displayed properly.

```
Imports System
Imports System.Data
Imports System.Data.SqlClient
Imports System.Web.UI
Imports System.Web.UI.WebControls

Namespace Proj03Web
    Public Class ViewEvents
        Inherits System.Web.UI.Page


        Protected rptList As Repeater

        Sub Page_Load(Src As Object, e As EventArgs)

            Dim DB as New AtWorkUtilities.Database()
            Dim DS As DataSet = DB.GetDataSet("sp_RetrieveAllEvents")
            rptList.DataSource = DS
            rptList.DataBind()

            db.Close()
        End Sub
    End Class
End Namespace
```

Listing 3.7 Viewevents.aspx.vb

The stored procedure being used here retrieves all the events from the table and translates the type of event into a Yes or No based on whether the event is recurring or not. The code for the stored procedure is shown here:

```
CREATE PROCEDURE dbo.sp_RetrieveAllEvents
AS
SELECT *,
IsRecurrence = (CASE RecurrenceType WHEN 'N' THEN 'No'  ELSE 'Yes' END)
FROM tblEvents
ORDER BY EventStartDate
GO
```

The Case statement here is actually part of SQL Server's language and shows a Yes when any type of recurring event is being used. This makes it easier to display the data, since we don't have to do any verification along the way. This is the easiest way to write code, especially when you are doing data binding to a Repeater control.

In order to use this page, you'll need to create a *bin* directory for the DLLs used by this Web application, if you haven't done so already. Be sure to put both the AtWorkUtilities and the new CalendarObjects assemblies into this directory before trying this application.

Creating the Event Data Entry Windows

In the last two projects, we've been doing a bit of duplicate effort to handle adding and editing records. When you think about it, the two functions are fairly similar. In an update, you simply populate the form with the existing data. In this application, we're going to combine the code for adding and updating records for this application. We'll start by building the data entry form, creating the separate add and edit pages, and then build the code-behind file that will be shared between the two files.

Building the Data Entry Form

The first step is to build the shared HTML form used in both add and update modes. This is just a series of ASP.NET Web controls that accept each piece of data for the event being entered. The code is shown in Listing 3.8, and this file is called Eventform.inc.

```
<form runat="server">
<input type="hidden" id="pkEventID" runat="server">
<input type="hidden" id="returnURL" runat="server">
<table cellspacing="5">
<tr class="tabletext">
    <td align="right">Name:</td>
    <td>
        <asp:textbox
            id="txtName"
            columns="50"
            maxlength="80"
            runat="server" /></td>
</tr>
<tr class="tabletext">
    <td valign="middle" align="right">Description:</td>
    <td>
        <asp:textbox
            id="txtDescription"
            rows="5"
            columns="40"
            wrap="true"
            textmode="Multiline"
            runat="server" /></td>
</tr>
<tr class="tabletext">
    <td align="right">Start Date:</td>
    <td>
        <asp:textbox
            id="txtEventStartDate"
            columns="10"
```

Listing 3.8 Entryform.inc

```
            maxlength="10"
            runat="server" />
        Time: <asp:textbox
            id="txtEventStartTime"
            columns="10"
            maxlength="10"
            runat="server" />
    </td>
</tr>

<tr class="tabletext">
    <td align="right">End Date:</td>
    <td>
        <asp:textbox
            id="txtEventEndDate"
            columns="10"
            maxlength="10"
            runat="server" />
        Time: <asp:textbox
            id="txtEventEndTime"
            columns="10"
            maxlength="10"
            runat="server" />
    </td>
</tr>

<tr class="tabletext">
    <td align="right">Show on<br>Public View?</td>
    <td>
        <asp:checkbox
            id="chkIsPublic"
            runat="server" />
    </td>
</tr>

<tr class="tabletext"><td colspan=2> </td></tr>

<tr class="tabletext"><td colspan=2>
    <strong>Select type of event:</strong>
</td></tr>

<tr class="tabletext"><td colspan=2>
    <asp:radiobutton
        id="rdoRecurrenceNone"
        groupName="rdoRecurrence"
        value="N"
        checked
        runat="server" /> One-time Event
    </td>
</tr>
```

Listing 3.8   Entryform.inc (continued)

```
<tr class="tabletext"><td colspan=2>
    <asp:radiobutton
        id="rdoRecurrencePeriodic"
        groupName="rdoRecurrence"
        value="P"
        runat="server" /> Periodic Event - Repeat every
    <asp:textbox id="txtPeriodicAmount" runat="server" size="5"
/>  
    <asp:dropdownlist
        id="cboPeriodicCode"
        runat="server">
        <asp:listitem value="" selected> </asp:listitem>
        <asp:listitem value="d">day(s)</asp:listitem>
        <asp:listitem value="m">month(s)</asp:listitem>
        <asp:listitem value="q">quarter(s)</asp:listitem>
        <asp:listitem value="w">weekday(s)</asp:listitem>
        <asp:listitem value="ww">week(s)</asp:listitem>
        <asp:listitem value="yyyy">year(s)</asp:listitem>
    </asp:dropdownlist>
    </td>
</tr>

<tr class="tabletext">
    <td colspan=2>
    <asp:radiobutton
        id="rdoRecurrenceMonthlyLogical"
        groupName="rdoRecurrence"
        value="ML"
        runat="server" /> Monthly Event - Repeat on the
        <asp:dropdownlist
            id="cboLogicalMonthlyOrdinal"
            runat="server">
            <asp:listitem value="" selected> </asp:listitem>
            <asp:listitem value="1">1st</asp:listitem>
            <asp:listitem value="2">2nd</asp:listitem>
            <asp:listitem value="3">3rd</asp:listitem>
            <asp:listitem value="4">4th</asp:listitem>
            <asp:listitem value="5">5th</asp:listitem>
        </asp:dropdownlist>
        <asp:dropdownlist
            id="cboLogicalMonthlyDay"
            runat="server">
            <asp:listitem value="" selected> </asp:listitem>
            <asp:listitem value="1">Sunday</asp:listitem>
            <asp:listitem value="2">Monday</asp:listitem>
            <asp:listitem value="3">Tuesday</asp:listitem>
            <asp:listitem value="4">Wednesday</asp:listitem>
            <asp:listitem value="5">Thursday</asp:listitem>
            <asp:listitem value="6">Friday</asp:listitem>
            <asp:listitem value="7">Saturday</asp:listitem>
        </asp:dropdownlist>
```

Listing 3.8 Entryform.inc (continued)

```
         of the month.
      </td>
   </tr>


<tr class="tabletext">
   <td colspan=2>
   <asp:radiobutton
      id="rdoRecurrenceMonthlyActual"
      groupName="rdoRecurrence"
      value="MA"
      runat="server" /> Monthly Event - Repeat on the
      <asp:dropdownlist
         id="cboActualMonthlyDay"
         runat="server">
         <asp:listitem value="" selected> </asp:listitem>
         <asp:listitem value="1">1st</asp:listitem>
         <asp:listitem value="2">2nd</asp:listitem>
         <asp:listitem value="3">3rd</asp:listitem>
         <asp:listitem value="4">4th</asp:listitem>
         <asp:listitem value="5">5th</asp:listitem>
         <asp:listitem value="6">6th</asp:listitem>
         <asp:listitem value="7">7th</asp:listitem>
         <asp:listitem value="8">8th</asp:listitem>
         <asp:listitem value="9">9th</asp:listitem>
         <asp:listitem value="10">10th</asp:listitem>
         <asp:listitem value="11">11th</asp:listitem>
         <asp:listitem value="12">12th</asp:listitem>
         <asp:listitem value="13">13th</asp:listitem>
         <asp:listitem value="14">14th</asp:listitem>
         <asp:listitem value="15">15th</asp:listitem>
         <asp:listitem value="16">16th</asp:listitem>
         <asp:listitem value="17">17th</asp:listitem>
         <asp:listitem value="18">18th</asp:listitem>
         <asp:listitem value="19">19th</asp:listitem>
         <asp:listitem value="20">20th</asp:listitem>
         <asp:listitem value="21">21st</asp:listitem>
         <asp:listitem value="22">22nd</asp:listitem>
         <asp:listitem value="23">23rd</asp:listitem>
         <asp:listitem value="24">24th</asp:listitem>
         <asp:listitem value="25">25th</asp:listitem>
         <asp:listitem value="26">26th</asp:listitem>
         <asp:listitem value="27">27th</asp:listitem>
         <asp:listitem value="28">28th</asp:listitem>
         <asp:listitem value="29">29th</asp:listitem>
         <asp:listitem value="30">30th</asp:listitem>
         <asp:listitem value="31">31st</asp:listitem>
      </asp:dropdownlist>
      day of every month.
   </td>
</tr>

<tr class="tabletext">
```

Listing 3.8   Entryform.inc (continued)

```
      <td colspan=2>
      <asp:radiobutton
        id="rdoRecurrenceAnniversary"
        groupName="rdoRecurrence"
        value="A"
        runat="server" /> Anniversary - Repeat on this date:
      <asp:textbox
        id="txtAnniversaryDate"
        runat="server"
        size="10" />
      (MM/DD/YYYY format)
      </td>
   </tr>

   <tr class="tabletext"><td colspan=2> </td></tr>

   <tr class="tabletext"><td colspan=2>
      <strong>For all recurring events:</strong>
   </td></tr>
   <tr class="tabletext">
      <td align="right">Date to start repeating:</td>
      <td>
        <asp:textbox
           id="txtRecurrenceStartDate"
           columns="10"
           maxlength="10"
           runat="server" />
      </td>
   </tr>

   <tr class="tabletext">
      <td align="right">Date to stop repeating:</td>
      <td>
        <asp:textbox
           id="txtRecurrenceEndDate"
           columns="10"
           maxlength="10"
           runat="server" />
      </td>
   </tr>

   <tr class="tabletext"><td colspan=2> </td></tr>

   <tr class="tabletext">
      <td colspan=2 align=middle>
      <input type="submit" name="btnSubmit" runat="server" value="Save" />
      <input type="reset"  name="btnReset"  runat="server" value="Clear" />
      </td>
   </tr>
   </table>
   </form>
```

Listing 3.8   Entryform.inc (continued)

This is definitely the most complex form you've built so far, but it still uses the basic building blocks used in prior projects. Each of the fields matches with one of the database fields, with the exception of the fields handling the monthly events. Because we have two types of monthly events, we have two sets of controls, but only one set of database fields to hold the data. We'll sort things out when we create or edit a record and store the appropriate codes in the object. The options are the key to this application, since we'll be using them when we put data in the CalendarEvent object and determine which fields to store in the object.

Creating the Add and Update Event Pages

The next step is to build the ASPX files that are loaded for the add and update functions. These are simple files that only differ in the TITLE tag and the text shown on the page indicating what function is being done. The code for the Add Event page is shown in Listing 3.9, and the code for the Update Event page is shown in Listing 3.10.

```
<%@ Page Inherits="Proj03Web.EventDataEntry"
Src="eventdataentry.aspx.vb" %>
<html>
    <head>
       <title>Calendar Manager: Add New Event</title>
       <link href="styles.css" rel="stylesheet" type="text/css">
    </head>
    <body bgcolor="#FFFFFF">
    <p class="pageheading">Add New Event</p>

       <asp:label id="lblErrorMessage" class="errortext" runat="server" />

<!--#include file="Eventform.inc" -->
    </body>
</html>
```

Listing 3.9   Addevent.aspx

This page is just like the others we've built, except for the fact that it is linked to a style sheet instead of being included with a server-side include. The Update Event page is shown in Listing 3.10.

```
<%@ Page Inherits="Proj03Web.EventDataEntry"
Src="eventdataentry.aspx.vb" %>
<html>
    <head>
       <title>Calendar Manager: Update Event</title>
       <link href="styles.css" rel="stylesheet" type="text/css">
    </head>
    <body bgcolor="#FFFFFF">
```

Listing 3.10   Updateevent.aspx

```
    <p class="pageheading">Update Event</p>

    <asp:label id="lblErrorMessage" class="errortext" runat="server" />

<!-#include file="Eventform.inc" ->
    </body>
</html>
```

Listing 3.10   Updateevent.aspx (continued)

Besides the simple changes of text and TITLE tags, the other important thing to note on these files is the new @Page directive. Both pages point to the same code-behind file, called Eventdataentry.aspx.vb. This single code-behind file will have the capability to handle both adding and updating records.

Building the Code-Behind File

The next step, and probably the most involved, is to build the code-behind file for adding and updating records. While it follows a similar structure to the update routines in previous projects, there are some simple changes that tie the two pages together. The code-behind file is shown in Listing 3.11.

```
Imports System
Imports System.Data
Imports System.Data.SqlClient
Imports System.Web.UI
Imports System.Web.UI.WebControls

Namespace Proj03Web
    Public Class EventDataEntry
        Inherits System.Web.UI.Page
        Protected txtName As TextBox
        Protected txtDescription As TextBox
        Protected txtEventStartDate As TextBox
        Protected txtEventStartTime As TextBox
        Protected txtEventEndDate As TextBox
        Protected txtEventEndTime As TextBox
        Protected chkIsPublic As CheckBox
        Protected rdoRecurrenceNone As RadioButton
        Protected rdoRecurrencePeriodic As RadioButton
        Protected rdoRecurrenceMonthlyLogical As RadioButton
        Protected rdoRecurrenceMonthlyActual As RadioButton
        Protected rdoRecurrenceAnniversary As RadioButton
        Protected cboPeriodicCode As DropDownList
        Protected txtPeriodicAmount As TextBox
        Protected cboLogicalMonthlyOrdinal As DropDownList
```

Listing 3.11   Eventdataentry.aspx.vb

```
Protected cboLogicalMonthlyDay As DropDownList
Protected cboActualMonthlyDay As DropDownList
Protected txtAnniversaryDate As TextBox
Protected txtRecurrenceStartDate As TextBox
Protected txtRecurrenceEndDate As TextBox

Protected pkEventID As HTMLControls.HTMLInputHidden
Protected returnURL As HTMLControls.HTMLInputHidden
Protected lblErrorMessage As Label

Sub Page_Load(objSender As Object, objArgs As EventArgs)
    Dim DB As New AtWorkUtilities.Database()
    Dim i As Integer
    Dim strType As String
    Dim E As CalendarObjects.CalendarEvent
    Dim DR As DataRow

    If Not Page.IsPostBack Then
        returnURL.Value = Request.QueryString("rURL")
        If Request.QueryString("ID") <> "" Then
            pkEventID.Value = Request.QueryString("ID")
            E = New CalendarObjects.CalendarEvent(DB, _
                Request.QueryString("ID"))
            DR = E.GetRow()
            txtName.Text = DR("Name")
            txtDescription.Text = DR("Description")
            txtEventStartDate.Text = _
                DR("EventStartDate").ToShortDateString()
            txtEventStartTime.Text = _
                DR("EventStartTime").ToShortTimeString()
            txtEventEndDate.Text = _
                DR("EventEndDate").ToShortDateString()
            txtEventEndTime.Text = _
                DR("EventEndTime").ToShortTimeString()
            chkIsPublic.Checked = DR("IsPublic")
            Select Case DR("RecurrenceType")
                Case "N"
                    rdoRecurrenceNone.Checked = True
                Case "P"
                    rdoRecurrencePeriodic.Checked = True
                    txtPeriodicAmount.Text = DR("PeriodicAmount")
                    SelectFromList(cboPeriodicCode, _
                        DR("PeriodicCode"))
                Case "M"
                    If DR("MonthlyCode") = "L" Then
                        rdoRecurrenceMonthlyLogical.Checked = True
                        SelectFromList(cboLogicalMonthlyOrdinal, _
                            DR("MonthlyOrdinal"))
                        SelectFromList(cboLogicalMonthlyDay, _
                            DR("MonthlyDay"))
                    ElseIf DR("MonthlyCode") = "A" Then
```

Listing 3.11   Eventdataentry.aspx.vb (continued)

```
                            rdoRecurrenceMonthlyActual.Checked = True
                            SelectFromList(cboActualMonthlyDay, _
                                DR("MonthlyDay"))
                        End If
                    Case "A"
                        rdoRecurrenceAnniversary.Checked = True
                        txtAnniversaryDate.Text = _
                            DR("AnniversaryDate").ToShortDateString()

                End Select
                If DR("RecurrenceType") <> "N" Then
                    txtRecurrenceStartDate.Text = _
                        DR("RecurrenceStart").ToShortDateString()
                    If DR("RecurrenceEnd").ToString() <> "" Then
                        txtRecurrenceEndDate.Text = _
                            DR("RecurrenceEnd").ToShortDateString()
                    End If
                End If

            End If
        Else


            E = New CalendarObjects.CalendarEvent(DB)
            DR = E.GetRow()

            DR("Name") = txtName.Text
            DR("Description") = txtDescription.Text
            StoreDate(DR, "EventStartDate", txtEventStartDate)
            StoreDate(DR, "EventStartTime", txtEventStartTime)
            StoreDate(DR, "EventEndDate", txtEventEndDate)
            StoreDate(DR, "EventEndTime", txtEventEndTime)
            DR("IsPublic") = chkIsPublic.Checked

            If rdoRecurrenceNone.Checked Then
                DR("RecurrenceType") = "N"
            Else
                If rdoRecurrencePeriodic.Checked Then
                    StorePeriodicEvent(DR)
                ElseIf rdoRecurrenceMonthlyLogical.Checked Then
                    StoreLogicalMonthlyEvent(DR)
                ElseIf rdoRecurrenceMonthlyActual.Checked Then
                    StoreActualMonthlyEvent(DR)
                ElseIf rdoRecurrenceAnniversary.Checked Then
                    DR("RecurrenceType") = "A"
                    StoreDate(DR, "AnniversaryDate", _
                        txtAnniversaryDate)
                End If
            End If
            StoreDate(DR, "RecurrenceStart", txtRecurrenceStartDate)
            StoreDate(DR, "RecurrenceEnd", txtRecurrenceEndDate)
```

Listing 3.11 Eventdataentry.aspx.vb (continued)

```
             E.SaveRow(DR)
         If Not E.IsValid Then
            lblErrorMessage.Text = _
               E.ValidationError("<b>ERROR:</b> The following " _
                  & "errors were detected in your data:<br>", _
                  "&bull; {0}<br>", "")
      Else
         E.Save()
         '
         ' Clean up old event data once the new one is
         ' saved to the database. This eliminates the
         ' problem of cleaning out all the fields of
         ' old data.
         '
         If pkEventID.Value <> "" Then
            E = New CalendarObjects.CalendarEvent(DB, _
               pkEventID.Value)
            E.Delete()
         End If
         DB.Close()
         If returnURL.Value = "" Then
            Response.Redirect("viewevents.aspx")
         Else
            Response.Redirect(returnURL.Value)
         End If
      End If
   End If
End Sub

Private Sub StorePeriodicEvent(ByRef DR As DataRow)
   DR("RecurrenceType") = "P"
   DR("PeriodicCode") = cboPeriodicCode.SelectedItem.Value
   Try
      DR("PeriodicAmount") = Byte.Parse(txtPeriodicAmount.Text)
   Catch e As FormatException
      ' do nothing, object will handle validation
   End Try

End Sub

Private Sub StoreLogicalMonthlyEvent(ByRef DR As DataRow)
   DR("RecurrenceType") = "M"
   DR("MonthlyCode") = "L"
   Try
      DR("MonthlyOrdinal") = _
         Byte.Parse(cboLogicalMonthlyOrdinal.SelectedItem.Value)
   Catch e As FormatException
      ' do nothing, object will generate error
   End Try
```

Listing 3.11   Eventdataentry.aspx.vb (continued)

```
           Try
              DR("MonthlyDay") = _
                 Byte.Parse(cboLogicalMonthlyDay.SelectedItem.Value)
           Catch e As FormatException
              ' do nothing, object will generate error
           End Try

        End Sub


        Private Sub StoreActualMonthlyEvent(ByRef DR As DataRow)
           DR("RecurrenceType") = "M"
           DR("MonthlyCode") = "A"
           Try
              DR("MonthlyDay") = _
                 Byte.Parse(cboActualMonthlyDay.SelectedItem.Value)
           Catch e As FormatException
              ' do nothing, object will generate error
           End Try
    End Sub


        Private Sub StoreDate(ByRef DR As DataRow, _
           strName As String, txtInput As TextBox)
           Try
              DR(strName) = DateTime.Parse(txtInput.Text)
           Catch e As FormatException
              ' No code, object will handle
           End Try
        End Sub


        Private Sub SelectFromList(cboList As DropDownList, _
           strValue As String)

           Dim i As Integer

           For i = 0 To cboList.Items.Count
              If cboList.Items(i).Value = strValue Then
                 cboList.SelectedIndex = i
                 Exit For
              End If
           Next i

        End Sub

    End Class
End Namespace
```

Listing 3.11   Eventdataentry.aspx.vb (continued)

The major benefit of using the code-behind file in this way is the fact that we have removed half the code we would have needed otherwise. Any time you can remove duplicate code, you'll save yourself major headaches if you ever have to change the files.

We begin this file by declaring protected variables for each server control that we created in the last section. This is tedious, but absolutely required for the class to work properly. In non-postback mode, we are either showing an empty form or populating the form with existing data. For existing data, the ID name/value pair stored in the query string will have the current ID in it. If that value is missing, we assume that we are in add mode. We also read the value from the rURL query string variable, if it's there, and put it in the hidden-input field called returnURL. This will allow us, when necessary, to return to a different URL than the one for the View Events window. This makes our application more flexible and able to accept edit requests from other sources. We'll use this same code in the delete function.

In update mode, we have to populate the form with the existing data. We take the data from the DataRow and store it in each control. For the drop-down lists, we have to search through the list items to find the value that was in the database. This is done in the SelectFromList routine, since we have to repeat this process several times. We also have to deal with all the types of recurring events and populate the appropriate portions of the form based on what is in the database. The only real trick here is to show the date and time using the appropriate format.

Once the user has entered the data and clicked the Submit button, we go into postback mode. We can still determine if we're adding or editing a record by looking at the value of the event ID that was stored in the hidden-input field. For both editing and adding records, we create a new DataRow to fill. We do this because we have to worry about old data being in the record. For instance, if you change an event from being a recurring event to a one-time event, there may be leftover data in the record that is no longer required. Instead of saving the changes and trying to clean out the record, we simply create a new record. Once the data has been stored in the object and the validation passes, we save the new record and delete the old one. Since you are creating a new record on each change, this simplifies and shortens the code because we don't have to empty the old record of prior data.

As part of storing the data in the DataRow, we have a series of helper functions. These serve to simplify the code and make it easier to read. Most of the routines are fairly simple, but the StoreDate routine shown here deserves a bit of extra explanation.

```
Private Sub StoreDate(ByRef DR As DataRow, _
    strName As String, txtInput As TextBox)
    Try
        DR(strName) = DateTime.Parse(txtInput.Text)
    Catch e As FormatException
        ' No code, object will handle
    End Try
End Sub
```

This subroutine is designed to take data from a text box and store it as a date/time value. This requires parsing the data and watching for any possible formatting errors.

We had to deal with this problem when creating the contacts feature in the previous project. We look for FormatExceptions and if we find them, we don't load the data into the particular field. The Business object will then generate an error because the field is missing or incorrect.

This code could also be replaced with client-side JavaScript verifying that the data entered is of a particular type, or you could use a Validation control to verify it. However, the current solution lets us keep all the validation in one place in the CalendarEvent class. It's not the only solution, but it works fairly well.

Building the Delete Event Pages

Deleting an event is just like deleting any other object. If you want, you can copy your code from the previous project to build the pages shown here. The ASPX file is shown in Listing 3.12.

```
<%@ Page Inherits="Proj03Web.DeleteEvent" Src="deleteevent.aspx.vb" %>
<html>
   <head>
      <title>Calendar Manager: Delete Event</title>
      <link href="styles.css" rel="stylesheet" type="text/css">
   </head>
   <body bgcolor="#FFFFFF">
   <p class="pageheading">Delete Event</p>
   <p class="tabletext">Are you sure you want to delete this event?</p>
   <form runat="server">
   <input type="hidden" runat="server" id="pkEventID">
    <input type="hidden" runat="server" id="fkEventID">
    <input type="hidden" runat="server" id="returnURL">
    <p class="tabletext">
    <a href="javascript:document.forms[0].submit();">Yes</a>
      
    <a href="javascript:history.go(-1);">No</a>
    </p>
    </form>
    </body>
</html>
```

Listing 3.12   Deleteevent.aspx

As with the other ASPX files in this project, we are linking to the style sheet instead of including it. We've also added a third hidden-input field called returnURL. As mentioned earlier, this will hold the URL that this page should return to when it's completed its task. The code for this file is identical except for the name of the data we're deleting. The code-behind file is shown in Listing 3.13.

```
Imports System
Imports System.Data
Imports System.Data.SqlClient
Imports System.Web.UI
Imports System.Web.UI.WebControls

Namespace Proj03Web
    Public Class DeleteEvent
        Inherits System.Web.UI.Page

        Protected pkEventID As HTMLControls.HTMLInputHidden
        Protected fkEventID As HTMLControls.HTMLInputHidden

        Sub Page_Load(objSender As Object, objArgs As EventArgs)
            If Not Page.IsPostBack Then
                pkEventID.Value = Request.QueryString("ID")
                fkEventID.Value = Request.QueryString("pID")

            Else
                Dim DB As New AtWorkUtilities.Database()
                Dim E As New CalendarObjects.CalendarEvent(DB, _
                    pkEventID.Value)
                E.Delete()
                DB.Close()
                If returnURL.Value = "" Then
                    Response.Redirect("viewevents.aspx")
                Else
                    Response.Redirect(returnURL.Value)
                End If
            End If
        End Sub

    End Class
End Namespace
```

Listing 3.13   Deleteevent.aspx.vb

In this page, we populate the hidden-input fields in non-postback mode, and then use those values in postback mode to delete the correct event. When we're done, we redirect back to the View Event page or the return URL value specified, if appropriate.

This takes us to the end of the administration site. The next step is to build the calendar viewers, both monthly and daily views, and populate them with the events in the system.

Building the Monthly Calendar View

The next step, now that you have a way to enter and modify events, is to build the calendar viewer. We'll start with the monthly view and then build the daily view. We'll also be linking this application with the administration tool to make it easier to add and modify events. The monthly view is shown in Figure 3.3.

Figure 3.3 Monthly view of calendar.

Before you panic at the complexity of building a calendar from scratch, the bulk of this code is handled automatically by the Calendar control provided with ASP.NET. All you have to do is to figure out which events to show on each day. The Calendar control generates an event for each displayed day, and we can use that date with a stored procedure to determine which events should be shown.

Because we're using this control and it has a number of graphic features to configure, you might find it easier to build this page inside Visual Studio .NET as a new Web application. If your calendar doesn't look exactly like the one shown in the previous figure, don't worry about it. The important thing here is to make the events work correctly and populate the cells with the right events. You'll also need to link this page to the others that we've built in this project, as well as to the daily view, which you'll build next.

Creating the ASPX File

The first step in building this application is to add the Calendar control to the Web page. This control can take advantage of style sheets once you link them to the ASPX file. The style sheet that I'm using in my file is shown in Listing 3.14 and is called calendar_styles.css.

```
.text
{
   COLOR: #000000;
   FONT-FAMILY: Tahoma, Arial;
   FONT-SIZE: 9pt;
}

.calheading
{
   COLOR: #FFFFFF;
   FONT-FAMILY: Tahoma, Arial;
   FONT-WEIGHT: bold;
   FONT-SIZE: 9pt;
   BACKGROUND-COLOR: #AA0000;
   TEXT-ALIGN: center;
}
.celltext
{
   COLOR: #000000;
   FONT-FAMILY: Tahoma, Arial;
   FONT-SIZE: 8pt;
}
.celltext_gray
{
   COLOR: #000000;
   FONT-FAMILY: Tahoma, Arial;
   FONT-SIZE: 8pt;
   BACKGROUND-COLOR: #CCCCCC;
}
```

Listing 3.14   Calendar_styles.css

Once you have the style sheet created, you can link it to your ASPX file by dragging it from the Solution Explorer and dropping it into the ASPX file. This creates a LINK tag in the HTML view of the ASPX file. You'll also be able to use the CSSClass properties throughout the various controls, including the various styles used in the Calendar control.

Once you have the style sheet linked, you can add the Calendar control onto your page. Depending on the size of your monitor, you'll want to size the calendar accordingly. The easiest way to size the calendar is to set the size of each cell. The ASPX file is shown in Listing 3.15, complete with all the properties already set for you.

```
<%@ Page Inherits="Proj03Web.MonthlyCalendarView"
      Src="calendar_monthly.aspx.vb" %>
<HTML>
<HEAD>
```

Listing 3.15   Calendar_monthly.aspx

```
    <title>View Calendar - Month View</title>
    <link href="calendar_styles.css" type="text/css" rel="stylesheet">
</HEAD>
<body>
<p class="text">
<b>Actions:</b>
<a href="viewevents.aspx">View All Events</a>
 | 
<% Response.Write("<a href=""addevent.aspx?rURL=" _
    & Request.ServerVariables("SCRIPT_NAME") _
    & """>Add Event</a>")
%>
</p>
<form id="CalendarForm" method="post" runat="server">
    <asp:Calendar id="objCalendar" runat="server" ShowGridLines="True">
        <TodayDayStyle CssClass="celltext_gray" />
        <DayStyle HorizontalAlign="Left" Height="90px"
            Width="90px" CssClass="celltext" VerticalAlign="Top" />
        <DayHeaderStyle Height="15px" CssClass="calheading" />
        <TitleStyle Font-Size="16pt" Font-Names="Tahoma"
            Font-Bold="True" Height="25px" BackColor="White" />
        <OtherMonthDayStyle CssClass="celltext_gray" />
    </asp:Calendar>
</form>
</body>
</HTML>
```

Listing 3.15 Calendar_monthly.aspx (continued)

As you can see from this listing, we've added a little bit of extra HTML to connect this page with the event viewer that you built in the last section, as well as the page that allows you to add new events. Using the rURL parameter, you can instruct the Add Event page to return to this page when it's done adding the event.

For the Calendar control, there are a number of properties that you can set to change the style of the calendar. Most of the important ones are for the individual cells, but let's go through each of the styles being used here:

TodayDayStyle. The calendar knows what day it currently is, and the Today-DayStyle is used with that particular cell. In our case, we're going to shade this cell light gray, but otherwise leave it as-is.

DayStyle. This style is used for all cells in the table as a base style. TodayDayStyle uses these attributes and either builds on or overrides them. For this cell, we are positioning the data in the upper-left corner of the cell and setting the height and width to 90 pixels. If you have a larger monitor, you might want to use a larger amount. Since there are seven days in a week, if you have a 1024 x 768 monitor, you could easily use a width of 140 pixels without running past the edge of your monitor. At the time this project was written, there wasn't a way to automatically resize the calendar based on the size of the Web page. However, be sure to check the book's Web site at 10projectswithasp.net for any updates.

TitleStyle. This style formats the title of the calendar, which by default is the current month and year. At the time of this writing, this particular property did not accept a style from the style sheet. However, you can manually format this field using the various properties available, including font name, size, and so on.

OtherMonthDayStyle. This style is used for the days that are part of the previous and subsequent month shown on this view. We're using the same style for these cells and making them a shade of gray to help them stand out from the current month cells.

That takes care of the necessary calendar formatting. As mentioned before, don't worry too much about the formatting of the calendar. The important thing is to get the code-behind page working correctly so that the events are correctly populated. You can make the file pretty later.

Creating the Code-Behind File

The code-behind file for this page is shown in Listing 3.16. It includes all the logic to show the various recurring events. We'll go through each of the types of recurring events and review the logic to cover each type of event.

```vb
Imports System
Imports System.Data
Imports System.Data.SqlClient
Imports System.Web.UI
Imports System.Web.UI.WebControls
Imports System.Text
Imports Microsoft.VisualBasic
Namespace Proj03Web
    Public Class MonthlyCalendarView
        Inherits System.Web.UI.Page
        Protected WithEvents objCalendar As _
            System.Web.UI.WebControls.Calendar
        Private DB As AtWorkUtilities.Database

        Private Sub Page_Load(ByVal sender As System.Object, _
            ByVal e As System.EventArgs) Handles MyBase.Load

            DB = New AtWorkUtilities.Database()
            If Request.QueryString("date") <> "" Then
                objCalendar.TodaysDate = _
                    DateTime.Parse(Request.QueryString("date"))
            End If

        End Sub
```

Listing 3.16 Calendar_monthly.aspx.vb

```
   Private Sub _
      objCalendar_SelectionChanged(ByVal sender As System.Object, _
      ByVal e As System.EventArgs) _
      Handles objCalendar.SelectionChanged

      Response.Redirect("calendar_daily.aspx?date=" _
         & objCalendar.SelectedDate.ToShortDateString)

   End Sub

   Private Sub _
      objCalendar_DayRender(ByVal sender As Object, _
      ByVal e As System.Web.UI.WebControls.DayRenderEventArgs) _
      Handles objCalendar.DayRender
      Dim DR As SqlDataReader
      Dim strOutput As New StringBuilder()
      Dim dteCurrent As DateTime
      Dim blnShowEvent As Boolean
      Dim intDiff As Integer
      Dim intOffset As Integer
      Dim intDay As Integer
      Dim i As Integer
      Dim intCount As Integer = 0

      dteCurrent = e.Day.Date

      DR = DB.GetDataReader("sp_RetrieveOnetimeEvents '" _
         & dteCurrent.ToShortDateString & "'", True)

      While DR.Read()
         ' Reset event flag
         blnShowEvent = False

         ' One-time only events only show up on the day(s)
         ' they are scheduled.
         If DR("RecurrenceType") = "N" Then
            blnShowEvent = True
         Else
            Select Case DR("RecurrenceType")
               Case "P"
                  intDiff = DateDiff(DR("PeriodicCode"), _
                     DR("EventStartDate"), dteCurrent)
                  If DateAdd(DR("PeriodicCode"), _
                     intDiff, DR("EventStartDate")) = dteCurrent Then
                     blnShowEvent = True
                  End If

               Case "M"
                  If DR("MonthlyCode") = "A" Then
                     If Day(dteCurrent) = DR("MonthlyDay") Then
```

Listing 3.16 Calendar_monthly.aspx.vb (continued)

```vb
                                blnShowEvent = True
                            End If
                        ElseIf DR("MonthlyCode") = "L" Then
                            For i = 1 To 7
                                If Weekday(DateTime.Parse(Month(dteCurrent) _
                                    & "/" & i & "/" & Year(dteCurrent))) _
                                    = DR("MonthlyDay") Then
                                    Exit For
                                End If
                            Next i
                            intDay = Day(dteCurrent)
                            If (intDay - i) = _
                                (DR("MonthlyOrdinal") - 1) * 7 Then
                                blnShowEvent = True
                            End If
                        End If
                    Case "A"
                        If Month(dteCurrent) = _
                            Month(DR("AnniversaryDate"))
                            And Day(dteCurrent) = _
                                Day(DR("AnniversaryDate"))
                        Then
                            blnShowEvent = True
                        End If
                End Select
            End If
            If blnShowEvent Then
                intCount += 1
                If intCount <= 3 Then
                    strOutput.AppendFormat("<br>{0}", DR("Name"))
                ElseIf intCount = 4 Then
                    ' If more than 3 events are on this day, show
                    ' "More" and bail out since the calendar doesn't
                    ' have enough room to show everything.
                    strOutput.Append("<br>more...")
                    Exit While
                End If
            End If
        End While
        If strOutput.Length > 0 Then
            e.Cell.Controls.Add(New LiteralControl("<br>" _
                & strOutput.ToString))
        End If
        DR.Close()

    End Sub


    End Class
End Namespace
```

Listing 3.16   Calendar_monthly.aspx.vb (continued)

The key feature of this file is the support for the various events handled by the calendar. The first thing we do, however, is reference a series of assemblies. The one used here that we have not used before is the Microsoft.VisualBasic library. This library is referenced because we are using the DateAdd and DateDiff functions. There are currently no equivalents to these functions in the .NET Framework that support all the time units that DateAdd and DateDiff do. For this reason, we're referencing the old library to make these functions available.

We then create a Database object to be shared throughout the page. We also determine if the date parameter has been passed to this page. If so, we point the calendar to the date specified by using the TodaysDate property of the Calendar control.

The next logical event to be triggered is the DayRender event of the Calendar control. You will receive one DayRender event for each day shown in the calendar. We'll be using this to populate the cells in the calendar with events from the database. Working through this event, we first determine what day is being filled by looking at the event arguments' Day.Date property, which is stored in a temporary variable. We then create a SqlDataReader with all the potential events for this day by running the sp_RetrieveEventsByDay stored procedure, which is shown in Listing 3.17.

```
CREATE procedure sp_RetrieveEventsByDay
@DateInput datetime
as
select * from tblEvents
where (@DateInput between EventStartDate and EventEndDate)
or (@DateInput between RecurrenceStart and RecurrenceEnd)
or (@DateInput >= RecurrenceStart and RecurrenceEnd Is Null)
Order By EventStartTime
```

Listing 3.17   sp_RetrieveEventsByDay Stored Procedure

This routine accomplishes three tasks:

- Retrieves all the one-time events that occur during the date supplied.
- Retrieves all the recurring events that occur during the date supplied.
- Retrieves all the recurring events that have no ending date and that have a starting date before the date supplied.

Not all of the events returned will actually be shown on a given day; however, this list gives us a good sampling of the possible events that can occur on each day. Using the stored procedure to do some of the work simplifies some of the date logic in this page, but it doesn't eliminate all of it.

Once we have the data in the SqlDataReader, we loop through all the records. We keep a flag indicating whether the event currently being read should be shown in the cell. Any one-time event would not show up if it didn't occur on the date in question, so that's an automatic pass. For periodic events, we have to determine if the event's recurrence period occurs on the date given. For instance, an event that occurs every two weeks would only be displayed if the date being filled is a multiple of two weeks from the event starting date. The calculations performed here determine if this is the case, and if so, the event is shown. We determine the number of time units between the current date and the starting date of the event. We then add that amount back to the original date to see if we get the current date. If not, we know the date is not a multiple and we don't show the recurring event.

Monthly recurring events have two different modes: logical and actual. An actual recurring event occurs on the same day every month. This is easy to check, since we can look at the day of the event's start date and look at the current date to see if the day number is the same. For logical dates, we have to determine if, for instance, the day being shown is the third Thursday of the month in order for the event to be displayed. We first determine what the first day of the month is for the day in question. We then determine if the current date is the correct number of weeks following that date.

The final type of event is the anniversary, and with this, we simply have to verify that the month and day are the same as the Anniversary Date field. If so, the event is displayed.

In order to show the event, we add the events to a StringBuilder, each one preceded by a BREAK tag, separating the text onto more than one line. We then have to add a new control into the cell in order to show the text in the cell. If you simply set the Text property of the cell, the day number disappears. If there are more than three events on a particular day, we stop listing them and simply list More for any events after the third one. We also exit the loop that finds other events. Since we have a daily view that shows all the events for a day, we don't need to show everything in this view.

The last event we have to code is the SelectionChanged event, which will activate if you click the day number. Clicking the date will bring up the daily view of the calendar, which we'll build next. The code is fairly simple and uses a basic redirect to send you to the correct page. It also passes the date to show, which is made available through the objCalendar.SelectedDate property. This will let us properly show the date in the daily view.

The easiest way to test this page is to add a number of different events, if you haven't done so already. You can use the View Events page and the add event feature to add events that test each of the different types of recurrences. Once you're done testing, you can go on to the next section and build the daily view of the calendar.

Building the Daily Calendar View

The last page you'll be building for this application is the daily view of the calendar. This shows all the events on a particular day, their descriptions, and the starting and ending times. An example of this window is shown in Figure 3.4.

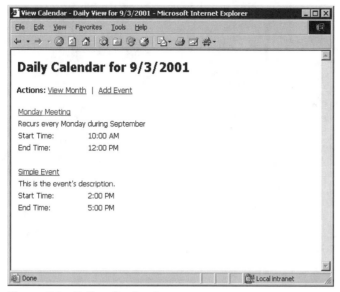

Figure 3.4 Daily calendar view.

The good thing about this view is that the logic is nearly identical to that of the monthly view. Any code that determines whether or not to show an event is the same. The differences are isolated to the display logic. In this mode, we want to show more information in a more formatted method. The ASPX file for this page is shown in Listing 3.18.

```
<%@ Page
      Inherits="Proj03Web.DailyCalendarView"
      Src="calendar_daily.aspx.vb" %>
<HTML>
<HEAD>
   <title>View Calendar - Daily View for
   <% = DateTime.Parse(Request.QueryString("date")).ToShortDateString %>
   </title>
   <link href="styles.css" type="text/css" rel="stylesheet">
</HEAD>
<body>
<p class="pageheading">Daily Calendar for
<% = DateTime.Parse(Request.QueryString("date")).ToShortDateString %>
</p>
<p class="text">
<b>Actions:</b>
```

Listing 3.18 Calendar_daily.aspx

```
<a href="calendar_monthly.aspx?date=<% = Request.QueryString("date")
%>">View Month</a>
 | 
<% Response.Write("<a href=""addevent.aspx?rURL=" _
   & Request.ServerVariables("SCRIPT_NAME") _
   & "?" _
   & Request.ServerVariables("QUERY_STRING") _
   & """>Add Event</a>")
%>
<p class="text">
<asp:label id="lblEvents" runat="server" />
</p>
</p>
</body>
</HTML>
```

Listing 3.18   Calendar_daily.aspx (continued)

This page dynamically sets the title of the page as well as the heading. It then has a label control where the events will be filled in at runtime. This allows us to do the bulk of the formatting in the code-behind file and then just dump in the text. We also format links pointing to both the monthly view of the calendar and the Add Event page, along with the return URL to bring us back to the daily calendar view when we're done adding events.

The code-behind file is shown in Listing 3.19 and is nearly identical to the one used in the monthly view, so we won't need to go through all the date logic again.

```
Imports System
Imports System.Data
Imports System.Data.SqlClient
Imports System.Web.UI
Imports System.Web.UI.WebControls
Imports System.Text
Imports Microsoft.VisualBasic
Namespace Proj03Web
    Public Class DailyCalendarView
        Inherits System.Web.UI.Page
        Private DB As AtWorkUtilities.Database
        Protected lblEvents As Label

        Private Sub Page_Load(ByVal sender As System.Object, _
            ByVal e As System.EventArgs) Handles MyBase.Load

            Dim DR As SqlDataReader
            Dim strOutput As New StringBuilder()
            Dim dteCurrent As DateTime
            Dim blnShowEvent As Boolean
```

Listing 3.19   Calendar_daily.aspx.vb

```
      Dim intDiff As Integer
      Dim intOffset As Integer
      Dim intDay As Integer
      Dim i As Integer
      Dim intCount As Integer = 0

      DB = New AtWorkUtilities.Database()
      lblEvents.Text = "test"


      dteCurrent = DateTime.Parse(Request.QueryString("date"))

      DR = DB.GetDataReader("sp_RetrieveEventsByDay '" _
         & dteCurrent.ToShortDateString & "'", True)

      While DR.Read()
         ' Reset event flag
         blnShowEvent = False

         ' One-time only events only show up on the day(s)
         ' they are scheduled.
         If DR("RecurrenceType") = "N" Then
            blnShowEvent = True
         Else
            Select Case DR("RecurrenceType")
               Case "P"
                  intDiff = DateDiff(DR("PeriodicCode"), _
                     DR("EventStartDate"), dteCurrent)
                  If DateAdd(DR("PeriodicCode"), _
                     intDiff, DR("EventStartDate")) = dteCurrent Then
                     blnShowEvent = True
                  End If

               Case "M"
                  If DR("MonthlyCode") = "A" Then
                     If Day(dteCurrent) = DR("MonthlyDay") Then
                        blnShowEvent = True
                     End If
                  ElseIf DR("MonthlyCode") = "L" Then
                     For i = 1 To 7
                        If Weekday(DateTime.Parse(Month(dteCurrent) _
                           & "/" & i & "/" & Year(dteCurrent))) _
                           = DR("MonthlyDay") Then
                           Exit For
                        End If
                     Next i
                     intDay = Day(dteCurrent)
                     If (intDay - i) = _
                        (DR("MonthlyOrdinal") - 1) * 7 Then
                        blnShowEvent = True
                     End If
```

Listing 3.19 Calendar_daily.aspx.vb (continued)

```vb
                            End If
                Case "A"
                    If Month(dteCurrent) = _
                        Month(DR("AnniversaryDate"))
                        And Day(dteCurrent) = _
                            Day(DR("AnniversaryDate"))
                    Then
                        blnShowEvent = True
                    End If
            End Select
        End If
        If blnShowEvent Then
            intCount += 1
            strOutput.AppendFormat("<tr class=tabletext>" _
                & "<td colspan=2>" _
                & "<b><a href=""updateevent.aspx?id={0}" _
                & "&rURL={1}"">{2}</a></b></td></tr>", _
                DR("pkEventID"), _
                Request.ServerVariables("SCRIPT_NAME") & "?" _
                & Request.ServerVariables("QUERY_STRING"), DR("Name"))
            strOutput.AppendFormat("<tr class=tabletext>" _
                &colspan=2>" _
                & "{0}</td></tr>", DR("Description"))
            strOutput.AppendFormat("<tr class=tabletext>" _
                & "<td>Start Time:</td>" _
                & "<td>{0}</td></tr>", _
                DR("EventStartTime").ToShortTimeString())
            strOutput.AppendFormat("<tr class=tabletext>" _
                & "<td>End Time:</td>" _
                & "<td>{0}</td></tr>", _
                DR("EventEndTime").ToShortTimeString())

            strOutput.Append("<tr class=tabletext>")
            strOutput.Append("<td colspan=2> </td></tr>")
        End If
    End While
    If intCount > 0 Then
        lblEvents.Text = "<table cellpadding=3 cellspacing=0>" _
            & strOutput.ToString() & "</table>"
    Else
        lblEvents.Text = "<b>No events are scheduled for today.</b>"
    End If
End Sub


End Class
End Namespace
```

Listing 3.19   Calendar_daily.aspx.vb (continued)

We're using the same stored procedure for this page, except we only have to render the events for a single day. Once we've found all the events, we append them to the StringBuilder object we created. We also include table rows and table cells to better align the data. If we find events, the final bit of code adds the initial TABLE tag and the closing TABLE tag. If no events are found, the appropriate message is displayed.

This view is rather plain, so feel free to spruce it up with additional HTML, graphics, and so on. You might also want to make the window a pop-up window instead of a full page. Again, the hard part is the date logic, which is already working.

Wrap Up

This application gave you another way to manage data using a calendar. There are many other features that you can add to this calendar, but the code you built in this project should have given you a good idea as to where you can go next. You might want to consider allowing multiple users to add events, and a calendar would show each user's personal events instead of just one big list. However, the things learned here will benefit you in other projects in this book.

In Project 4, you'll build an application that will let you determine how much traffic your web sites are receiving. You'll build a Web Service to periodically gather the logs into a database, and you'll build an ASP.NET application to analyze the traffic patterns.

Building the Web Log Analyzer

In this project, we'll build an application that can be used to archive and analyze the Web logs produced by the IIS Web Service. If logging is enabled for a particular site, every hit that the Web server receives is recorded as a new line in the Web server's current log file. Since a given Web server can potentially receive thousands and even millions of hits each day, both the number of log files and their size can be enormous. Therefore, we need to pay special attention to the performance of our application. For example, we don't want to parse the Web logs on-the-fly whenever a user wants an analysis report, since the page itself would invariably time out while trying to parse and analyze the logs for a high-traffic site.

By default, IIS and most other popular Web servers record their log files in W3C Extended Log File Format, although log files can also be recorded in NCSA (National Center for Supercomputing Applications) Common Log File Format, Microsoft's IIS Log File Format, recorded directly to a database using ODBC Logging, or using a custom log file format through the use of extension mechanisms provided by IIS. Our log parser must therefore have an extensible architecture (which can easily be achieved through inheritance) so that these other formats can be supported. For this project, we will focus on parsing the default W3C Extended Log File Format, and leave the other formats as an exercise for the reader.

THE PROBLEM

Web log files can provide a great deal of information about the people visiting your site, but managing all the log files can be difficult.

THE SOLUTION

Build a set of applications to import, analyze, and report on the log data.

Project Background

By now, you should be familiar with the way ASP.NET works and with assemblies in general. In this project, you will create a Windows Service application to handle log collection and parsing, thus freeing our ASP.NET application for more useful tasks, such as analyzing the logs and deciding which Web server's logs will be collected.

A Windows Service application, (also known as an NT Service), is a long-running application that can be started as soon as the server starts, does not require any interaction with a user, and can continue to run even when no user is logged on. These characteristics make a Windows Service application the perfect solution for collecting and parsing the log entries into our database for later analysis. Building a successful Windows Service application, however, requires a greater degree of responsibility on the part of the programmer than other types of applications, partly because of these benefits and partly because of the limitations they impose. For example, Windows Service applications run in their own desktop, which is not available to the logged in user, and as a result, any dialog boxes or error messages raised by your service will go unanswered and undetected. To the user, it will appear as if the service has hung. In addition, a service's work is usually done on a different thread than the one used to start the service, which is the main reason previous versions of Visual Basic could not create this type of application.

Windows Service applications are controlled by the Service Control Manager (SCM), which imposes some additional restrictions. The SCM requires all Windows Services to support a specific set of actions, such as Start, Stop, and Pause/Resume, and calls these methods in your component to perform the appropriate action. Specifically, the Start method must finish its initialization and return to the caller (the SCM) within 30 seconds. Because of this, the code you put in the Start method: 1) cannot be debugged and 2) should be as concise as possible. This usually results in the Start method containing only the code necessary to begin a timer or start another thread, which then performs the bulk of the work that the service provides.

Debugging a Windows Service application also requires some extra steps by the developer since they do not run in the user's desktop environment. To debug a Windows Service application, you must first create and run an installer and then start the service. After that, you can use Visual Studio's Debug Processes command to attach to the process. Once these steps have been completed, you can set breakpoints, step through code, and perform any other debugging tasks required.

In this project, we'll create four different Visual Studio projects in our solution:

WebLogParser. This component is a Class Library project responsible for the actual parsing of individual log files. The project consists of two main classes and seven supporting classes. The two main classes are an abstract (MustInherit) LogParser component, which defines a specific set of methods that all inherited parsers should support, and our implementation of the W3CExtLogParser, which parses files in the W3C Extended Log File Format.

WebLogDataAccess. This Class Library project encapsulates all of the direct communications with our database. It is shared (privately, not through the Global Assembly Cache) between our Windows Service application that collects the log files and the ASP.NET application that performs analysis on the collected logs.

WebLogCollector. This is the Windows Service project responsible for collecting the log entries to the database. The log collector queries the directories specified by IIS and registered through our ASP.NET application for log sources (individual log files), and hands each source off to the LogParser for processing.

Project04. This is our ASP.NET Web application project, which presents the user interface and supports interaction with the other components.

Before we begin, let's first set up a new SQL Server 2000 database to hold our log information. If you're using SQL Server 7.0, you will need to make some adjustments to your database for the BigInt fields and cascading deletes. In SQL Server 7.0, the BigInt fields can be specified as either numeric or decimal to hold a large range of values, and cascading deletes can be implemented through the use of triggers.

To build this application, you'll be performing these steps:

1. Set up the database and database objects.
2. Build the WebLogParser project to parse your web log files.
3. Build the WebLogDataAccess project to provide access to the database for your other applications.
4. Build the WebLogCollector project to periodically import logs into the database.
5. Build the Web application to view the analysis results.

 ## You Will Need

✔ **Windows 2000**

✔ **Internet Information Server 5.0 with .NET Framework installed**

✔ **Visual Studio .NET**

✔ **SQL Server 2000 or 7.0**

✔ **Internet Information Server 5.0 log files**

Setting Up the Database

First, start SQL Server Enterprise Manager and establish a connection to the server that you will use. Then right-click the Databases folder and select New Database. I've given my database the name ASPNetProject04 in the database properties window, but you can name it anything you want—just remember to adjust the connection string in the application configuration file. After you've named your database, click OK, and locate the database in the Enterprise Manager window.

Right-click your new database in the Enterprise Manager window, and select Properties. Click the Options tab in the resulting dialog box. Make sure that the following items are selected, and then click OK.

■ ANSI NULL default
■ Recursive triggers

- Auto close
- Auto shrink

Our database will initially consist of eight tables: LogSite, LogSource, URIStem, URIQuery, Host, Referer, Cookie, and UserAgent. Notice that we're not creating a separate table for individual log entries. These tables will be created dynamically and will hold the entries for individual sites that are registered for collection through the ASP.NET application. This is done because the entries in each of these tables can potentially number in the millions, and we may want to later optimize the file groups where these tables are stored to enhance our application's performance.

Creating the LogSite Table

The LogSite table contains the list of Web sites and computers that we want the log collector to collect entries for. Create the table with the following field definitions (shown in Figure 4.1):

- ID, uniqueidentifier, not null, primary key, default value = NEWID(), isrowguid = true
- MachineName, nvarchar(15), not null

  This is the computer where the Web server resides. This field supports a single ASP.NET application and log collector service to collect logs from across a Web farm, if necessary.

- SiteIndex, smallint, not null

  This is the unique site index used by IIS to identify a particular Web site.

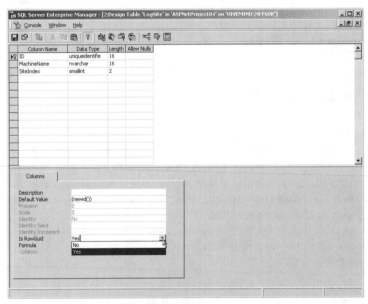

Figure 4.1   LogSite table design view.

Note that we're not storing the Log File directory in the database. This information is obtained by our WebLogDataAccess project from a much more authoritative data store, the IIS MetaBase.

Creating the LogSource Table

The LogSource table will contain the list of log files found in directories that are registered by the ASP.NET application, as well as the current status of the collection-and-parsing operation. This way, the ASP.NET application can easily check to see if a particular log file has been processed (and by which log collector service instance), is currently being processed, is pending, or contains errant log entries, which prevents it from being fully processed. Create the LogSource table with the following field definitions (shown in Figure 4.2):

- ID, uniqueidentifier, not null, primary key, default value = NEWID(), isrowguid = true

- Site, uniqueidentifier, not null, foreign key references LogSite ([ID])

  This field will be our foreign key to the LogSite table.

- FilePath, nvarchar(512), not null

  This field holds the full path (which can be a UNC path) to the individual log file to be parsed. It is declared as nvarchar since filenames can contain Unicode characters.

- Status, varchar(20), not null, default value = 'PENDING'

  This field holds the current status of this log file, which will be used by the log collector and the ASP.NET application.

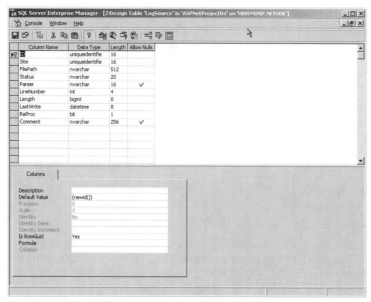

Figure 4.2 LogSource table design view.

- Parser, nvarchar(15), allow null

  This identifies the computer that is currently responsible for parsing this log file. This prevents multiple instances of the log collector service running on separate computers from processing the same log file. Again, it is declared as nvarchar since computer names can contain Unicode characters.

- LineNumber, int, not null, default value = 0

  This contains the last line number that has been processed by the log parser. If an error occurs while processing a log file, you can easily determine the offending line by looking at the value in this field. This is also used when the log collector service has been stopped before it finished processing a particular log file to determine where to start processing the next time it is started.

- Length, bigint, not null, default value = 0

  This holds the length of the log file in bytes. Since files on Windows 2000 can be larger than 2 GB, this number can exceed the range of values defined in an int SQL data type. If you are using a database that does not support the bigint data type, such as SQL Server 7.0, make this field a numeric data type that can handle large integer values.

- LastWrite, datetime, not null

  This contains the last time that the log file was written to.

- ReProc, bit, not null, default value = 0

  This indicates whether the log file should be reprocessed after an error occurs. Sometimes, IIS will lock the file after it has been created but before any entries have been written. This will cause an IOException in the log parser. By setting this value to True, however, we can allow the log collector to try to reprocess the file on the next pass (after IIS has released the lock).

- Comment, nvarchar(1024), allow null, default value = 'This file has not yet been processed'

  This holds either a comment provided by the log collector service or the cause of the error, if one occurs while processing a log file.

Creating the Other Tables

The URIStem, URIQuery, Host, Referer, Cookie, and UserAgent tables are used to store large text information that is frequently repeated, which can drastically reduce the size of the tables that are used to hold entry data and improve the overall performance of the application.

Create the URIStem table with the following field definitions (shown in Figure 4.3):

- ID, uniqueidentifier, not null, primary key, default value = NEWID(), isrowguid = true

- [cs-uri-stem], nvarchar(512), not null

  This field holds the stem portion of the URL (the part up to the query string). At a maximum, there will be one entry for each file in your site and each unfulfilled request (404 error) for the sites that you have registered. The stem portion of a URL can contain UTF-8 (Unicode) characters, which is why we've defined this as nvarchar.

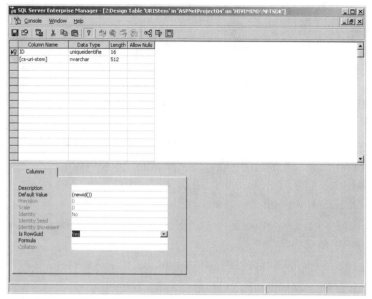

Figure 4.3   URIStem table design view.

Create the URIQuery table with the following field definitions (shown in Figure 4.4):

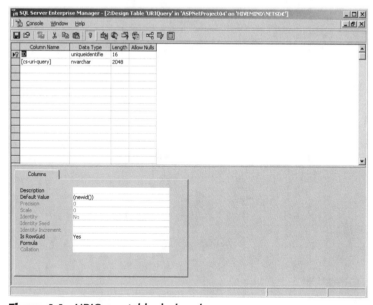

Figure 4.4   URIQuery table design view.

- ID, uniqueidentifier, not null, primary key, default value = NEWID(), isrowguid = true

- [cs-uri-query], nvarchar(2048), not null

    This field holds the query portion of the URL (the query string). Query strings can be as long as 2 K, but are usually fairly short (less than 100-200 characters). The query portion of a URL can contain UTF-8 (Unicode) characters, which is why we've defined this as nvarchar.

Create the Host table with the following field definitions (shown in Figure 4.5):

- ID, uniqueidentifier, not null, primary key, default value = NEWID(), isrowguid = true

- [cs-host], nvarchar(256), not null

    This field holds the host name of your site, which is usually the DNS name, but it can be an IP address or "localhost."

Create the Referer table with the following field definitions (shown in Figure 4.6):

- ID, uniqueidentifier, not null, primary key, default value = NEWID(), isrowguid = true

- [cs(Referer)], nvarchar(512), not null

    This field holds the referring URL.

Create the Cookie table with the following field definitions (shown in Figure 4.7):

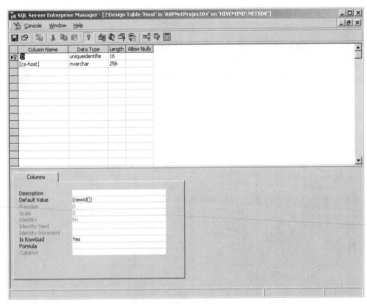

Figure 4.5   Host table design view.

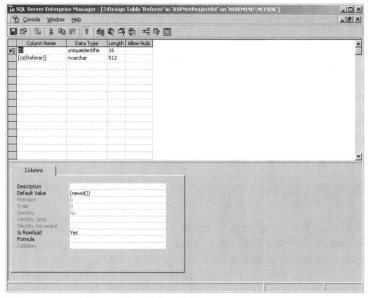

Figure 4.6   Referer table design view.

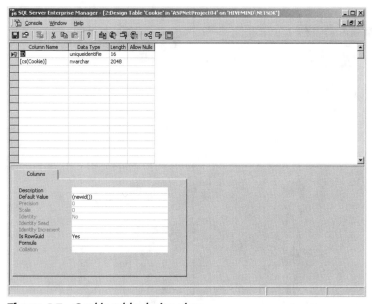

Figure 4.7   Cookie table design view.

- ID, uniqueidentifier, not null, primary key, default value = NEWID(), isrowguid = true

- [cs(Cookie)], nvarchar(2048), not null

  This field holds the cookies sent by the browser.

Create the UserAgent table with the following field definitions (shown in Figure 4.8):

- ID, uniqueidentifier, not null, primary key, default value = NEWID(), isrowguid = true

- [cs(User-Agent)], nvarchar(256), not null

  This field holds the user agent (the browser type) strings sent by the client's browser.

You probably have noticed that we're using the same field names in our database as those used in the W3C Extended Log File Format by IIS. This isn't necessary, but it does simplify the identification of which database field goes with which log file field.

Creating the Stored Procedures

The WebLogDataAccess project will make use of several stored procedures to perform its tasks. In the SQL Server Enterprise Manager, expand the database node, right-click the Stored Procedures item, and then click New Stored Procedure to begin creating each of the following stored procedures.

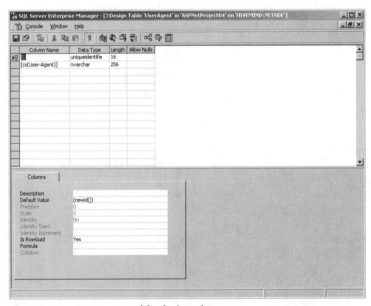

Figure 4.8 UserAgent table design view.

The registerSite Stored Procedure

This procedure is called whenever the ASP.NET application requests a new site to be registered for collection. The stored procedure is defined in Listing 4.1.

```
CREATE  PROCEDURE [dbo].[registerSite] (
 @SiteID uniqueidentifier = NULL OUTPUT,
 @MachineName nvarchar(15),
 @SiteIndex smallint
) AS
BEGIN TRAN
DECLARE @tmpID uniqueidentifier
DECLARE @TableName nvarchar(25)
DECLARE @SQLStatement nvarchar(2000)

IF (ISNULL(@MachineName, N'') = N'')
 RAISERROR(N'The machine name ''%s'' is invalid.', 16, 1, @MachineName)
IF (ISNULL(@SiteIndex, 0) < 1)
 RAISERROR(N'The site index ''%hd'' is invalid.', 16, 1, @SiteIndex)

IF (@@ERROR <> 0) GOTO EXIT_BATCH

IF EXISTS(SELECT [ID] FROM LogSite WHERE [MachineName] = @MachineName
 AND [SiteIndex] = @SiteIndex)
 BEGIN
  SELECT @tmpID = [ID] FROM LogSite WHERE [MachineName] = @MachineName
   AND [SiteIndex] = @SiteIndex
  GOTO EXIT_BATCH
 END

IF (@SiteID IS NULL)
 SET @tmpID = NEWID()
ELSE
 SET @tmpID = @SiteID

INSERT INTO [LogSite] ([ID], [MachineName], [SiteIndex])
 VALUES (@tmpID, @MachineName, @SiteIndex)

SET @TableName = @MachineName + N'W3SVC' + CONVERT(nvarchar(5),
 @SiteIndex)

-- This will dynamically create the table
-- used to hold individual log entries.
IF EXISTS(SELECT * FROM dbo.sysobjects WHERE [ID] =
OBJECT_ID(@TableName)
 AND OBJECTPROPERTY([ID], N'IsUserTable') = 1)
 BEGIN
  SET @SQLStatement = N'DROP TABLE ' + @TableName
  EXECUTE sp_executesql @SQLStatement
```

Listing 4.1 registerSite stored procedure

```
   SET @SQLStatement = N'DROP VIEW vw_' + @TableName
    EXECUTE sp_executesql @SQLStatement
   END


-- Dynamically construct our SQL statement
 SET @SQLStatement = N'CREATE TABLE [' + @TableName + '] (
  [ID] uniqueidentifier ROWGUIDCOL NOT NULL PRIMARY KEY CLUSTERED
  DEFAULT (NEWID()), [Source] [uniqueidentifier] NOT NULL FOREIGN
  KEY REFERENCES LogSource ([ID]) ON DELETE CASCADE, [date-time]
  datetime NULL, [c-ip] int NULL, [cs-username] nvarchar(36) NULL,
  [s-sitename] varchar(12) NULL, [s-computername] nvarchar(15) NULL,
  [s-ip] int NULL, [s-port] int NULL, [cs-method] varchar(10) NULL,
  [cs-uri-stem] uniqueidentifier NULL FOREIGN KEY REFERENCES URIStem
  ([ID]), [cs-uri-query] uniqueidentifier NULL FOREIGN KEY REFERENCES
  URIQuery ([ID]), [sc-status] smallint NULL, [sc-win32-status] int NULL,
  [sc-bytes] int NULL, [cs-bytes] int NULL, [time-taken] int NULL,
  [cs-version] varchar(20) NULL, [cs-host] uniqueidentifier NULL FOREIGN
  KEY REFERENCES Host ([ID]), [cs(User-Agent)] uniqueidentifier NULL
  FOREIGN KEY REFERENCES UserAgent ([ID]), [cs(Cookie)]
  uniqueidentifier NULL FOREIGN KEY REFERENCES Cookie ([ID]),
  [cs(Referer)] uniqueidentifier NULL FOREIGN KEY REFERENCES Referer
  ([ID])) ON [PRIMARY]'

EXECUTE sp_executesql @SQLStatement

SET @SQLStatement = 'CREATE VIEW vw_' + @TableName + ' AS SELECT
  [ID], [date-time], CONVERT(varchar(15), CONVERT(varchar(3), [c-ip]
  & 255) + ''.'' + CONVERT(varchar(3), (([c-ip] & 65280) / 256)) +
  ''.'' + CONVERT(varchar(3), (([c-ip] & 16711680) / 65536)) + ''.'' +
  CONVERT(varchar(3), (([c-ip] & 2130706432) / 16777216) + ((CONVERT(
  smallint, SIGN([c-ip])) & -32768) / -32768 * 128)) AS [c-ip],
  [cs-username], [s-sitename], [s-computername], CONVERT(varchar(15),
  CONVERT(varchar(3), [s-ip] & 255) + ''.'' + CONVERT(varchar(3), ((
  [s-ip] & 65280) / 256)) + ''.'' + CONVERT(varchar(3), (([s-ip] &
  16711680) / 65536)) + ''.'' + CONVERT(varchar(3), (([s-ip] &
  2130706432) / 16777216) + ((CONVERT(smallint, SIGN([s-ip])) &
  -32768) / -32768 * 128)) AS [s-ip], [s-port], [cs-method],
  [cs-uri-stem], [cs-uri-query], [sc-status], [sc-win32-status],
  [sc-bytes], [cs-bytes], [time-taken], [cs-version], [cs-host],
  [cs(User-Agent)], [cs(Cookie)], [cs(Referer)] FROM ' + @TableName

EXECUTE sp_executesql @SQLStatement

EXIT_BATCH:
IF (@@ERROR <> 0)
  BEGIN
   ROLLBACK TRAN
   SET @SiteID = NULL
  END
```

Listing 4.1 registerSite stored procedure (continued)

```
ELSE
 BEGIN
  COMMIT TRAN
  SET @SiteID = @tmpID
 END
```

Listing 4.1   registerSite stored procedure (continued)

The unregisterSite Stored Procedure

This procedure is the opposite of the registerSite stored procedure. It is called when the ASP.NET application no longer needs to collect the log files for a given site. The stored procedure is defined in Listing 4.2.

```
CREATE  PROCEDURE [dbo].[unregisterSite] (
 @SiteID uniqueidentifier
) AS
BEGIN TRAN
DECLARE @SQLStatement nvarchar(2000)
DECLARE @MachineName nvarchar(15)
DECLARE @SiteIndex smallint
DECLARE @TableName nvarchar(25)

-- First delete the entries from the child table so as
-- not to cause any Foreign key constraint violations.
DELETE FROM LogSource WHERE [Site] = @SiteID
-- Then select the machine name and site index from the
-- log site table that corresponds to this registered
-- site so we can build our SQL statement dynamically.
SELECT @MachineName = [MachineName], @SiteIndex = [SiteIndex] FROM
 LogSite WHERE [ID] = @SiteID
-- Remove the site entry.
DELETE FROM LogSite WHERE [ID] = @SiteID

SET @TableName = @MachineName + N'W3SVC' + CONVERT(nvarchar(5),
 @SiteIndex)

-- And finally, drop the entries table for this site.
IF EXISTS(SELECT * FROM dbo.sysobjects WHERE [ID] =
OBJECT_ID(@TableName)
 AND OBJECTPROPERTY([ID], N'IsUserTable') = 1)
 BEGIN
  SET @SQLStatement = N'DROP TABLE ' + @TableName
  EXECUTE sp_executesql @SQLStatement
```

Listing 4.2   unregisterSite stored procedure

```
    SET @SQLStatement = N'DROP VIEW vw_' + @TableName
    EXECUTE sp_executesql @SQLStatement
  END

EXIT_BATCH:
IF (@@ERROR <> 0)
  BEGIN
   ROLLBACK TRAN
  END
ELSE
  BEGIN
   COMMIT TRAN
  END
```

Listing 4.2   unregisterSite stored procedure (continued)

The getRegisteredSites Stored Procedure

This procedure is used by the log collector service (through our data-access component) to retrieve the list of sites for which logs need to be collected. It is also used by the ASP.NET application to retrieve the list of available sites on a specific computer. The stored procedure is defined in Listing 4.3.

```
CREATE PROCEDURE dbo.getRegisteredSites    (
  @MachineName nvarchar(15) = NULL
) AS
IF (@MachineName IS NULL)
  SELECT [ID], [MachineName], [SiteIndex], CONVERT(nvarchar(25),
   [MachineName] + N'W3SVC' + CONVERT(nvarchar(5), [SiteIndex])) AS
   [EntriesTable], CONVERT(nvarchar(256), NULL) AS [SiteName],
   CONVERT(nvarchar(512), NULL) As [LogFileDirectory], CONVERT(bit, 1)
   AS [Registered] FROM [LogSite] ORDER BY [MachineName], [SiteIndex]
ELSE
  SELECT [ID], [MachineName], [SiteIndex], CONVERT(nvarchar(25),
   [MachineName] + N'W3SVC' + CONVERT(nvarchar(5), [SiteIndex])) AS
   [EntriesTable], CONVERT(nvarchar(256), NULL)
   AS [SiteName], CONVERT(nvarchar(512), NULL) As [LogFileDirectory],
   CONVERT(bit, 1) AS [Registered] FROM [LogSite]
   WHERE [MachineName] = @MachineName ORDER BY [SiteIndex]
RETURN
```

Listing 4.3   getRegisteredSites stored procedure

The next few stored procedures are used by the log collector service to add, retrieve, and update the list of available log sources (individual log files). The ASP.NET application uses the getSources stored procedure to show the user a list of sources and their status for a given site.

The addSource Stored Procedure

This procedure is used by the log collector service to add a new log source that was detected in the file system. Notice that we're setting the transaction isolation level to Serializable for the duration of this procedure. This way, we can make sure that two instances of the log collector service, running on different computers, cannot add the same log source twice. If this type of attempt is made, the second (unsuccessful) operation will receive the correct log source ID in the output parameter. The stored procedure is defined in Listing 4.4.

```sql
CREATE PROCEDURE dbo.addSource (
 @SourceID uniqueidentifier = NULL OUTPUT,
 @Site uniqueidentifier,
 @FilePath nvarchar(512),
 @Status nvarchar(20) = N'PENDING',
 @Parser nvarchar(15) = NULL,
 @LineNumber int = 0,
 @Length bigint = 0,
 @LastWrite datetime,
 @ReProc bit = 0,
 @Comment nvarchar(256) = N'This file has not yet been processed.'
) AS
SET TRANSACTION ISOLATION LEVEL SERIALIZABLE
BEGIN TRAN

IF EXISTS(SELECT * FROM [LogSource] WHERE [FilePath] = @FilePath
 AND [Site] = @Site)
 SELECT @SourceID = [ID] FROM [LogSource] WHERE [FilePath] = @FilePath
 AND [Site] = @Site
ELSE
 INSERT INTO [LogSource] ([ID], [Site], [FilePath], [Status], [Parser],
 [LineNumber], [Length], [LastWrite], [ReProc], [Comment]) VALUES
 (@SourceID, @Site, @FilePath, @Status, @Parser, @LineNumber,
 @Length, @LastWrite, @ReProc, @Comment)

IF (@@ERROR <> 0)
 BEGIN
  ROLLBACK TRAN
  SET @SourceID = NULL
 END
ELSE
 BEGIN
  COMMIT TRAN
 END
SET TRANSACTION ISOLATION LEVEL READ COMMITTED
```

Listing 4.4   addSource stored procedure

The updateSource Stored Procedure

This procedure is used by the log collector service to update a log source in response to processing activity or activity that was detected in the file system. The stored procedure is defined in Listing 4.5.

```
CREATE PROCEDURE dbo.updateSource (
  @SourceID uniqueidentifier OUTPUT,
  @Site uniqueidentifier,
  @FilePath nvarchar(512),
  @Status nvarchar(20),
  @Parser nvarchar(15),
  @LineNumber int,
  @Length bigint,
  @LastWrite datetime,
  @ReProc bit,
  @Comment nvarchar(256) = NULL
) AS
BEGIN TRAN

UPDATE [LogSource] SET [ID] = @SourceID, [Site] = @Site,
  [FilePath] = @FilePath, [Status] = @Status, [Parser] = @Parser,
  [LineNumber] = @LineNumber, [Length] = @Length,
  [LastWrite] = @LastWrite, [ReProc] = @ReProc,
  [Comment] = @Comment WHERE [ID] = @SourceID
IF (@@ERROR <> 0)
  BEGIN
    ROLLBACK TRAN
  END
ELSE
  BEGIN
    COMMIT TRAN
  END
RETURN
```

Listing 4.5   updateSource stored procedure

The getSources Stored Procedure

This procedure is used by the log collector service upon initialization to retrieve a list of log sources that are already registered in the database. It is also used by the ASP.NET application to retrieve a list of log sources and their status for a particular site. The stored procedure is defined in Listing 4.6.

```
CREATE PROCEDURE dbo.getSources (
 @SiteID uniqueidentifier = NULL
) AS
IF (@SiteID IS NULL)
 SELECT [LogSource].[ID], [Site], [FilePath], [Status], [Parser],
  [LineNumber], [Length], [LastWrite], [ReProc], [Comment] FROM
  [LogSource] INNER JOIN [LogSite] ON
  [LogSource].[Site] = [LogSite].[ID] ORDER BY [LogSite].[SiteIndex]
ELSE
 SELECT [ID], [Site], [FilePath], [Status], [Parser], [LineNumber],
  [Length], [LastWrite], [ReProc], [Comment] FROM [LogSource]
  WHERE [Site] = @SiteID ORDER BY [FilePath]
```

Listing 4.6   getSources stored procedure

The addEntry Stored Procedure

The following stored procedure is used by the log collector service to add individual log entries to the database. The log entry table is selected dynamically by the procedure. IIS stores its log files as plain text, but to reduce the size of the data stored in the logs, most of the fields are reduced to their numeric equivalents. The stored procedure is defined in Listing 4.7.

```
CREATE PROCEDURE dbo.addEntry (
 @EntryTable nvarchar(25) = NULL OUTPUT,
 @Source uniqueidentifier,
 @SourceLine int,
 @dateTime datetime = NULL,
 @cIp int = NULL,
 @csUsername nvarchar(36) = NULL,
 @sSitename varchar(12) = NULL,
 @sComputername nvarchar(15) = NULL,
 @sIp int = NULL,
 @sPort int = NULL,
 @csMethod varchar(10) = NULL,
 @csUriStem nvarchar(512) = NULL,
 @csUriQuery nvarchar(2048) = NULL,
 @scStatus smallint = NULL,
 @scWin32Status int = NULL,
 @scBytes int = NULL,
 @csBytes int = NULL,
 @timeTaken int = NULL,
 @csVersion varchar(20) = NULL,
 @csHost nvarchar(256) = NULL,
 @csUserAgent nvarchar(256) = NULL,
```

Listing 4.7   addEntry stored procedure

```
  @csCookie nvarchar(2048) = NULL,
  @csReferer nvarchar(512) = NULL
) AS
SET NOCOUNT ON
BEGIN TRAN

DECLARE @SQLStatement nvarchar(2000)
DECLARE @ParamDefinitions nvarchar(2000)
DECLARE @tmpCsUriStem uniqueidentifier
DECLARE @tmpCsUriQuery uniqueidentifier
DECLARE @tmpCsHost uniqueidentifier
DECLARE @tmpCsUserAgent uniqueidentifier
DECLARE @tmpCsCookie uniqueidentifier
DECLARE @tmpCsReferer uniqueidentifier

SELECT @tmpCsUriStem = [ID] FROM [URIStem]
 WHERE [cs-uri-stem] = @csUriStem
SELECT @tmpCsUriQuery = [ID] FROM [URIQuery]
 WHERE [cs-uri-query] = @csUriQuery
SELECT @tmpCsHost = [ID] FROM [Host]
 WHERE [cs-host] = @csHost
SELECT @tmpCsUserAgent = [ID] FROM [UserAgent]
 WHERE [cs(User-Agent)] = @csUserAgent
SELECT @tmpCsCookie = [ID] FROM [Cookie]
 WHERE [cs(Cookie)] = @csCookie
SELECT @tmpCsReferer = [ID] FROM [Referer]
 WHERE [cs(Referer)] = @csReferer

IF ((@csUriStem IS NOT NULL) AND (@tmpCsUriStem IS NULL))
 BEGIN
  SET @tmpCsUriStem = NEWID()
  INSERT INTO URIStem ([ID], [cs-uri-stem])
   VALUES (@tmpCsUriStem, @csUriStem)
  IF (@@ERROR <> 0) GOTO EXIT_BATCH
 END
IF ((@csUriQuery IS NOT NULL) AND (@tmpCsUriQuery IS NULL))
 BEGIN
  SET @tmpCsUriQuery = NEWID()
  INSERT INTO URIQuery ([ID], [cs-uri-query])
   VALUES (@tmpCsUriQuery, @csUriQuery)
  IF (@@ERROR <> 0) GOTO EXIT_BATCH
 END
IF ((@csHost IS NOT NULL) AND (@tmpCsHost IS NULL))
 BEGIN
  SET @tmpCsHost = NEWID()
  INSERT INTO Host ([ID], [cs-host])
   VALUES (@tmpCsHost, @csHost)
  IF (@@ERROR <> 0) GOTO EXIT_BATCH
 END
IF ((@csUserAgent IS NOT NULL) AND (@tmpCsUserAgent IS NULL))
```

Listing 4.7 addEntry stored procedure (continued)

```
    BEGIN
     SET @tmpCsUserAgent = NEWID()
     INSERT INTO UserAgent ([ID], [cs(User-Agent)])
      VALUES (@tmpCsUserAgent, @csUserAgent)
     IF (@@ERROR <> 0) GOTO EXIT_BATCH
    END
  IF ((@csCookie IS NOT NULL) AND (@tmpCsCookie IS NULL))
   BEGIN
     SET @tmpCsCookie = NEWID()
     INSERT INTO Cookie ([ID], [cs(Cookie)])
      VALUES (@tmpCsCookie, @csCookie)
     IF (@@ERROR <> 0) GOTO EXIT_BATCH
   END
  IF ((@csReferer IS NOT NULL) AND (@tmpCsReferer IS NULL))
   BEGIN
     SET @tmpCsReferer = NEWID()
     INSERT INTO Referer ([ID], [cs(Referer)])
      VALUES (@tmpCsReferer, @csReferer)
     IF (@@ERROR <> 0) GOTO EXIT_BATCH
   END

  IF (@EntryTable IS NULL)
   SELECT @EntryTable = CONVERT(nvarchar(25), [MachineName] +
    N'W3SVC' + CONVERT(nvarchar(5), [SiteIndex])) FROM [LogSite]
    INNER JOIN [LogSource] ON [LogSite].[ID] = [LogSource].[Site]
    WHERE [LogSource].[ID] = @Source

  IF (@EntryTable IS NULL)
   BEGIN
     RAISERROR(N'No site is defined for this source.', 16, 1)
     GOTO EXIT_BATCH
   END

  SET NOCOUNT OFF

  SET @SQLStatement = N'INSERT INTO ' + @EntryTable + '
   ([Source], [date-time], [c-ip], [cs-username], [s-sitename],
   [s-computername], [s-ip], [s-port], [cs-method], [cs-uri-stem],
   [cs-uri-query], [sc-status], [sc-win32-status], [sc-bytes], [cs-bytes],
   [time-taken], [cs-version], [cs-host], [cs(User-Agent)], [cs(Cookie)],
   [cs(Referer)]) VALUES (@Source, @dateTime, @cIp,
   @csUsername, @sSiteName, @sComputername, @sIp, @sPort,
   @csMethod, @tmpCsUriStem, @tmpCsUriQuery, @scStatus,
   @scWin32Status, @scBytes, @csBytes, @timeTaken,
   @csVersion, @tmpCsHost, @tmpCsUserAgent, @tmpCsCookie,
   @tmpCsReferer)'
  SET @ParamDefinitions = N'@Source uniqueidentifier,
   @SourceLine int, @dateTime datetime, @cIp int,
   @csUsername nvarchar(36), @sSitename varchar(12),
   @sComputername nvarchar(15), @sIp int, @sPort int,
```

Listing 4.7 addEntry stored procedure (continued)

```
   @csMethod varchar(10), @tmpCsUriStem uniqueidentifier,
   @tmpCsUriQuery uniqueidentifier, @scStatus smallint,
   @scWin32Status int, @scBytes int, @csBytes int,
   @timeTaken int, @csVersion varchar(20), @tmpCsHost uniqueidentifier,
   @tmpCsUserAgent uniqueidentifier, @tmpCsCookie uniqueidentifier,
   @tmpCsReferer uniqueidentifier'

EXECUTE sp_executesql @SQLStatement, @ParamDefinitions,
   @Source, @SourceLine, @dateTime, @cIp, @csUsername,
   @sSitename, @sComputername, @sIp, @sPort, @csMethod,
   @tmpCsUriStem, @tmpCsUriQuery, @scStatus,
   @scWin32Status, @scBytes, @csBytes, @timeTaken,
   @csVersion, @tmpCsHost, @tmpCsUserAgent, @tmpCsCookie,
   @tmpCsReferer

SET NOCOUNT ON

UPDATE [LogSource] SET [LineNumber] = @SourceLine
  WHERE [ID] = @Source

EXIT_BATCH:
IF (@@ERROR <> 0)
  ROLLBACK TRAN
ELSE
  COMMIT TRAN
```

Listing 4.7   addEntry stored procedure (continued)

The scrubDatabase Stored Procedure

This utility procedure can be used while you are testing the log collector service to scrub the database between test runs. The stored procedure is defined in Listing 4.8.

```
CREATE PROCEDURE scrubDatabase (
  @IncludeSiteRegistrations bit = 0
) AS
BEGIN TRAN
DECLARE @TableName nvarchar(25)
DECLARE @SQLStatement nvarchar(2000)
DECLARE sites CURSOR LOCAL FORWARD_ONLY READ_ONLY
  FOR SELECT CONVERT(nvarchar(25), [MachineName] + N'W3SVC' +
  CONVERT(nvarchar(5), [SiteIndex])) AS [TableName] FROM [LogSite]

OPEN sites
FETCH NEXT FROM sites INTO @TableName
```

Listing 4.8   scrubDatabase stored procedure

```
WHILE @@FETCH_STATUS = 0
 BEGIN
  IF EXISTS(SELECT * FROM dbo.sysobjects WHERE [ID] =
   OBJECT_ID(@TableName) AND OBJECTPROPERTY([ID],
  N'IsUserTable') = 1)
   BEGIN
    IF (@IncludeSiteRegistrations = 1)
     BEGIN
      SET @SQLStatement = N'DROP TABLE ' + @TableName
      EXECUTE sp_executesql @SQLStatement
      SET @SQLStatement = N'DROP VIEW vw_' + @TableName
      EXECUTE sp_executesql @SQLStatement
     END
    ELSE
     BEGIN
      SET @SQLStatement = N'DELETE FROM ' + @TableName
      EXECUTE sp_executesql @SQLStatement
     END
   END
  FETCH NEXT FROM sites INTO @TableName
 END

DELETE FROM URIStem
DELETE FROM URIQuery
DELETE FROM Host
DELETE FROM Referer
DELETE FROM Cookie
DELETE FROM UserAgent
DELETE FROM LogSource
IF (@IncludeSiteRegistrations = 1)
 DELETE FROM LogSite

IF (@@ERROR <> 0)
 ROLLBACK TRAN
ELSE
 COMMIT TRAN
```

Listing 4.8   scrubDatabase stored procedure (continued)

Finally, let's go ahead and define some of the reports that will be available to our ASP.NET application. The SQL for these reports may be a bit hard to follow, so I would suggest downloading the code for these items from the Web site. In all of these, we are using dynamically defined queries and the sp_executesql stored procedure, so the report will work for any given site's log entry table. The four reports are HitsByClient, HitsByUserAgent, PageHitsByFrequency, and RequestsForExecutables. The complete stored procedures are shown in Listings 4.9, 4.10, 4.11, and 4.12.

```
CREATE PROCEDURE HitsByClient (
 @TableName nvarchar(25),
 @StartDate datetime = NULL,
 @EndDate datetime = NULL
) AS
DECLARE @SQLStatement nvarchar(2000)
DECLARE @ParamDefs nvarchar(2000)

SET @SQLStatement = 'SELECT DISTINCT [c-ip] AS [Client IP], CONVERT(
 nvarchar(512), NULL) AS [Client Domain], COUNT([c-ip]) AS Hits,
 CONVERT(nvarchar(10), CONVERT(decimal(5, 3), (CONVERT(decimal(24, 4),
 COUNT([c-ip])) / CONVERT(decimal(24, 4), (SELECT SUM(a.Hits) AS Total
 FROM (SELECT DISTINCT [c-ip] AS [Client IP], COUNT([c-ip]) AS [Hits]
 FROM vw_' + @TableName + ' a WHERE a.[date-time] BETWEEN CONVERT(
 datetime, @StartDate) AND CONVERT(datetime, @EndDate) AND NOT
 a.[c-ip] IS NULL GROUP BY [c-ip]) AS a)) * 100))) + ''%'' AS
 [Percentage] FROM vw_' + @TableName + ' WHERE [date-time] BETWEEN
 CONVERT(datetime, @StartDate) AND CONVERT(datetime, @EndDate) AND
 NOT [c-ip] IS NULL GROUP BY [c-ip] ORDER BY [c-ip]'
SET @ParamDefs = '@StartDate datetime, @EndDate datetime'

IF (@StartDate IS NULL) SET @StartDate = CONVERT(datetime, '1/1/1753')
IF (@EndDate IS NULL) SET @EndDate = CONVERT(datetime,
 '12/31/9999 11:59:59')

EXECUTE sp_executesql @SQLStatement, @ParamDefs, @StartDate, @EndDate
```

Listing 4.9   HitsByClient stored procedure

```
CREATE PROCEDURE HitsByUserAgent (
 @TableName nvarchar(25),
 @StartDate datetime = NULL,
 @EndDate datetime = NULL
) AS
DECLARE @SQLStatement nvarchar(2000)
DECLARE @ParamDefs nvarchar(2000)

SET @SQLStatement = 'SELECT DISTINCT UserAgent.[cs(User-Agent)] AS
 [User Agent / Browser Type], COUNT(UserAgent.[cs(User-Agent)]) AS
 Hits, CONVERT(nvarchar(10), CONVERT(decimal(5, 3), CONVERT(
 decimal(24, 4), COUNT(UserAgent.[cs(User-Agent)]))) / CONVERT(
 decimal(24, 4), (SELECT SUM(a.Hits) AS Total FROM (SELECT DISTINCT
 UserAgent.[cs(User-Agent)] AS [User Agent / Browser Type], COUNT(
 UserAgent.[cs(User-Agent)]) AS [Hits] FROM vw_' + @TableName + ' i LEFT
 JOIN UserAgent ON i.[cs(User-Agent)] = UserAgent.[ID] WHERE
 i.[date-time] BETWEEN CONVERT(datetime, @StartDate) AND CONVERT(
```

Listing 4.10   HitsByUserAgent stored procedure

```
datetime, @EndDate) AND NOT i.[cs(User-Agent)] IS NULL GROUP BY
UserAgent.[cs(User-Agent)]) AS a)) * 100)) + ''%'' AS Percentage
FROM vw_' + @TableName + ' a LEFT JOIN UserAgent ON a.[cs(User-Agent)]
= UserAgent.[ID] WHERE a.[cs(User-Agent)] IS NOT NULL AND a.[date-time]
BETWEEN CONVERT(datetime, @StartDate) AND CONVERT(datetime, @EndDate)
GROUP BY UserAgent.[cs(User-Agent)] ORDER BY UserAgent.[cs(User-
Agent)]'
SET @ParamDefs = '@StartDate datetime, @EndDate datetime'

IF (@StartDate IS NULL) SET @StartDate = CONVERT(datetime, '1/1/1753')
IF (@EndDate IS NULL) SET @EndDate = CONVERT(datetime,
 '12/31/9999 11:59:59')

EXECUTE sp_executesql @SQLStatement, @ParamDefs, @StartDate, @EndDate
```

Listing 4.10 HitsByUserAgent stored procedure (continued)

```
CREATE PROCEDURE PageHitsByFrequency (
 @TableName nvarchar(25),
 @StartDate datetime = NULL,
 @EndDate datetime = NULL
) AS
DECLARE @SQLStatement nvarchar(2000)
DECLARE @ParamDefs nvarchar(2000)

SET @SQLStatement = 'SELECT DISTINCT URIStem.[cs-uri-stem] AS
 [Request URL], COUNT(URIStem.[cs-uri-stem]) AS Hits,
 CONVERT(nvarchar(10), CONVERT(decimal(5, 3), (CONVERT(
 decimal(24, 4), COUNT(URIStem.[cs-uri-stem])) / CONVERT(
 decimal(24, 4), (SELECT SUM(a.Hits) AS Total FROM (SELECT
 DISTINCT URIStem.[cs-uri-stem], COUNT(URIStem.[cs-uri-stem])
 AS [Hits] FROM vw_' + @TableName + ' a INNER JOIN URIStem ON
 a.[cs-uri-stem] = URIStem.[ID] WHERE a.[date-time] BETWEEN
 CONVERT(datetime, @StartDate) AND CONVERT(datetime, @EndDate)
 GROUP BY URIStem.[cs-uri-stem]) AS a)) * 100))) + ''%'' AS
 [Percentage of Hits] FROM vw_' + @TableName + ' a INNER JOIN
 URIStem ON a.[cs-uri-stem] = URIStem.[ID] WHERE a.[date-time]
 BETWEEN CONVERT(datetime, @StartDate) AND CONVERT(datetime,
 @EndDate) GROUP BY URIStem.[cs-uri-stem] HAVING CONVERT(
 decimal(5, 3), (CONVERT(decimal(24, 4), COUNT(
 URIStem.[cs-uri-stem])) / CONVERT(decimal(24, 4), (SELECT
 SUM(a.Hits) AS Total FROM (SELECT DISTINCT URIStem.[cs-uri-stem]
 AS [Page Request], COUNT(URIStem.[cs-uri-stem]) AS [Hits] FROM
 vw_' + @TableName + ' a INNER JOIN URIStem ON a.[cs-uri-stem] =
 URIStem.[ID] WHERE a.[date-time] BETWEEN CONVERT(datetime,
 @StartDate) AND CONVERT(datetime, @EndDate) GROUP BY
```

Listing 4.11 PageHitsByFrequency stored procedure

```
    URIStem.[cs-uri-stem]) AS a)) * 100)) > 1 ORDER BY
    URIStem.[cs-uri-stem]'

SET @ParamDefs = '@StartDate datetime, @EndDate datetime'

IF (@StartDate IS NULL) SET @StartDate = CONVERT(datetime, '1/1/1753')
IF (@EndDate IS NULL) SET @EndDate = CONVERT(datetime,
    '12/31/9999 11:59:59')

EXECUTE sp_executesql @SQLStatement, @ParamDefs, @StartDate, @EndDate
```

Listing 4.11   PageHitsByFrequency stored procedure (continued)

```
CREATE PROCEDURE RequestsForExecutables (
 @TableName nvarchar(25),
 @StartDate datetime = NULL,
 @EndDate datetime = NULL
) AS
DECLARE @SQLStatement nvarchar(4000)
DECLARE @ParamDefs nvarchar(2000)

SET @SQLStatement = 'SELECT DISTINCT [c-ip] AS [Client IP], CASE WHEN
 URIQuery.[cs-uri-query] IS NULL THEN URIStem.[cs-uri-stem] ELSE
 URIStem.[cs-uri-stem] + ''?'' + URIQuery.[cs-uri-query] END AS [URL],
 a.[sc-status] AS [Result Code] FROM vw_' + @TableName + ' a INNER JOIN
 URIStem ON a.[cs-uri-stem] = URIStem.[ID] LEFT JOIN URIQuery ON
 a.[cs-uri-query] = URIQuery.[ID] WHERE a.[sc-status] >= 400 AND
 (CASE WHEN URIQuery.[cs-uri-query] IS NULL THEN URIStem.[cs-uri-stem]
 ELSE URIStem.[cs-uri-stem] + ''?'' + URIQuery.[cs-uri-query] END) LIKE
 ''%.exe'' OR (CASE WHEN URIQuery.[cs-uri-query] IS NULL THEN
 URIStem.[cs-uri-stem] ELSE URIStem.[cs-uri-stem] + ''?'' +
 URIQuery.[cs-uri-query] END) LIKE ''%.exe?%'' OR (CASE WHEN
 URIQuery.[cs-uri-query] IS NULL THEN URIStem.[cs-uri-stem] ELSE
 URIStem.[cs-uri-stem] + ''?'' + URIQuery.[cs-uri-query] END) LIKE
 ''%.dll'' OR (CASE WHEN URIQuery.[cs-uri-query] IS NULL THEN
 URIStem.[cs-uri-stem] ELSE URIStem.[cs-uri-stem] + ''?'' +
 URIQuery.[cs-uri-query] END) LIKE ''%.dll?%'' OR (CASE WHEN
 URIQuery.[cs-uri-query] IS NULL THEN URIStem.[cs-uri-stem] ELSE
 URIStem.[cs-uri-stem] + ''?'' + URIQuery.[cs-uri-query] END) LIKE
 ''%.ida'' OR (CASE WHEN URIQuery.[cs-uri-query] IS NULL THEN
 URIStem.[cs-uri-stem] ELSE URIStem.[cs-uri-stem] + ''?'' +
```

Listing 4.12   RequestsForExecutables stored procedure

```
URIQuery.[cs-uri-query] END) LIKE ''%.ida?%'' OR (CASE WHEN
URIQuery.[cs-uri-query] IS NULL THEN URIStem.[cs-uri-stem] ELSE
URIStem.[cs-uri-stem] + ''?'' + URIQuery.[cs-uri-query] END) LIKE
''%.bat'' OR (CASE WHEN URIQuery.[cs-uri-query] IS NULL THEN
URIStem.[cs-uri-stem] ELSE URIStem.[cs-uri-stem] + ''?'' +
URIQuery.[cs-uri-query] END) LIKE ''%.bat?%'' OR (CASE WHEN
URIQuery.[cs-uri-query] IS NULL THEN URIStem.[cs-uri-stem] ELSE
URIStem.[cs-uri-stem] + ''?'' + URIQuery.[cs-uri-query] END) LIKE
''%.com'' OR (CASE WHEN URIQuery.[cs-uri-query] IS NULL THEN
URIStem.[cs-uri-stem] ELSE URIStem.[cs-uri-stem] + ''?'' +
URIQuery.[cs-uri-query] END) LIKE ''%.com?%'' OR (CASE WHEN
URIQuery.[cs-uri-query] IS NULL THEN URIStem.[cs-uri-stem] ELSE
URIStem.[cs-uri-stem] + ''?'' + URIQuery.[cs-uri-query] END) LIKE
''%.bat'' OR (CASE WHEN URIQuery.[cs-uri-query] IS NULL THEN
URIStem.[cs-uri-stem] ELSE URIStem.[cs-uri-stem] + ''?'' +
URIQuery.[cs-uri-query] END) LIKE ''%.bat?%'' AND a.[date-time]
BETWEEN CONVERT(datetime, @StartDate) AND CONVERT(datetime, @EndDate)
ORDER BY [sc-status], [c-ip]'

SET @ParamDefs = '@StartDate datetime, @EndDate datetime'

IF (@StartDate IS NULL) SET @StartDate = CONVERT(datetime, '1/1/1753')
IF (@EndDate IS NULL) SET @EndDate = CONVERT(datetime,
 '12/31/9999 11:59:59')

EXECUTE sp_executesql @SQLStatement, @ParamDefs, @StartDate, @EndDate
```

Listing 4.12 RequestsForExecutables stored procedure (continued)

Now, we are ready to begin setting up our development environment. The first project that we will set up will be the ASP.NET Web application, although it will be the last to be developed. After all, we need to have some data in the database before we can successfully use the application. Setting it up first in the development environment will automatically make it the startup project for debugging purposes, since none of the other project types (the two Class Libraries and our Windows Service) can be directly debugged in the Visual Studio environment by using the Start Debugging command or the F5 keyboard shortcut. The logical steps we'll follow to complete this project are as follows:

1. Create the Web Application in IIS and a new ASP.NET Web Application project in Visual Studio .NET.

2. Create and build the WebLogParser Class Library project.

3. Create and build the WebLogDataAccess Class Library project.

4. Create, build, install, and test the LogCollector Windows Service project.

5. Develop, build, and test the ASP.NET Web Application.

Setting Up the Development Environment

Visual Studio .NET can automatically create the IIS application folder that we will use if you have previously set it up to do so. By default, when Visual Studio .NET is installed, it will create a share point (shared folder) for the Default Web Site root directory in IIS, which it uses to create and access new applications. However, if you want to use a different Web site to develop this application or want to locate your data files in a directory that is not accessible through the wwwroot$ shared folder, you must set up your application manually using the Internet Service Manager console. In that case, follow these steps to create a new application:

1. Create a new directory on your computer to hold the ASP.NET application's Web files.

2. Start Internet Service Manager.

3. Right-click the Web site you've chosen to contain this application, and select New —> Virtual Directory.

4. In the introductory screen of the wizard, click the Next button.

5. The second page of the wizard (shown in Figure 4.9) prompts you for an alias for your virtual directory. I would suggest a name of Project04. Type the alias, and click the Next button.

6. The next step of the wizard (shown in Figure 4.10) is where you specify the physical directory that you created in step 1. Type the path or browse to this directory, and then click the Next button.

7. On the last screen of the wizard, verify that the Read and Run Scripts permissions check boxes are selected, and then click the Next and Finish buttons to create the virtual directory.

8. You should now see your new virtual directory listed in the left panel of the Internet Services Manager. If you don't, click the Refresh button on the toolbar. Right-click the virtual directory you created, and select Properties. The dialog box shown in Figure 4.11 will appear.

Figure 4.9   Virtual directory alias screen.

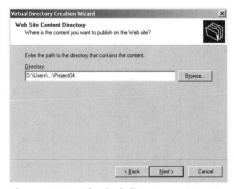

Figure 4.10   Physical directory entry screen.

9. IIS should have automatically created your virtual directory as a Web Application, but if it hasn't, you can click the Create button to have one created for you. Next, click the Directory Security tab shown in Figure 4.12.

10. Since Web logs can sometimes contain sensitive data and the ADSI IIS MetaBase queries performed by our WebLogDataAccess component require an administrator's security context in order to run successfully, we want to make sure that an anonymous user cannot access our site and that all requests to our site are authenticated. Click the Edit button under the heading Anonymous Access and Authentication Control to see the dialog box shown in Figure 4.13.

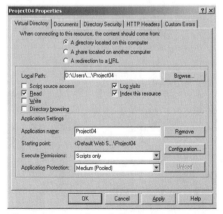

Figure 4.11   Virtual directory properties dialog box.

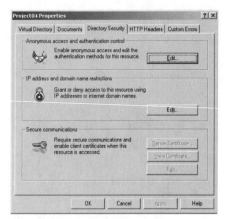

Figure 4.12   Directory Security tab.

11. It is important that you make sure that the Anonymous access check box is *not selected*. As you can see in Figure 4.13, I have also selected all of the authentication types supported by IIS under the Authenticated Access heading.

12. Now that you have your IIS Web Application set up, close Internet Services Manager. Next, start Visual Studio .NET, and select File —> New —> Project. Select the ASP.NET Web Application project type from the list of available Visual Basic projects, and type the name of the virtual directory you created in step 5, as shown in Figure 4.14.

13. Visual Studio .NET automatically creates your application's project files and a *bin* directory for us and sets the appropriate properties. After it has completed initializing your project, the Solution Explorer window should look like the one shown in Figure 4.15.

Figure 4.13   Authentication Methods dialog box.

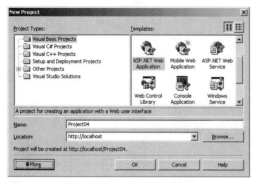

Figure 4.14   ASP.NET Web Application project dialog box.

14. Before you continue creating the other project types, open the AssemblyInfo.vb file, and set the assembly's attributes as you have done in previous projects. For the AssemblyTitle attribute, type ASP.NET At Work - Web Log Analyzer.

15. At this point, you can close the source code windows in Visual Studio .NET and start creating the other project types. To do this, choose File —> Add Project —> New Project. Select the Class Library project type from the list of available Visual Basic projects, and use the name WebLogParser for the project name, as shown in Figure 4.16.

Figure 4.15   Solution Explorer after creating our initial project.

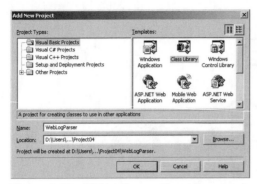

Figure 4.16   WebLogParser Class Library project dialog box.

16. Again, set the AssembyInfo.vb information for this project so you don't have to worry about it later. This time, use the assembly title ASP.NET At Work - Web Log Parser Component.

17. Now add a new Class Library project to your solution, as you did in step 15, and name it WebLogDataAccess, as shown in Figure 4.17. After the project is added to the solution, set its AssemblyInfo.vb information as before, but use the assembly title ASP.NET At Work - Web Log Data Access Component.

18. Add a new Windows Service project to your solution named WebLogCollector, as shown in Figure 4.18, and set its assembly information using the assembly title ASP.NET At Work - Web Log Collector Windows Service.

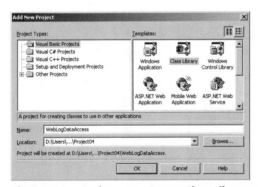

Figure 4.17   WebLogDataAccess Class Library project dialog box.

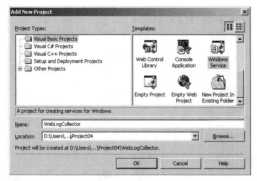

Figure 4.18   WebLogCollector Windows Service project dialog box.

19. After all of these steps have been completed, your Solution Explorer window should appear as the one shown in Figure 4.19. At this point, click the Save button on the toolbar to save our initial solution configuration.

You might be wondering why I decided to separate the log parser component from the log collector service instead of simply adding these classes to the log collector. I did this because the two components represent distinct pieces of functionality that are not entirely reliant upon each other. The log parser is generic enough that it could conceivably be used outside the context of collecting log entries into a database.

Figure 4.19   Solution Explorer window.

Developing the WebLogParser Project

The WebLogParser component has one single responsibility: to successfully parse a single log file. *Successfully* is the key word here. This project will consist of a series of classes and web pages, the first of which handles the errors in the application.

The ParseException Class

Since log files of a specific type are supposed to be in a specific and well-defined format, our component should be able to read and understand that format. Unfortunately, if a user manually edits a log file, the file is truncated or corrupted, or IIS changes the fields or format midstream, Web log files can and often do contain errant entries that do not correspond to this well-defined format. In this case, the WebLogParser needs to notify its user, usually another component, that an exception occurred from which it could not recover. Therefore, our first class in the WebLogParser project is the Parse-Exception. Now that your development environment is initialized, select the Class1.vb file in the WebLogParser project, and rename it ParseException.vb. The complete code listing for this class can be found in Listing 4.13.

```
Option Strict On
Option Explicit On


Imports System.Runtime.Serialization

'
' Notice that we are marking our exception class as "Serializable". This
' will allow the exception to be thrown across process and/or machine
' boundaries, if necessary. However, if we add any internal state to our
' exception (which we are in this class) that is not present in the base
' exception, it is VERY important to also add the deserialization
' constructor and override the GetObjectData method so that these members
' can also be serialized.
'
<Serializable()> Public Class ParseException
  Inherits ApplicationException

  ' This variable holds the file name being
  ' parsed where the exception occurred.
  Private _strFileName As String
  ' This variable holds the line number
  ' where the exception occurred.
  Private _intLineNumber As Integer


    '
  ' The following three constructors are pretty standard for exceptions,
  ' and allow the exception to be created with or without a message, and
  ' optionally include an "inner" exception that may have caused this
```

Listing 4.13   Code for ParseException.vb

```
' exception to occur. For example, if a ParseException occurs, it
' could be because another exception occurred as well, such as an
' IOException.
'
Public Sub New()

 MyBase.New()
 Me._strFileName = String.Empty
 Me._intLineNumber = 0

End Sub

Public Sub New(ByVal message As String)

 ' Notice that we are forwarding the following
 ' constructors to one of our custom constructors.
 Me.New(message, String.Empty, 0, Nothing)

End Sub

Public Sub New(ByVal message As String, ByVal inner As Exception)

 Me.New(message, String.Empty, 0, inner)

End Sub


' The next two constructors are specific to the ParseException class.
' These allow us to notify the user which log file and line number
' was currently being parsed when the exception occurred.
'
Public Sub New(ByVal message As String, ByVal fileName As String, _
 ByVal lineNumber As Integer)

 Me.New(message, String.Empty, 0, Nothing)

End Sub

Public Sub New(ByVal message As String, ByVal fileName As String, _
 ByVal lineNumber As Integer, ByVal inner As Exception)

 MyBase.New(message, inner)
 Me._strFileName = fileName
 Me._intLineNumber = lineNumber

End Sub


' This is our deserialization constructor. The Common Language Runtime
' automatically calls this constructor to "rebuild" our object when it
```

Listing 4.13 Code for ParseException.vb (continued)

```vb
' is thrown across process or machine boundaries.
'
Protected Sub New(ByVal info As SerializationInfo, _
 ByVal context As StreamingContext)

 MyBase.New(info, context)
 Me._strFileName = info.GetString("FileName")
 Me._intLineNumber = info.GetInt32("LineNumber")

End Sub


'
' This is our implementation of the ISerializable interface which is
' also implemented by our base class, ApplicationException. This is
' called by the Common Language Runtime remoting infrastructure when
' our exception needs to be thrown to another process or machine, and
' allows us to serialize our internal state information.
'
Overrides Sub GetObjectData(ByVal info As SerializationInfo, _
 ByVal context As StreamingContext)

 MyBase.GetObjectData(info, context)
 info.AddValue("FileName", Me._strFileName)
 info.AddValue("LineNumber", Me._intLineNumber)

End Sub


'
' This read-only property overrides the default message provided by
' the ApplicationException base class to include information specific
' to parsing exceptions.
'
Public Overrides ReadOnly Property Message() As String
 Get
  Dim strMessage As String
  strMessage = String.Format("FileName = ""{0}""", LineNumber = {1}", _
   Me._strFileName, Me._intLineNumber)
  Return MyBase.Message & Environment.NewLine & strMessage
 End Get
End Property

'
```

Listing 4.13   Code for ParseException.vb (continued)

```
' This read-only property allows a component that catches
' this exception to determine the filename that was being
' parsed when the exception occurred.
'
Public ReadOnly Property FileName() As String
 Get
   Return Me._strFileName
 End Get
End Property


'
' This read-only property allows a component that catches this
exception
' to determine the line number in the file where the exception
occurred.
'
Public ReadOnly Property LineNumber() As Integer
 Get
   Return Me._intLineNumber
 End Get
End Property

End Class
```

Listing 4.13   Code for ParseException.vb (continued)

Almost any operation can potentially throw an exception (an error), but when our users (other components) are using the log parser, we can assume that they are not interested the file system, security, or I/O (input/output) operations. They're interested in parsing a file. After the other component has a valid reference to a log parser component, this will be the only exception that can be thrown. This way, the other component does not need to trap for IOException, SecurityException, or other types of exceptions that can be thrown while working with the file system; instead, they can trap for a single ParseException and use the InnerException property if they are interested in more detail.

First, we set the Option Strict and Option Explicit flags, which can assist in detecting certain types of errors that can prevent our project from compiling successfully and also prevent certain runtime errors. We will use these flags in all of the classes in this project. To set these flags globally for a specific project, right-click the project in the Solution Explorer, select Properties, and navigate to the Build property section in the project properties dialog box, as shown in Figure 4.20.

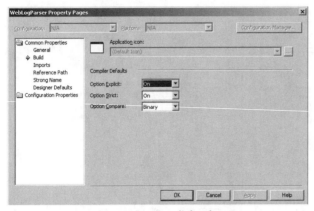

Figure 4.20   Project properties dialog box.

Next, we import the System.Runtime.Serialization namespace into this class. This namespace contains the class definitions for SerializationInfo and StreamingContext that we will use in one of our constructors.

This class inherits its base functionality from the more generic ApplicationException class defined in the System namespace. The ApplicationException class is serializable, so we also mark our exception as serializable as well, which will allow it to be thrown across processes and computer boundaries, if necessary.

We declare two private fields to hold information specific to our exception. The first, _strFileName, is used to hold the name of the file that was being parsed when the exception occurred, and the second, _intLineNumber, is used to hold the line number the parser was on when the exception was thrown.

.NET NAMING GUIDELINES

The .NET Framework Naming Guidelines discourage the use of Hungarian notation (the str, int, bln, and other types of variable-name prefixes that indicate the type of variable being used), preferring instead that variable names indicate semantics, not type. However, I know from experience that this is a difficult habit to break for VB and C++ developers. In this project, we will continue to use Hungarian notation for readability, but only for private fields and procedure-level variables.

The ParseException class implements six separate constructors. The first three are standard constructors that are defined for nearly every exception in the runtime. The following two constructors are specific to our exception and allow the parser component to specify the filename and line number that it was parsing when the exception occurred, and optionally, the inner exception that caused this ParseException. The W3CExtLogParser that we will build for this project uses only these two constructors. The next and final constructor requires a bit of explanation.

The base class, ApplicationException, defines a protected constructor, which accepts a SerializationInfo object and StreamingContext structure. This constructor is called automatically by the .NET Remoting Infrastructure to reconstruct an exception that has been thrown across a process or computer boundary. Stored within the Serialization-Info are the local field values used to restore this object's state on the other side of the boundary. This type of constructor is known as a *deserialization constructor*, and works in conjunction with the GetObjectData method, also defined in this class, which is called on this side of the boundary to store the current state into the SerializationInfo object.

The next three read-only properties allow the component that catches this type of exception to determine the file and line number where the exception occurred and retrieve the exception's message. Notice that we're overriding the default message property provided by our base class so that we can provide information specific to this type of exception in the message sent to the user.

The FieldDefinitionCollection Class

Every log file that can be parsed by one of our LogParser components is assumed to be a flat-file text database consisting of a number of well-defined fields and their values. Therefore, every LogParser component recognizes and can provide parsing services for a specific schema. The callers of our parser components might be interested in the format of that schema so they can adjust their internal settings accordingly. The Field-DefinitionCollection class implements a read-only string collection that provides the caller with the field names defined in the current schema. To create the FieldDefinitionCollection class in Visual Studio .NET, right-click the Log Parser project in Solution Explorer, and select Add —> Add Class. In the Add New Item dialog box, name your class FieldDefinitionCollection.vb (shown in Figure 4.21), and then click Open. The complete code for this class is shown in Listing 4.14.

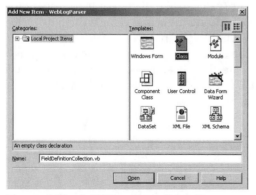

Figure 4.21   Add New Class dialog box.

```
Option Strict On
Option Explicit On

' This is our implementation of a strongly-typed read-only string
' collection to contain the list of fields defined in the schema.
<Serializable()> Public Class FieldDefinitionCollection
  Inherits ReadOnlyCollectionBase

  Public Sub New(ByVal schemaDefinition() As String)
    Me.InnerList.AddRange(schemaDefinition)
  End Sub

  ' This is used to retrieve an individual field from the list.
  Default Public ReadOnly Property Item(ByVal index As Integer) As String
    Get
      Return CStr(Me.InnerList(index))
    End Get
  End Property

End Class
```

Listing 4.14   Code for FieldDefinitionCollection.vb

As you can see from the listing, we are inheriting our class from the abstract base class ReadOnlyCollectionBase, which greatly simplifies the development of our own read-only collection. Again, we're marking this class as serializable, but unlike the ParseException, in this case we don't need to perform any extra steps to serialize this object's internal state.

The EntryDataCollection Class

We also need to define a collection to hold the entry data for each entry parsed by the log parser. This entry data consists of a name/value pair, with the name corresponding to the field name in the schema, and the value being the actual value written to the log file. The values themselves are declared as type Object since we can perform some data optimization in our parser to represent the actual log data value (a text string) as a more appropriate data type for that field (date, time, IP address, and so on). Add a new class to your Log Parser project named EntryDataCollection.vb, and enter the code shown in Listing 4.15 to implement this class.

```
Option Strict On
Option Explicit On

Imports System.Collections
Imports System.Collections.Specialized
```

Listing 4.15   Code for EntryDataCollection.vb

```
Imports System.Runtime.Serialization

<Serializable()> Public Class EntryDataCollection
 Inherits NameObjectCollectionBase


 '
 ' Our constructor takes the current log parser's schema as
 ' well as an array of field values to construct the collection.
 '
 Public Sub New(ByVal schema As FieldDefinitionCollection, _
  ByVal logData() As Object)

  Dim intIndex As Integer

  ' If the number of fields in the schema do not match
  ' the number of field values, throw an exception.
  If schema.Count <> logData.Length Then
   Throw New ArgumentException("The number of defined fields " & _
    "do not match the number of fields provided.")
  End If

  ' Initialize our collection to contain each key/value pair.
  For intIndex = 0 To schema.Count - 1
   BaseAdd(schema(intIndex), logData(intIndex))
  Next

  ' And finally, mark the collection as read only.
  MyBase.IsReadOnly = True

 End Sub


 '
 ' This default read-only property retrieves a single key/value
 ' pair given the key of the entry you wish to retrieve.
 '
 Default Public ReadOnly Property Item(ByVal key As String) _
  As DictionaryEntry
  Get
   Return New DictionaryEntry(key, MyBase.BaseGet(key))
  End Get
 End Property


 '
 ' This default read-only property retrieves a single key/value
 ' pair given the index of the entry you wish to retrieve.
 '
 Default Public ReadOnly Property Item(ByVal index As Integer) _
  As DictionaryEntry
  Get
   If index > MyBase.Count - 1 Then
```

Listing 4.15   Code for EntryDataCollection.vb (continued)

```
      Return New DictionaryEntry(String.Empty, Nothing)
    Else
      Return New DictionaryEntry(MyBase.Keys(index), _
      MyBase.BaseGet(index))
    End If
  End Get
End Property


'
' This read-only property retrieves a single value
' given the key of the value you wish to retrieve.
'
Public ReadOnly Property Values(ByVal key As String) As Object
  Get
    Return MyBase.BaseGet(key)
  End Get
End Property


'
' This read-only property retrieves a single value
' given the index of the value you wish to retrieve.
'
Public ReadOnly Property Values(ByVal index As Integer) As Object
  Get
    Return Item(index).Value
  End Get
End Property

End Class
```

Listing 4.15 Code for EntryDataCollection.vb (continued)

As before, we're inheriting this collection from an abstract base collection class, this time the NameObjectCollectionBase, which implements most of the functionality we want.

The ParsedEntryEventArgs Class

In order to keep our log parser component as self-contained, generic, and extensible as possible, we use events to notify our caller when each individual entry has been parsed and of periodic progress updates while parsing a file. This removes any need to reference a data-access component in the log parser, since it may be used in circumstances that do not involve storing the entries in a database.

The log parser component defines three events, two of which are generic and apply to all types of log parsers, and a third, which is specific to the W3C Extended Log File Format. The first of the generic events is the ParsedEntry event, which is raised for each relevant entry in the log file. This event carries with it two custom pieces of information: the line number in the log file where the entry was found, and the fields included in the entry. Create the ParsedEntryEventArgs class with the filename ParsedEntryEventArgs.vb, and add the complete code listing shown in Listing 4.16.

```vb
Option Strict On
Option Explicit On


<Serializable()> Public Class ParsedEntryEventArgs
 Inherits EventArgs

 ' This variable contains the line number where this entry was found.
 Private _intLineNumber As Integer
 ' This variable contains the individual fields for this entry.
 Private _objEntryData As EntryDataCollection


 '

 ' This constructor accepts a line number and an array of objects
 ' that are passed back to the log parser's event recipients. The
 ' array of objects represent the values in each field of the log's
 ' schema definition.
 '
 Public Sub New(ByVal lineNumber As Integer, _
  ByVal entry As EntryDataCollection)

  Me._intLineNumber = lineNumber
  Me._objEntryData = entry

 End Sub


 '

 ' This returns the line number to the class that receives this event.
 '
 Public ReadOnly Property LineNumber() As Integer
  Get
   Return Me._intLineNumber
  End Get
 End Property


 '

 ' ...and this returns the entry data to the class that receives this
 ' event.
 '
 Public ReadOnly Property Entry() As EntryDataCollection
  Get
   Return Me._objEntryData
  End Get
 End Property

End Class
```

Listing 4.16   Code for ParsedEntryEventArgs.vb

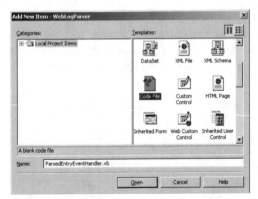

Figure 4.22 New Project Item dialog box.

The ParsedEntryEventHandler Delegate

The event logging system in the .NET Framework relies upon two types of classes. The first is the EventArgs class or classes derived from System.EventArgs, which we have already created; the second is the EventHandler delegate type, which contains the method signature of the event and (internally) a list of callers to be notified. To create our ParsedEntryEventHandler delegate in Visual Studio .NET, right-click the project in Solution Explorer and select Add —> New Item. In the New Project Item dialog box, select the generic code file from the list of available templates (shown in Figure 4.22), name the file ParsedEntryEventHandler.vb, and click Open. The complete listing for this file is shown in Listing 4.17.

```
<Serializable()> Public Delegate Sub ParsedEntryEventHandler( _
  ByVal sender As Object, ByVal e As ParsedEntryEventArgs)
```

Listing 4.17 Code for ParsedEntryEventHandler.vb

The ParseProgressEventArgs Class

The second generic event that all log parsers should support is the ParseProgress event. This event is raised by a log parser after a predetermined number of lines in the log file have been read (but not necessarily parsed . . . you'll understand why later in this project). This event contains a read-write property called Cancel that allows the event recipient to cancel further processing. Add a new class to the WebLogParser project named ParseProgressEventArgs.vb, and enter the code contained in Listing 4.18.

```
Option Strict On
Option Explicit On

<Serializable()> Public Class ParseProgressEventArgs
 Inherits EventArgs

 Private _intLineNumber As Integer
 Private _blnCancel As Boolean
 Private _blnFinal As Boolean

 '
 ' This is the normal constructor that is called
 ' during periodic progress update events.
 '
 Public Sub New(ByVal lineNumber As Integer)

  Me.New(lineNumber, False)

 End Sub

 '
 ' This constructor is called by the log parser
 ' when it has finished processing all of the
 ' entries in a particular log file.
 '
 Public Sub New(ByVal lineNumber As Integer, _
  ByVal final As Boolean)

  Me._intLineNumber = lineNumber
  Me._blnFinal = final
  Me._blnCancel = False

 End Sub

 '
 ' This read-only property allows the event
 ' recipient to determine the line number the
 ' parser is on during periodic progress updates.
 '
 Public ReadOnly Property LineNumber() As Integer
  Get
   Return Me._intLineNumber
  End Get
 End Property

 '
 ' This read-only property is set to true when
 ' the log parser has finished processing the
 ' log file. It can be used by the event recipient
 ' along with line number to determine to total
```

Listing 4.18   Code for ParseProgressEventArgs.vb

```
' number of lines in the file.
'
Public ReadOnly Property Final() As Boolean
 Get
  Return Me._blnFinal
 End Get
End Property


'
' This property allows the event recipient to
' cancel further processing of the log file.
'
Public Property Cancel() As Boolean
 Get
  Return Me._blnCancel
 End Get
 Set(ByVal Value As Boolean)
  Me._blnCancel = Value
 End Set
End Property

End Class
```

Listing 4.18   Code for ParseProgressEventArgs.vb (continued)

The ParseProgressEventHandler Delegate

This delegate is required in order for the object to periodically send back progress reports on the status of the parsing being done. Add a new code file to the WebLog-Parser project named ParseProgressEventHandler.vb to hold the delegate for this event, and add the code in Listing 4.19.

```
<Serializable()> Public Delegate Sub ParseProgressEventHandler( _
  ByVal sender As Object, ByVal e As ParseProgressEventArgs)
```

Listing 4.19   Code for ParseProgressEventHandler.vb

The SchemaChangedEventArgs Class

The third event that our log parser component supports is specific to the W3C Extended Log File parser. Log files in the W3C Extended Log File Format support a variable number of log fields, which can be modified through the Internet Service Manager console. The number and type of fields are known as the log file's schema, and when this schema is changed, IIS writes a number of comment entries that allow log processors to pick up the new field definitions. We want to notify our callers that this schema change has taken place so they can adjust accordingly. To support this event, add a new class file to your WebLogParser project named SchemaChangedEventArgs.vb, and enter the code shown in Listing 4.20.

```
Option Strict On
Option Explicit On


<Serializable()> Public Class SchemaChangedEventArgs
 Inherits EventArgs

 ' This contains the new field definitions in the log file.
 Private _objNewSchema As FieldDefinitionCollection
 ' This contains the former field definitions in the log file.
 Private _objOldSchema As FieldDefinitionCollection


 '
 ' This constructor accepts two string arrays corresponding to
 ' the new field definitions and the old field definitions that
 ' are used to set our internal state.
 '
 Protected Friend Sub New(ByVal newSchema As FieldDefinitionCollection, _
  ByVal oldSchema As FieldDefinitionCollection)

  If (newSchema Is Nothing) Then
   Me._objNewSchema = New FieldDefinitionCollection(New String() {})
  Else
   Me._objNewSchema = newSchema
  End If

  If (oldSchema Is Nothing) Then
   Me._objOldSchema = New FieldDefinitionCollection(New String() {})
  Else
   Me._objOldSchema = oldSchema
  End If

 End Sub


 '
 ' This returns the read-only list of new
 ' fields defined for the log file.
 '
 Public ReadOnly Property NewSchema() As FieldDefinitionCollection
  Get
   Return Me._objNewSchema
  End Get
```

Listing 4.20   Code for SchemaChangedEventArgs.vb

```
    End Property

    `
    ` This returns the read-only list of old
    ` fields defined for the log file.
    `
    Public ReadOnly Property OldSchema() As FieldDefinitionCollection
      Get
        Return Me._objOldSchema
      End Get
    End Property

End Class
```

Listing 4.20   Code for SchemaChangedEventArgs.vb (continued)

The SchemaChangedEventHandler Delegate

This event handler is required in order for the class to handle any log file schema changes, as discussed prior to the previous listing. Add a new code file to the project named SchemaChangedEventHandler.vb to hold this event's delegate, and enter the code shown in Listing 4.21.

```
<Serializable()> Public Delegate Sub SchemaChangedEventHandler( _
  ByVal sender As Object, ByVal e As SchemaChangedEventArgs)
```

Listing 4.21   Code for SchemaChangedEventHandler.vb

The LogParser Class

Now we're ready to get down to the business of parsing log files. Each type of log file format will have its own parsing mechanism and file format that it understands, but these parsers will always share a common set of functionality. To support this, we create a generic abstract log-parser class called LogParser.vb that can implement this common functionality. Only the Parse and ParseAt methods of this class need to be implemented by derived classes. The complete code listing for the LogParser.vb file is shown in Listing 4.22.

```
Option Strict On
Option Explicit On
```

Listing 4.22   Code for LogParser.vb

```vb
Imports System.IO
Imports System.Threading

Public MustInherit Class LogParser
 Inherits System.ComponentModel.Component

 Protected _strFilePath As String
 Protected _intProgressInterval As Integer
 Protected _intCurrentLine As Integer
 Protected _objSchema As FieldDefinitionCollection

 ' This variable is used to prevent re-entrancy in our log
 ' parser component. Log parsers which derive from this class
 ' should set this variable to True as soon as their Parse or
 ' ParseAt methods are called and before they raise any events.
 Protected _blnParsing As Boolean

 Public Event ParsedEntry As ParsedEntryEventHandler
 Public Event ParseProgress As ParseProgressEventHandler

 Protected Sub New(ByVal filePath As String, _
  ByVal progressInterval As Integer)

  Me._strFilePath = filePath
  Me._intProgressInterval = progressInterval
  Me._intCurrentLine = 0
  Me._objSchema = New FieldDefinitionCollection(New String() {})
  Me._blnParsing = False

 End Sub


 '
 ' This method is used to create one of the following
 ' LogParser types, depending on the filename passed in.
 ' W3CExtLogParser
 ' IISLogParser
 ' NCSALogParser
 '
 Public Shared Function Create(ByVal filePath As String, _
  ByVal progressInterval As Integer) As LogParser

  Dim objFileInfo As FileInfo
  Dim strFileName As String
  Dim strFileExt As String

  If filePath = Nothing Then Throw New ArgumentNullException("filePath")

  If Not File.Exists(filePath) Then
   Throw New FileNotFoundException("The log file was not found.", _
    filePath)
```

Listing 4.22   Code for LogParser.vb (continued)

```
    Else
      filePath = Path.GetFullPath(filePath)
    End If

    objFileInfo = New FileInfo(filePath)
    strFileName = objFileInfo.Name.ToLower()
    strFileExt = objFileInfo.Extension.ToLower()

    If strFileName.StartsWith("nc") Then
      Throw New NotImplementedException("The NCSA Log File Parser " & _
        "has not been implemented.")
    ElseIf strFileName.StartsWith("in") Then
      Throw New NotImplementedException("The IIS Log File Parser " & _
        "has not been implemented.")
    Else
      Return New W3CExtLogParser(filePath, progressInterval)
    End If

  End Function


  '
  ' Components that inherit from LogParser can use
  ' this method to raise the ParsedEntry event.
  '
  Protected Sub OnParsedEntry(ByVal sender As Object, _
    ByVal e As ParsedEntryEventArgs)

    RaiseEvent ParsedEntry(sender, e)

  End Sub


  '
  ' Components that inherit from LogParser can use
  ' this method to raise the ParseProgress event.
  '
  Protected Sub OnParseProgress(ByVal sender As Object, _
    ByVal e As ParseProgressEventArgs)

    RaiseEvent ParseProgress(sender, e)

  End Sub


  '
  ' This read-only property retrieves the name of the file being
  ' parsed, or an empty string if the name has not been set by
  ' the concrete log parser class.
  '
  Public Overridable ReadOnly Property FileName() As String
    Get
      If Me._strFilePath = Nothing Then
```

Listing 4.22   Code for LogParser.vb (continued)

```vb
      Return String.Empty
    Else
      Return Me._strFilePath
    End If
  End Get
End Property


'
' This read-only property retrieves the current schema in
' use by the log parser. That is, the list of fields it
' recognizes.
'
Public Overridable ReadOnly Property Schema() _
 As FieldDefinitionCollection

 Get
  Return Me._objSchema
 End Get

End Property


'
' This property retrieves or sets the number of lines read by
' the log parser before each ParseProgress event is raised.
'
' NOTE: Even though the log parser component operates in a
'      single thread, we must still synchronize access to
'      the _intProgressInterval field because our callers
'      may be multi-threaded, as is the case with the
'      log collector service.
'
Public Overridable Property ProgressInterval() As Integer
 Get
  Return Me._intProgressInterval
 End Get
 Set(ByVal Value As Integer)
  Monitor.Enter(Me)
  Me._intProgressInterval = Value
  Monitor.Exit(Me)
 End Set
End Property


'
' This method, when overridden by a derived class, starts
' processing log entries from the beginning of the file.
'
Public MustOverride Sub Parse()


'
' This method, when overridden by a derived class,
```

Listing 4.22   Code for LogParser.vb (continued)

```
' starts processing log entries at the specified line.
'
Public MustOverride Sub ParseAt(ByVal lineNumber As Integer)

End Class
```

Listing 4.22   Code for LogParser.vb (continued)

One important point to notice about this class is that it inherits from System.ComponentModel.Component. Since we've taken care to allow our other classes to be used through .NET's Remoting Infrastructure, this class should also be remotable. However, unlike the other classes, this type is only remotable by reference and not by value.

The W3CExtLogParser Class

Now we can work on a concrete implementation of a log parser - the W3CExtLogParser class, which is responsible for parsing log files in the W3C Extended Log File Format. Add a new class to the WebLogParser project named W3CExtLogParser.vb, and enter the code shown in Listing 4.23 to implement this class.

```
Option Strict On
Option Explicit On

Imports System.IO ' This is used for file handling operations.
Imports System.Net ' This is used to import the IPAddress structure.
Imports System.Threading ' This is used for synchronization.
Imports System.Globalization ' This is used for the NumberStyles enum.
Imports System.Text.RegularExpressions

Public Class W3CExtLogParser
 Inherits LogParser

 '
 ' This static regular expression is pre-compiled for enhanced
 ' performance. This particular expression is responsible for picking
 ' up new field def's and setting the current schema in use.
 '
 Private Shared ReadOnly rxpW3CSchemaDef As Regex = New Regex( _
  "^#Fields:(?:\s+(?<Field>\S+))*\s*$", RegexOptions.Compiled Or _
  RegexOptions.Singleline)

 '
 ' This static regular expression is pre-compiled for enhanced
 ' performance. This particular expression is responsible for
 ' reading in the actual field values that are logged.
```

Listing 4.23   Code for W3CExtLogParser.vb

```
'
Private Shared ReadOnly rxpW3CFieldValues As Regex = New Regex( _
  "^(?:\s*(?<Value>\S+))*\s*$", RegexOptions.Compiled Or _
  RegexOptions.Singleline)


'
' This event is used to notify the caller
' that a new schema has been set.
'
Public Event SchemaChanged As SchemaChangedEventHandler


'
' This is our class constructor, which simply
' calls the base class constructor and exits.
'
Public Sub New(ByVal filePath As String, _
  ByVal progressInterval As Integer)

  MyBase.New(filePath, progressInterval)

End Sub


'
' This method allows components that inherit from
' W3CExtLogParser to raise the SchemaChanged event.
'
Protected Sub OnSchemaChanged(ByVal sender As Object, _
  ByVal e As SchemaChangedEventArgs)

  RaiseEvent SchemaChanged(sender, e)

End Sub


'
' When this method is called, the log parser will begin
' parsing entries at the beginning of the file.
'
Public Overrides Sub Parse()

  ParseAt(0)

End Sub


'
' When this method is called, the log parser will
' begin parsing entries at the specified line.
'
Public Overrides Sub ParseAt(ByVal lineNumber As Integer)

  Dim strTextReader As StreamReader
```

Listing 4.23   Code for W3CExtLogParser.vb (continued)

```
Dim strLine As String
Dim blnInvalid As Boolean
Dim objProgressEventArgs As ParseProgressEventArgs

' This prevents re-entrancy, since it is possible that
' calling code can call Parse() during the ParsedEntry,
' ParseProgress or SchemaChanged events.
Monitor.Enter(Me)
Try
 If Me._blnParsing Then Return
 Me._blnParsing = True
Finally
 Monitor.Exit(Me)
End Try

' We want to make sure that if an error occurs, the parsing
' flag is set to False.
Try

 strTextReader = File.OpenText(FileName)

 Do

   ' If the next character is a Unicode NULL, then
   ' we've reached the end of the logical file.
   If strTextReader.Peek() = 0 Then Exit Do

   strLine = strTextReader.ReadLine()

   ' Also, if the next line is Nothing, we've
   ' reached the end of the physical file.
   If Not (strLine = Nothing) Then

    Me._intCurrentLine += 1

    ' If the progress interval is less than 1, then don't raise any
    ' progress updates until the entire file has been processed.
    If ProgressInterval > 0 Then

     ' If we're currently at a ProgressInterval line, then raise
     ' the ProgressInterval event and allow our caller to cancel
     ' further processing.
     If (Me._intCurrentLine Mod ProgressInterval) = 0 Then

      objProgressEventArgs = New ParseProgressEventArgs( _
       Me._intCurrentLine)
      OnParseProgress(Me, objProgressEventArgs)

      If objProgressEventArgs.Cancel = True Then
       Return
```

Listing 4.23   Code for W3CExtLogParser.vb (continued)

```
            End If

            ' Reading a file in a loop like this can be very processor
            ' intensive, so force our thread to sleep for at least 50
            ' milliseconds after every ProgressInterval lines.
            Try
              Thread.Sleep(50)
            Catch exc As ThreadInterruptedException
            End Try

          End If

        End If

        ' The ParseAt method should only start processing
        ' log entries after the specified line number.
        If Me._intCurrentLine > lineNumber Then

          ' Sleep for 5 milliseconds between
          ' each line to reduce CPU usage.
          Try
            Thread.Sleep(5)
          Catch exc As ThreadInterruptedException
          End Try

          ' Next, attempt to parse the current line.
          Try
            ParseLine(strLine)
            blnInvalid = False
          Catch exc As ParseException
            '
            ' Allow a single invalid log entry to pass through
            ' without throwing an error.
            '
            ' This can often be caused by changing the information
            ' that logged in mid-stream. IIS will immediately start
            ' writing the new schema header (#Software: ...) even
            ' though the current line has not been completely written
            '
            If blnInvalid = False Then
              blnInvalid = True
            Else
              Throw exc
            End If
          End Try

        Else
          ' Even if we've specified a starting position at which
          ' to begin reading log entries, we still need to parse
          ' schema changes so that the current schema can be
          ' used when actual parsing begins.
```

Listing 4.23   Code for W3CExtLogParser.vb (continued)

```
        If strLine.StartsWith("#") Then ParseComment(strLine)
      End If

   End If

 Loop While Not (strLine = Nothing)


  ' After the entire file has been processed, raise the ParseProgress
  ' event with the Final flag set to True, this notifies our caller
  ' that no additional entries will be parsed from this log file.
  objProgressEventArgs = New ParseProgressEventArgs( _
   Me._intCurrentLine, True)
  OnParseProgress(Me, objProgressEventArgs)

Catch exc As IOException

  ' An IOException can occur if IIS is currently holding
  ' a lock on the file or the file is in a binary format.
  Throw New ParseException("The file could not be opened as a " & _
   "text file. This could possibly be a binary file or is " & _
   "in the process of being written.", FileName, _
   Me._intCurrentLine, exc)

Catch exc As ParseException

  Throw New ParseException("The number of fields found in the " & _
   "log file do not match the number of fields declared in the " & _
   "header.", FileName, Me._intCurrentLine)

Catch exc As Exception

  ' Any other types of exceptions are unexpected,
  ' and should be treated generically.
  Throw New ParseException("An error occured while parsing the " & _
   "log file.", FileName, Me._intCurrentLine, exc)

Finally

  ' Make sure that our file is closed before we exit.
  If Not (strTextReader Is Nothing) Then
   strTextReader.Close()
  End If


  ' And set the parsing flag to false so that our
  ' caller can reparse this file, if necessary.
  Monitor.Enter(Me)
  Me._blnParsing = False
  Monitor.Exit(Me)

End Try
```

Listing 4.23   Code for W3CExtLogParser.vb (continued)

```
End Sub

'
' This method is responsible for parsing individual lines
' in the log file. W3C Extended Logs begin all of its
' comment lines with the character "#".
'
Private Sub ParseLine(ByVal logLine As String)

 If logLine.StartsWith("#") Then
  ParseComment(logLine)
 Else
  ParseEntry(logLine)
 End If

End Sub

'
' This method is responsible for parsing the comment lines
' in the log file that begin with the character "#".
'
Private Sub ParseComment(ByVal logComment As String)
 Dim rxpMatch As Match
 Dim rxpCaptures As CaptureCollection
 Dim objSchemaChanged As SchemaChangedEventArgs
 Dim strFields() As String
 Dim objSchema As FieldDefinitionCollection
 Dim intIndex As Integer

 ' IIS can write a number of different comments, but the only
 ' one we're interested in is the #Fields: schema definition
 ' comment.
 rxpMatch = rxpW3CSchemaDef.Match(logComment)
 If rxpMatch.Success() Then
  rxpCaptures = rxpMatch.Groups("Field").Captures
  strFields = New String(rxpCaptures.Count - 1) {}

  ' Fill the string array with the field
  ' names in the captures collection
  For intIndex = 0 To rxpCaptures.Count - 1
   strFields(intIndex) = rxpCaptures(intIndex).Value
  Next

  ' Create a new schema based on these fields.
  objSchema = New FieldDefinitionCollection(strFields)

  objSchemaChanged = New SchemaChangedEventArgs(objSchema, _
   Me._objSchema)
  OnSchemaChanged(Me, objSchemaChanged)
```

Listing 4.23   Code for W3CExtLogParser.vb (continued)

```vb
    ' Set the new schema for this instance.
    Me._objSchema = objSchema
  End If

End Sub

'
' This method is responsible for parsing individual
' log entries that contain actual values.
'
Private Sub ParseEntry(ByVal logEntry As String)

  Dim rxpCaptures As CaptureCollection
  Dim objParsedEntry As ParsedEntryEventArgs
  Dim objData() As Object
  Dim strFieldName As String
  Dim strFieldValue As String
  Dim intIndex As Integer

  rxpCaptures = rxpW3CFieldValues.Match(logEntry). _
   Groups("Value").Captures
  If rxpCaptures.Count = 0 Then
   ' Empty line.
   Return
  ElseIf rxpCaptures.Count = Schema.Count Then

   objData = New Object(rxpCaptures.Count - 1) {}

   Try

    For intIndex = 0 To objData.Length - 1
     strFieldName = Schema(intIndex)
     strFieldValue = rxpCaptures(intIndex).Value
     If strFieldValue = Nothing Then strFieldValue = "-"

     ' These fields are recognized and can be optimized for storage.
     Select Case strFieldName
      Case "date"
       objData(intIndex) = Date.ParseExact(strFieldValue, _
        "yyyy-MM-dd", New DateTimeFormatInfo()).Date
      Case "time"
       objData(intIndex) = Date.ParseExact(strFieldValue, _
        "HH:mm:ss", New DateTimeFormatInfo()).TimeOfDay
      Case "c-ip", "s-ip"
       If strFieldValue <> "-" Then
        objData(intIndex) = IPAddress.Parse( _
         strFieldValue).Address
       End If
      Case "cs-username"
       If (strFieldValue <> "-") And (strFieldValue <> "()") Then
```

Listing 4.23   Code for W3CExtLogParser.vb (continued)

```
        strFieldValue = Left(strFieldValue, 36)
        objData(intIndex) = strFieldValue
      End If
    Case "s-sitename"
      If (strFieldValue <> "-") Then
        strFieldValue = Left(strFieldValue, 12)
        objData(intIndex) = strFieldValue
      End If
    Case "s-computername"
      If (strFieldValue <> "-") Then
        strFieldValue = Left(strFieldValue, 16)
        objData(intIndex) = strFieldValue
      End If
    Case "s-port", "sc-win32-status", "sc-bytes", "cs-bytes", _
      "time-taken"
      If strFieldValue <> "-" Then
        objData(intIndex) = Integer.Parse(strFieldValue, _
          NumberStyles.None)
      End If
    Case "cs-method"
      If (strFieldValue <> "-") Then
        strFieldValue = Left(strFieldValue, 10)
        objData(intIndex) = strFieldValue
      End If
    Case "cs-uri-stem", "cs(Referer)"
      If strFieldValue <> "-" Then
        strFieldValue = Left(strFieldValue, 512)
        objData(intIndex) = strFieldValue
      End If
    Case "cs-uri-query"
      If (strFieldValue <> "-") And _
        (strFieldValue.StartsWith("|") = False) Then
        strFieldValue = Left(strFieldValue, 2048)
        objData(intIndex) = strFieldValue
      End If
    Case "sc-status"
      If strFieldValue <> "-" Then
        objData(intIndex) = Short.Parse(strFieldValue, _
          NumberStyles.None)
      End If
    Case "cs-version"
      If (strFieldValue <> "-") Then
        strFieldValue = Left(strFieldValue, 20)
        objData(intIndex) = strFieldValue
      End If
    Case "cs-host", "cs(User-Agent)"
      If (strFieldValue <> "-") Then
        strFieldValue = Left(strFieldValue, 256)
        objData(intIndex) = strFieldValue
      End If
```

Listing 4.23   Code for W3CExtLogParser.vb (continued)

```
      Case "cs(Cookie)"
       If (strFieldValue <> "-") Then
        strFieldValue = Left(strFieldValue, 2048)
        objData(intIndex) = strFieldValue
       End If
      Case "s-user-time", "s-kernel-time"
        If strFieldValue <> "-" Then
         objData(intIndex) = Decimal.Parse(strFieldValue. _
          Substring(0, strFieldValue.Length - 1))
        End If
      Case "s-page-faults", "s-total-procs", "s-active-procs", _
       "s-stopped-procs"
       If strFieldValue <> "-" Then
        objData(intIndex) = Integer.Parse(strFieldValue)
       End If
      Case Else
        ' Any other fields should be stored as text.
        objData(intIndex) = strFieldValue
     End Select

   Next

   ' Raise the ParsedEntry event so our caller can do something
   ' with this entry. (In this case, store it in a database.)
   objParsedEntry = New ParsedEntryEventArgs( _
    Me._intCurrentLine, New EntryDataCollection(Schema, objData))
   OnParsedEntry(Me, objParsedEntry)

  Catch exc As Exception

   Throw exc

  End Try

 Else

  Throw New ParseException()

 End If

 End Sub

End Class
```

Listing 4.23   Code for W3CExtLogParser.vb (continued)

By now, you have a complete implementation of a log parser that can parse logs in the W3C Extended Log File Format. If you have the time and inclination, you might want to also implement the IIS Log File Format and NCSA Common Log File Format using the generic LogParser component as a base.

The WebLogParser project has no external references, and is generic enough that it can be used in several contexts other than the Web Log Analyzer that you are building in this project. It is also designed to be easily extensible, so you can add your own custom log parsers without the necessity of modifying the code in this project.

Our next step is to add data handling to our Web log analyzer application.

Developing the WebLogDataAccess Project

The WebLogDataAccess project will be referenced by both the Web Log Collector service as well as the ASP.NET application used to analyze those logs. This project consists of a single class, named Database.vb. This is not the same Database class that you have used in previous projects, however, since most of our database access in this project involves parametric stored procedures.

Your Database class will be capable of accessing two different types of data stores. The first and most obvious is the SQL Server database we created at the beginning of this project. The second is the IIS MetaBase, which is used to retrieve authoritative information for the location of the log file directories. It is also used to display a list of available sites on a specific computer that you can register and un-register for collection. To access the IIS MetaBase, you will be using the Directory Services IIS Provider, so your WebLogDataAccess project will need to reference the System.DirectoryServices.dll assembly. To add this reference to your project, right-click the WebLogDataAccess project or the References node beneath it, and select Add Reference. In the Add New Reference dialog box, shown in Figure 4.23, select the System.DirectoryServices.dll assembly from the .NET tab, and click Select to add the reference to your project.

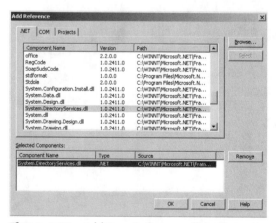

Figure 4.23 Add New Reference dialog box.

You will also need to reference the WebLogParser project, since the Database class uses the EntryDataCollection defined in that project to add entries to the database. With the Add New Reference dialog box open, click the Projects tab, and select the WebLogParser project. Then click Select to add the reference to the WebLogDataAccess project.

After your references are set up, add the Database.vb class file (if you have not already done so), and enter the code shown in Listing 4.24 to implement this class.

```
Option Strict On
Option Explicit On

Imports System.Data
Imports System.Data.SqlClient
Imports System.DirectoryServices
Imports System.IO
Imports System.Runtime.InteropServices
Imports WebLogParser

Public Class Database

'
' This string is the only state that this class holds, and it
' is set in the class constructor. To make the class completely
' stateless (for example, if you wanted to modify it to become
' a "ServicedComponent" for installation in COM+ Services) you
' would need to add a ConnectionString argument to each of the
' methods in this class.
'
Private _strConnectionString As String


'
' Our constructor takes a connection string as an argument,
' and will attempt to open a database connection with it.
' If this is not successful, then the error is thrown to the
' caller.
'
Public Sub New(ByVal connectionString As String)
 Dim dbConnection As SqlConnection

 dbConnection = New SqlConnection(connectionString)
 Try
  dbConnection.Open()
 Finally
  dbConnection.Close()
  dbConnection.Dispose()
 End Try

 ' Only if the above was successful do we store the
 ' connection string information in our module-level
 ' variable
```

Listing 4.24   Code for Database.vb

```vb
    Me._strConnectionString = connectionString

End Sub

Private Function Connection() As SqlConnection

 Return New SqlConnection(Me._strConnectionString)

End Function

Private Function StoredProcedure(ByVal procedureName As String) _
 As SqlCommand

 Dim dbCommand As SqlCommand

 dbCommand = New SqlCommand(procedureName, Connection())
 dbCommand.CommandType = CommandType.StoredProcedure

 Return dbCommand

End Function

'
' This method is used by our ASP.NET application to show the virtual
' sites on a given machine and whether or not they are enabled for
' log collection.
'
Public Function GetAvailableSites(ByVal machineName As String) _
 As DataTable

 Dim iisWebService As DirectoryEntry
 Dim iisWebServer As DirectoryEntry
 Dim tblSite As DataTable
 Dim dvwSiteView As DataView
 Dim tblRow As DataRow

 If machineName = Nothing Then
  Throw New ArgumentNullException("machineName")
 End If

 tblSite = GetRegisteredSites(machineName)

 Try
  iisWebService = New DirectoryEntry(String.Format( _
   "IIS://{0}/W3SVC", machineName))
 Catch exc As COMException
  '
  ' If the ASP.NET application user does not have sufficient access
  ' to the specified machine, do not show the list of sites
  ' registered and do not allow them to view analysis data.
```

Listing 4.24   Code for Database.vb (continued)

```
'
tblSite.Rows.Clear()
tblSite.AcceptChanges()
Return tblSite
End Try


dvwSiteView = New DataView(tblSite)
Try

  For Each iisWebServer In iisWebService.Children

    ' We declare these variables here because they are
    ' only used in the context of this For...Next loop.
    Dim shtIndex As Short
    Dim strSiteName As String
    Dim strLogBaseDir As String
    Dim strLogSubDir As String
    Dim strLogDir As String

    Try
      If iisWebServer.SchemaClassName = "IIsWebServer" Then
        shtIndex = CShort(iisWebServer.Name)
        strLogSubDir = String.Format("W3SVC{0}", shtIndex)
        strSiteName = CStr(iisWebServer.Properties( _
          "ServerComment")(0))
        strLogBaseDir = Environment.ExpandEnvironmentVariables( _
          CStr(iisWebServer.Properties("LogFileDirectory")(0)))
        strLogDir = Path.Combine(strLogBaseDir, strLogSubDir)

        If Environment.MachineName <> machineName Then
          ' Convert this to a UNC path in the form
          ' \\machineName\driveletter$\relativepath
          strLogSubDir = strLogDir.Substring(3, strLogDir.Length - 3)
          strLogBaseDir = Path.DirectorySeparatorChar & _
            Path.DirectorySeparatorChar & machineName & _
            Path.DirectorySeparatorChar & Path.GetPathRoot( _
            strLogDir).Substring(0, 1) & "$" & _
            Path.DirectorySeparatorChar
          strLogDir = Path.Combine(strLogBaseDir, strLogSubDir)
        End If

        dvwSiteView.RowFilter = "[MachineName] = " & _
          Clean(machineName) & " AND [SiteIndex] = " & shtIndex

        If dvwSiteView.Count = 0 Then
          ' Add this site as an unregistered site.
          tblRow = tblSite.NewRow()
          tblRow.BeginEdit()
          tblRow("ID") = Guid.NewGuid()
          tblRow("MachineName") = machineName
```

Listing 4.24   Code for Database.vb (continued)

```
        tblRow("SiteIndex") = shtIndex
        tblRow("EntriesTable") = DBNull.Value
        tblRow("SiteName") = strSiteName
        tblRow("LogFileDirectory") = strLogDir
        tblRow("Registered") = False
        tblRow.EndEdit()
        tblSite.Rows.Add(tblRow)
      End If

    End If

  Finally
    iisWebServer.Dispose()
  End Try

 Next

 Finally
  dvwSiteView.Dispose()
  iisWebService.Dispose()
 End Try

 tblSite.AcceptChanges()
 tblSite.DefaultView.RowFilter = "[MachineName] = " & _
  Clean(machineName)
 tblSite.DefaultView.Sort = "SiteIndex"

 Return tblSite

End Function


' See GetRegisteredSites(String)
'
Public Function GetRegisteredSites() As DataTable

  Return GetRegisteredSites(Nothing)

End Function

'
' This method is used by the log collector service to retrieve a
' list of sites that our ASP.NET application wants to collect
' logs for.
'
Public Function GetRegisteredSites(ByVal machineName As String) _
  As DataTable

  Dim dbAdapter As SqlDataAdapter
  Dim dbCommand As SqlCommand
```

Listing 4.24   Code for Database.vb (continued)

```
Dim prmMachineName As SqlParameter
Dim tblSite As DataTable
Dim tblRow As DataRow

tblSite = New DataTable("LogSite")

dbCommand = StoredProcedure("getRegisteredSites")

' Set up our parameter, if any was specified.
prmMachineName = New SqlParameter("@MachineName", _
 SqlDbType.NVarChar, 15)
If Not machineName = Nothing Then
 If machineName.Length > 0 Then
  prmMachineName.Value = Left(machineName, 15)
 End If
End If

dbCommand.Parameters.Add(prmMachineName)
dbAdapter = New SqlDataAdapter(dbCommand)

Try
 dbAdapter.Fill(tblSite)
Finally
 ' Release all of our unmanaged resources.
 dbAdapter.Dispose()
 dbCommand.Connection.Close()
 dbCommand.Connection.Dispose()
 dbCommand.Dispose()
End Try

' Fill out the other information required by the log collector
' service that is not suitable for storage in the database from
' a different data store...the IIS MetaBase.
For Each tblRow In tblSite.Rows

 Dim iisWebServer As DirectoryEntry = Nothing
 Dim strMachineName As String
 Dim shtIndex As Short
 Dim strSiteName As String
 Dim strLogBaseDir As String
 Dim strLogDir As String
 Dim strLogSubDir As String
 Dim strADsPath As String

 strMachineName = CStr(tblRow("MachineName"))
 shtIndex = CShort(tblRow("SiteIndex"))
 strLogSubDir = String.Format("W3SVC{0}", shtIndex)
 ' Build the ADsPath to this site in the MetaBase.
 strADsPath = String.Format("IIS://{0}/W3SVC/{1}", _
  strMachineName, shtIndex)
```

Listing 4.24   Code for Database.vb (continued)

```
  Try
    iisWebServer = New DirectoryEntry(strADsPath)
    strSiteName = CStr(iisWebServer.Properties("ServerComment")(0))
    strLogBaseDir = Environment.ExpandEnvironmentVariables( _
      CStr(iisWebServer.Properties("LogFileDirectory")(0)))
    strLogDir = Path.Combine(strLogBaseDir, strLogSubDir)
    If Environment.MachineName <> strMachineName Then
      ' Convert this to a UNC path in the form
      ' \\machineName\driveletter$\relativepath
      strLogSubDir = strLogDir.Substring(3, strLogDir.Length - 3)
      strLogBaseDir = Path.DirectorySeparatorChar & _
        Path.DirectorySeparatorChar & strMachineName & _
        Path.DirectorySeparatorChar & Path.GetPathRoot( _
        strLogDir).Substring(0, 1) & "$" & _
        Path.DirectorySeparatorChar
      strLogDir = Path.Combine(strLogBaseDir, strLogSubDir)
    End If

    tblRow.BeginEdit()
    tblRow("SiteName") = strSiteName
    tblRow("LogFileDirectory") = strLogDir
    tblRow.EndEdit()
  Catch exc As Exception
    ' If an error occurs, then there's no way that
    ' we can retrieve the log file directory. In
    ' this case, delete the row from the result set.
    tblRow.Delete()
  Finally
    If Not iisWebServer Is Nothing Then
      iisWebServer.Dispose()
    End If
  End Try

Next

tblSite.AcceptChanges()
tblSite.DefaultView.Sort = "[SiteIndex]"

Return tblSite

End Function


'
' This method is used by the ASP.NET application
' to register a web site for collection.
'
Public Sub RegisterSite(ByVal siteID As Guid, ByVal machineName _
  As String, ByVal siteIndex As Short)

  Dim dbCommand As SqlCommand
```

Listing 4.24   Code for Database.vb (continued)

```
dbCommand = StoredProcedure("registerSite")
dbCommand.Parameters.Add("@SiteID", siteID)
dbCommand.Parameters("@SiteID").Direction = _
 ParameterDirection.InputOutput
dbCommand.Parameters.Add("@MachineName", machineName)
dbCommand.Parameters.Add("@SiteIndex", siteIndex)

dbCommand.Connection.Open()
Try
 dbCommand.ExecuteNonQuery()
Finally
 dbCommand.Connection.Close()
 dbCommand.Connection.Dispose()
 dbCommand.Dispose()
End Try

End Sub

'
' This method is used by the ASP.NET application
' to un-register a web site for collection.
'
Public Sub UnregisterSite(ByVal siteID As Guid)

 Dim dbCommand As SqlCommand

 dbCommand = StoredProcedure("unregisterSite")
 dbCommand.Parameters.Add("@SiteID", siteID)

 dbCommand.Connection.Open()
 Try
  dbCommand.ExecuteNonQuery()
 Finally
  dbCommand.Connection.Close()
  dbCommand.Connection.Dispose()
  dbCommand.Dispose()
 End Try

End Sub

'
' This method is used by the ASP.NET application to
' retrieve the site table name for a specific site ID.
'
Public Function GetSiteTable(ByVal siteID As Guid) As String

 Dim dbCommand As SqlCommand
 Dim dbReader As SqlDataReader
 Dim strTableName As String
```

Listing 4.24   Code for Database.vb (continued)

```vb
    dbCommand = New SqlCommand("SELECT [MachineName] + " & _
     "N'W3SVC' + CONVERT(nvarchar(5), [SiteIndex]) FROM " & _
     "LogSite WHERE [ID] = '" & siteID.ToString("B") & "'", _
     Connection())

    dbCommand.Connection.Open()
    Try
     dbReader = dbCommand.ExecuteReader(CommandBehavior.SingleRow)
     If dbReader.Read() Then
      strTableName = CStr(dbReader(0))
     End If
    Finally
     dbReader.Close()
     dbCommand.Connection.Close()
     dbCommand.Connection.Dispose()
     dbCommand.Dispose()
    End Try

    If strTableName = Nothing Then
     Return String.Empty
    Else
     Return strTableName
    End If

   End Function

   '
   ' This method is used by the ASP.NET application
   ' to run analysis reports.
   '
   Public Function RunReport(ByVal reportName As String, ByVal tableName _
    As String, ByVal startDate As Date, ByVal endDate As Date) _
    As DataTable

    Dim dbCommand As SqlCommand
    Dim dbAdapter As SqlDataAdapter
    Dim tblReport As DataTable

    tblReport = New DataTable(reportName)
    dbCommand = StoredProcedure(reportName)
    dbCommand.Parameters.Add("@TableName", tableName)
    dbCommand.Parameters.Add("@StartDate", startDate)
    dbCommand.Parameters.Add("@EndDate", endDate)

    dbAdapter = New SqlDataAdapter(dbCommand)
    Try
     dbAdapter.Fill(tblReport)
    Finally
     dbAdapter.Dispose()
     dbCommand.Connection.Close()
```

Listing 4.24   Code for Database.vb (continued)

```
      dbCommand.Connection.Dispose()
      dbCommand.Dispose()
    End Try

    Return tblReport

  End Function

  '
  ' This method is used by the log collector to initially
  ' retrieve all of the log sources stored in the database.
  '
  Public Function GetAllLogSources() As DataTable

    Dim dbAdapter As SqlDataAdapter
    Dim dbCommand As SqlCommand
    Dim tblSource As DataTable

    tblSource = New DataTable("LogSource")

    dbCommand = StoredProcedure("getSources")
    dbAdapter = New SqlDataAdapter(dbCommand)

    Try
      dbAdapter.Fill(tblSource)
    Finally
      ' Release unmanaged resources.
      dbAdapter.Dispose()
      dbCommand.Connection.Close()
      dbCommand.Connection.Dispose()
      dbCommand.Dispose()
    End Try

    Return tblSource

  End Function

  '
  ' This method is used by the ASP.NET application to retrieve
  ' a list of log sources defined for a specific site.
  '
  Public Function GetLogSources(ByVal siteID As Guid) As DataTable

    Dim dbAdapter As SqlDataAdapter
    Dim dbCommand As SqlCommand
    Dim tblSource As DataTable

    tblSource = New DataTable("LogSource")

    dbCommand = StoredProcedure("getSources")
```

Listing 4.24   Code for Database.vb (continued)

```
  dbCommand.Parameters.Add("@SiteID", siteID)

  dbAdapter = New SqlDataAdapter(dbCommand)

  Try
   dbAdapter.Fill(tblSource)
  Finally
   ' Release unmanaged resources
   dbAdapter.Dispose()
   dbCommand.Connection.Close()
   dbCommand.Connection.Dispose()
   dbCommand.Dispose()
  End Try

  Return tblSource

End Function

'
' This is used to add the common parameters for the source
' Add and Update operations
'
Private Sub AddParameters(ByVal command As SqlCommand, ByVal tblRow _
  As DataRow)

  Dim params() As SqlParameter = New SqlParameter(9) {}
  Dim param As SqlParameter

  params(0) = New SqlParameter("@SourceID", SqlDbType.UniqueIdentifier)
  params(0).Direction = ParameterDirection.InputOutput
  params(0).Value = tblRow("ID")
  params(1) = New SqlParameter("@Site", SqlDbType.UniqueIdentifier)
  params(1).Value = tblRow("Site")
  params(2) = New SqlParameter("@FilePath", SqlDbType.NVarChar, 512)
  params(2).Value = tblRow("FilePath")
  params(3) = New SqlParameter("@Status", SqlDbType.NVarChar, 20)
  params(3).Value = tblRow("Status")
  params(4) = New SqlParameter("@Parser", SqlDbType.NVarChar, 16)
  params(4).Value = tblRow("Parser")
  params(5) = New SqlParameter("@LineNumber", SqlDbType.Int)
  params(5).Value = tblRow("LineNumber")
  params(6) = New SqlParameter("@Length", SqlDbType.BigInt)
  params(6).Value = tblRow("Length")
  params(7) = New SqlParameter("@LastWrite", SqlDbType.DateTime)
  params(7).Value = tblRow("LastWrite")
  params(8) = New SqlParameter("@ReProc", SqlDbType.Bit)
  params(8).Value = tblRow("ReProc")
  params(9) = New SqlParameter("@Comment", SqlDbType.NVarChar, 256)
  params(9).Value = tblRow("Comment")
```

Listing 4.24   Code for Database.vb (continued)

```
For Each param In params
  command.Parameters.Add(param)
Next

End Sub


'
' This method is used by the log collector to synchronize it's
' local (offline) Source table with the database and check if
' if another service has taken over processing of this log source.
'
Public Sub GetSource(ByVal sourceID As Guid, ByRef tblRow As DataRow)

  Dim dbCommand As SqlCommand
  Dim dbAdapter As SqlDataAdapter
  Dim tblSource As DataTable

  tblSource = New DataTable("LogSource")

  dbCommand = New SqlCommand("SELECT * FROM LogSource WHERE " & _
    "[ID] = '" & sourceID.ToString("B") & "'", Connection())
  dbAdapter = New SqlDataAdapter(dbCommand)

  Try
    dbAdapter.Fill(tblSource)
  Finally
    dbAdapter.Dispose()
    dbCommand.Connection.Close()
    dbCommand.Connection.Dispose()
    dbCommand.Dispose()
  End Try

  If tblSource.Rows.Count > 0 Then
    tblRow.BeginEdit()
    tblRow.ItemArray = CType(tblSource.Rows(0).ItemArray.Clone(), _
      Object())
    tblRow.EndEdit()
  Else
    tblRow.Delete()
  End If

  tblSource.Dispose()

End Sub


'
' This method is used by the log collector service whenever
' IIS writes a new log file, as well as during source initialization
'
Public Function AddSource(ByVal tblRow As DataRow) As Guid
```

Listing 4.24   Code for Database.vb (continued)

```vb
 Dim retVal As Guid = Guid.Empty
 Dim dbCommand As SqlCommand

 dbCommand = StoredProcedure("addSource")

 AddParameters(dbCommand, tblRow)

 dbCommand.Connection.Open()
 Try
  dbCommand.ExecuteNonQuery()
  retVal = CType(dbCommand.Parameters(0).Value, Guid)
 Finally
  ' Release unmanaged resources
  dbCommand.Connection.Close()
  dbCommand.Connection.Dispose()
  dbCommand.Dispose()
 End Try

 Return retVal

End Function

'
' This method is used by the log collector service whenever
' IIS writes a batch of entries to disk (updating the LastWriteTime)
' and during source initialization.
'
Public Sub UpdateSource(ByVal tblRow As DataRow)

 Dim dbCommand As SqlCommand

 dbCommand = StoredProcedure("updateSource")
 AddParameters(dbCommand, tblRow)

 dbCommand.Connection.Open()
 Try
  dbCommand.ExecuteNonQuery()
 Finally
  ' Release unmanaged resources
  dbCommand.Connection.Close()
  dbCommand.Connection.Dispose()
  dbCommand.Dispose()
 End Try

End Sub

'
' This method is used by the log collector service
' to add an individual log entry to the database.
'
```

Listing 4.24   Code for Database.vb (continued)

```
' NOTE: If you add other log parsers, you will need
'    to change this method to support those log
'    parser's fields.
'
Public Function AddLogEntry(ByVal sourceID As Guid, ByVal sourceLine _
As Integer, ByVal entryTable As String, _
ByVal entry As EntryDataCollection) As String

    Dim dbCommand As SqlCommand
    Dim prms() As SqlParameter = New SqlParameter(22) {}
    Dim prm As SqlParameter
    Dim dtmEntryDate As Date
    Dim strReturn As String

    dbCommand = StoredProcedure("addEntry")

    ' Add all of the parameters that our addEntry stored procedure
    ' supports. If you add other log parsers, you will need to map
    ' their fields to the equivalent stored procedure parameter
    ' here.
    prms(0) = New SqlParameter("@EntryTable", SqlDbType.NVarChar, 25)
    prms(0).Direction = ParameterDirection.Output
    prms(0).Value = entryTable
    prms(1) = New SqlParameter("@Source", SqlDbType.UniqueIdentifier)
    prms(1).Value = sourceID
    prms(2) = New SqlParameter("@SourceLine", SqlDbType.Int)
    prms(2).Value = sourceLine
    prms(3) = New SqlParameter("@dateTime", SqlDbType.DateTime)
    If entry("date").Value Is Nothing Then
      If Not entry("time").Value Is Nothing Then
       dtmEntryDate = New Date(CType(entry("time").Value, _
        TimeSpan).Ticks)
      End If
    Else
      dtmEntryDate = CDate(entry("date").Value)
      If Not entry("time").Value Is Nothing Then
       dtmEntryDate = dtmEntryDate.Add( _
        CType(entry("time").Value, TimeSpan))
      End If
    End If
    prms(3).Value = dtmEntryDate
    prms(4) = New SqlParameter("@cIp", SqlDbType.Int)
    prms(4).Value = entry("c-ip").Value
```

Listing 4.24 Code for Database.vb (continued)

```vb
prms(5) = New SqlParameter("@csUsername", SqlDbType.NVarChar, 36)
prms(5).Value = entry("cs-username").Value
prms(6) = New SqlParameter("@sSitename", SqlDbType.VarChar, 12)
prms(6).Value = entry("s-sitename").Value
prms(7) = New SqlParameter("@sComputername", SqlDbType.NVarChar, 16)
prms(7).Value = entry("s-computername").Value
prms(8) = New SqlParameter("@sIp", SqlDbType.Int)
prms(8).Value = entry("s-ip").Value
prms(9) = New SqlParameter("@sPort", SqlDbType.Int)
prms(9).Value = entry("s-port").Value
prms(10) = New SqlParameter("@csMethod", SqlDbType.VarChar, 10)
prms(10).Value = entry("cs-method").Value
prms(11) = New SqlParameter("@csUriStem", SqlDbType.NVarChar, 512)
prms(11).Value = entry("cs-uri-stem").Value
prms(12) = New SqlParameter("@csUriQuery", SqlDbType.NVarChar, 2048)
prms(12).Value = entry("cs-uri-query").Value
prms(13) = New SqlParameter("@scStatus", SqlDbType.SmallInt)
prms(13).Value = entry("sc-status").Value
prms(14) = New SqlParameter("@scWin32Status", SqlDbType.Int)
prms(14).Value = entry("sc-win32-status").Value
prms(15) = New SqlParameter("@scBytes", SqlDbType.Int)
prms(15).Value = entry("sc-bytes").Value
prms(16) = New SqlParameter("@csBytes", SqlDbType.Int)
prms(16).Value = entry("cs-bytes").Value
prms(17) = New SqlParameter("@timeTaken", SqlDbType.Int)
prms(17).Value = entry("time-taken").Value
prms(18) = New SqlParameter("@csVersion", SqlDbType.VarChar, 20)
prms(18).Value = entry("cs-version").Value
prms(19) = New SqlParameter("@csHost", SqlDbType.NVarChar, 256)
prms(19).Value = entry("cs-host").Value
prms(20) = New SqlParameter("@csUserAgent", SqlDbType.NVarChar, 256)
prms(20).Value = entry("cs(User-Agent)").Value
prms(21) = New SqlParameter("@csCookie", SqlDbType.NVarChar, 2048)
prms(21).Value = entry("cs(Cookie)").Value
prms(22) = New SqlParameter("@csReferer", SqlDbType.NVarChar, 512)
prms(22).Value = entry("cs(Referer)").Value


For Each prm In prms
 dbCommand.Parameters.Add(prm)
Next


' Execute the command and retrieve the value of our output parameter.
dbCommand.Connection.Open()
```

Listing 4.24 Code for Database.vb (continued)

```
   Try
     dbCommand.ExecuteNonQuery()
     strReturn = CStr(dbCommand.Parameters("@EntryTable").Value)
   Finally
     ' Release all of our unmanaged resources.
     dbCommand.Connection.Close()
     dbCommand.Connection.Dispose()
     dbCommand.Dispose()
   End Try


   Return strReturn


 End Function


 Private Function Clean(ByVal Value As String) As String
   Return "'" & Replace(Value, "'", "''") & "'"
 End Function


End Class
```

Listing 4.24   Code for Database.vb (continued)

Developing the WebLogCollector Project

Now that we have all of the supporting projects in place, we can develop, install, and test our Windows Service application and have it start collecting the log files while we're working on the ASP.NET application.

Begin by adding references to the WebLogCollector project (as we did for the WebLogDataAccess project) for both the WebLogParser and WebLogDataAccess projects so that we can use the classes they provide.

We want to add an application configuration file to our Windows Service so that it can retrieve configuration settings at runtime. To add this file, right-click the WebLog-Collector project, and select Add —> New Item. In the Add New Item dialog box, select the Application Configuration File template, as shown in Figure 4.24, and click Open. Then add the settings for this file as they appear in Listing 4.25.

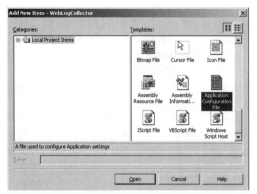

Figure 4.24 Add New Item dialog box (Application Configuration File).

```
<?xml version="1.0" encoding="utf-8" ?>
<configuration>
 <appSettings>
  <add key="ConnectionString"
   value="server=localhost;database=ASPNetProject04;uid=sa;pwd=;" />
  <add key="ProgressInterval" value="200" />
  <add key="ProgressIntervalUNC" value="50" />
  <add key="PollingIntervalForSiteRegistration" value="120" />
  <add key="WaitToAttachDebugger" value="30" />
 </appSettings>
</configuration>
```

Listing 4.25 Configuration settings for app.config

The first setting in this file is the connection string used to create the database connection in the Database class. This is self-explanatory and will not be gone over in detail here.

The second and third settings are the number of lines that will be read in each log file before the log parser component raises the ParseProgress event. Although we will not be doing it in this project, if you set the Web Log Collector service to run using a domain administrator account, it will be able to collect log files from multiple computers, even across a Web farm. However, network access is often much slower than local disk access, so we set the progress interval used for UNC paths to a quarter of its local path equivalent.

The fourth setting is used by our service to accept communication from the ASP.NET application through the database. Since our service cannot constantly monitor the LogSite table in the database for changes, as it can with log file directories, we poll the database every two minutes (120 seconds) to see if any new sites have been registered for collection or if any sites have been unregistered.

The fifth setting is used to attach a debugger to the service before it performs any real work. As mentioned at the beginning, the OnStart method has only 30 seconds to complete any initialization and exit back to the SCM, which makes it nearly impossible to set breakpoints and step through the initialization. Therefore, since your OnStart method will only load configuration settings and start the worker thread, the worker thread itself is where we need to begin any debugging.

A service cannot be started inside of Visual Studio .NET, since it needs to run in a different desktop environment and under the context of the SCM. Instead, whenever we want to debug our service, we need to start it from the Services console, and then use the Debug —> Processes menu command to attach to the running process. The WaitToAttachDebugger setting tells the worker thread how many seconds you want it to wait so you can attach to the process and set breakpoints before it does any processing (or encounters errors and crashes).

The LogCollector Class

You should currently have three files displayed in the Solution Explorer window for the WebLogCollector project: App.config, AssemblyInfo.vb, and Service1.vb. Select the Service1.vb file in Solution Explorer, and rename it LogCollector.vb. After clicking Enter, double-click the file to open the Windows Service application in Component-Design view, and then click the designer surface.

The Properties window should now appear as it does in Figure 4.25. Set the properties as indicated in Table 4.1.

Figure 4.25   Properties window.

Table 4.1   Property Settings

NAME	VALUE
(Name)	LogCollector
AutoLog	True
CanHandlePowerEvent	False
CanPauseAndContinue	True
CanShutdown	False
CanStop	True
ServiceName	Web Log Collector

To ensure that our code can build successfully, switch to code view using either the hyperlink on the designer surface or the leftmost button in Solution Explorer. Locate and expand (if it is collapsed) the Component Designer Generated Code section. Inside the Shared Sub Main() method, you will see a line, as shown in Listing 4.26.

```
ServicesToRun = New System.ServiceProcess.ServiceBase() {New
Service1()}
```

Listing 4.26   Component Designer Generated Code (before modification)

Change this line so that it matches the one shown in Listing 4.27. Then collapse the Component Designer Generated Code section, save the file, and close the code window. You should now be back on the designer surface. If not, double-click the LogCollector.vb file in Solution Explorer to open it.

```
ServicesToRun = New System.ServiceProcess.ServiceBase() _
   {New LogCollector()}
```

Listing 4.27   Component Designer Generated Code (after modification)

In the properties window shown in Figure 4.25, there is an Add Installer hyperlink towards the bottom. In your properties window, click that link to have Visual Studio automatically add an installer to your project, which you can use later to install the Web Log Collector service into the SCM.

Figure 4.26   ServiceProcessInstaller property settings.

Visual Studio will automatically add a new file named ProjectInstaller.vb to your project, and you should now see the ProjectInstaller component design surface, which contains a ServiceProcessInstaller and ServiceInstaller component. Select the Service-ProcessInstaller component so that its properties are displayed in the Properties window, and change them to the ones shown in Figure 4.26.

Now select the ServiceInstaller component, and set its properties to the ones shown in Figure 4.27.

Before we can test our installers, we need to save the file. Right-click the WebLog-Collector project, and select Properties. In the WebLogCollector Property Pages window, the Startup object may still reference Service1, so we need to set this to Sub Main to have our component compile correctly. After you have set this, close the Property Pages window, and, on the Build menu, click Build WebLogCollector.

Figure 4.27   ServiceInstaller property settings.

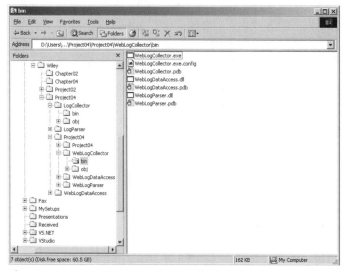

Figure 4.28   Contents of WebLogCollector\bin directory.

Before we progress any further, we want to make sure that our service can be successfully installed and uninstalled. To do this, we need to use one of the command-line utilities included with the .NET Framework. Start Windows Explorer, and navigate to the directory where the WebLogCollector project is stored. In that directory should be a *bin* directory where your project was built, as shown in Figure 4.28.

In your Start menu inside the Visual Studio .NET Tools folder, there should be a link to the Visual Studio .NET Command Prompt, which sets up a number of environmental variables in your PATH environment variable. This is where the command-line tools provided by Visual Studio .NET and the .NET Framework can be located. Click this link to open the Command Prompt window, and set these variables.

Then, navigate to the folder you located in Windows Explorer using the cd (change directory) command. You might need to access the drive and press the Enter key first if the folder is located on a different drive. Do a directory listing to make sure you've located the correct folder. This directory listing should be similar to the one shown in Figure 4.29.

Figure 4.29   Directory listing of WebLogCollector\bin directory.

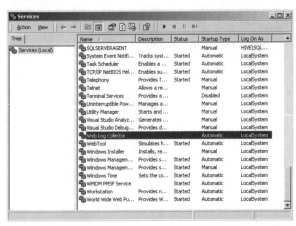

Figure 4.30   Services console with the Web Log Collector service.

Now run the install utility using the following command line:

```
installutil.exe -i WebLogCollector.exe
```

If everything went successfully, your command line should now show The Commit phase completed successfully. The transacted install has completed. You can verify this by opening the Services Control Panel console and locating the Web Log Collector service, as shown in Figure 4.30.

 Do not start the service yet, since it has not been developed.

If you plan to have your Web Log Collector service access log files from multiple computers, you can open the Service Properties window by double-clicking the service in the Services console, navigating to the Log On tab, and changing the account this service runs to an account with domain administrator privileges and the Log On as a Service user right.

After you have finished, close these windows and begin developing the LogCollector class. We no longer need the LogCollector.vb design view, so this window can also be closed. Open the LogCollector.vb file in code view, and add the flags and Imports directives shown in Listing 4.28.

```
Option Strict On
Option Explicit On


Imports System.Data
Imports System.ServiceProcess
Imports System.Threading
Imports System.Collections
```

Listing 4.28   Option flags and imports directives for LogCollector.vb

```
Imports System.Configuration
Imports System.IO
Imports WebLogDataAccess
Imports WebLogParser
```

Listing 4.28   Option flags and imports directives for LogCollector.vb (continued)

Leave the Component Designer Generated Code section alone for now. We will be modifying the OnStart and OnStop methods later. Add the class-level variables and EntryType enumeration shown in Listing 4.29.

```
Private Enum EntryType As Integer
 Warning = EventLogEntryType.Warning
 [Error] = EventLogEntryType.Error
 Info = EventLogEntryType.Information
End Enum

' Service Configuration Defaults
Private Const defaultProgressInterval As Integer = 200
Private Const defaultConnectionString As String = "server=(local);" & _
 "database=ASPNetProject04;uid=sa;pwd=;"
Private Const defaultPollingInterval As Integer = 120

' Service Configuration Fields
Private _fswConfigWatcher As FileSystemWatcher
Private _clsDataAccess As Database
Private _intProgressInterval As Integer
Private _intProgressIntervalUNC As Integer
Private _intPollingInterval As Integer
Private _intWaitToAttachDebugger As Integer

' Service Control Field
Private _blnStop As Boolean

' Thread used to do the bulk of our service's work.
Private _thrWorker As Thread

' This Hashtable contains FileSystemWatcher components for each
' site that the service can parse logs for. This allows us to
' update the "Sources" table dynamically, rather than having to
' get a list of files in the directory on each pass.
Private _htbWatcher As Hashtable

' This timer is used to poll the "GetRegisteredSites" method.
' The ASP.NET application can add and remove sites to be parsed.
' Note that we need to fully qualify the name since the
```

Listing 4.29   Class member variables and types

```
' System.Threading namespace also contains a Timer definition
Private _tmrPoll As System.Timers.Timer

' This holds the SourceID of the current log source being parsed.
Private _fldSourceID As Guid
' This holds the table name for the current
' site that we're processing a file for.
Private _strTableName As String

' This holds our local table of sites
' that are registered for collection.
Private _tblSites As DataTable

' This holds our local table of log sources
' that are registered for collection.
Private _tblSources As DataTable
```

Listing 4.29   Class member variables and types (continued)

As soon as our service starts, we want it to load the application configuration from the configuration file we added earlier, register a FileSystemWatcher object on the configuration file (so that we can detect and pick up any new changes made while the service is running), start the worker thread (which will perform the bulk of the service's work), and then return to the SCM. The OnStart, OnStop, and supporting methods to load and register a FileSystemWatcher for our configuration file are shown in Listing 4.30.

```
'
' This method checks the configuration file for relevant settings that
' apply to the service. Included are the progress intervals, which
' control the number of log lines that are read before the service is
' polled for a stop command, and the connection string used to connect
' to the database.
'
Private Sub LoadConfiguration()

 Dim clsDataAccess As Database
 Dim fswConfigWatcher As FileSystemWatcher
 Dim config As ConfigurationSettings
 Dim strConnectionString As String
 Dim strProgressInterval As String
 Dim strProgressIntervalUNC As String
 Dim strPollingInterval As String
 Dim strWaitToAttachDebugger As String
 Dim intProgressInterval As Integer
 Dim intProgressIntervalUNC As Integer
 Dim intPollingInterval As Integer
```

Listing 4.30   OnStart, OnStop, and configuration methods

```
Dim intWaitToAttachDebugger As Integer

Dim strFilter As String = Process.GetCurrentProcess().MainModule. _
 ModuleName

config = New ConfigurationSettings()

strConnectionString = config.AppSettings("ConnectionString")
strProgressInterval = config.AppSettings("ProgressInterval")
strProgressIntervalUNC = config.AppSettings("ProgressIntervalUNC")
strPollingInterval = config.AppSettings( _
 "PollingIntervalForSiteRegistration")
strWaitToAttachDebugger = config.AppSettings( _
 "WaitToAttachDebugger")

Try
 intProgressInterval = Integer.Parse(strProgressInterval)
 If intProgressInterval < 1 Or intProgressInterval > 1000 Then
  Throw New FormatException()
 End If
Catch exc As Exception
 Log(EntryType.Warning, exc, "The application configuration " & _
  "file contains an invalid progress interval ""{0}"". " & _
  "Expected a numeric integer between 1 and 1000. The " & _
  "default progress interval will be used instead.", _
  strProgressInterval)
 intProgressInterval = defaultProgressInterval
End Try

Try
 intProgressIntervalUNC = Integer.Parse(strProgressIntervalUNC)
 If intProgressIntervalUNC < 1 Or intProgressIntervalUNC > 1000 Then
  Throw New FormatException()
 End If
Catch exc As Exception
 Log(EntryType.Warning, exc, "The application configuration " & _
  "file contains an invalid UNC progress interval ""{0}"". " & _
  "Expected a numeric integer between 1 and 1000. The default " & _
  "UNC progress interval will be used instead.", _
  strProgressIntervalUNC)
 If intProgressInterval < 4 Then
  intProgressIntervalUNC = 1
 Else
  intProgressIntervalUNC = CInt(0.25 * intProgressInterval)
 End If
End Try

Try
 intPollingInterval = Integer.Parse(strPollingInterval)
 If intPollingInterval < 30 Then
```

Listing 4.30 OnStart, OnStop, and configuration methods (continued)

```
   Throw New ArgumentOutOfRangeException( _
    "PollingIntervalForSiteRegistration")
  End If
 Catch exc As Exception
  Log(EntryType.Warning, exc, "The application configuration " & _
   "file contains an invalid polling interval for site " & _
   "registrations. Expected a numeric positive integer " & _
   "of 30 or greater. The default polling interval of " & _
   "120 seconds (two minutes) will be used instead.", _
   strPollingInterval)
  intPollingInterval = defaultPollingInterval
 End Try


 Try
  intWaitToAttachDebugger = Integer.Parse(strWaitToAttachDebugger)
  If intWaitToAttachDebugger < 0 Then
   intWaitToAttachDebugger = 0
  End If
 Catch exc As Exception
  intWaitToAttachDebugger = 30
 End Try


 If strConnectionString = "" Then
  strConnectionString = defaultConnectionString
 End If
 Try
  clsDataAccess = New Database(strConnectionString)
 Catch exc As Exception
  Log(EntryType.Error, exc, "The application configuration file " & _
   "contains an invalid database connection string. This " & _
   "MUST be corrected for the service to run correctly.")
  Throw
 End Try


 ' If we've gotten this far, then we're OK. The following
 ' will watch our configuration file for any changes so we
 ' can reload on demand.

 ' Synchronize access to class-level fields for thread safety.
 Monitor.Enter(Me)
 Try
  If Me._fswConfigWatcher Is Nothing Then
   fswConfigWatcher = New FileSystemWatcher(Environment. _
    CurrentDirectory, strFilter)
   fswConfigWatcher.NotifyFilter = NotifyFilters.LastWrite
   AddHandler fswConfigWatcher.Changed, _
    AddressOf ConfigurationChanged
   fswConfigWatcher.EnableRaisingEvents = True
   Me._fswConfigWatcher = fswConfigWatcher
  End If
```

Listing 4.30   OnStart, OnStop, and configuration methods (continued)

```vb
    Me._clsDataAccess = clsDataAccess
    Me._intProgressInterval = intProgressInterval
    Me._intProgressIntervalUNC = intProgressIntervalUNC
    Me._intPollingInterval = intPollingInterval
    Me._intWaitToAttachDebugger = intWaitToAttachDebugger
  Finally
   Monitor.Exit(Me)
  End Try

End Sub


' This method stops the service from watching for configuration
changes.
'
Private Sub UnloadConfiguration()

 Monitor.Enter(Me)
 If Not (_fswConfigWatcher Is Nothing) Then
  Me._fswConfigWatcher.EnableRaisingEvents = False
  RemoveHandler Me._fswConfigWatcher.Changed, _
   AddressOf ConfigurationChanged
  Me._fswConfigWatcher.Dispose()
  Me._fswConfigWatcher = Nothing
 End If
 Monitor.Exit(Me)

End Sub


' This method is activated by the configuration watcher component every
' time our service's configuration has changed. Note that this is
called
' on a different thread than the main ones in which our service runs.
'
Private Sub ConfigurationChanged(ByVal sender As Object, ByVal e _
 As FileSystemEventArgs)

 Try
  LoadConfiguration()
 Catch exc As Exception
  Log(EntryType.Warning, exc, "The former application " & _
   "configuration settings were valid, but the new " & _
   "configuration is not. The old configuration will " & _
   "continue to be used until the service is stopped.")
 End Try

End Sub


' This helper routine writes events to the event log.
```

Listing 4.30 OnStart, OnStop, and configuration methods (continued)

```vb
'
Private Sub Log(ByVal entryType As EntryType, ByVal exc As Exception, _
 ByVal formatMessage As String, ByVal ParamArray params() As Object)

 Dim strFormatted As String
 Dim strErrorInfo As String = String.Empty

 Do Until exc Is Nothing
  strErrorInfo = strErrorInfo & exc.GetType().Name & vbNewLine & _
   exc.Message & vbNewLine & "StackTrace:" & vbNewLine & _
   exc.StackTrace & vbNewLine
  exc = exc.InnerException
 Loop
 strFormatted = String.Format(formatMessage, params) & vbNewLine & _
  strErrorInfo
 EventLog.WriteEntry(Me.ServiceName, strFormatted, _
  CType(entryType, EventLogEntryType))

End Sub

'
' The SCM calls this method to start the service.
'
Protected Overrides Sub OnStart(ByVal args() As String)

 Dim thrWorker As ThreadStart

 ' Set the process priority so that we don't interfere
 ' with a user currently working on the machine.
 System.Diagnostics.Process.GetCurrentProcess().PriorityClass = _
  ProcessPriorityClass.BelowNormal

 ' Load the current configuration (if valid) and start
 ' watching the configuration file for any changes. If
 ' the configuration file is invalid, then this will
 ' throw an exception and our service will not start.
 LoadConfiguration()

 ' This variable is queried by our worker thread when
 ' it's at a place where it can stop, in response to
 ' a command received from the SCM.
 Me._blnStop = False
 Me._blnInit = False
 thrWorker = New ThreadStart(AddressOf Worker)
 Me._thrWorker = New Thread(thrWorker)
 Me._thrWorker.Start()

 ' Wait until the thread has actually started running before exiting.
 While Not Me._thrWorker.IsAlive
  Thread.Sleep(0)
 End While
```

Listing 4.30 OnStart, OnStop, and configuration methods (continued)

```
    End Sub


    '
    ' The SCM calls this method to stop our service
    '
    Protected Overrides Sub OnStop()
     Dim item As Object

     ' After these three lines execute, the next time the worker thread
     ' polls this field, it will know that a stop request has been sent
     ' and should proceed to shut down as quickly as possible.
     Monitor.Enter(Me)
     Me._blnStop = True
     Monitor.Exit(Me)

     ' Make sure that the worker thread exists, is alive and running.
     If Not Me._thrWorker Is Nothing Then
       If Me._thrWorker.IsAlive Then

        If Me._thrWorker.ThreadState = ThreadState.Suspended Or _
         Me._thrWorker.ThreadState = ThreadState.SuspendRequested Then
         ' If we're stopping from a "Paused" state, the worker thread
         ' will be suspended and can't respond to our stop request.
         ' In this case resume the thread so it can respond.
         Me._thrWorker.Resume()
        ElseIf Me._thrWorker.ThreadState = ThreadState.WaitSleepJoin Then
         ' During processing, the worker thread often goes to "sleep" to
         ' reduce the amount of apparent CPU cycles consumed for a given
         ' operation. If the thread is currently in this state, wake it
         ' up so that it can respond to our stop request. Note that this
         ' will cause a ThreadInterruptedException in the thread, sort of
         ' the thread's way of throwing a temper tantrum at being
         ' awakened from a deep sleep. :)
         Me._thrWorker.Interrupt()
        End If

        ' Now that the thread is awake (groggy, but awake), let's
        ' wait up to 25 seconds for it to finish any clean-up tasks
        ' and exit.
        If Not Me._thrWorker.Join(25000) Then
         ' The above method will return "False" if the thread is not
         ' responding to our stop request. In this case, log a warning
         ' that we're about to forcibly abort the thread, and an error
         ' when the thread finally dies.
         Log(EntryType.Warning, Nothing, "The log collector is not " & _
          "responding to the stop request. Attempting to abort.")
         Me._thrWorker.Abort()
         ' Wait until the thread dies.
         While Me._thrWorker.IsAlive
          Thread.Sleep(5)
```

Listing 4.30   OnStart, OnStop, and configuration methods (continued)

```
      End While
      Log(EntryType.Error, Nothing, "The log collector has been " & _
      "terminated.")
    End If
  End If
 End If


UnloadConfiguration()


End Sub
```

Listing 4.30   OnStart, OnStop, and configuration methods (continued)

There are several thread-management statements in the code, such as Monitor.Enter, Interrupt, and Thread.Sleep. At any given point in time, the Web Log Collector service may have several threads running. The thread-management statements allow us to control these threads and synchronize access to shared information inside the class.

The next two methods, shown in Listing 4.31, are called by the SCM when a user pauses or continues this service.

```
'
' The SCM calls this method to suspend our service.
'
Protected Overrides Sub OnPause()
  ' When our service is paused, we still want to respond to file system
  ' changed events, but we want to stop processing log files.

  ' This suspends the worker thread so
  ' it will no longer process log files.
  If Not Me._thrWorker Is Nothing Then
   If Me._thrWorker.IsAlive Then
    ' Even though the thread is alive, it could very possibly be
    ' in "sleep" mode. If this is the case, we need to interrupt
    ' the thread so we can place it in "Suspend" mode.
    If Me._thrWorker.ThreadState = ThreadState.WaitSleepJoin Then
     Me._thrWorker.Interrupt()
     ' If we've interrupted the thread, wait until
     ' it's running again before we suspend.
     While Not Me._thrWorker.ThreadState = ThreadState.Running
      Thread.Sleep(0)
     End While
    End If

    ' Double-check to make sure the thread is not already suspended
    ' (it shouldn't be) and then suspend it.
    If Me._thrWorker.ThreadState <> ThreadState.Suspended And _
    Me._thrWorker.ThreadState <> ThreadState.SuspendRequested Then
```

Listing 4.31   OnPause and OnContinue methods

```
      Me._thrWorker.Suspend()
    End If
   End If
 End If

End Sub


'
' The SCM calls this method to resume our service.
'
Protected Overrides Sub OnContinue()
  ' This method will only be invoked by the SCM after a pause request.
  ' We can safely assume that the thread is either a) suspended or b)
  ' suspending.

  ' This will allow the suspended worker
  ' thread to start running again.
  If Not Me._thrWorker Is Nothing Then
    If Me._thrWorker.IsAlive Then
      ' Double-check to make sure the thread is suspended, and then
      ' resume it.
      If Me._thrWorker.ThreadState = ThreadState.Suspended Or _
        Me._thrWorker.ThreadState = ThreadState.SuspendRequested Then
        Me._thrWorker.Resume()
      End If
    End If
  End If

End Sub
```

Listing 4.31   OnPause and OnContinue methods (continued)

Now we can set up the event-handling methods that this service will use to respond to changes in log file directories and parsing operations. The code for these methods is shown in Listing 4.32.

```
'
' This is a helper method for setting DataView filters.
'
Private Function Clean(ByVal value As Object) As String
  ' Note that value is declared as Object since we may
  ' be passing either a String or Guid to this function.
  Return "'" & Replace(value.ToString(), "'", "''") & "'"
End Function


'
' This method is called by one of our FileSystemWatcher
```

Listing 4.32   Watcher and LogParser event handlers

```
' components is the Hashtable whenever IIS creates a new
' log file, and will always be called on a different thread
' than our worker process. To handle this event, we only
' want to update our locally cached copy of the "LogSource"
' table.
'
Private Sub Watcher_OnCreated(ByVal sender As Object, ByVal e _
  As FileSystemEventArgs)

  ' This holds our filtered view of the Sites table
  Dim dvwSite As DataView
  Dim fldSiteID As Guid
  Dim fldSourceID As Guid
  Dim fldProposedID As Guid
  Dim tblRow As DataRow

  ' This is the file that was added.
  Dim strFileName As String = e.FullPath
  ' And this is directory that our Watcher component is watching
  Dim strLogFileDir As String = Path.GetDirectoryName(strFileName)
  Dim dtmLastWrite As Date = CDate(File.GetLastWriteTime(strFileName). _
   ToString())
  Dim lngFileLength As Long = New FileInfo(strFileName).Length

  ' Create and filter our view of the "Sites" table so we
  ' can retrieve the SiteID that this source was added to.
  dvwSite = New DataView(Me._tblSites)
  dvwSite.RowFilter = "LogFileDirectory = " & Clean(strLogFileDir)
  If dvwSite.Count > 0 Then
    fldSiteID = CType(dvwSite.Item(0).Row("ID"), Guid)
  End If
  ' Release any unmanaged resources the dataview may be holding.
  dvwSite.Dispose()

  ' Lock access to this class, since we don't want another
  ' thread modifying the "Sources" table while we are.
  Monitor.Enter(Me)
  Try
    ' Add a row to our locally cached "Sources" table for this site.
    fldProposedID = Guid.NewGuid()
    tblRow = Me._tblSources.NewRow()
    tblRow.BeginEdit()
    tblRow("ID") = fldProposedID
    tblRow("Site") = fldSiteID
    tblRow("FilePath") = strFileName
    tblRow("Status") = "PENDING"
    tblRow("Parser") = DBNull.Value
    tblRow("LineNumber") = 0
    tblRow("Length") = lngFileLength
    tblRow("LastWrite") = dtmLastWrite
```

Listing 4.32 Watcher and LogParser event handlers (continued)

```
    tblRow("ReProc") = False
    tblRow("Comment") = "This log file has not yet been processed."
    tblRow.EndEdit()
    ' Update the database to include this file.
    Try
      ' If another LogCollector service running on a different machine
      ' has already caught and processed this event, then the source
      ' will already exist in the database. In this case, the SourceID
      ' will be different than the one we assigned. Make sure that we
      ' use the correct one.
      fldSourceID = Me._clsDataAccess.AddSource(tblRow)
      If Guid.op_Inequality(fldSourceID, fldProposedID) Then
        Me._clsDataAccess.GetSource(fldSourceID, tblRow)
      End If
      Me._tblSources.Rows.Add(tblRow)
      ' If everything went OK, accept the
      ' changes to the "Sources" table.
      Me._tblSources.AcceptChanges()
    Catch exc As Exception
      Log(EntryType.Warning, exc, "One of the IIS Web Servers " & _
        "being monitored added a new log file ""{0}"". This log " & _
        "file will not be processed by this log collector since it " & _
        "could not be added to the database.", e.FullPath)
      Me._tblSources.RejectChanges()
    End Try
    Finally
      Monitor.Exit(Me)
    End Try


    ' If the worker thread is currently sleeping,
    ' wake it up to process the new entries.
    If Me._thrWorker.IsAlive Then
      If Me._thrWorker.ThreadState = ThreadState.WaitSleepJoin Then
        Me._thrWorker.Interrupt()
      End If
    End If


End Sub


    '
    ' This method is called by one of our FileSystemWatcher components
    ' whenever IIS changes the LastWrite time of a log file. We're pretty
    ' much guaranteed that this won't happen for every entry since IIS
    ' collects a number of entries internally before flushing them to disk.
    '
    Private Sub Watcher_OnChanged(ByVal sender As Object, ByVal e _
      As FileSystemEventArgs)

      ' This holds our filtered view of the Sources table
      Dim dvwSrc As DataView
```

Listing 4.32   Watcher and LogParser event handlers (continued)

```
Dim fldSourceID As Guid
Dim fldStatus As String
Dim tblRow As DataRow

' This is the file that was added.
Dim strFileName As String = e.FullPath
Dim dtmLastWrite As Date = CDate(File.GetLastWriteTime(strFileName). _
 ToString())
Dim lngFileLength As Long = New FileInfo(strFileName).Length

Monitor.Enter(Me)
Try
 ' Locate the Guid associated with this source file.
 dvwSrc = New DataView(Me._tblSources)
 dvwSrc.RowFilter = "FilePath = " & Clean(strFileName)
 If dvwSrc.Count = 0 Then
  dvwSrc.Dispose()
  Monitor.Exit(Me)
  ' Forward this the the created method.
  Watcher_OnCreated(sender, e)
  Monitor.Enter(Me)
  Return
 Else
  tblRow = dvwSrc.Item(0).Row
  fldSourceID = CType(tblRow("ID"), Guid)
  fldStatus = CStr(tblRow("Status"))
  tblRow.BeginEdit()
  tblRow("LastWrite") = dtmLastWrite
  tblRow("Length") = lngFileLength
  ' If this file has already been processed, make sure we process
  ' it again to get the new log entries that were written.
  If fldStatus = "PROCESSED" Or fldStatus = "ERROR" Then
   tblRow("Status") = "PENDING"
   tblRow("ReProc") = False
   tblRow("Comment") = "This log file is waiting to be " & _
    "re-processed."
   ' Regardless of which machine processed
   ' it, it's now up for grabs.
   tblRow("Parser") = DBNull.Value
  End If
  tblRow.EndEdit()
  ' Update the database for this file.
  Try
   Me._clsDataAccess.UpdateSource(tblRow)
   tblRow.AcceptChanges()
  Catch exc As Exception
   Log(EntryType.Warning, exc, "A database error occurred " & _
    "while updating the log source entry for ""{0}""." , _
    strFileName)
   tblRow.RejectChanges()
  End Try
```

Listing 4.32   Watcher and LogParser event handlers (continued)

```
      End If
      dvwSrc.Dispose()
    Finally
      Monitor.Exit(Me)
    End Try


    ' If the worker thread is currently sleeping,
    ' wake it up to process the new entries.
    If Me._thrWorker.IsAlive Then
      If Me._thrWorker.ThreadState = ThreadState.WaitSleepJoin Then
       Me._thrWorker.Interrupt()
      End If
    End If

  End Sub


  '
  ' This method is called by one of our FileSystemWatcher components
  ' whenever a user renames a log file. This will prevent the log
  ' collector from re-parsing a file unnecessarily.
  '
  Private Sub Watcher_OnRenamed(ByVal sender As Object, ByVal e _
    As RenamedEventArgs)

    Dim dvwSrc As DataView
    Dim tblRow As DataRow
    Dim fldSourceID As Guid
    Dim strNewFileName As String = e.FullPath
    Dim strOldFileName As String = e.OldFullPath

    Monitor.Enter(Me)
    Try
      ' Locate the Guid associated with this source file.
      dvwSrc = New DataView(Me._tblSources)
      dvwSrc.RowFilter = "FilePath = " & Clean(strOldFileName)
      If dvwSrc.Count = 0 Then
       dvwSrc.Dispose()
       Monitor.Exit(Me)
        ' Forward this the the created method.
       Watcher_OnCreated(sender, e)
       Monitor.Enter(Me)
       Return
      Else
       tblRow = dvwSrc.Item(0).Row
       fldSourceID = CType(tblRow("ID"), Guid)
       tblRow.BeginEdit()
       tblRow("FilePath") = strNewFileName
       tblRow.EndEdit()
        ' Update the database for this file.
       Try
        Me._clsDataAccess.UpdateSource(tblRow)
```

Listing 4.32   Watcher and LogParser event handlers (continued)

```
      tblRow.AcceptChanges()
    Catch exc As Exception
      Log(EntryType.Warning, exc, "A database error occurred " & _
        "while renaming the log source entry ""{0}"" to ""{1}"".", _
        strOldFileName, strNewFileName)
      tblRow.RejectChanges()
    End Try
   End If
   dvwSrc.Dispose()
 Finally
   Monitor.Exit(Me)
 End Try


 ' Note that we don't wake up the worker thread, since
 ' this type of change does not require processing.

End Sub


'
' The log LogParser component that we're using calls this event
' every time it has parsed a new entry. This alleviates the parser
' from having to deal with any type of database activity whatsoever.
' After all, it doesn't care what you do with the entry, it just
' parses them. Also note that we have to supply the SourceID, since
' that is implementation-specific (relies on the database). The log
' parser is only concerned with file paths and entries.
'
Private Sub LogParser_ParsedEntry(ByVal sender As System.Object, _
 ByVal e As ParsedEntryEventArgs)

 Dim dvwSrc As DataView
 Dim tblRow As DataRow

 Monitor.Enter(Me)
 Try
   Me._strTableName = Me._clsDataAccess.AddLogEntry( _
     Me._fldSourceID, e.LineNumber, Me._strTableName, e.Entry)
   Try
     Thread.Sleep(5) ' Sleep to reduce CPU usage.
   Catch exc As ThreadInterruptedException
   End Try

   dvwSrc = New DataView(Me._tblSources)
   dvwSrc.RowFilter = "ID = " & Clean(Me._fldSourceID)
   If dvwSrc.Count > 0 Then
     tblRow = dvwSrc.Item(0).Row
```

Listing 4.32 Watcher and LogParser event handlers (continued)

```
      tblRow.BeginEdit()
      tblRow("LineNumber") = e.LineNumber
      tblRow.EndEdit()
      tblRow.AcceptChanges()
    End If
    dvwSrc.Dispose()
  Finally
    Monitor.Exit(Me)
  End Try

End Sub

'

' After every "ProgressInterval" number of lines are read (not parsed),
' or between files, whichever comes first, the log parser component
will
' call this method to check if it should stop parsing. This allows the
' log parser to respond to service stop requests.
'
Private Sub LogParser_ParseProgressUpdate(ByVal sender _
  As System.Object, ByVal e As ParseProgressEventArgs)

  Dim dvwSrc As DataView
  Dim tblRow As DataRow

  e.Cancel = Me._blnStop

  Monitor.Enter(Me)
  Try
    dvwSrc = New DataView(Me._tblSources)
    dvwSrc.RowFilter = "ID = " & Clean(Me._fldSourceID)
    If dvwSrc.Count > 0 Then
      tblRow = dvwSrc.Item(0).Row
      tblRow.BeginEdit()
      tblRow("LineNumber") = e.LineNumber
      tblRow.EndEdit()
      tblRow.AcceptChanges()
    End If
    dvwSrc.Dispose()
  Finally
    Monitor.Exit(Me)
  End Try

End Sub
```

Listing 4.32   Watcher and LogParser event handlers (continued)

After each polling interval, the log collector queries the database for new or removed sites. The methods in Listing 4.33 implement this functionality.

```
'
' This routine retrieves the list of web servers our ASP.NET
' application has told us to collect the logs for. We need
' to poll this method occasionally to watch for new registered
' sites.
'
Private Sub GetRegisteredSites()

 Dim tblSites As DataTable
 Dim dvwSite As DataView
 Dim tblSiteRow As DataRow
 Dim fldSiteID As Guid
 Dim dvwSrc As DataView
 Dim tblSrcRow As DataRow

 Dim strLogFileDir As String
 Dim fswWatcher As FileSystemWatcher

 Dim rowIndex As Integer
 Dim item As Object
 Dim blnHasChanges As Boolean = False

 Monitor.Enter(Me)

 Try
  ' First, stop the timer if it exists.
  If Not Me._tmrPoll Is Nothing Then
   Me._tmrPoll.Enabled = False
  End If

  Me._tblSites = Me._clsDataAccess.GetRegisteredSites()
  ' If we have a source row for a site that the ASP.NET application
  ' has unregistered for collection. Make sure we remove it from our
  ' internal sources table as well as remove the Watcher that is
  ' watching the log file directory.
  For Each tblSrcRow In Me._tblSources.Rows

   fldSiteID = CType(tblSrcRow("Site"), Guid)

   dvwSite = New DataView(Me._tblSites)
   dvwSite.RowFilter = "ID = " & Clean(fldSiteID)

   If dvwSite.Count = 0 Then
    strLogFileDir = Path.GetDirectoryName( _
     CStr(tblSrcRow("FilePath")))
    tblSrcRow.Delete()
    If Me._htbWatcher.Contains(strLogFileDir) Then
```

Listing 4.33   Site updates and polling interval methods

```
      fswWatcher = CType(Me._htbWatcher(strLogFileDir), _
        FileSystemWatcher)
      fswWatcher.EnableRaisingEvents = False
      RemoveHandler fswWatcher.Changed, AddressOf Watcher_OnChanged
      RemoveHandler fswWatcher.Created, AddressOf Watcher_OnCreated
      RemoveHandler fswWatcher.Renamed, AddressOf Watcher_OnRenamed
      fswWatcher.Dispose()
      Me._htbWatcher.Remove(strLogFileDir)
     End If
   End If

   dvwSite.Dispose()

 Next

 ' Iterate through the sites table looking for
 ' any sites for which we do not have sources.
 For Each tblSiteRow In Me._tblSites.Rows

   fldSiteID = CType(tblSiteRow("ID"), Guid)
   strLogFileDir = CStr(tblSiteRow("LogFileDirectory"))

   dvwSrc = New DataView(Me._tblSources)
   dvwSrc.RowFilter = "Site = " & Clean(fldSiteID)

   ' If no sources exist for this particular
   ' site, it may have just been registered.
   If dvwSrc.Count = 0 Then
     If Not Me._htbWatcher.Contains(strLogFileDir) Then
       InitializeSourcesForSite(tblSiteRow)

       ' Start the worker thread so it can process these new logs
       If Me._thrWorker.ThreadState = ThreadState.WaitSleepJoin Then
         Me._thrWorker.Interrupt()
       End If
     End If
   End If

   ' Add a watcher, if necessary, to watch for
   ' changes in this site's log file directory.
   If Not Me._htbWatcher.Contains(strLogFileDir) Then
     fswWatcher = New FileSystemWatcher(strLogFileDir)
     fswWatcher.NotifyFilter = NotifyFilters.FileName Or _
       NotifyFilters.LastWrite
     AddHandler fswWatcher.Changed, AddressOf Watcher_OnChanged
     AddHandler fswWatcher.Created, AddressOf Watcher_OnCreated
     AddHandler fswWatcher.Renamed, AddressOf Watcher_OnRenamed
     fswWatcher.EnableRaisingEvents = True
     Me._htbWatcher.Add(strLogFileDir, fswWatcher)
   End If
```

Listing 4.33 Site updates and polling interval methods (continued)

```
        dvwSrc.Dispose()

    Next

    ' Before we exit, set our timer for the next polling interval.
    If Me._tmrPoll Is Nothing Then
      Me._tmrPoll = New System.Timers.Timer( _
        CDbl(Me._intPollingInterval) * 1000)
      AddHandler Me._tmrPoll.Elapsed, AddressOf Timer_Elapsed
    End If
    Me._tmrPoll.Enabled = True

  Finally
    Monitor.Exit(Me)
  End Try

End Sub


'
' This is the event that is called after our polling timer has elapsed
'
Private Sub Timer_Elapsed(ByVal sender As Object, ByVal e As _
  System.Timers.ElapsedEventArgs)

  GetRegisteredSites()

End Sub


'
' This is called whenever a new site is registered for collection
' or when no Sources currently exist for a registered site and no
' watchers are currently set up for the site's log file directory.
'
Private Sub InitializeSourcesForSite(ByVal tblSiteRow As DataRow)

  Dim strLogFileDir As String
  Dim strFiles() As String
  Dim intIndex As Integer
  Dim strFileName As String
  Dim fldSiteID As Guid
  Dim fldProposedID As Guid
  Dim fldSourceID As Guid
  Dim tblRow As DataRow
  Dim lngFileLength As Long
  Dim dtmLastWrite As Date

  strLogFileDir = CStr(tblSiteRow("LogFileDirectory"))
  fldSiteID = CType(tblSiteRow("ID"), Guid)

  ' We're only interested in *.log files.
```

Listing 4.33   Site updates and polling interval methods (continued)

```
    strFiles = Directory.GetFiles(strLogFileDir, "*.log")


    ' For each *.log file found in the directory,
    ' add an entry to our Sources table.
    For intIndex = 0 To strFiles.Length - 1
      strFileName = strFiles(intIndex)
      lngFileLength = New FileInfo(strFileName).Length
      dtmLastWrite = CDate(File.GetLastWriteTime(strFileName).ToString())


      fldProposedID = Guid.NewGuid()


      tblRow = Me._tblSources.NewRow()
      tblRow.BeginEdit()
      tblRow("ID") = fldProposedID
      tblRow("Site") = fldSiteID
      tblRow("FilePath") = strFileName
      tblRow("Status") = "PENDING"
      tblRow("Parser") = DBNull.Value
      tblRow("LineNumber") = 0
      tblRow("Length") = lngFileLength
      tblRow("LastWrite") = dtmLastWrite
      tblRow("ReProc") = False
      tblRow("Comment") = "This log file has not yet been processed."
      tblRow.EndEdit()
      ' Update the database to include this log source.
      Try
        fldSourceID = Me._clsDataAccess.AddSource(tblRow)
        If Guid.op_Inequality(fldProposedID, fldSourceID) Then
          Me._clsDataAccess.GetSource(fldSourceID, tblRow)
        End If
        Me._tblSources.Rows.Add(tblRow)
        Me._tblSources.AcceptChanges()
      Catch exc As Exception
        Log(EntryType.Warning, exc, "A database error occurred while " & _
          "adding the log source found at ""{0}"". This log file " & _
          "will not be processed by this log collector since it " & _
          "could not be added to the database.", strFileName)
        Me._tblSources.RejectChanges()
      End Try


    Next


End Sub
```

Listing 4.33   Site updates and polling interval methods (continued)

When our worker thread starts, the first thing it has to do is get a list of all the sources already registered in the database, check each log file directory for new files, add them to the database or update the database with new file lengths (since the service itself might have been stopped when a new log was created or entries written), and finally create FileSystemWatcher components for each of the log file directories that it monitors. This method is expensive in terms of performance, so fortunately, it is only called once each time the service starts. The SourceInitialization method is shown in Listing 4.34.

```
'
' This method is expensive, and fortunately it is only called once,
' when the service starts. It first retrieves a list of sources that
are
' already defined in the database. Then it checks the log file
directory
' for any new sources that are not yet registered. This way, it can
pick
' up and register any log sources that have been added while the
service
' was stopped.
'
Private Sub SourceInitialization()

  Dim strDirs As System.Collections.Specialized.StringCollection
  Dim strLogFileDir As String
  Dim tblRow As DataRow
  Dim dvwSrc As DataView
  Dim tblRowFromDV As DataRow
  Dim strFiles() As String
  Dim strFileName As String
  Dim lngFileLength As Long
  Dim dtmLastWrite As Date
  Dim fldSiteID As Guid
  Dim fldProposedID As Guid
  Dim fldSourceID As Guid
  Dim intIndex As Integer

  strDirs = New System.Collections.Specialized.StringCollection()

  Monitor.Enter(Me)
  Try
   Me._tblSources = Me._clsDataAccess.GetAllLogSources()
   For Each tblRow In Me._tblSources.Rows
    If Me._blnStop = True Then Exit For
    strLogFileDir = Path.GetDirectoryName(CStr(tblRow("FilePath")))
    ' Check to see if we've already processed
    ' the directory this file is contained in.
    If Not strDirs.Contains(strLogFileDir) Then
     fldSiteID = CType(tblRow("Site"), Guid)
```

Listing 4.34 SourceInitialization method

```
' We're only interested in *.log files.
strFiles = Directory.GetFiles(strLogFileDir, "*.log")

' For each *.log file found in the directory,
' add an entry to our Sources table or update
' the table with the actual last write time
' length.
For intIndex = 0 To strFiles.Length - 1
 strFileName = strFiles(intIndex)
 lngFileLength = New FileInfo(strFileName).Length
 dtmLastWrite = CDate(File.GetLastWriteTime(strFileName). _
 ToString())

 dvwSrc = New DataView(Me._tblSources)
 dvwSrc.RowFilter = "Site = " & Clean(fldSiteID) & _
  " AND FilePath = " & Clean(strFileName)
 If dvwSrc.Count = 0 Then
  ' The file found in the directory is
  ' not registered in the database.
  fldProposedID = Guid.NewGuid()

  tblRowFromDV = dvwSrc.AddNew().Row
  tblRowFromDV.BeginEdit()
  tblRowFromDV("ID") = fldProposedID
  tblRowFromDV("Site") = fldSiteID
  tblRowFromDV("FilePath") = strFileName
  tblRowFromDV("Status") = "PENDING"
  tblRowFromDV("Parser") = DBNull.Value
  tblRowFromDV("LineNumber") = 0
  tblRowFromDV("Length") = lngFileLength
  tblRowFromDV("LastWrite") = dtmLastWrite
  tblRowFromDV("ReProc") = False
  tblRowFromDV("Comment") = "This log file has not yet " & _
   "been processed."
  tblRowFromDV.EndEdit()
  ' Update the database to include this log source.
  Try
   fldSourceID = Me._clsDataAccess.AddSource(tblRowFromDV)
   If Guid.op_Inequality(fldProposedID, fldSourceID) Then
    Me._clsDataAccess.GetSource(fldSourceID, tblRowFromDV)
   End If
   Me._tblSources.Rows.Add(tblRow)
   Me._tblSources.AcceptChanges()
  Catch exc As Exception
   Log(EntryType.Warning, exc, "A database error " & _
    "occurred while adding the log source found at " & _
    """{0}""". This log file will not be processed by " & _
    "this log collector since it could not be added " & _
    "to the database.", strFileName)
   Me._tblSources.RejectChanges()
```

Listing 4.34   SourceInitialization method (continued)

```
      End Try
    Else
     Dim dtmOldLastWrite As Date
     Dim lngOldFileLength As Long
     Dim strOldStatus As String

     tblRowFromDV = dvwSrc.Item(0).Row
     ' Note that we convert this to a string before converting
     ' it to a date. This way, we can compare it to the
     ' LastWriteTime in dtmLastWrite with equal precision.
     dtmOldLastWrite = CDate( _
      tblRowFromDV("LastWrite").ToString())
     lngOldFileLength = CLng(tblRowFromDV("Length"))
     strOldStatus = CStr(tblRowFromDV("Status"))

     ' Only update the database if the last
     ' write time or length has changed.
     If dtmOldLastWrite < dtmLastWrite Or lngOldFileLength < _
      lngFileLength Then
      tblRowFromDV.BeginEdit()
      tblRowFromDV("LastWrite") = dtmLastWrite
      tblRowFromDV("Length") = lngFileLength
      If strOldStatus = "PROCESSED" Or _
       strOldStatus = "ERROR" Then
       tblRowFromDV("Status") = "PENDING"
       tblRowFromDV("ReProc") = False
       tblRowFromDV("Parser") = DBNull.Value
       tblRowFromDV("Comment") = "This log file is " & _
        "waiting to be re-processed."
      End If
      tblRowFromDV.EndEdit()
      ' Update the database
      Try
       Me._clsDataAccess.UpdateSource(tblRowFromDV)
       Me._tblSources.AcceptChanges()
      Catch exc As Exception
       Log(EntryType.Warning, exc, "A database error " & _
        "occurred while updating the log source entry " & _
        "for ""{0}""." , strFileName)
       Me._tblSources.RejectChanges()
      End Try
     End If

    End If

   Next

   strDirs.Add(strLogFileDir)

  End If
```

Listing 4.34 SourceInitialization method (continued)

```
    Next
  Finally
    Monitor.Exit(Me)
  End Try

End Sub
```

Listing 4.34 SourceInitialization method (continued)

The Worker method that starts everything rolling is shown in Listing 4.35.

```
'
' This method is used by the worker thread to write log parsing
' errors to the database and synchronize them with our local
' table
'
Private Sub WriteLogError(ByVal exc As Exception, ByVal tblRow _
  As DataRow, ByVal reProc As Boolean)

  Dim strComment As String
  Dim e As Exception

  tblRow.BeginEdit()
  tblRow("Status") = "ERROR"
  tblRow("Parser") = Environment.MachineName
  tblRow("ReProc") = reProc
  e = exc
  strComment = String.Empty
  Do Until e Is Nothing
    strComment = strComment & String.Format("{0} - {1}" & _
    vbNewLine, e.GetType().Name, e.Message)
    e = e.InnerException
  Loop
  tblRow("Comment") = Left(strComment, 1024)
  tblRow.EndEdit()
  Me._clsDataAccess.UpdateSource(tblRow)
  tblRow.AcceptChanges()

End Sub

'
' This method is basically an infinite loop that performs our
' service's work. If a stop command is received from the SCM
' the blnStop variable will be True and the loop will exit.
'
Private Sub Worker()
```

Listing 4.35 WriteLogError and Worker methods

```
Dim fswWatcher As FileSystemWatcher
Dim AbstractParser As LogParser
Dim Parser As W3CExtLogParser
Dim item As Object
Dim dvwSrc As DataView
Dim tblSrcRow As DataRow
Dim fldSourceID As Guid
Dim strStatus As String
Dim strParser As String
Dim intIndex As Integer
Dim intInterval As Integer
Dim strFileName As String
Dim intStartAt As Integer


' During debugging, we want to pause for a specified number of
' seconds right here to give us time to attach a debugger.
Try
 Thread.Sleep(Me._intWaitToAttachDebugger * 1000)
Catch exc As ThreadInterruptedException
 ' This will only be executed if the user stops
 ' the service before the interval runs out.
 If Me._blnStop = True Then Return
End Try


' Initialize the Hashtable
Me._htbWatcher = New Hashtable(1024)
Try
 ' Initialize the Sources table
 SourceInitialization()
 ' Initialize the Sites table and Polling Timer
 GetRegisteredSites()
Catch exc As Exception
 If Not Me._tblSites Is Nothing Then
  Me._tblSites.Dispose()
  Me._tblSites = Nothing
 End If
 If Not Me._tblSources Is Nothing Then
  Me._tblSources.Dispose()
  Me._tblSources = Nothing
 End If
 If Not Me._tmrPoll Is Nothing Then
  RemoveHandler _tmrPoll.Elapsed, AddressOf Timer_Elapsed
  Me._tmrPoll.Enabled = False
  Me._tmrPoll.Dispose()
  Me._tmrPoll = Nothing
 End If
 Me._htbWatcher = Nothing
 ' Catch ANY error that might occur and write
 ' an error event to the event log.
 Log(EntryType.Error, exc, "The log collector service's worker " & _
```

Listing 4.35 WriteLogError and Worker methods (continued)

```
    "thread terminated abnormally.")
  Return
End Try

' We now know that the service is initialized.
Log(EntryType.Info, Nothing, "The log collector service has " & _
  "initialized.")
' If any unexpected error occurs, exit gracefully.
Try

  ' This loop will continue to run as long as our service is active.
  Do

    Try

      If Me._blnStop = True Then Exit Do

      dvwSrc = New DataView(Me._tblSources)
      Try
        dvwSrc.RowFilter = "(Status = 'PENDING') OR ((Status = " & _
          "'PROCESSING') AND (Parser = " & _
          Clean(Environment.MachineName) & ")) OR (ReProc = 1)"
        dvwSrc.Sort = "Site"

        If dvwSrc.Count = 0 Then
          ' Sleep until we pick up new changes.
          Thread.Sleep(Timeout.Infinite)
          Exit Try
        End If

        For intIndex = 0 To dvwSrc.Count - 1

          If intIndex > dvwSrc.Count - 1 Then Exit For
          tblSrcRow = dvwSrc.Item(intIndex).Row
          If tblSrcRow.RowState = DataRowState.Deleted Then Exit For
          fldSourceID = CType(tblSrcRow("ID"), Guid)
          Me._clsDataAccess.GetSource(fldSourceID, tblSrcRow)
          If tblSrcRow.RowState = DataRowState.Deleted Then Exit For

          strStatus = CStr(tblSrcRow("Status"))
          If TypeOf tblSrcRow("Parser") Is DBNull Then
            strParser = String.Empty
          Else
            strParser = CStr(tblSrcRow("Parser"))
          End If

          If strStatus = "PENDING" Or (strStatus = "PROCESSING" _
            And strParser = Environment.MachineName) Then

            intStartAt = CInt(tblSrcRow("LineNumber"))
```

Listing 4.35 WriteLogError and Worker methods (continued)

```
Try
 strFileName = CStr(tblSrcRow("FilePath"))
 If strFileName.StartsWith("\\") Then
  intInterval = Me._intProgressIntervalUNC
 Else
  intInterval = Me._intProgressInterval
 End If
 AbstractParser = LogParser.Create( _
  CStr(tblSrcRow("FilePath")), intInterval)
Catch exc As NotImplementedException
 Log(EntryType.Warning, exc, "The log file at " & _
  """{0}"" is in a format that is not recognized " & _
  "by any of the installed log parsers.", strFileName)
 WriteLogError(exc, tblSrcRow, False)
 Exit For
Catch exc As Exception
 Log(EntryType.Warning, exc, "Could not create a " & _
  "parser for the log file ""{0}"". Perhaps the " & _
  "log file does not exist or access was denied.", _
  strFileName)
 WriteLogError(exc, tblSrcRow, False)
 Exit For
End Try

Try
 Me._fldSourceID = fldSourceID
 tblSrcRow.BeginEdit()
 tblSrcRow("Status") = "PROCESSING"
 tblSrcRow("Parser") = Environment.MachineName
 tblSrcRow("ReProc") = False
 tblSrcRow("Comment") = "This log file is currently " & _
  "being processed."
 tblSrcRow.EndEdit()
 Me._clsDataAccess.UpdateSource(tblSrcRow)
 tblSrcRow.AcceptChanges()
 If TypeOf AbstractParser Is W3CExtLogParser Then
  Parser = CType(AbstractParser, W3CExtLogParser)
  AddHandler Parser.ParsedEntry, _
   AddressOf LogParser_ParsedEntry
  AddHandler Parser.ParseProgress, _
   AddressOf LogParser_ParseProgressUpdate
  Parser.ParseAt(intStartAt)
  RemoveHandler Parser.ParsedEntry, _
   AddressOf LogParser_ParsedEntry
  RemoveHandler Parser.ParseProgress, _
   AddressOf LogParser_ParseProgressUpdate
  Parser.Dispose()
  Parser = Nothing
 End If
 tblSrcRow.BeginEdit()
```

Listing 4.35 WriteLogError and Worker methods (continued)

```
            tblSrcRow("Status") = "PROCESSED"
            tblSrcRow("Parser") = Environment.MachineName
            tblSrcRow("ReProc") = False
            tblSrcRow("Comment") = "This log file was " & _
              "processed successfully."
            tblSrcRow.EndEdit()
            Me._clsDataAccess.UpdateSource(tblSrcRow)
            tblSrcRow.AcceptChanges()
            Log(EntryType.Info, Nothing, "Successfully " & _
              "processed the log file at ""{0}"".", _
              CStr(tblSrcRow("FilePath")))
          Catch exc As IOException
            Log(EntryType.Warning, exc, "An error occurred " & _
              "while parsing the log file ""{0}"".", strFileName)
            WriteLogError(exc, tblSrcRow, True)
          Catch exc As Exception
            Log(EntryType.Warning, exc, "An error occurred " & _
              "while parsing the log file ""{0}"".", strFileName)
            WriteLogError(exc, tblSrcRow, False)
          End Try
        End If

      Next

    Finally
      dvwSrc.Dispose()
    End Try

    If Me._blnStop = True Then Exit Do

    Thread.Sleep(50)

  Catch err As ThreadInterruptedException
    ' Do nothing. Evidently another thread wants us to start again.
  Finally
    If Not Parser Is Nothing Then
      ' Clean-up before we end.
      RemoveHandler Parser.ParsedEntry, _
        AddressOf LogParser_ParsedEntry
      RemoveHandler Parser.ParseProgress, _
        AddressOf LogParser_ParseProgressUpdate
      Parser.Dispose()
      Parser = Nothing
    End If
  End Try

  Loop

Catch exc As Exception
```

Listing 4.35   WriteLogError and Worker methods (continued)

```
' Catch ANY error that might occur and write
' an error event to the event log.
Log(EntryType.Error, exc, "The log collector service's worker " & _
  "thread terminated abnormally.")

Finally

  Monitor.Enter(Me)
  Try
    Dim dict As DictionaryEntry
    For Each item In Me._htbWatcher
      dict = CType(item, DictionaryEntry)
      fswWatcher = CType(dict.Value, FileSystemWatcher)
      fswWatcher.EnableRaisingEvents = False
      RemoveHandler fswWatcher.Changed, AddressOf Watcher_OnChanged
      RemoveHandler fswWatcher.Created, AddressOf Watcher_OnCreated
      RemoveHandler fswWatcher.Renamed, AddressOf Watcher_OnRenamed
      fswWatcher.Dispose()
      dict.Value = Nothing
    Next
    Me._tblSites.Dispose()
    Me._tblSources.Dispose()
    Me._tmrPoll.Enabled = False
    RemoveHandler Me._tmrPoll.Elapsed, AddressOf Timer_Elapsed
    Me._tmrPoll.Dispose()
    Me._tblSources = Nothing
    Me._tblSites = Nothing
    Me._htbWatcher = Nothing
    Me._tmrPoll = Nothing
  Finally
    Monitor.Exit(Me)
  End Try

  End Try

End Sub

End Class
```

Listing 4.35   WriteLogError and Worker methods (continued)

You now have a fully functional log collector. If you have not yet done so, build the project using the Build —> Build WebLogCollector menu command (you will need to select the project in Solution Explorer first). You can install your service using the technique discussed previously (if you have uninstalled it), using the Installutil.exe command-line utility.

To debug your service, set the breakpoints that you want and open the Services console. If you set the application configuration file settings as I did in this project, you will have 30 seconds after the service starts to attach the debugger before it starts running at full speed. You can increase the WaitToAttachDebugger setting at this point if you think it will take longer.

Next, start the service, and switch back to the Visual Studio .NET environment. Choose the Debug —> Processes menu command. After a few seconds, it will show you the current processes running in your user context. At the bottom of this dialog box is a check box pertaining to system processes that are running. After selecting the check box, locate your WebLogCollector.exe process, click Attach, and then click OK. Click OK again to attach the Visual Studio debugger.

When you are satisfied that your Web Log Collector service is running smoothly, you should stop the service before continuing with the ASP.NET Web Application project. We will be using the Start Debugging command (or F5, if you prefer to use keyboard shortcuts) to debug the ASP.NET Web Application, and it will not build correctly if the service is running when you compile the project. This is because the Visual Studio environment recompiles all of the projects in the solution when you press F5. If the service is running, it will not be allowed to overwrite the currently running program.

Developing the Web Application Project

Before we jump into developing the Project04 (ASP.NET Web Application) project, let's cover a few basic details. First, our ASP.NET project needs to reference both the WebLogParser and WebLogDataAccess projects we created previously. Add those references through the Add References shortcut menu (accessed by right-clicking the project).

Recall that when we set up our Web Application project in Internet Services Manager, we cleared the Allow anonymous access check box because we wanted all the users of this site to be at least an administrator on the computer where the Web server resides, and a domain administrator if they are analyzing logs from other computers. The reason that this is necessary is because our Database class accesses the IIS MetaBase for information instead of the SQL Server database. By default, the MetaBase restricts access to many of its properties and objects to users in the Administrators group.

However, ASP.NET provides its own security system, which can override the security defined in Internet Services Manager. The method by which ASP.NET manages security is through the Web.config file. If you open that file now, you should notice two configuration sections marked by the authentication and authorization tags. These configuration settings determine how ASP.NET handles security for your Web site.

By default, the Authorization section contains an entry that allows all users to access the Web site, anonymous or not. If you were to build your project right now, you would notice that regardless of the settings in Internet Services Manager, everyone would have access to your site. To correct this, remove the tag that says <allow users="*" />, and add the following entries to this section.

```
<allow roles="BUILTIN\Administrators" />
<deny users="*" />
```

This tells the ASP.NET runtime to allow any member of the BUILTIN\Administrators group (including domain administrators) to access the site, but to deny all other users.

One other configuration setting that we need to add to this file is our appSettings section and connection string, as follows:

```
<appSettings>
 <add key="ConnectionString"
  value="server=localhost;database=ASPNetProject04;uid=sa;pwd=;" />
</appSettings>
```

To make this setting easily available through an application variable, open the Global.asax file in code view and add the following method:

```
Sub Application_Start(ByVal sender As Object, ByVal e As EventArgs)
  Application("Connection") = _
    ConfigurationSettings.AppSettings("ConnectionString")
End Sub
```

The Default Page

When you create a new ASP.NET Web Application project using Visual Basic, it will automatically add a default style sheet to your project. Open that now, replace the anchor tag entries with the following styles and add the .ReportButton CSS class. Then save and close the Styles.css file.

```
A:link {
 text-decoration: none;
 color: #333399;
}

A:visited {
 text-decoration: none;
 color: #333399;
}

A:active {
 text-decoration: none;
 color: #333399;
}

A:hover {
 text-decoration: none;
 color: #3333ff;
}
```

```
.ReportButton {
 font-weight: bold;
 width: 3.5in;
 height: 0.3in;
 background-color: #e9e9ff;
 border: 1px solid #000080;
}
```

Now open the Default.aspx page in HTML view, and add the code shown in Listing 4.36. The formatting may look a bit odd because I am constrained to the size of this page.

```
<%@ Page Language="vb" AutoEventWireup="false"
  Codebehind="Default.aspx.vb" Inherits="Project04.DefaultPage"%>
<!DOCTYPE HTML PUBLIC "-//W3C//DTD HTML 4.0 Transitional//EN">
<html>
 <head>
  <title></title>
  <meta name="GENERATOR" content="Microsoft Visual Studio.NET 7.0">
  <meta name="CODE_LANGUAGE" content="Visual Basic 7.0">
  <meta name="vs_defaultClientScript" content="JavaScript">
  <meta name="vs_targetSchema"
   content="http://schemas.microsoft.com/intellisense/ie5">
  <link rel="stylesheet" href="Styles.css">
 </head>
 <body ms_positioning="GridLayout">
  <form id="Form1" method="post" runat="server">
   <input type="hidden" id="OldMachineNameField" runat="server">
   <table cellpadding="0" cellspacing="0" border="0" width="100%"
    height="100%">
    <tr>
     <td height="100" align="middle">
      <h1>
       Web Site Log Collection
      </h1>
     </td>
    </tr>
    <tr>
    <tr>
     <td align="middle" valign="top">
      <table cellpadding="0" cellspacing="5" width="600">
       <tr>
        <td>
         <table cellpadding="0" cellspacing="0">
          <tr>
           <td>
            Machine NetBIOS Name:
           </td>
           <td>
            <asp:textbox id="MachineNameField" runat="server"
```

Listing 4.36   HTML for the Default.aspx file

```
                    maxlength="15"></asp:textbox>
              </td>
              <td>
                <asp:button id="UpdateMachine" runat="server"
                text="Update Machine"></asp:button>
              </td>
            </tr>
          </table>
        </td>
      </tr>
      <tr>
        <td>
<asp:datagrid id="AvailableSitesGrid" cellpadding="0"
 cellspacing="5" gridlines="None" bordercolor="#000080"
 borderstyle="Solid" borderwidth="2px"
 backcolor="#e9e9ff" horizontalalign="Center"
 runat="server" autogeneratecolumns="False"
 width="100%">
 <columns>
  <asp:templatecolumn headertext="Site Index"
   headerstyle-verticalalign="Bottom"
   headerstyle-horizontalalign="Center"
   itemstyle-horizontalalign="Center"
   itemstyle-verticalalign="Top"
   headerstyle-wrap="False"
   sortexpression="SiteIndex">
   <itemtemplate>
<asp:label id="SiteID" runat="server"
 text='<%# DataBinder.Eval(Container.DataItem, "ID", "{0}") %>'
 visible="False"></asp:label>
<asp:label id="SiteIndex" runat="server"
 text='<%# DataBinder.Eval(Container.DataItem, "SiteIndex", "{0}") %>'>
</asp:label>
   </itemtemplate>
  </asp:templatecolumn>
  <asp:templatecolumn headerstyle-verticalalign="Bottom"
   itemstyle-verticalalign="Top" sortexpression="SiteName">
   <headertemplate>
    <table cellspacing="0" cellpadding="0" width="100%"
    border="0">
    <tr>
     <td>
      Site Name
     </td>
    </tr>
    <tr>
     <td>
      Log File Directory
     </td>
    </tr>
```

Listing 4.36   HTML for the Default.aspx file (continued)

```
          </table>
        </headertemplate>
        <itemtemplate>
         <table cellspacing="0" cellpadding="0" width="100%"
          border="0">
          <tr>
           <td nowrap>
            <%# DataBinder.Eval(Container.DataItem, "SiteName") %>
           </td>
          </tr>
          <tr>
           <td nowrap>
        <%# DataBinder.Eval(Container.DataItem, "LogFileDirectory") %>
           </td>
          </tr>
         </table>
        </itemtemplate>
      </asp:templatecolumn>
      <asp:templatecolumn headertext="Registered"
       headerstyle-verticalalign="Bottom"
       headerstyle-horizontalalign="Center"
       itemstyle-horizontalalign="Center" itemstyle-verticalalign="Top"
       headerstyle-wrap="False" sortexpression="Registered">
       <itemtemplate>
<asp:checkbox id="Registered" runat="server"
 checked='<%# DataBinder.Eval(Container.DataItem,"Registered","{0}")
%>'>
</asp:checkbox>
       </itemtemplate>
      </asp:templatecolumn>
      <asp:templatecolumn headerstyle-horizontalalign="Center"
       itemstyle-horizontalalign="Center"
       itemstyle-verticalalign="Top">
       <headertemplate>
        <table cellspacing="0" cellpadding="0" width="100%"
         border="0">
         <tr>
          <td nowrap align="middle">
           Log Source
          </td>
         </tr>
         <tr>
          <td nowrap align="middle">
           Status
          </td>
         </tr>
        </table>
       </headertemplate>
       <itemtemplate>
<a
```

Listing 4.36   HTML for the Default.aspx file (continued)

```
href='<%#DataBinder.Eval(Container.DataItem,"ID","Sources.aspx?ID={0}")%
>'>
Status</a>
    </itemtemplate>
  </asp:templatecolumn>
 </columns>
</asp:datagrid>
        </td>
      </tr>
      <tr>
       <td align="right">
        <asp:button id="UpdateRegistrations" runat="server"
         text="Update Registrations"></asp:button>
       </td>
      </tr>
     </table>
    </td>
   </tr>
  </table>
 </form>
</body>
</html>
```

Listing 4.36 HTML for the Default.aspx file (continued)

Before you add the code for this file, switch to Design view so that the Visual Studio environment automatically places our server Web controls in the code-behind file. Then open the Default.aspx page in code view, and add the information shown in Listing 4.37.

 Do not modify the Web Form Designer generated code, even though it is not shown in the listing.

```
Option Strict On
Option Explicit On

Imports WebLogDataAccess

Public Class DefaultPage
 Inherits System.Web.UI.Page

 Protected WithEvents MachineNameField As _
  System.Web.UI.WebControls.TextBox
 Protected WithEvents SiteID As System.Web.UI.WebControls.Label
 Protected WithEvents SiteIndex As System.Web.UI.WebControls.Label
```

Listing 4.37 Code for Default.aspx.vb

```
Protected WithEvents Registered As System.Web.UI.WebControls.CheckBox
Protected WithEvents UpdateRegistrations As _
 System.Web.UI.WebControls.Button
Protected WithEvents AvailableSitesGrid As _
 System.Web.UI.WebControls.DataGrid
Protected WithEvents UpdateMachine As System.Web.UI.WebControls.Button
Protected WithEvents OldMachineNameField As _
 System.Web.UI.HtmlControls.HtmlInputHidden
Private objDatabase As Database

Protected Sub Page_Load(ByVal sender As System.Object, _
 ByVal e As System.EventArgs) Handles MyBase.Load

 objDatabase = New Database(Application("Connection").ToString())
 If Page.IsPostBack = False Then
  OldMachineNameField.Value = Environment.MachineName
  ReBind()
  MachineNameField.Text = OldMachineNameField.Value
 End If

End Sub

Private Sub UpdateRegistrations_Click(ByVal sender As Object, _
 ByVal e As System.EventArgs) Handles UpdateRegistrations.Click

 Dim dgiRow As DataGridItem
 Dim strSiteID As String
 Dim strSiteIndex As String
 Dim siteID As Guid
 Dim strMachineName As String
 Dim shtSiteIndex As Short
 Dim blnRegister As Boolean

 Trace.Write("UpdateRegistrations_Click", "Called")
 For Each dgiRow In AvailableSitesGrid.Items
  blnRegister = _
   CType(dgiRow.Cells(2).FindControl("Registered"), CheckBox).Checked
  strSiteID = _
   CType(dgiRow.Cells(0).FindControl("SiteID"), Label).Text.Trim()
  strSiteIndex = _
   CType(dgiRow.Cells(0).FindControl("SiteIndex"), Label).Text.Trim()
  siteID = New Guid(strSiteID)
  strMachineName = OldMachineNameField.Value
  shtSiteIndex = Short.Parse(strSiteIndex)
  If blnRegister Then
   objDatabase.RegisterSite(siteID, strMachineName, shtSiteIndex)
  Else
   objDatabase.UnregisterSite(siteID)
  End If
 Next
```

Listing 4.37   Code for Default.aspx.vb (continued)

```
   ReBind()

End Sub

Private Sub UpdateMachine_Click(ByVal sender As System.Object, _
  ByVal e As System.EventArgs) Handles UpdateMachine.Click

 Dim strOldValue As String
 strOldValue = OldMachineNameField.Value
 OldMachineNameField.Value = MachineNameField.Text
 Try
  ReBind()
  MachineNameField.ForeColor = Color.Black
 Catch
  OldMachineNameField.Value = strOldValue
  ReBind()
  MachineNameField.ForeColor = Color.Red
 End Try

End Sub

Private Sub ReBind()

 AvailableSitesGrid.DataSource = _
   objDatabase.GetAvailableSites(OldMachineNameField.Value)
 AvailableSitesGrid.DataBind()

End Sub

End Class
```

Listing 4.37   Code for Default.aspx.vb (continued)

The Sources Page

Now add a new Web form to your project named Sources.aspx. This page will be used to view the parsing status of individual log files. After you have added it to your project, open the page in HTML view, and add the code shown in Listing 4.38.

```
<%@ Page Language="vb" Trace="True" AutoEventWireup="false"
  Codebehind="Sources.aspx.vb" Inherits="Project04.Sources"%>
<!DOCTYPE HTML PUBLIC "-//W3C//DTD HTML 4.0 Transitional//EN">
<html>
 <head>
  <title></title>
```

Listing 4.38   HTML for Sources.aspx

```
   <meta name="GENERATOR" content="Microsoft Visual Studio.NET 7.0">
   <meta name="CODE_LANGUAGE" content="Visual Basic 7.0">
   <meta name="vs_defaultClientScript" content="JavaScript">
   <meta name="vs_targetSchema"
    content="http://schemas.microsoft.com/intellisense/ie5">
   <link rel="stylesheet" href="Styles.css">
 </head>
 <body ms_positioning="GridLayout">
  <form id="Sources" method="post" runat="server">
   <table cellpadding="0" cellspacing="0" border="0" width="100%"
    height="100%">
    <tr>
     <td height="100" align="middle">
      <h1>
       Web Site Log Entry Sources
      </h1>
      <h3>
       <asp:hyperlink id="ViewReports" runat="server"
        navigateurl="">View Reports</asp:hyperlink>
      </h3>
     </td>
    </tr>
    <tr>
    <tr>
     <td align="middle" valign="top">
      <asp:datagrid id="LogSourcesGrid" runat="server"
       enableviewstate="False" cellpadding="0" cellspacing="10"
       borderwidth="2px" borderstyle="Solid" bordercolor="#000080"
       backcolor="#e9e9ff" gridlines="None"
       autogeneratecolumns="False" allowpaging="True"
       pagesize="10" pagerstyle-mode="NumericPages"
       allowsorting="True" width="700">
       <columns>
        <asp:templatecolumn headertext="File Name"
         headerstyle-horizontalalign="Center"
         headerstyle-verticalalign="Bottom"
         headerstyle-wrap="False" itemstyle-wrap="False"
         itemstyle-verticalalign="Top" sortexpression="FilePath">
         <itemtemplate>
          <%# GetFileName(Container.DataItem) %>
         </itemtemplate>
        </asp:templatecolumn>
        <asp:templatecolumn headerstyle-horizontalalign="Center"
         headerstyle-verticalalign="Bottom"
         headerstyle-wrap="False" itemstyle-wrap="False"
         itemstyle-verticalalign="Top"
         itemstyle-horizontalalign="Center">
         <headertemplate>
          <table cellpadding="0" width="500" border="0">
           <tr>
```

Listing 4.38   HTML for Sources.aspx (continued)

```
                <td nowrap align="left" width="33%">
                  Status
                </td>
                <td nowrap align="middle" width="33%">
                  Parser
                </td>
                <td nowrap align="right" width="33%">
                  Lines
                </td>
              </tr>
              <tr>
                <td align="middle" colspan="3">
                  Comment
                </td>
              </tr>
            </table>
          </headertemplate>
          <itemtemplate>
            <table cellspacing="0" cellpadding="0" width="500"
              border="0">
              <tr>
                <td nowrap align="left" width="33%">
                <%# DataBinder.Eval(Container.DataItem, "Status") %>
                </td>
                <td nowrap align="middle" width="33%">
                <%# DataBinder.Eval(Container.DataItem, "Parser") %>
                </td>
                <td nowrap align="right" width="33%">
              <%# DataBinder.Eval(Container.DataItem, "LineNumber") %>
                </td>
              </tr>
              <tr bgcolor="#ffffe9">
                <td colspan="3">
                <%# DataBinder.Eval(Container.DataItem, "Comment") %>
                </td>
              </tr>
            </table>
          </itemtemplate>
        </asp:templatecolumn>
      </columns>
    </asp:datagrid>
    </td>
  </tr>
  </table>
  </form>
  </body>
</html>
```

Listing 4.38   HTML for Sources.aspx (continued)

Once this has been entered, switch to Design view so that Visual Studio can set up our Web controls in the code-behind file. Then switch to code view, and enter the code shown in Listing 4.39. Again, the Web Form Designer Generated Code is hidden and it should not be modified.

```
Option Strict On
Option Explicit On

Imports WebLogDataAccess
Imports System.IO

Public Class Sources
 Inherits System.Web.UI.Page
 Protected WithEvents ViewReports As System.Web.UI.WebControls.HyperLink
 Protected WithEvents LogSourcesGrid As _
  System.Web.UI.WebControls.DataGrid

 Private Sub Page_Load(ByVal sender As System.Object, _
  ByVal e As System.EventArgs) Handles MyBase.Load

  Dim siteID As Guid
  Dim objDatabase As Database

  objDatabase = New Database(Application("Connection").ToString())

  If Not Page.IsPostBack Then
   If Not (Request.QueryString("ID") = Nothing) Then
    Try
     siteID = New Guid(Request.QueryString("ID"))
    Catch
     Response.Redirect("default.aspx", True)
     Return
    End Try
   Else
    Response.Redirect("default.aspx", True)
   End If
  Else
   siteID = New Guid(Request.QueryString("ID"))
  End If

  ViewReports.NavigateUrl = "reports.aspx?ID=" & _
   Server.UrlEncode(siteID.ToString())
  LogSourcesGrid.DataSource = objDatabase.GetLogSources(siteID)
  LogSourcesGrid.DataBind()

 End Sub

 Private Sub LogSourcesGrid_PageIndexChanged(ByVal source As Object, _
  ByVal e As System.Web.UI.WebControls.DataGridPageChangedEventArgs) _
  Handles LogSourcesGrid.PageIndexChanged
```

Listing 4.39 Code for Sources.aspx.vb

```
 If e.NewPageIndex < LogSourcesGrid.PageCount Then
  LogSourcesGrid.CurrentPageIndex = e.NewPageIndex
 End If
 LogSourcesGrid.DataBind()

End Sub

Protected Function GetFileName(ByVal item As Object) As String

 Return Path.GetFileName(CStr( _
  CType(item, DataRowView).Row("FilePath")))

End Function

End Class
```

Listing 4.39 Code for Sources.aspx.vb (continued)

Now that we can view the list of available and registered sites on this computer (and others) and can view the current status of each log file as it is being parsed, the third and final page in our site will allow us to view the Web log analysis reports that we defined through stored procedures in the database.

Add a new Web form to your project named Reports.aspx, switch to HTML view, and enter the code shown in Listing 4.40.

```
<%@ Page Language="vb" AutoEventWireup="false"
  Codebehind="Reports.aspx.vb" Inherits="Project04.Reports"%>
<!DOCTYPE HTML PUBLIC "-//W3C//DTD HTML 4.0 Transitional//EN">
<html>
 <head>
  <title></title>
  <meta name="GENERATOR" content="Microsoft Visual Studio.NET 7.0">
  <meta name="CODE_LANGUAGE" content="Visual Basic 7.0">
  <meta name="vs_defaultClientScript" content="JavaScript">
  <meta name="vs_targetSchema"
   content="http://schemas.microsoft.com/intellisense/ie5">
  <link rel="stylesheet" href="Styles.css">
 </head>
 <body ms_positioning="GridLayout">
  <form id="Reports" method="post" runat="server">
   <asp:label id="TableNameField" runat="server"
    visible="False"></asp:label>
   <table cellpadding="0" cellspacing="0" border="0" width="100%"
    height="100%">
    <tr>
     <td height="100" align="middle">
      <h1>
```

Listing 4.40 HTML for Reports.aspx

```
   Web Log Analysis Reports
  </h1>
  <h3 id="ReportTitle" runat="server">
  </h3>
 </td>
</tr>
<tr>
 <td valign="top" style="PADDING-RIGHT: 5px;
  PADDING-LEFT: 5px;PADDING-BOTTOM: 5px;PADDING-TOP: 5px">
  <asp:panel id="ReportSelection" runat="server">
   <table cellspacing="5" cellpadding="0" align="center"
    border="0">
    <tr>
     <td colspan="4">
      <p>
       Please enter the dates for which the report should
       be run, and then select a report type from the
       list below.
      </p>
      <p>
       To run the report for all dates, leave the fields
       empty.
      </p>
     </td>
    </tr>
    <tr>
     <td nowrap>
      Start Date:
     </td>
     <td>
      <asp:textbox id="StartDateField" runat="server"
       maxlength="10"></asp:textbox>
     </td>
     <td nowrap align="right">
      End Date:
     </td>
     <td>
      <asp:textbox id="EndDateField" runat="server"
       maxlength="10"></asp:textbox>
     </td>
    </tr>
   </table>
   <table cellspacing="5" cellpadding="0" align="center"
    border="0">
    <tr>
     <td>
      <asp:button id="HitsByClient" runat="server"
       text="Hits by Client IP"
       cssclass="ReportButton"></asp:button>
     </td>
```

Listing 4.40   HTML for Reports.aspx (continued)

```
        </tr>
        <tr>
         <td>
          <asp:button id="HitsByUserAgent" runat="server"
          text="Hits by User Agent"
          cssclass="ReportButton"></asp:button>
         </td>
        </tr>
        <tr>
         <td>
          <asp:button id="RequestsForExecutables" runat="server"
          text="Requests to run executables on the server"
          cssclass="ReportButton"></asp:button>
         </td>
        </tr>
        <tr>
         <td>
          <asp:button id="PageHitsByFrequency" runat="server"
          text="Most Frequent Page Hits"
          cssclass="ReportButton"></asp:button>
         </td>
        </tr>
       </table>
      </asp:panel>
      <asp:panel id="ReportView" runat="server" visible="False">
       <table cellspacing="5" cellpadding="0" align="center"
       border="0">
        <tr>
         <td align="middle">
          <asp:button id="ReturnHomeButton" runat="server"
          text="Return to the Report Selection Page"
          cssclass="ReportButton"></asp:button>
         </td>
        </tr>
        <tr>
         <td align="middle">
          <asp:datagrid id="ReportViewGrid" runat="server"
          cellpadding="2" cellspacing="0"
          horizontalalign="Center"
          autogeneratecolumns="True"></asp:datagrid>
         </td>
        </tr>
       </table>
      </asp:panel>
     </td>
    </tr>
   </table>
  </form>
 </body>
</html>
```

Listing 4.40   HTML for Reports.aspx (continued)

As before, switch to Design view first, then open the page in code view, and add the code in Listing 4.41.

```vb
Option Strict On
Option Explicit On

Imports System.Net
Imports WebLogDataAccess
Imports System.Data.SqlClient
Imports System.Runtime.Remoting.Messaging

Public Class Reports
  Inherits System.Web.UI.Page
  Protected WithEvents StartDateField As
System.Web.UI.WebControls.TextBox
  Protected WithEvents EndDateField As System.Web.UI.WebControls.TextBox
  Protected WithEvents HitsByClient As System.Web.UI.WebControls.Button
  Protected WithEvents RequestsForExecutables As _
    System.Web.UI.WebControls.Button
  Protected WithEvents PageHitsByFrequency As _
    System.Web.UI.WebControls.Button
  Protected WithEvents HitsByUserAgent As
System.Web.UI.WebControls.Button
  Private objDatabase As Database
  Protected WithEvents TableNameField As System.Web.UI.WebControls.Label
  Private dtmStartDate As Date
  Protected WithEvents ReportSelection As System.Web.UI.WebControls.Panel
  Protected WithEvents ReportViewGrid As _
    System.Web.UI.WebControls.DataGrid
  Protected WithEvents ReportView As System.Web.UI.WebControls.Panel
  Protected WithEvents ReturnHomeButton As _
    System.Web.UI.WebControls.Button
  Private dtmEndDate As Date
  Protected WithEvents ReportTitle As _
    System.Web.UI.HtmlControls.HtmlGenericControl
  Private htcCallbacks As Hashtable

  Private Sub Page_Load(ByVal sender As System.Object, _
    ByVal e As System.EventArgs) Handles MyBase.Load

    Dim dbCommand As SqlCommand
    Server.ScriptTimeout = 300

    objDatabase = New Database(CStr(Application("Connection")))

    If Not Page.IsPostBack Then
      TableNameField.Text = objDatabase.GetSiteTable( _
        New Guid(Request.QueryString("ID")))
      dtmStartDate = Date.Parse("1/1/1753")
      dtmEndDate = Date.Parse("12/31/9999 11:59:59")
    Else
```

Listing 4.41   Code for Reports.aspx.vb

```
  Try
    dtmStartDate = Date.Parse(StartDateField.Text)
  Catch
    StartDateField.Text = String.Empty
    dtmStartDate = Date.Parse("1/1/1753")
  End Try
  Try
    dtmEndDate = Date.Parse(EndDateField.Text)
  Catch
    EndDateField.Text = String.Empty
    dtmEndDate = Date.Parse("12/31/9999 11:59:59")
  End Try
  If dtmEndDate < dtmStartDate Then
    Dim dtmSwap As Date = dtmEndDate
    dtmEndDate = dtmStartDate
    dtmStartDate = dtmSwap
  End If
 End If

End Sub

Private Sub HitsByClient_Click(ByVal sender As System.Object, _
 ByVal e As System.EventArgs) Handles HitsByClient.Click

 Dim tblReport As DataTable
 Dim tblRow As DataRow
 Dim strDomain As String
 Dim strIPAddress As String

 tblReport = objDatabase.RunReport("HitsByClient", _
  TableNameField.Text.Trim(), dtmStartDate, dtmEndDate)
 For Each tblRow In tblReport.Rows
  strIPAddress = CStr(tblRow("Client IP"))
  strDomain = Dns.Resolve(strIPAddress).HostName
  tblRow.BeginEdit()
  tblRow("Client Domain") = strDomain
  tblRow.EndEdit()
  tblRow.AcceptChanges()
 Next

 ReportTitle.InnerText = "Hits By Client from " & _
  dtmStartDate.ToShortDateString() & " to " & _
  dtmEndDate.ToShortDateString()

 ReportSelection.Visible = False
 ReportView.Visible = True

 ReportViewGrid.DataSource = tblReport
 ReportViewGrid.DataBind()
```

Listing 4.41   Code for Reports.aspx.vb (continued)

```
   End Sub

   Private Sub HitsByUserAgent_Click(ByVal sender As System.Object, _
    ByVal e As System.EventArgs) Handles HitsByUserAgent.Click

    Dim tblReport As DataTable

    tblReport = objDatabase.RunReport("HitsByUserAgent", _
     TableNameField.Text.Trim(), dtmStartDate, dtmEndDate)

    ReportTitle.InnerText = "Hits By User Agent from " & _
     dtmStartDate.ToShortDateString() & " to " & _
     dtmEndDate.ToShortDateString()

    ReportSelection.Visible = False
    ReportView.Visible = True

    ReportViewGrid.DataSource = tblReport
    ReportViewGrid.DataBind()

   End Sub

   Private Sub ReturnHomeButton_Click(ByVal sender As Object, _
    ByVal e As System.EventArgs) Handles ReturnHomeButton.Click

    ReportSelection.Visible = True
    ReportView.Visible = False

   End Sub

   Private Sub RequestsForExecutables_Click(ByVal sender As Object, _
    ByVal e As System.EventArgs) Handles RequestsForExecutables.Click

    Dim tblReport As DataTable

    tblReport = objDatabase.RunReport("RequestsForExecutables", _
     TableNameField.Text.Trim(), dtmStartDate, dtmEndDate)

    ReportTitle.InnerText = "Requests for Executables from " & _
     dtmStartDate.ToShortDateString() & " to " & _
     dtmEndDate.ToShortDateString()

    ReportSelection.Visible = False
    ReportView.Visible = True

    ReportViewGrid.DataSource = tblReport
    ReportViewGrid.DataBind()

   End Sub
```

Listing 4.41   Code for Reports.aspx.vb (continued)

```
Private Sub PageHitsByFrequency_Click(ByVal sender As Object, _
  ByVal e As System.EventArgs) Handles PageHitsByFrequency.Click

Dim tblReport As DataTable

tblReport = objDatabase.RunReport("PageHitsByFrequency", _
  TableNameField.Text.Trim(), dtmStartDate, dtmEndDate)

ReportTitle.InnerText = "Most Frequently Requested Pages from " & _
  dtmStartDate.ToShortDateString() & " to " & _
  dtmEndDate.ToShortDateString()

ReportSelection.Visible = False
ReportView.Visible = True

ReportViewGrid.DataSource = tblReport
ReportViewGrid.DataBind()

End Sub

End Class
```

Listing 4.41   Code for Reports.aspx.vb (continued)

Congratulations! You are now ready to build your project, start the Web log collector, and analyze log files. There are a couple of things I would like to call to your attention in this last code listing. Notice that the first thing we do when the page loads is set the ScriptTimeout server setting to 300 seconds (5 minutes). This is necessary because the queries that are involved in presenting these reports must sometimes read through millions of individual log entries, and even on a fast server with plenty of memory, this can often take a while.

The second item I'd like to call to your attention is the HitsByClient report. The query itself only deals with information found in the log entries (namely, the client IP address), but most people aren't used to navigating through IP addresses and would like a name to associate it with. In this case, we're using the Dns class in the System.Net namespace to do a reverse-name lookup for the given IP addresses so we can display the domain name along with the IP address to the user.

Wrap Up

In this project, you built a generic, remotable log parser component that you can easily extend and reuse in your own projects; a multithreaded Windows Service application, which can be used either to collect log files from multiple computers into a database, or can be used on multiple computers to collect logs from a single, high-traffic server;

a database component to encapsulate communication with a database; and an ASP.NET application, which ties these together into a single, coherent application.

In addition, we've used several technologies that are not traditionally in the domain of ASP programmers, such as multithreading, directory services, I/O, and serialization.

In Project 5, you'll be building an application to consolidate and track errors that are detected in ASP.NET applications. This application will give you an easy way to track, report, and solve these problems.

Building the ASP.NET Error Manager

No matter how much we would like to think otherwise, even the most proficient writers among us write code that contains bugs. For most computer users, the perceived quality of any application is determined by a number of important factors, including (but not limited to):

- Personal usefulness

- Appearance and navigability

- Availability

- The ability to gracefully handle and quickly recover from errors

In this project, you will learn how to make your ASP.NET applications more robust and available by implementing an error manager that traps and records unexpected errors in your applications and presents you and your users with options for resolution.

In fact, this project is not really an application per se, but rather is a collection of techniques and an add-on that you can use to make your own sites more robust.

THE PROBLEM

Errors occur on various Web sites that you manage, but unless you read all the files, you don't know about them to fix them.

THE SOLUTION

Build an ASP.NET application to manage errors fed to it by other applications to make it easier to find and solve problems.

Project Background

If you have been using ASP.NET for any length of time, you are already familiar with pages similar to the one shown in Figure 5.1. Some would say it is too familiar. To us programmers, this is often useful information as long as we can access the source and correct the problem. To users, however, it would most certainly brand your application as one containing bugs. Fortunately, ASP.NET gives us the ability to present something more user-friendly.

To build this application, you will need to install the SMTP mail server component bundled with IIS, or you can comment out the sections in the following code that use the SmtpMail.NET class.

The steps we will be completing in this project are:

1. Set up the development environment.

2. Create and install a custom event log to hold the recorded exceptions. You will be using this rather than a database.

3. Create the ErrorManager directory, and include a page so you can view the event data from your custom log.

4. Create the Error directory, and develop your custom error pages in it.

5. Modify the Web.config file using the <location> attribute to secure the Error-Manager directory, and redirect common errors to the custom error pages.

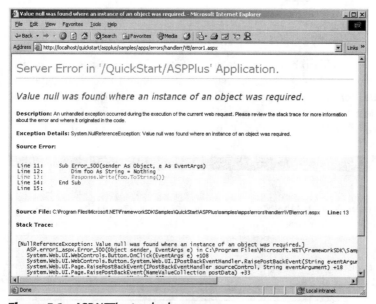

Figure 5.1   ASP.NET's standard error page.

6. Modify the Global.asax file to trap unhandled errors in the application, notify site administrators, and write the error information to your custom event log.

7. Develop a page containing bugs with which to test your work.

You Will Need

✔ **Windows 2000**

✔ **Internet Information Server 5.0 with .NET Framework installed**

✔ **Visual Studio .NET**

✔ **SQL Server 2000 or 7.0**

✔ **Ability to send SMTP e-mail messages from your server or another server**

Setting Up the Development Environment

First, you need to create a new Web application in IIS to contain your project. Follow these steps to create the new application:

1. Create a new directory on your computer for your Project 5 files. Keep track of this folder, as you will need to navigate to it using the command-line later in this project to install your event log.

2. Start Internet Service Manager.

3. Right-click the Default Web Site, and select New —> Virtual Directory.

4. Click the next button on the introductory screen, name your new Web Project05, and click Next.

5. The next step of the wizard (shown in Figure 5.2) is where you specify the physical directory you created in step 1. Type or browse to the directory, and then click the Next button.

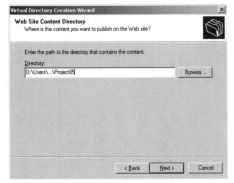

Figure 5.2   Physical directory entry screen.

Figure 5.3   Virtual Directory properties dialog box.

6. On the next screen, verify that the Read and Run Scripts permissions are selected, and then click the Next button.

7. On the final screen, click Finish to have your new virtual directory and application created.

8. Locate your new virtual directory in the left-hand tree pane of Internet Service Manager, right-click it, and choose Properties from the menu. The dialog box shown in Figure 5.3 appears.

9. If the application was not created automatically, click Create to have IIS create a new application for your virtual directory. You can tell if the application was created by looking at the name of the application. If it is grayed out, no application was created for you.

10. Click OK to exit the properties dialog box, and close Internet Service Manager.

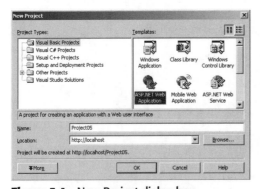

Figure 5.4   New Project dialog box.

Figure 5.5   Solution Explorer window.

Open the Visual Studio .NET development environment, and choose File —> New —> Project to display the New Project dialog box, shown in Figure 5.4. You can now set up the initial ASP.NET Web Application configuration in your virtual directory by following the next few steps:

1. First, delete the default WebForm1.aspx page that was automatically generated, as we won't be using it in this project.

2. Your Solution Explorer window should now appear as it does in Figure 5.5.

```vb
Imports System.Reflection
Imports System.Runtime.InteropServices


' General Information about an assembly is controlled through the
' following set of attributes. Change these attribute values to
' modify the information associated with an assembly.


' Review the values of the assembly attributes

<Assembly: AssemblyTitle("ASP.NET At Work - Error Manager Application")>
<Assembly: AssemblyDescription("This assembly contains utility " _
    & "classes for use with Eric Smith's book, ASP.NET " _
    & "at Work: 10 Projects You Can Build with ASP.NET.")>
<Assembly: AssemblyCompany("Northstar Computer Systems")>
<Assembly: AssemblyProduct("ASP.NET At Work")>
<Assembly: AssemblyCopyright("Copyright 2001 by Northstar " _
    & "Computer Systems. All Rights Reserved.")>
<Assembly: AssemblyTrademark("Copyright 2001 by Northstar " _
    & "Computer Systems. All Rights Reserved.")>
<Assembly: CLSCompliant(True)>
```

Listing 5.1   Code for AssemblyInfo.vb

```
'The following GUID is for the ID of the typelib if this project is
'exposed to COM
<Assembly: Guid("3A1F4647-0E2C-46A2-944D-359DCEA58FF0")>

' Version information for an assembly
' consists of the following four values:
'
'    Major Version
'    Minor Version
'    Build Number
'    Revision
'
' You can specify all the values or you can default the Build
' and Revision Numbers by using the '*' as shown below:

<Assembly: AssemblyVersion("5.0.*")>
```

Listing 5.1   Code for AssemblyInfo.vb (continued)

3. Open the AssemblyInfo.vb file, and enter the assembly-level attributes as you have done in previous projects. The assembly title for this project is ASP.NET At Work - Error Manager. The complete listing for my AssemblyInfo.vb file appears as shown in Listing 5.1.

4. Since we will be creating a new event log resource in our application, we will need an installer for it. Most installers are found in the System.Configuration.Install assembly, so you will need to reference that assembly in your application. Right-click Project05 in Solution Explorer, and select Add Reference.

5. Locate the System.Configuration.Install.dll assembly in the .NET tab, and click Select to add the reference, as shown in Figure 5.6.

You are now ready to begin development. First, we need to create an Error directory and ErrorManager directory to hold your custom error pages and the ErrorManager Event Viewer page, respectively, which you will develop later. Right-click Project05 in the Solution Explorer, and select Add —> New Folder. Name it either Error or Error-Manager, and repeat the process for the other folder.

The first thing we will add to the application is an event log component and its installer, so that you can quickly create your custom event source for logging errors. Double-click the Global.asax file in Solution Explorer. A blank designer surface is displayed in which you can add components.

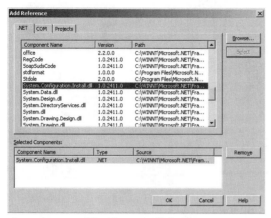

Figure 5.6   Add Reference dialog box.

The Toolbox is located on the left-hand side of the Visual Studio .NET environment as a slide-out window with a hammer-and-wrench icon. Open your Toolbox, and several sliding buttons are displayed. Click the Components button. A window opens, as shown in Figure 5.7.

Double-click the EventLog component to add an instance to the Global.asax designer surface. If it is not enclosed in a box on the designer surface, click it. You should now see the initial configuration shown in Figure 5.8 in your properties window.

Figure 5.7   Toolbox window.

Figure 5.8   EventLog component initial properties.

Now modify these properties so that they appear like the ones shown in Figure 5.9.

You might have noticed in Figures 5.8 and 5.9 an Add Installer link at the bottom of the properties window. This link is automatically added by some application components whenever a component requires installation before it can be used (rather than XCOPY deployment). Click the link now to have Visual Studio .NET add the appropriate installer for you, then change the EventLogInstaller component properties to the ones shown in Figure 5.10.

Figure 5.9   EventLog component properties.

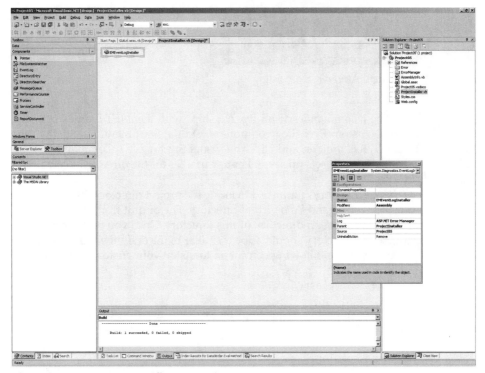

Figure 5.10 EventLogInstaller properties.

Now save the solution using the Save All button on the toolbar, and build the project. The next step is to install the new EventLog component and verify it using the Windows NT Event Viewer.

Installing the Event Log Component

One of the great things about .NET is the ability for components that create or use custom resources to store their own installation information. For example, if you were to examine the ProjectInstaller.vb file that was added to your project when you selected Add Installer, you would notice an attribute called RunInstaller on the class. This allows Windows Installer 2.0 and custom utilities like the Installutil.exe command-line application we're about to use to recognize that a particular class requires a special setup. When these utilities are invoked, they examine the classes contained within an assembly, look for the RunInstaller attribute, and automatically run the installation contained within those classes. This allows just about any program you design to store all of the setup information needed to successfully install it and the resources it uses on a user's system, such as databases, performance counters, event logs, and so on.

Figure 5.11   Project05\bin directory listing.

You will be using a command-line utility that ships with the .NET Framework SDK to install your new custom EventLog component. On the Start menu, navigate to the Visual Studio .NET Tools folder, and click the Visual Studio .NET Command Prompt link. This command prompt sets up several path variables for the directories containing the various utilities.

Use the cd (change directory) command to locate the project directory that you set up to contain your project files and Web virtual directory. The output from your last build should be located in the *bin* sub-directory of this directory. Once you have done this, a directory listing in that directory should appear similar to the one shown in Figure 5.11.

In that directory, type the following command to install your custom event log.

```
installutil.exe -i Project05.dll
```

After you have installed the event log, the last two lines on the command-line should read:

```
The Commit phase completed successfully.
```

```
The transacted install has completed.
```

Double-check this through the Event Viewer. On the command-line, type the following command and press the Enter key to start the Event Viewer.

```
eventvwr.msc
```

You should now see an Event Viewer console window containing your new error manager event log, shown in Figure 5.12.

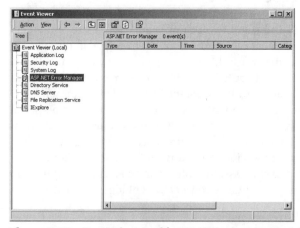

Figure 5.12   Event Viewer with ASP.NET error manager log.

The event log is now installed and ready to receive events. Close the Event Viewer for now, and let's work on the ErrorManager default page.

Building the ErrorManager Default Page

Right-click the ErrorManager directory you created earlier, and select Add —> Add Web Form. In the resulting dialog box, name it DefaultPage.aspx, and click Open.

Creating pages named Default.aspx is a bit tricky in Visual Basic (VB), since Default is a reserved keyword and Visual Studio .NET will name the class in the code-behind with the same name as the page, minus the extension. In this case, it's even more complicated, because before you're finished with this project, you will have two pages named Default.aspx in your site, which would normally also cause naming ambiguities in the assembly. Initially, we create the default page with the name DefaultPage.aspx so that it will give that name (DefaultPage) to our code-behind class. Now, rename the page in Solution Explorer to Default.aspx, and open the page in both HTML view and code view.

On the tabs in Visual Studio .NET's source windows, the filenames for both the code-behind file and the ASPX page are now Default.aspx.vb and Default.aspx, respectively, but the class that is referred to and defined in the code-behind file is still DefaultPage.

Switch to the HTML view, and take a look at the first line, the @ Page directive. At the end of that line, notice that the page currently inherits from the following:

```
Inherits="Project05.DefaultPage"
```

Modify it so that it reads as follows, and then switch to code view.

```
Inherits="Project05.ErrorManager.DefaultPage"
```

In code view, add the following two uncommented lines—the first before the class definition, and the second after it.

```
Namespace ErrorManager
' Class definition follows...
'...
' Class definition above...
End Namespace
```

By defining this DefaultPage class in a separate namespace, we avoid the naming ambiguities that would otherwise occur later when we add a DefaultPage to the main Web.

Now switch back to HTML view, and type the complete listing shown in Listing 5.2.

```
<%@ Page Language="vb" AutoEventWireup="false"
   Codebehind="Default.aspx.vb"
   Inherits="Project05.ErrorManager.DefaultPage" %>
<!DOCTYPE HTML PUBLIC "-//W3C//DTD HTML 4.0 Transitional//EN">
<html>
```

Listing 5.2   HTML for ErrorManager/Default.aspx

```
<head>
 <title>ASP.NET Error Manager</title>
 <meta name="GENERATOR" content="Microsoft Visual Studio.NET 7.0">
 <meta name="CODE_LANGUAGE" content="Visual Basic 7.0">
 <meta name="vs_defaultClientScript" content="JavaScript">
 <meta name="vs_targetSchema"
  content="http://schemas.microsoft.com/intellisense/ie5">
 <link rel="stylesheet" href="../Styles.css">
</head>
<body ms_positioning="FlowLayout">
 <form id="Default" method="post" runat="server">
  <table cellpadding="0" cellspacing="0" border="0" width="100%">
   <tr>
    <td align="middle">
     <h1>
      ASP.NET Error Manager
     </h1>
    </td>
   </tr>
   <tr>
    <td align="middle">
     <h4>
      <asp:label id="EMStatus" runat="server">The ASP.NET Error
      Manager is currently NOT installed.</asp:label>
     </h4>
    </td>
   </tr>
   <tr>
    <td align="middle">
     <asp:button id="EMClear" runat="server"
     text="Clear the current log" visible="False"></asp:button>
    </td>
   </tr>
   <tr id="EMEvents" runat="server">
    <td>
     <asp:datalist id="EMDataList" runat="server"
     enableviewstate="False" backcolor="#e9e9ff"
     itemstyle-backcolor="#e9e9ff"
     alternatingitemstyle-backcolor="#f9f9ff"
     bordercolor="#000080" borderstyle="Solid" borderwidth="2px"
     cellpadding="2" cellspacing="0" horizontalalign="Center">
     <itemtemplate>
      <table cellspacing="0" cellpadding="0" width="100%"
       border="0">
       <tr>
        <td nowrap align="left">
        <%# DataBinder.Eval(Container.DataItem, "EntryType") %>
        </td>
        <td nowrap align="left">
         <%# DataBinder.Eval(Container.DataItem, "Source") %>
```

Listing 5.2   HTML for ErrorManager/Default.aspx (continued)

```
                  </td>
                  <td nowrap align="right">
                <%# DataBinder.Eval(Container.DataItem, "TimeGenerated", _
                       "{0:MM-dd-yyyy HH:mm:ss}") %>
                  </td>
                </tr>
                <tr>
                  <td colspan="3">
                   <%# GetHtmlMessage(Container.DataItem) %>
                  </td>
                </tr>
              </table>
            </itemtemplate>
            <separatortemplate>
             <hr width="100%" noshade size="1">
            </separatortemplate>
          </asp:datalist>
        </td>
      </tr>
    </table>
  </form>
 </body>
</html>
```

Listing 5.2   HTML for ErrorManager/Default.aspx (continued)

This page sets up an ASP:DataList Web server control to display the entries contained in the event log, if the event log is installed.

Next, switch to the code-behind file, and type the complete listing shown in Listing 5.3 (do not modify the Web Forms Designer generated code section, however).

```
Option Strict On
Option Explicit On


Imports System.Diagnostics


Namespace ErrorManager
 Public Class DefaultPage
  Inherits System.Web.UI.Page
  Protected WithEvents EMDataList As System.Web.UI.WebControls.DataList
  Protected WithEvents EMClear As System.Web.UI.WebControls.Button
  Protected WithEvents EMEvents As _
   System.Web.UI.HtmlControls.HtmlTableRow
  Protected WithEvents EMStatus As System.Web.UI.WebControls.Label
  Private blnInstalled As Boolean = HasErrorManager()


  Private Sub Page_Load(ByVal sender As System.Object, _
```

Listing 5.3   Code for ErrorManager/Default.aspx.vb

```
    ByVal e As System.EventArgs) Handles MyBase.Load

    Dim evtEM As EventLog

    '
    ' If the custom event log is not installed, do
    ' not show the data list or the "Clear" button.
    '
    If blnInstalled = False Then
      EMStatus.Text = "The ASP.NET Error Manager is currently " & _
       "NOT installed."
      EMEvents.Visible = False
      EMClear.Visible = False
      Return
    End If


    '
    ' Otherwise, show both and bind the data list
    ' to the event log entries collection.
    '
    EMStatus.Text = "The ASP.NET Error Manager is currently installed."
    EMEvents.Visible = True
    EMClear.Visible = True

    evtEM = New EventLog("ASP.NET Error Manager")

    EMDataList.DataSource = evtEM.Entries
    EMDataList.DataBind()

    evtEM.Dispose()

  End Sub

  '
  ' This method is used as a check to
  ' see if the custom event log exists.
  '
  Friend Function HasErrorManager() As Boolean
    Return EventLog.Exists("ASP.Net Error Manager")
  End Function


  '
  ' This method converts NewLines in the event log
  ' entry message into <br> tags so they will look
  ' at least somewhat formatted.
  '
  Protected Function GetHtmlMessage(ByVal item As Object) As String
    Dim entry As EventLogEntry
    If TypeOf item Is EventLogEntry Then
      entry = CType(item, EventLogEntry)
```

Listing 5.3   Code for ErrorManager/Default.aspx.vb (continued)

```
        Return entry.Message.Replace(Environment.NewLine, "<br>")
      End If
    End Function


    '
    ' This method is used to clear
    ' the event log of all entries.
    '
    Private Sub EMClear_Click(ByVal sender As Object, _
      ByVal e As System.EventArgs) Handles EMClear.Click

      Dim evtEM As EventLog

      evtEM = New EventLog("ASP.NET Error Manager")
      evtEM.Clear()

      EMDataList.DataSource = evtEM.Entries
      EMDataList.DataBind()

      evtEM.Dispose()

    End Sub

  End Class
End Namespace
```

Listing 5.3   Code for ErrorManager/Default.aspx.vb (continued)

That's all there is to it. You now have all the necessary code to view and clear your custom event log. When the page loads, the first thing it does is check to see if the event log exists. If not, it will make both the button used to clear the log and the data list that is used to display it invisible (thus removing it from the HTML output).

After that initial check, it binds the data list to the EventLog Entries property, which contains the collection of individual entries, and then releases any unmanaged resources that may be held by the evtEM event log component.

Of course, you could make this as fancy as you want by adding the Error, Warning, and Information graphics, and sorting, filtering, and paging to the data list, but I'll leave that to your capable hands.

The next step is to add a plain text file to this directory that can hold our email template. Right-click the ErrorManager directory, and select Add —> Add New Item. Then select the text file template, name it ErrorEMail.txt, and click OK.

Type the following text in the file, and save it. This will be the default email that is sent to an administrator when a site failure occurs.

```
<html>
<head>
<title>An Error Occurred On Your Site</title>
```

```
<style>
body {
 font-family: Verdana;
 font-size: 10pt;
}
table {
 font-family: Verdana;
 font-size: 10pt;
}
</style>
</head>
<body>
<p>A visitor encountered an error while browsing your site. The visitor
was successfully redirected to a custom error page and did not see the
details of the error.</p>

<p>The error details are as follows:</p>

<blockquote>%CUSTOM_INSERT%</blockquote>

<p>Please correct the cause of this error as soon as possible.</p>

<p><font size="2">THIS MESSAGE WAS SENT BY AN AUTOMATED SYSTEM. DO
 NOT REPLY.</font></p>
</body>
</html>
```

Next, we'll tackle the custom error pages in HTTP status code order . . .

Building the Error/Denied Page

This is the page that visitors will see when they attempt to access a protected resource with incorrect authorization. Select the Error folder in Solution Explorer, right-click it, and select Add —> New Web Form. Name the page Denied.aspx, and then click Open.

Switch to HTML view for the Denied.aspx page, and type the code as it is shown in Listing 5.4.

```
<%@ Page Language="vb" AutoEventWireup="false"
  Codebehind="Denied.aspx.vb"
  Inherits="Project05.Error.Denied" %>
<!DOCTYPE HTML PUBLIC "-//W3C//DTD HTML 4.0 Transitional//EN">
<html>
 <head>
  <title>Access to the requested page was denied...</title>
  <meta name="GENERATOR" content="Microsoft Visual Studio.NET 7.0">
  <meta name="CODE_LANGUAGE" content="Visual Basic 7.0">
  <meta name="vs_defaultClientScript" content="JavaScript">
  <meta name="vs_targetSchema"
```

Listing 5.4   HTML for Error/Denied.aspx

```
      content="http://schemas.microsoft.com/intellisense/ie5">
  <link rel="stylesheet" href="../Styles.css">
</head>
<body ms_positioning="FlowLayout">
  <form id="Denied" method="post" runat="server">
    <table cellpadding="0" cellspacing="0" border="0" width="100%"
      height="100%">
    <tr>
      <td valign="top" align="middle" height="42">
        <h1>
          Access to the requested page was denied
        </h1>
      </td>
    </tr>
    <tr>
      <td valign="top">
        <p>
          Some parts of this site are secured and are therefore not
          available to the general public. If you have received this
          message in error, our site administrators have already been
          notified and will correct the problem as soon as possible.
        </p>
        <p>
          <asp:label id="ContactUs" runat="server"
            font-size="1.3em">Please feel free to contact our customer
            service department regarding this issue at
            <nobr>1-800-555-5555</nobr>, or use the form below to send
            us an <nobr>e-mail</nobr> message.</asp:label>
        </p>
      </td>
    </tr>
    <tr>
      <td valign="top" align="middle">
        <table cellpadding="0" cellspacing="5" border="0"
          id="EMailForm" runat="server">
        <tr>
          <td colspan="3">
            <asp:validationsummary id="Summary" runat="server"
            displaymode="BulletList"
            headertext="Please correct the following and try again:"
            showsummary="True"></asp:validationsummary>
          </td>
        </tr>
        <tr>
          <td>
            E-Mail Address:
          </td>
          <td>
            <asp:textbox id="EMailFrom" runat="server"
              maxlength="255" width="3in"></asp:textbox>
```

Listing 5.4 HTML for Error/Denied.aspx (continued)

```
    </td>
    <td>
     <asp:requiredfieldvalidator id="EMailFromRequired"
     runat="server" controltovalidate="EMailFrom"
     errormessage="Your e-mail address is required for reply"
     display="Static">*</asp:requiredfieldvalidator>
    </td>
   </tr>
   <tr>
    <td>
     Subject:
    </td>
    <td>
     <asp:textbox readonly="True" id="EMailSubject"
     runat="server" maxlength="255"
     width="3in"></asp:textbox>
    </td>
    <td rowspan="3">
      
    </td>
   </tr>
   <tr>
    <td valign="top">
     Message:
    </td>
    <td valign="top">
     <asp:textbox id="EMailMessage" runat="server"
     rows="10" textmode="MultiLine"
     width="3in"></asp:textbox>
    </td>
   </tr>
   <tr>
    <td colspan="2" align="right">
     <asp:button id="SendButton" runat="server"
     text="Send Now"></asp:button>
    </td>
   </tr>
  </table>
  <table cellpadding="0" cellspacing="0" border="0"
  align="center" id="SuccessNotice" runat="server">
   <tr>
    <td>
     Your message was sent successfully. In 10 seconds,
     you will be redirected to the public home page.
     If the redirect does not work, please use the link
     at the bottom of this page.
    </td>
   </tr>
  </table>
 </td>
```

Listing 5.4   HTML for Error/Denied.aspx (continued)

```
     </tr>
     <tr>
      <td valign="bottom" align="middle">
       <a href="/default.aspx">Return to the public home page</a>
      </td>
     </tr>
    </table>
   </form>
  </body>
</html>
```

Listing 5.4   HTML for Error/Denied.aspx (continued)

This page explains to users that parts of the site are secure and that an administrator has been notified of the access attempt, and gives the visitor an opportunity to contact customer service regarding this event.

The code-behind for this page is shown in Listing 5.5.

```
Option Strict On
Option Explicit On

Imports System.Web.Mail

Namespace [Error]
Public Class Denied
 Inherits System.Web.UI.Page
 Protected WithEvents Summary As _
   System.Web.UI.WebControls.ValidationSummary
 Protected WithEvents EMailFrom As System.Web.UI.WebControls.TextBox
 Protected WithEvents EMailFromRequired As _
   System.Web.UI.WebControls.RequiredFieldValidator
 Protected WithEvents EMailSubject As System.Web.UI.WebControls.TextBox
 Protected WithEvents EMailMessage As System.Web.UI.WebControls.TextBox
 Protected WithEvents ContactUs As System.Web.UI.WebControls.Label
 Protected WithEvents EMailForm As System.Web.UI.HtmlControls.HtmlTable
 Protected WithEvents SuccessNotice As _
   System.Web.UI.HtmlControls.HtmlTable
 Protected WithEvents SendButton As System.Web.UI.WebControls.Button

 Private Sub Page_Load(ByVal sender As System.Object, _
  ByVal e As System.EventArgs) Handles MyBase.Load

  Dim strTo As String

  SuccessNotice.Visible = False

  `
```

Listing 5.5   Code for Error/Denied.aspx.vb

```
' If we're not set up to send e-mail, don't offer it.
'
strTo = CStr(Application("CustomerServiceEMail"))
If strTo = Nothing Then
 ContactUs.Text = "Please feel free to contact our " & _
  "customer service department regarding this issue at " & _
  "<nobr>1-800-555-5555</nobr>."
 EMailForm.Visible = False
 Return
End If

EMailSubject.Text = "Access Denied to Page """ & _
 Request.QueryString("aspxerrorpath") & """"

If Not Page.IsPostBack Then
 '
 ' Pre-validate so the asterisk shows up.
 '
 EMailFromRequired.Validate()
 Summary.Visible = False
Else
 If Not Page.IsValid Then
  Summary.Visible = True
  Return
 End If
End If

End Sub


'
' This sends the e-mail and then notifies the visitor and redirects
' them to the default page.
'
Private Sub SendButton_Click(ByVal sender As Object, _
 ByVal e As System.EventArgs) Handles SendButton.Click

 Dim strTo As String
 Dim emlMsg As MailMessage
 Dim emlSender As SmtpMail

 strTo = CStr(Application("CustomerServiceEMail"))
 If Not strTo = Nothing Then

  emlMsg = New MailMessage()
  emlMsg.To = CStr(Application("CustomerServiceEMail"))
  emlMsg.From = EMailFrom.Text.Trim()
  emlMsg.Subject = EMailSubject.Text
  emlMsg.BodyFormat = MailFormat.Text
  emlMsg.Body = EMailMessage.Text
```

Listing 5.5 Code for Error/Denied.aspx.vb (continued)

```
   Try
    emlSender = New SmtpMail()
    Try
     emlSender.Send(emlMsg)
     '
     ' If the mail was sent successfully, redirect
     ' back to the home page after 10 seconds.
     '
     Response.AppendHeader("Refresh", _
      "10;URL=/Project05/Default.aspx")
     EMailForm.Visible = False
     SuccessNotice.Visible = True
    Catch
    End Try
   Finally
    emlSender = Nothing
   End Try

  End If

 End Sub
End Class
End Namespace
```

Listing 5.5 Code for Error/Denied.aspx.vb (continued)

This code sets up the visual details of the page based upon the server configuration's current capabilities and then responds when the Send Now button is clicked.

 NOTE **The square brackets around the namespace name Error are required because Error is a reserved keyword. You can use keywords as parameters, properties, method names, and so on as long as they are qualified in this way.**

Building the Error/NotFound Page

This page is almost identical to the Denied page, with some minor changes in the wording in the page. Within the Error directory, add another Web Forms page named NotFound.aspx, and in HTML view, type the code shown in Listing 5.6.

```
<%@ Page Language="vb" AutoEventWireup="false"
  Codebehind="NotFound.aspx.vb"
  Inherits="Project05.Error.NotFound" %>
```

Listing 5.6 HTML for Error/NotFound.aspx

```
<!DOCTYPE HTML PUBLIC "-//W3C//DTD HTML 4.0 Transitional//EN">
<html>
 <head>
  <title>The page you were looking for was not found...</title>
  <meta name="GENERATOR" content="Microsoft Visual Studio.NET 7.0">
  <meta name="CODE_LANGUAGE" content="Visual Basic 7.0">
  <meta name="vs_defaultClientScript" content="JavaScript">
  <meta name="vs_targetSchema"
   content="http://schemas.microsoft.com/intellisense/ie5">
  <link rel="stylesheet" href="../Styles.css">
 </head>
 <body ms_positioning="FlowLayout">
  <form id="NotFound" method="post" runat="server">
   <table cellpadding="0" cellspacing="0" border="0" width="100%"
   height="100%">
   <tr>
    <td valign="top" align="middle" height="42">
     <h1>
      The page you were looking for was not found
     </h1>
    </td>
   </tr>
   <tr>
    <td valign="top">
     <p>
      Like any popular Internet property, this site is always
      under construction. Sometimes when we make these changes
      our customers temporarily find some broken links in our
      site.  Our site administrators are now aware that
      the page you were looking for is not available and may
      implement an automatic redirect to the correct page.
     </p>
     <p>
      <asp:label id="ContactUs" runat="server"
      font-size="1.3em">Let us help you find what you were
      looking for by using the form below to send us an e-mail.
      Alternatively, you may contact our customer service
      department at <nobr>1-800-555-5555</nobr>.</asp:label>
     </p>
    </td>
   </tr>
   <tr>
    <td valign="top" align="middle">
     <table cellpadding="0" cellspacing="5" border="0"
      id="EMailForm" runat="server">
      <tr>
       <td colspan="3">
       <asp:validationsummary id="Summary" runat="server"
       displaymode="BulletList"
       headertext="Please correct the following and try again:"
```

Listing 5.6   HTML for Error/NotFound.aspx (continued)

```
    showsummary="True"></asp:validationsummary>
   </td>
 </tr>
 <tr>
  <td>
   E-Mail Address:
  </td>
  <td>
   <asp:textbox id="EMailFrom" runat="server"
    maxlength="255" width="3in"></asp:textbox>
  </td>
  <td>
   <asp:requiredfieldvalidator id="EMailFromRequired"
   runat="server" controltovalidate="EMailFrom"
   errormessage="Your e-mail address is required for reply"
   display="Static">*</asp:requiredfieldvalidator>
  </td>
 </tr>
 <tr>
  <td>
   Subject:
  </td>
  <td>
   <asp:textbox readonly="True" id="EMailSubject"
   runat="server" maxlength="255"
   width="3in"></asp:textbox>
  </td>
  <td rowspan="3">
    
  </td>
 </tr>
 <tr>
  <td valign="top">
   Message:
  </td>
  <td valign="top">
   <asp:textbox id="EMailMessage" runat="server"
   rows="10" textmode="MultiLine"
   width="3in"></asp:textbox>
  </td>
 </tr>
 <tr>
  <td colspan="2" align="right">
   <asp:button id="SendButton" runat="server"
   text="Send Now"></asp:button>
  </td>
 </tr>
</table>
<table cellpadding="0" cellspacing="0" border="0"
 align="center" id="SuccessNotice" runat="server">
```

Listing 5.6   HTML for Error/NotFound.aspx (continued)

```
      <tr>
       <td>
        Your message was sent successfully. In 10 seconds,
        you will be redirected to the public home page. If
        the redirect does not work, please use the link at the
        bottom of this page.
       </td>
      </tr>
     </table>
    </td>
   </tr>
   <tr>
    <td valign="bottom" align="middle">
     <a href="/default.aspx">Return to the public home page</a>
    </td>
   </tr>
  </table>
 </form>
 </body>
</html>
```

Listing 5.6   HTML for Error/NotFound.aspx (continued)

The complete listing for the associated code-behind file is shown in Listing 5.7.

```
Option Strict On
Option Explicit On

Imports System.Web.Mail

Namespace [Error]
Public Class NotFound
 Inherits System.Web.UI.Page
 Protected WithEvents ContactUs As System.Web.UI.WebControls.Label
 Protected WithEvents Summary As _
  System.Web.UI.WebControls.ValidationSummary
 Protected WithEvents EMailFrom As System.Web.UI.WebControls.TextBox
 Protected WithEvents EMailFromRequired As _
  System.Web.UI.WebControls.RequiredFieldValidator
 Protected WithEvents EMailSubject As System.Web.UI.WebControls.TextBox
 Protected WithEvents EMailMessage As System.Web.UI.WebControls.TextBox
 Protected WithEvents EMailForm As System.Web.UI.HtmlControls.HtmlTable
 Protected WithEvents SuccessNotice As _
  System.Web.UI.HtmlControls.HtmlTable
 Protected WithEvents SendButton As System.Web.UI.WebControls.Button

 Private Sub Page_Load(ByVal sender As System.Object, _
  ByVal e As System.EventArgs) Handles MyBase.Load
```

Listing 5.7   Code for Error/NotFound.aspx.vb

```vb
    Dim strTo As String

    SuccessNotice.Visible = False

    '
    ' If we're not set up to send e-mail, don't offer it.
    '
    strTo = CStr(Application("CustomerServiceEMail"))
    If strTo = Nothing Then
     ContactUs.Text = "Our customer service department can be " & _
       "contacted at <nobr>1-800-555-5555</nobr> and would be " & _
       "happy to help you find what you were looking for."
     EMailForm.Visible = False
     Return
    End If

    EMailSubject.Text = "File Not Found Looking For """ & _
      Request.QueryString("aspxerrorpath") & """"

    If Not Page.IsPostBack Then
      '
      ' Pre-validate so the asterisk shows up.
      '
      EMailFromRequired.Validate()
      Summary.Visible = False
    Else
      If Not Page.IsValid Then
       Summary.Visible = True
       Return
      End If
    End If

End Sub

'
' This sends the e-mail and then notifies the visitor and redirects
' them to the default page.
'
Private Sub SendButton_Click(ByVal sender As Object, _
 ByVal e As System.EventArgs) Handles SendButton.Click

  Dim strTo As String
  Dim emlMsg As MailMessage
  Dim emlSender As SmtpMail

  strTo = CStr(Application("CustomerServiceEMail"))
  If Not strTo = Nothing Then

    emlMsg = New MailMessage()
    emlMsg.To = CStr(Application("CustomerServiceEMail"))
    emlMsg.From = EMailFrom.Text.Trim()
```

Listing 5.7   Code for Error/NotFound.aspx.vb (continued)

```
    emlMsg.Subject = EMailSubject.Text
    emlMsg.BodyFormat = MailFormat.Text
    emlMsg.Body = EMailMessage.Text

  Try
   emlSender = New SmtpMail()
   Try
    emlSender.Send(emlMsg)
    '
    ' If the mail was sent successfully, redirect
    ' back to the home page after 10 seconds.
    '
    Response.AppendHeader("Refresh", _
     "10;URL=/Project05/Default.aspx")
    EMailForm.Visible = False
    SuccessNotice.Visible = True
   Catch
   End Try
  Finally
   emlSender = Nothing
  End Try

  End If

  End Sub

End Class
End Namespace
```

Listing 5.7   Code for Error/NotFound.aspx.vb (continued)

Building the Error/Problem Page

Users will see this page if an untrapped error occurs within any page on the site. This
is similar to the other error pages, again with some changes in wording. Select the
Error directory, and add a new Web Forms page named Problem.aspx. Switch to
HTML view, and type the code as shown in Listing 5.8.

```
<%@ Page Language="vb" AutoEventWireup="false"
  Codebehind="Problem.aspx.vb" Inherits="Project05.Error.Problem" %>
<!DOCTYPE HTML PUBLIC "-//W3C//DTD HTML 4.0 Transitional//EN">
<html>
 <head>
```

Listing 5.8   HTML for Error/Problem.aspx

```
   <title>We are experiencing a problem with our site...</title>
   <meta name="GENERATOR" content="Microsoft Visual Studio.NET 7.0">
   <meta name="CODE_LANGUAGE" content="Visual Basic 7.0">
   <meta name="vs_defaultClientScript" content="JavaScript">
   <meta name="vs_targetSchema"
    content="http://schemas.microsoft.com/intellisense/ie5">
   <link rel="stylesheet" href="../Styles.css">
  </head>
  <body ms_positioning="FlowLayout">
   <form id="Problem" method="post" runat="server">
    <table cellpadding="0" cellspacing="0" border="0" width="100%"
     height="100%">
     <tr>
      <td valign="top" align="middle" height="42">
       <h1>
        We're sorry, but...
       </h1>
       <h3>
        we seem to be having a problem with our site.
       </h3>
      </td>
     </tr>
     <tr>
      <td valign="top">
       <p>
        <asp:label id="ContactUs" runat="server"
        font-size="1.3em">If this problem persists, please contact
        our customer service department at
        <nobr>1-800-555-5555</nobr> or use the form below to
        e-mail our customer service and information technology
        help desks. Please note that the error has been recorded,
        and a site administrator has been dispatched to correct
        it.</asp:label>
       </p>
      </td>
     </tr>
     <tr>
      <td valign="top" align="middle">
       <table cellpadding="0" cellspacing="5" border="0"
        id="EMailForm" runat="server">
        <tr>
         <td colspan="3">
          <asp:validationsummary id="Summary" runat="server"
          displaymode="BulletList"
          headertext="Please correct the following and try again:"
          showsummary="True"></asp:validationsummary>
         </td>
        </tr>
```

Listing 5.8   HTML for Error/Problem.aspx (continued)

```
   <tr>
    <td>
     E-Mail Address:
    </td>
    <td>
     <asp:textbox id="EMailFrom" runat="server"
     maxlength="255" width="3in"></asp:textbox>
    </td>
    <td>
     <asp:requiredfieldvalidator id="EMailFromRequired"
     runat="server" controltovalidate="EMailFrom"
     errormessage="Your e-mail address is required for reply"
     display="Static">*</asp:requiredfieldvalidator>
    </td>
   </tr>
   <tr>
    <td>
     Subject:
    </td>
    <td>
     <asp:textbox readonly="True" id="EMailSubject"
     runat="server" maxlength="255"
     width="3in"></asp:textbox>
    </td>
    <td rowspan="3">
      
    </td>
   </tr>
   <tr>
    <td valign="top">
     Message:
    </td>
    <td valign="top">
     <asp:textbox id="EMailMessage" runat="server"
     rows="10" textmode="MultiLine"
     width="3in"></asp:textbox>
    </td>
   </tr>
   <tr>
    <td colspan="2" align="right">
     <asp:button id="SendButton" runat="server"
     text="Send Now"></asp:button>
    </td>
   </tr>
 </table>
<table cellpadding="0" cellspacing="0" border="0"
 align="center" id="SuccessNotice" runat="server">
  <tr>
   <td>
```

Listing 5.8 HTML for Error/Problem.aspx (continued)

```
          Your message was sent successfully. In 10 seconds, you
          will be redirected to the public home page. If the
          redirect does not work, please use the link at the
          bottom of this page.
        </td>
      </tr>
    </table>
    </td>
  </tr>
  <tr>
  <td valign="bottom" align="middle">
  <a href="/default.aspx">Return to the public home page</a>
  </td>
  </tr>
  </table>
  </form>
 </body>
</html>
```

Listing 5.8   HTML for Error/Problem.aspx (continued)

The code-behind for this page is shown in Listing 5.9 (except for the Web Forms Designer Generated Code, which should not be modified).

```
Option Strict On
Option Explicit On

Imports System.Web.Mail

Namespace [Error]

 Public Class Problem
  Inherits System.Web.UI.Page

  Protected WithEvents ContactUs As System.Web.UI.WebControls.Label
  Protected WithEvents Summary As _
   System.Web.UI.WebControls.ValidationSummary
  Protected WithEvents EMailFrom As System.Web.UI.WebControls.TextBox
  Protected WithEvents EMailFromRequired As _
   System.Web.UI.WebControls.RequiredFieldValidator
  Protected WithEvents EMailSubject As System.Web.UI.WebControls.TextBox
  Protected WithEvents EMailMessage As System.Web.UI.WebControls.TextBox
  Protected WithEvents SendButton As System.Web.UI.WebControls.Button
  Protected WithEvents EMailForm As System.Web.UI.HtmlControls.HtmlTable
  Protected WithEvents SuccessNotice As _
   System.Web.UI.HtmlControls.HtmlTable


  Private Sub Page_Load(ByVal sender As System.Object, _
   ByVal e As System.EventArgs) Handles MyBase.Load
```

Listing 5.9   Code for Error/Problem.aspx.vb

```
Dim strTo As String

SuccessNotice.Visible = False

'
' If we're not set up to send e-mail, don't offer it.
'
strTo = CStr(Application("CustomerServiceEMail"))
If strTo = Nothing Then
 ContactUs.Text = "If this problem persists, please contact " & _
  "our customer service department at " & _
  "<nobr>1-800-555-5555</nobr>."
 EMailForm.Visible = False
 Return
End If

EMailSubject.Text = "Internal Server Error In """ & _
 Request.QueryString("aspxerrorpath") & """"

If Not Page.IsPostBack Then
 '
 ' Pre-validate so the asterisk shows up.
 '
 EMailFromRequired.Validate()
 Summary.Visible = False
Else
 If Not Page.IsValid Then
  Summary.Visible = True
  Return
 End If
End If

End Sub

'
' This sends the e-mail and then notifies the visitor and redirects
' them to the default page.
'
Private Sub SendButton_Click(ByVal sender As Object, _
 ByVal e As System.EventArgs) Handles SendButton.Click

 Dim strTo As String
 Dim emlMsg As MailMessage
 Dim emlSender As SmtpMail

 strTo = CStr(Application("CustomerServiceEMail"))
 If Not strTo = Nothing Then

  emlMsg = New MailMessage()
  emlMsg.To = CStr(Application("CustomerServiceEMail"))
```

Listing 5.9   Code for Error/Problem.aspx.vb (continued)

```
      emlMsg.From = EMailFrom.Text.Trim()
      emlMsg.Subject = EMailSubject.Text
      emlMsg.BodyFormat = MailFormat.Text
      emlMsg.Body = EMailMessage.Text

    Try
      emlSender = New SmtpMail()
      Try
        emlSender.Send(emlMsg)
        '
        ' If the mail was sent successfully, redirect
        ' back to the home page after 10 seconds.
        '
        Response.AppendHeader("Refresh", _
          "10;URL=/Project05/Default.aspx")
        EMailForm.Visible = False
        SuccessNotice.Visible = True
      Catch
      End Try
    Finally
      emlSender = Nothing
    End Try

    End If

  End Sub

End Class

End Namespace
```

Listing 5.9   Code for Error/Problem.aspx.vb (continued)

Now that you're finished with the subdirectories, let's go ahead and secure the ErrorManager directory and then add error handling to the Global.asax code.

Setting the Configuration

Open the Web.config file in the Source Code window, and locate the customErrors tag. This tag should read as follows:

```
<customErrors mode="RemoteOnly" />
```

This means that visitors from any computer other than "localhost" will see a stripped-down error page, while you will see the source code where the error occurred, the stack trace, and so on.

In order to test our custom error pages, change the line shown previously to read as follows:

```
<customErrors mode="On" defaultRedirect="/Project05/Error/Problem.aspx">
 <error statusCode="403" redirect="/Project05/Error/Denied.aspx" />
 <error statusCode="404" redirect="/Project05/Error/NotFound.aspx" />
 <error statusCode="500" redirect="/Project05/Error/Problem.aspx" />
</customErrors>
```

That's all there is to implementing custom error pages. The error pages can be ASP, aspx, htm, and so on, and can be branded to appear consistent with the rest of your site.

Now let's secure the ErrorManager directory so that only administrators can access the Event Log. Then you'll add your custom application-specific settings to the configuration file. Move to the bottom of this file, and between the </system.web> and </configuration> tags add the following code, replacing the values "email.address@domain.com" with your own email address.

```
</system.web> <!-- This is already here, don't add -->
<location path="ErrorManager">
 <system.web>
  <authorization>
   <allow roles="BUILTIN\Administrators" />
   <deny users="*" />
  </authorization>
 </system.web>
</location>
<!-- Custom application-specific settings
    for the ASP.NET Error Manager -->
<appSettings>
 <add key="AdministratorEMail" value="email.address@domain.com" />
 <add key="CustomerServiceEMail" value="email.address@domain.com" />
 <add key="ErrorManagerEventLog" value="ASP.NET Error Manager" />
</appSettings>
</configuration> <!-- This is already here, don't add -->
```

By inserting this location tag, you can override the default configuration for specific subdirectories. It is available for use in the ASP.NET configuration files as well as in the rest of the .NET runtime, including Windows Forms applications and the like. By making this change, we are overriding the default authorization configuration to specify that members of the BUILTIN\Administrators groups are permitted to access that directory, while everyone else is denied.

Now, save the Web.config file, and open the Global.asax file in code view.

Adding Global Error Handling at the Application Level

The Global.asax file is the second line of defense against errors, but it is also the last place where the exception that caused the error is available. The first line of defense is in the page itself, and the last is in the pages specified in the <customErrors> section of the configuration file.

With the Global.asax file open in code view, modify it so that it contains the code shown in Listing 5.10 (leaving the Component Designer Generated Code section alone).

```vb
Option Strict On
Option Explicit On

Imports System.Web
Imports System.Web.Mail
Imports System.Web.SessionState
Imports System.Text
Imports System.Diagnostics
Imports System.Configuration
Imports System.IO

Public Class Global
  Inherits System.Web.HttpApplication

#Region " Component Designer Generated Code "

  Public Sub New()
    MyBase.New()

    'This call is required by the Component Designer.
    InitializeComponent()

    'Add any initialization after the InitializeComponent() call

  End Sub
 Friend WithEvents EMEventLog As System.Diagnostics.EventLog

 'Required by the Component Designer
 Private components As System.ComponentModel.Container

 'NOTE: The following procedure is required by the Component Designer
 'It can be modified using the Component Designer.
 'Do not modify it using the code editor.
 <System.Diagnostics.DebuggerStepThrough()> Private Sub
InitializeComponent()
  Me.EMEventLog = New System.Diagnostics.EventLog()
  CType(Me.EMEventLog,
System.ComponentModel.ISupportInitialize).BeginInit()
  '
  'EMEventLog
  '
  Me.EMEventLog.Log = "ASP.NET Error Manager"
  Me.EMEventLog.Source = "Project05"
  CType(Me.EMEventLog,
System.ComponentModel.ISupportInitialize).EndInit()
```

Listing 5.10   Code for Global.asax.vb

```
  End Sub

#End Region

'
' This routine is called only once during the life of the application.
' Here is where we want to initialize the Application variables that
' we want to remain in memory throughout the life of the application.
'
Sub Application_Start(ByVal sender As Object, ByVal e As EventArgs)

  Dim strPath As String
  Dim strErrorEMail As String
  Dim frdReader As StreamReader


  '
  ' Here, we read in our text file and use it as a template for the
  ' error e-mails that we will generate. Notice that the path to the
  ' file is in the ErrorManager directory. This allows us to put
  ' semi-sensitive (the ErrorManager URL, in this case) information
  ' in the file without worrying that it can be downloaded directly
  ' by a casual user.
  '
  ' Some tips for extending this application would be to make the
  ' file an XML template with a stylesheet to construct the HTML,
  ' as well as storing a FileSystemWatcher object in the Application
  ' to pick up changes to the file and re-read it.
  '
  strPath = Server.MapPath("/Project05/ErrorManager/ErrorEMail.txt")


  '
  ' First, make sure the file exists.
  '
  If File.Exists(strPath) Then


    '
    ' In the next few lines, we open, read, and close the file.
    ' If an error occurs, we ignore it, since it is really not
    ' that important to have the template.
    '
    Try
     frdReader = File.OpenText(strPath)
     Try
      strErrorEMail = frdReader.ReadToEnd()
     Finally
      frdReader.Close()
     End Try
    Catch
    End Try
```

Listing 5.10   Code for Global.asax.vb (continued)

```vb
  If strErrorEMail = Nothing Then

    '
    ' This will execute if an error occurred while reading the
    ' file. The only important that we're looking for when we
    ' send the e-mail is the string %CUSTOM_INSERT%, which is
    ' what we will replace with the actual error information.
    '
    strErrorEMail = "%CUSTOM_INSERT%"
  End If
  Application("ErrorEMail") = strErrorEMail

End If

'
' This is a constant value. It should never change and should not be
' configurable. Basically, it identifies this particular application
' from others that may be writing their events to the same Event Log.
'
Application("ErrorManagerLogSource") = "Project05"

End Sub

'
' Implementing this routine allows us to pick up any changes to the
' configuration as soon as the user makes them. This prevents us
' from having to restart the application whenever a configuration
' change takes place.
'
Sub Application_BeginRequest(ByVal sender As Object, _
ByVal e As System.EventArgs) Handles MyBase.BeginRequest

  ' Fires at the beginning of each request

  Dim cfg As ConfigurationSettings

  '
  ' These are the custom settings recognized by our application.
  '
  cfg = New ConfigurationSettings()
  Application.Lock()
  Application("AdministratorEMail") = _
    cfg.AppSettings("AdministratorEMail")
  Application("CustomerServiceEMail") = _
    cfg.AppSettings("CustomerServiceEMail")
  Application("SmtpHost") = cfg.AppSettings("SmtpHost")
  Application("ErrorManagerEventLog") = _
    cfg.AppSettings("ErrorManagerEventLog")
  Application.UnLock()

End Sub
```

Listing 5.10   Code for Global.asax.vb (continued)

```
'
' This is the second line of defense against unhandled errors. This
' is called when the page itself cannot adequately recover from an
' error in order to continue processing.
'
Sub Application_Error(ByVal sender As Object, ByVal e As EventArgs)

  ' Fires when an error occurs.

  Dim exc As Exception
  Dim sbError As StringBuilder
  Dim evtEM As EventLog
  Dim strLog As String
  Dim strSource As String
  Dim strKey As String
  Dim strEMail As String
  Dim emlMsg As MailMessage
  Dim strMsg As String
  Dim objSmtp As SmtpMail


  '
  ' Get the error that occurred.
  '
  exc = Server.GetLastError
  If Not exc Is Nothing Then

    sbError = New StringBuilder(4096)


    '
    ' Build a string containing the list of exceptions
    ' that occurred and information about each. We're
    ' using a StringBuilder because it performs better
    ' at concatenation than String, since concatenation
    ' on normal strings always involve a copy operation.
    '
    Do Until exc Is Nothing
      sbError.AppendFormat("Exception Type: {0}{1}", _
        exc.GetType().Name, Environment.NewLine)
      sbError.AppendFormat("Message: {0}{1}", _
        exc.Message, Environment.NewLine)
      sbError.AppendFormat("Source: {0}{1}", _
        exc.Message, Environment.NewLine)
      sbError.AppendFormat("Target: {0}{1}", _
        exc.TargetSite, Environment.NewLine)
      sbError.AppendFormat("Stack Trace: {0}{1}{1}", _
        exc.StackTrace, Environment.NewLine)
      exc = exc.InnerException
    Loop

    '
```

Listing 5.10   Code for Global.asax.vb (continued)

```
' If either no log was specified, or no source was specified,
' don't attempt to write to the event log.
'
strLog = CStr(Application("ErrorManagerEventLog"))
If Not (strLog = Nothing) Then

  '
  ' Make sure the specified Event Log exists on the system.
  '
  If EventLog.Exists(strLog) Then

    evtEM = New EventLog(strLog)

    Try

      strSource = CStr(Application("ErrorManagerLogSource"))

      If Not (strSource = Nothing) Then

        '
        ' If a log source was specified and the log exists, but
        ' the source doesn't, then create it on the fly.
        '
        If Not evtEM.SourceExists(strSource) Then

          evtEM.CreateEventSource(CStr(Application( _
          "ErrorManagerLogSource")), strLog)

        End If

        '
        ' Write the error information to the event log.
        '
        evtEM.Source = strSource
        evtEM.WriteEntry(sbError.ToString(), _
        EventLogEntryType.Error)

      End If

    Finally

      evtEM.Dispose()

    End Try

  End If

End If

'
```

Listing 5.10 Code for Global.asax.vb (continued)

```vb
      ' If you do not have the Smtp component of IIS installed on
      ' your server, comment out the following If...Then block.
      '
      ' This sends an e-mail to the administrator for the site,
      ' specified in the web.config file and using the IIS SMTP
      ' service.
      '
      strEMail = CStr(Application("AdministratorEMail"))
      '
      ' First, make sure we have an address to send to. We'll
      ' assume that if the address is not empty or null, it's
      ' an e-mail address. You could actually do a Regular
      ' Expression match to make sure.
      '
      If Not strEMail = Nothing Then
        If strEMail <> "" Then

          strMsg = CStr(Application("ErrorEMail"))

          '
          ' Flesh out the message properties.
          '
          emlMsg = New MailMessage()
          With emlMsg
            .To = strEMail
            .From = "webserver@mydomain.com"
            .Subject = "A visitor encountered an error on your site."
            .Priority = MailPriority.High
            .BodyFormat = MailFormat.Html
            .Body = strMsg.Replace("%CUSTOM_INSERT%", sbError.ToString())
          End With

          '
          ' ...and finally, send the message.
          '
          objSmtp = New SmtpMail()
          Try
            objSmtp.Send(emlMsg)
          Catch
          End Try
          objSmtp = Nothing

        End If
      End If

    End If

    '
    ' At this point, the visitor will be redirected to our custom error
    ' page.
```

Listing 5.10   Code for Global.asax.vb (continued)

```
    `

    End Sub

    End Class
```

Listing 5.10   Code for Global.asax.vb (continued)

Here, you are loading a template email file upon application startup and setting the
source value that will be used with this particular application (other ASP.NET applications may specify that sources be placed in the ASP.NET Error Manager event log).

On each request, you are loading the application-specific configuration settings.
This is a quick operation, since ASP.NET caches the configuration file and only reloads
it when it changes.

Finally, we are trapping any unhandled errors that may occur in our application and
tracing the exception chain and stack to be written to the event log. In addition, we're
notifying the site administrator that an error has occurred so that he or she can take
appropriate action.

Building the Page with Bugs and Testing It

Now you can have fun building a page with bugs, broken links, and so on in order to
test the integrity of the error-handling backbone. Feel free to design your own, but I
made the following by creating a new DefaultPage.aspx page at the root of the project
directory and renaming it Default.aspx. The complete code listing is shown for the
HTML view and the code-behind (except for the generated code) in Listing 5.11.

```
<%@ Page Language="vb" AutoEventWireup="false"
  Codebehind="Default.aspx.vb" Inherits="Project05.DefaultPage"%>
<!DOCTYPE HTML PUBLIC "-//W3C//DTD HTML 4.0 Transitional//EN">
<html>
 <head>
  <title></title>
  <meta name="GENERATOR" content="Microsoft Visual Studio.NET 7.0">
  <meta name="CODE_LANGUAGE" content="Visual Basic 7.0">
  <meta name="vs_defaultClientScript" content="JavaScript">
  <meta name="vs_targetSchema"
   content="http://schemas.microsoft.com/intellisense/ie5">
  <link rel="stylesheet" href="Styles.css">
 </head>
 <body ms_positioning="GridLayout">
  <form id="Default" method="post" runat="server">
```

Listing 5.11   Code for Default.aspx.vb

```
    <h1>
     Error Handling Test Page
    </h1>
    <p>
     Hi, I'm a buggy application. :)
    </p>
    <p>
     <a href="SomewhereOverTheRainbow.aspx">Here's a link to
      something you're really interested in.</a>
    </p>
    <p>
     <asp:label id="MyLabel" runat="server">To crash, or not
      to crash, that is the question.</asp:label>
    </p>
    <p>
     <a href="ErrorManager/Somepage.aspx">Would you like to
      see something strange and mystical?</a>
    </p>
    <p>
     <asp:button id="MyButton" runat="server"
      text="Orange Crash"></asp:button>
    </p>
   </form>
  </body>
</html>
```

Listing 5.11 HTML for Default.aspx.

```
Option Strict On
Option Explicit On

Public Class DefaultPage
 Inherits System.Web.UI.Page
 Protected WithEvents MyLabel As System.Web.UI.WebControls.Label
 Protected WithEvents MyButton As System.Web.UI.WebControls.Button

 Private Sub Page_Load(ByVal sender As System.Object, _
  ByVal e As System.EventArgs) Handles MyBase.Load
   'Put user code to initialize the page here
 End Sub

 Private Sub MyButton_Click(ByVal sender As Object, _
  ByVal e As System.EventArgs) Handles MyButton.Click

  Dim bytA As Byte
  Dim bytR As Byte
  Dim bytG As Byte
  Dim bytB As Byte
  bytA = MyLabel.ForeColor.A
  bytR = MyLabel.ForeColor.R
```

Listing 5.11   Code for Default.aspx.vb (continued)

```
    bytG = MyLabel.ForeColor.G
    bytB = MyLabel.ForeColor.B
    bytA = 0
    bytR = bytR + CByte(96) ' One of these is likely to cause an
    bytG = (bytG + CByte(64)) Mod CByte(240) ' overflow at some
    bytB = bytB + CByte(32) ' point.
    MyLabel.ForeColor = Color.FromArgb(bytA, bytR, bytG, bytB)


  End Sub


End Class
```

Listing 5.11   Code for Default.aspx.vb (continued)

Wrap Up

In this project, you built a comprehensive error handler for your site, created and manipulated an event log, and used the <location> configuration attribute to configure a specific subdirectory while inheriting most of the parent directory's settings. In addition, you used data binding in the ErrorManager/Default page to bind to nontraditional data sources, such as collections, and used the SmtpMail system class to send emails from the Web.

In Project 6, you'll be building an online store, complete with user interfaces for both the customer and the administrator.

Building the Online Store Application

In this project, you will be building an online store. E-commerce continues to be a big money-maker on the Internet, and being able to build an e-commerce site without the cost and learning curve associated with an application such as Commerce Server is a valuable commodity.

THE PROBLEM

You need to create an online store for your company's products, and you do not have much time to get it rolled out. You also need to provide the managers with a virtual back door to site information, such as customer orders, product sales, and product sale statistics.

THE SOLUTION

Using Visual Studio .NET, ASP.NET and the Northwind Traders database, you can quickly get the online store up and running.

Project Background

Today, there are millions of examples of different types of e-commerce applications on the Internet. You have most likely purchased a book from Amazon.com or purchased office supplies from OfficeDepot.com. In this online store application, you will be duplicating the base functionality of a site similar to Amazon or Office Depot.

From a consumer standpoint, every e-commerce site on the Internet has the following features:

- View products and product details
- Add products to a shopping cart
- View shopping cart details
- Perform a checkout process
- Enter shipping and billing information
- View an invoice

From an administrative standpoint, some useful features could include:

- View product sales history
- View customer order history
- View demographic sales data

Figure 6.1 is an example of the complete user interface for the online store created in the project.

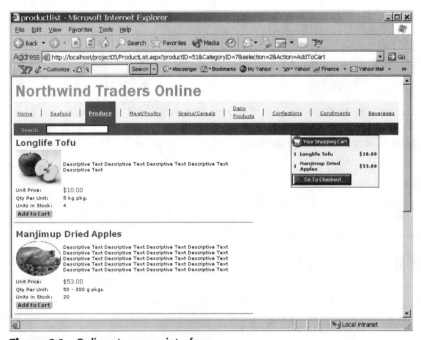

Figure 6.1   Online store user interface.

The project is broken down into several steps that will allow you to complete it rapidly, and give you the opportunity to expand on the design once you are completed. The following list explains how you will attack the creation of the online store:

1. Modify the sample database to include new tables specific to the store.

2. Create Insert, Select and Update stored procedures for common tasks.

3. Create Views in SQL Server to access the data.

4. Create the classes in your project that can be considered the data access layer and the business logic layer.

5. Create ASP.NET user controls that make up the functionality and user interface for the store, using the classes created.

6. Create the ASP.NET and add the user controls to them, to complete the user interface.

By encapsulating the data access into stored procedures, it will be very easy to implement SQL Server security once the project is complete. There is no ad-hoc queries in the classes or code-behind in the project.

Since the sky is the limit on both the user interface and the administrative areas, I will include some suggestions on how you could further enhance the site from both a consumer and administrative standpoint as we are creating it. If you have ever used an e-commerce site on the Web, you will already have a good idea of what you like and don't like; this site will be designed for easy customization.

 ## You Will Need

✔ **Windows 2000**

✔ **Internet Information Server 5.0 with .NET Framework installed**

✔ **Visual Studio .NET**

✔ **SQL Server 7.0 or 2000**

✔ **Northwind Traders sample database from SQL Server**

Setting Up the Development Environment

This project will be built using just the Visual Studio .NET environment and Visual Basic .NET as the language. Because this project is not dependent on anything you have done in previous projects, you do not need to worry about using any of those files.

Follow these steps to create your project file and Web site in IIS.

1. Start Visual Studio .NET.

2. From the Start page, click the New Project button.

3. Select ASP.NET from the list of templates.

4. Type project06 in the Name box.

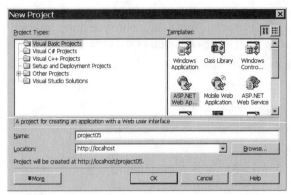

Figure 6.2 New Project dialog box.

5. Set the Location field to the location of your IIS computer, which could be your local computer. If it is, leave the default localhost option selected.

6. Click the OK button.

Figure 6.2 is an example of what your New Project dialog box should look like.

Setting Up the Database

This project will use the Northwind Traders database in SQL Server as a starting point for formatting tables and data. Since the Northwind Traders application that ships with Microsoft Access is actually a desktop version of an e-commerce application, the structure of the database is perfectly suited for our needs in the online store. We will not use all of the tables, and some of the tables that we borrow will need to be slightly modified.

Figure 6.3 is a diagram of the database you will be using.

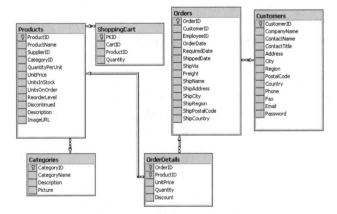

Figure 6.3 Online store database diagram.

Table 6.1 The ShoppingCart Table

FIELD NAME	DATA TYPE	LENGTH	NULLS	DESCRIPTION
PKID	Int	4	No	Primary Key, Identity column
CartID	VarChar	50	No	Shopping cart ID, based on GUID created in the application
ProductID	Int	4	No	Foreign key to the Products table. When the user adds an item to the shopping cart, the product ID is stored here.
Quantity	Int	4	No	You will write code to keep track of the number of unique products that are added to the cart.

All of the tables exist in the Northwind Traders database with the exception of the ShoppingCart table. The ShoppingCart table will be a temporary storage area for the users' data as they add items to their shopping cart. Once the shopping cart information is turned into an actual order, the data will be removed from the shopping cart. Table 6.1 describes the ShoppingCart table.

The Products table will need to be modified to allow for a URL field for the product image and a description of the product. Table 6.2 lists the two fields you will need to add to the end of the Products table.

Table 6.2 Additional Fields Added to the Products Table

FIELD NAME	DATA TYPE	LENGTH	NULLS	DESCRIPTION
Description	Varchar	500	No	Description of the product. This is the main marketing information that the user will see about the product.
ImageURL	Varchar	150	No	The URL of the image to be displayed for the product.

There are other fields, but we will not be using them in this project. When the project is completed, you can determine if you want to remove those fields from the database or add functionality to the application that takes advantage of those fields.

Writing the Views and Stored Procedures

Because you expect many users to be using the online store, all of the data access will be accomplished through stored procedures and views in SQL Server. There will be no methods that directly access any of the base tables. If you are not familiar with SQL Server security, then this may not make sense. In SQL Server, each table would need Insert, Update, Select, and Delete permissions in order to give the user access to the data. This over complicates security. If you create stored procedures that access the base tables, you can just set the Execute permission on the stored procedures, and leave the base tables inaccessible from the outside world. You should always set up your data access in this way, since it is the only way to guarantee that users do not have access to your base table data.

The vw_Cart_Products view is responsible for displaying the product information, quantity, and price in the small shopping cart and big shopping cart user controls, as shown in Listing 6.1. This view also returns the total amount due for the number of products for which you have orders. The total will be displayed in the small cart user control that we'll create later in this project.

```
CREATE VIEW dbo.vw_Cart_Products AS
SELECT
dbo.ShoppingCart.Quantity,
dbo.ShoppingCart.CartID, dbo.ShoppingCart.ProductID,
dbo.Products.ProductName, dbo.Products.UnitPrice,
dbo.Products.Description, dbo.ShoppingCart.Quantity *
dbo.Products.UnitPrice AS TotalDue,
dbo.Products.QuantityPerUnit
FROM
   dbo.ShoppingCart INNER JOIN
   dbo.Products ON dbo.ShoppingCart.ProductID =
   dbo.Products.ProductID
```

Listing 6.1 vw_Cart_Products view

The vw_Categories_Products view is responsible for displaying the product information, quantity, and price in the small shopping cart and big shopping cart user controls, as shown in Listing 6.2.

```
CREATE VIEW dbo.vw_Categories_Products AS
SELECT TOP 100 PERCENT dbo.Categories.CategoryID,
dbo.Categories.CategoryName, dbo.Products.ProductName,
dbo.Products.UnitPrice, dbo.Products.QuantityPerUnit,
dbo.Products.UnitsInStock, dbo.Products.ProductID,
dbo.Products.Discontinued, dbo.Products.Description,
dbo.Products.ImageURL, dbo.Products.UnitsOnOrder,
dbo.Products.ReorderLevel
FROM
  dbo.Categories INNER JOIN
  dbo.Products ON dbo.Categories.CategoryID =
  dbo.Products.CategoryID
WHERE    (dbo.Products.Discontinued <> 1)
ORDER BY dbo.Categories.CategoryName,
dbo.Products.ProductName
```

Listing 6.2   vw_Categories_Products view

The sp_Update_Customer stored procedure takes the customer data and updates the information in the customers table, as shown in Listing 6.3.

```
CREATE PROCEDURE sp_Update_Customer
  (@CustomerID        nvarchar(50), @CompanyName nvarchar(40),
  @ContactName nvarchar(30), @ContactTitle nvarchar(30),
  @Address nvarchar(60), @City nvarchar(15),
  @Region nvarchar(15), @PostalCode nvarchar(10),
  @Country nvarchar(15), @Phone nvarchar(24),
  @Fax nvarchar(24), @Email nvarchar(50),
  @Password nvarchar(50))
AS UPDATE Customers
SET
  CompanyName = @CompanyName,
  ContactName = @ContactName, ContactTitle = @ContactTitle,
  Address = @Address, City = @City, Region = @Region,
  PostalCode = @PostalCode, Country = @Country,
  Phone = @Phone, Fax = @Fax, Email = @Email,
  [Password] = @Password
WHERE
  CustomerID = @CustomerID
```

Listing 6.3   sp_Update_Customer stored procedure

The sp_Add_To_Cart stored procedure takes the GUID created in the application and inserts a row in the ShoppingCart table based on the product the user has selected, as shown in Listing 6.4.

```
CREATE PROCEDURE sp_Add_To_Cart
  @CartID varchar(50), @ProductID int, @Quantity int
AS
Insert into ShoppingCart(CartID, ProductID, Quantity)
 Values(@CartID, @ProductID, @Quantity)
```

Listing 6.4 sp_Add_To_Cart stored procedure

The sp_Authenticate stored procedure takes the username and password that the user enters and returns the CustomerID to the calling procedure, as shown in Listing 6.5.

```
CREATE PROCEDURE sp_Authenticate
  @Username nvarchar(50), @Password nvarchar(50),
  @CustomerID nvarchar(50) OUTPUT
AS
  Select @CustomerID = CustomerID
  from Customers
  Where Email = @Username and Password = @password
```

Listing 6.5 sp_Authenticate stored procedure

The sp_Delete_Cart_Item stored procedure deletes a row or rows from the ShoppingCart table based on the CartID and the ProductID passed to the procedure, as shown in Listing 6.6.

```
CREATE PROCEDURE sp_Delete_Cart_Item
  @CartID varchar(50), @ProductID int
As
  Delete from ShoppingCart
  Where CartID = @CartID AND ProductID = @ProductID
```

Listing 6.6 sp_Delete_Cart_Item stored procedure

The sp_Get_Cart stored procedure returns all the rows in the vw_Cart_Products view based on the CartID passed to the procedure, as shown in Listing 6.7.

```
CREATE PROCEDURE sp_Get_Cart
  @cartID varchar(50)
AS
  Select * from vw_Cart_Products
  Where CartID = @cartID
  return @@rowcount
```

Listing 6.7 sp_Get_Cart stored procedure

The sp_Get_Cart_Item_Count returns the number of unique products in the shopping cart. The ItemCount output will be incremented in values of 1 and used as the value to either update the Quantity field in the ShoppingCart table or insert a new row if the count returns zero, as shown in Listing 6.8.

```
CREATE PROCEDURE sp_Get_Cart_Item_Count
  @CartID varchar(50),
  @ProductID int,
  @ItemCount int OUTPUT
AS
  Select @ItemCount = Quantity
  From ShoppingCart
  Where ProductID = @ProductID and CartID = @CartID
```

Listing 6.8   sp_Get_Cart_Item_Count stored procedure

The sp_Get_Cart_Total returns the sum value of the products in the user's shopping cart, as shown in Listing 6.9.

```
CREATE Procedure sp_Get_Cart_Total
  @CartID varchar(50),
  @CartSum money OUTPUT
AS
  SELECT @CartSum = SUM(UnitPrice * Quantity)
  FROM vw_Cart_Products
  WHERE CartID = @CartID
```

Listing 6.9   sp_Get_Cart_Total stored procedure

The sp_Get_Categories stored procedure returns the categories and displays them in the main menu for the Web site, as shown in Listing 6.10.

```
CREATE PROCEDURE sp_Get_Categories
AS
  Select CategoryID, CategoryName, Description
  From Categories
  Order By CategoryID DESC
```

Listing 6.10   sp_Get_Categories stored procedure

The sp_Get_Customer stored procedure returns the customer details based on the CustomerID passed to the procedure, as shown in Listing 6.11.

```
CREATE PROCEDURE sp_Get_Customer
  @CustomerID varchar(50) AS
  Select * from Customers
  Where CustomerID = @CustomerID
```

Listing 6.11   sp_Get_Customer stored procedure

The sp_Get_Product_Details stored procedure returns the product details from the vw_Categories_Products view based on the ProductID passed to the procedure, as shown in Listing 6.12.

```
CREATE PROCEDURE sp_Get_Product_Details
  @productID int
AS
Select * from vw_Categories_Products
Where productID = @productID
return @@rowcount
```

Listing 6.12   sp_Get_Product_Details stored procedure

The sp_Get_Products_By_Category stored procedure returns the list of products based on the CategoryID passed to the stored procedure. The data returned is used in the ProductList.ascx user control to list the available products, as shown in Listing 6.13.

```
CREATE PROCEDURE sp_Get_Products_By_Category
  @categoryID int
AS
  Select * from vw_Categories_Products
  Where CategoryID = @categoryID
  return @@rowcount
```

Listing 6.13   sp_Get_Products_By_Category stored procedure

The sp_Insert_Customer stored procedure inserts a new customer into the Customers table, as shown in Listing 6.14. This procedure is used if the user attempts to check out and they do not exist in the database.

```
CREATE PROCEDURE sp_Insert_Customer
  (@CustomerID nvarchar(50),
  @CompanyName nvarchar(40), @ContactName nvarchar(30),
  @ContactTitle nvarchar(30),@Address nvarchar(60),
```

Listing 6.14   sp_Insert_Customer stored procedure

```
    @City nvarchar(15), @Region nvarchar(15),
    @PostalCode nvarchar(10), @Country nvarchar(15),
    @Phone nvarchar(24), @Fax nvarchar(24),
    @Email nvarchar(50), @Password nvarchar(50))
AS
INSERT INTO Customers
    (CustomerID, CompanyName, ContactName, ContactTitle,
    Address, City, Region, PostalCode, Country, Phone,
    Fax, Email, Password)
VALUES
    (@CustomerID, @CompanyName, @ContactName, @ContactTitle,
    @Address, @City, @Region, @PostalCode, @Country, @Phone,
    @Fax, @Email, @Password)
```

Listing 6.14   sp_Insert_Customer stored procedure (continued)

The sp_Insert_Order stored procedure inserts a new order into the database, as shown in Listing 6.15. This is the final step in the checkout process.

```
CREATE PROCEDURE sp_Insert_Order
    (@CustomerID nvarchar(50),
    @EmployeeID int, @OrderDate datetime,
    @RequiredDate datetime, @ShippedDate datetime,
    @ShipVia int, @Freight money,
    @ShipName nvarchar(40), @ShipAddress nvarchar(60),
    @ShipCity nvarchar(15), @ShipRegion nvarchar(15),
    @ShipPostalCode nvarchar(10), @ShipCountry nvarchar(15))
AS
    INSERT INTO Orders
    (CustomerID, EmployeeID, OrderDate, RequiredDate,
    ShippedDate, ShipVia, Freight, ShipName, ShipAddress,
    ShipCity, ShipRegion, ShipPostalCode, ShipCountry)
VALUES
    (@CustomerID, @EmployeeID, @OrderDate,@RequiredDate,
    @ShippedDate, @ShipVia, @Freight, @ShipName,
    @ShipAddress, @ShipCity, @ShipRegion, @ShipPostalCode,
    @ShipCountry)
```

Listing 6.15   sp_Insert_Order stored procedure

The sp_Insert_Order_Details stored procedure inserts a row of data for each line item in the shopping cart, as shown in Listing 6.16. Once the actual order is inserted, the order details are added to the database and the checkout process ends.

```
CREATE PROCEDURE sp_Insert_Order_Details
   @ProductID int, @UnitPrice money,
   @Quantity smallint, @Discount real)
AS
  INSERT INTO OrderDetails
   (ProductID, UnitPrice, Quantity, Discount)
VALUES
   (@ProductID, @UnitPrice, @Quantity, 0)
```

Listing 6.16   sp_Insert_Order_Details stored procedure

The sp_Update_Cart_Item stored procedure updates the quantity of items for a product in the cart, as shown in Listing 6.17. This is necessary so that the same product is not listed multiple times by accident. The output from the sp_Get_Cart_Item_Count stored procedure is used to determine if items for a particular product exist in the ShoppingCart table. It they do, then the return value is incremented by one and the count in the table is updated.

```
CREATE PROCEDURE sp_Update_Cart_Item
   @CartID varchar(50), @ProductID int, @Quantity int
AS
  Update ShoppingCart Set Quantity = @Quantity
   Where CartID = @CartID and ProductID = @ProductID
```

Listing 6.17   sp_Update_Cart_Item stored procedure

Creating the Online Store User Interface

The way in which we are going to approach the design of the online store is through a heavy use of user controls. User controls are similar to include files or ActiveX controls in that they encapsulate functionality that can be reused over and over again without any modifications being made to the underlying code. The nice thing about user controls is that they can be designed visually, which is the opposite of include files, and they require no overhead, like ActiveX controls. Once you create a user control, you can drag it from your Solution Explorer on to a Web form, and it will run as if it is part of that form. Web forms have an *aspx* extension, while user controls have an *ascx* extension. You may have seen documentation that refers to user controls as *pagelets*, but in this project we will refer to them as user controls, since there has been no official alternate name given to them.

Once you have completed the online store application, you will be able to quickly modify the look and feel by changing the user controls and the main style sheet. Since there will be no server code written in any of the Web forms and all of the functionality will be encapsulated inside the user controls and code-behind, the changes you need to make to the application will be minimal in order to make it useful in your environment.

To begin creating the application, you need to add the Web forms, user controls, and class files to your solution. Table 6.3 lists the Web forms that you need to add to your solution and gives a description of what they do. To add the Web forms to your application, repeat the following steps for each of the Web forms listed in Table 6.3.

1. Right-click the project name.
2. Click Add.
3. Click Add Web Form.
4. In the Add New Item dialog box, type the name of the Web form.
5. Click the OK button. The Web form will now be in your Solution Explorer.

Once you have added the Web forms to your application, you will need to add the user controls encapsulating the user interface and interaction with the database. To add the user controls to your application, repeat the following steps for each of the user controls listed in Table 6.4.

1. Right-click the project name.
2. Click Add.
3. Click Add Web User Control.
4. In the Add New Item dialog box, type the name of the user control.
5. Click the OK button. The user control will now be in your Solution Explorer.

Table 6.3   Web Forms to Be Added to the Online Store Application

NAME	DESCRIPTION
Default.aspx	Home page for the online store
Productslist.aspx	Lists the products based on the category the user selects
Userlogin.aspx	Prompts for username and password before the checkout process occurs
Userhistory.aspx	Displays the previous orders of the user
Userprofile.aspx	Displays the billing information for the user
Checkout.aspx	Displays the shopping cart before the user completes the order
Verify.aspx	Allows user to modify billing information before completing the order

Table 6.4 User Controls to Be Added to the Online Store Application

NAME	DESCRIPTION
_BigCart.ascx	Lists the products and prices before the final checkout occurs
_CategoriesMenu.ascx	Displays the categories of products for sale
_CustomerDetails.ascx	Data entry for customer information
_Login.ascx	Login logic
_NoMenuHeader.ascx	Header to display during checkout or whenever you do not want the categories listed
_ProductList.ascx	Product information with image
_SiteHeader.ascx	Header for each page; contains the company name but can include advertising banners
_SmallCart.ascx	Small version of the shopping cart that is displayed on every page
_VerifyDetails.ascx	Verification of user details and cart items

The application logic will reside in three classes: Customers, Products, and ShoppingCart. Table 6.5 lists the class files that you will need to add to your solution and gives a description of what they will do. To add the class files to your application, repeat the following steps for each of the class files listed in Table 6.5.

1. Right-click the *bin* directory in Solution Explorer.
2. Click Add Class.
3. In the Add New Item dialog box, type the name of the class file.
4. Click the OK button. The class file will now be in your Solution Explorer.

Table 6.5 Class Files to Be Added to the Online Store Application

NAME	DESCRIPTION
Customers	All data-access code and logic for customer information
Products	All data-access code and logic for working with products
ShoppingCart	All data-access code and logic for manipulating the shopping cart

Now that all the files you need to get started are added to your solution, we can start working on the data-access code for the online store.

Writing the Data-Access Layer

Before we write any code in the Web forms, we need to write the data-access code that will populate the user controls. Once we write all of the code in the class files, we can then write the code in the user controls that use the class files. There are three class files that are used from the main online store: Products, Customers, and ShoppingCart.

Creating the Products Class

The Products class contains two methods that handle access to the Categories and Products tables in the database. The first method, GetAllCategories, retrieves all of the rows in the Categories table in the database. The Categories table maps to the Products table, which contains all of the available products for which the user can shop. The second method, GetProductsByCategory, accepts a ProductID parameter, which is used to return the set of products that correspond to the selected category. Both of the methods return a SQLDataReader object. The SQLDataReader is used to return read-only, forward-only sets of data. Since you do not need to navigate these data sets, the SQL-DataReader object is perfectly suited for returning the records needed. Listing 6.18 is the complete Products class code. Notice that we are creating a namespace called Proj06Web. This will be used in each class that you create, ensuring uniqueness across the assembly created for this project.

```
' Import the SQLClient namespace
Imports System.Data.SqlClient

' Use the unique namespace for this application
Namespace Proj06Web
  '
  ' Name the Class
  Public Class Products
  '    '
  Function GetAllCategories() As SqlDataReader
    ' Get all products as return a dataset to the caller
    ' uses sp_Get_Products stored proc to return all
    ' of the products
    '
    ' Create the connection
    Dim cn As SqlConnection
    cn = New _
    SqlConnection(ConfigurationSettings.AppSettings("ConnectionString"))
    '
    ' Create a SQLCommand object with the stored procedure
    ' that we will be executing
    Dim cmd As SqlCommand = _
```

Listing 6.18 Products class

```vbnet
  New SqlCommand("sp_Get_Categories", cn)
  cmd.CommandType = _
   CommandType.StoredProcedure
   '
   ' Open the connection
   cn.Open()
   '
   ' Call the executeReader method to return the DataReader
   ' back to the caller
   Return cmd.ExecuteReader(CommandBehavior.CloseConnection)
 End Function

 Function GetProductsByCategory(ByVal categoryID As Integer) _
  As SqlDataReader
  ' Return all of the products for a particular category
  '
  ' Create the connection
  Dim cn As SqlConnection
  cn = New _
  SqlConnection(ConfigurationSettings.AppSettings("ConnectionString"))
  '
  ' Create a SQLCommand object with the stored procedure
  ' that we will be executing
  Dim cmd As SqlCommand = _
  New SqlCommand("sp_Get_Products_By_Category", cn)
  cmd.CommandType = CommandType.StoredProcedure
  '
  ' Create a new Parameter and pass the CategoryID
  Dim paramCategoryID As SqlParameter = _
   New SqlParameter("@CategoryID", SqlDbType.Int, 4)
  paramCategoryID.Value = categoryID
  cmd.Parameters.Add(paramCategoryID)
  '
  ' Open the connection
  cn.Open()
  '
  ' Call the executeReader method to return the DataReader
  ' back to the caller
  Return cmd.ExecuteReader(CommandBehavior.CloseConnection)

 End Function
 End Class
End Namespace
```

Listing 6.18   Products class (continued)

Creating the Customers Class

The Customers class contains the methods that pertain to the shopper. Once a person using the online store decides to purchase items, he or she needs to enter billing and address information. The process of checking out begins with the entry of a username and password. The Authenticate method in the Customers class takes a username and password parameter and returns the customer's unique ID from the database. If the customer does not exist in the database, then the form that allows the user to enter his or her billing information is presented. Once the user enters his or her personal information, the AddEditCustomer method is called, with all of the parameters, to insert the new record into the Customers table in the database. The AddEditCustomer method can either add a new customer or update existing customer information. Since the parameters passed for adding a new customer are the same as the parameters needed to update existing information, an AddNew parameter is passed indicating whether or not the user is updating or adding information. Listing 6.19 is the complete Customers class. You can see in the comments the individual steps that are taken during each method call.

```
Imports System.Data.SqlClient

Namespace Proj06Web
 Public Class Customers

 Function Authenticate(ByVal Username As String, _
  ByVal Password As String) As String
    '
    ' Check to see if this user exists in the database of customers,
    ' if not, just return a blank string, if true,
    ' then return the customerID from the database
    ' and redirect to address verification pages
    '
    Dim cn As SqlConnection
    cn = New _
      SqlConnection(ConfigurationSettings.AppSettings("ConnectionString"))
    cn.Open()

    Dim cmd As SqlCommand = New SqlCommand("sp_Authenticate", cn)
    cmd.CommandType = CommandType.StoredProcedure

    Dim paramUsername As SqlParameter = _
        New SqlParameter("@Username", SqlDbType.NVarChar, 50)
    paramUsername.Value = Username
    cmd.Parameters.Add(paramUsername)

    Dim paramPassword As SqlParameter = _
        New SqlParameter("@Password", SqlDbType.NVarChar, 50)
```

Listing 6.19 Customers class

```vb
    paramPassword.Value = Password
    cmd.Parameters.Add(paramPassword)


    Dim paramCustomerID As SqlParameter = _
        New SqlParameter("@CustomerID", SqlDbType.NVarChar, 50)
    paramCustomerID.Direction = ParameterDirection.Output
    cmd.Parameters.Add(paramCustomerID)

    cmd.ExecuteNonQuery()

    If Not IsDBNull(paramCustomerID.Value) Then
      Return CType(paramCustomerID.Value, String)
    Else
      Return ""
    End If

End Function

Function AddEditCustomer(ByVal Username As String, _
    ByVal Password As String, ByVal CompanyName As String, _
    ByVal ContactName As String, ByVal ContactTitle As String, _
    ByVal Address As String, ByVal City As String, _
    ByVal Region As String, ByVal PostalCode As String, _
    ByVal Country As String, ByVal Phone As String, _
    ByVal Fax As String, ByVal AddNew As Boolean) As Boolean

  ' Create a new connection object
  ' based on information stored in the Web.Config file
  Dim cn As SqlConnection
  cn = New _
    SqlConnection(ConfigurationSettings.AppSettings("ConnectionString"))
  '
  ' Delcare a new Command object
  Dim cmd As SqlCommand
  ' if the AddNew paramater = True, then add a new customer, if the
  ' value is False, then specify the Update stored procedure
  If AddNew = True Then
    cmd = New SqlCommand("sp_Insert_Customer", cn)
  Else
    cmd = New SqlCommand("sp_Update_Customer", cn)
  End If
  ' set the Command type to Stored Procedure
  cmd.CommandType = CommandType.StoredProcedure
  '
  ' Create parameters for each value in the stored procedure
  ' and set the value based on the parameters passed to the procedure
  '
```

Listing 6.19 Customers class (continued)

```
Dim paramUsername As SqlParameter = _
    New SqlParameter("@CustomerID", SqlDbType.NVarChar, 50)
  paramUsername.Value = Username
  cmd.Parameters.Add(paramUsername)
  '
Dim paramPassword As SqlParameter = _
    New SqlParameter("@Password", SqlDbType.NVarChar, 50)
paramPassword.Value = Password
cmd.Parameters.Add(paramPassword)
  '
Dim paramCompanyName As SqlParameter = _
    New SqlParameter("@CompanyName", SqlDbType.NVarChar, 50)
paramCompanyName.Value = CompanyName
cmd.Parameters.Add(paramCompanyName)
  '
Dim paramContactName As SqlParameter = _
    New SqlParameter("@ContactName", SqlDbType.NVarChar, 50)
paramContactName.Value = ContactName
cmd.Parameters.Add(paramContactName)
  '
Dim paramContactTitle As SqlParameter = _
    New SqlParameter("@ContactTitle", SqlDbType.NVarChar, 50)
paramContactTitle.Value = ContactTitle
cmd.Parameters.Add(paramContactTitle)
  '
Dim paramAddress As SqlParameter = _
    New SqlParameter("@Address", SqlDbType.NVarChar, 50)
paramAddress.Value = Address
cmd.Parameters.Add(paramAddress)
  '
Dim paramCity As SqlParameter = _
    New SqlParameter("@City", SqlDbType.NVarChar, 50)
paramCity.Value = City
cmd.Parameters.Add(paramCity)
  '
Dim paramRegion As SqlParameter = _
    New SqlParameter("@Region", SqlDbType.NVarChar, 50)
paramRegion.Value = Region
cmd.Parameters.Add(paramRegion)
  '
Dim paramPostalCode As SqlParameter = _
    New SqlParameter("@PostalCode", SqlDbType.NVarChar, 50)
paramPostalCode.Value = PostalCode
cmd.Parameters.Add(paramPostalCode)
  '

Dim paramCountry As SqlParameter = _
```

Listing 6.19   Customers class (continued)

```
        New SqlParameter("@Country", SqlDbType.NVarChar, 50)
    paramCountry.Value = Country
    cmd.Parameters.Add(paramCountry)
    '
    Dim paramPhone As SqlParameter = _
        New SqlParameter("@Phone", SqlDbType.NVarChar, 50)
    paramPhone.Value = Phone
    cmd.Parameters.Add(paramPhone)
    '
    Dim paramFax As SqlParameter = _
        New SqlParameter("@Fax", SqlDbType.NVarChar, 50)
    paramFax.Value = Fax
    cmd.Parameters.Add(paramFax)
    '
    Dim paramEmail As SqlParameter = _
        New SqlParameter("@Email", SqlDbType.NVarChar, 50)
    paramEmail.Value = Username
    cmd.Parameters.Add(paramEmail)
    '
    ' Open the connection
    cn.Open()
    ' Execute the query
    cmd.ExecuteNonQuery()
    ' Close the connection
    cn.Close()
End Function
    '
Function GetCustomerInfo(ByVal CustomerID As String) As SqlDataReader
    ' Get the customer details from the database based on the CustomerID
    ' passed to the methos
    '
    ' Create a connection to the database
    Dim cn As SqlConnection
    cn = New _
       SqlConnection(ConfigurationSettings.AppSettings("ConnectionString"))
    '
    ' Create command object of type stored procedure
    Dim cmd As New SqlCommand("sp_Get_Customer", cn)
    cmd.CommandType = CommandType.StoredProcedure
    '
    ' Create the parameter object that holds the CustomerID
    Dim paramCustomerID As SqlParameter = _
        New SqlParameter("@CustomerID", SqlDbType.NVarChar, 50)
    paramCustomerID.Value = CustomerID
    cmd.Parameters.Add(paramCustomerID)
    '
    ' Open the database
    cn.Open()
    '
```

Listing 6.19 Customers class (continued)

```
   ' Execute the command, returning the DataReader
   Return cmd.ExecuteReader(CommandBehavior.CloseConnection)
  End Function

  End Class


End Namespace
```

Listing 6.19   Customers class (continued)

Creating the ShoppingCart Class

The ShoppingCart class is the most important class in the whole project. Keeping track of what the user wants to buy is critical to the success of the application. In this online store, the items added to the shopping cart are stored in SQL Server. Each time the user clicks the Add To Cart button on the ProductsList Web form, the application checks to see if a cart for this current session exists. If it does, it adds the item to the database based on the current Cart ID. If a cart ID does not exist, then a new Cart ID is created and the product is added to the ShoppingCart table in the database. This logic is contained in the GetCartID function. If a Cart ID does not exist when the GetCartID method is called, then a new Cart ID is created and stored in a cookie. Once a user checks out, the cart information is removed from the database—it is only valid for the current session.

Another important feature is that when a user clicks the Add To Cart button, a new row is not added to the ShoppingCart table if the product being added already exists in the table. The GetItemCount takes care of this problem, which would be duplicate products for the same shopper. Each time an item is added to the cart, a check is made to see if the product being added already exists in the current shopping cart. If the item exists, the Quantity field from the table is returned, and this number is then incremented by one and passed back to the table to reflect the new quantity for the product. The UpdateCartQuantity method handles updating the Quantity field in the ShoppingCart table. The method has a Boolean parameter named OverWrite. If the Over-Write value is True, then the user is on the CheckOut Web form and shopper has updated the total quantity on the line item for the shopping cart. If the value is False, then the quantity parameter passed to the method is used to update the table. This normally occurs when the Add To Cart button is clicked from the ProductList page. Listing 6.20 is the complete ShoppingCart class. The comments in the code further explain the steps that occur in each of the methods.

```
Imports System.Data.SqlClient
Imports System.Web
Imports System.Web.Configuration
```

Listing 6.20   ShoppingCart class

```
Namespace Proj06Web
Public Class ShoppingCart

 Function GetCartID() As String
  ' Generate a random cart ID for this session
  ' if one does
  ' not exist in the cookie CartID
  '
  ' Get the current HTTP context
  Dim ctx As HttpContext = HttpContext.Current
  '
  ' Check the cookie on the machine for a cartID
  '
  If ctx.Request.Cookies("CartID") Is Nothing Then
   Dim cartID As Guid = Guid.NewGuid()
   '
   ' Write the new CartID to a cookie
   '
   ctx.Response.Cookies("CartID").Value = cartID.ToString
   ' Return the CartID as a string
   '
   Return cartID.ToString
  Else
   ' A cookie exists, so return the
   ' CartID stored in the cookie
   Return ctx.Request.Cookies("CartID").Value.ToString
  End If
 End Function

 Function UpdateCartQuantity(ByVal ProductID As Integer, _
   ByVal Qty As Integer, _
   ByVal CartID As String, _
   ByVal OverWrite As Boolean) As Boolean
  '
  ' Create the connection
  '
  Dim cn As SqlConnection
  cn = New _
  SqlConnection(ConfigurationSettings.AppSettings("ConnectionString"))
  '
  ' Create a new SQLCommand object of type Stored Procedure
  Dim cmd As SqlCommand
  cmd = New SqlCommand()
  cmd.CommandType = CommandType.StoredProcedure
  cmd.Connection = cn
  '
  ' First, check and see if there are already existing
  ' items with the same productID
```

Listing 6.20 ShoppingCart class (continued)

```
' If OverWrite = True, that means the update is
' coming from the BigCart page,
' so the user changed a quantity in the textbox,
' so we need to overwrite the value in
' Quantity, not add to it
'
Dim CurrentItemCount As Integer = _
   GetItemCount(CartID, ProductID)
'
If CurrentItemCount > 0 Then
 ' we need to update the existing quantity,
 ' not add a new item
 ' Increment the CurrentyItemCount returned
 ' with the Quantity they are adding
 If OverWrite = True Then
   Qty = Qty
 Else
   Qty = Qty + CurrentItemCount
 End If
 cmd.CommandText = "sp_Update_Cart_Item"
Else
 ' we need to insert a new record for this item
 cmd.CommandText = "sp_Add_To_Cart"
End If
'
' The parameters are generic, so fill the values
'
Dim paramProductID As SqlParameter = _
 New SqlParameter("@ProductID", SqlDbType.Int, 4)
paramProductID.Value = ProductID
cmd.Parameters.Add(paramProductID)
'
Dim paramQty As SqlParameter = _
 New SqlParameter("@Quantity", SqlDbType.Int, 4)
paramQty.Value = Qty
cmd.Parameters.Add(paramQty)
'
Dim paramCartID As SqlParameter = _
 New SqlParameter("@CartID", SqlDbType.VarChar, 50)
paramCartID.Value = CartID
cmd.Parameters.Add(paramCartID)
'
' Open the connection
cn.Open()
' Execute the query that returns no records
cmd.ExecuteNonQuery()
' close the connection
cn.Close()
```

Listing 6.20 ShoppingCart class (continued)

```
 End Function

 Function GetCart(ByVal CartID As String) As SqlDataReader
   '
   ' Return the contents of the cart based on the CartID passed
   ' to the method
   '
   Dim cn As SqlConnection
   cn = New _
     SqlConnection(ConfigurationSettings.AppSettings("ConnectionString"))
   cn.Open()
   ' Create the command object
   '
   Dim cmd As New SqlCommand("sp_Get_Cart", cn)
   cmd.CommandType = CommandType.StoredProcedure
   ' Fill the CartID parameter
   '
   Dim paramCartID As SqlParameter = _
     New SqlParameter("@CartID", SqlDbType.VarChar, 50)
   paramCartID.Value = CartID
   cmd.Parameters.Add(paramCartID)
   '
   ' Return the DataReader with the cart contents and close the
 connection
   Return cmd.ExecuteReader(CommandBehavior.CloseConnection)
 End Function


 Public Function GetCartSum(ByVal cartID As String) As Decimal
   '
   ' Return the sum dollar value of the contents of a cart
   '
   ' Create the connection object
   Dim cn As SqlConnection
   cn = New _
     SqlConnection(ConfigurationSettings.AppSettings("ConnectionString"))
   '
   ' Create the new command object of type stored procedure
   Dim cmd As SqlCommand = _
     New SqlCommand("sp_Get_Cart_Total", cn)
   cmd.CommandType = CommandType.StoredProcedure
   '
   ' Create the parameters for the CartID
   Dim paramCartID As SqlParameter = _
     New SqlParameter("@CartID", SqlDbType.VarChar, 50)
   paramCartID.Value = cartID
   cmd.Parameters.Add(paramCartID)
   '
   ' Create an Output parameter for CartSum which will return the sum
   ' value of the products in the cart
```

Listing 6.20   ShoppingCart class (continued)

```
Dim paramSum As SqlParameter = _
  New SqlParameter("@CartSum", SqlDbType.Money, 8)
paramSum.Direction = ParameterDirection.Output
cmd.Parameters.Add(paramSum)
'
' Open the connection
cn.Open()
'
' Execute the query
cmd.ExecuteNonQuery()
'
' Close the connection
cn.Close()
'
' Return the outpur parameter as a string value
Return CType(paramSum.Value, String)
End Function

Function GetItemCount(ByVal CartID As String, _
    ByVal ProductID As Integer) As Integer
' Return the number od unique products in the shopping
' cart based on the CartID and ProductID passed
'
' Create a connection
Dim cn As SqlConnection
cn = New _
  SqlConnection(ConfigurationSettings.AppSettings("ConnectionString"))
'
' Create the command object of type stored procedure
Dim cmd As SqlCommand = New _
  SqlCommand("sp_Get_Cart_Item_Count", cn)
cmd.CommandType = CommandType.StoredProcedure
'
' Create the input paramters for the CartID and ProductID
Dim paramCartID As SqlParameter = _
  New SqlParameter("@CartID", SqlDbType.VarChar, 50)
paramCartID.Value = CartID
cmd.Parameters.Add(paramCartID)
'
Dim paramProductID As SqlParameter = _
  New SqlParameter("@ProductID", SqlDbType.Int, 4)
paramProductID.Value = ProductID
cmd.Parameters.Add(paramProductID)
'
' Create the ItemCount output parameter to hold the
' return values for the number of products in the current cart
Dim paramItemCount As SqlParameter = _
  New SqlParameter("@ItemCount", SqlDbType.Int, 4)
paramItemCount.Direction = ParameterDirection.Output
cmd.Parameters.Add(paramItemCount)
'
```

Listing 6.20 ShoppingCart class (continued)

```
' Open the connection
cn.Open()
'
' Execute the query
cmd.ExecuteNonQuery()
'
' Close the connection
cn.Close()
'
' Check the return value, if a null is returned, then
' the item count is zero, else convert the return value to
' an integer and return it to the caller
If IsDBNull(paramItemCount.Value) Then
 Return 0
Else
 Return Convert.ToInt32(paramItemCount.Value)
End If
'
End Function


Function RemoveFromCart(ByVal ProductID As Integer, _
ByVal CartID As String) As Boolean
'
' Remove an item from the cart based on the productID
' This is used in the BigCart user control when the user updates or
' removes items from the cart before checkout
'
' Create the connection object
Dim cn As SqlConnection
cn = New _
 SqlConnection(ConfigurationSettings.AppSettings("ConnectionString"))
'
' Create the command object of type stored procedure
Dim cmd As SqlCommand = _
 New SqlCommand("sp_Delete_Cart_Item", cn)
cmd.CommandType = CommandType.StoredProcedure
'
' Create the parameter objects for the CartID and ProductID
Dim paramCartID As SqlParameter = _
 New SqlParameter("@CartID", SqlDbType.VarChar, 50)
paramCartID.Value = CartID
cmd.Parameters.Add(paramCartID)

Dim paramProductID As SqlParameter = _
 New SqlParameter("@ProductID", SqlDbType.Int, 4)
paramProductID.Value = ProductID
cmd.Parameters.Add(paramProductID)

'
' Open the connection
cn.Open()
'
```

Listing 6.20 ShoppingCart class (continued)

```
    ` Execute the query
    cmd.ExecuteNonQuery()
    `

    ` Close the connection
    cn.Close()
    `

  End Function

  End Class

End Namespace
```

Listing 6.20   ShoppingCart class (continued)

Now that you have all of the code written for the classes used by the user controls, you can build your application to make sure that there are no errors. Since you have been using the Visual Studio .NET IDE, any typos or undeclared variables would have been caught as you were writing your code. As you went through the code in the classes, you can see that there is nothing too complex here. As with any application, you need to insert, update, and delete records. A few of the methods return output parameters for dollar sums or item counts, but the bulk of the code is straightforward, simple data access.

Creating the User Controls

The reusability of user controls makes them perfect for any Web application. Up to this point, you have created the database and written all the code to access the data. From here on out, the project consists of user interface design. By creating user controls to encapsulate the basic functionality of the online store, it is easy to add features to individual Web forms. Just as you would create ActiveX controls in Visual Basic containing all the application logic for the tasks they were created for, you will do the same with user controls. Each user control created will contain all of the code that it needs to perform its task, so placing the controls anywhere on any Web form will not include any additional coding. It is a simple drag-and-drop programming model. In the past, Visual Interdev was not the easiest tool to use when creating reusable Web interfaces. Because the editor in Interdev did not allow you to visually create reusable components, it was difficult to make any of your code truly reusable. If you have ever used include files to encapsulate functionality, then you know that placement had to be perfect for the end result to look good, and while designing, you did not really have a good idea of what the final page was going to look like.

In the online store, user controls will handle the logic of the application. As previously mentioned, all of the code will be in the code-behind pages of your user controls. The only server script that will be in the actual aspx pages will be data-binding instructions. For a developer who is used to a Visual Basic-like development environment, the

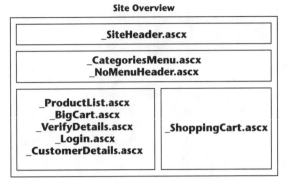

Figure 6.4 Online store page architecture.

code-behind concept is one of the coolest things that you will ever use as an ASP.NET developer. With full support for autocomplete and on-the-fly error checking, your coding efficiency for Web applications will skyrocket.

This section covers the creation of each user control that makes up the online store. To give you an idea of where we are going with this, Figure 6.4 shows you the basic layout of the final product. The Web forms that you added earlier will contain HTML tables to position the location of the user controls. For example, Default.aspx will contain an HTML table with two rows across the top and two columns. The top row will hold the _SiteHeader.ascx user control; the second row will contain the _Categories-Menu.ascx user control; the left column will contain the _ProductList.ascx user control; and the right column will contain the _ShoppingCart.ascx.

As you are writing the code for the user controls, you can quickly test them by dragging them from Solution Explorer on to a Web form and then running the application. An important thing to remember is that since the code is not script, you will need to rebuild the application if you modify any code in the classes or in the code-behind pages. To rebuild the application, right-click the project name in Solution Explorer and select Rebuild.

Creating _SiteHeader.ascx

Each page on the site should contain a header. The _SiteHeader.ascx user control in the online store contains the name of our store, Northwind Traders Online. Every e-commerce site on the Internet is different, and you might want to include things such as advertising or banner ads to catch the user's attention on each page. This user control in Listing 6.21 contains no code-behind; it is simply for display.

Creating _CategoriesMenu.ascx

The _CategoriesMenu.ascx user control is extremely important. This user control encapsulates the main navigation for the Web site. Based on the item the user selects from the menu, the _ProductsList.ascx user control reads the query string passed in the URL and looks for a CategoryID passed from the _CategoriesMenu.ascx user control. The control is created using a DataList bound control. When the control is loaded, it looks for the SelectedIndex property to determine what column the user selected. The SelectedItemTemplate and the ItemTemplate portions of the bound control contain the same bound columns—the CategoryID and the CategoryName. The only difference is the SelectedItemStyle, which displays the selected column in a different color so the user can visually see where he or she is at in the navigation.

To improve upon this design, you might want to make the menu vertical instead of horizontal. We are using the Categories table in the Northwind Traders database, which has about eight categories. By making the menu horizontal, the amount of data that can be displayed across the top of the screen is limited. If your store has 50 categories, then a vertical menu would be your only option. The nice thing about the DataList control is the RepeatDirection property, which can be either Horizontal or Vertical, making it easy to change the look of the menu without having to change any of the code.

Another improvement would be to add the OutputCache parameter to the top of the control. Using the OutputCache directive, you can specify when a page expires, where the cache for the page should be located, and what parameter to use to indicate the cache should be refreshed. The following example tells the page to cache for 10 seconds and to not contain a parameter that would cause the page to be cleared from the cache.

```
<%@ OutputCache Duration="10" VaryByParam="none" %>
```

The Duration property is in seconds, so if you know that the data in the menu will not be updated often, you could set the output cache to look something like this:

```
<%@ OutputCache Duration="7200" Location="Any"
      VaryByParam="CategoryID;Selection" %>
```

```
<%@ Control Language="vb" AutoEventWireup="false" _
Codebehind="_SiteHeader.ascx.vb" Inherits="project06.C_SiteHeader" _
TargetSchema="http://schemas.microsoft.com/intellisense/ie5" %>
<P>
<TABLE id="Table1" width="100%" border="0">
 <TR>
  <TD class="SiteHeader">Northwind Traders Online</TD>
 </TR>
</TABLE>
</P>
```

Listing 6.21 Code for _SiteHeader.ascx user control

This will cause the user control to be cached for two hours and force the cache to be updated if the Selection item in the query string changes. The Location property can be Client, Server, Downstream, or Any, based on where you want the cache to be located. If you decide to use the OutputCache directive in a user control, then the Location and VaryByParam properties are required. Listing 6.22 is the HTML and data-binding code for the user control.

```
<%@ Control Language="vb" AutoEventWireup="false" _
  Codebehind="_CategoriesMenu.ascx.vb" _
  Inherits="project06.C_CategoriesMenu" _
  TargetSchema="http://schemas.microsoft.com/intellisense/ie5" %>
<TABLE>
 <TR>
 <TD style="WIDTH: 624px">
 <asp:DataList id="DataList1"
  runat="server"
  RepeatDirection="Horizontal"
  SelectedItemStyle-BackColor="#006666"
  Height="16px" BackColor="LemonChiffon"
  SelectedIndex="0"
  CellPadding="8" Width="507px">

  <SelectedItemStyle BackColor="#006666"></SelectedItemStyle>

  <SelectedItemTemplate>
   <asp:HyperLink
   id="Hyperlink4"
   runat="server"
   NavigateUrl='<%# "productlist.aspx?CategoryID=" &amp; _
   DataBinder.Eval(Container.DataItem, "CategoryID") _
    &amp; "&amp;selection=" &amp; Container.ItemIndex %>' _
    Text='<%# DataBinder.Eval(Container.DataItem, "CategoryName") %>' _
    CssClass="selected">
    </asp:HyperLink>
  </SelectedItemTemplate>

  <ItemTemplate>
   <asp:HyperLink
   id="Hyperlink3"
   runat="server"
   NavigateUrl='<%# "productlist.aspx?CategoryID=" _
   &amp; DataBinder.Eval(Container.DataItem, "CategoryID") _
   &amp; "&amp;selection=" &amp; Container.ItemIndex %>' _
   Text='<%# DataBinder.Eval(Container.DataItem, "CategoryName") %>'_
   CssClass="notselected">
   </asp:HyperLink>
  </ItemTemplate>
 </asp:DataList>
 </TD>
```

Listing 6.22   Code for _CategoriesMenu.ascx user control

```
   </TR>
   <TR>
   <TD>
   <asp:Label id="Label1" runat="server">Search</asp:Label>
   <asp:TextBox id="SearchText"></asp:TextBox>
   </TD>
   </TR>
</TABLE>
```

Listing 6.22   Code for _CategoriesMenu.ascx user control (continued)

The code-behind for _CategoriesMenu.ascx.vb contains the logic that tells the DataList control what item to select. It does this by looking at the Selection parameter passed in the query string. All of the code is contained in the Page_Load event. Since the user is selecting an item in the DataList, the page gets refreshed each time a selection is made. When an item is selected, the selection is passed in the query string. Based on the index, a category in the DataList control is highlighted with a different color.

To load the data into the DataList control, the GetAllCategories method is called from the Products class. Once the method returns the SQLDataReader object containing the categories, the DataBind method is called after the DataSource property is set to the SQLDataReader object. Listing 6.23 contains the code in the Page_Load event for the _CategoriesMenu.ascx.vb class.

```
Private Sub Page_Load(ByVal sender As System.Object, _
   ByVal e As System.EventArgs) Handles MyBase.Load
   '
   ' Check the selection parameter in the querystring, and if
   ' it contains a value, set the seletedindex of the menu to
   ' the correct option
   If Request.Params("selection") <> "" Then
      DataList1.SelectedIndex = Request.Params("selection")
   End If
   '
   ' If the Action parameter in the querystring is CheckOut,
   ' then they user is viewing the full shopping cart, and you
   ' should not have a default category selected in the menu
   If Request.Params("Action") = "CheckOut" Then
      DataList1.SelectedIndex = -1
   End If
   '
   ' Declare an instance of the Products class
   Dim cat As Proj06Web.Products = New Proj06Web.Products()
   '
   ' Call the GetAllCategories method and bind the results
   ' to the data list
   With DataList1
      .DataSource = cat.Get_All_Categories()
      .DataBind()
   End With
End Sub
```

Listing 6.23   Code for _CategoriesMenu.ascx.vb class

Figure 6.5   Testing the Categories Menu user control.

Once you have completed the _CategoriesMenu user control, you can drag it to any of the Web forms that you have in your solution, rebuild the solution, and view the Web form in the browser. You should see the categories from the database in an easy-to-read vertical menu, as Figure 6.5 demonstrates.

Creating _ProductsList.ascx

The products displayed are based on what the user selects from the list of categories on the main menu. The _ProductsList.ascx user control uses a DataList control, such as _CategoriesMenu.ascx user control, to repeat the product data retrieved from the database. This user control contains an image for each product listed and passes an Action item to the query string. If the value of the Action item is AddToCart, then the _ShoppingCart.ascx user control will pick up on that indicator and add the selected item to the cart. You should be seeing how the user controls you are creating are working together to make the user interface work. Once you have completed the _ProductsList user control, you will have the main menu and the list of products working together to output the data to the user. Once the _SmallCart user control is completed, it will perform the process of adding items to the ShoppingCart table based on what the Products List user control is passing to the query string.

All of the data-binding code is straightforward; the important code that tells the shopping cart to add the selected item is in the AddToCart image. I have highlighted that code in bold in Listing 6.24, which is the complete code for this user control.

```
<%@ Control Language="vb" AutoEventWireup="false" _
  Codebehind="_ProductList.ascx.vb" Inherits="project06.C_ProductList" _
  TargetSchema="http://schemas.microsoft.com/intellisense/ie5" %>

<asp:DataList id="DataList1" RepeatColumns="1" _
      runat="server" Height="466px">
 <ItemTemplate>
 <TABLE border="0">
  <TR><TD class="ProductName" colSpan="3">
    <%# DataBinder.Eval(Container.DataItem, "ProductName") %>
  </TD></TR>
  <TR>
   <TD><A href='ProductDetails.aspx?productID=<%# _
     DataBinder.Eval(Container.DataItem, "ProductID") %>'>
     <IMG height="75" src='images/<%# DataBinder.Eval_
      (Container.DataItem,"ImageURL") %>' _
     width="100" border="0"></A>
```

Listing 6.24   Code for _ProductList.ascx user control

```
       </TD>
       <TD class="ProductDescription">
        <%# DataBinder.Eval(Container.DataItem, "Description") %>
       </TD>
      <TR>
       <TD class="ProductNormal">Unit Price:</TD>
       <TD class="ProductPrice">
        <%# DataBinder.Eval(Container.DataItem, _
         "UnitPrice", "{0:c}") %>
       </TD>
      </TR>
      <TR>
       <TD class="ProductNormal">Qty Per Unit:</TD>
       <TD class="ProductNormal">
        <%# DataBinder.Eval(Container.DataItem, _
         "QuantityPerUnit") %>
       </TD>
      </TR>
      <TR><TD class="ProductNormal">Units in Stock:</TD>
       <TD class="ProductNormal">
        <%# DataBinder.Eval(Container.DataItem, _
         "UnitsInStock") %></TD>
      </TR>
      <TR><TD>
        <A href='ProductList.aspx?productID=<%# DataBinder.Eval_
         (Container.DataItem,"ProductID")%>&CategoryID=_
          <%# DataBinder.Eval(Container.DataItem, _
          "CategoryID") %>&selection=<%=Request.Params_
          ("selection") %>&Action=AddToCart'>
        <IMG alt="Add to Cart" src="images/addtocart.gif" border="0">
        </A>
       </TD>
      </TR>
     </TABLE><HR>
    </ItemTemplate>
   </asp:DataList>
```

Listing 6.24   Code for _ProductList.ascx user control (continued)

The code-behind for the _ProductList user control is encapsulated in the Page_Load event. Based on the CategoryID passed in the query string, a list of products is returned by calling the Get_Products_By_Cateogry method in the Products class. Because there is no way to prevent a CategoryID from being passed in the query string, if a user attempts to modify the query string and leave the CategoryID empty, we force a 1 in the CategoryID to display the default products for the CategoryID of 1. Listing 6.25 is the code for _ProductsList.ascx.vb.

```
Private Sub Page_Load(ByVal sender As System.Object, _
  ByVal e As System.EventArgs) Handles MyBase.Load
  '
  ' Load Products list into the DataList control
  ' Calls stored proc sp_Get_Products_By_Category
  Dim categoryID As String = Request.Params("categoryID")
  If categoryID = "" Then categoryID = 1
  ' If the CategoryID is not empty, then create
  ' an instance of the Products class and call the
  ' GetProductsByCategory method and bind the results
  ' to the data list
  If categoryID <> "" Then
    Dim p As Proj06Web.Products = _
    New Proj06Web.Products()
    With DataList1
    .DataSource = p.Get_Products_By_Category(categoryID)
    .DataBind()
    End With
  End If
End Sub
```

Listing 6.25   ProductsList.ascx.vb code listing

Now that the user control to list the products is created, you can test it by rebuilding the solution and dragging the _ProductsList.ascx user control from Solution Explorer on to the test form containing the Menu user control you created earlier. Figure 6.6 is an example of what your test form should look like once both controls are added and you select an item from the menu.

Don't worry about the fonts and colors at this point. Later on in the project you will create the style sheet that makes everything look good. In the HTML code you are writing for the user controls, there are classes in certain HTML tags indicating what formatting to apply once the style sheets are added to the aspx pages.

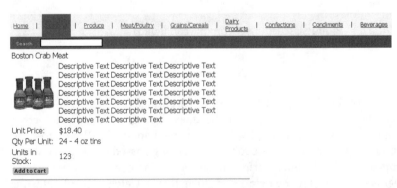

Figure 6.6   Testing the Menu and Products List user controls.

Creating _SmallCart.ascx

The _SmallCart user control displays the product name, quantity, and total price of the products that the user has decided to purchase. In the _ProductsList user control that you created earlier, I highlighted the code in bold that passes the ProductID and the AddToCart action in the query string. The code-behind for the _SmallCart user control checks the query string, and if the AddToCart action exists, it calls a method to update the ShoppingCart table in the database, return a new SQLDataReader object containing this user's cart data, and binds that data to the DataList control. This user control uses the FooterTemplate item to display a Check Out image. Once the online store is completed, the _SmallCart user control is displayed on each page the user views up until the point of checking out. When the user decides he or she is done shopping, he or she can click the Check Out image, which passes the CheckOut action in the query string and redirects to the CheckOut.aspx page. Listing 6.26 is the complete HTML code for the _SmallCart user control.

```
<%@ Control Language="vb" AutoEventWireup="false" _
  Codebehind="_SmallCart.ascx.vb" _
  Inherits="project06.C_SmallCart" _
  TargetSchema="http://schemas.microsoft.com/intellisense/ie5"%>

<asp:DataList id="DataList1"
  runat="server"
  BackColor="LemonChiffon"
  BorderColor="DarkGreen"
  BorderWidth="1px"
  BorderStyle="Groove">
<HeaderTemplate>
  <IMG src="images/carttop.gif">
</HeaderTemplate>
<FooterTemplate>
  <a href="checkout.aspx?Action=CheckOut">
   <IMG src="images/cartbottom.gif">
  </a>
</FooterTemplate>
<ItemTemplate>
  <TABLE border="0">
   <TR>
    <TD class="SmallCart" width="5">
      <%# DataBinder.Eval(Container.DataItem, "Quantity")%>
    </TD>
     <TD class="SmallCart" align="left" width="120">
     <%# DataBinder.Eval(Container.DataItem, "ProductName")%>
    </TD>
     <TD class="SmallCart" align="right" width="45">
      <%# DataBinder.Eval(Container.DataItem, "TotalDue", "{0:c}") %>
     </TD>
   </TR>
  </TABLE>
</ItemTemplate>
</asp:DataList>
```

Listing 6.26   Code for _SmallCart.ascx user control

The code that updates the ShoppingCart table in the database is encapsulated in the Page_Load event. When a user clicks an item in the _ProductsList user control, three items are passed in the query string: Action, CategoryID, and ProductID. When a user clicks the Add To Cart image, the query string will look something like this:

```
ProductList.aspx?productID=55&CategoryID=6&selection=3&Action=AddToCart
```

The Page_Load event reads the Action parameter in the query string, and if the Action parameter is AddToCart, then the UpdateCartQuantity method is called from a new instance of the ShoppingCart class. Once the item is added to the cart, the GetCart method is called, and the DataSource property of the DataList control is set to the SQL-DataReader object that the method returns. Then the DataBind method is called, and the shopping cart display is updated. Listing 6.27 is the code-behind for the _SmallCart user control.

```vb
Private Sub Page_Load(ByVal sender As System.Object, _
   ByVal e As System.EventArgs) Handles MyBase.Load
   ' Declare a new instance of the ShoppingCart class
   Dim s As Proj06Web.ShoppingCart = _
     New Proj06Web.ShoppingCart()
   '
   ' No matter what, we need a shopping cartID
   Dim cartID As String = s.GetCartID()
   If Request.Params("Action") = "AddToCart" Then
      '
      ' Need to get the query string and add the
      ' items to the page
      Dim strCat = Request.Params("CategoryID")
      Dim strProd = Request.Params("ProductID")
      '
      ' When the page loads on the small cart,
      ' the quantity
      ' is always 1, since this only gets called from the AddToCart
      ' image on the ProductsList page
      s.UpdateCartQuantity(CInt(strProd), 1, cartID, False)
   End If
   '
   ' Load Products list into the DataList control
   ' Calls stored proc sp_Shopping_Cart
   If cartID <> "" Then
      With DataList1
      .DataSource = s.GetCart(cartID)
      .DataBind()
      End With
   End If
End Sub
```

Listing 6.27   _SmallCart.ascx.vb code

Figure 6.7   _SmallCart user control.

Figure 6.7 displays an example of the _SmallCart user control once a few items are added to it.

Creating _BigCart.ascx

The _BigCart.ascx user control is displayed to the shopper during the checkout process. This user control is a little more complicated than the previous user controls you have created, mainly because it includes a Checkbox control that the user can click to indicate the removal of an item from the shopping cart and a Textbox control that the user can use to change the quantity of the items being purchased. The design of the user control is not the hard part; it is the actual code-behind that is a little more complex than the data-binding process that occurs during the Page_Load event in the previous controls that we created.

Listing 6.28 is the partial HTML code for the _BigCart user control. The listing is quite long, so I thought it better to just display the data-binding code, which is really the important part. To give you an idea of what the grid looks like at design time, Figure 6.8 shows you the complete grid in the IDE. When we explore the code-behind, you will see the code that handles the events for the buttons on the user control. There is also a Label control on the form that will output any error information back to the user if an error occurs during the update process the cart goes through when an item is deleted or a quantity is changed.

Check Out						
Remove	Quantity	Product Name	Qty Per Unit	Unit Price	Total Due	
☐	Datab	Databound	Databound	Databound	Databound	Update Cart
☐	Datab	Databound	Databound	Databound	Databound	
☐	Datab	Databound	Databound	Databound	Databound	Proceed to Checkout
☐	Datab	Databound	Databound	Databound	Databound	Label
☐	Datab	Databound	Databound	Databound	Databound	
Please review your selections, if you make any changes, click the Update Cart button to refresh the list of items.						
[ErrorMessage]						

Figure 6.8   _BigCart.ascx at design time.

```
<asp:datagrid id="DataGrid1" Height="118px"
  AutoGenerateColumns="False" runat="server"
  CssClass="checkout" Width="615px"
  DataKeyField="Quantity">
<Columns>

 <asp:TemplateColumn HeaderText="Remove">
  <ItemTemplate>
   <asp:CheckBox id="Delete" runat="server" />
  </ItemTemplate>
 </asp:TemplateColumn>

 <asp:TemplateColumn HeaderText="Quantity">
  <ItemTemplate>
   <asp:TextBox id=Quantity runat="server"
    Text='<%# DataBinder.Eval(Container.DataItem, "Quantity")%>'
       width="40px" Columns="4">
   </asp:TextBox>
  </ItemTemplate>
 </asp:TemplateColumn>

 <asp:TemplateColumn>
  <ItemTemplate>
   <asp:Label id=ProductID runat="server"
    Text='<%# DataBinder.Eval(Container.DataItem, "ProductID")%>'
    Visible="False" Width="298px">
   </asp:Label>
  </ItemTemplate>
 </asp:TemplateColumn>

 <asp:BoundColumn
   DataField="ProductName"
   HeaderText="Product Name">
 </asp:BoundColumn>

 <asp:BoundColumn
   DataField="QuantityPerUnit"
   HeaderText="Qty Per Unit">
 </asp:BoundColumn>

 <asp:BoundColumn
   DataField="UnitPrice"
   HeaderText="Unit Price" DataFormatString="{0:c}">
 </asp:BoundColumn>

 <asp:BoundColumn
   DataField="TotalDue"
   HeaderText="Total Due" DataFormatString="{0:c}">
 </asp:BoundColumn>
</Columns>
</asp:datagrid></TD>
```

Listing 6.28   _BigCart.ascx code

The code-behind for the _BigCart user control is a little more complicated due to the fact that we are allowing the user to modify each row in the grid. Once the user chooses to either delete an item or modify the quantity, he or she clicks the Update Cart button, and the ShoppingCart table in the database is updated. If you were to write this code in ASP, it could be a little more complicated, but since the DataGrid control has some additional functionality to make processes like this possible, the code you need to write is simple. We will break down the code-behind for this user control by each event that occurs, since the code is quite lengthy and deserves proper explaining.

Listing 6.29 is the code for the Page_Load event. Like each Page_Load event up until now, this is straightforward data binding. A new instance of the ShoppingCart class is created, and if there is data in the ShoppingCart table, then the SQLDataReader that is returned is bound to the DataGrid grid control by setting the DataSource property and calling the DataBind method.

```
Private Sub Page_Load(ByVal sender As System.Object, _
  ByVal e As System.EventArgs) Handles MyBase.Load

  If Not IsPostBack Then
    Dim CartID As String = _
    Request.Cookies("CartID").Value.ToString()
    '
    ' If the CartID is not empty, then fill the DataGrid with
    ' the current cart data in the database
    If CartID <> "" Then
      Dim s As Proj06Web.ShoppingCart = _
      New Proj06Web.ShoppingCart()
      ' Call the GetCart method and bind the
      ' results to the DataGrid
      DataGrid1.DataSource = _
        s.GetCart(CartID)
      DataGrid1.DataBind()
      ' Display the Total Order Amount in the label
      Label1.Text = "Total Order Amount: " _
        & FormatNumber(s.GetCartSum(CartID), 2)
    End If
  End If
End Sub
```

Listing 6.29 Page_Load event for the _BigCart.ascx

The UpdateButton control on the form handles updating the ShoppingCart table with any changes that the user makes to the items displayed in the grid. There are three items for each row in the grid that are important to this method: the ProductID field, the Delete check box, and the Quantity text box. In order to determine if the user has either selected the Delete check box or modified the value in the Quantity text box, you need to iterate through the collection of rows in the grid and use the FindControl method of Items collection in the grid. Using the FindControl method for each row, compare the value of the original quantity in the textbox to the current quantity. This is accomplished by setting the DataKeyField property equal to the item in the grid that you want to key on. In Listing 6.28, you defined the DataKeyField for the DataGrid control with the following code:

```
<asp:datagrid id="DataGrid1" Height="118px"
    AutoGenerateColumns="False" runat="server"
    CssClass="checkout" Width="615px"
    DataKeyField="Quantity">
```

Because the DataGrid control has a DataKeyField property, you are saved the additional work of creating hidden fields or otherwise figuring out how to keep track of values that have changed. This means that the actual data-access code that updates or deletes items from the cart only occurs if the user is requesting it.

To determine if the user is requesting to remove a product from the shopping cart, the checked property of the Checkbox control is examined. If the property is True, then the RemoveFromCart method is called, the ProductID for that row is passed, and the item is removed.

Listing 6.30 is the complete code for the UpdateButton_Click event.

```
Private Sub UpdateButton_Click(ByVal sender As System.Object, _
ByVal e As System.EventArgs) Handles UpdateButton.Click
'
' Make sure the ErrorMessage label is not visible
ErrorMessage.Visible = False
'
Dim CartID As String = _
 Request.Cookies("CartID").Value.ToString
Dim s As Proj06Web.ShoppingCart = _
 New Proj06Web.ShoppingCart()
Dim Looper As Long
Dim strMsg As String

Try
  ' Loop thru the collection of items in the DataGrid
  '
  For Looper = 0 To DataGrid1.Items.Count - 1
    ' Declare a variable for each type of control
    ' that you need to evaluate
    '
    Dim DeletedCheckbox As CheckBox
    Dim UpdatedQty As TextBox
    Dim ProductID As Label
    ' Set the controls that need to be evaluated to each type that
    ' is in the DataGrid using the FindControl method
    ProductID = DataGrid1.Items(Looper).FindControl("ProductID")
    DeletedCheckbox = DataGrid1.Items(Looper).FindControl("Delete")
    UpdatedQty = DataGrid1.Items(Looper).FindControl("Quantity")
    '
```

Listing 6.30 UpdateButton_Click event handler

```
' Make sure the value in the textbox is a number
' before updating the qty
If IsNumeric(UpdatedQty.Text) And CInt(UpdatedQty.Text) > 0 Then
  If Convert.ToInt32(UpdatedQty.Text) <> _
  Convert.ToInt32(DataGrid1.DataKeys(Looper)) Then
    ' Call the UpdateCartQuantity method if the number in the
    ' Quantity Texbox control is different than the original value
    s.UpdateCartQuantity(CInt(ProductID.Text), _
      CInt(UpdatedQty.Text), CartID, True)
  End If
End If
' If the user put a 0 in the Qty box, then make it a Delete
If DeletedCheckbox.Checked = True _
  Or CInt(UpdatedQty.Text) = 0 Then
  ' Call the RemoveFromCart method to delete the Cart Item
  s.RemoveFromCart(CInt(ProductID.Text), CartID)
End If
Next
Catch ex1 As Exception
' If an error occurs, make the ErrorMessage label visible
' and fill it with the error string
With ErrorMessage
  .Visible = True
  .Text = ex1.Message.ToString
End With
Finally
' No matter what, the cart needs to be filled with the current cart
' data, even if an error occured
With DataGrid1
  .DataSource = s.GetCart(Request.Cookies("CartID").Value.ToString)
  .DataBind()
End With
' Display the Total Order Amount in the Label control
Label1.Text = "Total Order Amount: " & _
  FormatNumber(s.GetCartSum(CartID), 2)
End Try
End Sub
```

Listing 6.30 UpdateButton_Click event handler (continued)

Creating _CustomerDetailsAdd.ascx

The _CustomerDetails user control is a basic data entry form that enables users to add or update their personal information. This user control introduces validation controls that notify users if they have not entered the correct data in the data entry fields.

Listing 6.31 is a partial listing of the _CustomerDetails user control demonstrating the different types of validation controls in use.

The RequiredFieldValidator control is straightforward. Once you add this control to your form, you specify a control to validate and an error message.

The RegularExpressionValidator control is more complex and gives you complete control over the type of data that is entered into the control you want to validate. Like the RequiredFieldValidator control, you must set the ControlToValidate property to a valid control on your form. The difference is in how you validate the expression. The .NET Framework has an extensive regular-expression syntax that can be used in many different scenarios, one of them being data validation. By using the regular-expression syntax, you can define how data should look in the control. We are using regular-expression syntax to define an email address that validates the EmailTextBox control. When you add a RegularExpressionValidator control to a form, the properties dialog box gives you several options for predefined expressions, such as phone numbers for different locales, email addresses, and URLs. Most of the bases are covered with the predefined offerings, but if something does not match your needs, you can customize the property as you see fit.

The third type of validation control on the user control is the CompareValidator control. This control is perfectly suited for the password data entry fields. In order to make sure that the user re-enters the password in the Password2 text box, add the CompareValidator to the form, and set the ControlToValidate property to Password2 and the ControlToCompare property to the Password1 text box. The control will automatically check that both fields are the same before the data is submitted to the server for processing.

```
<TD>Company Name:</TD>
<TD><asp:textbox id="Company" Width="208px" runat="server">
</asp:textbox></TD>


<TD><asp:requiredfieldvalidator id="RequiredFieldValidator1"
 runat="server" ControlToValidate="Company"
 ErrorMessage="Company name required">
</asp:requiredfieldvalidator></TD>


<TD>Email Address:</TD>
<TD><asp:textbox id="Email" Width="208px" runat="server">
</asp:textbox></TD>
<TD>
<asp:RegularExpressionValidator id="RegularExpressionValidator1"
 runat="server" ErrorMessage="Invalid email address"
 ControlToValidate="Email"
 ValidationExpression="\w+([-+.]\w+)*@\w+([-.]\w+)*\.\w+([-.]\w+)*">
</asp:RegularExpressionValidator></TD>



<TD>Re-Enter Password:</TD>
<TD><asp:textbox id="Password2" Width="208px" runat="server">
</asp:textbox></TD>
```

Listing 6.31 Partial _CustomerDetailsAdd.ascx HTML

```
<TD><asp:comparevalidator id="CompareValidator1"
 runat="server" ControlToValidate="Password2"
 ErrorMessage="Passwords do not match"
 ControlToCompare="Password1">
</asp:comparevalidator></TD>
```

Listing 6.31   Partial _CustomerDetailsAdd.ascx HTML (continued)

The code-behind for the _CustomerDetailsAdd user control is contained in two events: the Page_Load event and the SaveButton_Click event. The SaveButton_Click event does the basic reading of the data in the text box controls and passes them to the AddEditCustomer method in the Customers class. This either adds new customer information or updates an existing customer's profile. If a cookie containing the CustomerID exists on the computer, then the method assumes that the user has already logged in and is attempting to update his or her profile information. If this is the case, then the AddNew Boolean value that tells the method in the class to call the Update stored procedure is set to False, ensuring that the existing data is updated and a new record is not added. If the CustomerID cookie does not exist, then the AddNew Boolean value is set to True, and the AddEditCustomer method uses the appropriate stored procedure to add a new record to the Customers table.

The Page_Load event only runs if the CustomerID cookie exists on the computer. The event checks for the cookie, and if a CustomerID exists, then the user has either already logged in on this session or in a previous session. If this is the case, then the GetCustomerInfo method in the Customers class is called, and the SQLDataReader object that is returned is used to populate the controls on the page with the customer's data. The only way the user can get to this screen is after a login attempt, so no matter what, you are guaranteed that a cookie containing the CustomerID will either exist or not exist—there is no way an order can get lost in the process of the user attempting a login or updating profile information. Listing 6.32 is the complete listing for the _CustomerDetailsAdd.ascx.vb class.

```
Private Sub SaveButton_Click(ByVal sender As System.Object, _
  ByVal e As System.EventArgs) Handles SaveButton.Click
  ' make sure the page is valid and
  ' save the data to the database
  Dim c As Proj06Web.Customers = _
    New Proj06Web.Customers()
  ' Set a true/false switch to determine if this
  ' is an update or an add new
  Dim CustID As String = _
    Request.Cookies("CustomerID").Value.ToString
  '
  Dim AddNew As Boolean
  If CustID = "" Then
```

Listing 6.32   _CustomerDetailsAdd.ascx.vb

```
      AddNew = True
   Else
      AddNew = False
   End If
   '
   If c.AddEditCustomer(Email.Text.ToString.Trim, _
    Password1.Text.ToString.Trim, Company.Text.ToString.Trim, _
    Contact.Text.ToString.Trim, Title.Text.ToString.Trim, _
    Address.Text.ToString.Trim, City.Text.ToString.Trim, _
    State.Text.ToString.Trim, PostalCode.Text.ToString.Trim, _
    Country.Text.ToString.Trim, Phone.Text.ToString.Trim, _
    Fax.Text.ToString.Trim, AddNew) Then
      '
      ' Save the CustomerID as the cookie
      context.Response.Cookies("CustomerID").Value = _
        Email.Text.ToString
      '
      ' Go to the page that allows the user to verify their details
      Response.Redirect("verify.aspx?CustomerID=" & _
        Email.Text.ToString)
   End If
End Sub

Private Sub Page_Load(ByVal sender As System.Object, _
  ByVal e As System.EventArgs) Handles MyBase.Load

  Dim CustID As String = _
    Request.Cookies("CustomerID").Value.ToString
  If CustID <> "" Then
    ' a customerID value exisits as a cookie, so the user needs
    ' to update their existing profile, and not add a new profile.
    Dim c As Proj06Web.Customers = _
     New Proj06Web.Customers()
    ' Get the customer details, and fill the textboxes
    Dim rdr As SqlDataReader = _
    c.GetCustomerInfo(CustID)
    ' call the Read method of the SQLDataReader object
    ' to retrieve the fields
  While rdr.Read
    Company.Text = Convert.ToString(rdr("CompanyName"))
    Contact.Text = Convert.ToString(rdr("ContactName"))
    Address.Text = Convert.ToString(rdr("Address"))
    City.Text = Convert.ToString(rdr("City"))
    State.Text = Convert.ToString(rdr("Region"))
    PostalCode.Text = Convert.ToString(rdr("PostalCode"))
    Country.Text = Convert.ToString(rdr("Country"))
    Phone.Text = Convert.ToString(rdr("Phone"))
    Fax.Text = Convert.ToString(rdr("Fax"))
```

Listing 6.32   _CustomerDetailsAdd.ascx.vb (continued)

```
    Email.Text = Convert.ToString(rdr("Email"))
    ' set the email to read only, since this is
    ' the customer ID
    Email.ReadOnly = True
  End While
  End If
End Sub
```

Listing 6.32   _CustomerDetailsAdd.ascx.vb (continued)

A cool feature to add at this juncture would be the ability for a customer to have multiple addresses. In Commerce Server 2000, a single customer can have more than one shipping address. You can customize this feature even further by allowing a customer to break out a single order into multiple addresses. If you add an Address table to the database, you can add an Add New Address button on this user control and link the user to a new screen where a new address can be added. During the checkout process, you could list the available addresses in a DataList control and using an OptionButton control, let users choose the address they want shipments to go to and update the Orders table with that address.

Creating _VerifyDetails.ascx

The _VerifyDetails user control is the last step in the checkout process. Once the user logs in, he or she verifies their address and billing information and is presented with the option of modifying this information or completing the order. This user control consists of read-only label controls that display the user information from the Customers table in the database. Listing 6.33 is the _VerifyDetails.ascx code.

```
<%@ Control Language="vb" AutoEventWireup="false"
   Codebehind="_VerifyDetails.ascx.vb"
   Inherits="project06.C_VerifyDetails"
   TargetSchema="http://schemas.microsoft.com/intellisense/ie5" %>
<TABLE id="Table1" cellSpacing="1" cellPadding="1"
    width="417" border="0" height="456">
  <TR>
    <TD class="siteheader" colSpan="2">
    Verify Customer Information</TD>
  </TR>
  <TR>
   <TD style="WIDTH: 379px"></TD>
  </TR>
  <TR>
   <TD style="WIDTH: 379px; HEIGHT: 20px">
   <HR style="COLOR: #669999" width="100%" SIZE="1"></TD>
```

Listing 6.33   _VerifyDetails.ascx code

```
   </TR>
  <TR>
   <TD>
<TABLE id="Table2">
 <TR>
  <TD class="ProductNormal">Company: </TD>
  <TD><asp:Label CssClass="MediumRed14" id="Company"
     Width="216px" runat="server">
    </asp:Label></TD></TR>
 <TR>
  <TD class="ProductNormal">Contact Name: </TD>
  <TD><asp:Label CssClass="MediumRed14" id="Contact"
     Width="216px" runat="server">
   </asp:Label></TD></TR>
 <TR>
  <TD class="ProductNormal">Address:</TD>
  <TD><asp:Label CssClass="MediumRed14" id="Address"
     Width="216px" runat="server">
   </asp:Label></TD></TR>
 <TR>
  <TD class="ProductNormal">City:</TD>
  <TD><asp:Label CssClass="MediumRed14" id="City"
    Width="216px" runat="server">
   </asp:Label></TD></TR>
 <TR>
  <TD class="ProductNormal">Region:</TD>
  <TD><asp:Label CssClass="MediumRed14" id="RegionName"
     Width="216px" runat="server">
   </asp:Label></TD></TR>
 <TR>
  <TD class="ProductNormal">Postal Code:</TD>
  <TD><asp:Label CssClass="MediumRed14" id="PostalCode"
    Width="216px" runat="server">
   </asp:Label></TD></TR>
 <TR>
  <TD class="ProductNormal">Country:</TD>
  <TD><asp:Label CssClass="MediumRed14" id="Country"
     Width="216px" runat="server">
   </asp:Label></TD></TR>
 <TR>
  <TD class="ProductNormal">Phone:</TD>
  <TD><asp:Label CssClass="MediumRed14" id="Phone"
    Width="216px" runat="server">
   </asp:Label></TD></TR>
 <TR>
  <TD class="ProductNormal">Fax:</TD>
  <TD><asp:Label CssClass="MediumRed14" id="Fax"
    Width="216px" runat="server">
   </asp:Label></TD></TR>
```

Listing 6.33 _VerifyDetails.ascx code (continued)

```
<TR>
  <TD class="ProductNormal">Email:</TD>
  <TD><asp:Label CssClass="MediumRed14" id="Email"
    Width="216px" runat="server">
    </asp:Label></TD></TR>
</TABLE>
  </TD>
</TR>
<TR>
  <TD style="WIDTH: 379px">
   <HR style="COLOR: #009999" width="100%" SIZE="1">
  </TD>
</TR>
<TR><TD style="WIDTH: 379px">
    <asp:Button id="CheckOutButton" runat="server"
    Width="133px" Text="Submit Order>
    </asp:Button> </TD></TR>
<TR><TD style="WIDTH: 379px"></TD>
</TR>
<TR>
  <TD style="WIDTH: 379px">
   <asp:Button id="ChangeProfile"
     runat="server" Text="Change Information">
   </asp:Button></TD>
</TR>
</TABLE>
```

Listing 6.33   _VerifyDetails.ascx code (continued)

The code-behind for the _VerifyDetails user control consists of the Page_Load event, which loads the user information from the Customers table, and the ChangeProfile_Click event, which redirects the shopper to the profile data-entry form if personal information needs to be modified. The Page_Load event creates an instance of the Customers class and calls the GetCustomerInfo method to return a SQL-DataReader object, which binds the results to the label controls. The DataField property for each label control is set to the appropriate field from the table. Listing 6.34 is the complete listing for the _VerifyDetails.ascx.vb class.

```
Private Sub Page_Load(ByVal sender As System.Object, _
    ByVal e As System.EventArgs) Handles MyBase.Load

  ' Load the information from the customers database to let the user
  ' verify address information
  Dim c As Proj06Web.Customers = _
    New Proj06Web.Customers()
```

Listing 6.34   _VerifyDetails.ascx.vb code

```
 Dim rdr As SqlDataReader = _
  c.GetCustomerInfo(Request.Cookies("CustomerID").Value.ToString)

 While rdr.Read
   Company.Text = Convert.ToString(rdr("CompanyName"))
   Contact.Text = Convert.ToString(rdr("ContactName"))
   Address.Text = Convert.ToString(rdr("Address"))
   City.Text = Convert.ToString(rdr("City"))
   RegionName.Text = Convert.ToString(rdr("Region"))
   PostalCode.Text = Convert.ToString(rdr("PostalCode"))
   Country.Text = Convert.ToString(rdr("Country"))
   Phone.Text = Convert.ToString(rdr("Phone"))
   Fax.Text = Convert.ToString(rdr("Fax"))
   Email.Text = Convert.ToString(rdr("Email"))
 End While

End Sub

Private Sub ChangeProfile_Click(ByVal sender As System.Object, _
  ByVal e As System.EventArgs) Handles ChangeProfile.Click
  ' The user has determined that they need to modify their information,
  ' so redirect them to the profile page
  Response.Redirect("userprofile.aspx")
End Sub
```

Listing 6.34   _VerifyDetails.ascx.vb code (continued)

When you create an actual online store, you will need to include some type of credit card verification. This user control would most likely encapsulate that functionality. You might want to include the type of credit card and the credit card number so users can view this information one last time and modify it if need be before completing the order.

Creating _Login.ascx

The _Login user control is your basic login screen. Once the user decides that the information in the shopping cart is what he or she wants, he or she proceeds to the login screen. If the user has already shopped at the online store, the username and password can be entered and the login attempted. If a user has not shopped here before, clicking the Register button displays the user profile data entry screen you created earlier. This user control uses RequiredFieldValidator controls to force the user to enter a username and password, but since the Register button would cause the validation events to occur, you need to set the CausesValidation property of the Register button to False so the click event can occur. If you are a Visual Basic 6 developer, the CausesValidation property behaves the same in ASP.NET as it did in VB6. Listing 6.35 is the _Login user control code listing.

```
<%@ Control Language="vb" AutoEventWireup="false"
    Codebehind="_Login.ascx.vb"
    Inherits="project06.C_Login"
    TargetSchema="http://schemas.microsoft.com/intellisense/ie5" %>
<TABLE class="ProductNormal" id="Table1">
 <TR>
  <TD style="WIDTH: 96px"></TD>
  <TD style="WIDTH: 236px">
     Returning customers, please log in.
  </TD>
 </TR>
 <TR>
  <TD>User Name:</TD>
  <TD style="WIDTH: 236px">
     <asp:TextBox id="Username" runat="server">
     </asp:TextBox>
  </TD>
  <TD>
     <asp:RequiredFieldValidator id="RequiredFieldValidator1"
       runat="server" ErrorMessage="RequiredFieldValidator"
       Width="198px" ControlToValidate="Username">
    Please enter a User Name</asp:RequiredFieldValidator>
  </TD>
 </TR>
 <TR>
  <TD>Password:</TD>
  <TD style="WIDTH: 236px">
     <asp:TextBox id="Password" runat="server">
     </asp:TextBox>
  </TD>
  <TD>
     <asp:RequiredFieldValidator id="RequiredFieldValidator2"
       runat="server" ErrorMessage="RequiredFieldValidator"
       ControlToValidate="Password">
    Please enter a Password</asp:RequiredFieldValidator>
  </TD>
 </TR>
 <TR>
  <TD>
     <asp:Button id="LoginButton" runat="server"
       Width="115px" Text="Log In">
     </asp:Button>
  </TD>
 </TR>
 <TR>
  <TD>
     <asp:Label id="LoginError" runat="server"
       Width="181px" ForeColor="Red">
     </asp:Label>
  </TD>
```

Listing 6.35   _Login.ascx code listing

```
</TR>
 <TR>
  <TD style="WIDTH: 236px">
     If you are a new customer, click here to register.
  </TD>
 </TR>
 <TR>
  <TD style="WIDTH: 236px">
     <asp:Button id="RegisterButton" runat="server"
      CausesValidation="False">
     </asp:Button>
  </TD>
 </TR>
</TABLE>
```

Listing 6.35 _Login.ascx code listing (continued)

The code-behind for the _Login user control is simple. Once the user clicks the Login button, the Authenticate method in the Customers class is called, using the username and password entered as the parameters. If the user exists in the database, he or she is redirected to the Verify.aspx page to complete the checkout process. If this user does not exist in the database, the LoginError label control notifies him or her that the login attempt was unsuccessful. From this point, the user can either try to log in again or click the Register button and get redirected to the Userprofile.aspx page and enter new customer information. The Action parameter with the Add value lets the Userprofile.aspx page know that this is a new user and not an existing user attempting to update his or her profile information. The _CustomerDetailsAdd.ascx user control also performs an additional check for the CustomerID cookie to verify that the user is adding a new record and not updating previous information. Listing 6.36 is the complete listing for the _Login.ascx.vb code.

```
Private Sub LoginButton_Click(ByVal sender As System.Object, _
  ByVal e As System.EventArgs) Handles LoginButton.Click

  Dim c As Proj06Web.Customers = _
    New Proj06Web.Customers()

  Dim CustomerID As String = _
    c.Authenticate(Username.Text, Password.Text)

  If CustomerID <> "" Then
    context.Response.Cookies("CustomerID").Value = _
      CustomerID.ToString
    Response.Redirect("verify.aspx?CustomerID=" & CustomerID)
  Else
```

Listing 6.36 _Login.ascx.vb code

```
    LoginError.Text = "You are not in the database"
  End If
End Sub

Private Sub RegisterButton_Click(ByVal sender As System.Object, _
  ByVal e As System.EventArgs) Handles RegisterButton.Click
    Response.Redirect("userprofile.aspx?Action=Add")
End Sub
```

Listing 6.36   _Login.ascx.vb code (continued)

Creating _NoMenuHeader.ascx

The final user control that needs to be created is the _NoMenuHeader user control. This user control is used on the Verify.aspx and Checkout.aspx pages to replace the Categories menu that would normally be across the top of the page. When users are in the checkout process, they should not have the ability to continue shopping. To ensure that they do not, we remove the Categories menu and give them no way to return back to shopping. Listing 6.37 is the code for the _NoMenuHeader user control. There is no code-behind for this control; it is simply for display purposes.

```
<TABLE id="Table1" style="WIDTH: 100%; HEIGHT: 51px" cellSpacing="1"
  cellPadding="1" width="100%" border="0">
 <TR>
   <TD bgColor="#336600"> </TD>
 </TR>
 <TR>
   <TD bgColor="#cccc66"> </TD>
 </TR>
</TABLE>
```

Listing 6.37   _NoMenuHeader.ascx code

Creating the Style Sheet

The style sheet that covers the whole application is presented in Listing 6.38. Up until now, each HTML element and ASP.NET Web control had either the class or CssClass property set with a style class. Each of the Web forms will need the relative link to this style sheet to unify the look and feel of the Web site. To change the colors and fonts, you can just change this style sheet and the site will be updated. There are several areas in the user controls where the colors of the controls are hard-coded, but that can also be included in the style sheet, along with border style settings for tables and any other visual features you want to add to improve the look and feel of your online store.

```
body
{
      font-size: 11px;
      font-weight:bolder;
      color: navy;
      font-family: Verdana;
}

.checkout
{
      font-size: 11px;
      font-weight:normal ;
      color:Black ;
      font-family: Verdana;
}

.selected
{
      font-size: 11px;
      font-weight:bolder;
      color: white;
      font-family: Verdana;
      background-color: #006666;
}
.notselected
{
      font-size: 10px;
      font-weight:normal;
      color: maroon;
      font-family: Verdana;
      background-color: LemonChiffon;

}
.ProductName
{
      font-weight: bold;
      font-size: 18px;
      color: maroon;
      font-family: Verdana, Tahoma;
}
.ProductDescription
{
      font-size: 10px;
      color: black;
      font-family: Verdana, Tahoma;
}
```

Listing 6.38   Main.css style sheet code

```
.ProductPrice
{
     font-size: 12px;
     color: maroon;
     font-family: Verdana, Tahoma;
}
.ProductNormal
{
     font-size: 10px;
     color: black;
     font-family: Verdana, Tahoma;
}
.SiteHeader
{
     font-family: Franklin Gothic Medium;
     color: #999933;
     font-size: 36;
     font-weight:bold
}
 .SmallCart
{
     font-size: 10px;
     color: maroon;
     font-weight:bold;
     font-family: Verdana, Tahoma;
}
.MediumRed14
{
     font-size: 14px;
     color: maroon;
     font-family: Verdana, Tahoma;
}
.UserProfile
{
     font-size: 10px;
     color: Navy;
     font-family: Verdana, Tahoma;
}
```

Listing 6.38 Main.css style sheet code (continued)

Creating the Web Forms

Earlier, I mentioned that once the user controls were created, it would simply be a matter of dragging and dropping the controls on to the Web forms in the correct location. Each of the Web forms that you added to the project will have almost the exact same layout. The basic idea here is that you want the design to be in the user controls and not the Web forms, so the less work in the Web forms, the better.

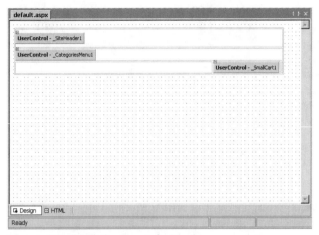

Figure 6.9   Default.aspx at design time.

Instead of going right into the HTML code that makes up each page, take a look at Figure 6.9. This figure displays the basic structure of the page. The image represents the Default.aspx page, but the HTML table that controls the positioning of the user controls is the same for each Web form.

The process of adding user controls to the Web forms is the same as adding any other control. Drag and drop the control to the desired location on the page. If you add a table to each of the Web forms, then it is just a matter of setting the correct width of the rows and columns. Listing 6.39 is the HTML output for the Default.aspx page represented in Figure 6.9. The code in bold indicates the code that is added to the ASP.NET form once the user controls are added.

```
<%@ Register TagPrefix="uc1" TagName="_productlist"
Src="_productlist.ascx" %>
<%@ Register TagPrefix="uc1" TagName="_SiteHeader"
Src="_SiteHeader.ascx" %>
<%@ Register TagPrefix="uc1" TagName="_SmallCart" Src="_SmallCart.ascx"
%>
<%@ Page Language="vb" AutoEventWireup="false"
Codebehind="default.aspx.vb"
     Inherits="project06._default" %>
<%@ Register TagPrefix="uc1" TagName="_CategoriesMenu"
Src="_CategoriesMenu.ascx" %>
<!DOCTYPE HTML PUBLIC "-//W3C//DTD HTML 4.0 Transitional//EN">
<HTML>
  <HEAD>
    <title>Project06 - Online Store Home</title>
    <meta name="GENERATOR" content="Microsoft Visual Studio.NET 7.0">
```

Listing 6.39   HTML code for default.aspx

```
        <meta name="CODE_LANGUAGE" content="Visual Basic 7.0">
        <meta name="vs_defaultClientScript" content="JavaScript">
        <meta name="vs_targetSchema"
           content="http://schemas.microsoft.com/intellisense/ie5">

        <LINK rel="stylesheet" type="text/css" href="main.css">

</HEAD>
  <body MS_POSITIONING="GridLayout">
    <form id="Form1" method="post" runat="server">
      <TABLE id="Table1">
      <TR>
        <TD class="siteheader" style="HEIGHT: 40px" colSpan="3">

<uc1:_SiteHeader id=_SiteHeader1 runat="server"></uc1:_SiteHeader>
        </TD>

      </TR>
      <TR>
        <TD style="HEIGHT: 1px" colSpan="3">

<uc1:_CategoriesMenu id=_CategoriesMenu1
runat="server"></uc1:_CategoriesMenu>
        </TD>

        <TR>
        <TD style="WIDTH: 435px" vAlign=top align=left></TD>
        <TD vAlign=top align=left>

<uc1:_SmallCart id=_SmallCart1 runat="server"></uc1:_SmallCart>
        </TD>

        <TD vAlign=top align=top></TD>
      </TR>
    </TABLE>
    </form>
  </body>
</HTML>
```

Listing 6.39   HTML code for default.aspx (continued)

First, when you add a user control to a Web form, the Register directive is added to the top of the Web form. The Register directive notifies the page that there are user controls on the page. It specifies the TagPrefix for the user control and sets the location of the actual control in the Web directory. The ID property for each user control added is incremented by one for each instance of the same control, so if you added the _Small-Cart user control more than once on the same page, you would have _SmallCart1,

_SmallCart2, and so on. The second item to notice is the style sheet link. Each Web form needs the style sheet to correctly set the fonts and colors for the elements in each user control.

To complete the user interface, Table 6.6 lists the remaining Web forms and the user controls that need to be added to each form. If you refer to Figure 6.4 earlier in this project, you can get a refresher on the goal for the page setup. The Location column in the table refers to either Top, Middle, Left, or Right, which specifies the location in the HTML table where the user control is to be added.

Now that you have added the user controls to their respective Web forms, you can work on positioning and any other formatting issues you might have. The final step in creating the online store is doing a final build to make sure all the assemblies are up-to-date. Once the solution is built, you can run the store and then start thinking of what you can do next to improve on the design to meet your specific needs.

Table 6.6   Web Forms and User Control Location

WEB FORM	USER CONTROL	LOCATION
ProductsList.aspx	_SiteHeader.ascx	Top
	_CategoriesMenu.ascx	Middle
	_ProductsList.ascx	Left
	_SmallCart.ascx	Right
Checkout.aspx	_SiteHeader.ascx	Top
	_CategoriesMenu.ascx	Middle
	_BigCart.ascx	Left
UserLogin.aspx	_SiteHeader.ascx	Top
	_NoMenuHeader.ascx	Middle
	_Login,ascx	Left
UserProfile.aspcx	_SiteHeader.ascx	Top
	_NoMenuHeader.ascx	Middle
	_CustomerDetailsAdd.ascx	Left
Verify.aspx	_SiteHeader.ascx	Top
	_NoMenuHeader.ascx	Middle
	_VerifyDetails.ascx	Left

Wrap Up

In this project, you went through all of the steps necessary to create an online e-commerce application. Using the thousands of e-commerce applications across the Internet as an example, you now have the base functionalities that all e-commerce applications must have:

- Browsing items for sale
- Adding items to a shopping cart
- Performing a checkout process

To enhance this version of the online store, you can add features such as a Wish List, which is becoming more popular on the larger e-commerce sites, banner advertising, and targeted marketing features, like an Also Bought user control that could check what other people have purchased when the user adds an item to the shopping cart. There is no limit when it comes to features you can add, so by examining what exists on the Internet and what your requirements are, the architecture of the site makes it easy to implement new features without major redesign or modification to existing code.

In Project 7, you'll begin building the Team Network system, an application that will provide project tracking, file sharing, and discussion forums.

Teamwork Network:
The Infrastructure

One of the more interesting aspects of the Internet is how it has made *virtual corporations* a reality. Instead of hiring people to do jobs, you add people as needed to perform certain tasks. This is especially true among independent contractors like myself. I work with a client on a project, and then we all go our separate ways. If I need help doing something, I bring people in to do those tasks. The problem with all this collaboration, however, is the sheer number of places information can get lost. You might have some information in your email program, some printed on paper on your desk, some files stored on various computers, and lots of phone calls, for which there is really no record.

In this project, you'll start building the Teamwork Network system. This application provides three major features: project tracking, file sharing, and discussion forums.

These three subsystems are integrated in a complex infrastructure, which you'll build in this project. While there aren't a lot of heavy concepts, there are quite a few files to build and a number of features to implement. Besides the three major subsystems, you'll also be implementing a user login system, a team manager, and a messaging component that allows for system- and user-generated messages to be kept in the system outside of regular email. A customized home page will consolidate information from the three subsystems onto a single page for the user, and a search utility will enable the user to search for content in all the subsystems. You'll also see how to expand the system to add on other features later.

If you want to see the system operational, be sure to visit the Web site at www.teamworknetwork.com. I intend to keep this site running as a public-development project that you can discuss at the book's Web site: www.10projectswithasp.net. We'll add new features as time goes on to make this site useful for everyone.

THE PROBLEM

Online collaboration requires a variety of components in order to work well, and each component requires the purchase of expensive software to do even the simplest collaboration tasks.

THE SOLUTION

An ASP.NET application that provides file sharing, project tracking, discussion forums, and an overall infrastructure supporting additional subsystems in the future.

Project Background

Before you start building the key components of the application, you have to build the infrastructure first. This infrastructure is common in many applications that you will build. Most applications have to have a user authentication method of some sort. In this application, you'll be building a structure that allows members (the term for users in this application) to be added to any number of teams. Data in the project, file sharing, and discussion forum systems will all be related to the teams created by members. The team leader can add and remove members at will. When a member is added or removed, a message is generated automatically and sent to the member. I chose to create a separate system for messaging instead of sending the messages to external email programs. By keeping the messages internal to the system, you could change the web site to a secure one using SSL (Secure Socket Layer) and provide even better security for the messages being sent.

To build this application, you'll need to complete these tasks:

1. Design the database tables.
2. Create the stored procedures used in the application.
3. Build the business objects.
4. Build the application's Web pages.

 ## You Will Need

✔ **Windows 2000**

✔ **Internet Information Server 5.0 with .NET Framework installed**

✔ **Visual Studio .NET**

✔ **SQL Server 2000 or 7.0**

✔ **SQL Server client utilities, including SQL Server Enterprise Manager and Query Analyzer**

Designing the Tables

There are four tables that you'll be building for this portion of the application:

tblMembers. Each user of the system has a member record in this table.

tblMessages. Messages sent to other members are stored in this table.

tblTeams. Members can create and be added to an unlimited number of teams. This table stores the team description and name.

tblTeamMembers. This join table links the tblMembers table and tblTeams table to support a many-to-many relationship between the two tables.

Table 7.1 shows the fields for the tblMembers table, which is the largest of the four tables. It contains all the required and optional profile information for each member.

The required fields are integral to making the system work. The email address is required so that if you want to email a person and verify that they exist, you have that capability. The username and email address will both be verified to make sure that a user has only one account and that no duplicate usernames are allowed. We'll take care of this through a pair of stored procedures that you'll write later in the project.

The next table to build is the tblMessages table, which stores internal emails sent between users. The fields for this table are shown in Table 7.2.

Table 7.1 tblMembers Table Definition

FIELD NAME	SQL DATA TYPE	LENGTH	OTHER
pkMemberID	int	N/A	Identity, Primary Key, Not Null
FirstName	varchar	40	Not Null
LastName	varchar	40	Not Null
Email	varchar	100	Not Null
UserName	varchar	20	Not Null
Password	varchar	20	Not Null
DisplayProfile	char	1	Not Null, Default 'P'
HomePage	varchar	100	
HomePhone	varchar	40	
WorkPhone	varchar	40	
MobilePhone	varchar	40	
Fax	varchar	40	
AboutMe	text	N/A	

Table 7.2   tblMessages Table Definition

FIELD NAME	SQL DATA TYPE	LENGTH	OTHER
pkMessageID	int	N/A	Identity, Primary Key, Not Null
fkMessageToMemberID	int	N/A	Not Null
fkMessageFromMemberID	int	N/A	Not Null
MessageDate	datetime	N/A	Not Null
MessageSubject	varchar	80	Not Null
MessageText	text	N/A	
MessageRead	bit	N/A	

All the fields except the actual text message are required in this table. The two foreign keys point to the tblMembers table so that a message can be linked to its sender and recipient. Each message also has a MessageRead field indicating whether the user has actually opened and read the message. The user can keep messages in the system indefinitely, and a good opportunity for expansion would be to add on a message folder system. This would involve adding another foreign key to this table and adding a new table called tblMessageFolders that might look like one in Table 7.3.

This is just one place you could expand the application. I'll be pointing out more of these opportunities throughout this and the next three projects.

The third table you need to build is used to keep records of the teams that have been created in the system. Teams are the basis for the other applications in the system. Files, discussions, and projects can be made available publicly to everyone or just to particular teams. Any user can create a team, but the team owner is solely responsible for adding users to his or her teams. The table definition is shown in Table 7.4.

The fkLeaderID foreign key points to the tblMembers table. This identifies the leader of the team so that user can maintain the team record and team members. The next table to build is tblTeamMembers, and it joins the tblTeams table with the tblMembers table in a many-to-many relationship that allows each user to be on many teams and each team to have many users. The table definition for tblTeamMembers is shown in Table 7.5.

Table 7.3   tblMessageFolders Proposed Table Definition

FIELD NAME	SQL DATA TYPE	LENGTH	OTHER
pkFolderID	int	N/A	Identity, Primary Key, Not Null
Name	varchar	80	Not Null
Description	text	N/A	

Table 7.4   tblTeams Table Definition

FIELD NAME	SQL DATA TYPE	LENGTH	OTHER
pkTeamID	int	N/A	Identity, Primary Key, Not Null
fkLeaderID	int	N/A	Not Null
Name	varchar	80	Not Null
Description	text	N/A	

Table 7.5   tblTeams Table Definition

FIELD NAME	SQL DATA TYPE	LENGTH	OTHER
pkTeamMemberID	int	N/A	Identity, Primary Key, Not Null
fkTeamID	int	N/A	Not Null
fkMemberID	int	N/A	Not Null

We use a separate primary key here to make it easier to remove records using our object infrastructure, which relies on a unique primary key to function properly. You could also use the two foreign keys together as a primary key, since SQL Server and most other databases will allow you to use multiple fields together as a primary key to a table.

Creating the Stored Procedures

This database makes heavier use of stored procedures to handle several complicated tasks directly on the server instead of retrieving lots of data to be processed manually. For the features covered in this project, you will be building a total of 10 stored procedures:

sp_CheckForDuplicateEMail. Determines whether the selected email address already exists in the system.

sp_CheckForDuplicateUserName. Determines whether the selected username already exists in the system.

sp_CheckForTeamDelete. Teams can only be deleted when all the related records have been removed. This stored procedure, which will be modified as we work through the other projects, returns the number of related records in each table (currently just the tblTeamMembers table) so that the Delete Team function can determine whether or not it can delete the team.

sp_CheckLogin. Determines if the username and password match a member's record in the database. If so, the member's ID is returned.

sp_CheckProfileVisibility. Each user has the option to make his or her profile information public, available to teammates only, or private. This stored procedure determines whether a user can see another's profile.

sp_RetrieveAllMembers. Returns a list of all members. This stored procedure is bound to several pages used to select members for sending messages and joining teams.

sp_RetrieveMessageCountByMember. Returns the number of old and new messages for a particular member.

sp_RetrieveMessagesByMember. Returns all messages for a particular member, as well as indicators showing whether the message is new or not.

sp_RetrieveTeamMembers. Retrieves information about all team members for a given team.

sp_RetrieveTeamsByMember. Retrieves all the teams that a given member leads.

These stored procedures are broken into two logical categories: verification stored procedures and retrieval stored procedures. We'll work through each category in turn.

Building the Verification Stored Procedures

The first stored procedure we need to build is the sp_CheckForDuplicateEmail stored procedure. The code is shown in Listing 7.1.

This stored procedure returns the number of times a given email address occurs in the system. This stored procedure is checked when a new member is added to the system and should return a zero if the address does not exist. The Member class will view the DuplicateCount to make sure that this is the case, and if not, will generate a validation error.

```
CREATE PROCEDURE dbo.sp_CheckForDuplicateEmail
@Email varchar(100)
AS
SELECT COUNT(*) As DuplicateCount
FROM tblMembers
WHERE Lower(Email) = Lower(@Email)
```

Listing 7.1 sp_CheckForDuplicateEmail

The next stored procedure does basically the same thing, but with the username selected by a potential member. The code for sp_CheckForDuplicateUserName is shown in Listing 7.2.

```
CREATE PROCEDURE dbo.sp_CheckForDuplicateUserName
@UserName varchar(20)
AS
SELECT COUNT(*) As DuplicateCount
FROM tblMembers
WHERE Lower(UserName) = Lower(@UserName)
```

Listing 7.2   sp_CheckForDuplicateUserName

Again, the Member class checks the result of this stored procedure before allowing a new record into the system. The result of this routine is far more critical than the email address, but both will help keep the member records more reliable and free of duplicates.

The next stored procedure is modified as we add other subsystems to the site. It returns the number of related records to a given team. The ASP.NET code looks at the results of this stored procedure before attempting to delete a team. This prevents data-integrity errors from occurring and keeps the database clean. The code for sp_CheckForTeamDelete is shown in Listing 7.3.

This routine returns an additional field for each table that we check as we add more subsystems to the application in the next few projects.

```
CREATE PROCEDURE dbo.sp_CheckForTeamDelete
@TeamID int
AS
SELECT TeamMembers =
  (SELECT COUNT(*) FROM tblTeamMembers WHERE fkTeamID = @TeamID)
```

Listing 7.3   sp_CheckForTeamDelete

Our login-verification routine, sp_CheckLogin, is next on the list to build. The code is shown in Listing 7.4.

```
CREATE PROCEDURE dbo.sp_CheckLogin
@UserName varchar(20),
@Password varchar(20)
AS
SELECT *
FROM tblMembers
WHERE Lower(UserName) = Lower(@UserName)
AND Lower(Password) = Lower(@Password)
```

Listing 7.4   sp_CheckLogin

I made the decision to make usernames and passwords case-insensitive, as we did in the two routines checking for duplicate fields. In this routine, we return a record if we find one that matches the username and password entered. This information is then used in a variety of ways for the application.

The next stored procedure to build is called sp_CheckProfileVisibility and is the most complicated one of the lot. The code is shown in Listing 7.5.

```
CREATE PROCEDURE dbo.sp_CheckProfileVisibility
@ViewerID int,
@ProfileID int
AS
SELECT 'T' As IsProfileVisible
FROM tblMembers
WHERE pkMemberID = @ProfileID
AND
  (DisplayProfile = 'P'
  OR
  @ViewerID = @ProfileID
  OR
  (DisplayProfile = 'T' AND
  @ViewerID IN
   (SELECT DISTINCT fkMemberID
   FROM tblTeamMembers
   WHERE fkTeamID IN
     (SELECT DISTINCT fkTeamID
     FROM tblTeamMembers
     WHERE fkMemberID = @ProfileID)
     )
   )
  )
```

Listing 7.5 sp_CheckProfileVisibility

This routine returns a single value if the user wanting to see the profile (@ViewerID) is able to see the profile selected (@ProfileID). The only way this can happen is if one of these conditions occurs:

- The viewer and the profile represent the same member
- A member's profile has been marked as public
- A member's profile is marked as visible to team members, and the viewer is on a team with the member in question.

The nested SQL here checks all three conditions in one fell swoop instead of manually looking through a bunch of records. I always tell my SQL Server students to take as much advantage of the server as possible. It can handle this sort of dirty work much faster than you can manually in ASP.NET.

Building the Retrieval Stored Procedures

The next set of stored procedures to build retrieve information. Most of them are used in combination with ASP.NET Repeater controls, so we have to do some extra formatting in the stored procedure to save ourselves work in the Repeater control. Again, let the database do the extra work, and if you have to pull back an extra field, it's definitely worth it, as you'll soon see.

The first retrieval stored procedure to build is sp_RetrieveAllMembers. The code is shown in Listing 7.6.

This stored procedure returns all the member information already formatted for display by the Repeater control. We concatenate the last and first names into a new field, return a Yes or No for whether the profile is public (this routine doesn't need to worry about team membership), and a URL that points to the member-profile viewer. We'll populate this into the repeater, and if the profile is not visible, the URL will be empty and will not create a link on the page.

```
CREATE PROCEDURE dbo.sp_RetrieveAllMembers
AS
SELECT *,
LastName + ', ' + FirstName As MemberName,
ProfileVisible =
 (CASE DisplayProfile
 WHEN 'P'
 THEN 'Yes'
 ELSE 'No'
 END),
ProfileURL =
 (CASE DisplayProfile
 WHEN 'P'
 THEN '<a href="member_view.aspx?id='
 + convert(varchar, pkMemberID) + '">'
 ELSE ''
 END)

FROM tblMembers
ORDER BY LastName, FirstName
```

Listing 7.6 sp_RetrieveAllMembers

The next stored procedure is sp_RetrieveMessageCountByMember, and the code is shown in Listing 7.7.

```
CREATE PROCEDURE dbo.sp_RetrieveMessageCountByMember
@MemberID int
AS
SELECT NewCount =
  (SELECT COUNT(*) FROM tblMessages
  WHERE fkMessageToMemberID = @MemberID AND MessageRead = 0),
OldCount =
  (SELECT COUNT(*) FROM tblMessages
  WHERE fkMessageToMemberID = @MemberID And MessageRead = 1)
```

Listing 7.7 sp_RetrieveMessageCountByMember

This simple routine counts each type of message and returns two fields for the My Home Page code to format a statement similar to the following:

```
You have 2 new messages and 3 old messages.
```

The next routine returns all the messages for a particular user, as well as a graphic URL pointing to either a new message icon or an empty spacer graphic. This way, we can drop the URL into an image tag instead of having to do a lot of extra manipulation. The code for sp_RetrieveMessagesByMember is shown in Listing 7.8.

Again, we're letting the database do some of our formatting work by selecting either a visible or invisible graphic, based on whether the message is new or old. The CASE statement used in this and several of the other stored procedures is part of SQL Server's TransactSQL language and can make programming a lot easier. We also join the tblMessages table with the tblMembers table to generate the recipient's name of the message for display.

When we need to show the members of a team, the sp_RetrieveTeamMembers routine will take care of all the data retrieval for us. The code is shown in Listing 7.9.

```
CREATE PROCEDURE dbo.sp_RetrieveMessagesByMember
@MemberID int
AS
SELECT MSG.*,
     M.LastName + ', ' + M.FirstName As MessageFrom,
     MessageIndicator = (CASE MessageRead WHEN 0 THEN 'newmessage.gif'
ELSE 'spacer.gif' END),
     MessageIndicatorText = (CASE MessageRead WHEN 0 THEN 'New Message'
ELSE '' END)
FROM tblMembers M, tblMessages MSG
WHERE MSG.fkMessageFromMemberID = M.pkMemberID
AND MSG.fkMessageToMemberID = @MemberID
ORDER BY MSG.MessageDate DESC
```

Listing 7.8 sp_RetrieveMessagesByMember

```
CREATE PROCEDURE dbo.sp_RetrieveTeamMembers
@TeamID int
AS
SELECT pkTeamMemberID,
M.LastName + ', ' + M.FirstName As MemberName,
M.UserName As UserName
FROM tblMembers M, tblTeamMembers TM
WHERE TM.fkTeamID = @TeamID
AND TM.fkMemberID = M.pkMemberID
ORDER BY M.LastName, M.FirstName
```

Listing 7.9   sp_RetrieveTeamMembers

Like the previous routine that retrieved the member name for messages, we retrieve the member name to show on the team listing.

The final stored procedure we need to write is sp_RetrieveTeamsByMember, and the code for this is shown in Listing 7.10. This is just a basic SELECT statement with a parameter. However, it does have a sort, so making it a stored procedure is always a good idea.

With the stored procedures out of the way, it's time to build the business objects we need to make this system work. These objects all build on what you did in Project 3, with a few minor changes along the way.

```
CREATE PROCEDURE dbo.sp_RetrieveTeamsByMember
@MemberID int
AS
SELECT *
FROM tblTeams
WHERE fkLeaderID = @MemberID
ORDER BY Name
```

Listing 7.10   sp_RetrieveTeamsByMember

Building the Business Objects

The next thing we'll be doing is building the objects that manipulate each type of data in the system. As in Project 3, we put most of the functionality into the BaseServices class and simply inherit from it for each entity. We have made a few minor changes to the Database and BaseServices classes to make them a bit more flexible for the type of work we need to do in this section.

Creating the Database Class

The AtWorkUtilities.Database class code is shown in Listing 7.11. The one change to this class is that the GetDataReader method has an optional parameter to skip the initial Read() call. Some of the pages in this system use stored procedures that only return a single row or none at all. We need to be able to view the return value from the Read() function to determine whether or not we can look at the data. Adding the parameter as optional ensures that any code using the previous version of the Database class will still work. The new code is highlighted in bold for easy reference.

```
Imports System.Data.SqlClient
Imports System.Configuration

Public Class Database
  Private m_cnDB As SqlConnection


  ' This constructor reads the application configuration
  ' file (Web.config for web applications) for a string
  ' called ConnectionString. If it's not there, an exception
  ' is thrown. Otherwise, the connection is made.
  '
  Public Sub New()
   Dim objCnf As ConfigurationSettings
   If objCnf.AppSettings("ConnectionString") = "" Then
     Throw New Exception("Connection string not found " _
       & "in application configuration file.")
   Else
     m_cnDB = New _
       SqlConnection(objCnf.AppSettings("ConnectionString").ToString)
     m_cnDB.Open()
   End If
  End Sub


  '
  ' This constructor accepts a connection string as input
  ' and makes a connection to that SQL Server.
  '
  Public Sub New(ByVal ConnectionString As String)
   m_cnDB = New SqlConnection(ConnectionString)
   m_cnDB.Open()
  End Sub


  '
  ' In case there are other objects that need the live
  ' connection, make it available through a read-only
  ' property.
  '
  Public ReadOnly Property Connection() As SqlConnection
```

Listing 7.11   Database.vb class

```
Get
 Return m_cnDB
End Get
End Property


' Run a query that does not return records.
'
Public Function Execute(ByVal SQL As String) As Integer
 Dim lngRecords As Integer
 Dim cmdQuery As New SqlCommand()
 cmdQuery.Connection = m_cnDB
 cmdQuery.CommandText = SQL
 cmdQuery.CommandType = CommandType.Text
 lngRecords = cmdQuery.ExecuteNonQuery()
End Function


' Run a stored procedure that does not return records.
'
Public Function ExecuteStoredProc(ByVal SQL As String) As Integer
 Dim lngRecords As Integer
 Dim cmdQuery As New SqlCommand()
 cmdQuery.Connection = m_cnDB
 cmdQuery.CommandText = SQL
 cmdQuery.CommandType = CommandType.StoredProcedure
 lngRecords = cmdQuery.ExecuteNonQuery()
End Function


' Run a query that returns records in the form
' of a SqlDataReader.
'
Public Function GetDataReader(ByVal SQL As String, _
 Optional ByVal blnSkipRead As Boolean = False) As SqlDataReader

 Dim cmdQuery As New SqlCommand()
 Dim dr As SqlDataReader
 cmdQuery.Connection = m_cnDB
 cmdQuery.CommandText = SQL
 cmdQuery.CommandType = CommandType.Text
 dr = cmdQuery.ExecuteReader
 If Not blnSkipRead Then dr.Read()
 Return dr
End Function


' Run a query that returns records in the form
```

Listing 7.11   Database.vb class (continued)

```
' of a DataSet.
'
Public Function GetDataSet(ByVal SQL As String) As DataSet
 Dim da As New SqlDataAdapter(SQL, m_cnDB)
 Dim ds As New DataSet("Results")
 da.Fill(ds)
 Return ds
End Function


 '
 ' Close the database connection.
 '
 Public Sub Close()
  m_cnDB.Close()
 End Sub
End Class
```

Listing 7.11   Database.vb class (continued)

The BaseServices class has a new method added to it called CheckRequiredField. This verifies that a required text field is both populated and less than the maximum length allowed. It is typically called by an object's validation routine and helps remove a lot of duplicate code. The code for this is highlighted in bold in Listing 7.12.

```
Imports System.Text
Imports System.Data
Imports System.Data.SqlClient
Imports AtWorkUtilities

Public MustInherit Class BaseServices
  Private m_arrErrors As ArrayList
  Protected m_DB As Database
  Protected m_DA As SqlDataAdapter
  Protected m_CB As SqlCommandBuilder
  Protected m_DS As DataSet


  '
  ' This constructor should be overloaded and called
  ' by each derived class. It sets up the protected
  ' objects available to all derived classes for handling
  ' database activities.
  '
  Protected Sub New(ByVal DB As Database, ByVal strSQL As String)
   m_DB = DB
   m_DA = New SqlDataAdapter(strSQL, m_DB.Connection)
   m_CB = New SqlCommandBuilder(m_DA)
   m_DS = New DataSet()
```

Listing 7.12   BaseServices.vb class

```
    m_DA.Fill(m_DS)
End Sub


' The DataSet will have either zero rows or one row
' so we simply return the current row in the dataset.
' This code makes it easier to get at the data instead
' of having to duplicate the full hierarchy in the
' calling code. For empty DataSets, we return an empty
' row that can be populated.
'
Public Function GetRow() As DataRow
  If m_DS.Tables(0).Rows.Count > 0 Then
    Return m_DS.Tables(0).Rows(0)
  Else
    Return m_DS.Tables(0).NewRow()
  End If
End Function


'
' This routine accepts a data row as input and stores
' the data into the dataset. In cases where the row
' is new, we add the new row to the DataSet. If the
' DataSet has data in it, we read the data row and
' replace each field in the DataSet one column at a
' time.
'
Protected Sub SaveRow(ByVal dr As DataRow)
  Dim val As DataColumn
  '
  ' Handle new row
  '
  If m_DS.Tables(0).Rows.Count = 0 Then
    m_DS.Tables(0).Rows.Add(dr)
    Exit Sub
  End If


  '
  ' Handle existing row
  '
  m_DS.Tables(0).Rows(0).BeginEdit()
  For Each val In m_DS.Tables(0).Columns
    m_DS.Tables(0).Rows(0).Item(val) = dr.Item(val)
  Next
  m_DS.Tables(0).Rows(0).EndEdit()
End Sub


'
' Adds another validation error to the array list
```

Listing 7.12   BaseServices.vb class (continued)

```
' object. This saves some work for the calling/inheriting
' class.
'
Protected Sub AddError(ByVal strInput As String)
 If m_arrErrors Is Nothing Then
   m_arrErrors = New ArrayList()
 End If
 m_arrErrors.Add(strInput)
End Sub


'
' This method empties the array list of any previous errors
' that had been detected.
'
Protected Sub ClearErrors()
 If m_arrErrors Is Nothing Then
   m_arrErrors = New ArrayList()
 Else
   m_arrErrors.Clear()
 End If
End Sub


'
' This method formats the array into a message that can be
' used in a message box.
'
Public Function ValidationError( _
 Optional ByVal Header As String = _
   "The following errors were detected in your data:" & vbCrLf, _
 Optional ByVal ItemFormat As String = "- {0}" & vbCrLf, _
 Optional ByVal Footer As String = "") As String
 Dim strMessage As New StringBuilder()
 Dim strErr As String

 If m_arrErrors.Count > 0 Then
   strMessage.Append(Header)
   For Each strErr In m_arrErrors
    strMessage.AppendFormat(ItemFormat, strErr)
   Next
   strMessage.Append(Footer)
   Return strMessage.ToString
 Else
   Return ""
 End If
End Function


'
' Provides access to the list of errors that were detected
' during the validation process. This is used for applications
' that need custom error messages.
```

Listing 7.12   BaseServices.vb class (continued)

```vb
'
Public ReadOnly Property ValidationErrors() As ArrayList
Get
 Return m_arrErrors
End Get
End Property


'
' Indicates whether any validation errors were detected
' as the data was stored into the object.
'
Public ReadOnly Property IsValid() As Boolean
Get
 Return (m_arrErrors.Count = 0)
End Get
End Property


Protected Sub CheckRequiredField(ByVal DR As DataRow, _
 ByVal strField As String, _
 ByVal strFieldDesc As String, _
 ByVal intLength As Integer)

 If IsDBNull(DR(strField)) Then
   AddError(strFieldDesc & " is a required field.")
 Else
   If DR(strField).Length <= 0 Then
    AddError(strFieldDesc & " is a required field.")
   ElseIf DR(strField).Length > intLength Then
    AddError(strFieldDesc & " must be less than " _
      & intLength.ToString & " characters long.")
   End If
 End If

 End Sub
End Class
```

Listing 7.12   BaseServices.vb class (continued)

All that work we did in Project 3 will pay off here since we'll be using exactly the same structure for each of our objects: Member, Team, TeamMember, and Message. We'll also be creating the corresponding exception classes, which all look the same, except for the name. Because of space considerations, I won't be showing all four of those classes here, but they will be available as part of the finished application.

Creating the Member Class

The first entity class we need is the Member class. The code for this class is shown in Listing 7.13.

```
Imports AtWorkUtilities
Imports System.Data.SqlClient

Public Class Member
  Inherits BaseServices


  '
  ' If no arguments are supplied, build a separate
  ' database connection for this object.
  '
  Public Sub New()
   MyBase.New(New Database(), "SELECT * FROM tblMembers WHERE 1=0")
  End Sub


  '
  ' If database connection is supplied, store it
  ' in the private connection variable for this
  ' object.
  '
  Public Sub New(ByVal db As Database)
   MyBase.New(db, "SELECT * FROM tblMembers WHERE 1=0")
  End Sub


  '
  ' If both database and ID are supplied, retrieve
  ' data into the object from the database.
  '
  Public Sub New(ByVal db As Database, _
   ByVal ID As Integer)

   MyBase.New(db, "SELECT * FROM tblMembers WHERE pkMemberID = " _
     & ID.ToString)

  End Sub


  '
  ' Verify that all data validation rules have been
  ' met. Any errors get stored into the errors collection
  ' inherited from the BaseServices class.
  '
  Public Sub Validate()
   Dim dr As DataRow

   ClearErrors()
   For Each dr In m_DS.Tables(0).Rows
     If dr.RowState = DataRowState.Added _
     Or dr.RowState = DataRowState.Modified Then
      ValidateRow(dr)
     End If
```

Listing 7.13   Member.vb class

```
   Next

End Sub

'
' Checks an individual row for validation rule
' compliance. Any errors are added to the errors
' collection.
'
Private Sub ValidateRow(ByVal dr As DataRow)
 Dim drCount As SqlDataReader

 CheckRequiredField(dr, "LastName", "Last name", 40)
 CheckRequiredField(dr, "FirstName", "First name", 40)
 CheckRequiredField(dr, "Email", "E-mail address", 100)
 CheckRequiredField(dr, "UserName", "User name", 20)
 CheckRequiredField(dr, "Password", "Password", 20)
 If IsDBNull(dr("pkMemberID")) Then
   drCount = m_DB.GetDataReader("sp_CheckForDuplicateEmail '" _
     & dr("EMail") & "'")
   If drCount("DuplicateCount") > 0 Then
    AddError("E-mail address already exists in system.")
   End If
   drCount.Close()

   drCount = m_DB.GetDataReader("sp_CheckForDuplicateUserName '" _
     & dr("UserName") & "'")
   If drCount("DuplicateCount") > 0 Then
    AddError("User name already exists in system.")
   End If
   drCount.Close()
 End If

End Sub

'
' The base Save method stores the DataRow into the
' DataSet, whether it's a new or existing row. The
' rest of this routine handles specific validation
' for this type of data.
'
Public Overloads Sub SaveRow(ByVal dr As DataRow)
 MyBase.SaveRow(dr)
 Validate()

End Sub

'
' We separate the SaveRow method from the Save method
```

Listing 7.13   Member.vb class (continued)

```
' to give us a chance to handle any validation. We have
' a verification here that the data is good before we
' continue, however.
'
Public Sub Save()

  If Not Me.IsValid Then
     Throw New MemberException(Me.ValidationError)
     Exit Sub
  End If

  m_DA.Update(m_DS)
End Sub


'
' Since we only have a single row in our DataSet,
' delete it and then update the database with the
' change.
'
Public Sub Delete()
  If m_DS.Tables(0).Rows.Count > 0 Then
    m_DS.Tables(0).Rows(0).Delete()
    m_DA.Update(m_DS)
  End If
End Sub

End Class
```

Listing 7.13   Member.vb class (continued)

The ValidateRow routine is the most unique thing about this class, so let's go through it in detail. We first use our new CheckRequiredField method to take care of all the required text fields. We then call our two verification procedures when adding a new record to make sure that the username and email address don't already exist in the system. If either one exists, we generate an error and reject the change. Other than that code, the object is basically the same as the others we've done in the past.

Creating the Message Class

The Message class is the next one we need to build. The code for this class is shown in Listing 7.14.

```
Imports AtWorkUtilities
Imports System.Data.SqlClient

Public Class Message
```

Listing 7.14   Message.vb class

```
Inherits BaseServices


'
' If no arguments are supplied, build a separate
' database connection for this object.
'
Public Sub New()
 MyBase.New(New Database(), "SELECT * FROM tblMessages WHERE 1=0")
End Sub


'
' If database connection is supplied, store it
' in the private connection variable for this
' object.
'
Public Sub New(ByVal db As Database)
 MyBase.New(db, "SELECT * FROM tblMessages WHERE 1=0")
End Sub


'
' If both database and ID are supplied, retrieve
' data into the object from the database.
'
Public Sub New(ByVal db As Database, _
 ByVal ID As Integer)

 MyBase.New(db, "SELECT * FROM tblMessages WHERE pkMessageID = " _
   & ID.ToString)

End Sub


'
' Verify that all data validation rules have been
' met. Any errors get stored into the errors collection
' inherited from the BaseServices class.
'
Public Sub Validate()
 Dim dr As DataRow

 ClearErrors()
 For Each dr In m_DS.Tables(0).Rows
   If dr.RowState = DataRowState.Added _
   Or dr.RowState = DataRowState.Modified Then
    ValidateRow(dr)
   End If
 Next

End Sub

'
```

Listing 7.14   Message.vb class (continued)

```
' Checks an individual row for validation rule
' compliance. Any errors are added to the errors
' collection.
'
Private Sub ValidateRow(ByVal dr As DataRow)
  If IsDBNull(dr("fkMessageToMemberID")) Then
    AddError("Message destination is missing.")
  End If
  If IsDBNull(dr("fkMessageFromMemberID")) Then
    AddError("Message source is missing.")
  End If
  CheckRequiredField(dr, "MessageSubject", "Subject", 80)
  If IsDBNull(dr("MessageDate")) Then
    AddError("Message date is missing.")
  End If
  If IsDBNull(dr("MessageRead")) Then
    AddError("Message read flag is missing.")
  End If
End Sub


' The base Save method stores the DataRow into the
' DataSet, whether it's a new or existing row. The
' rest of this routine handles specific validation
' for this type of data.
'
Public Overloads Sub SaveRow(ByVal dr As DataRow)
  MyBase.SaveRow(dr)
  Validate()

End Sub


' We separate the SaveRow method from the Save method
' to give us a chance to handle any validation. We have
' a verification here that the data is good before we
' continue, however.
'
Public Sub Save()

  If Not Me.IsValid Then
    Throw New MessageException(Me.ValidationError)
    Exit Sub
  End If

  m_DA.Update(m_DS)
End Sub

'
```

Listing 7.14 Message.vb class (continued)

```
' Since we only have a single row in our DataSet,
' delete it and then update the database with the
' change.
'
Public Sub Delete()
 If m_DS.Tables(0).Rows.Count > 0 Then
   m_DS.Tables(0).Rows(0).Delete()
   m_DA.Update(m_DS)
 End If
End Sub


End Class
```

Listing 7.14 Message.vb class (continued)

We use the IsDBNull function to check all the non-text fields and verify that they are populated before saving this object. One good addition to this object would be to create some simplified methods for sending messages to users. It would break the pattern of this object as compared to the others, but you might want to think about doing it to make your code shorter elsewhere.

Building the Team Class

The Team class is simpler than the other two since it has fewer fields. The code is shown in Listing 7.15.

```
Imports AtWorkUtilities
Imports System.Data.SqlClient

Public Class Team
  Inherits BaseServices


  '
  ' If no arguments are supplied, build a separate
  ' database connection for this object.
  '
  Public Sub New()
   MyBase.New(New Database(), "SELECT * FROM tblTeams WHERE 1=0")
  End Sub


  '
  ' If database connection is supplied, store it
  ' in the private connection variable for this
  ' object.
```

Listing 7.15 Team.vb class

```
`
Public Sub New(ByVal db As Database)
 MyBase.New(db, "SELECT * FROM tblTeams WHERE 1=0")
End Sub


`
' If both database and ID are supplied, retrieve
' data into the object from the database.
`
Public Sub New(ByVal db As Database, _
 ByVal ID As Integer)

 MyBase.New(db, "SELECT * FROM tblTeams WHERE pkTeamID = " _
   & ID.ToString)

End Sub


`
' Verify that all data validation rules have been
' met. Any errors get stored into the errors collection
' inherited from the BaseServices class.
`
Public Sub Validate()
 Dim dr As DataRow

 ClearErrors()
 For Each dr In m_DS.Tables(0).Rows
   If dr.RowState = DataRowState.Added _
   Or dr.RowState = DataRowState.Modified Then
    ValidateRow(dr)
   End If
 Next

End Sub


`
' Checks an individual row for validation rule
' compliance. Any errors are added to the errors
' collection.
`
Private Sub ValidateRow(ByVal dr As DataRow)
 If IsDBNull(dr("fkLeaderID")) Then
   AddError("Team leader is missing.")
 End If
 CheckRequiredField(dr, "Name", "Team name", 80)
End Sub


`
' The base Save method stores the DataRow into the
```

Listing 7.15   Team.vb class (continued)

```
' DataSet, whether it's a new or existing row. The
' rest of this routine handles specific validation
' for this type of data.
'
Public Overloads Sub SaveRow(ByVal dr As DataRow)
 MyBase.SaveRow(dr)
 Validate()

End Sub


'
' We separate the SaveRow method from the Save method
' to give us a chance to handle any validation. We have
' a verification here that the data is good before we
' continue, however.
'
Public Sub Save()

 If Not Me.IsValid Then
    Throw New TeamException(Me.ValidationError)
   Exit Sub
 End If


 m_DA.Update(m_DS)
End Sub


'
' Since we only have a single row in our DataSet,
' delete it and then update the database with the
' change.
'
Public Sub Delete()
 If m_DS.Tables(0).Rows.Count > 0 Then
   m_DS.Tables(0).Rows(0).Delete()
   m_DA.Update(m_DS)
 End If
End Sub

End Class
```

Listing 7.15 Team.vb class (continued)

Other than the team name and leader, the other fields are already taken care of. Like the other classes, this one includes a TeamException class that follows the same pattern as the other custom exception classes we've created. If someone tries to save an invalid record, that exception will be thrown to prevent it from happening.

Building the TeamMember Class

The final class we need to build is the TeamMember class. This class represents the intersection of the members with teams. We'll use this object to add records to the tbl-TeamMember table when we add members to teams later in the project. The code is shown in Listing 7.16. The only validation we do here is to make sure both the team ID and member ID are populated.

```vb
Imports AtWorkUtilities
Imports System.Data.SqlClient

Public Class TeamMember
  Inherits BaseServices


  '
  ' If no arguments are supplied, build a separate
  ' database connection for this object.
  '
  Public Sub New()
   MyBase.New(New Database(), "SELECT * FROM tblTeamMembers WHERE 1=0")
  End Sub


  '
  ' If database connection is supplied, store it
  ' in the private connection variable for this
  ' object.
  '
  Public Sub New(ByVal db As Database)
    MyBase.New(db, "SELECT * FROM tblTeamMembers WHERE 1=0")
  End Sub


  '
  ' If both database and ID are supplied, retrieve
  ' data into the object from the database.
  '
  Public Sub New(ByVal db As Database, _
   ByVal ID As Integer)

   MyBase.New(db,
"SELECT * FROM tblTeamMembers WHERE pkTeamMemberID = " _
      & ID.ToString)

  End Sub


  '
  ' Verify that all data validation rules have been
  ' met. Any errors get stored into the errors collection
  ' inherited from the BaseServices class.
  '
```

Listing 7.16   TeamMember.vb class

```
Public Sub Validate()
 Dim dr As DataRow

 ClearErrors()
 For Each dr In m_DS.Tables(0).Rows
   If dr.RowState = DataRowState.Added _
   Or dr.RowState = DataRowState.Modified Then
    ValidateRow(dr)
   End If
 Next

End Sub


'
' Checks an individual row for validation rule
' compliance. Any errors are added to the errors
' collection.
'
Private Sub ValidateRow(ByVal dr As DataRow)
 If IsDBNull(dr("fkTeamID")) Then
   AddError("Team number is missing.")
 End If
 If IsDBNull(dr("fkMemberID")) Then
   AddError("Member number is missing.")
 End If
End Sub


'
' The base Save method stores the DataRow into the
' DataSet, whether it's a new or existing row. The
' rest of this routine handles specific validation
' for this type of data.
'
Public Overloads Sub SaveRow(ByVal dr As DataRow)
 MyBase.SaveRow(dr)
 Validate()

End Sub


'
' We separate the SaveRow method from the Save method
' to give us a chance to handle any validation. We have
' a verification here that the data is good before we
' continue, however.
'
Public Sub Save()

 If Not Me.IsValid Then
   Throw New TeamMemberException(Me.ValidationError)
```

Listing 7.16 TeamMember.vb class (continued)

```
      Exit Sub
   End If


   m_DA.Update(m_DS)
End Sub


' Since we only have a single row in our DataSet,
' delete it and then update the database with the
' change.
'
Public Sub Delete()
 If m_DS.Tables(0).Rows.Count > 0 Then
   m_DS.Tables(0).Rows(0).Delete()
   m_DA.Update(m_DS)
 End If
End Sub

End Class
```

Listing 7.16   TeamMember.vb class (continued)

With the business objects done, it's time to start building some Web pages.

Building the Web Pages

This is by far the largest application you've built in the book to date, and we're only getting started. The pages you build in this project will enable you to add the other subsystems in Projects 8, 9, and 10, as well as expand the system for your own features later. We are going to be building all of these logical functions using ASP.NET pages:

- General page structure, intelligent toolbar, style sheet, and so on
- Member profile creation and editing
- Log in/log out functionality
- Viewing, sending, replying, and deleting messages
- Creating, updating, and deleting teams
- Adding and deleting team members

All of these functions are common to nearly every Web application in one way or another, so this will give you a good base for building your own applications. The web page layout of the application is shown in Figure 7.1.

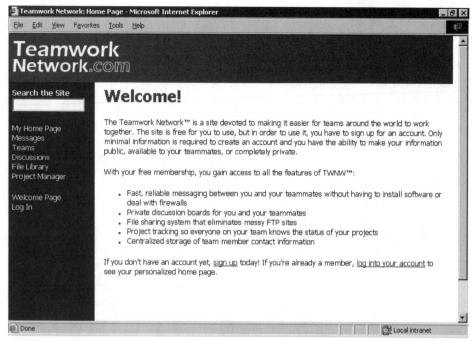

Figure 7.1 Teamwork Network web page layout.

This page gives some general information about what the site offers and how to get started. Note the toolbar on the left showing Log In as an option. Once you're logged in, that toolbar will change to say Log Out. We'll be building an ASP.NET user control to take care of the toolbar, the header information, and the footer. As we work through each of the other functional areas, you'll be seeing more pictures of what is to come. In addition, you can visit this site live at www.teamworknetwork.com and use all the features that you're building right now.

Creating the Page Infrastructure

The first thing you have to do is create the overall page design. I've already done this work for you, but feel free to change the graphics, colors, or text. The HTML for the home page is shown in Listing 7.17 so you can get a feel for the structure.

```
<!DOCTYPE HTML PUBLIC "-//W3C//DTD HTML 4.0 Transitional//EN">
<html>
<head>
   <title>Teamwork Network: Home Page</title>
   <link href="styles.css" rel="stylesheet" type="text/css">
```

Listing 7.17 HTML source code for home page

```
</head>

<body>

<table width="100%" cellpadding=3 cellspacing=0>
<tr class="pagebanner">
<td colspan="3">
<img src="images/logo.gif" width="213" height="60" vspace="5" border="0"
alt="">
</td>
</tr>
<tr>
<td class="sidebar" width="140">
<form action="search.aspx" method="post">
<p><b>Search the Site</b><br>
<input type="text" name="txtSearch" size="15"></p>
</form>
<p>
<a href="homepage.aspx" class="sidebar_link">My Home Page</a><br>
<a href="messages.aspx" class="sidebar_link">Messages</a><br>
<a href="teams.aspx" class="sidebar_link">Teams</a><br>
<a href="discussions.aspx" class="sidebar_link">Discussions</a><br>
<a href="files.aspx" class="sidebar_link">File Library</a><br>
<a href="projects.aspx" class="sidebar_link">Project Manager</a><br>
</p>
<p>
<a href="default.aspx" class="sidebar_link">Welcome Page</a><br>
<span id="PageHeader_lblLogin"><a href="login.aspx"
class="sidebar_link">Log In</a></span><br>
</p>
</td>
<td width="5"><img src="images/spacer.gif" width="5" height="400"
border="0" alt=""></td>
<td valign="top">
<table width="600">
<tr>
<td valign="top" width="600">
<p class="pageheading">Welcome!</p>
<p class="text">The Teamwork Network&trade; is a site devoted to making
it easier for
teams around the world to work together. The site is free for you to
use, but in order
to use it, you have to sign up for an account. Only minimal information
is required to
create an account and you have the ability to make your information
public, available to
your teammates, or completely private.
</p>
```

Listing 7.17 HTML source code for home page (continued)

```
<p class="text">With your free membership, you gain access to all the
features of TWNW&trade;:</p>
<ul class="text">
<li>Fast, reliable messaging between you and your teammates without
having to install software or deal with firewalls</li>
<li>Private discussion boards for you and your teammates
<li>File sharing system that eliminates messy FTP sites
<li>Project tracking so everyone on your team knows the status of your
projects
<li>Centralized storage of team member contact information
</ul>
<p class="text">If you don't have an account yet, <a
href="member.aspx">sign up</a> today!
If you're already a member, <a href="login.aspx">log into your
account</a> to see your
personalized home page.
</p>
</td>
</tr>
</table>


</td>
</tr>
<tr>
<td class="sidebar"></td>
<td></td>
<td class="copyright">
<hr noshade>
Copyright &copy 2001 by Northstar Computer Systems.<br>
Comments, questions, or problems? Contact the <a
href="mailto:webmaster@northcomp.com">webmaster</a>.
</td>
</tr>
</table>
</body>
</html>
```

Listing 7.17   HTML source code for home page (continued)

Before you start madly typing HTML, you're going to build some files to make this site easier to maintain. First, we're going to build the style sheet. This sheet is shown in Listing 7.18 and follows the pattern of the one we did in Project 3.

```
<style type="text/css" title="Application Style Sheet">
<!--
BODY
{
     background-color : White;
     margin-top : 0px;
     margin-left : 0px;
}
.pagebanner
{
     FONT-FAMILY: Tahoma, Arial;
     FONT-SIZE: 16pt;
     FONT-WEIGHT: bold;
     background-color : #800000;
}
.sidebar
{
     background-color : #000040;
     vertical-align : top;
     font-family : Tahoma, Arial;
     font-size : 10pt;
     color : White;
     padding-left : 5px;
     padding-top : 10px;
}
.sidebar_link
{
     font-family : Tahoma, Arial;
     font-size : 10pt;
     color : White;

}
A.sidebar_link:link {
     text-decoration:none;
}
A.sidebar_link:visited {
     text-decoration:none;
}
A.sidebar_link:hover {
     color:#FFFF00;
     text-decoration:underline;
}

.pageheading
{
     COLOR: #800000;
     FONT-FAMILY:Tahoma, Arial;
     FONT-SIZE: 20pt;
     font-weight : bold;
}
```

Listing 7.18   styles.css

```
.subheading
{
    COLOR: #800000;
    FONT-FAMILY:Tahoma, Arial;
    FONT-SIZE: 14pt;
    font-weight : bold;
}

.text
{
    COLOR: #000000;
    FONT-FAMILY: Tahoma, Arial;
    FONT-SIZE: 10pt;
}
.copyright
{
  COLOR: #000000;
  FONT-FAMILY: Tahoma, Arial;
  FONT-SIZE: 7pt;
}
.errortext
{
  COLOR: #FF0000;
  FONT-FAMILY: Tahoma, Arial;
  FONT-SIZE: 10pt;
}

.tableheading
{
  COLOR: #FFFFFF;
  FONT-FAMILY: Tahoma, Arial;
  FONT-WEIGHT: bold;
  FONT-SIZE: 9pt;
  BACKGROUND-COLOR: #800000;
  TEXT-ALIGN: center;
}
.tabletext
{
  COLOR: #000000;
  FONT-FAMILY: Tahoma, Arial;
  FONT-SIZE: 9pt;
}
.tabletext_gray
{
  COLOR: #000000;
  FONT-FAMILY: Tahoma, Arial;
  FONT-SIZE: 9pt;
  BACKGROUND-COLOR: #CCCCCC;
}

-->
</style>
```

Listing 7.18   styles.css (continued)

We'll be linking this style sheet to each page in the application instead of using a #include directive. If you visit the site or run this code, you'll see that the banner on the top is dark red and the side toolbar is dark blue. Feel free to change the colors here, as they will be immediately reflected throughout the rest of the site. My advice: If you're going to use style sheets, use the tags consistently everywhere and you'll never be sorry you used CSS.

The next step is to build the Toolbar user control. This works in a similar way to a server-side include, except for the fact that you write this code like an ASP.NET page, complete with events and everything. We'll be using two user controls for the site: one for the header and toolbar, and another for the footer. The user control is broken into two files: an ASCX file containing the HTML and other ASP.NET server controls, and a .VB file that is the Visual Basic .NET code behind the scenes. The ASCX file for the header is called Header.ascx and is shown in Listing 7.19.

```
<%@ Control ClassName="Header" Inherits="TWNW.PageHeader"
Src="header.ascx.vb" %>
<table width="100%" cellpadding=3 cellspacing=0>
<tr class="pagebanner">
<td colspan="3">
<img src="images/logo.gif" width="213" height="60" vspace="5" border="0"
alt="">
</td>
</tr>
<tr>
<td class="sidebar" width="140">
<form action="search.aspx" method="post">
<p><b>Search the Site</b><br>
<input type="text" name="txtSearch" size="15"></p>
</form>
<p>
<a href="homepage.aspx" class="sidebar_link">My Home Page</a><br>
<a href="messages.aspx" class="sidebar_link">Messages</a><br>
<a href="teams.aspx" class="sidebar_link">Teams</a><br>
<a href="discussions.aspx" class="sidebar_link">Discussions</a><br>
<a href="files.aspx" class="sidebar_link">File Library</a><br>
<a href="projects.aspx" class="sidebar_link">Project Manager</a><br>
</p>
<p>
<a href="default.aspx" class="sidebar_link">Welcome Page</a><br>
<asp:label id="lblLogin" runat="server" /><br>
</p>
</td>
<td width="5"><img src="images/spacer.gif" width="5" height="400"
border="0" alt=""></td>
<td valign="top">
```

Listing 7.19   header.ascx

The only way you can tell that this is a user control and not a standard ASP.NET page is in the @Control directive at the top of the page. This directive works in a similar fashion to the @Page directive, but is used with user controls like this one. One other restriction is that you can't have HTML page-layout elements, such as the HTML, HEAD, or BODY tags. The Visual Basic .NET code for this page is stored in Header. ascx.vb and is shown in Listing 7.20.

```vb
Imports System
Imports System.Web.UI
Imports System.Web.UI.WebControls
Imports System.Data
Imports TWNWObjects

Namespace TWNW
  Public Class PageHeader
    Inherits UserControl

    Protected WithEvents lblLogin As Label

    Private Sub Page_Load(ByVal sender As System.Object, _
      ByVal e As System.EventArgs) Handles MyBase.Load

    Dim strCookie As String
    Dim strURL As String
    Dim strAction As String
    If (Request.Cookies("mID") Is Nothing) Then
      strURL = "login.aspx"
      strAction = "In"
    Else
      If Request.Cookies("mID").Value <> "" Then
        Dim DB As New AtWorkUtilities.Database()
        Dim M As New Member(DB, _
         Request.Cookies("mID").Value)
        Dim DR As DataRow = M.GetRow()
        strURL = "logout.aspx"
        strAction = "Off " & DR("UserName")
        DB.Close()
      Else
        strURL = "login.aspx"
        strAction = "In"
      End If
    End If
    lblLogin.Text = "<a href=""" & strURL _
      & """ class=""sidebar_link"">Log " _
      & strAction & "</a>"
    End Sub
  End Class
End Namespace
```

Listing 7.20   header.ascx.vb

This file introduces the use of cookies in this application. We are using a single cookie named mID, which holds the member's unique ID. By keeping this in a cookie, we don't have to worry about passing it to every single page. We can also do some simple security checks by looking at the value of the cookie to see if it is visible or not. If not, we send the user to the Login page.

We also dynamically change the Log in/log out link based on whether or not the cookie is visible. This gives us a good way to keep users posted as to what their current status is, whether they are logged in or not, and with what user ID. It is designed to look similar to the Log Off feature on the Windows Start menu.

The other user control we need to build is the footer, which closes out the tables and shows the copyright. This copyright date will always be current, since we're using the current date to determine the year. The ASCX file is shown in Listing 7.21. Since there is no code required to make this page work, no VB file is needed.

```
<%@ Control ClassName="Footer" EnableViewstate="false" %>
</td>
</tr>
<tr>
<td class="sidebar"></td>
<td></td>
<td class="copyright">
<hr noshade>
Copyright &copy <% = Year(Now) %> by Northstar Computer Systems.<br>
Comments, questions, or problems? Contact the
<a href="mailto:webmaster@northcomp.com">webmaster</a>.
</td>
</tr>
</table>
```

Listing 7.21   footer.ascx

This is a simple file that takes care of its little bit of ASP.NET code using the <% = symbols commonly used in ASP. It works fine here, as well, so now my site will never have an out-of-date copyright on it.

The last step is to put these controls into the Default.aspx page that serves as the Welcome page. The code for the Default.aspx file is shown in Listing 7.22. Again, there is no important code-behind, so no VB file is needed here. The lines you should notice here are highlighted in bold.

```
<%@ Register Tagprefix="TWNW" Tagname="Header" Src="Header.ascx" %>
<%@ Register Tagprefix="TWNW" Tagname="Footer" Src="Footer.ascx" %>
<!DOCTYPE HTML PUBLIC "-//W3C//DTD HTML 4.0 Transitional//EN">
<html>
<head>
```

Listing 7.22   default.aspx

```
  <title>Teamwork Network: Home Page</title>
  <link href="styles.css" rel="stylesheet" type="text/css">
</head>

<body>
<TWNW:Header id="PageHeader" runat="server" />
<table width="600">
<tr>
<td valign="top" width="600">
<p class="pageheading">Welcome!</p>
<p class="text">The Teamwork Network&trade; is a site devoted to making
it easier for
teams around the world to work together. The site is free for you to
use, but in order
to use it, you have to sign up for an account. Only minimal information
is required to
create an account and you have the ability to make your information
public, available to
your teammates, or completely private.
</p>

<p class="text">With your free membership, you gain access to all the
features of TWNW&trade;:</p>
<ul class="text">
<li>Fast, reliable messaging between you and your teammates without
having to install software or deal with firewalls</li>
<li>Private discussion boards for you and your teammates
<li>File sharing system that eliminates messy FTP sites
<li>Project tracking so everyone on your team knows the status of your
projects
<li>Centralized storage of team member contact information
</ul>
<p class="text">If you don't have an account yet, <a
href="member.aspx">sign up</a> today!
If you're already a member, <a href="login.aspx">log into your
account</a> to see your
personalized home page.
</p>
</td>
</tr>
</table>

<TWNW:Footer id="PageFooter" runat="server" />

</body>
</html>
```

Listing 7.22   default.aspx (continued)

The text on the page is really up to you and is just a suggestion. The important code is at the top of the page where we register the user controls that we want to use. We specify the tag prefix and the control name, which is then used later in the page to refer to each type of control. We also have to specify the source of the code for the control stored in the ASCX file.

User controls are a good way to combine the modularity of server-side includes with the event-driven code model of ASP.NET pages.

Building Login and Logout Functionality

The next step is to allow an existing member to log into the system and log out when he or she is done using the system. This is a simple page to build and takes care of setting and releasing the mID cookie as needed. When it is running, the Login page looks like Figure 7.2 and resembles similar pages on other sites.

This page does have another hidden feature. If you attempt to go to a page like the My Home Page link, you must first be logged in to view it. The home page checks for that cookie; if it is missing, you are redirected to the Login page, where you get a slightly different message, courtesy of the URL parameters provided.

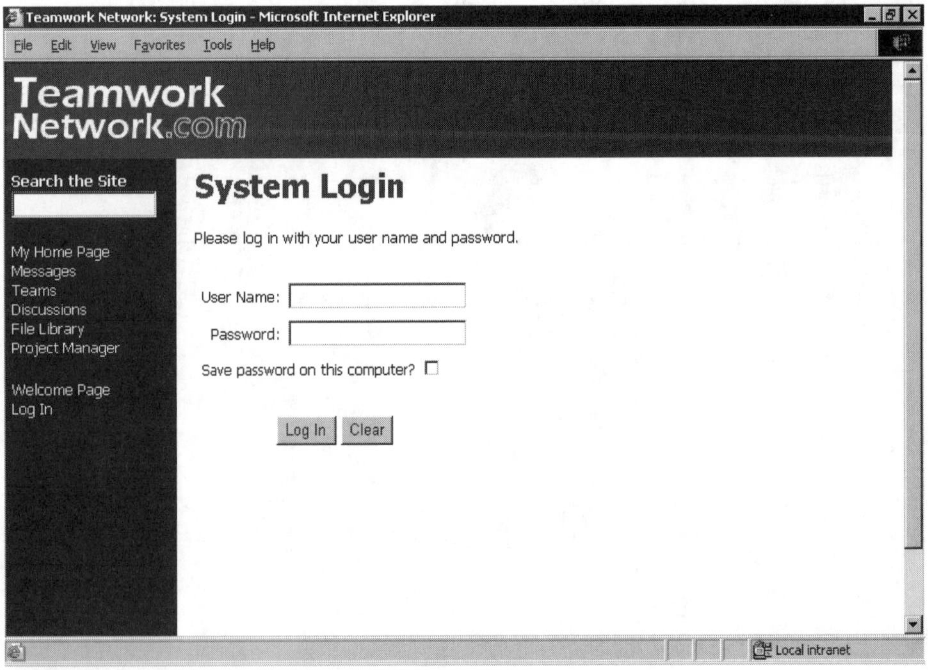

Figure 7.2 Login page.

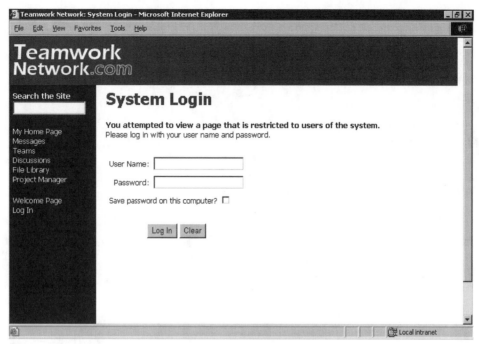

Figure 7.3 Login page after attempt to read protected page.

The error message displays the explanatory text shown in Figure 7.3, and the URL looks like the following:

```
login.aspx?msg=403&rURL=/twnw/homepage.aspx?
```

The home page redirected the user to the Login page and passed a value for the msg variable (message) and a value for the rURL variable (return URL). The 403 error message is the standard HTML response for security errors. We use this number to indicate that the user tried to go somewhere he or she shouldn't have, and the Login page generates the appropriate message. The return URL is provided so that once the user has logged in, he or she is sent back to the original page. This is a nice touch that saves the user an extra click or two.

The Login.aspx file is shown in Listing 7.23.

```
<%@ Page Inherits="TWNW.Login" Src="login.aspx.vb" %>
<%@ Register Tagprefix="TWNW" Tagname="Header" Src="Header.ascx" %>
<%@ Register Tagprefix="TWNW" Tagname="Footer" Src="Footer.ascx" %>
<!DOCTYPE HTML PUBLIC "-//W3C//DTD HTML 4.0 Transitional//EN">
```

Listing 7.23 login.aspx

```
<html>
<head>
  <title>Teamwork Network: System Login</title>
  <link href="styles.css" rel="stylesheet" type="text/css">
</head>

<body>
<TWNW:Header id="PageHeader" runat="server" />
<form runat="server">
<input type="hidden" runat="server" id="returnURL">
<table width="600">
<tr>
  <td valign="top" width="600">
  <p class="pageheading">System Login</p>
  <asp:label id="lblErrorMessage" class="errortext" runat="server" />
  <asp:label id="lblMessage" class="text" runat="server" />
  <table cellspacing="5">
  <tr class="text"><td colspan="2"> </td></tr>
  <tr class="text">
   <td align="right">User Name:</td>
   <td>
   <asp:textbox
     id="txtUserName"
     columns="20"
     maxlength="20"
     runat="server" />
   </td>
  </tr>
  <tr class="text">
   <td align="right">Password:</td>
   <td>
   <asp:textbox
     id="txtPassword"
     textmode="Password"
     columns="20"
     maxlength="20"
     runat="server" />
   </td>
  </tr>
  <tr class="tabletext">
   <td colspan="2">Save password on this computer?
   <asp:checkbox
     id="chkSavePassword"
     runat="server" />
   </td>
  </tr>
  <tr class="text"><td colspan="2"> </td></tr>
  <tr class="text">
   <td colspan=2 align=middle>
```

Listing 7.23 login.aspx (continued)

```
    <input type="submit"
      name="btnLogin"
      runat="server"
      value="Log In" />
    <input type="reset"
      name="btnReset"
      runat="server"
      value="Clear" />
    </td>
  </tr>

  </table>
</td>
</tr>
</table>
</form>
<TWNW:Footer id="PageFooter" runat="server" />

</body>
</html>
```

Listing 7.23   login.aspx (continued)

This is a basic HTML form making use of the user controls we built in the last section. We have some hidden-label controls that are populated with the messages in the previous figure. The code behind this page is in Login.aspx.vb and is shown in Listing 7.24.

```
Imports System
Imports System.Data
Imports System.Data.SqlClient
Imports System.Web.UI
Imports System.Web.UI.WebControls
Imports TWNWObjects

Namespace TWNW
  Public Class Login
    Inherits System.Web.UI.Page

    Protected txtUserName As TextBox
    Protected txtPassword As TextBox
    Protected chkSavePassword As CheckBox
    Protected returnURL As HTMLControls.HTMLInputHidden

    Protected lblMessage As Label
```

Listing 7.24   login.aspx.vb

```
    Protected lblErrorMessage As Label

    Sub Page_Load(objSender As Object, objArgs As EventArgs)
      Dim DB As New AtWorkUtilities.Database()
      Dim DR As SqlDataReader
      Dim strMessage As String

      If Not Page.IsPostBack Then
        If Not (Request.QueryString("rURL") Is Nothing) Then
          returnURL.Value = Request.QueryString("rURL")
        End If

        If Not (Request.QueryString("msg") Is Nothing) Then
          Select Case Request.QueryString("msg")
            Case "403"
              strMessage = "<b>You attempted to view a page that " _
              & "is restricted to users of the system.</b><br>"
          End Select
        End If
        lblMessage.Text = strMessage _
          & "Please log in with your user " _
          & "name and password."
      Else
        DR = DB.GetDataReader("sp_CheckLogin '" _
          & txtUserName.Text & "', '" _
          & txtPassword.Text & "'", True)
        If DR.Read() Then
          Response.Cookies("mID").Value = DR("pkMemberID").ToString()
          If chkSavePassword.Checked Then
            Response.Cookies("mID").Expires = _
              DateTime.Now.AddMonths(3)
          End If
          DR.Close()
          If returnURL.Value = "" Then
            Response.Redirect("homepage.aspx")
          Else
            Response.Redirect(returnURL.Value)
          End If
        Else
          lblErrorMessage.Text = _
            "Invalid user name and/or password.<br>"
          DR.Close()
        End If
      End If
    End Sub

  End Class
End Namespace
```

Listing 7.24 login.aspx.vb (continued)

When the page is first loaded, we populate hidden fields with the return URL that may have been provided to us. If no return URL is supplied, the field stays empty, which is also a valid condition. If a message code was provided, we display the appropriate message in the label control. When the user submits the form data, we look at the database to see if the user ID and password match a member in the system; if not, we generate an error message. If the user ID and password match, we store the member ID in the mID cookie and then redirect the user to either the return URL or to the user's personal home page.

Logging out of the system is easier and involves removing the mID cookie and showing a message to the user. The Logout.aspx file is shown in Listing 7.25 and only contains HTML. The Logout.aspx.vb file is shown in Listing 7.26 and takes care of removing the cookie.

```
<%@ Page Inherits="TWNW.Logout" Src="logout.aspx.vb" %>
<%@ Register Tagprefix="TWNW" Tagname="Header" Src="Header.ascx" %>
<%@ Register Tagprefix="TWNW" Tagname="Footer" Src="Footer.ascx" %>
<!DOCTYPE HTML PUBLIC "-//W3C//DTD HTML 4.0 Transitional//EN">
<html>
<head>
  <title>Teamwork Network: Log Out</title>
  <link href="styles.css" rel="stylesheet" type="text/css">
</head>

<body>
<TWNW:Header id="PageHeader" runat="server" />
<table width="500">
<tr>
<td valign="top">
<p class="pageheading">Log Out Successful</p>
<p class="text">
You have been logged out of the Teamwork Network system. When you close
and
reopen your browser, you will need to log in again. To log in again now,
<a href="login.aspx">click here</a>.
</p>
</td></tr>
</table>

<TWNW:Footer id="PageFooter" runat="server" />

</body>
</html>
```

Listing 7.25   logout.aspx

This text is displayed once the user's cookie has been removed. The code is shown in Listing 7.26.

```
Imports System
Imports System.Web.UI
Imports System.Web.UI.WebControls

Namespace TWNW
  Public Class Logout
    Inherits Page

    Private Sub Page_Load(ByVal sender As System.Object, _
      ByVal e As System.EventArgs) Handles MyBase.Load

      Response.Cookies("mID").Value = Nothing
      Response.Cookies("mID").Expires = Nothing

    End Sub
  End Class
End Namespace
```

Listing 7.26   logout.aspx.vb

I'm always using Login and Logout pages in administrative sites, and I'm sure you do, too. This is one thing you can add as a generic form in most applications with only minor modifications.

Creating the Member Maintenance Page

The next page to build enables users to both create and update a member profile. This page uses the technique introduced in Project 3 that combines both the creation and edit process into a single page. In our site, we provide two different links. On the Welcome page, the user can create a profile. Then, once the user is logged in, he or she can link to the page to edit his or her record. The page is shown in Figure 7.4.

If you bring the page up in creation mode, the title on the page changes, since it is a label control. However, the title of the page in the HEAD of the page can't change, since it is static in the page. It would be nice if these could be made consistent, but it is not something we need to be concerned with at this time.

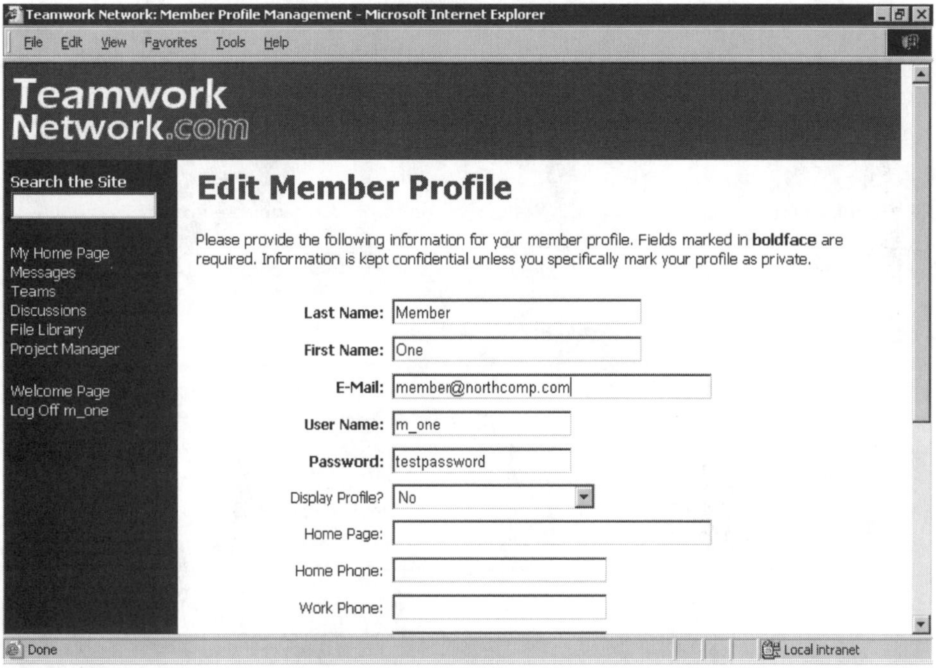

Figure 7.4   Edit Member Profile page.

The code for the Member.aspx file is shown in Listing 7.27.

```
<%@ Page Inherits="TWNW.MemberCreate" Src="member.aspx.vb" %>
<%@ Register Tagprefix="TWNW" Tagname="Header" Src="Header.ascx" %>
<%@ Register Tagprefix="TWNW" Tagname="Footer" Src="Footer.ascx" %>
<!DOCTYPE HTML PUBLIC "-//W3C//DTD HTML 4.0 Transitional//EN">
<html>
<head>
  <title>Teamwork Network: Member Profile Management</title>
  <link href="styles.css" rel="stylesheet" type="text/css">
</head>
<body>
<TWNW:Header id="PageHeader" runat="server" />
<table width="600">
```

Listing 7.27   member.aspx

```
<tr>
<td valign="top" width="600">

<p><asp:label id="lblPageTitle" class="pageheading" runat="server"
/></p>
<p class="text">
Please provide the following information for your member profile.
Fields marked in <strong>boldface</strong> are required. Information is
kept confidential unless you specifically mark your profile as private.
</p>
<asp:label id="lblErrorMessage" class="errortext" runat="server" />

<form runat="server">
<input type="hidden" runat="server" id="pkMemberID">
<input type="hidden" runat="server" id="returnURL">

<table cellspacing="5">
<tr class="tabletext">
  <td align="right"><strong>Last Name:</strong></td>
  <td>
  <asp:textbox
    id="txtLastName"
    columns="30"
    maxlength="40"
    runat="server" />
  </td>
</tr>
<tr class="tabletext">
  <td align="right"><strong>First Name:</strong></td>
  <td>
  <asp:textbox
    id="txtFirstName"
    columns="30"
    maxlength="40"
    runat="server" />
  </td>
</tr>
<tr class="tabletext">
  <td align="right"><strong>E-Mail:</strong></td>
  <td>
  <asp:textbox
    id="txtEMail"
    columns="40"
    maxlength="100"
    runat="server" />
  </td>
</tr>
<tr class="tabletext">
```

Listing 7.27 member.aspx (continued)

```
    <td align="right"><strong>User Name:</strong></td>
    <td>
    <asp:textbox
     id="txtUserName"
     columns="20"
     maxlength="20"
     runat="server" />
    </td>
</tr>
<tr class="tabletext">
    <td align="right"><strong>Password:</strong></td>
    <td>
    <asp:textbox
     id="txtPassword"
     columns="20"
     maxlength="20"
     runat="server" />
    </td>
</tr>
<tr class="tabletext">
    <td valign="middle" align="right">Display Profile?</td>
    <td>
    <asp:dropdownlist
     id="cboDisplayProfile"
     runat="server">
    <asp:listitem value="P" selected="True">Yes</asp:listitem>
    <asp:listitem value="T" >Yes, Team members only</asp:listitem>
    <asp:listitem value="N" >No</asp:listitem>
    </asp:dropdownlist>
    </td>
</tr>

<tr class="tabletext">
    <td align="right">Home Page:</td>
    <td>
    <asp:textbox
     id="txtHomePage"
     columns="40"
     maxlength="100"
     runat="server" />
    </td>
</tr>
<tr class="tabletext">
    <td align="right">Home Phone:</td>
    <td>
    <asp:textbox
     id="txtHomePhone"
```

Listing 7.27   member.aspx (continued)

```
    columns="25"
    maxlength="40"
    runat="server" />
  </td>
</tr>
<tr class="tabletext">
  <td align="right">Work Phone:</td>
  <td>

  <asp:textbox
   id="txtWorkPhone"
   columns="25"
   maxlength="40"
   runat="server" />
  </td>
</tr>
<tr class="tabletext">
  <td align="right">Mobile Phone:</td>
  <td>
  <asp:textbox
   id="txtMobilePhone"
   columns="25"
   maxlength="40"
   runat="server" />
  </td>
</tr>
<tr class="tabletext">
  <td align="right">Fax Number:</td>
  <td>
  <asp:textbox
   id="txtFax"
   columns="25"
   maxlength="40"
   runat="server" />
  </td>
</tr>

<tr class="tabletext">
  <td valign="middle" align="right">
  More information about me:
  </td>
  <td>
  <asp:textbox
   id="txtAboutMe"
   rows="5"
   columns="40"
   wrap="true"
   textmode="Multiline"
   runat="server" />
  </td>
```

Listing 7.27   member.aspx (continued)

```
</tr>
<tr class="tabletext">
  <td colspan=2 align=middle>
  <input type="submit"
   name="btnSubmit"
   runat="server"
   value="Save" />
  <input type="reset"
   name="btnReset"
   runat="server"
   value="Clear" />
  </td>
</tr>
</table>
</form>
</td>
</tr>
</table>
<TWNW:Footer id="PageFooter" runat="server" />
</body>
</html>
```

Listing 7.27   member.aspx (continued)

We have generic text describing the function of this page, which is relevant in both adding and updating mode. We have hidden fields for the return URL and the member ID for update mode. We're also using user controls to provide the common header and footer on the page.

The code-behind file is called Member.aspx.vb and is shown in Listing 7.28.

```
Imports System
Imports System.Data
Imports System.Data.SqlClient
Imports System.Web
Imports System.Web.UI
Imports System.Web.UI.WebControls
Imports TWNWObjects

Namespace TWNW
  Public Class MemberCreate
    Inherits System.Web.UI.Page

    Protected txtLastName As TextBox
    Protected txtFirstName As TextBox
    Protected txtEMail As TextBox
```

Listing 7.28   member.aspx.vb

```
Protected txtUserName As TextBox
Protected txtPassword As TextBox
Protected cboDisplayProfile As DropDownList
Protected txtHomePage As TextBox
Protected txtHomePhone As TextBox
Protected txtWorkPhone As TextBox
Protected txtMobilePhone As TextBox
Protected txtFax As TextBox
Protected txtAboutMe As TextBox

Protected pkMemberID As HTMLControls.HTMLInputHidden
Protected returnURL As HTMLControls.HTMLInputHidden

Protected lblPageTitle As Label
Protected lblErrorMessage As Label

Sub Page_Load(objSender As Object, objArgs As EventArgs)
  Dim DB As New AtWorkUtilities.Database()
  Dim i As Integer
  Dim strType As String
  Dim M As Member
  Dim DR As DataRow
  Dim objCookie As HTTPCookie
  objCookie = Request.Cookies("mID")

  If Not Page.IsPostBack Then
   returnURL.Value = Request.QueryString("rURL")
   If objCookie Is Nothing Then
     lblPageTitle.Text = "Create Member Profile"
   Else
     lblPageTitle.Text = "Edit Member Profile"
     M = New Member(DB, objCookie.Value)
     DR = M.GetRow()
     pkMemberID.Value = DR("pkMemberID").ToString()
     txtLastName.Text = DR("LastName").ToString()
     txtFirstName.Text = DR("FirstName").ToString()
     txtEMail.Text = DR("EMail").ToString()
     txtUserName.Text = DR("UserName").ToString()
     txtPassword.Text = DR("Password").ToString()
     SelectFromList(cboDisplayProfile, _
      DR("DisplayProfile"))
     txtHomePage.Text = DR("HomePage").ToString()
     txtHomePhone.Text = DR("HomePhone").ToString()
     txtWorkPhone.Text = DR("WorkPhone").ToString()
     txtMobilePhone.Text = DR("MobilePhone").ToString()
     txtFax.Text = DR("Fax").ToString()
     txtAboutMe.Text = DR("AboutMe").ToString()
   End If
```

Listing 7.28   member.aspx.vb (continued)

```
      Else
        If pkMemberID.Value = "" Then
          M = New Member(DB)
        Else
          M = New Member(DB, pkMemberID.Value)
        End If
        DR = M.GetRow()
        DR("LastName") = txtLastName.Text
        DR("FirstName") = txtFirstName.Text
        DR("Email") = txtEMail.Text
        DR("UserName") = txtUserName.Text
        DR("Password") = txtPassword.Text
        DR("DisplayProfile") = cboDisplayProfile.SelectedItem.Value
        DR("HomePage") = txtHomePage.Text
        DR("HomePhone") = txtHomePhone.Text
        DR("WorkPhone") = txtWorkPhone.Text
        DR("MobilePhone") = txtMobilePhone.Text
        DR("Fax") = txtFax.Text
        DR("AboutMe") = txtAboutMe.Text

        M.SaveRow(DR)
        If Not M.IsValid Then
          lblErrorMessage.Text = _
            M.ValidationError("<b>ERROR:</b> The following " _
              & "errors were detected in your data:<br>", _
              "&bull; {0}<br>", "")
        Else
          M.Save()
          DB.Close()
          If returnURL.Value = "" Then
            If pkMemberID.Value = "" Then
              Response.Redirect("member_created.aspx")
            Else
              Response.Redirect("member_updated.aspx")
            End If
          Else
            Response.Redirect(returnURL.Value)
          End If

        End If
      End If
End Sub

Private Sub SelectFromList(cboList As DropDownList, _
  strValue As String)

  Dim i As Integer
```

Listing 7.28   member.aspx.vb (continued)

```
      For i = 0 To cboList.Items.Count
       If cboList.Items(i).Value = strValue Then
         cboList.SelectedIndex = i
         Exit For
       End If
      Next i


    End Sub


   End Class
End Namespace
```

Listing 7.28   member.aspx.vb (continued)

This file follows the same pattern as the one we did in Project 3. When the page is first loaded, we look to see if the cookie value is present. If not, we assume that we are creating a new record and change the page accordingly. In update mode, we request the member profile using the Member object and then populate the fields. We have copied the helper function, SelectFromList, to automatically select the list item that matches the value in the database. When the user clicks the Save button, the data is stored in the DataRow and then put back into the Member object to be saved. When the operation is complete, the user is sent to one of two pages: Member_created.aspx or Member_updated.aspx. These pages tell the user that the data has either been created or updated. These pages are included in the source code, but won't be shown here for space considerations. These pages could be consolidated into a single page, but this is really up to you.

The next step is to build the messaging system, which allows the member to be notified of important events and team membership changes.

Building the Messaging System

The messaging system built into this application is designed to let members communicate and be informed about what is going on in the system. When members are added and removed from teams, the members in question will be notified through this system. The system can also be used to send team members messages and so on. Most of the work is done in the Message object, but we have to build the Web pages supporting the logical functions.

Viewing Messages

The first page to build is the Message Viewing page. This page uses a Repeater control for looping through the messages and a DataSet object behind the scenes to provide the data to be shown. The ASPX file is shown in Listing 7.29.

```
<%@ Page Inherits="TWNW.MessagesViewAll" Src="messages.aspx.vb" %>
<%@ Register Tagprefix="TWNW" Tagname="Header" Src="Header.ascx" %>
<%@ Register Tagprefix="TWNW" Tagname="Footer" Src="Footer.ascx" %>


<!DOCTYPE HTML PUBLIC "-//W3C//DTD HTML 4.0 Transitional//EN">
<html>
<head>
    <title>Teamwork Network: View All Messages</title>
  <link href="styles.css" rel="stylesheet" type="text/css">
</head>

<body leftmargin=0 topmargin=0>
<TWNW:Header id="PageHeader" runat="server" />
<p class="pageheading">View All Messages</p>
<p class="text"><a href="message_choose.aspx">Send a Message</a></p>
<asp:label id="lblMessage" class="text" runat="server" />

<asp:Repeater id="rptList" runat="server">
  <HeaderTemplate>
  <table cellpadding="4" cellspacing="0" width="100%">
  <tr class="tableheading">
  <td width="5%"></td>
  <td width="25%">From</td>
  <td width="30%">Subject</td>
  <td width="20%">Date</td>
  <td width="20%">Actions</td>
  </tr>
  </HeaderTemplate>
  <ItemTemplate>
  <tr class="tabletext">
  <td><img src="images/<%# DataBinder.Eval(Container.DataItem, _
   "MessageIndicator") %>" height="16" width="16"
   alt="<%# DataBinder.Eval(Container.DataItem, _
   "MessageIndicatorText") %>"></td>
  <td valign="top"><%# DataBinder.Eval(Container.DataItem, _
   "MessageFrom") %></td>
  <td valign="top"><%# DataBinder.Eval(Container.DataItem, _
   "MessageSubject") %></td>
  <td valign="top" align="center">
  <%# DataBinder.Eval(Container.DataItem, _
   "MessageDate").ToShortDateString %>
  <%# DataBinder.Eval(Container.DataItem, _
   "MessageDate").ToShortTimeString %>

  </td>
```

Listing 7.29 messages.aspx

```
   <td valign="top" align="center">
   <a href="message_read.aspx?id=<%# DataBinder.Eval(Container.DataItem, _
     "pkMessageID") %>">Read</a>  
   <a href="message_create.aspx?id=<%#
DataBinder.Eval(Container.DataItem, _
     "pkMessageID") %>">Reply</a>  
   <a href="message_delete.aspx?id=<%#
DataBinder.Eval(Container.DataItem, _
     "pkMessageID") %>">Delete</a>
   </td>
   </tr>
   </ItemTemplate>
   <AlternatingItemTemplate>
   <tr class="tabletext_gray">
   <td><img src="images/<%#DataBinder.Eval(Container.DataItem, _
     "MessageIndicator") %>" height="16" width="16"
     alt="<%# DataBinder.Eval(Container.DataItem, _
     "MessageIndicatorText") %>"></td>
   <td valign="top"><%# DataBinder.Eval(Container.DataItem, _
     "MessageFrom") %></td>
   <td valign="top"><%# DataBinder.Eval(Container.DataItem, _
     "MessageSubject") %></td>
   <td valign="top" align="center">
   <%# DataBinder.Eval(Container.DataItem, _
     "MessageDate").ToShortDateString %>
   <%# DataBinder.Eval(Container.DataItem, _
     "MessageDate").ToShortTimeString %>
   </td>
   <td valign="top" align="center">
   <a href="message_read.aspx?id=<%# DataBinder.Eval(Container.DataItem, _
     "pkMessageID") %>">Read</a>  
   <a href="message_create.aspx?id=<%#
DataBinder.Eval(Container.DataItem, _
     "pkMessageID") %>">Reply</a>  
   <a href="message_delete.aspx?id=<%#
DataBinder.Eval(Container.DataItem, _
     "pkMessageID") %>">Delete</a>
   </td>
   </tr>
   </AlternatingItemTemplate>
   <FooterTemplate>
   </table>
   </FooterTemplate>
</asp:Repeater>
```

Listing 7.29   messages.aspx (continued)

```
</body>
</html>
<TWNW:Footer id="PageFooter" runat="server" />
</body>
</html>
```

Listing 7.29 messages.aspx (continued)

This page has links to several other pages that you'll be creating in this section:

message_choose.aspx. Selects a member to send a message to.

message_delete.aspx. Deletes a message.

message_read.aspx. Displays a message.

message_create.aspx. Users can reply to and create new messages.

When populated with some messages, this page looks similar to the one shown in Figure 7.5.

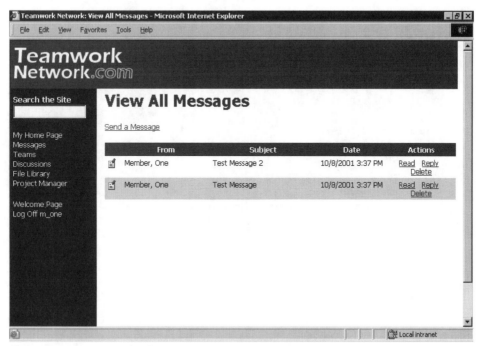

Figure 7.5 Message Viewing page.

New messages are indicated by the icon on the left side of the page. When you open a message, the code will update the record to mark the message as read, at which point, the icon will be replaced by a transparent graphic that fills the space.

The code behind this file is shown in Listing 7.30.

```vb
Imports System
Imports System.Data
Imports System.Data.SqlClient
Imports System.Web
Imports System.Web.UI
Imports System.Web.UI.WebControls
Imports TWNWObjects

Namespace TWNW
  Public Class MessagesViewAll
    Inherits System.Web.UI.Page

    Protected lblMessage As Label
    Protected rptList As Repeater

    Sub Page_Load(objSender As Object, objArgs As EventArgs)
      If (Request.Cookies("mID") Is Nothing) Then
        Response.Redirect("login.aspx?msg=403&rURL=" _
          & Request.ServerVariables("SCRIPT_NAME") _
          & "?" _
          & Request.ServerVariables("QUERY_STRING"))
      End If

      Dim DB As New AtWorkUtilities.Database()
      Dim objCookie As HTTPCookie
      objCookie = Request.Cookies("mID")

      Dim DS As DataSet = _
        DB.GetDataSet("sp_RetrieveMessagesByMember " _
        & objCookie.Value.ToString())
      If DS.Tables(0).Rows.Count = 0 Then
        lblMessage.Text = _
          "<b>There are no messages in your mailbox.</b>"
      Else
        rptList.DataSource = DS
        rptList.DataBind()
      End If
      db.Close()
    End Sub
  End Class
End Namespace
```

Listing 7.30   messages.aspx.vb

We've used similar code before, but we have made one change here. If there are no messages to show, we don't bind to the Repeater control. Instead, we show a message in a label control and shut things down. This looks better than an empty grid, in my opinion, and is easy to do.

The code at the top of the Page_Load event makes sure that we are logged in before we view this page. Since everything is keyed to the mID cookie, if it's not there, we run into errors. Therefore, we send the user to the Login page first. We build a return URL that includes the current script name and query string so the user can come back when he or she is done logging into the system.

Sending Messages

The next logical page to build will let you create a new message. Since we're using numeric IDs for members, we have simplified the user-selection process by showing a list of users and allowing the user to pick from that list. This accomplishes a couple of key things. First of all, there is no possibility that a message can't be delivered. It also prevents users from spamming everyone in the system since they can only send one message at a time.

The first page we need to build is the Message_choose.aspx page, which is shown in Figure 7.6.

For users with public or team-readable profiles, the Yes link will be active and will take you to the Member_view page, shown in Figure 7.7.

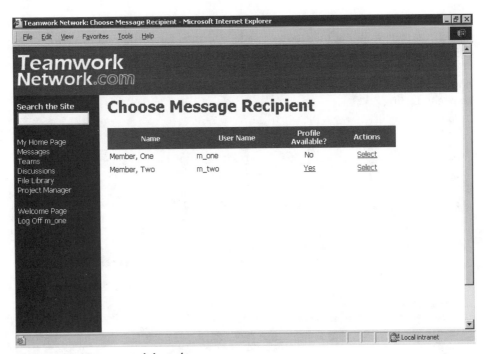

Figure 7.6 Message recipient chooser.

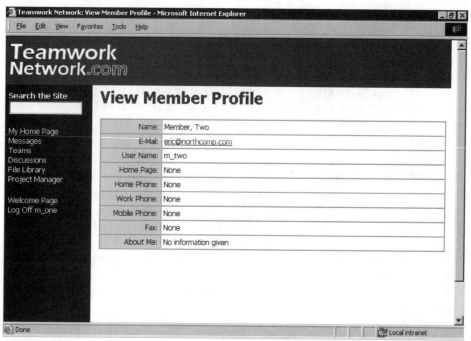

Figure 7.7　Member Profile viewer.

We'll start by building the Chooser page, and then build the Profile Viewer page before moving on to the actual message-creation section. The Message_choose.aspx file is shown in Listing 7.31. It also uses a Repeater control and lets the stored procedure populate a great deal of the data. The code-behind file is fairly straightforward and is shown in Listing 7.32.

```
<%@ Page Inherits="TWNW.MessageChoose" Src="message_choose.aspx.vb" %>
<%@ Register Tagprefix="TWNW" Tagname="Header" Src="Header.ascx" %>
<%@ Register Tagprefix="TWNW" Tagname="Footer" Src="Footer.ascx" %>


<!DOCTYPE HTML PUBLIC "-//W3C//DTD HTML 4.0 Transitional//EN">
<html>
<head>
    <title>Teamwork Network: Choose Message Recipient</title>
  <link href="styles.css" rel="stylesheet" type="text/css">
</head>

<body leftmargin=0 topmargin=0>
<TWNW:Header id="PageHeader" runat="server" />
<p class="pageheading">Choose Message Recipient</p>
<asp:Repeater id="rptList" runat="server">
  <HeaderTemplate>
```

Listing 7.31　message_choose.aspx

```
    <table cellpadding="4" cellspacing="0" width="500">
    <tr class="tableheading">
    <td width="30%">Name</td>
    <td width="30%">User Name</td>
    <td width="20%">Profile Available?</td>
    <td width="20%">Actions</td>
    </tr>
    </HeaderTemplate>
    <ItemTemplate>
    <tr class="tabletext">
    <td valign="top"><%# DataBinder.Eval(Container.DataItem, _
     "MemberName") %></td>
    <td valign="top"><%# DataBinder.Eval(Container.DataItem, _
     "UserName") %></td>
    <td valign="top" align="middle"><%#
DataBinder.Eval(Container.DataItem, _
     "ProfileURL") %><%# DataBinder.Eval(Container.DataItem, _
     "ProfileVisible") %></a></td>
    <td valign="top" align="middle">
    <a href="message_create.aspx?TM=<%#
DataBinder.Eval(Container.DataItem, _
     "pkMemberID") %>">Select</a>
    </td>
    </tr>
    </ItemTemplate>
    <AlternatingItemTemplate>
    <tr class="tabletext">
    <td valign="top"><%# DataBinder.Eval(Container.DataItem, _
     "MemberName") %></td>
    <td valign="top"><%# DataBinder.Eval(Container.DataItem, _
     "UserName") %></td>
    <td valign="top" align="middle"><%#
DataBinder.Eval(Container.DataItem, _
     "ProfileURL") %><%# DataBinder.Eval(Container.DataItem, _
     "ProfileVisible") %></a></td>
    <td valign="top" align="middle">
    <a href="message_create.aspx?TM=<%#
DataBinder.Eval(Container.DataItem, _
     "pkMemberID") %>">Select</a>
    </td>
    </tr>
    </AlternatingItemTemplate>
    <FooterTemplate>
    </table>
    </FooterTemplate>
</asp:Repeater>
</body>
</html>
<TWNW:Footer id="PageFooter" runat="server" />
</body>
</html>
```

Listing 7.31 message_choose.aspx (continued)

The Choose link points to the Message_create.aspx page and provides the TM argument indicating the member to whom the message should be sent. The code-behind file is shown in Listing 7.32.

```
Imports System
Imports System.Data
Imports System.Data.SqlClient
Imports System.Web
Imports System.Web.UI
Imports System.Web.UI.WebControls
Imports TWNWObjects

Namespace TWNW
  Public Class MessageChoose
    Inherits System.Web.UI.Page

    Protected lblMessage As Label
    Protected rptList As Repeater

    Sub Page_Load(objSender As Object, objArgs As EventArgs)
      Dim DB As New AtWorkUtilities.Database()
      Dim objCookie As HTTPCookie
      objCookie = Request.Cookies("mID")

      Dim DS As DataSet = _
        DB.GetDataSet("sp_RetrieveAllMembers")
      rptList.DataSource = DS
      rptList.DataBind()
      db.Close()
    End Sub
  End Class
End Namespace
```

Listing 7.32   message_choose.aspx.vb

Before moving on to the actual Message Creation page, let's show the Member Profile page. The code is essentially transferring a Member object's data into a readable format. The ASPX file is shown in Listing 7.33 and is fairly unremarkable. The code-behind file uses a few new features that we need to cover.

```
<%@ Page Inherits="TWNW.MemberView" Src="member_view.aspx.vb" %>
<%@ Register Tagprefix="TWNW" Tagname="Header" Src="Header.ascx" %>
<%@ Register Tagprefix="TWNW" Tagname="Footer" Src="Footer.ascx" %>


<!DOCTYPE HTML PUBLIC "-//W3C//DTD HTML 4.0 Transitional//EN">
```

Listing 7.33   member_view.aspx

```
<html>
<head>
    <title>Teamwork Network: View Member Profile</title>
  <link href="styles.css" rel="stylesheet" type="text/css">
</head>

<body leftmargin=0 topmargin=0>
<TWNW:Header id="PageHeader" runat="server" />
<p class="pageheading">View Member Profile</p>

<table width="600" cellspacing="0" cellpadding="4" border="1">
<tr>
  <td width="100" class="tabletext_gray" align="right">Name:</td>
  <td width="500" class="tabletext">
   <asp:label id="lblName" runat="server" />
  </td>
</tr>
<tr>
  <td width="100" class="tabletext_gray" align="right">E-Mail:</td>
  <td width="500" class="tabletext">
   <asp:label id="lblEMail" runat="server" />
  </td>
</tr>
<tr>
  <td width="100" class="tabletext_gray" align="right">User Name:</td>
  <td width="500" class="tabletext">
   <asp:label id="lblUserName" runat="server" />
  </td>
</tr>

<tr>
  <td width="100" class="tabletext_gray" align="right">Home Page:</td>
  <td width="500" class="tabletext">
   <asp:label id="lblHomePage" runat="server" />
  </td>
</tr>
<tr>
  <td width="100" class="tabletext_gray" align="right">Home Phone:</td>
  <td width="500" class="tabletext">
   <asp:label id="lblHomePhone" runat="server" />
  </td>
</tr>
<tr>
  <td width="100" class="tabletext_gray" align="right">Work Phone:</td>
  <td width="500" class="tabletext">
   <asp:label id="lblWorkPhone" runat="server" />
  </td>
</tr>
```

Listing 7.33   member_view.aspx (continued)

```
<tr>
  <td width="100" class="tabletext_gray" align="right">Mobile
Phone:</td>
  <td width="500" class="tabletext">
   <asp:label id="lblMobilePhone" runat="server" />
  </td>
</tr>
<tr>
  <td width="100" class="tabletext_gray" align="right">Fax:</td>
  <td width="500" class="tabletext">
   <asp:label id="lblFax" runat="server" />
  </td>
</tr>
<tr>
  <td width="100" class="tabletext_gray" align="right">About Me:</td>
  <td width="500" class="tabletext" valign="top">
   <asp:label id="lblAboutMe" runat="server" />
  </td>
</tr>

</table>

</body>
</html>
<TWNW:Footer id="PageFooter" runat="server" />
</body>
</html>
```

Listing 7.33 member_view.aspx (continued)

When we show the data, we don't want a member putting some malicious JavaScript or HTML code in their profile, so we use the Server.HTMLEncode method to render any HTML ineffective. We also change all the new line characters in the About Me field into <BR> tags so that the otherwise invisible line breaks are visible on a web page. Otherwise, they would be considered white space and not visible to the user on the web page. The code-behind file is shown in Listing 7.34.

```
Imports System
Imports System.Data
Imports System.Data.SqlClient
Imports System.Web
Imports System.Web.UI
Imports System.Web.UI.WebControls
Imports TWNWObjects

Namespace TWNW
```

Listing 7.34 member_view.aspx.vb

```
Public Class MemberView
 Inherits Page

 Protected lblName As Label
 Protected lblEMail As Label
 Protected lblUserName As Label
 Protected lblHomePage As Label
 Protected lblHomePhone As Label
 Protected lblWorkPhone As Label
 Protected lblMobilePhone As Label
 Protected lblFax As Label
 Protected lblAboutMe As Label

 Sub Page_Load(objSender As Object, objArgs As EventArgs)
   Dim DB As New AtWorkUtilities.Database()
   Dim blnShowProfile As Boolean = False
   Dim SDR As SqlDataReader = _
    DB.GetDataReader("sp_CheckProfileVisibility " _
      & Request.Cookies("mID").Value & ", " _
      & Request.QueryString("ID"), True)
   If SDR.Read() Then
    blnShowProfile = (SDR("IsProfileVisible") = "T")
   End If
   SDR.Close()

   Dim M As New Member(DB, Request.QueryString("ID"))
   Dim DR As DataRow = M.GetRow()

   lblName.Text = DR("LastName").ToString _
    & ", " & DR("FirstName").ToString
   lblUserName.Text = DR("UserName").ToString
   If blnShowProfile Then
    If DR("EMail").ToString <> "" Then
      lblEMail.Text = "<a href=""mailto:" _
      & DR("EMail").ToString _
      & """>" & DR("EMail").ToString _
      & "</a>"
    Else
      lblEMail.Text = "None"
    End If

    If DR("HomePage").ToString <> "" Then
      lblHomePage.Text = "<a href=""" _
      & DR("HomePage").ToString
    Else
      lblHomePage.Text = "None"
    End If

    If DR("HomePhone").ToString <> "" Then
```

Listing 7.34   member_view.aspx.vb (continued)

```
      lblHomePhone.Text = DR("HomePhone").ToString
  Else
      lblHomePhone.Text = "None"
  End If

  If DR("WorkPhone").ToString <> "" Then
      lblWorkPhone.Text = DR("WorkPhone").ToString
  Else
      lblWorkPhone.Text = "None"
  End If

  If DR("MobilePhone").ToString <> "" Then
      lblMobilePhone.Text = DR("MobilePhone").ToString
  Else
      lblMobilePhone.Text = "None"
  End If

  If DR("Fax").ToString <> "" Then
      lblFax.Text = DR("Fax").ToString
  Else
      lblFax.Text = "None"
  End If

  If DR("AboutMe").ToString <> "" Then
      Dim strTemp As String
      strTemp = DR("AboutMe").ToString
      strTemp = Server.HTMLEncode(strTemp)
      strTemp = _
        strTemp.Replace(Environment.NewLine, "<br>")
      lblAboutMe.Text = _
        strTemp
  Else
      lblAboutMe.Text = "No information given"
  End If

Else
  lblEMail.Text = "<i>Hidden</i>"
  lblHomePage.Text = "<i>Hidden</i>"
  lblHomePhone.Text = "<i>Hidden</i>"
  lblWorkPhone.Text = "<i>Hidden</i>"
  lblMobilePhone.Text = "<i>Hidden</i>"
  lblFax.Text = "<i>Hidden</i>"
  lblAboutMe.Text = "<i>Hidden/i>"
```

Listing 7.34 member_view.aspx.vb (continued)

```
      End If

    db.Close()
  End Sub
End Class
End Namespace
```

Listing 7.34   member_view.aspx.vb (continued)

When we're showing the data, we are also careful not to show any private profile information and instead show the word Hidden. Email and home page links are turned into active links by employing a little extra HTML here.

The next step in sending a message is to prompt the user for the message text. We already know where it's going since the user clicked the Choose link to go to the Message_create.aspx file. On this page, new messages can be written as well as replies to existing messages. When you reply to a message, a copy of the old message is placed into the body of the message, as shown in Figure 7.8.

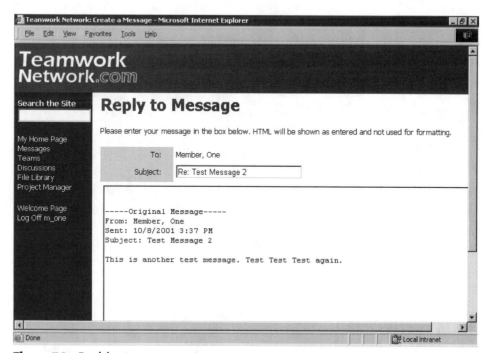

Figure 7.8   Replying to a message.

When I designed this system, I tried to make it as much like a regular email system as possible to make it easier to understand and use. This is just another feature in which you see the similarities. The code is shown in Listing 7.35.

```
<%@ Page Inherits="TWNW.MessagesCreate" Src="message_create.aspx.vb" %>
<%@ Register Tagprefix="TWNW" Tagname="Header" Src="Header.ascx" %>
<%@ Register Tagprefix="TWNW" Tagname="Footer" Src="Footer.ascx" %>
<!DOCTYPE HTML PUBLIC "-//W3C//DTD HTML 4.0 Transitional//EN">
<html>
<head>
  <title>Teamwork Network: Create a Message</title>
  <link href="styles.css" rel="stylesheet" type="text/css">
</head>
<body>
<TWNW:Header id="PageHeader" runat="server" />
<p><asp:label id="lblPageTitle" class="pageheading" runat="server"
/></p>
<p class="text">
Please enter your message in the box below. HTML will be shown as
entered and
not used for formatting.
</p>
<asp:label id="lblErrorMessage" class="errortext" runat="server" />

<form runat="server">
<input type="hidden" runat="server" id="returnURL">
<input type="hidden" runat="server" id="fkMessageToMemberID">

<table width="600" cellspacing="0" cellpadding="5">
<tr>
  <td width="100" class="tabletext_gray" align="right">To:</td>
  <td width="500" class="tabletext">
  <asp:label
    id="lblMessageTo"
    runat="server" />
  </td>
</tr>
<tr class="tabletext">
  <td width="100" class="tabletext_gray" align="right">Subject:</td>
  <td width="500" class="tabletext">
  <asp:textbox
    id="txtMessageSubject"
    columns="30"
    maxlength="80"
    runat="server" />
  </td>
</tr>
<tr class="tabletext">
  <td colspan="2">
```

Listing 7.35   message_create.aspx

```
    <asp:textbox
     id="txtMessageText"
     rows="15"
     columns="80"
     wrap="true"
     textmode="Multiline"
     runat="server" />
    </td>
  </tr>
  <tr class="tabletext">
    <td colspan=2 align=middle>
    <input type="submit"
     name="btnSubmit"
     runat="server"
     value="Save" />
    <input type="reset"
     name="btnReset"
     runat="server"
     value="Clear" />
    </td>
  </tr>
  </table>
  </form>
  <TWNW:Footer id="PageFooter" runat="server" />
  </body>
  </html>
```

Listing 7.35   message_create.aspx (continued)

This form was actually created by tweaking the Member Editor page you built earlier. If you copy and paste, be sure to double-check your variable names or you're going to be in trouble. The code-behind file is shown in Listing 7.36.

```
Imports System
Imports System.Data
Imports System.Data.SqlClient
Imports System.Web
Imports System.Web.UI
Imports System.Web.UI.WebControls
Imports TWNWObjects

Namespace TWNW
  Public Class MessagesCreate
    Inherits System.Web.UI.Page
```

Listing 7.36   message_create.aspx.vb

```
Protected returnURL As HTMLControls.HTMLInputHidden
Protected fkMessageToMemberID As HTMLControls.HTMLInputHidden

Protected lblMessageTo As Label
Protected txtMessageSubject As TextBox
Protected txtMessageText As TextBox

Protected lblPageTitle As Label
Protected lblErrorMessage As Label

Sub Page_Load(objSender As Object, objArgs As EventArgs)
  Dim DB As New AtWorkUtilities.Database()
  Dim M As Member
  Dim MS As Message
  Dim DR, DRF As DataRow
  Dim objCookie As HTTPCookie
  objCookie = Request.Cookies("mID")

  If Not Page.IsPostBack Then
   returnURL.Value = Request.QueryString("rURL")
   If Request.QueryString("ID") <> "" Then
    '
    ' If ID is provided, do a reply
    '
    lblPageTitle.Text = "Reply to Message"
    MS = New Message(DB, Request.QueryString("ID"))
    DR = MS.GetRow()
    M = New Member(DB, DR("fkMessageFromMemberID"))
    DRF = M.GetRow()
    lblMessageTo.Text = DRF("LastName") & ", " & DRF("FirstName")
    fkMessageToMemberID.Value = DRF("pkMemberID").ToString
    If DR("MessageSubject").ToString.IndexOf("Re:") < 0 Then
     txtMessageSubject.Text = "Re: " & DR("MessageSubject")
    Else
     txtMessageSubject.Text = DR("MessageSubject")
    End If
    txtMessageText.Text = Environment.NewLine _
     & Environment.NewLine _
     & Environment.NewLine _
     & "-----Original Message-----" _
     & Environment.NewLine _
     & "From: " & DRF("LastName") & ", " & DRF("FirstName") _
     & Environment.NewLine _
     & "Sent: " & DR("MessageDate").ToShortDateString _
     & " " & DR("MessageDate").ToShortTimeString _
     & Environment.NewLine _
     & "Subject: " & DR("MessageSubject") _
     & Environment.NewLine _
     & Environment.NewLine _
     & DR("MessageText")
```

Listing 7.36   message_create.aspx.vb (continued)

```
        ElseIf Request.QueryString("TM") <> "" Then
          lblPageTitle.Text = "Create New Message"
          M = New Member(DB, Request.QueryString("TM"))
          DR = M.GetRow()
          lblMessageTo.Text = DR("LastName") & ", " & DR("FirstName")
          fkMessageToMemberID.Value = DR("pkMemberID").ToString
          M = Nothing
        End If
      Else
        MS = New Message(DB)
        DR = MS.GetRow()
        DR("fkMessageFromMemberID") = _
          Int16.Parse(Request.Cookies("mID").Value)
        DR("fkMessageToMemberID") = _
          Int16.Parse(fkMessageToMemberID.Value)
        DR("MessageDate") = DateTime.Now()
        DR("MessageRead") = 0
        DR("MessageSubject") = txtMessageSubject.Text
        DR("MessageText") = txtMessageText.Text
        MS.SaveRow(DR)
        If Not MS.IsValid Then
          lblErrorMessage.Text = _
          MS.ValidationError("<b>ERROR:</b> The following " _
            & "errors were detected in your data:<br>", _
            "&bull; {0}<br>", "")
        Else
          MS.Save()
          DB.Close()
          If returnURL.Value = "" Then
           Response.Redirect("messages.aspx")
          Else
           Response.Redirect(returnURL.Value)
          End If
        End If
      End If
    End Sub

    Private Sub SelectFromList(cboList As DropDownList, _
      strValue As String)

      Dim i As Integer

      For i = 0 To cboList.Items.Count
        If cboList.Items(i).Value = strValue Then
          cboList.SelectedIndex = i
          Exit For
        End If
      Next i

    End Sub

  End Class
End Namespace
```

Listing 7.36   message_create.aspx.vb (continued)

This page has quite a bit going on, so it's best to follow through one path at a time. The query string gives us a hint as to whether we are replying to a message or creating a new message. If a value for ID is supplied in the query string, that is the message to which we are replying, and we take the appropriate path. If ID is missing but TM is supplied, we are creating a new message to a particular member, and the member ID is supplied in the query string.

When replying to a message, most of the code here handles filling up the message entry area with the previous message. This is similar to many email programs so that it's easier to see the history of an email. This code also generates a Re: as part of the subject line if one doesn't already exist. This code uses several of the objects, including the Member and Message objects in order to pull up information to populate the message. For a new message, the only thing that needs to be done is to store the destination member ID in the hidden-input field and show the destination member's name on the form. Generating the message is a matter of filling in the Message object with all the relevant fields. When we're done, we send the user back to the message viewer or to the previous page through the return URL parameter supplied earlier.

Reading a Message

Now that we have the ability to send messages, we need to build the Message_ read.aspx page so that we can read the message. This page is formatted in a similar way to the member profile page and shows all the message information and provides a way for the user to reply to the message. The message text is encoded so that HTML doesn't interfere with the layout of the page.

The ASPX file, called Message_read.aspx, is shown in Listing 7.37.

```
<%@ Page Inherits="TWNW.MessagesRead" Src="message_read.aspx.vb" %>
<%@ Register Tagprefix="TWNW" Tagname="Header" Src="Header.ascx" %>
<%@ Register Tagprefix="TWNW" Tagname="Footer" Src="Footer.ascx" %>


<!DOCTYPE HTML PUBLIC "-//W3C//DTD HTML 4.0 Transitional//EN">
<html>
<head>
    <title>Teamwork Network: Read Message</title>
  <link href="styles.css" rel="stylesheet" type="text/css">
</head>

<body leftmargin=0 topmargin=0>
<TWNW:Header id="PageHeader" runat="server" />
<p class="pageheading">Read Message</p>
<asp:label id="lblActions" runat="server" />

<table width="600" cellspacing="0" cellpadding="4" border="1">
<tr>
  <td width="100" class="tabletext_gray" align="right">From:</td>
  <td width="500" class="tabletext">
```

Listing 7.37 message_read.aspx

```
      <asp:label id="lblMessageFrom" runat="server" />
    </td>
  </tr>
  <tr>
    <td width="100" class="tabletext_gray" align="right">Subject:</td>
    <td width="500" class="tabletext">
      <asp:label id="lblMessageSubject" runat="server" />
    </td>
  </tr>
  <tr>
    <td width="100" class="tabletext_gray" align="right">Date:</td>
    <td width="500" class="tabletext">
      <asp:label id="lblMessageDate" runat="server" />
    </td>
  </tr>
  <tr>
    <td width="600" class="tabletext" colspan="2">
      <asp:label id="lblMessage" runat="server" />
    </td>
  </tr>
</table>

</body>
</html>
<TWNW:Footer id="PageFooter" runat="server" />
</body>
</html>
```

Listing 7.37   message_read.aspx (continued)

For the most part, this page is just a big form with labels instead of text boxes. The more interesting code is in the code behind the scenes, shown in Listing 7.38.

```
Imports System
Imports System.Data
Imports System.Data.SqlClient
Imports System.Web
Imports System.Web.UI
Imports System.Web.UI.WebControls
Imports TWNWObjects

Namespace TWNW
  Public Class MessagesRead
    Inherits Page

    Protected lblMessageFrom As Label
```

Listing 7.38   message_read.aspx.vb

```
    Protected lblMessageSubject As Label
    Protected lblMessageDate As Label
    Protected lblMessage As Label
    Protected lblActions As Label

    Sub Page_Load(objSender As Object, objArgs As EventArgs)
      Dim DB As New AtWorkUtilities.Database()
      Dim M As New Message(DB, Request.QueryString("ID"))
      Dim DR As DataRow = M.GetRow()
      DR("MessageRead") = True
      M.SaveRow(DR)
      M.Save()

      Dim MF As New Member(DB, DR("fkMessageFromMemberID"))
      Dim DRM As DataRow = MF.GetRow()

      lblMessageFrom.Text = DRM("LastName") & ", " & DRM("FirstName")
      lblMessageSubject.Text = Server.HTMLEncode(DR("MessageSubject"))
      lblMessageDate.Text = DR("MessageDate").ToShortDateString _
      & " " & DR("MessageDate").ToShortTimeString
      lblMessage.Text = _
      Server.HTMLEncode(DR("MessageText")).Replace(Environment.NewLine, _
      "<br>")
      lblActions.Text = "<p class=""text"">" _
        & "<a href=""messages.aspx"">Return to Message List</a>" _
        & " | " _
        & "<a href=""message_choose.aspx"">Create a New Message</a>" _
        & " | " _
        & "<a href=""message_create.aspx?id=" _
        & Request.QueryString("ID") _
        & """>Reply to Message</a>" _
        & " | " _
        & "<a href=""message_delete.aspx?id=" _
        & Request.QueryString("ID") _
        & """>Delete Message</a></p>"

      db.Close()
    End Sub
  End Class
End Namespace
```

Listing 7.38 message_read.aspx.vb (continued)

The message ID is passed through the query string and is loaded by way of a Message object. We then take the data from the GetRow method and populate it into the form. You should also note that we are generating the action links manually here, since we have to build them using the values that came from the query string. The label control holds the output that we concatenate together.

The interesting thing about this code is that before we show the message, we update the record to indicate that the message has been read. This quick save takes care of changing the icon when the user comes back to the list window. Because the Message object takes care of most of the work for us, there's not a lot of extra code here.

Deleting Messages

Now that you've got messages in your mailbox, you're going to need to delete them. The Delete Message function is short and doesn't have a lot of fluff to it. In fact, the ASPX file is a single line long:

```
<%@ Page Inherits="TWNW.MessagesDelete" Src="message_delete.aspx.vb" %>
```

The VB code is shown in Listing 7.39, and isn't much longer.

```
Imports System
Imports System.Web
Imports TWNWObjects

Namespace TWNW
  Public Class MessagesDelete
    Inherits System.Web.UI.Page

    Sub Page_Load(objSender As Object, objArgs As EventArgs)
      Dim DB As New AtWorkUtilities.Database()
      Dim M As New Message(DB, Request.QueryString("ID"))
      M.Delete()
      db.Close()
      Response.Redirect("messages.aspx")
    End Sub
  End Class
End Namespace
```

Listing 7.39 message_delete.aspx.vb

We now need to get the message ID from the query string, load it into the Message object, and call the Delete method. We then send the user back to the Message Listing page, since that's the logical place to go next. This page has no confirmation step since the messages being generated in the system are generally not worth keeping. However, you could modify the message list to generate a quick JavaScript message giving the user the chance to cancel the deletion.

Building the Team Management Features

The next step is to build the team management features. A team is a group of members selected by a member (known as the leader) to work together. Teams are used throughout the site to group files, discussions, and projects. We'll have pages to view a member's teams, add, modify, and delete teams, as well as manage the people on the teams. The first page we'll start with is the team viewer, showing the teams that a particular member leads.

View Teams Page

We'll start with the View All Teams page that shows the teams that you as the person viewing the page lead. The ASPX file code is shown in Listing 7.40. Like the other list windows, we're using a Repeater control here along with a stored procedure to generate our output.

```
<%@ Page Inherits="TWNW.TeamsViewAll" Src="teams.aspx.vb" %>
<%@ Register Tagprefix="TWNW" Tagname="Header" Src="Header.ascx" %>
<%@ Register Tagprefix="TWNW" Tagname="Footer" Src="Footer.ascx" %>
<!DOCTYPE HTML PUBLIC "-//W3C//DTD HTML 4.0 Transitional//EN">
<html>
<head>
     <title>Teamwork Network: View All Teams</title>
  <link href="styles.css" rel="stylesheet" type="text/css">
</head>

<body leftmargin=0 topmargin=0>
<TWNW:Header id="PageHeader" runat="server" />
<p class="pageheading">View All Teams</p>
<p class="text"><a href="team_create.aspx">Create a Team</a></p>
<asp:label id="lblMessage" class="text" runat="server" />

<asp:Repeater id="rptList" runat="server">
  <HeaderTemplate>
  <table cellpadding="4" cellspacing="0" width="100%">
  <tr class="tableheading">
  <td width="30%">Name</td>
  <td width="40%">Description</td>
  <td width="30%">Actions</td>
  </tr>
  </HeaderTemplate>
  <ItemTemplate>
  <tr class="tabletext">
  <td valign="top"><%# DataBinder.Eval(Container.DataItem, _
    "Name") %></td>
  <td valign="top"><%# DataBinder.Eval(Container.DataItem, _
    "Description") %></td>
  <td valign="top" align="center">
  <a href="teammembers.aspx?id=<%# DataBinder.Eval(Container.DataItem, _
    "pkTeamID") %>">Manage Members</a>  
  <a href="team_create.aspx?id=<%# DataBinder.Eval(Container.DataItem, _
    "pkTeamID") %>">Update</a>  
  <a href="team_delete.aspx?id=<%# DataBinder.Eval(Container.DataItem, _
    "pkTeamID") %>">Delete</a>
```

Listing 7.40   teams.aspx

```
        </td>
        </tr>
        </ItemTemplate>
        <AlternatingItemTemplate>
        <tr class="tabletext">
        <td valign="top"><%# DataBinder.Eval(Container.DataItem, _
          "Name") %></td>
        <td valign="top"><%# DataBinder.Eval(Container.DataItem, _
          "Description") %></td>
        <td valign="top" align="center">
        <a href="teammembers.aspx?id=<%# DataBinder.Eval(Container.DataItem, _
          "pkTeamID") %>">Manage Members</a>
        <a href="team_create.aspx?id=<%# DataBinder.Eval(Container.DataItem, _
          "pkTeamID") %>">Update</a>  
        <a href="team_delete.aspx?id=<%# DataBinder.Eval(Container.DataItem, _
          "pkTeamID") %>">Delete</a>  
        </td>
        </tr>
        </AlternatingItemTemplate>
        <FooterTemplate>
        </table>
        </FooterTemplate>
</asp:Repeater>
</body>
</html>
<TWNW:Footer id="PageFooter" runat="server" />
</body>
</html>
```

Listing 7.40   teams.aspx (continued)

There's really nothing new here, but we do create links to the Teammembers.aspx file, Team_create.aspx, and Team_delete.aspx, all of which we'll cover in this project. The VB code for this page is shown in Listing 7.41.

```
Imports System
Imports System.Data
Imports System.Data.SqlClient
Imports System.Web
Imports System.Web.UI
Imports System.Web.UI.WebControls
Imports TWNWObjects

Namespace TWNW
  Public Class TeamsViewAll
```

Listing 7.41   teams.aspx.vb

```
    Inherits System.Web.UI.Page

    Protected lblMessage As Label
    Protected rptList As Repeater

    Sub Page_Load(objSender As Object, objArgs As EventArgs)
      If (Request.Cookies("mID") Is Nothing) Then
       Response.Redirect("login.aspx?msg=403&rURL=" _
         & Request.ServerVariables("SCRIPT_NAME") _
         & "?" _
         & Request.ServerVariables("QUERY_STRING"))
      End If

      Dim DB As New AtWorkUtilities.Database()
      Dim objCookie As HTTPCookie
      objCookie = Request.Cookies("mID")

      Dim DS As DataSet = _
        DB.GetDataSet("sp_RetrieveTeamsByMember " _
        & objCookie.Value.ToString())
      If DS.Tables(0).Rows.Count = 0 Then
        lblMessage.Text _
        = "<b>You do not currently manage any teams.</b>"
      Else
        rptList.DataSource = DS
        rptList.DataBind()
      End If
      db.Close()
    End Sub
  End Class
End Namespace
```

Listing 7.41   teams.aspx.vb (continued)

Like the message viewer, we first verify that the user is logged in. If not, we send him or her to the Login page with the appropriate message. We then retrieve the teams for the member viewing the page. If there are teams already, those are shown in the Repeater control. Otherwise, a message is displayed to the user indicating that no teams exist.

This page gives us a place to begin building the other features of the site that maintain the team records. The Team_create.aspx file is the next one to be built, and the ASPX file is shown in Listing 7.42.

```
<%@ Page Inherits="TWNW.TeamsCreate" Src="team_create.aspx.vb" %>
<%@ Register Tagprefix="TWNW" Tagname="Header" Src="Header.ascx" %>
<%@ Register Tagprefix="TWNW" Tagname="Footer" Src="Footer.ascx" %>
```

Listing 7.42   team_create.aspx

```
<!DOCTYPE HTML PUBLIC "-//W3C//DTD HTML 4.0 Transitional//EN">
<html>
<head>
  <title>Teamwork Network: Team Management</title>
  <link href="styles.css" rel="stylesheet" type="text/css">
</head>
<body>
<TWNW:Header id="PageHeader" runat="server" />
<table width="600">
<tr>
<td valign="top" width="600">

<p><asp:label id="lblPageTitle" class="pageheading" runat="server"
/></p>
<asp:label id="lblErrorMessage" class="errortext" runat="server" />

<form runat="server">
<input type="hidden" runat="server" id="pkTeamID">
<input type="hidden" runat="server" id="returnURL">

<table cellspacing="5">
<tr class="tabletext">
  <td align="right">Name:</td>
  <td>
  <asp:textbox
   id="txtName"
   columns="30"
   maxlength="80"
   runat="server" />
  </td>
</tr>
<tr class="tabletext">
  <td valign="middle" align="right">
  Description:
  </td>
  <td>
  <asp:textbox
   id="txtDescription"
   rows="5"
   columns="40"
   wrap="true"
   textmode="Multiline"
   runat="server" />
  </td>
</tr>
<tr class="tabletext">
  <td colspan=2 align=middle>
  <input type="submit"
   name="btnSubmit"
```

Listing 7.42   team_create.aspx (continued)

```
      runat="server"
      value="Save" />
    <input type="reset"
     name="btnReset"
     runat="server"
     value="Clear" />
    </td>
  </tr>
</table>
</form>
</td>
</tr>
</table>
<TWNW:Footer id="PageFooter" runat="server" />
</body>
</html>
```

Listing 7.42   team_create.aspx (continued)

This page is used for both adding new teams and updating existing ones. Since the tblTeams table itself is short, this page is simple. The VB code is shown in Listing 7.43 and is called Team_create.aspx.vb.

```
Imports System
Imports System.Data
Imports System.Data.SqlClient
Imports System.Web
Imports System.Web.UI
Imports System.Web.UI.WebControls
Imports TWNWObjects

Namespace TWNW
  Public Class TeamsCreate
    Inherits System.Web.UI.Page

    Protected txtName As TextBox
    Protected txtDescription As TextBox

    Protected pkTeamID As HTMLControls.HTMLInputHidden
    Protected returnURL As HTMLControls.HTMLInputHidden

    Protected lblPageTitle As Label
    Protected lblErrorMessage As Label

    Sub Page_Load(objSender As Object, objArgs As EventArgs)
```

Listing 7.43   team_create.aspx.vb

```
      Dim DB As New AtWorkUtilities.Database()
      Dim T As Team
      Dim DR As DataRow
      Dim objCookie As HTTPCookie
      objCookie = Request.Cookies("mID")

    If Not Page.IsPostBack Then
      returnURL.Value = Request.QueryString("rURL")
      If Request.QueryString("ID") <> "" Then
        lblPageTitle.Text = "Edit Team Profile"
        T = New Team(DB, Request.QueryString("ID"))
        DR = T.GetRow()
        pkTeamID.Value = DR("pkTeamID").ToString()
        txtName.Text = DR("Name").ToString()
        txtDescription.Text = DR("Description").ToString()
      Else
        lblPageTitle.Text = "Create New Team"
      End If
    Else
      If pkTeamID.Value = "" Then
        T = New Team(DB)
      Else
        T = New Team(DB, pkTeamID.Value)
      End If
      DR = T.GetRow()
      DR("fkLeaderID") = objCookie.Value
      DR("Name") = txtName.Text
      DR("Description") = txtDescription.Text
      T.SaveRow(DR)
      If Not T.IsValid Then
        lblErrorMessage.Text = _
        T.ValidationError("<b>ERROR:</b> The following " _
          & "errors were detected in your data:<br>", _
          "&bull; {0}<br>", "")
      Else
        T.Save()
        DB.Close()
        If returnURL.Value = "" Then
         Response.Redirect("teams.aspx")
        Else
         Response.Redirect(returnURL.Value)
        End If
      End If
    End If
  End Sub
  End Class
End Namespace
```

Listing 7.43   team_create.aspx.vb (continued)

Like the other data entry pages you've built in this project, we use the query string to determine if we are adding or editing a team record. For edits, we retrieve the team, populate the form with the appropriate data, and store the unique ID in the hidden field for later. When the user fills in the information and clicks Save, we use the Team object to store the data in the database. The only required fields are the leader ID and the name. The name can be entered by the user on the form you'll build. The other information comes from the user's cookie and is added to the database through this code.

The next page we need to build is the Delete Team page. A team can only be deleted if there are no related records in any of the tables. As we add more subsystems, we will be changing the stored procedure used in this page before the deletion takes place. By using the stored procedure, we avoid having to change this file later. The ASPX file for the Delete Team function is shown in Listing 7.44.

```
<%@ Page Inherits="TWNW.TeamsDelete" Src="team_delete.aspx.vb" %>
<%@ Register Tagprefix="TWNW" Tagname="Header" Src="Header.ascx" %>
<%@ Register Tagprefix="TWNW" Tagname="Footer" Src="Footer.ascx" %>
<!DOCTYPE HTML PUBLIC "-//W3C//DTD HTML 4.0 Transitional//EN">
<html>
<head>
  <title>Teamwork Network: Team Management</title>
  <link href="styles.css" rel="stylesheet" type="text/css">
</head>
<body>
<TWNW:Header id="PageHeader" runat="server" />
<p class="pageheading">Delete Team</p>
<p class="text">Are you sure you want to delete this team?</p>
<form runat="server" id="deleteTeam">
<input type="hidden" runat="server" id="pkTeamID">
<input type="hidden" runat="server" id="returnURL">
<p class="text">
<a href="javascript:document.deleteTeam.submit();">Yes</a>
  
<a href="javascript:history.go(-1);">No</a>
</p>
</form>
<TWNW:Footer id="PageFooter" runat="server" />
</body>
</html>
```

Listing 7.44   team_delete.aspx

The code behind this page is shown in Listing 7.45 and is called Team_delete. aspx.vb. This file follows the same pattern as the Event Deletion page we built in Project 3.

We call the stored procedure to determine if this team can be deleted. If it can't, we send the user to the Team_delete_failed.aspx page, which informs them that all related records must be removed before a team can be deleted. This page is included in the application, but won't be shown here for space reasons. For a team that can be deleted, we use the Delete function on the Team object and then send the user back to either the team listing or the URL supplied when the Team_delete.aspx page was called.

```
Imports System
Imports System.Data
Imports System.Data.SqlClient
Imports System.Web.UI
Imports System.Web.UI.WebControls
Imports TWNWObjects

Namespace TWNW
  Public Class TeamsDelete
   Inherits System.Web.UI.Page

   Protected pkTeamID As HTMLControls.HTMLInputHidden
   Protected returnURL As HTMLControls.HTMLInputHidden

   Sub Page_Load(objSender As Object, objArgs As EventArgs)
     If Not Page.IsPostBack Then
      pkTeamID.Value = Request.QueryString("ID")
      returnURL.Value = Request.QueryString("rURL")
     Else
      Dim DB As New AtWorkUtilities.Database()
      Dim DR As SqlDataReader = _
        DB.GetDataReader("sp_CheckForTeamDelete " _
        & pkTeamID.Value)
      If DR("TeamMembers") > 0 Then
        DR.Close()
        Response.Redirect("team_delete_failed.aspx")
      Else
        DR.Close()
        Dim T As New Team(DB, pkTeamID.Value)
        T.Delete()
        DB.Close()
        If returnURL.Value = "" Then
         Response.Redirect("teams.aspx")
        Else
         Response.Redirect(returnURL.Value)
        End If
      End If
     End If
   End Sub
  End Class
End Namespace
```

Listing 7.45   team_delete.aspx.vb

Now that we have created the team, we can add members to it. To do this, we have a page nearly identical to the page used to select people to email. In this case, we choose to add them to the team. The first page we see is the Teammembers.aspx page showing the current members of a selected team. That code is shown in Listing 7.46.

```
<%@ Page Inherits="TWNW.TeamMembersViewAll" Src="teammembers.aspx.vb" %>
<%@ Register Tagprefix="TWNW" Tagname="Header" Src="Header.ascx" %>
<%@ Register Tagprefix="TWNW" Tagname="Footer" Src="Footer.ascx" %>


<!DOCTYPE HTML PUBLIC "-//W3C//DTD HTML 4.0 Transitional//EN">
<html>
<head>
     <title>Teamwork Network: View Team Members</title>
  <link href="styles.css" rel="stylesheet" type="text/css">
</head>

<body leftmargin=0 topmargin=0>
<TWNW:Header id="PageHeader" runat="server" />
<p class="pageheading">View Team Members</p>
<p class="text">
<a href="teammember_add.aspx?tID=<% = Request.QueryString("ID") %>">Add
a New Member</a>
</p>
<asp:label id="lblMessage" class="text" runat="server" />

<asp:Repeater id="rptList" runat="server">
  <HeaderTemplate>
  <table cellpadding="4" cellspacing="0" width="500">
  <tr class="tableheading">
  <td width="40%">Name</td>
  <td width="40%">User Name</td>
  <td width="20%">Actions</td>
  </tr>
  </HeaderTemplate>
  <ItemTemplate>
  <tr class="tabletext">
  <td valign="top"><%# DataBinder.Eval(Container.DataItem, _
    "MemberName") %></td>
  <td valign="top"><%# DataBinder.Eval(Container.DataItem, _
    "UserName") %></td>
  <td valign="top" align="center">
  <a href="teammember_delete.aspx?id=<%#
DataBinder.Eval(Container.DataItem, _
    "pkTeamMemberID") %>">Delete</a>
  </td>
  </tr>
  </ItemTemplate>
  <AlternatingItemTemplate>
  <tr class="tabletext">
  <td valign="top"><%# DataBinder.Eval(Container.DataItem, _
```

Listing 7.46   teammembers.aspx

```
    "MemberName") %></td>
  <td valign="top"><%# DataBinder.Eval(Container.DataItem, _
    "UserName") %></td>
  <td valign="top" align="center">
  <a href="teammember_delete.aspx?id=<%#
DataBinder.Eval(Container.DataItem, _
    "pkTeamMemberID") %>">Delete</a>
  </td>
  </tr>
  </AlternatingItemTemplate>
  <FooterTemplate>
  </table>
  </FooterTemplate>
</asp:Repeater>
</body>
</html>
<TWNW:Footer id="PageFooter" runat="server" />
</body>
</html>
```

Listing 7.46   teammembers.aspx (continued)

The Repeater control makes light work of the formatting and looping, so we use it again here. The VB code for this page follows the same pattern as the Teams.aspx code and is shown in Listing 7.47.

```
Imports System
Imports System.Data
Imports System.Data.SqlClient
Imports System.Web
Imports System.Web.UI
Imports System.Web.UI.WebControls
Imports TWNWObjects

Namespace TWNW
  Public Class TeamMembersViewAll
    Inherits System.Web.UI.Page

    Protected lblMessage As Label
    Protected rptList As Repeater

    Sub Page_Load(objSender As Object, objArgs As EventArgs)
      Dim DB As New AtWorkUtilities.Database()

      Dim DS As DataSet = _
        DB.GetDataSet("sp_RetrieveTeamMembers " _
```

Listing 7.47   teammembers.aspx.vb

```
      & Request.QueryString("ID"))
     If DS.Tables(0).Rows.Count = 0 Then
      lblMessage.Text = "<b>This team currently has no members.</b>"
     Else
      rptList.DataSource = DS
      rptList.DataBind()
     End If
     db.Close()
   End Sub
  End Class
End Namespace
```

Listing 7.47   teammembers.aspx.vb (continued)

We read the ID parameter from the query string and use that value to determine which team's members we are retrieving. The rest of the work is done in the stored procedure that returns the name of each member and their username in the system.

To add a new member to the team, we first navigate to the Teammember_add.aspx file, where all the current members are listed, along with links to their profiles. This page works exactly like the Message_choose.aspx file, so we'll leave out the listing here. Once you pick a user from this list, you are sent to the Teammember_addsave. aspx page, where he or she is added to the tblTeamMembers table. The ASPX file is a one-directive file, shown here:

```
<%@ Page Inherits="TWNW.TeamMemberAddSave"
     Src="teammember_addsave.aspx.vb" %>
```

The code-behind file is shown in Listing 7.48.

```
Imports System
Imports System.Web
Imports System.Data
Imports TWNWObjects

Namespace TWNW
  Public Class TeamMemberAddSave
   Inherits System.Web.UI.Page

   Sub Page_Load(objSender As Object, objArgs As EventArgs)
    Dim DB As New AtWorkUtilities.Database()
    Dim T As New Team(DB, Request.QueryString("tID"))

    Dim TM As New TeamMember(DB)
    Dim DR As DataRow = TM.GetRow()
    DR("fkTeamID") = Request.QueryString("tID")
```

Listing 7.48   teammember_add.aspx.vb

```
        DR("fkMemberID") = Request.QueryString("ID")
        TM.SaveRow(DR)
        TM.Save()
        '
        ' Confirm addition with a message to the new
        ' team member.
        '
        Dim M As New Message(DB)
        Dim DRM As DataRow = M.GetRow()
        Dim DT As DataRow = T.GetRow()
        Dim intTeamID As Integer
        DRM("MessageDate") = DateTime.Now()
        DRM("fkMessageFromMemberID") = _
          Int16.Parse(Request.Cookies("mID").Value)
        DRM("fkMessageToMemberID") = Request.QueryString("ID")
        DRM("MessageRead") = 0
        DRM("MessageSubject") = "Addition to " & DT("Name") & " Team"
        DRM("MessageText") = "You have been added to the " _
          & DT("Name") & " team by the team leader. Contact the " _
          & "team leader for more information."
        M.SaveRow(DRM)
        M.Save()
        intTeamID = DR("fkTeamID")
        DB.Close()
        Response.Redirect("teammembers.aspx?id=" & intTeamID.ToString)
      End Sub
    End Class
End Namespace
```

Listing 7.48 teammember_add.aspx.vb (continued)

Most of the code here is designed to send a message to the new team member informing him or her of this fact. We use the Message object, but we have to retrieve some information from the tblTeams table about the team so that we can generate an appropriate message to the user. When done, we return to the team member listing so we can add another team member, if necessary.

When a team member needs to be removed, we have a page that performs the deletion. The ASPX file is a one-line file, shown here:

```
<%@ Page Inherits="TWNW.TeamMemberDelete"
    Src="teammember_delete.aspx.vb" %>
```

The code behind this page is nearly identical to the Add function code in the structure, but the function is exactly the opposite. The code is shown in Listing 7.49 and is called Teammember_delete.aspx.vb.

```
Imports System
Imports System.Web
Imports System.Data
Imports TWNWObjects

Namespace TWNW
  Public Class TeamMemberDelete
    Inherits System.Web.UI.Page

    Sub Page_Load(objSender As Object, objArgs As EventArgs)
      Dim DB As New AtWorkUtilities.Database()
      Dim TM As New TeamMember(DB, Request.QueryString("ID"))
      Dim DR As DataRow = TM.GetRow()
      Dim M As New Message(DB)
      Dim DRM As DataRow = M.GetRow()
      Dim T As New Team(DB, DR("fkTeamID"))
      Dim DT As DataRow = T.GetRow()
      Dim intTeamID As Integer
      DRM("MessageDate") = DateTime.Now()
      DRM("fkMessageFromMemberID") =
       Int16.Parse(Request.Cookies("mID").Value)
      DRM("fkMessageToMemberID") = DR("fkMemberID")
      DRM("MessageRead") = 0
      DRM("MessageSubject") = "Removal From " & DT("Name") & " Team"
      DRM("MessageText") = "You have been removed from the " _
       & DT("Name") & " team by the team leader. Contact the " _
       & "team leader to be added back to the team."
      M.SaveRow(DRM)
      M.Save()
      intTeamID = DR("fkTeamID")
      TM.Delete()
      DB.Close()
      Response.Redirect("teammembers.aspx?id=" & intTeamID.ToString)
    End Sub
  End Class
End Namespace
```

Listing 7.49   teammember_delete.aspx.vb

We remove the user from the team and then send the user a message informing him or her of this fact. The user is then sent back to the Team Member viewer to continue working.

Wrap Up

This project should have given you a good idea of the infrastructure needed to create a multiuser application like the Teamwork Network that we're building. Many of the features are common to other applications on the Web, and knowing how to build them will give you a boost in the right direction when it's time to build your own systems.

As was mentioned in the introduction of this project, you can see this application running live at www.teamworknetwork.com. As new features are introduced, we'll make announcements on this site and make the code available at the book's Web site, www.10projectswithasp.net. The code you built in this project will, for the most part, remain constant throughout the rest of the book. Any changes will be noted, and the final version of the code made available with the book will have the latest edition of all the files.

In the next project, you'll build the discussion forum portion of the application. This threaded discussion system is similar to ones you've probably seen on other web sites. The discussions in this application will be linked to the teams to which you belong so that members of other teams can't see your discussions.

Teamwork Network: Discussion Boards

In the last project, you built the infrastructure for the Teamwork Network application. In this project, you'll help solve the problem that most of us struggle with today: too many messaging systems. I can get voice mail at four different places: home, work, cell phone, and an integrated messaging system. I get email at one mail box, but I have thousands of messages archived from past projects and client contacts. Most people have several email accounts: one for home, one at work, and maybe another for a home-based business.

The solution you're going to build to help alleviate this problem is a discussion board. With it you'll be able to post and reply to messages from your teammates on various projects. Instead of losing information or relying on everyone to get an email that you send, messages will be permanently archived in the discussion boards.

If you want to see the system live and operational, visit the project Web site at www. teamworknetwork.com. I intend to keep this site running as a public-development project that you can discuss at the book's Web site: www.10projectswithasp.net. We'll add new features as time goes on to make this site useful for everyone.

THE PROBLEM

Too many messaging systems cause you to misplace or lose messages and not have a reliable way to share knowledge generated through email conversations.

THE SOLUTION

A discussion-forum feature integrated into the Teamwork Network to keep a running record of all conversations held by members of a team.

Project Background

Discussion boards have been on the Internet much longer than the World Wide Web that we take for granted today. Usenet news groups have been used for years, but most of the early news readers didn't let you see the "threads" of discussion. A thread consists of an original message and all the replies to that message. Some news readers allow you to see multiple levels of replies, but our system will keep things a bit less complex. When a message is posted, any replies to that message will be kept together through foreign keys in the database tables that you'll build.

To build this application, you'll need to complete these tasks:

1. Design the database tables.
2. Create the stored procedures used in the application.
3. Build the business objects.
4. Build the application's Web pages.

You Will Need

✔ **Windows 2000**

✔ **Internet Information Server 5.0 with .NET Framework installed**

✔ **Visual Studio .NET**

✔ **SQL Server 2000 or 7.0**

✔ **SQL Server client utilities, including SQL Server Enterprise Manager and Query Analyzer**

✔ **The code from Project 7**

Building the Database Objects

The first thing you need to do is add the tables that will support this system: tblPosts and tblMemberHistory. Each message is called a *post*, and a primary/foreign key relationship within the table will allow us to keep track of messages and their replies, which is commonly called a *discussion thread*. Most newsgroup systems allow you to see the tree that is built by a message and all the replies. In this system, you'll see the original message and the replies on the same page.

The tblMemberHistory table is designed to keep track of each member's usage of the system. As the user views each discussion board, this activity is logged according to the user's team number. This will make it possible for the user's home page to display whether or not there are new messages since the member's last visit. Since all activity in this table will be handled with a rather complex stored procedure, we won't be building a business object for it. We will, however, need a stored procedure to contain the update.

Creating the tblPosts Table

The tblPosts table is the main table that we need to make all this work. The structure of the table is shown in Table 8.1.

Each message will be automatically assigned a unique ID number for its pkPostID. Every message must have an author, which is a foreign key to the tblMembers table. While most messages will be associated with a particular team, members of the system will also be able to post to a public forum discussion area. In this case, the team ID will be zero or Null. Any initial messages in a thread won't have an original posting number, so that field is also left as zero or Null. The other fields are self-explanatory.

Creating the tblMemberHistory Table

The second table we need to build will hold each member's activity log for each of the subsystems in the Teamwork Network. This table is specifically designed to let us show what's new since the user's last visit to a particular part of the site. The table structure is shown in Table 8.2.

Table 8.1 tblPosts Table Design

FIELD NAME	SQL DATA TYPE	LENGTH	OTHER
pkPostID	int	N/A	Primary Key, Identity, Not Null
fkAuthorID	int	N/A	Not Null
fkTeamID	int	N/A	
fkOriginalPostID	int	N/A	
PostDate	datetime	N/A	Not Null
Subject	varchar	80	Not Null
MessageText	text	N/A	Not Null

Table 8.2 tblMemberHistory Table Design

FIELD NAME	SQL DATA TYPE	LENGTH	OTHER
pkHistoryID	int	N/A	Identity, Primary Key, Not Null
fkMemberID	int	N/A	Not Null
fkTeamID	int	N/A	Not Null
Subsystem	char	1	Not Null
LastVisit	datetime	N/A	Default: getdate()

This table will hold a record for each subsystem for each user. If a user visits the discussion board for Team 5, a record will be placed here for that particular team's discussion board. In the other projects, you'll use this table for other types of data tracking. We only have a single record per member, per team, and per section. The stored procedure we create will take care of either inserting a new record or updating an existing one. This keeps the table as small as possible and removes a lot of duplicate records that might otherwise appear.

With these tables out of the way, we can build our stored procedures next. We'll be using a lot of the techniques you learned in the previous project to make data binding easier.

Creating the Stored Procedures

This feature requires a total of four stored procedures, all of which are designed to display data to the user in various formats. The first stored procedure is used on the main Discussions page, which is shown in Figure 8.1.

This page shows all of the member's teams that have active discussions. If a team does not have any messages posted (which will probably be a rare occurrence), it will not be displayed in this view. This page is generated through the use of a view and a stored procedure that joins to it. The view's SQL code is shown in Listing 8.1.

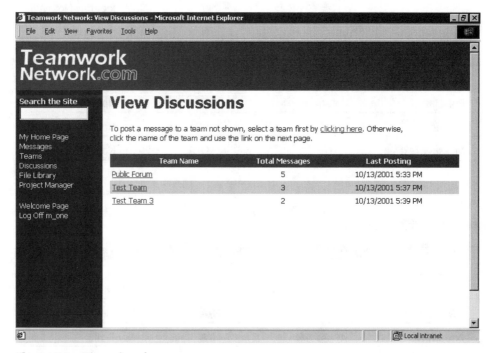

Figure 8.1 Discussions home page.

```
CREATE VIEW dbo.vw_DiscussionList
AS
SELECT   ISNULL(fkTeamID, 0) AS fkTeamID,
COUNT(*) AS TotalMessageCount,
MAX(PostDate) AS LastPostDate
FROM     dbo.tblPosts
GROUP BY fkTeamID
```

Listing 8.1   vw_DiscussionList view

Because we're using the grouping to do some of our work here, it was easier to design the stored procedure by first creating a view of the tblPosts table. Here, we count the number of messages by team number and also show the latest posting for that team. We then take this information and join it to the tblMembers table in the sp_RetrieveDiscussionsByMember stored procedure, shown in Listing 8.2.

```
CREATE PROCEDURE dbo.sp_RetrieveDiscussionsByMember
@MemberID int
AS
SELECT '<a href="posts_view.aspx?tID='
  + convert(varchar, IsNull(fkTeamID, '')) + '">'
  + IsNull(T.Name, 'Public Forum')
  + '</a>' As TeamName, V.*
FROM tblTeams T, vw_DiscussionList V
WHERE V.fkTeamID *= T.pkTeamID
AND (V.fkTeamID IN
  (SELECT fkTeamID FROM tblTeamMembers WHERE fkMemberID = @MemberID)
OR V.fkTeamID = 0)
ORDER BY TeamName
GO
```

Listing 8.2   sp_RetrieveDiscussionsByMember

The primary purpose of this stored procedure is to generate a link that ties the list of forums to the page that shows the user the current threads for each team. It's easier to generate this code here than in the page, since the page is built using a Repeater control. We join the team name and ID to the view we created to create the integrated view shown in the previous figure.

The next stored procedure is designed to show discussion threads on a per-team basis. This page is shown in Figure 8.2.

Each original message (not replies) is shown in this view in reverse chronological order. The user can click the subject line to go to the message thread. The code for this stored procedure is shown in Listing 8.3.

```
CREATE procedure sp_RetrieveOriginalPostsByTeam
@TeamID int
AS
select M.LastName + ', ' + M.FirstName As Author,
  '<a href="posts_read.aspx?pID='
  + convert(varchar, pkPostID)
  + '&tID=' + convert(varchar, @TeamID)
  + '">'
  + P.Subject
  + '</a>' As Subject,
  P.*
FROM tblPosts P, tblMembers M
WHERE IsNull(fkTeamID, 0) = @TeamID
AND P.fkAuthorID = M.pkMemberID
AND fkOriginalPostID IS NULL
ORDER BY PostDate DESC
```

Listing 8.3 sp_RetrieveOriginalPostsByTeam

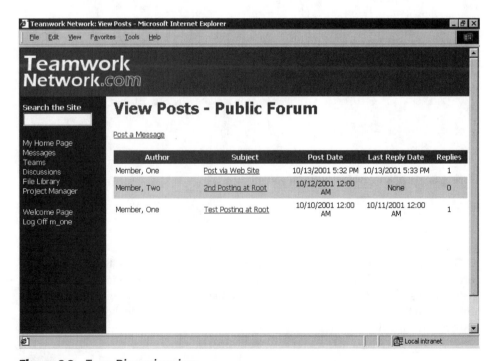

Figure 8.2 Team Discussion view.

We only want to show the original messages, so we specifically look for messages that have null fkOriginalPostID fields. We then join the table with the tblMembers table so that we can display each user's name next to his or her post. We sort the messages in reverse order by date so that the newest ones are listed at the top of the page. This listing also shows the number of replies, as well as the date of the last reply. This is done using a second stored procedure, shown in Listing 8.4.

```
CREATE PROCEDURE dbo.sp_RetrieveStatisticsByPost
@PostID int
AS
SELECT COUNT(*) As ReplyCount,
Max(PostDate) As LastReplyDate
FROM tblPosts
WHERE fkOriginalPostID = @PostID
```

Listing 8.4   sp_RetrieveStatisticsByPost

We'll be building this view manually, since we need to run another stored procedure for each post number that we show as an original post. This makes our ASP.NET code longer, but it makes this view possible without extensively complex database code.

The next page we build shows the original message and any replies. An example of this is shown in Figure 8.3.

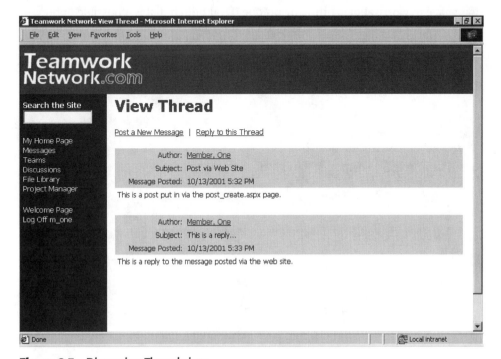

Figure 8.3   Discussion Thread view.

Clicking a user's name here will bring up the user's profile, using the page we built in the previous project. This way, a user can find out who posted the message and possibly send the user a message directly instead of posting to the discussion forum. A user viewing this page also has the option to post a new message to this team's discussion board or reply to this thread.

The stored procedure used to create this view is shown in Listing 8.5.

```
CREATE procedure sp_RetrieveThreadByPostID
@PostID int
as
select '<a href="member_view.aspx?id='
  + convert(varchar, M.pkMemberID)
  + '">' + M.LastName + ', ' + M.FirstName + '</a>' As Author,
  P.*
FROM tblPosts P, tblMembers M
WHERE P.fkAuthorID = M.pkMemberID
AND (pkPostID = @PostID OR fkOriginalPostID = @PostID)
ORDER BY PostDate ASC
```

Listing 8.5 sp_RetrieveThreadByPostID

This stored procedure looks for both original messages and replies, and sorts them in chronological order. Since the original post logically comes before any replies, we don't have to worry about sorting by unique ID, although that is a possible option.

The last stored procedure we need to build for the discussion board system is the stored procedure updating a member's history record for each team's discussion board. This stored procedure is shown in Listing 8.6.

```
CREATE PROCEDURE dbo.sp_UpdateMemberDiscussionHistory
@MemberID int,
@TeamID int
AS
DECLARE @RecordCount int
SELECT @RecordCount = COUNT(*) FROM tblMemberHistory
WHERE fkMemberID = @MemberID
AND fkTeamID = @TeamID
AND Subsystem = 'D'

IF @RecordCount > 0
BEGIN
  UPDATE tblMemberHistory
  SET LastVisit = getdate()
  WHERE fkMemberID = @MemberID
  AND fkTeamID = @TeamID
  AND Subsystem = 'D'
```

Listing 8.6 sp_UpdateMemberDiscussionHistory

```
END
ELSE
BEGIN
  INSERT INTO tblMemberHistory
  (fkMemberID, fkTeamID, Subsystem)
  VALUES
  (@MemberID, @TeamID, 'D')
END
GO
```

Listing 8.6 sp_UpdateMemberDiscussionHistory (continued)

This stored procedure first checks to see if the member has a discussion board history for a particular team's message board, with a zero standing for the public discussion area. If a record already exists, the existing record's timestamp is updated. Otherwise, a new record is added. Because all the work is done in the stored procedure, we can call the procedure from our ASP.NET page and not have to deal with a separate object to handle the logic.

With the stored procedures built, it's time to build our business objects: Post and PostException.

Building the Business Objects

Since we only have a single entity to build in this project, we only have two business objects to build. A Post object represents the entity, and any errors it generates are Post-Exception objects. The Post object follows the same pattern as the previous objects we've built, but we have added a bit of intelligence to it. Instead of making the ASP.NET page populate all of the fields, the object adds a time/date stamp to the message automatically if the row is saved and no data is in the field. This saves you some effort and gives you a model for similar situations with other objects.

The code for the Post class is shown in Listing 8.7.

```
Imports AtWorkUtilities
Imports System.Data.SqlClient


Public Class Post
  Inherits BaseServices


  '
  ' If no arguments are supplied, build a separate
  ' database connection for this object.
  '
```

Listing 8.7 Post.vb class

```
Public Sub New()
 MyBase.New(New Database(), "SELECT * FROM tblPosts WHERE 1=0")
End Sub


' If database connection is supplied, store it
' in the private connection variable for this
' object.
'
Public Sub New(ByVal db As Database)
 MyBase.New(db, "SELECT * FROM tblPosts WHERE 1=0")
End Sub


'
' If both database and ID are supplied, retrieve
' data into the object from the database.
'
Public Sub New(ByVal db As Database, _
 ByVal ID As Integer)

 MyBase.New(db, "SELECT * FROM tblPosts WHERE pkPostID = " _
   & ID.ToString)

End Sub


'
' Verify that all data validation rules have been
' met. Any errors get stored into the errors collection
' inherited from the BaseServices class.
'
Public Sub Validate()
 Dim dr As DataRow

 ClearErrors()
 For Each dr In m_DS.Tables(0).Rows
   If dr.RowState = DataRowState.Added _
   Or dr.RowState = DataRowState.Modified Then
    ValidateRow(dr)
   End If
 Next

End Sub


'
' Checks an individual row for validation rule
' compliance. Any errors are added to the errors
' collection.
'
Private Sub ValidateRow(ByVal dr As DataRow)
```

Listing 8.7 Post.vb class (continued)

```
      If IsDBNull(dr("fkTeamID")) Then
        AddError("Team number is missing.")
      End If
      If IsDBNull(dr("fkAuthorID")) Then
        AddError("Author number is missing.")
      End If
      CheckRequiredField(dr, "Subject", "Subject", 80)
      If IsDBNull(dr("PostDate")) Then
        AddError("Message date is missing.")
      End If
      CheckRequiredField(dr, "MessageText", _
        "Message text", Int32.MaxValue)
    End Sub


    '
    ' The base Save method stores the DataRow into the
    ' DataSet, whether it's a new or existing row. The
    ' rest of this routine handles specific validation
    ' for this type of data.
    '
    Public Overloads Sub SaveRow(ByVal dr As DataRow)
      If IsDBNull(dr("PostDate")) Then
        dr("PostDate") = Now()
      End If
      MyBase.SaveRow(dr)
      Validate()

    End Sub


    '
    ' We separate the SaveRow method from the Save method
    ' to give us a chance to handle any validation. We have
    ' a verification here that the data is good before we
    ' continue, however.
    '
    Public Sub Save()

      If Not Me.IsValid Then
        Throw New PostException(Me.ValidationError)
        Exit Sub
      End If

      m_DA.Update(m_DS)
    End Sub


    '
    ' Since we only have a single row in our DataSet,
    ' delete it and then update the database with the
    ' change.
```

Listing 8.7   Post.vb class (continued)

```
    `
    Public Sub Delete()
     If m_DS.Tables(0).Rows.Count > 0 Then
       m_DS.Tables(0).Rows(0).Delete()
       m_DA.Update(m_DS)
     End If
    End Sub

End Class
```

Listing 8.7   Post.vb class (continued)

The validation rules are applied in the ValidateRow method. We check to make sure that all required foreign keys are supplied and that the subject of the post and some text is supplied. Since we're using a large text field, we still use the CheckRequired-Field routine we built in the previous project, but we use the maximum value by referencing the largest value for the 32-bit integer data type, which has the same value as the maximum length of a text field in SQL Server.

In the SaveRow method, we check to see if the PostDate field has been filled in. If it hasn't, we assume this is a new message and supply the current date and time before going into the validation routine. Again, this saves the ASP.NET page from having to do something with this field. The reason we have to do this here instead of using the database is that when the SqlCommandBuilder writes the database code, it is apparently unaware of any database defaults that may exist. If you leave a Not Null field null, even if the database has a default, an error is generated. This problem should be fixed by the time Visual Studio .NET is released, but it's something to watch in your own coding.

The PostException class follows the same pattern as our other custom exception classes and is shown in Listing 8.8.

```
Public Class PostException
  Inherits Exception

  Public Sub New()
    MyBase.New()
  End Sub

  Public Sub New(ByVal Message As String)
    MyBase.New(Message)
  End Sub

  Public Sub New(ByVal Message As String, ByVal baseError As Exception)
    MyBase.New(Message, baseError)
  End Sub

End Class
```

Listing 8.8   PostException.vb class

The only time we currently generate one of these exceptions is if the data in the Post object is saved and validation errors still exist. Other than that, we are proactive in checking for errors and should never see this type of exception generated in our application.

With the business objects created, we can start building the Web pages for this portion of the application.

Building the Web Pages

There are a total of four new ASP.NET pages you'll be building in this section. You'll also be making a minor change to the Team Viewing page you built in the previous project.

The first page you'll be building shows the list of teams that have any discussions going on in them. As long as at least one message is posted, the discussion will show up. This page is also the first one a user will see, since it is linked to the Discussions link on the main toolbar. The page is called Discussions.aspx, and the code for it is shown in Listing 8.9.

```
<%@ Page Inherits="TWNW.Discussions" Src="discussions.aspx.vb" %>
<%@ Register Tagprefix="TWNW" Tagname="Header" Src="Header.ascx" %>
<%@ Register Tagprefix="TWNW" Tagname="Footer" Src="Footer.ascx" %>
<!DOCTYPE HTML PUBLIC "-//W3C//DTD HTML 4.0 Transitional//EN">
<html>
<head>
      <title>Teamwork Network: View Discussions</title>
  <link href="styles.css" rel="stylesheet" type="text/css">
</head>

<body leftmargin=0 topmargin=0>
<TWNW:Header id="PageHeader" runat="server" />
<p class="pageheading">View Discussions</p>
<p class="text">
To post a message
to the public discussion forum, you can
<a href="post_create.aspx?tID=0">click here</a>.<br>
To post a message to a team not shown,
select a team first by
<a href="teams.aspx">clicking here</a>. <br>
Otherwise, click the name of the team
below to read and post messages<br>
to that team's discussion board.</p>
<asp:label id="lblMessage" class="text" runat="server" />
<asp:Repeater id="rptList" runat="server">
  <HeaderTemplate>
  <table cellpadding="4" cellspacing="0" width="600">
  <tr class="tableheading">
  <td width="40%">Team Name</td>
```

Listing 8.9 discussions.aspx

```
  <td width="20%">Total Messages</td>
  <td width="40%">Last Posting</td>
  </tr>
  </HeaderTemplate>
  <ItemTemplate>
  <tr class="tabletext">
  <td valign="top">
  <%# DataBinder.Eval(Container.DataItem, "TeamName") %>
  </td>
  <td valign="top" align="center">
  <%# DataBinder.Eval(Container.DataItem, _
   "TotalMessageCount") %>
  </td>
  <td valign="top" align="center">
  <%# DataBinder.Eval(Container.DataItem, _
   "LastPostDate").ToShortDateString %>
  <%# DataBinder.Eval(Container.DataItem, _
   "LastPostDate").ToShortTimeString %>
  </td>

  </tr>
  </ItemTemplate>
  <AlternatingItemTemplate>
  <tr class="tabletext_gray">
  <td valign="top">
  <%# DataBinder.Eval(Container.DataItem, "TeamName") %>
  </td>
  <td valign="top" align="center">
  <%# DataBinder.Eval(Container.DataItem, _
   "TotalMessageCount") %>
  </td>
  <td valign="top" align="center">
  <%# DataBinder.Eval(Container.DataItem, _
   "LastPostDate").ToShortDateString %>
  <%# DataBinder.Eval(Container.DataItem, _
   "LastPostDate").ToShortTimeString %>
  </td>
  </tr>
  </AlternatingItemTemplate>
  <FooterTemplate>
  </table>
  </FooterTemplate>
</asp:Repeater>
</body>
</html>
<TWNW:Footer id="PageFooter" runat="server" />
</body>
</html>
```

Listing 8.9 discussions.aspx (continued)

As with many of the other grids we've been building, we are using a Repeater control to show the information. There is a bit of HTML at the top pointing users in the right direction for posting new messages if the teams that a member has joined are not listed. We show the team name, the total number of postings, and the date that someone last posted to the team's discussion board. This way, users can quickly see if they need to visit the board.

The code behind this page is shown in Listing 8.10.

```vb
Imports System
Imports System.Data
Imports System.Web
Imports System.Web.UI
Imports System.Web.UI.WebControls
Imports TWNWObjects


Namespace TWNW
  Public Class Discussions
    Inherits Page


    Protected lblMessage As Label
    Protected rptList As Repeater


    Sub Page_Load(objSender As Object, objArgs As EventArgs)
      If (Request.Cookies("mID") Is Nothing) Then
        Response.Redirect("login.aspx?msg=403&rURL=" _
          & Request.ServerVariables("SCRIPT_NAME") _
          & "?" _
          & Request.ServerVariables("QUERY_STRING"))
      End If


      Dim DB As New AtWorkUtilities.Database()
      Dim DS As DataSet = _
        DB.GetDataSet("sp_RetrieveDiscussionsByMember " _
        & Request.Cookies("mID").Value)
      If DS.Tables(0).Rows.Count = 0 Then
        lblMessage.Text = "<b>There are no posts by any " _
          & "of your teams.</b>"
      Else
        rptList.DataSource = DS
        rptList.DataBind()
      End If
      db.Close()
    End Sub
  End Class
End Namespace
```

Listing 8.10   discussions.aspx.vb

Because the information shown here is restricted to members of the system, we check to make sure the person is logged into the system before doing anything else. We then retrieve the team listing from the database using the stored procedure we built earlier. If there are no posts in any of the teams (a rare occurrence), we display an appropriate message to the user. Otherwise, we bind to the data set, which already has links built into the data coming out of the database. This makes our job here much easier and keeps us from having to manually render this table.

Once the user has chosen a team's discussion board (or the public forum) to view, the Posts_view.aspx page is displayed. This page shows all the original messages in the board, along with their date and author. Users can click an original message to view the messages in that thread. The ASPX file is shown in Listing 8.11.

```
<%@ Page Inherits="TWNW.PostsView" Src="posts_view.aspx.vb" %>
<%@ Register Tagprefix="TWNW" Tagname="Header" Src="Header.ascx" %>
<%@ Register Tagprefix="TWNW" Tagname="Footer" Src="Footer.ascx" %>
<!DOCTYPE HTML PUBLIC "-//W3C//DTD HTML 4.0 Transitional//EN">
<html>
<head>
     <title>Teamwork Network: View Posts</title>
  <link href="styles.css" rel="stylesheet" type="text/css">
</head>

<body leftmargin=0 topmargin=0>
<TWNW:Header id="PageHeader" runat="server" />
<asp:label id="lblPageTitle" class="pageheading" runat="server" />
<p class="text">
<a href="post_create.aspx?tID=<% = Request.QueryString("tID") %>">Post a
Message</a></p>
<table cellpadding="4" cellspacing="0" width="100%">
<tr class="tableheading">
  <td width="25%">Author</td>
  <td width="25%">Subject</td>
  <td width="20%">Post Date</td>
  <td width="20%">Last Reply Date</td>
  <td width="10%">Replies</td>
</tr>
<asp:label id="lblContent" runat="server" />
</table>
</body>
</html>
<TWNW:Footer id="PageFooter" runat="server" />
</body>
</html>
```

Listing 8.11   posts_view.aspx

On this particular page, we have to build the table since we have to call a second stored procedure for each thread that we show. We already built the stored procedure, so we just have to call it at the appropriate time. When we build the HTML, we'll put it into the label control in the middle of the table on the page. This gives us our headers and basic table structure when we show the various rows.

The code behind this page is shown in Listing 8.12 and uses a lot of the features demonstrated in the first project to generate the output.

```vb
Imports System
Imports System.Data
Imports System.Data.SqlClient
Imports System.Web
Imports System.Web.UI
Imports System.Web.UI.WebControls
Imports TWNWObjects


Namespace TWNW
  Public Class PostsView
    Inherits Page

    Protected lblPageTitle As Label
    Protected lblContent As Label

    Sub Page_Load(objSender As Object, objArgs As EventArgs)
      Dim strColor As String = "tabletext"

      If (Request.Cookies("mID") Is Nothing) Then
        Response.Redirect("login.aspx?msg=403&rURL=" _
          & Request.ServerVariables("SCRIPT_NAME") _
          & "?" _
          & Request.ServerVariables("QUERY_STRING"))
      End If


      Dim DB As New AtWorkUtilities.Database()
      Dim DBR As New AtWorkUtilities.Database()
      Dim SD, SDR As SqlDataReader
      If Int16.Parse(Request.QueryString("tID")) > 0 Then
        Dim T As New Team(DB, Request.QueryString("tID"))
        Dim DR As DataRow = T.GetRow()
        lblPageTitle.Text = "View Posts - " & DR("Name")
        DB.Execute("sp_UpdateMemberDiscussionHistory " _
          & Request.Cookies("mID").Value & ", " _
          & Request.QueryString("tID"))
      Else
        lblPageTitle.Text = "View Posts - Public Forum"
        DB.Execute("sp_UpdateMemberDiscussionHistory " _
          & Request.Cookies("mID").Value & ", 0")
      End If
      SD = DB.GetDataReader("sp_RetrieveOriginalPostsByTeam " _
        & Request.QueryString("tID"), True)
      Dim SB As New System.Text.StringBuilder()
      Do While SD.Read()
```

Listing 8.12   posts_view.aspx.vb

```
      SB.AppendFormat("<tr class=""{0}"">", _
        strColor)
      SB.AppendFormat("<td>{0}</td>", _
        SD("Author"))
      SB.AppendFormat("<td>{0}</td>", _
        SD("Subject"))
      SB.AppendFormat("<td align=""center"">{0} {1}</td>", _
        SD("PostDate").ToShortDateString, _
        SD("PostDate").ToShortTimeString)
      SDR = DBR.GetDataReader("sp_RetrieveStatisticsByPost " _
        & SD("pkPostID"))
      If SDR("LastReplyDate").ToString() = "" Then
        SB.Append("<td align=""center"">None</td>")
      Else
        SB.AppendFormat("<td align=""center"">{0} {1}</td>", _
          SDR("LastReplyDate").ToShortDateString, _
          SDR("LastReplyDate").ToShortTimeString)
      End If
      SB.AppendFormat("<td align=""center"">{0}</td>", _
        SDR("ReplyCount"))
      SDR.Close()
      SB.Append("</tr>" & Environment.NewLine)
      If strColor = "tabletext" Then
        strColor = "tabletext_gray"
      Else
        strColor = "tabletext"
      End If
    Loop
    DB.Close()
    DBR.Close()
    lblContent.Text = SB.ToString()
  End Sub
  End Class
End Namespace
```

Listing 8.12   posts_view.aspx.vb (continued)

We start by verifying that the user has logged into the system. This prevents someone who has bookmarked the page from getting back in without a valid username and password. We then create two different Database objects: one to show the threads and the other to get the counts. We'll be using the SqlDataReader object here, but we can only have a single SqlDataReader open at a time with a given connection.

Next, we look at the value of the tID value in the query string. If it is absent or zero, we are going to view the public forum. Otherwise, we are looking at a particular team's discussion board. At this time, we call the stored procedure to update this member's history record for this particular board. This is the only place we call this stored procedure, so there's no point in making a separate business object to call it.

We then start looping through the threads found in the database for this team. Each one is shown in a separate row, and when we get to the cells that show the number of replies and the last reply date, we call our second stored procedure, get the values, and then close the second SqlDataReader object. Since the database itself can't generate this sort of drill-down information in a straightforward way, this method works well.

Once we're done looping through all the records and building the HTML into our StringBuilder object, we put the output into the label control that we added to the ASPX file. This displays the output to the user and gives the user the opportunity to select a thread to view, which is handled by the next page we need to cover. The user can also post a message to this team's discussion board by clicking the link at the top of the page. We'll build this page after the thread viewer.

Once the user has selected a thread to view, we show the user the Posts_read.aspx page, which is shown in Listing 8.13. This page uses the Repeater control, but not in the wide table-style view we've been using in most of the other pages. We're also not using an alternating row template here since every row looks the same.

```
<%@ Page Inherits="TWNW.PostsReadThread" Src="posts_read.aspx.vb" %>
<%@ Register Tagprefix="TWNW" Tagname="Header" Src="Header.ascx" %>
<%@ Register Tagprefix="TWNW" Tagname="Footer" Src="Footer.ascx" %>
<!DOCTYPE HTML PUBLIC "-//W3C//DTD HTML 4.0 Transitional//EN">
<html>
<head>
     <title>Teamwork Network: View Thread</title>
  <link href="styles.css" rel="stylesheet" type="text/css">
</head>

<body leftmargin=0 topmargin=0>
<TWNW:Header id="PageHeader" runat="server" />
<p class="pageheading">View Thread</p>
<p class="text">
<a href="post_create.aspx?tid=<% = Request("tid") %>">Post
a New Message</a>
 | 
<%
Response.Write("<a href=""post_create.aspx?tid=" _
  & Request.QueryString("tid") _
  & "&pid=" _
  & Request.QueryString("pid") _
  & """>Reply to this Thread</a>")
%>
</p>
<asp:label id="lblMessage" class="text" runat="server" />
<asp:Repeater id="rptList" runat="server">
  <HeaderTemplate>
  <table cellpadding="4" cellspacing="0" width="600">
  </HeaderTemplate>
  <ItemTemplate>
  <tr class="tabletext_gray">
  <td align="right" width="20%">Author:</td>
```

Listing 8.13 posts_read.aspx

```
  <td width="80%">
  <%# DataBinder.Eval(Container.DataItem, "Author") %>
  </td>
  </tr>
  <tr class="tabletext_gray">
  <td align="right">Subject:</td>
  <td>
  <%# DataBinder.Eval(Container.DataItem, "Subject") %>
  </td>
  </tr>
  <tr class="tabletext_gray">
  <td align="right">Message Posted:</td>
  <td>
  <%# DataBinder.Eval(Container.DataItem, _
   "PostDate").ToShortDateString %>
  <%# DataBinder.Eval(Container.DataItem, _
   "PostDate").ToShortTimeString %>
  </td>
  </tr>
  <tr class="tabletext">
  <td colspan="2">
  <%# Server.HTMLEncode(DataBinder.Eval( _
   Container.DataItem, _
   "MessageText")) %>
  </td>
  </tr>
  </ItemTemplate>
  <SeparatorTemplate>
  <tr><td colspan=2> </td></tr>
  </SeparatorTemplate>
  <FooterTemplate>
  </table>
  </FooterTemplate>
</asp:Repeater>
</body>
</html>
<TWNW:Footer id="PageFooter" runat="server" />
</body>
</html>
```

Listing 8.13   posts_read.aspx (continued)

This page starts with the standard header information and provides two links: one to create a new message in this team's board, and another to post a reply to this thread. Since all replies are to the original message, we don't need a separate link for each reply. We then set up the table where the message data will be shown. For the actual message text, we prevent members from putting up malicious (intentional or otherwise) HTML by using the Server.HTMLEncode method on the data being shown. Note that this particular field doesn't bind directly to the field using the <%# symbol. Instead, we use the Response.Write method to print the values from the bound data, but first route it through our HTMLEncode function. This gives us the benefit of fixing the data without having to build the table manually.

The code behind this page follows the same pattern as most other data-bound pages, and is shown in Listing 8.14.

```vb
Imports System
Imports System.Data
Imports System.Web
Imports System.Web.UI
Imports System.Web.UI.WebControls
Imports TWNWObjects

Namespace TWNW
  Public Class PostsReadThread
    Inherits Page

    Protected lblMessage As Label
    Protected rptList As Repeater

    Sub Page_Load(objSender As Object, objArgs As EventArgs)
      If (Request.Cookies("mID") Is Nothing) Then
        Response.Redirect("login.aspx?msg=403&rURL=" _
          & Request.ServerVariables("SCRIPT_NAME") _
          & "?" _
          & Request.ServerVariables("QUERY_STRING"))
      End If

      Dim DB As New AtWorkUtilities.Database()
      Dim DS As DataSet = _
        DB.GetDataSet("sp_RetrieveThreadByPostID " _
        & Request.QueryString("pid"))
      If DS.Tables(0).Rows.Count = 0 Then
        lblMessage.Text = "<b>There are no messages in " _
          & "this thread.</b>"
      Else
        rptList.DataSource = DS
        rptList.DataBind()
      End If
      db.Close()
    End Sub
  End Class
End Namespace
```

Listing 8.14   posts_read.aspx.vb

The stored procedure does most of the work here in formatting the links to the member profiles. All we have to do is present the data in a readable format. We also make sure that there are messages in the thread to prevent any errors from occurring. Since the only legitimate way to get to this page is by clicking a link from the previous page, any errors are going to come from out-of-date page references where messages may have been manually deleted.

The final page we need to build allows users to post new messages or replies to existing threads. The ASPX file is shown in Listing 8.15.

```
<%@ Page Inherits="TWNW.PostCreate" Src="post_create.aspx.vb" %>
<%@ Register Tagprefix="TWNW" Tagname="Header" Src="Header.ascx" %>
<%@ Register Tagprefix="TWNW" Tagname="Footer" Src="Footer.ascx" %>
<!DOCTYPE HTML PUBLIC "-//W3C//DTD HTML 4.0 Transitional//EN">
<html>
<head>
  <title>Teamwork Network: Post a Message</title>
  <link href="styles.css" rel="stylesheet" type="text/css">
</head>
<body>
<TWNW:Header id="PageHeader" runat="server" />
<table width="600">
<tr>
<td valign="top" width="600">

<p><asp:label id="lblPageTitle" class="pageheading" runat="server"
/></p>
<asp:label id="lblErrorMessage" class="errortext" runat="server" />

<form runat="server">
<input type="hidden" runat="server" id="fkTeamID">
<input type="hidden" runat="server" id="fkOriginalPostID">

<table cellspacing="5">
<tr class="tabletext">
  <td align="right">Subject:</td>
  <td>
  <asp:textbox
   id="txtSubject"
   columns="40"
   maxlength="80"
   runat="server" />
  </td>
</tr>
<tr class="tabletext">
  <td valign="middle" align="right">
  Message Text:
  </td>
  <td>
  <asp:textbox
```

Listing 8.15   post_create.aspx

```
    id="txtMessageText"
    rows="15"
    columns="60"
    wrap="true"
    textmode="Multiline"
    runat="server" />
  </td>
</tr>
<tr class="tabletext">
  <td colspan=2 align=middle>
  <input type="submit"
   name="btnSubmit"
   runat="server"
   value="Save" />
  <input type="reset"
   name="btnReset"
   runat="server"
   value="Clear" />
  </td>
</tr>
</table>
</form>
</td>
</tr>
</table>
<TWNW:Footer id="PageFooter" runat="server" />
</body>
</html>
```

Listing 8.15   post_create.aspx (continued)

This page is similar to the Message Creation page we built in the last project, with some changes to the field names and visible text. We only need two visible boxes on the page: the subject and the message text. The member's cookie holds their member ID number, and the hidden-input fields allow us to hold the team ID number (passed in through the query string) and the thread's original message ID number, if any.

The code behind this page is shown in Listing 8.16.

```
Imports System
Imports System.Data
Imports System.Data.SqlClient
Imports System.Web
Imports System.Web.UI
Imports System.Web.UI.WebControls
Imports TWNWObjects
```

Listing 8.16   post_create.aspx.vb

```
Namespace TWNW
  Public Class PostCreate
    Inherits System.Web.UI.Page

    Protected txtSubject As TextBox
    Protected txtMessageText As TextBox

    Protected fkTeamID As HTMLControls.HTMLInputHidden
    Protected fkOriginalPostID As HTMLControls.HTMLInputHidden

    Protected lblPageTitle As Label
    Protected lblErrorMessage As Label

    Sub Page_Load(objSender As Object, objArgs As EventArgs)
      Dim DB As New AtWorkUtilities.Database()
      Dim P As Post
      Dim DR As DataRow
      Dim objCookie As HTTPCookie
      objCookie = Request.Cookies("mID")

      If Not Page.IsPostBack Then
        fkTeamID.Value = Request.QueryString("tID")
        If Request.QueryString("pID") = "" Then
          `
          ' New message to team
          lblPageTitle.Text = "Post New Message"
        Else
          `
          ' Reply to existing message
          lblPageTitle.Text = "Reply to Message"
          fkOriginalPostID.Value = Request.QueryString("pID")
        End If
      Else
        P = New Post(DB)
        DR = P.GetRow()
        DR("fkAuthorID") = Int16.Parse(objCookie.Value)
        If fkOriginalPostID.Value <> "" Then
          DR("fkOriginalPostID") = Int16.Parse(fkOriginalPostID.Value)
        End If
        DR("fkTeamID") = Int16.Parse(fkTeamID.Value)
        DR("Subject") = txtSubject.Text
        DR("MessageText") = txtMessageText.Text
        P.SaveRow(DR)
        If Not P.IsValid Then
          lblErrorMessage.Text = _
            P.ValidationError("<b>ERROR:</b> The following " _
              & "errors were detected in your data:<br>", _
              "&bull; {0}<br>", "")
```

Listing 8.16 post_create.aspx.vb (continued)

```
      Else
        P.Save()
        DB.Close()
        Response.Redirect("posts_view.aspx?tid=" _
          & fkTeamID.Value)
      End If
    End If
  End Sub
  End Class
End Namespace
```

Listing 8.16   post_create.aspx.vb (continued)

When the page is first shown, we determine if we're creating a new message in a board or a reply to an existing thread. We store the appropriate values in the hidden-input fields and then let the user type the message.

When we save the data, we store it in our new Post object, which sets the posting date. If any data is missing, those errors are returned from the object and displayed to the user. Otherwise, we save the posting and go back to the discussion-board thread viewer (Posts_view.aspx). If you want, you can go back to the thread so the user can see his or her message.

Note that there is no provision made for editing or deleting an existing post. These may be features you want to add to your own system. The Post object already supports these features since it follows the same design pattern as the other objects we've built. You just need to modify this page to repopulate the form if the post is being edited, just as you did in previous portions of this application. You could also restrict editing and posting to the original writer of the message.

The reason that I didn't provide this feature is data integrity. If you delete the first message in a thread, the other replies will be unlinked. Since deletions would probably be somewhat rare, I leave this up to the system administrator to do manually if the need should arise.

With all those pages done, we still need to make one change to the Teams.aspx page so that users can pick a team to post a message to if no messages exist. It also provides another way into the system from a different location. The new Teams.aspx page is shown in Listing 8.17 with the changes highlighted in bold.

```
<%@ Page Inherits="TWNW.TeamsViewAll" Src="teams.aspx.vb" %>
<%@ Register Tagprefix="TWNW" Tagname="Header" Src="Header.ascx" %>
<%@ Register Tagprefix="TWNW" Tagname="Footer" Src="Footer.ascx" %>
<!DOCTYPE HTML PUBLIC "-//W3C//DTD HTML 4.0 Transitional//EN">
<html>
<head>
  <title>Teamwork Network: View All Teams</title>
```

Listing 8.17   teams.aspx

```
  <link href="styles.css" rel="stylesheet" type="text/css">
</head>

<body leftmargin=0 topmargin=0>
<TWNW:Header id="PageHeader" runat="server" />
<p class="pageheading">View All Teams</p>
<p class="text"><a href="team_create.aspx">Create a Team</a></p>
<asp:label id="lblMessage" class="text" runat="server" />

<asp:Repeater id="rptList" runat="server">
  <HeaderTemplate>
  <table cellpadding="4" cellspacing="0" width="100%">
  <tr class="tableheading">
  <td width="30%">Name</td>
  <td width="30%">Description</td>
  <td width="40%">Actions</td>
  </tr>
  </HeaderTemplate>
  <ItemTemplate>
  <tr class="tabletext">
  <td valign="top"><%# DataBinder.Eval(Container.DataItem, _
    "Name") %></td>
  <td valign="top"><%# DataBinder.Eval(Container.DataItem, _
    "Description") %></td>
  <td valign="top" align="center">
  <a href="teammembers.aspx?id=<%# DataBinder.Eval(Container.DataItem, _
    "pkTeamID") %>">Manage Members</a>  
  <a href="post_create.aspx?tid=<%# DataBinder.Eval(Container.DataItem, _
    "pkTeamID") %>">Post Message</a>  
  <a href="team_create.aspx?id=<%# DataBinder.Eval(Container.DataItem, _
    "pkTeamID") %>">Update</a>  
  <a href="team_delete.aspx?id=<%# DataBinder.Eval(Container.DataItem, _
    "pkTeamID") %>">Delete</a>
  </td>
  </tr>
  </ItemTemplate>
  <AlternatingItemTemplate>
  <tr class="tabletext_gray">
  <td valign="top"><%# DataBinder.Eval(Container.DataItem, _
    "Name") %></td>
  <td valign="top"><%# DataBinder.Eval(Container.DataItem, _
    "Description") %></td>
  <td valign="top" align="center">
  <a href="teammembers.aspx?id=<%# DataBinder.Eval(Container.DataItem, _
    "pkTeamID") %>">Manage Members</a>  
  <a href="post_create.aspx?tid=<%# DataBinder.Eval(Container.DataItem, _
    "pkTeamID") %>">Post Message</a>  
```

Listing 8.17 teams.aspx (continued)

```
   <a href="team_create.aspx?id=<%# DataBinder.Eval(Container.DataItem, _
    "pkTeamID") %>">Update</a>  
   <a href="team_delete.aspx?id=<%# DataBinder.Eval(Container.DataItem, _
    "pkTeamID") %>">Delete</a>
   </td>
   </tr>
   </AlternatingItemTemplate>
   <FooterTemplate>
   </table>
   </FooterTemplate>
</asp:Repeater>
</body>
</html>
<TWNW:Footer id="PageFooter" runat="server" />
</body>
</html>
```

Listing 8.17 teams.aspx (continued)

We're adding another link here so that users can post a message to the team discussion board. Users choose any team within the Teamwork Network of which they are a member. We'll be adding more links to this page as we add more subsystems to this application.

Wrap Up

In a single table, you built a threaded discussion board for your collaboration system. There are lots of commercial packages that have discussion boards included, but I never found one that fit my requirements exactly. By spending a bit more time and building the system ourselves, we've gained a number of advantages. Most packaged solutions won't give you this flexibility, but sometimes the amount of time required to build a system like this outweighs the convenience of prepackaged software. Just remember that you always have the option to build it yourself if the packaged software doesn't meet your needs.

In Project 9, you'll build the file sharing system for the Teamwork Network application. As team files can get scattered across a network, having a common web site where your team members can post files makes them easier to share and track.

Teamwork Network: File Libraries

With the infrastructure and discussion boards out of the way, the next step in the collaboration system is file sharing. While you can attach files to an email and send them to someone, this is not always the most practical solution. When I'm on the road, for example, I hate dealing with email since I often get large attachments that take forever to download. I also get several copies of the same attachment from different people on the same team, just to make sure that I got a copy. There are also problems with sites that do not allow attachments or that limit the size of them due to bandwidth reasons. Furthermore, there is the inevitable problem of forgetting where you put a file that someone sent you and having to bother that person again to get a new copy.

The solution you'll be building in this project can be used to upload files to the Web server, store them in virtual folders for your team, and allow other users on the team to download the files. You can also keep extensive notes on each file you post. Folders are used to organize your files in a simple one-level hierarchy, and they can be updated or deleted by the owners.

If you want to see the system live, visit the Web site at www.teamworknetwork.com. I intend to keep this site running as a public-development project that users can discuss at the book's Web site: www.10projectswithasp.net. We'll add new features as time goes on to make this site useful for everyone.

THE PROBLEM

Sharing files is often difficult for technological and organizational reasons. Teams spread out often don't have a central location for depositing their files for collaboration.

THE SOLUTION

A file-sharing feature integrated into the Teamwork Network to provide a virtual file system for team members. Files can be organized into folders for even more usefulness, and team members will be notified of any new files added to file libraries to which they have access.

Project Background

File sharing systems allow you to centralize important files so that everyone knows where they are kept. These systems also handle file security and determine who can read and write to these files. One type of file sharing system is also known as a source control system. These applications, which include Visual SourceSafe, also keep track of revisions and prevent more than one person from editing a file simultaneously. In this project, you'll build a similar system that allows team members to store files and share them with their teammates. The system will prevent other teams from retrieving these files. While there is no version control in the application, it's something that you could add at a later date.

To build this application, you'll need to complete these tasks:

1. Design the database tables.

2. Create the stored procedures used in the application.

3. Build the business objects.

4. Build the application's Web pages.

You Will Need

✔ **Windows 2000**

✔ **Internet Information Server 5.0 with .NET Framework installed**

✔ **Visual Studio .NET**

✔ **SQL Server 2000 or 7.0**

✔ **SQL Server client utilities, including SQL Server Enterprise Manager and Query Analyzer**

✔ **The code from Project 7 and 8**

Building the Database Objects

This portion of the system requires two tables: tblFiles and tblFolders. Each of these tables will include team and individual member ownership information, as well as basic information about each entity. While we will be accepting uploaded files, the folder structure is completely a virtual one; that is, the files will all be stored in the same directory on the disk. The folders will simply serve to organize the files visually.

The tblFiles table is shown in Table 9.1.

Each file will be tagged with a team and folder ID number. Files can be placed at the root of a team's file directory, in which case the folder ID will be zero. Any files that are in the public file directory have a team ID of zero. The name of the file is its original name when loaded into the system, without any directory or drive information stored, so this filename: C:\Data\AtWork\Test.xls is stored as: Test.xls.

The file size is in bytes and will be formatted for display into the logical unit for the amount (gigabyte, megabyte, kilobyte, byte). The StoredAs field records the new physical pathname to the file when it is stored on the server. For security purposes, the real filename is hidden and a random one is generated. This helps remove the possibility of duplicate filenames, as you'll see later in the project. We store the date the file is created and also the member ID of the person who uploaded the file. This is so that the owner of the file can remove it, if necessary.

The second table we need is the tblFolders table, which is somewhat smaller but just as important. The structure is shown in Table 9.2.

Table 9.1   tblFiles Table Design

FIELD NAME	SQL DATA TYPE	LENGTH	OTHER
pkFileID	int	N/A	Identity, Primary Key, Not Null
fkTeamID	int	N/A	Not Null
fkFolderID	int	N/A	Not Null
Name	varchar	120	Not Null
Description	text	N/A	
FileSize	bigint	N/A	Not Null
StoredAs	varchar	120	Not Null
UploadDate	datetime	N/A	Not Null
fkCreatorID	int	N/A	Not Null

Table 9.2   tblFolders Table Design

FIELD NAME	SQL DATA TYPE	LENGTH	OTHER
pkFileID	int	N/A	Identity, Primary Key, Not Null
fkTeamID	int	N/A	Not Null
Name	varchar	120	Not Null
Description	text	N/A	
CreationDate	datetime	N/A	Not Null
fkCreatorID	int	N/A	Not Null

We are keeping a link to the team from both the folder and any files. This makes it possible to have files that are not in folders and that are at the root of a team's file directory. Without the separate team ID on each file, we wouldn't be able to find the files later.

With the tables created, we can now build our stored procedures. The first stored procedure retrieves the total number of files and the last file's upload date based on the team number. This data is shown on the Files.aspx page, which is linked to the main toolbar. The code is shown in Listing 9.1.

```
CREATE PROCEDURE dbo.sp_RetrieveTotalFilesByTeam
@TeamID int
AS
SELECT COUNT(*) AS TotalFileCount,
MAX(UploadDate) As LastUploadDate
FROM tblFiles
WHERE fkTeamID = @TeamID
```

Listing 9.1   sp_RetrieveTotalFilesByTeam

This, like the view of the discussions, shows how many files are in a team's file directories and if any content has been added. The user's home page will alert him or her to new content in the file directory, but this is a view of the total.

The next stored procedure is used when we view the folders in a particular team's file directory. The code is shown in Listing 9.2.

```
CREATE PROCEDURE dbo.sp_RetrieveFoldersByTeam
@TeamID int
AS
SELECT *
FROM tblFolders
WHERE fkTeamID = @TeamID
ORDER BY Name
```

Listing 9.2   sp_RetrieveFoldersByTeam

As we loop through the folders returned by this stored procedure, we retrieve statistics on them using the sp_RetrieveFolderStatistics stored procedure. This stored procedure returns the number of files in the folder. This saves the user time in having to go into the folder to see what's there. The code for this stored procedure is shown in Listing 9.3.

```
CREATE PROCEDURE dbo.sp_RetrieveFolderStatistics
@FolderID int
AS
SELECT COUNT(*) As TotalFileCount,
Max(UploadDate) As LastUploadDate
FROM tblFiles
WHERE fkFolderID = @FolderID
```

Listing 9.3 sp_RetrieveFolderStatistics

We'll use this stored procedure for each folder that we display in the Folder viewer. On the same page, we'll display any files at the root level using the stored procedure shown in Listing 9.4.

```
CREATE PROCEDURE dbo.sp_RetrieveFilesByTeamByFolder
@TeamID int,
@FolderID int
AS
SELECT *
FROM tblFiles
WHERE fkTeamID = @TeamID
AND fkFolderID = @FolderID
ORDER BY Name
```

Listing 9.4 sp_RetrieveFilesByTeamByFolder

This routine retrieves files based on a team and folder number. This stored procedure is only used to display files when we are also displaying the folders for a particular team. When we view the files in a particular folder, we use a different stored procedure that isn't concerned with the team number. That stored procedure is shown in Listing 9.5.

```
CREATE PROCEDURE dbo.sp_RetrieveFilesByFolder
@FolderID int
AS
SELECT *
FROM tblFiles
WHERE fkFolderID = @FolderID
ORDER BY Name
```

Listing 9.5 sp_RetrieveFilesByFolder

This routine is straightforward and is used whenever we are viewing the contents of a folder. Any files in the folder will be listed, along with any relevant actions that the user can take with the files.

There are two stored procedures that we'll write to help manage the content for the user's personalized home page. The first stored procedure updates the member's history record when he or she views the file library for a particular team. This stored procedure follows the pattern of the one used for the discussion boards and is shown in Listing 9.6.

```
CREATE PROCEDURE dbo.sp_UpdateMemberFileHistory
@MemberID int,
@TeamID int
AS
DECLARE @RecordCount int
SELECT @RecordCount = COUNT(*) FROM tblMemberHistory
WHERE fkMemberID = @MemberID
AND fkTeamID = @TeamID
AND Subsystem = 'F'

IF @RecordCount > 0
BEGIN
  UPDATE tblMemberHistory
  SET LastVisit = getdate()
  WHERE fkMemberID = @MemberID
  AND fkTeamID = @TeamID
  AND Subsystem = 'F'
END
ELSE
BEGIN
  INSERT INTO tblMemberHistory
  (fkMemberID, fkTeamID, Subsystem)
  VALUES
  (@MemberID, @TeamID, 'F')
END
```

Listing 9.6 sp_UpdateMemberFileHistory

We either insert a history record or update an existing one when we view the files for a particular team. We then use the results of this routine on the member's personalized home page to show which teams have new files. This is done using the stored procedure shown in Listing 9.7.

```
CREATE PROCEDURE dbo.sp_RetrieveNewFilesByMember
@MemberID int,
@TeamID int
AS
DECLARE @LastVisit datetime
```

Listing 9.7 sp_RetrieveNewFilesByMember

```
SELECT @LastVisit = LastVisit
FROM tblMemberHistory
WHERE fkTeamID = @TeamID
AND fkMemberID = @MemberID
AND Subsystem = 'F'

SELECT COUNT(*) AS NewFileCount,
MAX(UploadDate) As LastUploadDate
FROM tblFiles
WHERE fkTeamID = @TeamID
AND UploadDate >= IsNull(@LastVisit, '1-1-1900 12:00 AM')
```

Listing 9.7   sp_RetrieveNewFilesByMember (continued)

Like its counterpart in the discussion board project, this routine determines when the member's last visit to a particular file library was and returns the number of files added since that date. Once the user visits that file library, the visit timestamp will be updated and the home page will change accordingly.

With the database and stored procedure work done, it's time to build the business objects for this portion of the application.

Building the Business Objects

This subsystem requires a total of four business objects: File, Folder, FileException, and FolderException. Each one is based on the model we created and have been using in this application. We've continued to use the SaveRow method to store certain default values in the data before handling validation. Other than that and the differences in validation between File and Folder, these objects work almost identically to the other ones we've created.

The File object is first on our list, and the code is shown in Listing 9.8.

```
Imports AtWorkUtilities
Imports System.Data.SqlClient

Public Class File
  Inherits BaseServices


    '
    ' If no arguments are supplied, build a separate
    ' database connection for this object.
    '
  Public Sub New()
```

Listing 9.8   File.vb class

```
    MyBase.New(New Database(), "SELECT * FROM tblFiles WHERE 1=0")
  End Sub


  '
  ' If database connection is supplied, store it
  ' in the private connection variable for this
  ' object.
  '
  Public Sub New(ByVal db As Database)
   MyBase.New(db, "SELECT * FROM tblFiles WHERE 1=0")
  End Sub


  '
  ' If both database and ID are supplied, retrieve
  ' data into the object from the database.
  '
  Public Sub New(ByVal db As Database, _
   ByVal ID As Integer)

   MyBase.New(db, "SELECT * FROM tblFiles WHERE pkFileID = " _
     & ID.ToString)

  End Sub


  '
  ' Verify that all data validation rules have been
  ' met. Any errors get stored into the errors collection
  ' inherited from the BaseServices class.
  '
  Public Sub Validate()
   Dim dr As DataRow

   ClearErrors()
   For Each dr In m_DS.Tables(0).Rows
     If dr.RowState = DataRowState.Added _
     Or dr.RowState = DataRowState.Modified Then
       ValidateRow(dr)
     End If
   Next

  End Sub


  '
  ' Checks an individual row for validation rule
  ' compliance. Any errors are added to the errors
  ' collection.
  '
  Private Sub ValidateRow(ByVal dr As DataRow)
```

Listing 9.8   File.vb class (continued)

```vb
    If IsDBNull(dr("fkTeamID")) Then
      AddError("Team number is missing.")
    End If
    If IsDBNull(dr("fkFolderID")) Then
      AddError("Folder number is missing.")
    End If
    CheckRequiredField(dr, "Name", "Filename", 120)
    CheckRequiredField(dr, "StoredAs", "Destination filename", 120)
    If IsDBNull(dr("FileSize")) Then
      AddError("File size is missing.")
    End If
    If IsDBNull(dr("UploadDate")) Then
      AddError("Message date is missing.")
    End If
    If IsDBNull(dr("fkCreatorID")) Then
      AddError("Owner's member number is missing.")
    End If
  End Sub


  '
  ' The base Save method stores the DataRow into the
  ' DataSet, whether it's a new or existing row. The
  ' rest of this routine handles specific validation
  ' for this type of data.
  '
  Public Overloads Sub SaveRow(ByVal dr As DataRow)
   If IsDBNull(dr("fkTeamID")) Then
     dr("fkTeamID") = 0
   End If
   If IsDBNull(dr("fkFolderID")) Then
     dr("fkFolderID") = 0
   End If
   If IsDBNull(dr("UploadDate")) Then
     dr("UploadDate") = Now()
   End If
   MyBase.SaveRow(dr)
   Validate()

  End Sub


  '
  ' We separate the SaveRow method from the Save method
  ' to give us a chance to handle any validation. We have
  ' a verification here that the data is good before we
  ' continue, however.
  '
  Public Sub Save()

   If Not Me.IsValid Then
```

Listing 9.8 File.vb class (continued)

```
        Throw New FileException(Me.ValidationError)
      Exit Sub
    End If


  m_DA.Update(m_DS)
  End Sub


  '
  ' Since we only have a single row in our DataSet,
  ' delete it and then update the database with the
  ' change.
  '
  Public Sub Delete()
    If m_DS.Tables(0).Rows.Count > 0 Then
      m_DS.Tables(0).Rows(0).Delete()
      m_DA.Update(m_DS)
    End If
  End Sub

End Class
```

Listing 9.8   File.vb class (continued)

We fill in any missing default values in the DataRow passed back from the Web page, and then we verify that all required fields have been provided. The data is then stored to the tblFiles table. Any untrapped validation errors will generate a FileException error, and the class for this error type is shown in Listing 9.9.

```
Public Class FileException
  Inherits Exception

  Public Sub New()
    MyBase.New()
  End Sub

  Public Sub New(ByVal Message As String)
    MyBase.New(Message)
  End Sub

  Public Sub New(ByVal Message As String, ByVal baseError As Exception)
    MyBase.New(Message, baseError)
  End Sub

End Class
```

Listing 9.9   FileException.vb class

For the system to work properly, we have to manage folders inside the system. Each folder may or may not have files in it, but this object is primarily used to create, update, and delete folders from the system. Since files are not actually stored in folders, no physical I/O is required to move files around. The Web pages verify that a folder is not deleted if there are files in it. The code for the Folder class is shown in Listing 9.10.

```vb
Imports AtWorkUtilities
Imports System.Data.SqlClient

Public Class Folder
  Inherits BaseServices

    '
    ' If no arguments are supplied, build a separate
    ' database connection for this object.
    '
  Public Sub New()
    MyBase.New(New Database(), "SELECT * FROM tblFolders WHERE 1=0")
  End Sub


    '
    ' If database connection is supplied, store it
    ' in the private connection variable for this
    ' object.
    '
  Public Sub New(ByVal db As Database)
    MyBase.New(db, "SELECT * FROM tblFolders WHERE 1=0")
  End Sub


    '
    ' If both database and ID are supplied, retrieve
    ' data into the object from the database.
    '
  Public Sub New(ByVal db As Database, _
    ByVal ID As Integer)

    MyBase.New(db, "SELECT * FROM tblFolders WHERE pkFolderID = " _
      & ID.ToString)

  End Sub


    '
    ' Verify that all data validation rules have been
    ' met. Any errors get stored into the errors collection
```

Listing 9.10 Folder.vb class

```
' inherited from the BaseServices class.
'

Public Sub Validate()
 Dim dr As DataRow
 ClearErrors()
 For Each dr In m_DS.Tables(0).Rows
   If dr.RowState = DataRowState.Added _
   Or dr.RowState = DataRowState.Modified Then
     ValidateRow(dr)
   End If
 Next

End Sub


'

' Checks an individual row for validation rule
' compliance. Any errors are added to the errors
' collection.
'

Private Sub ValidateRow(ByVal dr As DataRow)
 If IsDBNull(dr("fkTeamID")) Then
   AddError("Team number is missing.")
 End If
 CheckRequiredField(dr, "Name", "Folder name", 80)
 If IsDBNull(dr("CreationDate")) Then
   AddError("Creation date is missing.")
 End If
 If IsDBNull(dr("fkCreatorID")) Then
   AddError("Owner's member number is missing.")
 End If
End Sub


'

' The base Save method stores the DataRow into the
' DataSet, whether it's a new or existing row. The
' rest of this routine handles specific validation
' for this type of data.
'

Public Overloads Sub SaveRow(ByVal dr As DataRow)
 If IsDBNull(dr("fkTeamID")) Then
   dr("fkTeamID") = 0
```

Listing 9.10 Folder.vb class (continued)

```
      End If
      If IsDBNull(dr("CreationDate")) Then
        dr("CreationDate") = Now()
      End If
      MyBase.SaveRow(dr)
      Validate()

    End Sub


    '
    ' We separate the SaveRow method from the Save method
    ' to give us a chance to handle any validation. We have
    ' a verification here that the data is good before we
    ' continue, however.
    '
    Public Sub Save()

      If Not Me.IsValid Then
         Throw New FolderException(Me.ValidationError)
         Exit Sub
      End If

      m_DA.Update(m_DS)
    End Sub


    '
    ' Since we only have a single row in our DataSet,
    ' delete it and then update the database with the
    ' change.
    '
    Public Sub Delete()
      If m_DS.Tables(0).Rows.Count > 0 Then
        m_DS.Tables(0).Rows(0).Delete()
        m_DA.Update(m_DS)
      End If
    End Sub

End Class
```

Listing 9.10 Folder.vb class (continued)

The last class you need to build is the FolderException class, which is generated for any untrapped validation errors detected in the Folder object. The code for this class is shown in Listing 9.11.

```
Public Class FolderException
   Inherits Exception

   Public Sub New()
     MyBase.New()
   End Sub

   Public Sub New(ByVal Message As String)
     MyBase.New(Message)
   End Sub

   Public Sub New(ByVal Message As String, ByVal baseError As Exception)
     MyBase.New(Message, baseError)
   End Sub

End Class
```

Listing 9.11   FolderException.vb class

As with the other applications, the FolderException class is difficult to generate based on the way we are validating and then displaying errors to the user. It's designed more as a safety device for other applications that you might build using these same objects or objects of this design.

With the business objects created, let's build some Web pages for this portion of the application.

Building the Web Pages

The Web pages in this section are broken into two logical groups: viewing pages and maintenance pages. The viewing pages are the ones used primarily by most users, but the maintenance pages are used to put actual data into the system. We'll cover each group in this section.

Creating the Viewing Pages

The first page we need to build is the main Files.aspx page, linked from the main toolbar. This page shows all of the file libraries for a member's team and the number of files in each. The page at runtime resembles Figure 9.1.

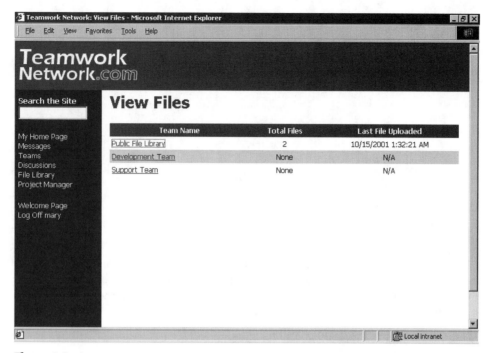

Figure 9.1   teams.aspx.

The ASPX file is shown in Listing 9.12, and the code behind it is shown in Listing 9.13. In order to show all the teams, regardless of the number of files, we are manually rendering this table and displaying it in a label control.

```
<%@ Page Inherits="TWNW.Files" Src="files.aspx.vb" %>
<%@ Register Tagprefix="TWNW" Tagname="Header" Src="Header.ascx" %>
<%@ Register Tagprefix="TWNW" Tagname="Footer" Src="Footer.ascx" %>
<!DOCTYPE HTML PUBLIC "-//W3C//DTD HTML 4.0 Transitional//EN">
<html>
<head>
    <title>Teamwork Network: View Files</title>
  <link href="styles.css" rel="stylesheet" type="text/css">
</head>

<body leftmargin=0 topmargin=0>
<TWNW:Header id="PageHeader" runat="server" />
<p class="pageheading">View Files</p>
<p class="text">
</p>
<table cellpadding="4" cellspacing="0" width="600">
<tr class="tableheading">
```

Listing 9.12   files.aspx

```
    <td width="40%">Team Name</td>
    <td width="20%">Total Files</td>
    <td width="40%">Last File Uploaded</td>
</tr>
<asp:label id="lblContent" runat="server" />
</table>
</body>
</html>
<TWNW:Footer id="PageFooter" runat="server" />
</body>
</html>
```

Listing 9.12   files.aspx (continued)

We set up the table headings here and leave space to fill in the content later. If there are no teams in the system, you'll get a heading here without any content. However, the public file library is always visible, so this page will have some content on it. The code behind this file is shown in Listing 9.13.

```
Imports System
Imports System.Data
Imports System.Web
Imports System.Web.UI
Imports System.Web.UI.WebControls
Imports System.Data.SqlClient
Imports TWNWObjects

Namespace TWNW
  Public Class Files
    Inherits Page

    Protected lblContent As Label

    Sub Page_Load(objSender As Object, objArgs As EventArgs)
      If (Request.Cookies("mID") Is Nothing) Then
        Response.Redirect("login.aspx?msg=403&rURL=" _
          & Request.ServerVariables("SCRIPT_NAME") _
          & "?" _
          & Request.ServerVariables("QUERY_STRING"))
      End If

      Dim DB As New AtWorkUtilities.Database()
      Dim DB2 As New AtWorkUtilities.Database()
      Dim DR As SqlDataReader
      Dim DR2 As SqlDataReader
      Dim strContent As New System.Text.StringBuilder()
```

Listing 9.13   pages.aspx.vb

```vb
        Dim strColor As String = "tabletext"


        '
        ' Check for any new postings in the member's teams
        ' or in the public forum.
        '
        DR = DB.GetDataReader("sp_RetrieveTeamsByMember " _
         & Request.Cookies("mID").Value, True)
        strContent.Append("<tr class=""tabletext"">")
        strContent.Append("<td><a href=""folder_view.aspx?tID=0"">")
        strContent.Append("Public File Library</a></td>")
        DR2 = DB2.GetDataReader("sp_RetrieveTotalFilesByTeam 0")
        If DR2("TotalFileCount") = 0 Then
         strContent.Append("<td align=middle>None</td>")
         strContent.Append("<td align=middle>N/A</td>")
        Else
         strContent.AppendFormat("<td align=middle>{0}</td>", _
           DR2("TotalFileCount"))
         strContent.AppendFormat("<td align=middle>{0}</td>", _
           DR2("LastUploadDate"))
        End If
        strContent.Append("</tr>")
        strContent.Append(Environment.NewLine)
        strColor = "tabletext_gray"
        DR2.Close()

        While DR.Read()
         strContent.AppendFormat("<tr class=""{0}""><td>", strColor)
         strContent.AppendFormat("<a href=""folder_view.aspx" _
           & "?tID={0}"">", _
           DR("pkTeamID"))
         strContent.AppendFormat("{0}</a></td>", DR("Name"))
         DR2 = DB2.GetDataReader("sp_RetrieveTotalFilesByTeam " _
           & DR("pkTeamID"))
         If DR2("TotalFileCount") = 0 Then
           strContent.Append("<td align=middle>None</td>")
           strContent.Append("<td align=middle>N/A</td>")
         Else
           strContent.AppendFormat("<td align=middle>{0}</td>", _
             DR2("TotalFileCount"))
           strContent.AppendFormat("<td align=middle>{0}</td>", _
             DR2("LastUploadDate"))
         End If
         strContent.Append("</tr>")
         If strColor = "tabletext" Then
           strColor = "tabletext_gray"
         Else
           strColor = "tabletext"
         End If
         strContent.Append(Environment.NewLine)
         DR2.Close()
        End While
```

Listing 9.13   pages.aspx.vb (continued)

```
        lblContent.Text = strContent.ToString()
        DR.Close()
    End Sub
  End Class
End Namespace
```

Listing 9.13   pages.aspx.vb (continued)

As with the other pages we've built that gather statistics for each displayed row, we now have to set up two separate database connections here. The primary connection, DB, will be used for the main loop. The DB2 connection will be used for gathering the necessary per-row statistics.

We start by adding the public file library entry to the table that we're building. We manually look up the number of files and the other statistics about this folder and add it to the grid. We then start looping through to the teams to which the member has been added and repeat the process. We link each folder's name to the Folder_view.aspx page that shows the folders and files within each team's file library. Since all files and folders have to be part of either a team file library or the public file library, we don't have any links on this page to add files or folders. Instead, users will have to navigate to their team's file library to accomplish these tasks.

The next page to build is the folder viewer. This page serves two separate functions. First, it shows the folders and any root-level files for a team's file library, as seen in Figure 9.2.

This page is also used to show the files within a particular folder once the user has selected one to view. That view is shown in Figure 9.3. In this view, we also provide a

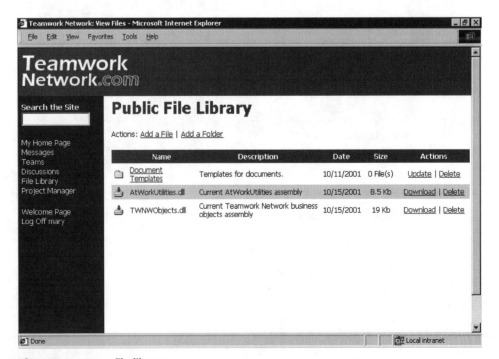

Figure 9.2   Team file library.

link back to the parent page to save the user from having to navigate back to that point. We are also showing only files in this view since folders cannot be hierarchical. If you wanted to add this feature, you could do it fairly easily by simply adding in the same code for this view as is used for the root view.

The ASPX file for this page is shown in Listing 9.14.

```
<%@ Page Inherits="TWNW.FoldersView" Src="folder_view.aspx.vb" %>
<%@ Register Tagprefix="TWNW" Tagname="Header" Src="Header.ascx" %>
<%@ Register Tagprefix="TWNW" Tagname="Footer" Src="Footer.ascx" %>
<!DOCTYPE HTML PUBLIC "-//W3C//DTD HTML 4.0 Transitional//EN">
<html>
<head>
   <title>Teamwork Network: View Files</title>
   <link href="styles.css" rel="stylesheet" type="text/css">
</head>

<body leftmargin=0 topmargin=0>
<TWNW:Header id="PageHeader" runat="server" />
<asp:label id="lblPageTitle" class="pageheading" runat="server" />
<asp:label id="lblActions" class="text" runat="server" />
<asp:label id="lblContent" runat="server" />
</body>
</html>
<TWNW:Footer id="PageFooter" runat="server" />
</body>
</html>
```

Listing 9.14 folder_view.aspx

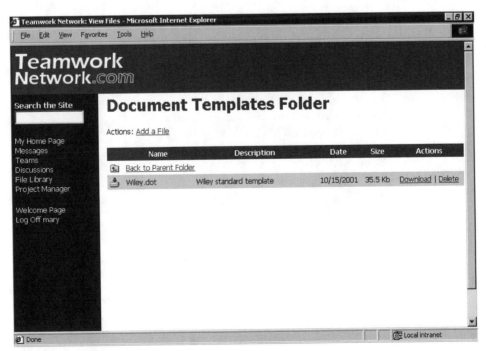

Figure 9.3 Folder viewer.

Since we're manually rendering all the tables in this page, the ASPX file is fairly short. The real code is in the Visual Basic (VB) file associated with this ASPX file. The code is shown in Listing 9.15.

```
Imports System
Imports System.Data
Imports System.Web
Imports System.Web.UI
Imports System.Web.UI.WebControls
Imports System.Data.SqlClient
Imports TWNWObjects


Namespace TWNW
  Public Class FoldersView
    Inherits Page

    Protected lblPageTitle As Label
    Protected lblActions As Label
    Protected lblContent As Label

    Sub Page_Load(objSender As Object, objArgs As EventArgs)
      If (Request.Cookies("mID") Is Nothing) Then
        Response.Redirect("login.aspx?msg=403&rURL=" _
          & Request.ServerVariables("SCRIPT_NAME") _
          & "?" _
          & Request.ServerVariables("QUERY_STRING"))
      End If

      Dim DB As New AtWorkUtilities.Database()
      Dim DB2 As New AtWorkUtilities.Database()
      Dim DR As SqlDataReader
      Dim DR2 As SqlDataReader
      Dim strSize As String

      Dim strContent As New System.Text.StringBuilder()
      Dim strOutput As New System.Text.StringBuilder()
      Dim strActions As New System.Text.StringBuilder()
      Dim strColor As String = "tabletext"
      Dim F As Folder
      Dim FDR As DataRow
      Dim intFolderID As Integer = 0
      Dim intTeamID As Integer = 0

      If Request.QueryString("fID") <> "" Then
        intFolderID = Int32.Parse(Request.QueryString("fID"))
      End If
```

Listing 9.15   folder_view.aspx.vb

```
If Request.QueryString("tID") <> "" Then
  intTeamID = Int32.Parse(Request.QueryString("tID"))
End If


If intFolderID > 0 Then
  F = New Folder(DB, intFolderID)
  FDR = F.GetRow()
  lblPageTitle.Text = FDR("Name") & " Folder"
  strActions.AppendFormat("<a href=""file_create.aspx?fID={0}", _
    intFolderID)
  strActions.AppendFormat(""">Add a File</a>")
ElseIf intTeamID = 0 Then
  lblPageTitle.Text = "Public File Library"
  strActions.AppendFormat("<a href=""file_create.aspx?tID={0}", _
    intTeamID)
  strActions.AppendFormat(""">Add a File</a>")
  strActions.Append("  | ")
  strActions.AppendFormat("<a href=""folder_create." _
    & "aspx?tID={0}", _
    intTeamID)
  strActions.AppendFormat(""">Add a Folder</a>")

ElseIf intTeamID > 0 Then
  Dim T As New Team(DB, intTeamID)
  Dim TDR As DataRow = T.GetRow()
  lblPageTitle.Text = TDR("Name") & " File Library"
  TDR = Nothing
  T = Nothing
  strActions.AppendFormat("<a href=""file_create.aspx?tID={0}", _
    intTeamID)
  strActions.AppendFormat(""">Add a File</a>")
  strActions.Append("  | ")
  strActions.AppendFormat("<a href=""folder_create." _
    & "aspx?tID={0}", _
    intTeamID)
  strActions.AppendFormat(""">Add a Folder</a>")
End If
lblActions.Text = "<p class=""text"">Actions: " _
  & strActions.ToString() _
  & "</p>"
'
' Folders are only displayed at the root directory
' since they cannot be nested. If the folder ID tag
' is missing, show any folders belonging to this team.
'
If intFolderID = 0 Then
  '
```

Listing 9.15   folder_view.aspx.vb (continued)

```
' Start by displaying any folders created for this team.
'
DB.Execute("sp_UpdateMemberFileHistory " _
  & Request.Cookies("mID").Value & ", " _
  & intTeamID.ToString())
DR = DB.GetDataReader("sp_RetrieveFoldersByTeam " _
  & intTeamID, True)

While DR.Read()
  strContent.AppendFormat("<tr class=""{0}"">", strColor)
  strContent.Append("<td><img src=""images/folder.gif"" " _
    & "height=16 width=16></td>")
  strContent.AppendFormat("<td><a href=""folder_view" _
    & ".aspx?fID={0}"">", _
    DR("pkFolderID"))
  strContent.AppendFormat("{0}</a></td>", DR("Name"))
  strContent.AppendFormat("<td>{0}</td>", DR("Description"))
  strContent.AppendFormat("<td align=center>{0}</td>", _
    DR("CreationDate").ToShortDateString())
  DR2 = DB2.GetDataReader("sp_RetrieveFolderStatistics " _
    & DR("pkFolderID"))
  strContent.Append("<td align=center>")
  strContent.AppendFormat("{0} File(s)</td>", _
    DR2("TotalFileCount"))
  strContent.Append("<td align=center>")
  If DR("fkCreatorID").ToString.Equals( _
  Request.Cookies("mID").Value) Then
    strContent.AppendFormat("<a href=""folder_create.aspx?" _
      & "id={0}"">Update</a>", DR("pkFolderID"))
    If DR2("TotalFileCount") = 0 Then
      strContent.Append(" | ")
      strContent.Append("<a href=""folder_delete.aspx?")
      strContent.AppendFormat("id={0}"">Delete</a>", _
        DR("pkFolderID"))
    End If
  Else
    strContent.Append("None")
  End If
  strContent.Append("</td>")
  strContent.Append("</tr>")
  If strColor = "tabletext" Then
    strColor = "tabletext_gray"
  Else
    strColor = "tabletext"
  End If
  strContent.Append(Environment.NewLine)
  DR2.Close()
```

Listing 9.15   folder_view.aspx.vb (continued)

```
    End While
    DR.Close()
  End If
  `
  ' Find any files created at the root level of the file system.
  `
  If intFolderID = 0 Then
    DR = DB.GetDataReader("sp_RetrieveFilesByTeamByFolder " _
      & intTeamID & ", 0", True)
  Else
    DR = DB.GetDataReader("sp_RetrieveFilesByFolder " _
      & intFolderID, True)
    strContent.AppendFormat("<tr class=""{0}"">", strColor)
    strContent.Append("<td>")
    strContent.Append("<img src=""images/folder_up.gif"" " _
      & "height=16 width=16>")
    strContent.Append("</td>")
    strContent.Append("<td colspan=5>")
    strContent.AppendFormat("<a href=""folder_view.aspx" _
      & "?tID={0}"">", _
      FDR("fkTeamID"))
    strContent.Append("Back to Parent Folder</a></td>")
    strContent.Append("</tr>")
    If strColor = "tabletext" Then
      strColor = "tabletext_gray"
    Else
      strColor = "tabletext"
    End If
  End If


  While DR.Read()
    strContent.AppendFormat("<tr class=""{0}"">", strColor)
    strContent.Append("<td><img src=""images/file.gif"" " _
      & "height=16 width=16></td>")
    strContent.AppendFormat("<td>{0}</td>", DR("Name"))
    strContent.AppendFormat("<td>{0}</td>", DR("Description"))
    strContent.AppendFormat("<td align=center>{0}</td>", _
      DR("UploadDate").ToShortDateString())
    If DR("FileSize") > 1024^3 Then
      strSize = Math.Round(DR("FileSize") / 1024^3, _
        1).ToString() & " Gb"
    ElseIf DR("FileSize") > 1024^2 Then
      strSize = Math.Round(DR("FileSize") / 1024^2, _
        1).ToString() & " Mb"
    ElseIf DR("FileSize") > 1024 Then
      strSize = Math.Round(DR("FileSize") / 1024, _
        1).ToString() & " Kb"
```

Listing 9.15   folder_view.aspx.vb (continued)

```
      Else
         strSize = DR("FileSize").ToString() & " bytes"
      End If


      strContent.AppendFormat("<td align=center>{0}</td>", strSize)
      strContent.Append("<td align=center>")
      strContent.AppendFormat("<a href=""file_download.aspx" _
         & "?id={0}"">Download</a>", _
         DR("pkFileID"))
      If DR("fkCreatorID").ToString.Equals( _
         Request.Cookies("mID").Value) Then
         strContent.Append(" | ")
         strContent.AppendFormat("<a href=""file_delete.aspx" _
          & "?id={0}"">Delete</a>", _
           DR("pkFileID"))
      End If
      strContent.Append("</td>")
      strContent.Append("</tr>")
      If strColor = "tabletext" Then
         strColor = "tabletext_gray"
      Else
         strColor = "tabletext"
      End If
      strContent.Append(Environment.NewLine)

   End While
   If strContent.ToString() <> "" Then
    strOutput.Append("<table cellpadding=4 " _
      & "cellspacing=0 width=""100%"">")
    strOutput.Append("<tr class=""tableheading"">")
    strOutput.Append("<td width=""5%""> </td>")
    strOutput.Append("<td width=""20%"">Name</td>")
    strOutput.Append("<td width=""35%"">Description</td>")
    strOutput.Append("<td width=""10%"">Date</td>")
    strOutput.Append("<td width=""10%"">Size</td>")
    strOutput.Append("<td width=""20%"">Actions</td>")
    strOutput.Append("</tr>")
    strOutput.Append(strContent.ToString())
    strOutput.Append("</table>")
    lblContent.Text = strOutput.ToString()
   Else
    lblContent.Text = "<p class=text><b>No files or folders " _
```

Listing 9.15 folder_view.aspx.vb (continued)

```
            & "have been added for this team.</b></p>"
        End If
        DR.Close()
    End Sub
  End Class
End Namespace
```

Listing 9.15   folder_view.aspx.vb (continued)

This code is somewhat more extensive, so let's go through some of the thinking behind it. When we are showing a team's file library, the previous page will be supplying just the team ID, represented in the query string by the tID value. When we click a folder, we are passing the folder ID to this page. When we are viewing the public file library, the team ID will be zero. We determine which case we're handling at the top of this page.

We then determine what links we should show. For both the root level and the folder level, we can add a file. However, we can only add a folder at the root file-library level, so we add the appropriate HTML to the label on the page reserved for this purpose. We also determine what the title of the page should be—whether it's the team's file library or a particular folder name. The title visible to the user on the page (not the one in the title bar of the page) changes as the page is loaded.

Next, we're ready to start showing folders and files. We start by determining if we should show folders at all, which we do if we're showing the folders in the team's file library. We add any existing folders, along with the relevant statistics, to a String-Builder object. We then look for any files located at this level and add them, as well. If we are showing a folder, the creator of the folder has the ability to change it or delete it if there are no files stored in it. These actions are added to the line dynamically, based on the database results.

As we're showing the files, we need to display the size. However, since we can have files of any size in our system, we have to be somewhat intelligent on how we display the file sizes. We can't show everything in bytes, since large files would be too wide to fit. We also can't just use megabytes, since small files would be shown in decimals. Instead, we create a graduated scale and show the appropriate unit based on size. Any files bigger than 1 GB are shown in gigabytes, files larger than 1 MB are shown in megabytes, and so on. We use the Round function to limit the decimal places to one digit for ease of reading. We'll use this same code when we display the details on each file on the next page.

The other thing we're doing as we display the files is dynamically determining what actions can be performed on them. Every file posted in the system can be downloaded, but only the owner of a file can delete it. We're not dealing with updating files here— any changes require that the file be removed and added again. Since we're dealing with files stored on the server as well, this is an easier approach to take.

When we get to the end, we only want to show the table if there are either files or folders to display. That's why we are adding the table headings to our content string at the end. If we were to show the headings and not have any content in the page, the output would look odd.

The next logical step for the user would be to download the file using the page shown in Figure 9.4.

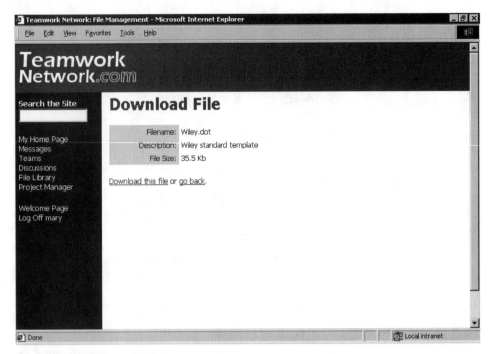

Figure 9.4 File Download page.

The downloading of files is handled by putting the file into a Web-accessible directory reserved for a particular member. The ASPX file for this is shown in Listing 9.16, but the important code is in Listing 9.17.

```
<%@ Page Inherits="TWNW.FileDownload" Src="file_download.aspx.vb" %>
<%@ Register Tagprefix="TWNW" Tagname="Header" Src="Header.ascx" %>
<%@ Register Tagprefix="TWNW" Tagname="Footer" Src="Footer.ascx" %>
<!DOCTYPE HTML PUBLIC "-//W3C//DTD HTML 4.0 Transitional//EN">
<html>
<head>
  <title>Teamwork Network: File Management</title>
  <link href="styles.css" rel="stylesheet" type="text/css">
</head>
<body>
<TWNW:Header id="PageHeader" runat="server" />
<p class="pageheading">Download File</p>
<table cellpadding="4" cellspacing="0" width="600">
<tr>
  <td class="tabletext_gray" align="right" width="20%">Filename:</td>
  <td class="tabletext" width="80%">
  <asp:label id="lblFilename" runat="server" />
```

Listing 9.16 file_download.aspx

```
      </td>
   </tr>
   <tr>
     <td class="tabletext_gray" align="right" width="20%">Description:</td>
     <td class="tabletext" width="80%">
     <asp:label id="lblDescription" runat="server" />
     </td>
   </tr>
   <tr>
     <td class="tabletext_gray" align="right" width="20%">File Size:</td>
     <td class="tabletext" width="80%">
     <asp:label id="lblSize" runat="server" />
     </td>
   </tr>
   </table>
   <asp:label id="lblDownload" runat="server" />
   <TWNW:Footer id="PageFooter" runat="server" />
   </body>
   </html>
```

Listing 9.16 file_download.aspx (continued)

We set up a table to display relevant details on the file selected by the user. The code behind this page populates the page and gets it ready to be downloaded by the user. This code is shown in Listing 9.17.

```
Imports System
Imports System.Data
Imports System.Data.SqlClient
Imports System.Web.UI
Imports System.Web.UI.WebControls
Imports System.IO
Imports TWNWObjects

Namespace TWNW
  Public Class FileDownload
    Inherits System.Web.UI.Page

    Protected lblFilename As Label
    Protected lblDescription As Label
    Protected lblSize As Label
    Protected lblDownload As Label

    Sub Page_Load(objSender As Object, objArgs As EventArgs)
      Const DOWNLOAD_DIR = "C:\Data\TWNW Downloads"
      Dim intFolderID As Integer
```

Listing 9.17 file_download.aspx.vb

```
      Dim strDownloadURL As String = "/twnwdownloads/"
      Dim strOutput As New Text.StringBuilder()

      Dim DB As New AtWorkUtilities.Database()
      Dim F As New TWNWObjects.File(DB, Request.QueryString("ID"))
      Dim DR As DataRow = F.GetRow()
      Dim strSize As String
      lblFilename.Text = DR("Name")
      lblDescription.Text = DR("Description")

      If DR("FileSize") > 1024^3 Then
        strSize = Math.Round(DR("FileSize") / 1024^3, 1).ToString() _
          & " Gb"
      ElseIf DR("FileSize") > 1024^2 Then
        strSize = Math.Round(DR("FileSize") / 1024^2, 1).ToString() _
          & " Mb"
      ElseIf DR("FileSize") > 1024 Then
        strSize = Math.Round(DR("FileSize") / 1024, 1).ToString() _
          & " Kb"
      Else
        strSize = DR("FileSize").ToString() & " bytes"
      End If
      lblSize.Text = strSize
      If Not IO.Directory.Exists(DOWNLOAD_DIR & "\member" _
        & Request.Cookies("mID").Value) Then
        IO.Directory.CreateDirectory(DOWNLOAD_DIR & "\member" _
          & Request.Cookies("mID").Value)
      End If
      IO.File.Copy(DR("StoredAs"), DOWNLOAD_DIR & "\member" _
        & Request.Cookies("mID").Value & "\" & DR("Name"), True)
      lblDownload.Text = "<p class=""text"">" _
        & "<a href=""/twnwdownloads/member" _
        & Request.Cookies("mID").Value & "/" & DR("Name") _
        & """>Download this file</a>" _
        & " or <a href=""javascript:history.go(-1);"">go back</a>.</p>"


      DB.Close()
    End Sub
  End Class
End Namespace
```

Listing 9.17   file_download.aspx.vb (continued)

In my test system, I have set up a directory known to Web users as /twnwdownload, but known to the server as physical pathname C:\Data\TWNW Downloads. Files are stored in a directory that is not directly accessible to the Web. This is a basic security precaution. However, when a user wants to download a file, we have to move a copy of the file to a Web-accessible directory. We do this using the IO.File object's Copy method. Remember that we stored both the original name of the file and the new name of the file. We simply copy the selected file from our storage area to the Web directory, but put it in a directory created on-the-fly (if necessary) for a particular member. This prevents one user from getting the same file as someone else and overwriting the other user's version. The user can then choose to download the file from the File_download.aspx page by clicking the link shown in the previous figure. When the user logs out, this temporary directory is removed; however, you could always create a Web service that periodically reviews directories and cleans out files that haven't been used in a while.

With the typical user's path through the system complete, let's add the pages to maintain the data in the system.

Creating the Maintenance Pages

The first maintenance page that we see when we navigate the system is the Folder Creation page. The ASPX file is shown in Listing 9.18.

```
<%@ Page Inherits="TWNW.FolderCreate" Src="folder_create.aspx.vb" %>
<%@ Register Tagprefix="TWNW" Tagname="Header" Src="Header.ascx" %>
<%@ Register Tagprefix="TWNW" Tagname="Footer" Src="Footer.ascx" %>
<!DOCTYPE HTML PUBLIC "-//W3C//DTD HTML 4.0 Transitional//EN">
<html>
<head>
  <title>Teamwork Network: Folder Management</title>
  <link href="styles.css" rel="stylesheet" type="text/css">
</head>
<body>
<TWNW:Header id="PageHeader" runat="server" />
<table width="600">
<tr>
<td valign="top" width="600">

<p><asp:label id="lblPageTitle" class="pageheading" runat="server"
/></p>
<asp:label id="lblErrorMessage" class="errortext" runat="server" />

<form runat="server">
<input type="hidden" runat="server" id="pkFolderID">
<input type="hidden" runat="server" id="fkTeamID">

<table cellspacing="5">
<tr class="tabletext">
  <td align="right">Name:</td>
  <td>
  <asp:textbox
```

Listing 9.18 folder_create.aspx

```
      id="txtName"
      columns="30"
      maxlength="80"
      runat="server" />
    </td>
</tr>
<tr class="tabletext">
    <td valign="middle" align="right">
    Description:
    </td>
    <td>
    <asp:textbox
      id="txtDescription"
      rows="5"
      columns="40"
      wrap="true"
      textmode="Multiline"
      runat="server" />
    </td>
</tr>
<tr class="tabletext">
    <td colspan=2 align=middle>
    <input type="submit"
      name="btnSubmit"
      runat="server"
      value="Save" />
    <input type="reset"
      name="btnReset"
      runat="server"
      value="Clear" />
    </td>
</tr>
</table>
</form>
</td>
</tr>
</table>
<TWNW:Footer id="PageFooter" runat="server" />
</body>
</html>
```

Listing 9.18   folder_create.aspx (continued)

This page follows the same pattern as most of the other data-entry pages we've done. In this system, we allow the folder name and description to be edited, so the code-behind page reflects this dual purpose, as shown in Listing 9.19.

```
Imports System
Imports System.Data
Imports System.Data.SqlClient
Imports System.Web
Imports System.Web.UI
Imports System.Web.UI.WebControls
Imports TWNWObjects

Namespace TWNW
  Public Class FolderCreate
    Inherits System.Web.UI.Page

    Protected pkFolderID As HTMLControls.HTMLInputHidden
    Protected fkTeamID As HTMLControls.HTMLInputHidden
    Protected txtName As TextBox
    Protected txtDescription As TextBox

    Protected lblPageTitle As Label
    Protected lblErrorMessage As Label

    Sub Page_Load(objSender As Object, objArgs As EventArgs)
      Dim DB As New AtWorkUtilities.Database()
      Dim F As Folder
      Dim DR As DataRow
      Dim objCookie As HTTPCookie
      objCookie = Request.Cookies("mID")

      If Not Page.IsPostBack Then
       If Request.QueryString("ID") <> "" Then
         lblPageTitle.Text = "Edit Folder"
         F = New Folder(DB, Request.QueryString("ID"))
         DR = F.GetRow()
         pkFolderID.Value = DR("pkFolderID").ToString()
         fkTeamID.Value = DR("fkTeamID").ToString()
         txtName.Text = DR("Name").ToString()
         txtDescription.Text = DR("Description").ToString()
       Else
         lblPageTitle.Text = "Create New Folder"
         fkTeamID.Value = Request.QueryString("tID")
       End If
      Else
        If pkFolderID.Value = "" Then
          F = New Folder(DB)
        Else
          F = New Folder(DB, pkFolderID.Value)
        End If
        DR = F.GetRow()
        DR("Name") = txtName.Text
        DR("Description") = txtDescription.Text
```

Listing 9.19   folder_create.aspx.vb

```
      DR("fkTeamID") = fkTeamID.Value
      DR("fkCreatorID") = objCookie.Value
      F.SaveRow(DR)
      If Not F.IsValid Then
        lblErrorMessage.Text = _
        F.ValidationError("<b>ERROR:</b> The following " _
          & "errors were detected in your data:<br>", _
          "&bull; {0}<br>", "")
      Else
        F.Save()
        DB.Close()
        Response.Redirect("folder_view.aspx?tID=" _
          & fkTeamID.Value)
      End If
    End If
  End Sub
  End Class
End Namespace
```

Listing 9.19   folder_create.aspx.vb (continued)

In edit mode, we populate the form fields and store our unique ID in the hidden-input field. In add mode, we only have to store the team ID that was passed in from a previous page. In both cases, we set the page title to be the action taking place.

Once the user has clicked the Save button, the data is taken from the form and placed in either a new Folder object or an existing one that is opened for editing. We then send the user back to the team file library as a final step.

If the user creates a folder in error or has an empty folder from which files have been deleted, the owner/creator of a folder has the option to delete it. The ASPX file for this is shown in Listing 9.20.

```
<%@ Page Inherits="TWNW.FolderDelete" Src="folder_delete.aspx.vb" %>
<%@ Register Tagprefix="TWNW" Tagname="Header" Src="Header.ascx" %>
<%@ Register Tagprefix="TWNW" Tagname="Footer" Src="Footer.ascx" %>
<!DOCTYPE HTML PUBLIC "-//W3C//DTD HTML 4.0 Transitional//EN">
<html>
<head>
  <title>Teamwork Network: Folder Management</title>
  <link href="styles.css" rel="stylesheet" type="text/css">
</head>
<body>
<TWNW:Header id="PageHeader" runat="server" />
<p class="pageheading">Delete Folder</p>
<p class="text">Are you sure you want to delete this folder?</p>
```

Listing 9.20   folder_delete.aspx

```
<form runat="server" id="deleteForm">
<input type="hidden" runat="server" id="pkFolderID">
<p class="text">
<a href="javascript:document.deleteForm.submit();">Yes</a>
  
<a href="javascript:history.go(-1);">No</a>
</p>
</form>
<TWNW:Footer id="PageFooter" runat="server" />
</body>
</html>
```

Listing 9.20   folder_delete.aspx (continued)

This page follows the same pattern as the other Delete pages that we've built in the Teamwork Network system. The code behind file is shown in Listing 9.21.

```
Imports System
Imports System.Data
Imports System.Data.SqlClient
Imports System.Web.UI
Imports System.Web.UI.WebControls
Imports TWNWObjects

Namespace TWNW
  Public Class FolderDelete
    Inherits System.Web.UI.Page

    Protected pkFolderID As HTMLControls.HTMLInputHidden

    Sub Page_Load(objSender As Object, objArgs As EventArgs)
      Dim intTeamID As Integer
      If Not Page.IsPostBack Then
       pkFolderID.Value = Request.QueryString("ID")
      Else
       Dim DB As New AtWorkUtilities.Database()
       Dim F As New Folder(DB, pkFolderID.Value)
       Dim DR As DataRow = F.GetRow()
       intTeamID = DR("fkTeamID")
       DR = Nothing
       F.Delete()
       DB.Close()
       Response.Redirect("folder_view.aspx?tID=" _
```

Listing 9.21   folder_delete.aspx.vb

```
         & intTeamID.ToString())
     End If
   End Sub
 End Class
End Namespace
```

Listing 9.21   folder_delete.aspx.vb (continued)

Our business object is doing most of the work for us here, but we do have to retrieve the team ID before removing the folder object. This returns the user to the team file library instead of to the home page or somewhere else.

Now that we can create and maintain folders, we need to create and delete files. The file-creation step is first, and the code for this function is shown in Listing 9.22. Take special note of the code marked in boldface, as we haven't covered it to this point in the book.

```
<%@ Page Inherits="TWNW.FileCreate" Src="file_create.aspx.vb" %>
<%@ Register Tagprefix="TWNW" Tagname="Header" Src="Header.ascx" %>
<%@ Register Tagprefix="TWNW" Tagname="Footer" Src="Footer.ascx" %>
<!DOCTYPE HTML PUBLIC "-//W3C//DTD HTML 4.0 Transitional//EN">
<html>
<head>
  <title>Teamwork Network: Add a File</title>
  <link href="styles.css" rel="stylesheet" type="text/css">
</head>
<body>
<TWNW:Header id="PageHeader" runat="server" />
<table width="600">
<tr>
<td valign="top" width="600">

<p class="pageheading">Add a File</p>
<asp:label id="lblErrorMessage" class="errortext" runat="server" />

<form enctype="multipart/form-data" runat="server">
<input type="hidden" runat="server" id="fkTeamID">
<input type="hidden" runat="server" id="fkFolderID">

<table cellspacing="5">

<tr class="tabletext">
  <td align="right">Filename:</td>
  <td>
  <input
   size="40"
```

Listing 9.22   file_create.aspx

```
      id="txtFilename"
      type="file"
      runat="server">
    </td>
  </tr>

  <tr class="tabletext">
    <td valign="middle" align="right">
    Description:
    </td>
    <td>
    <asp:textbox
      id="txtDescription"
      rows="10"
      columns="40"
      wrap="true"
      textmode="Multiline"
      runat="server" />
    </td>
  </tr>
  <tr class="tabletext">
    <td colspan=2 align=middle>
    <input type="submit"
      name="btnSubmit"
      runat="server"
      value="Save" />
    <input type="reset"
      name="btnReset"
      runat="server"
      value="Clear" />
    </td>
  </tr>
  </table>
  </form>
  </td>
  </tr>
  </table>
  <TWNW:Footer id="PageFooter" runat="server" />
  </body>
  </html>
```

Listing 9.22   file_create.aspx (continued)

This page looks, for the most part, like any other data-entry form we have built to date. However, note the code that is highlighted on bold in the previous listing. The FORM tag uses a different type of encoding, and we're using a different type of input box. Both features are required in order to let us upload files. When this page runs, it looks like Figure 9.5.

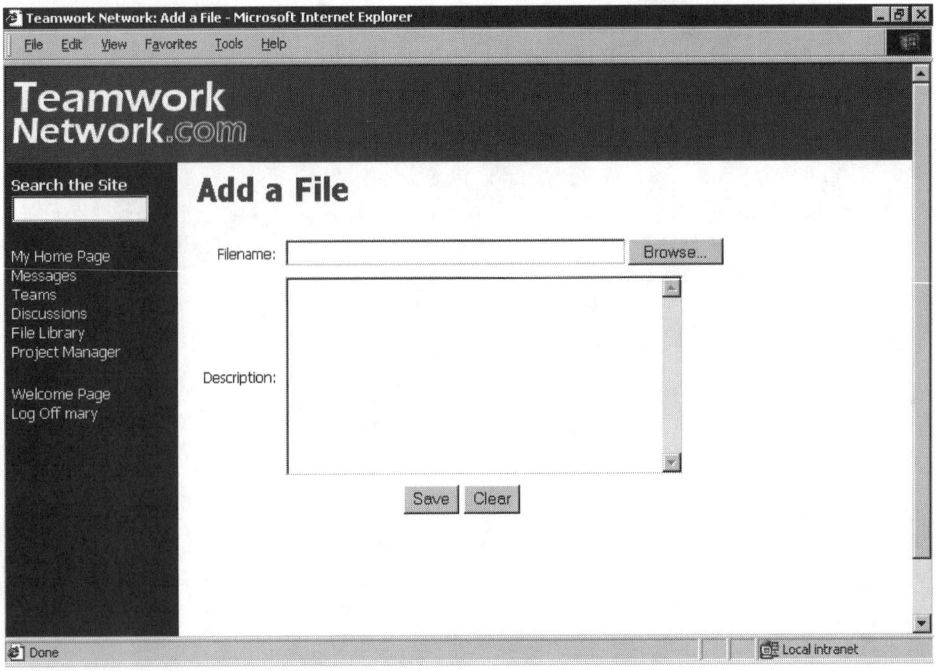

Figure 9.5 Add File dialog box.

Browsers that support uploading files via HTTP, which includes the current versions of all the major browsers, automatically add the Browse button. The part that had not been supported prior to .NET was the code that saves the uploaded file. This was previously handled by third-party components, which provided varying degrees of success. As you'll see in the next listing, handling uploaded files is now a piece of cake. Listing 9.23 shows the code behind this ASPX file.

```
Imports System
Imports System.Data
Imports System.Data.SqlClient
Imports System.Web
Imports System.Web.UI
Imports System.Web.UI.WebControls
Imports System.Text
Imports TWNWObjects

Namespace TWNW
  Public Class FileCreate
    Inherits System.Web.UI.Page
```

Listing 9.23 file_create.aspx.vb

```
Const UPLOAD_DIR = "C:\Data\TWNW Uploads\"
Protected txtName As TextBox
Protected txtFilename As HTMLControls.HTMLInputFile
Protected txtDescription As TextBox

Protected fkTeamID As HTMLControls.HTMLInputHidden
Protected fkFolderID As HTMLControls.HTMLInputHidden

Protected lblErrorMessage As Label

Sub Page_Load(objSender As Object, objArgs As EventArgs)
  Dim T As Team
  Dim FD As Folder
  Dim F As File
  Dim DB As New AtWorkUtilities.Database()

  If Not Page.IsPostBack Then
    If Request.QueryString("fID") <> "" Then
      FD = New Folder(DB, Request.QueryString("fID"))
      Dim FDR As DataRow = FD.GetRow()
      fkFolderID.Value = Request.QueryString("fID")
      fkTeamID.Value = FDR("fkTeamID")
      FDR = Nothing
      FD = Nothing
    Else
      fkFolderID.Value = 0
      fkTeamID.Value = Request.QueryString("tID")
    End If
  Else
    Dim strFilename As String
    Dim strOldname As String
    Dim strBasename As String
    Dim i As Integer
    strFilename = GenerateRandomFilename()
    strOldname = txtFilename.PostedFile.Filename
    For i = strOldname.Length - 1 To 0 Step -1
      If strOldname.Substring(i, 1) = "\" Then
        strBasename = strOldname.Substring(i + 1)
        Exit For
      End If
    Next i
    F = New File(DB)
    Dim DR As DataRow = F.GetRow()
    DR("fkTeamID") = fkTeamID.Value
    DR("fkFolderID") = fkFolderID.Value
    DR("Name") = strBaseName
    DR("Description") = txtDescription.Text.ToString()
    DR("FileSize") = txtFilename.PostedFile.ContentLength
    DR("StoredAs") = strFilename
```

Listing 9.23 file_create.aspx.vb (continued)

```
      DR("fkCreatorID") = Request.Cookies("mID").Value
      F.SaveRow(DR)
      If Not F.IsValid Then
        lblErrorMessage.Text = _
         F.ValidationError("<b>ERROR:</b> The following " _
          & "errors were detected in your data:<br>", _
          "&bull; {0}<br>", "")
      Else
        F.Save()
        txtFilename.PostedFile.SaveAs(strFilename)
        DB.Close()
        Response.Redirect("folder_view.aspx?tID=" _
         & fkTeamID.Value)
      End If


    End If
  End Sub

  Private Function GenerateRandomFilename() As String
    Const CHARS = _
     "ABCDEFGHIJKLMNOPQRSTUVWXYZabcdefghijklmnopqrstuvwxyz"
    Dim R As New Random(Environment.TickCount)
    Dim i As Integer
    Dim sb As New Text.StringBuilder(UPLOAD_DIR)
    For i = 1 To 20
      sb.Append(CHARS.ToString().Substring(R.Next(51) + 1), 1)
    Next i
    sb.Append(".dat")
    Return sb.ToString()
  End Function
 End Class
End Namespace
```

Listing 9.23   file_create.aspx.vb (continued)

We start by storing the folder ID and the team ID in the hidden-input fields on the form. If we don't have the team ID when the user chooses to load a file into a folder, we just look it up. The user is presented with the dialog box displayed in the previous figure and selects a file. After entering an optional description, the user clicks the Save button, and our page goes back to work. We first have to determine what the base name of the file is so that we can store this information in case someone wants to retrieve the file being uploaded. We then need to determine a unique name for the file for storage purposes in the Teamwork Network file archives. We can't use the existing filename, since this could conflict with another one. We also don't want to give any hint as to what the file actually is or have a potential name conflict, so we make up a random name. For even tighter security, you could use a component like ASPEncrypt to encrypt the files being stored. That would eliminate any possibility of someone not authorized for the file from getting the data. In the GenerateRandom-Filename function, we create a 20-character, random filename ending in .dat. We take the uploaded file and save it to our new filename in the archive directory specified by the UPLOAD_DIR constant. This directory has to be writable by the Web server, but it doesn't have to be accessible to anyone else. The download page reverses the process and takes the file from this directory, making it available for the user to download later.

The PostedFile property of the HTMLInputFile control gives us quite a bit of information, including the file size and the original name of the file, which we store in the File object. We also store the creator information from the current user's cookie and then put the file into the system.

As previously mentioned, handling file uploads used to be a pain, depending on the component that you had. This is completely painless and actually worked the first time I tried it out.

While we're not allowing a file to be edited, we are allowing it to be deleted by its owner. The ASPX file for this is nearly identical to the folder-deletion page and is shown in Listing 9.24.

```
<%@ Page Inherits="TWNW.FileDelete" Src="file_delete.aspx.vb" %>
<%@ Register Tagprefix="TWNW" Tagname="Header" Src="Header.ascx" %>
<%@ Register Tagprefix="TWNW" Tagname="Footer" Src="Footer.ascx" %>
<!DOCTYPE HTML PUBLIC "-//W3C//DTD HTML 4.0 Transitional//EN">
<html>
<head>
  <title>Teamwork Network: File Management</title>
  <link href="styles.css" rel="stylesheet" type="text/css">
</head>
<body>
<TWNW:Header id="PageHeader" runat="server" />
<p class="pageheading">Delete File</p>
<p class="text">Are you sure you want to delete this file?</p>
<form runat="server" id="deleteForm">
<input type="hidden" runat="server" id="pkFileID">
<p class="text">
<a href="javascript:document.deleteForm.submit();">Yes</a>
  
<a href="javascript:history.go(-1);">No</a>
</p>
</form>
<TWNW:Footer id="PageFooter" runat="server" />
</body>
</html>
```

Listing 9.24 file_delete.aspx

We take the file ID and store it in this form for when the user clicks the Yes link. The code behind this page is shown in Listing 9.25.

```
Imports System
Imports System.Data
Imports System.Data.SqlClient
Imports System.Web.UI
Imports System.Web.UI.WebControls
Imports System.IO
Imports TWNWObjects

Namespace TWNW
  Public Class FileDelete
    Inherits System.Web.UI.Page

    Protected pkFileID As HTMLControls.HTMLInputHidden

    Sub Page_Load(objSender As Object, objArgs As EventArgs)
      Dim intTeamID As Integer
      Dim intFolderID As Integer
      Const UPLOAD_DIR = "C:\Data\TWNW Uploads"
      If Not Page.IsPostBack Then
       pkFileID.Value = Request.QueryString("ID")
      Else
       Dim DB As New AtWorkUtilities.Database()
       Dim F As New TWNWObjects.File(DB, pkFileID.Value)
       Dim DR As DataRow = F.GetRow()
       intFolderID = DR("fkFolderID")
       intTeamID = DR("fkTeamID")
       Try
          IO.File.Delete(DR("StoredAs"))
       Catch e As Exception
          ' do nothing, let any non-existent files be ignored
       End Try
       DR = Nothing
       F.Delete()
       DB.Close()
       If intFolderID = 0 Then
          Response.Redirect("folder_view.aspx?tID=" _
           & intTeamID.ToString())
       Else
          Response.Redirect("folder_view.aspx?fID=" _
           & intFolderID.ToString())
       End If
      End If
    End Sub
  End Class
End Namespace
```

Listing 9.25 file_delete.aspx.vb

Just as with the Download page, we're using the System.IO library here to manipulate files. Once we've determined that the owner of the file has chosen to remove it, we create a File object to retrieve the pathname information. We then delete the copy of the file on the server and remove the database record. We then send the user back to either the team file library view or the folder view, depending on where the file was located.

The other thing we're doing here is using a Try block to ignore any errors that might occur when we're deleting files. This is done to avoid receiving errors when we try to delete a nonexistent file.

Modifying the Team Viewer

The next step is to make a minor change to the team-viewing page so that users viewing their teams can jump immediately to the file library to add or view files. The code-behind page did not change, but the changes to Teams.aspx, shown in Listing 9.26, are highlighted in bold.

```
<%@ Page Inherits="TWNW.TeamsViewAll" Src="teams.aspx.vb" %>
<%@ Register Tagprefix="TWNW" Tagname="Header" Src="Header.ascx" %>
<%@ Register Tagprefix="TWNW" Tagname="Footer" Src="Footer.ascx" %>
<!DOCTYPE HTML PUBLIC "-//W3C//DTD HTML 4.0 Transitional//EN">
<html>
<head>
    <title>Teamwork Network: View All Teams</title>
  <link href="styles.css" rel="stylesheet" type="text/css">
</head>

<body leftmargin=0 topmargin=0>
<TWNW:Header id="PageHeader" runat="server" />
<p class="pageheading">View All Teams</p>
<p class="text"><a href="team_create.aspx">Create a Team</a></p>
<asp:label id="lblMessage" class="text" runat="server" />

<asp:Repeater id="rptList" runat="server">
  <HeaderTemplate>
  <table cellpadding="4" cellspacing="0" width="100%">
  <tr class="tableheading">
  <td width="30%">Name</td>
  <td width="30%">Description</td>
  <td width="40%">Actions</td>
  </tr>
  </HeaderTemplate>
  <ItemTemplate>
  <tr class="tabletext">
  <td valign="top"><%# DataBinder.Eval(Container.DataItem, _
    "Name") %></td>
  <td valign="top"><%# DataBinder.Eval(Container.DataItem, _
```

Listing 9.26 teams.aspx changes

```
  "Description") %></td>
 <td valign="top" align="center">
 <a href="teammembers.aspx?id=<%# DataBinder.Eval(Container.DataItem, _
  "pkTeamID") %>">Manage Members</a>  
 <a href="folder_view.aspx?tid=<%# DataBinder.Eval(Container.DataItem, _
  "pkTeamID") %>">View Files</a><br>
 <a href="post_create.aspx?tid=<%# DataBinder.Eval(Container.DataItem, _
  "pkTeamID") %>">Post Message</a>  
 <a href="team_create.aspx?id=<%# DataBinder.Eval(Container.DataItem, _
  "pkTeamID") %>">Update</a>  
 <a href="team_delete.aspx?id=<%# DataBinder.Eval(Container.DataItem, _
  "pkTeamID") %>">Delete</a>
 </td>
 </tr>
 </ItemTemplate>
 <AlternatingItemTemplate>
 <tr class="tabletext_gray">
 <td valign="top"><%# DataBinder.Eval(Container.DataItem, _
  "Name") %></td>
 <td valign="top"><%# DataBinder.Eval(Container.DataItem, _
  "Description") %></td>
 <td valign="top" align="center">
 <a href="teammembers.aspx?id=<%# DataBinder.Eval(Container.DataItem, _
  "pkTeamID") %>">Manage Members</a>  
 <a href="folder_view.aspx?tid=<%# DataBinder.Eval(Container.DataItem, _
  "pkTeamID") %>">View Files</a><br>
 <a href="post_create.aspx?tid=<%# DataBinder.Eval(Container.DataItem, _
  "pkTeamID") %>">Post Message</a>  
 <a href="team_create.aspx?id=<%# DataBinder.Eval(Container.DataItem, _
  "pkTeamID") %>">Update</a>  
 <a href="team_delete.aspx?id=<%# DataBinder.Eval(Container.DataItem, _
  "pkTeamID") %>">Delete</a>
 </td>
 </tr>
 </AlternatingItemTemplate>
 <FooterTemplate>
 </table>
 </FooterTemplate>
</asp:Repeater>
</body>
</html>
<TWNW:Footer id="PageFooter" runat="server" />
</body>
</html>
```

Listing 9.26   teams.aspx changes (continued)

As in the previous project, we add another way to get to the file libraries from this page. This saves the user from having to first use the Files.aspx page.

Wrap Up

In this project, you used a number of new features of ASP.NET to make your work easier. You used the HTMLInputFile server control to upload files and the System.IO library to move files around inside the system. You used the Random class to build random strings of characters to generate obscure filenames, and you continued building using the business objects we've created for this and other applications in the book.

In Project 10, you will build the project tracking and time reporting feature of the Teamwork Network application. You'll be able to add projects with their related tasks, and be able to let your team record time for any of the tasks that you create.

Teamwork Network: Project Tracking

The last subsystem of the Teamwork Network application, which you'll be building in this project, is the project-tracking system. You can use this to manage projects and related tasks, as well as to track team member time on each task. This system even generates an invoice that can be used by a billing department to collect payment from the client. I have a similar system for my own business, and this system includes some enhancements that mine doesn't have.

If you want to see the system live, visit the Web site at www.teamworknetwork.com. I intend to keep this site running as a public-development project that users can discuss at the book's Web site: www.10projectswithasp.net. We'll add new features as time goes on to make this site useful for everyone.

THE PROBLEM

Tracking project work often involves lots of paper timesheets and other manual data-entry tasks. There is also little visibility among team members as to what the status of each task is during the course of a project.

THE SOLUTION

A Web-based project-tracking system that you can use to track the overall project, individual tasks, and each team member's time.

Project Background

As a consultant, the only thing I have to sell is my time. Without a reliable way of keeping track of my time on various projects, I can't keep track of the time I'm spending on my client's work. Most project planning utilities, such as Microsoft Project, do an excellent job of planning the work to be done, but a poor job of keeping track of the time expended so far. I'm happy using other applications to plan the work, but having a customized application like this one to keep track of projects, tasks, and the related time makes my job as a consultant much easier.

To build this application, you'll need to complete these tasks:

1. Design the database tables.
2. Create the stored procedures used in the application.
3. Build the business objects.
4. Build the application's Web pages.

You Will Need

✔ **Windows 2000**

✔ **Internet Information Server 5.0 with .NET Framework installed**

✔ **Visual Studio .NET**

✔ **SQL Server 2000 or 7.0**

✔ **SQL Server client utilities, including SQL Server Enterprise Manager and Query Analyzer**

✔ **The code from Projects 7, 8, and 9**

Reviewing the Functions

Since this subsystem is quite a bit larger than the other two, let's review the various functions first. The system is set up using three major entities: the project, the task, and the timecard. Each project can have any number of tasks and is associated with a particular team. Members who are on a team with projects can create timecards for the time they spend working on various tasks. Only the member who created the project can modify details about the project itself or add and remove tasks. Projects can only be removed if no tasks exist, and tasks can only be removed if no timecards have been entered.

The first page seen by the user is a list of the user's teams and the number of projects on each. This page is shown in Figure 10.1.

Any user can choose to create a new project by selecting a team and clicking Create New Project, shown on the individual team project viewer in Figure 10.2. All projects must be associated with a team, and this portion of the system has no public area. For ease of use, you have to first pick the team and then choose to create a new project. This ensures that the team number is automatically supplied by the link you click.

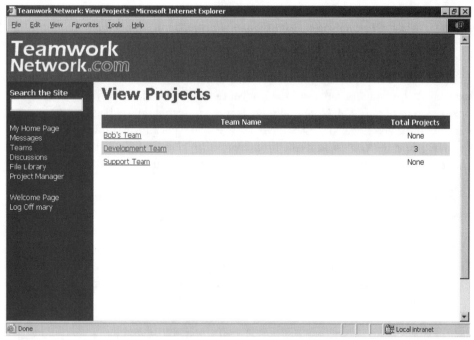

Figure 10.1   All Teams/Projects list.

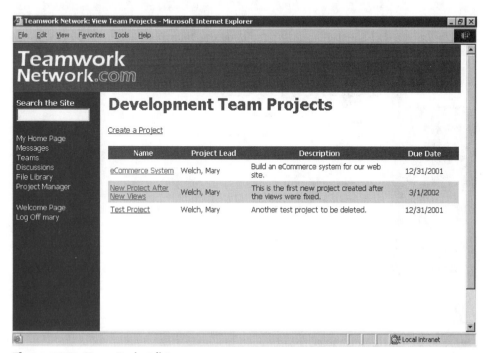

Figure 10.2   Team Project list.

From this page, the member has the option to create a new project or to pick a project to view. If the user chooses to create a new project, the page shown in Figure 10.3 will be displayed.

This page is used for both creating and editing projects. In this view, however, the form is empty except for a hidden field holding the team number. Once the project has been created, members can view the project details and tasks involved in the dialog box shown in Figure 10.4. Note that there is more information, such as project budget, current hours, and dollars spent, shown on this page. This information is automatically gathered from the tasks that make up the project. There is also a list of the available actions. These actions are only available to the owner of the project. Other users will see an empty box on this page.

At this level, the project owner can generate an invoice of all the time that has been recorded but not billed for yet. There is also an option to mark any unbilled items as billed once the invoice has been generated. The invoice page is shown in Figure 10.5.

This page is opened in a separate window and doesn't include all the header and graphic information normally shown on the system pages. This is intentional and makes it easier to print the page and add it to an invoice sent to a client.

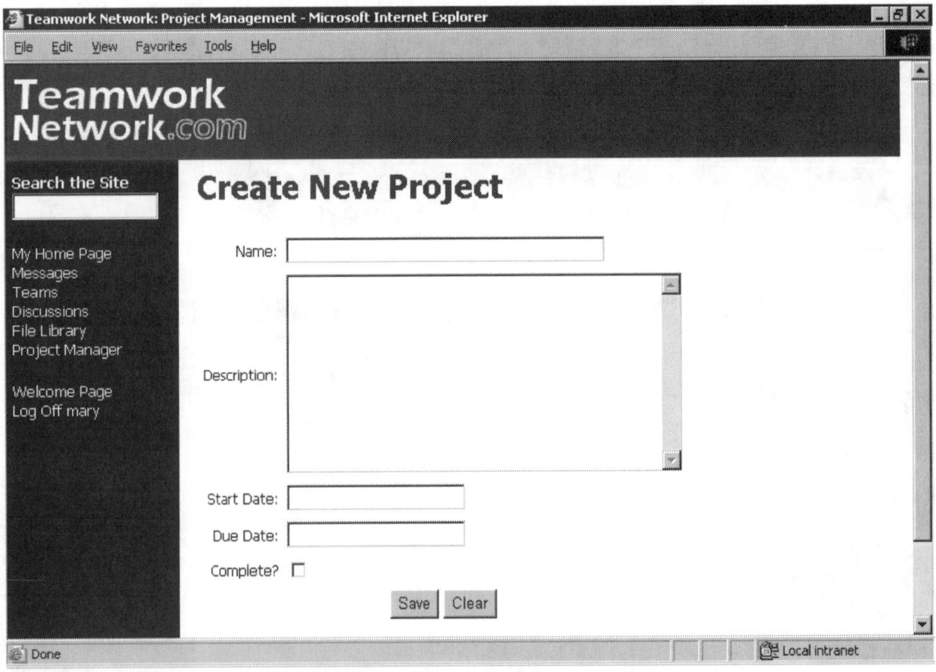

Figure 10.3   Create New Project page.

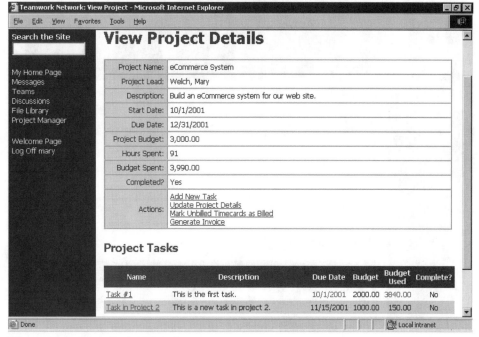

Figure 10.4   View Project Details page.

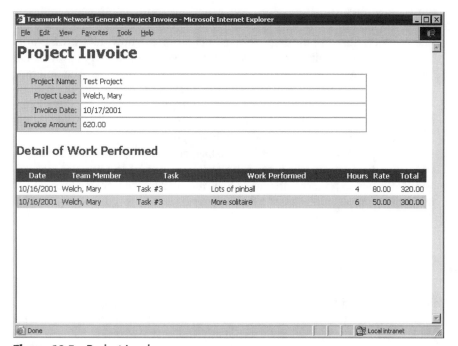

Figure 10.5   Project Invoice page.

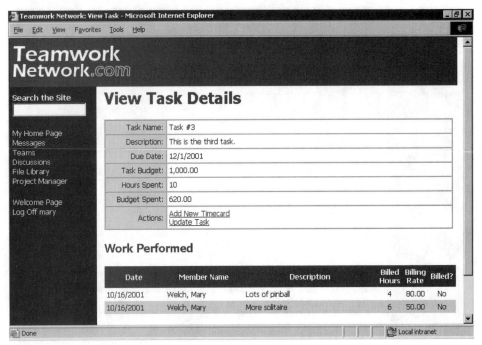

Figure 10.6   View Task Details page.

Once you're back on the View Project Details page, you can select a task to see the task details. The View Task Details page, shown in Figure 10.6, shows all the timecards that have been generated for this particular task, as well as some summary information.

All team members have the option to add a new timecard for this task. The timecard entry page is shown in Figure 10.7 and gathers the relevant work description to be printed on the invoice later. Each task is assigned a default hourly rate, and this value is automatically populated in the box, along with the timecard date. The user has the opportunity to change either of these values in this page.

In many of the windows, anomalous values are flagged in red. For instance, if a task or project is past due, the date is marked in red. If a task is over its budget, it's also marked. This helps call attention to problems that need to be resolved by the team leader.

With the review completed, let's build the tables and stored procedures required for this application.

Building the Database Objects

Three tables are required to make this subsystem function: tblProjects, tblTasks, and tblTimecards. Like the other tables you've built for this application, these new tables are also integrated into the framework you built in Project 7. We're using a number of views for this portion of the application to make it easier to get summary information, as well as the normal complement of stored procedures.

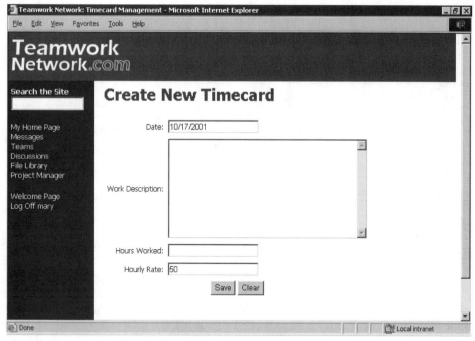

Figure 10.7   Create Timecard page.

Creating the Tables

The first step is to build the tables used in the system. The tblProjects table is shown in Table 10.1.

Table 10.1   tblProjects Table Design

FIELD NAME	SQL DATA TYPE	LENGTH	OTHER
pkProjectID	int	N/A	Identity, Primary Key, Not Null
fkTeamID	int	N/A	Not Null
fkCreatorID	int	N/A	Not Null
Name	varchar	80	Not Null
Description	text	N/A	
StartDate	datetime	N/A	Not Null
DueDate	datetime	N/A	Not Null
IsCompleted	bit	N/A	Not Null

Table 10.2   tblTasks Table Design

FIELD NAME	SQL DATA TYPE	LENGTH	OTHER
pkTaskID	int	N/A	Identity, Primary Key, Not Null
fkProjectID	int	N/A	Not Null
Name	varchar	80	Not Null
Description	text	N/A	
DueDate	datetime	N/A	Not Null
Budget	money	N/A	Not Null
DefaultHourlyRate	money	N/A	Not Null
IsCompleted	bit	N/A	Not Null

Each project is associated with a team and a member, who is considered the project lead. The other fields allow for as much or as little information as needed about the project. The DueDate field will be used to mark the project as late, when necessary. No budget information is kept at the project level; instead, the information is aggregated from the tasks table for display purposes.

The next table you need to build is the tblTasks table, and the design for it is shown in Table 10.2.

Because tasks can have varying rates, the total monetary figure for the budget is stored, not the number of hours. Each user is presumably aware of his or her billing rate and uses that (or the default value) when entering timecards. If you don't want the user to have control over what the billing rate is, you can leave that field off the Create Timecard page and supply it from this table when you save the timecard.

The final table we need holds the timecard entries made by members of the team on particular tasks. The table design is shown in Table 10.3.

Table 10.3   tblTimecards Table Design

FIELD NAME	SQL DATA TYPE	LENGTH	OTHER
pkTimecardID	int	N/A	Identity, Primary Key, Not Null
fkTaskID	int	N/A	Not Null
fkMemberID	int	N/A	Not Null
TimecardDate	datetime	N/A	Not Null
WorkDescription	text	N/A	Not Null
HourCount	money	N/A	Not Null
HourlyRate	money	N/A	Not Null
IsBilled	bit	N/A	Not Null

For each timecard, we keep track of how many hours were spent, what date they were used, and what the individual's hourly rate is. This way, we can generate project-status information to be shown at the task and project levels. We also require that a description of the member's work be stored in the timecard. This enables you to keep a running history of what has been accomplished by your team.

Creating the Views

We have two views that will help us aggregate billing and budget information for the task and project views. We do this to remove some of the more complex SQL code that would otherwise be required to get summary information, in addition to join to other tables.

The first view we create sums up the hours and dollars for timecards, grouped by task number. The code for this view is shown in Listing 10.1.

```
CREATE VIEW vw_SummarizeTimecardsByTask
AS
SELECT
  fkTaskID,
  SUM(HourCount) As HoursByTask,
  SUM(HourCount * HourlyRate) As TotalByTask
FROM tblTimecards
GROUP BY fkTaskID
```

Listing 10.1   vw_SummarizeTimecardsByTask

The second view we need is one step above this one and provides the total of hours and dollars by project. The code is shown in Listing 10.2.

```
CREATE VIEW dbo.vw_SummarizeTasksByProject
AS
SELECT
  T.fkProjectID,
  SUM(V.HoursByTask) AS HoursByProject,
  SUM(V.TotalByTask) AS TotalByProject
FROM dbo.tblTasks T INNER JOIN
   dbo.vw_SummarizeTimecardsByTask V ON T.pkTaskID = V.fkTaskID
GROUP BY T.fkProjectID
```

Listing 10.2   vw_SummarizeTasksByProject

You'll be seeing these views in a number of different places in the application as you work through the project.

Creating the Stored Procedures

As usual, we are making extensive use of stored procedures for this portion of the application. The primary reason we're doing this is to help remove some of the need to build grids manually. If we can get all the information from the database in the proper format, we can just feed it into the various Repeater controls instead of having to manually build all the tables; a few tables, however, will still have to be built manually.

The first stored procedure you need is used in the first page, where the teams are shown along with the number of projects for each. The code is shown in Listing 10.3.

```
CREATE PROCEDURE dbo.sp_RetrieveProjectCountByTeam
@TeamID int
AS
SELECT COUNT(*) AS Total
FROM tblProjects
WHERE fkTeamID = @TeamID
```

Listing 10.3   sp_RetrieveProjectCountByTeam

We're using the same stored procedure as that used in several other projects to determine what teams the member has joined, so we don't have to re-create that one here.

The next stored procedure we need to build returns all the projects for a particular team. We're doing a good deal of data formatting in this stored procedure to make it easier to display in the Web page. The code for this stored procedure is shown in Listing 10.4.

```
CREATE PROCEDURE dbo.sp_RetrieveProjectsByTeam
@TeamID int
AS
SELECT
  '<a href="project_view.aspx?id='
  + convert(varchar, pkProjectID)
  + '">'
  + P.Name
  + '</a>' As ProjectName,
P.*, M.LastName + ', ' + M.FirstName As ProjectLead
FROM tblProjects P, tblMembers M
WHERE fkTeamID = @TeamID
AND fkCreatorID = M.pkMemberID
ORDER BY P.Name
```

Listing 10.4   sp_RetrieveProjectsByTeam

This joins the projects table with the members table in order to retrieve the project lead's name. If you wanted to, you could create a link to the member viewer so that clicking the project leader's name would bring up his or her profile. Just copy the code used here to generate a link to the Project_view.aspx file and point to Member_view.aspx.

In order to show the Project Detail page, we have to run a fairly long query in order to gather the data required for the page. The code for this stored procedure is shown in Listing 10.5.

```
CREATE  procedure sp_RetrieveProjectDetails
@ProjectID int
AS
SELECT
  P.pkProjectID,
  P.fkTeamID,
  P.fkCreatorID,
  P.Name,
  M.LastName + ', ' + M.FirstName As ProjectLead,
  P.Description,
  P.StartDate,
  P.DueDate,
  P.IsCompleted,
  CompletedStatus = (CASE WHEN IsCompleted = 1 THEN 'Yes' ELSE 'No'
END),
  TaskCount = (SELECT COUNT(*) FROM tblTasks WHERE fkProjectID =
@ProjectID),
  ProjectBudget = CONVERT(varchar, (SELECT SUM(Budget) FROM tblTasks
WHERE fkProjectID = @ProjectID), 1),
  ProjectHours = IsNull((SELECT HoursByProject FROM
vw_SummarizeTasksByProject WHERE fkProjectID = @ProjectID), 0),
  ProjectTotal = CONVERT(varchar, IsNull((SELECT TotalByProject FROM
vw_SummarizeTasksByProject WHERE fkProjectID = @ProjectID), 0), 1)
FROM tblProjects P, tblMembers M
WHERE P.fkCreatorID = M.pkMemberID
AND P.pkProjectID = @ProjectID
```

Listing 10.5   sp_RetrieveProjectDetails

There are a number of subqueries in this routine, so let's go through it a little bit at a time. We first tie into the tblMembers table to get the project lead's name. As in the other stored procedure, you could change this to return a link to the member's profile. We return a text version of the completion status so that we can display Yes or No. We then calculate the number of tasks in the project. This value is used to determine whether or not the project can be deleted, since we don't allow deletions of projects once tasks have been added.

Next, we add up the task budgets to determine the overall project budget. Doing this summarization this way means less data entry and math for the team leader. Once the task budgets are entered, the project budget is just a summary of them.

We then use the view we created to determine how many hours and dollars have been expended on this project to date. Since there is a possibility that no time has been spent on this project, we have code that converts null values to zeroes. We also format the result using grouping symbols (commas) and two decimal places. We don't need to convert the number of hours, but we do check it for possible null results. All of these results are shown on the project viewer in the header of the page.

The next stored procedure returns all the tasks for a particular project. The code for it is shown in Listing 10.6.

```
CREATE PROCEDURE dbo.sp_RetrieveTasksByProject
@ProjectID int
AS
SELECT
  T.pkTaskID,
  T.fkProjectID,
  T.Name,
  '<a href="task_view.aspx?id='
   + convert(varchar, T.pkTaskID)
   + '">'
   + T.Name
   + '</a>' As TaskNameWithLink,
  T.Description,
  T.DueDate,
  DueDateStatus =
   (CASE
     WHEN DueDate < getdate()
     THEN '#FF0000'
     ELSE '#000000'
   END),
  T.Budget,
  TaskStatus = (CASE WHEN T.IsCompleted = 1 THEN 'Yes' ELSE 'No' END)
FROM tblTasks T
WHERE T.fkProjectID = @ProjectID
ORDER BY DueDate
```

Listing 10.6　sp_RetrieveTasksByProject

This routine, given a project number, returns all the tasks associated with that project. Besides returning the files, it also returns other status information that is used in the display. The DueDateStatus looks at whether the due date of the task has passed. If so, it returns a color code for red. This color code is used to change the color of the due date field in the list. The TaskStatus field changes the 0 or 1 of the IsCompleted field into a Yes or No for display purposes. We can use the data without having to do a lot of manual formatting.

Once the user selects a task, we have to show the details of that task. The stored procedure to perform this function is similar to the one used to retrieve the project details and is shown in Listing 10.7.

```
CREATE PROCEDURE sp_RetrieveTaskDetails
@TaskID int
as
select
  T.*,
  P.fkCreatorID,
  TaskBudget = CONVERT(varchar, Budget, 1),
  TaskHours = IsNull((SELECT HoursByTask FROM
vw_SummarizeTimecardsByTask WHERE fkTaskID = @TaskID), 0),
  TaskTotal = CONVERT(varchar, IsNull((SELECT TotalByTask FROM
vw_SummarizeTimecardsByTask WHERE fkTaskID = @TaskID), 0), 1),
  TimecardCount = (SELECT COUNT(*) FROM tblTimecards WHERE fkTaskID =
@TaskID)
FROM tblTasks T, tblProjects P
WHERE T.pkTaskID = @TaskID
AND T.fkProjectID = P.pkProjectID
```

Listing 10.7   sp_RetrieveTaskDetails

Instead of looking at the project summary view, we use the task summary view, which adds the timecards by task number. We take this information, accounting for any nulls that might exist for tasks without timecards, and use it in the Task Detail window.

The final stored procedure that we need retrieves the timecards for a particular task. We can show the work that has been accomplished for a particular task in the task viewer. The code for this stored procedure is shown in Listing 10.8.

```
CREATE PROCEDURE sp_RetrieveTimecardsByTask
@TaskID int,
@MemberID int
as
SELECT T.pkTimecardID,
M.LastName + ', ' + M.FirstName As MemberName,
CardDate =
  (CASE
  WHEN IsBilled = 0 AND
  (T.fkMemberID = @MemberID OR
  fkTaskID IN
  (SELECT pkTaskID FROM tblTasks WHERE fkProjectID IN
    (SELECT pkProjectID FROM tblProjects WHERE fkCreatorID = @MemberID)))
  THEN
  '<a href="tcard_create.aspx?id=' + convert(varchar, pkTimecardID) +
'">' + convert(varchar, TimecardDate, 101) + '</a>'
  ELSE
  convert(varchar, TimecardDate, 101)
  END),
```

Listing 10.8   sp_RetrieveTimecardsByTask

```
WorkDescription,
HourCount,
convert(varchar, HourlyRate, 1) as Rate,
IsBilled,
BilledStatus = (CASE WHEN T.IsBilled = 0 THEN 'No' ELSE 'Yes' END)
FROM tblTimecards T, tblMembers M
WHERE T.fkMemberID = M.pkMemberID
AND T.fkTaskID = @TaskID
ORDER BY TimecardDate
```

Listing 10.8   sp_RetrieveTimecardsByTask (continued)

As with some of the other bit fields, we change the IsBilled bit into a Yes or No, which is shown in the Repeater control. We also show the member name by joining to the tblMembers table. You see who has been working on the task without having to click any additional links. As with the other member names that we've shown, you could change this into a link to the Member Profile page.

This page also generates a link to the timecard editor only if the member viewing the information (supplied by the member ID parameter) is the creator of the timecard or is the project manager. In addition, the timecard has to be in an unbilled state. Otherwise, we would be changing history, and most accountants and CFOs get a bit upset about this. When viewing this page, unauthorized users will just see the date of the timecard and not the link.

We have another stored procedure that returns the total hours and total dollars expended to date on each task. This code is shown in Listing 10.9.

```
CREATE procedure sp_RetrieveTaskStatistics
@TaskID int
as
SELECT IsNull(HoursByTask, 0) As TaskHours, IsNull(TotalByTask, 0) As
TaskMoney
FROM vw_SummarizeTimecardsByTask
WHERE fkTaskID = @TaskID
```

Listing 10.9   sp_RetrieveTaskStatistics

This stored procedure is used as we loop through the tasks and display them and the related statistics to the user. You'll use this stored procedure later in the project when you build the task viewing page.

The next stored procedure we need to build retrieves timecards that have not been billed yet. This data is shown on the project invoice, and the code is shown in Listing 10.10.

```
CREATE PROCEDURE sp_RetrieveUnbilledTimecardsByProject
@ProjectID int
AS
SELECT
  TC.TimecardDate,
  M.LastName + ', ' + M.FirstName As MemberName,
  T.Name As TaskName,
  TC.WorkDescription,
  TC.HourCount,
  CONVERT(varchar, TC.HourlyRate, 1) As Rate,
  CONVERT(varchar, TC.HourlyRate * TC.HourCount, 1) As TimecardTotal
FROM tblTimecards TC, tblTasks T, tblMembers M
WHERE fkTaskID IN
  (SELECT pkTaskID FROM tblTasks WHERE fkProjectID = @ProjectID)
AND TC.fkTaskID = T.pkTaskID
AND TC.fkMemberID = M.pkMemberID
AND IsBilled = 0
```

Listing 10.10   sp_RetrieveUnbilledTimecardsByProject

We use this stored procedure to retrieve all timecards for a project that has not been billed for yet. The Project Invoice page uses this routine to display the invoice, which the team leader can then print. This is a particularly complex query, since we have to drill into the tasks table and find all the possible tasks in the timecards table. It's much easier to call the stored procedure from the ASP.NET page than to try to embed all this SQL code in the page.

Another stored procedure used in the invoicing process is the following, which determines what the invoice total should be by adding all the unbilled timecards. The code is shown in Listing 10.11.

```
CREATE PROCEDURE sp_RetrieveUnbilledTotalByProject
@ProjectID int
AS
SELECT CONVERT(varchar, IsNull(SUM(TC.HourlyRate * TC.HourCount), 0), 1)
As InvoiceTotal
FROM tblTimecards TC
WHERE fkTaskID IN
  (SELECT pkTaskID FROM tblTasks WHERE fkProjectID = @ProjectID)
AND IsBilled = 0
```

Listing 10.11   sp_RetrieveUnbilledTotalByProject

We'll use the single field returned from this stored procedure to populate the Invoice Total field when we build the project invoice.

The last stored procedure you need to build updates all unbilled timecards to a billed status on a per-project basis. The code is shown in Listing 10.12.

```
CREATE PROCEDURE sp_UpdateTimecardsByProject
@ProjectID int
AS
UPDATE tblTimecards
SET IsBilled = 1
WHERE IsBilled = 0
AND fkTaskID IN
  (SELECT pkTaskID FROM tblTasks WHERE fkProjectID = @ProjectID)
```

Listing 10.12   sp_UpdateTimecardsByProject

Once the team leader has determined that the billing has been done, he or she can select a page that calls this stored procedure, and everything that was shown as Unbilled will be changed to Billed. This function is restricted to the team leader for security reasons.

With the stored procedures out of the way, we can build the business objects for the subsystem.

Building the Business Objects

We have a total of six new objects to add to our Teamwork Network assembly: Project, Task, Timecard, and three corresponding exception classes. We are following the same design pattern for these objects as we have used in previous projects, so you should be able to quickly build these objects. The first object is the Project object, and its code is shown in Listing 10.13.

```
Imports AtWorkUtilities

Public Class Project
  Inherits BaseServices

  '
  ' If no arguments are supplied, build a separate
  ' database connection for this object.
  '
  Public Sub New()
   MyBase.New(New Database(), "SELECT * FROM tblProjects WHERE 1=0")
  End Sub

  '
  ' If database connection is supplied, store it
  ' in the private connection variable for this
  ' object.
  '
  Public Sub New(ByVal db As Database)
```

Listing 10.13   Project class

```
   MyBase.New(db, "SELECT * FROM tblProjects WHERE 1=0")
 End Sub


 '
 ' If both database and ID are supplied, retrieve
 ' data into the object from the database.
 '
 Public Sub New(ByVal db As Database, _
  ByVal ID As Integer)

   MyBase.New(db, "SELECT * FROM tblProjects WHERE pkProjectID = " _
     & ID.ToString)

 End Sub


 '
 ' Verify that all data validation rules have been
 ' met. Any errors get stored into the errors collection
 ' inherited from the BaseServices class.
 '
 Public Sub Validate()
  Dim dr As DataRow

  ClearErrors()
  For Each dr In m_DS.Tables(0).Rows
    If dr.RowState = DataRowState.Added _
    Or dr.RowState = DataRowState.Modified Then
     ValidateRow(dr)
    End If
  Next

 End Sub


 '
 ' Checks an individual row for validation rule
 ' compliance. Any errors are added to the errors
 ' collection.
 '
 Private Sub ValidateRow(ByVal dr As DataRow)
  If IsDBNull(dr("fkTeamID")) Then
    AddError("Team number is missing.")
  End If
  If IsDBNull(dr("fkCreatorID")) Then
    AddError("Owner's member number is missing.")
  End If
  CheckRequiredField(dr, "Name", "Project name", 80)
  If IsDBNull(dr("StartDate")) Then
    AddError("Project start date is missing.")
  End If
```

Listing 10.13 Project class (continued)

```
        If IsDBNull(dr("DueDate")) Then
          AddError("Project due date is missing.")
        End If
        If IsDBNull(dr("IsCompleted")) Then
          AddError("Completion flag is missing.")
        End If
      End Sub


    '
    ' The base Save method stores the DataRow into the
    ' DataSet, whether it's a new or existing row. The
    ' rest of this routine handles specific validation
    ' for this type of data.
    '
    Public Overloads Sub SaveRow(ByVal dr As DataRow)
      If IsDBNull(dr("IsCompleted")) Then
        dr("IsCompleted") = 0
      End If
      MyBase.SaveRow(dr)
      Validate()

    End Sub


    '
    ' We separate the SaveRow method from the Save method
    ' to give us a chance to handle any validation. We have
    ' a verification here that the data is good before we
    ' continue, however.
    '
    Public Sub Save()

      If Not Me.IsValid Then
          Throw New ProjectException(Me.ValidationError)
        Exit Sub
      End If

      m_DA.Update(m_DS)
    End Sub


    '
    ' Since we only have a single row in our DataSet,
    ' delete it and then update the database with the
    ' change.
    '
    Public Sub Delete()
      If m_DS.Tables(0).Rows.Count > 0 Then
        m_DS.Tables(0).Rows(0).Delete()
        m_DA.Update(m_DS)
      End If
    End Sub

End Class
```

Listing 10.13   Project class (continued)

We enforce our validation rules for the tblProjects table by way of this class. Unlike some other classes we've built, all fields but the Description field are required in this table, so we have to check them all. We use the SaveRow routine to default the IsCompleted field to a zero, but we populate the rest of the fields by way of our form.

The associated exception class is called ProjectException and is shown in Listing 10.14. This exception is only generated if an attempt is made to call the Save method while data-validation errors are present in the data.

```
Public Class ProjectException
  Inherits Exception

  Public Sub New()
   MyBase.New()
  End Sub

  Public Sub New(ByVal Message As String)
   MyBase.New(Message)
  End Sub

  Public Sub New(ByVal Message As String, ByVal baseError As Exception)
   MyBase.New(Message, baseError)
  End Sub

End Class
```

Listing 10.14   ProjectException class

The next object to build links the application to the tblTasks table. The Task class is shown in Listing 10.15.

```
Imports AtWorkUtilities

Public Class Task
  Inherits BaseServices

   `
   ` If no arguments are supplied, build a separate
   ` database connection for this object.
   `
  Public Sub New()
   MyBase.New(New Database(), "SELECT * FROM tblTasks WHERE 1=0")
  End Sub


   `
   ` If database connection is supplied, store it
   ` in the private connection variable for this
   ` object.
```

Listing 10.15   Task class

```
'
Public Sub New(ByVal db As Database)
 MyBase.New(db, "SELECT * FROM tblTasks WHERE 1=0")
End Sub


'
' If both database and ID are supplied, retrieve
' data into the object from the database.
'
Public Sub New(ByVal db As Database, _
 ByVal ID As Integer)

 MyBase.New(db, "SELECT * FROM tblTasks WHERE pkTaskID = " _
   & ID.ToString)

End Sub


'
' Verify that all data validation rules have been
' met. Any errors get stored into the errors collection
' inherited from the BaseServices class.
'
Public Sub Validate()
 Dim dr As DataRow

 ClearErrors()
 For Each dr In m_DS.Tables(0).Rows
   If dr.RowState = DataRowState.Added _
   Or dr.RowState = DataRowState.Modified Then
    ValidateRow(dr)
   End If
 Next

End Sub


'
' Checks an individual row for validation rule
' compliance. Any errors are added to the errors
' collection.
'
Private Sub ValidateRow(ByVal dr As DataRow)
 If IsDBNull(dr("fkProjectID")) Then
   AddError("Project number is missing.")
 End If
 CheckRequiredField(dr, "Name", "Task name", 80)
 If IsDBNull(dr("DueDate")) Then
   AddError("Task due date is missing.")
 End If
 If IsDBNull(dr("Budget")) Then
```

Listing 10.15 Task class (continued)

```
        AddError("Budget amount is missing.")
    End If
    If IsDBNull(dr("DefaultHourlyRate")) Then
        AddError("Default hourly rate is missing.")
    End If
    If IsDBNull(dr("IsCompleted")) Then
        AddError("Completion flag is missing.")
    End If
End Sub


'
' The base Save method stores the DataRow into the
' DataSet, whether it's a new or existing row. The
' rest of this routine handles specific validation
' for this type of data.
'
Public Overloads Sub SaveRow(ByVal dr As DataRow)
    If IsDBNull(dr("Budget")) Then
        dr("Budget") = 0
    End If
    If IsDBNull(dr("DefaultHourlyRate")) Then
        dr("DefaultHourlyRate") = 0
    End If
    If IsDBNull(dr("IsCompleted")) Then
        dr("IsCompleted") = 0
    End If
    MyBase.SaveRow(dr)
    Validate()

End Sub


'
' We separate the SaveRow method from the Save method
' to give us a chance to handle any validation. We have
' a verification here that the data is good before we
' continue, however.
'
Public Sub Save()

    If Not Me.IsValid Then
        Throw New TaskException(Me.ValidationError)
        Exit Sub
    End If

    m_DA.Update(m_DS)
End Sub


'
' Since we only have a single row in our DataSet,
' delete it and then update the database with the
' change.
```

Listing 10.15   Task class (continued)

```
`
Public Sub Delete()
  If m_DS.Tables(0).Rows.Count > 0 Then
    m_DS.Tables(0).Rows(0).Delete()
    m_DA.Update(m_DS)
  End If
End Sub


End Class
```

Listing 10.15   Task class (continued)

Like the Project class, all the fields of the Task object are required except for the Description field. Any missing fields are flagged as errors and are displayed on the Web page. While the budget and default hourly-rate fields are required, they can be zero. If, for instance, you have an internal project that doesn't really have a budget, you may want to assign a zero hourly rate but still track the number of hours spent. The SaveRow method defaults these two fields, as well as the IsCompleted field, to zero.

The associated exception is called TaskException and follows the same pattern as all the other custom exception classes we've built. The code for it is shown in Listing 10.16.

```
Public Class TaskException
  Inherits Exception

  Public Sub New()
   MyBase.New()
  End Sub

  Public Sub New(ByVal Message As String)
   MyBase.New(Message)
  End Sub

  Public Sub New(ByVal Message As String, ByVal baseError As Exception)
   MyBase.New(Message, baseError)
  End Sub

End Class
```

Listing 10.16   TaskException class

The final classes you need to build relate to the timecard feature of the application. The Timecard class is shown in Listing 10.17.

```
Imports AtWorkUtilities

Public Class Timecard
  Inherits BaseServices

  `
```

Listing 10.17   Timecard class

```
' If no arguments are supplied, build a separate
' database connection for this object.
'
Public Sub New()
 MyBase.New(New Database(), "SELECT * FROM tblTimecards WHERE 1=0")
End Sub


'
' If database connection is supplied, store it
' in the private connection variable for this
' object.
'
Public Sub New(ByVal db As Database)
 MyBase.New(db, "SELECT * FROM tblTimecards WHERE 1=0")
End Sub


'
' If both database and ID are supplied, retrieve
' data into the object from the database.
'
Public Sub New(ByVal db As Database, _
 ByVal ID As Integer)

 MyBase.New(db, "SELECT * FROM tblTimecards WHERE pkTimecardID = " _
   & ID.ToString)

End Sub


'
' Verify that all data validation rules have been
' met. Any errors get stored into the errors collection
' inherited from the BaseServices class.
'
Public Sub Validate()
 Dim dr As DataRow

 ClearErrors()
 For Each dr In m_DS.Tables(0).Rows
   If dr.RowState = DataRowState.Added _
   Or dr.RowState = DataRowState.Modified Then
    ValidateRow(dr)
   End If
 Next

End Sub


'
' Checks an individual row for validation rule
' compliance. Any errors are added to the errors
' collection.
```

Listing 10.17 Timecard class (continued)

```
'
Private Sub ValidateRow(ByVal dr As DataRow)
  If IsDBNull(dr("fkTaskID")) Then
    AddError("Task number is missing.")
  End If
  If IsDBNull(dr("fkMemberID")) Then
    AddError("Member number is missing.")
  End If
  CheckRequiredField(dr, "WorkDescription", _
    "Description of work", Int32.MaxValue)
  If IsDBNull(dr("TimecardDate")) Then
    AddError("Timecard date is missing.")
  End If
  If IsDBNull(dr("HourCount")) Then
    AddError("Number of hours is missing.")
  End If
  If IsDBNull(dr("HourlyRate")) Then
    AddError("Hourly rate is missing.")
  End If
End Sub


'
' The base Save method stores the DataRow into the
' DataSet, whether it's a new or existing row. The
' rest of this routine handles specific validation
' for this type of data.
'
Public Overloads Sub SaveRow(ByVal dr As DataRow)
  If IsDBNull(dr("HourlyRate")) Then
    dr("HourlyRate") = 0
  End If
  If IsDBNull(dr("IsBilled")) Then
    dr("IsBilled") = 0
  End If
  MyBase.SaveRow(dr)
  Validate()

End Sub


'
' We separate the SaveRow method from the Save method
' to give us a chance to handle any validation. We have
' a verification here that the data is good before we
' continue, however.
'
Public Sub Save()

  If Not Me.IsValid Then
    Throw New TimecardException(Me.ValidationError)
    Exit Sub
```

Listing 10.17   Timecard class (continued)

```
      End If

   m_DA.Update(m_DS)
   End Sub


   '
   ' Since we only have a single row in our DataSet,
   ' delete it and then update the database with the
   ' change.
   '
   Public Sub Delete()
    If m_DS.Tables(0).Rows.Count > 0 Then
      m_DS.Tables(0).Rows(0).Delete()
      m_DA.Update(m_DS)
    End If
   End Sub

End Class
```

Listing 10.17 Timecard class (continued)

Every field in this class is required, so we have to validate each one. For the large text field (WorkDescription), we use the maximum length in our CheckRequiredField routine, just in case the person creating the timecard is really verbose. We also default the hourly rate and the IsBilled fields to zero if they are left blank in the SaveRow routine.

The associated exception class is called TimecardException and is shown in Listing 10.18.

```
Public Class TimecardException
   Inherits Exception

   Public Sub New()
    MyBase.New()
   End Sub

   Public Sub New(ByVal Message As String)
    MyBase.New(Message)
   End Sub

   Public Sub New(ByVal Message As String, ByVal baseError As Exception)
    MyBase.New(Message, baseError)
   End Sub


End Class
```

Listing 10.18 TimecardException class

With the business objects done, be sure to rebuild the assembly and copy it to your Web directory. The next step is to build the Web pages for this application.

Building the Web Pages

Since there are quite a few Web pages for this application, we're going to break them into logical categories related to the main objects in the system: Project, Task, and Timecard. This should make it a bit easier to follow the flow of the application in this project. Because of the large amount of data we're dealing with in these objects, these pages are generally bigger than the others you've built so far. However, we are building on what you already know, so the code should still look familiar to you.

Creating the Project Pages

We start with the pages that view and maintain the projects in the system. The first page is the one linked to the main toolbar and is called Projects.aspx. The ASPX file is shown in Listing 10.19.

```
<%@ Page Inherits="TWNW.Projects" Src="projects.aspx.vb" %>
<%@ Register Tagprefix="TWNW" Tagname="Header" Src="Header.ascx" %>
<%@ Register Tagprefix="TWNW" Tagname="Footer" Src="Footer.ascx" %>
<!DOCTYPE HTML PUBLIC "-//W3C//DTD HTML 4.0 Transitional//EN">
<html>
<head>
     <title>Teamwork Network: View Projects</title>
  <link href="styles.css" rel="stylesheet" type="text/css">
</head>

<body leftmargin=0 topmargin=0>
<TWNW:Header id="PageHeader" runat="server" />
<p class="pageheading">View Projects</p>
<p class="text">
</p>
<table cellpadding="4" cellspacing="0" width="600">
<tr class="tableheading">
  <td width="80%">Team Name</td>
  <td width="20%">Total Projects</td>
</tr>
<asp:label id="lblContent" runat="server" />
</table>
</body>
</html>
<TWNW:Footer id="PageFooter" runat="server" />
</body>
</html>
```

Listing 10.19   projects.aspx

This page is designed to show just the team name and the number of projects associated with the team. This page performs two queries to do this, so we have to build the content table ourselves. We have a label control called lblContent into which we'll put the HTML that we generate in our code. The code behind this page is shown in Listing 10.20.

```
Imports System
Imports System.Data
Imports System.Web
Imports System.Web.UI
Imports System.Web.UI.WebControls
Imports System.Data.SqlClient
Imports TWNWObjects


Namespace TWNW
  Public Class Projects
    Inherits Page

    Protected lblContent As Label

    Sub Page_Load(objSender As Object, objArgs As EventArgs)
      If (Request.Cookies("mID") Is Nothing) Then
        Response.Redirect("login.aspx?msg=403&rURL=" _
          & Request.ServerVariables("SCRIPT_NAME") _
          & "?" _
          & Request.ServerVariables("QUERY_STRING"))
      End If

      Dim DB As New AtWorkUtilities.Database()
      Dim DB2 As New AtWorkUtilities.Database()
      Dim DR, DR2 As SqlDataReader
      Dim strContent As New System.Text.StringBuilder()
      Dim strColor As String = "tabletext"


      '
      ' Check for any new postings in the member's teams
      ' or in the public forum.
      '
      DR = DB.GetDataReader("sp_RetrieveTeamsByMember " _
        & Request.Cookies("mID").Value, True)
      While DR.Read()
        strContent.AppendFormat("<tr class=""{0}""><td>", strColor)
        strContent.AppendFormat("<a href=""projects_view.aspx" _
          & "?tID={0}"">", _
          DR("pkTeamID"))
        strContent.AppendFormat("{0}</a></td>", DR("Name"))
        DR2 = DB2.GetDataReader("sp_RetrieveProjectCountByTeam " _
          & DR("pkTeamID"))
        If DR2("Total") = 0 Then
          strContent.Append("<td align=middle>None</td>")
```

Listing 10.20   projects.aspx.vb

```
        Else
          strContent.AppendFormat("<td align=middle>{0}</td>", _
            DR2("Total"))
        End If
        strContent.Append("</tr>")
        If strColor = "tabletext" Then
          strColor = "tabletext_gray"
        Else
          strColor = "tabletext"
        End If
        strContent.Append(Environment.NewLine)
        DR2.Close()
      End While
      lblContent.Text = strContent.ToString()
      DR.Close()
    End Sub
  End Class
End Namespace
```

Listing 10.20   projects.aspx.vb (continued)

We use the sp_RetrieveTeamsByMember stored procedure as the outer loop of this page. For each team that we display, we need to look up the number of projects associated with that team. We use a second Database object here, since we can only have a single SqlDataReader open at a time per connection. We run the sp_RetrieveProject-CountByTeam stored procedure, get our result back, and put it into the HTML. Once we've displayed the data, we close the second SqlDataReader object and repeat the process.

The next page the user would see shows all the projects for a particular team. The code for this page is shown in Listing 10.21.

```
<%@ Page Inherits="TWNW.ProjectsView" Src="projects_view.aspx.vb" %>
<%@ Register Tagprefix="TWNW" Tagname="Header" Src="Header.ascx" %>
<%@ Register Tagprefix="TWNW" Tagname="Footer" Src="Footer.ascx" %>
<!DOCTYPE HTML PUBLIC "-//W3C//DTD HTML 4.0 Transitional//EN">
<html>
<head>
      <title>Teamwork Network: View Team Projects</title>
  <link href="styles.css" rel="stylesheet" type="text/css">
</head>

<body leftmargin=0 topmargin=0>
<TWNW:Header id="PageHeader" runat="server" />
<asp:label id="lblPageTitle" class="pageheading" runat="server" />
<p class="text">
<a href="project_create.aspx?tID=<% = Request.QueryString("tID")
```

Listing 10.21   projects_view.aspx

```
%>">Create a Project</a></p>
<table cellpadding="4" cellspacing="0" width="100%">
<tr class="tableheading">
  <td width="20%">Name</td>
  <td width="20%">Project Lead</td>
  <td width="40%">Description</td>
  <td width="20%">Due Date</td>
</tr>
<asp:label id="lblContent" runat="server" />
</table>
</body>
</html>
<TWNW:Footer id="PageFooter" runat="server" />
</body>
</html>
```

Listing 10.21   projects_view.aspx (continued)

We're using the same page-design model here to show the projects for the team so that we can show the due date in an alternate color. In some of the other pages, we'll do the same thing by way of the stored procedure. Both methods are shown here so that you can get ideas for your own applications.

At the top of the page, a link is displayed for users who want to create a new project. In order to create a new project, you need a team ID. By generating the link in this way, you force the team ID to always be supplied. This prevents errors later on.

The Visual Basic code behind this file is shown in Listing 10.22.

```
Imports System
Imports System.Data
Imports System.Data.SqlClient
Imports System.Web
Imports System.Web.UI
Imports System.Web.UI.WebControls
Imports TWNWObjects

Namespace TWNW
  Public Class ProjectsView
    Inherits Page

    Protected lblPageTitle As Label
    Protected lblContent As Label

    Sub Page_Load(objSender As Object, objArgs As EventArgs)
      Dim strColor As String = "tabletext"

      If (Request.Cookies("mID") Is Nothing) Then
        Response.Redirect("login.aspx?msg=403&rURL=" _
```

Listing 10.22   projects_view.aspx.vb

```
            & Request.ServerVariables("SCRIPT_NAME") _
            & "?" _
            & Request.ServerVariables("QUERY_STRING"))
        End If


        Dim DB As New AtWorkUtilities.Database()
        Dim objReader As SqlDataReader
        Dim T As New Team(DB, Request.QueryString("tID"))
        Dim DR As DataRow = T.GetRow()
        Dim strOutput As New System.Text.StringBuilder()
        Dim strFont As String = "#000000"


        lblPageTitle.Text = DR("Name") & " Projects"
        objReader = DB.GetDataReader("sp_RetrieveProjectsByTeam " _
         & Request.QueryString("tID"), True)
        Do While objReader.Read()
         strOutput.AppendFormat("<tr class=""{0}"">", _
            strColor)
         strOutput.AppendFormat("<td>{0}</td>", _
            objReader("ProjectName"))
         strOutput.AppendFormat("<td>{0}</td>", _
            objReader("ProjectLead"))
         strOutput.AppendFormat("<td>{0}</td>", _
            objReader("Description"))
         If DateTime.Compare(objReader("DueDate"), _
            DateTime.Now()) < 0 Then
            strFont = "#FF0000"
         Else
            strFont = "#000000"
         End If
         strOutput.Append("<td align=""center"">")
         strOutput.AppendFormat("<font color=""{0}"">{1}</font></td>", _
            strFont, objReader("DueDate").ToShortDateString)
         strOutput.Append("</tr>" & Environment.NewLine)
         If strColor = "tabletext" Then
            strColor = "tabletext_gray"
         Else
            strColor = "tabletext"
         End If
        Loop
        DB.Close()
        lblContent.Text = strOutput.ToString()
    End Sub
  End Class
End Namespace
```

Listing 10.22 projects_view.aspx.vb (continued)

This page uses the Team object to retrieve the name of the team. An ASP.NET label control is used to restrict the page title to the lower corner of the main area of the window. We then instruct the routine to retrieve the projects for the particular team being viewed and start building our table. We're marking any tasks that are late (due date is less than the current date) in red through Visual Basic code instead of directly in the stored procedure. When we're done building the table, we store it in the label control on the page.

Now a user can create a new project from this page. The code for the ASPX file is shown in Listing 10.23.

```
<%@ Page Inherits="TWNW.ProjectCreate" Src="project_create.aspx.vb" %>
<%@ Register Tagprefix="TWNW" Tagname="Header" Src="Header.ascx" %>
<%@ Register Tagprefix="TWNW" Tagname="Footer" Src="Footer.ascx" %>
<!DOCTYPE HTML PUBLIC "-//W3C//DTD HTML 4.0 Transitional//EN">
<html>
<head>
  <title>Teamwork Network: Project Management</title>
  <link href="styles.css" rel="stylesheet" type="text/css">
</head>
<body>
<TWNW:Header id="PageHeader" runat="server" />
<table width="600">
<tr>
<td valign="top" width="600">

<p><asp:label id="lblPageTitle" class="pageheading" runat="server"
/></p>
<asp:label id="lblErrorMessage" class="errortext" runat="server" />

<form runat="server">
<input type="hidden" runat="server" id="pkProjectID">
<input type="hidden" runat="server" id="fkTeamID">

<table cellspacing="5">
<tr class="tabletext">
  <td align="right">Name:</td>
  <td>
  <asp:textbox
    id="txtName"
    columns="40"
    maxlength="80"
    runat="server" />
  </td>
</tr>
<tr class="tabletext">
  <td valign="middle" align="right">
  Description:
  </td>
  <td>
```

Listing 10.23   project_create.aspx

```
  <asp:textbox
   id="txtDescription"
   rows="10"
   columns="40"
   wrap="true"
   textmode="Multiline"
   runat="server" />
  </td>
</tr>
<tr class="tabletext">
  <td align="right">Start Date:</td>
  <td>
  <asp:textbox
   id="txtStartDate"
   columns="20"
   maxlength="20"
   runat="server" />
  </td>
</tr>
<tr class="tabletext">
  <td align="right">Due Date:</td>
  <td>
  <asp:textbox
   id="txtDueDate"
   columns="20"
   maxlength="20"
   runat="server" />
  </td>
</tr>
<tr class="tabletext">
  <td align="right">Complete?</td>
  <td>
  <asp:checkbox
   id="chkIsComplete"
   value="Y"
   runat="server" />
  </td>
</tr>

<tr class="tabletext">
  <td colspan=2 align=middle>
  <input type="submit"
   name="btnSubmit"
   runat="server"
   value="Save" />
  <input type="reset"
   name="btnReset"
   runat="server"
   value="Clear" />
  </td>
```

Listing 10.23   project_create.aspx (continued)

```
</tr>
</table>
</form>
</td>
</tr>
</table>
<TWNW:Footer id="PageFooter" runat="server" />
</body>
</html>
```

Listing 10.23   project_create.aspx (continued)

This ASPX file is a standard data-entry form similar to the others we've built for the Teamwork Network application. We provide reasonable space for the dates required, since it's hard to have a maximum length for the date. October 21, 2001, is just as valid a date as 10/1/2001. Pick a reasonable amount, and let the code-behind and the object take care of the parsing and validation.

The code behind this page is shown in Listing 10.24.

```
Imports System
Imports System.Data
Imports System.Data.SqlClient
Imports System.Web
Imports System.Web.UI
Imports System.Web.UI.WebControls
Imports TWNWObjects

Namespace TWNW
  Public Class ProjectCreate
    Inherits System.Web.UI.Page

    Protected pkProjectID As HTMLControls.HTMLInputHidden
    Protected fkTeamID As HTMLControls.HTMLInputHidden
    Protected txtName As TextBox
    Protected txtDescription As TextBox
    Protected txtStartDate As TextBox
    Protected txtDueDate As TextBox
    Protected chkIsComplete As CheckBox

    Protected lblPageTitle As Label
    Protected lblErrorMessage As Label

    Sub Page_Load(objSender As Object, objArgs As EventArgs)
      Dim DB As New AtWorkUtilities.Database()
      Dim P As Project
      Dim DR As DataRow
      Dim objCookie As HTTPCookie
```

Listing 10.24   project_create.aspx.vb

```
objCookie = Request.Cookies("mID")

If Not Page.IsPostBack Then
 If Request.QueryString("ID") <> "" Then
   lblPageTitle.Text = "Edit Project"
   P = New Project(DB, Request.QueryString("ID"))
   DR = P.GetRow()
   pkProjectID.Value = DR("pkProjectID").ToString()
   fkTeamID.Value = DR("fkTeamID").ToString()
   txtName.Text = DR("Name").ToString()
   txtDescription.Text = DR("Description").ToString()
   txtStartDate.Text = DR("StartDate").ToShortDateString()
   txtDueDate.Text = DR("DueDate").ToShortDateString()
   chkIsComplete.Checked = DR("IsCompleted")
 Else
   lblPageTitle.Text = "Create New Project"
   fkTeamID.Value = Request.QueryString("tID")
 End If
Else
 If pkProjectID.Value = "" Then
   P = New Project(DB)
 Else
   P = New Project(DB, pkProjectID.Value)
 End If
 DR = P.GetRow()
 DR("Name") = txtName.Text
 DR("Description") = txtDescription.Text
 DR("fkTeamID") = fkTeamID.Value
 DR("fkCreatorID") = objCookie.Value
 Try
   DR("StartDate") = DateTime.Parse(txtStartDate.Text)
 Catch ex As Exception
 ' do nothing, object handles missing data
 End Try
 Try
   DR("DueDate") = DateTime.Parse(txtDueDate.Text)
 Catch ex As Exception
 ' do nothing, object handles missing data
 End Try
 DR("IsCompleted") = chkIsComplete.Checked
 P.SaveRow(DR)
 If Not P.IsValid Then
   lblErrorMessage.Text = _
     P.ValidationError("<b>ERROR:</b> The following " _
       & "errors were detected in your data:<br>", _
       "&bull; {0}<br>", "")
 Else
   P.Save()
   DB.Close()
   Response.Redirect("projects_view.aspx?tID=" _
```

Listing 10.24 project_create.aspx.vb (continued)

```
            & fkTeamID.Value)
        End If
      End If
    End Sub
  End Class
End Namespace
```

Listing 10.24   project_create.aspx.vb (continued)

We're going to use this page for both creating new projects and editing existing ones, so we need the code to load the form if an ID is supplied. For creating new projects, the previous page will pass a value for the tID value in the query string. For editing an existing project, a page will pass the ID of the project in the ID value in the query string. This keeps things simple, and there is no confusion as to what the value means at what time.

We populate the form and save data using the Project object. The team ID is passed between the modes of the form through the hidden-input field and is stored in the Project object along with the member ID of the user. The member ID comes from the cookie we created when the member logged in to the system. Other than those fields, the rest of the data comes directly from the input form. For the IsCompleted field, which is stored as a bit value in SQL Server, we can store a Visual Basic .NET True or False value in the DataRow. The DataRow will properly interpret a True or False value as a zero or one, respectively, and no further conversion is required. The same thing is true when we are loading the form with existing data. We set the Checked property of the check box equal to the IsCompleted value, and the box is marked or cleared accordingly.

Once members have added timecards to the system, the project lead has the option to generate an invoice. The Invoice page is shown without the normal page headers and footers for easier printing. The ASPX file is shown in Listing 10.25.

```
<%@ Page Inherits="TWNW.ProjectInvoice" Src="project_invoice.aspx.vb" %>
<!DOCTYPE HTML PUBLIC "-//W3C//DTD HTML 4.0 Transitional//EN">
<html>
<head>
     <title>Teamwork Network: Generate Project Invoice</title>
  <link href="styles.css" rel="stylesheet" type="text/css">
</head>

<body>
<p class="pageheading">Project Invoice</p>

<table width="600" cellspacing="0" cellpadding="4" border="1">
<tr>
  <td width="100" class="tabletext_gray" align="right">Project
Name:</td>
  <td width="500" class="tabletext">
   <asp:label id="lblName" runat="server" />
  </td>
```

Listing 10.25   project_invoice.aspx

```
    </tr>
    <tr>
     <td width="100" class="tabletext_gray" align="right">Project
Lead:</td>
     <td width="500" class="tabletext">
      <asp:label id="lblProjectLead" runat="server" />
     </td>
    </tr>
    <tr>
     <td width="100" class="tabletext_gray" align="right">Invoice
Date:</td>
     <td width="500" class="tabletext">
      <asp:label id="lblInvoiceDate" runat="server" />
     </td>
    </tr>
    <tr>
     <td width="100" class="tabletext_gray" align="right">Invoice
Amount:</td>
     <td width="500" class="tabletext">
      <asp:label id="lblInvoiceAmount" runat="server" />
     </td>
    </tr>
    </table>

    <asp:label id="lblMessage" class="text" runat="server" />
    <asp:Repeater id="rptList" runat="server">
     <HeaderTemplate>
     <p class="subheading">Detail of Work Performed</p>
     <table cellpadding="4" cellspacing="0" width="100%">
     <tr class="tableheading">
     <td width="5%">Date</td>
     <td width="20%">Team Member</td>
     <td width="20%">Task</td>
     <td width="35%">Work Performed</td>
     <td width="5%">Hours</td>
     <td width="5%">Rate</td>
     <td width="10%">Total</td>
     </tr>
     </HeaderTemplate>
     <ItemTemplate>
     <tr class="tabletext">
     <td align="center"><%# DataBinder.Eval(Container.DataItem, _
      "TimecardDate").ToShortDateString() %></td>
     <td><%# DataBinder.Eval(Container.DataItem, _
      "MemberName") %></td>
     <td><%# DataBinder.Eval(Container.DataItem, _
      "TaskName") %></td>
     <td><%# DataBinder.Eval(Container.DataItem, _
      "WorkDescription") %></td>
     <td align=center><%# DataBinder.Eval(Container.DataItem, _
```

Listing 10.25   project_invoice.aspx (continued)

```
 "HourCount") %></td>
<td align=right><%# DataBinder.Eval(Container.DataItem, _
 "Rate") %></td>
<td align=right><%# DataBinder.Eval(Container.DataItem, _
 "TimecardTotal") %></td>
</tr>
</ItemTemplate>
<AlternatingItemTemplate>
<tr class="tabletext_gray">
<td align="center"><%# DataBinder.Eval(Container.DataItem, _
 "TimecardDate").ToShortDateString() %></td>
<td><%# DataBinder.Eval(Container.DataItem, _
 "MemberName") %></td>
<td><%# DataBinder.Eval(Container.DataItem, _
 "TaskName") %></td>
<td><%# DataBinder.Eval(Container.DataItem, _
 "WorkDescription") %></td>
<td align=center><%# DataBinder.Eval(Container.DataItem, _
 "HourCount") %></td>
<td align=right><%# DataBinder.Eval(Container.DataItem, _
 "Rate") %></td>
<td align=right><%# DataBinder.Eval(Container.DataItem, _
 "TimecardTotal") %></td>
</tr>
</AlternatingItemTemplate>
<FooterTemplate>
</table>
</FooterTemplate>
</asp:Repeater>

</p>
</body>
</html>
```

Listing 10.25   project_invoice.aspx (continued)

This page is similar to the task viewer that you'll build later in that it shows all the timecards for a specific task. However, the difference is that it displays all the unbilled timecards for an entire project, sorted by date. The code behind this page is shown in Listing 10.26.

```
Imports System
Imports System.Data
Imports System.Data.SqlClient
Imports System.Web
Imports System.Web.UI
Imports System.Web.UI.WebControls
```

Listing 10.26   project_invoice.aspx.vb

```
Imports TWNWObjects

Namespace TWNW
  Public Class ProjectInvoice
    Inherits System.Web.UI.Page

    Protected lblMessage As Label
    Protected lblName As Label
    Protected lblProjectLead As Label
    Protected lblInvoiceDate As Label
    Protected lblInvoiceAmount As Label
    Protected rptList As Repeater

    Sub Page_Load(objSender As Object, objArgs As EventArgs)
      If (Request.Cookies("mID") Is Nothing) Then
        Response.Redirect("login.aspx?msg=403&rURL=" _
          & Request.ServerVariables("SCRIPT_NAME") _
          & "?" _
          & Request.ServerVariables("QUERY_STRING"))
      End If

      Dim DB As New AtWorkUtilities.Database()
      Dim DR As SqlDataReader = _
        DB.GetDataReader("sp_RetrieveProjectDetails " _
        & Request.QueryString("ID"))
      lblName.Text = DR("Name")
      lblProjectLead.Text = DR("ProjectLead")
      lblInvoiceDate.Text = DateTime.Now.ToShortDateString()
      DR.Close()
      DR = DB.GetDataReader("sp_RetrieveUnbilledTotalByProject " _
        & Request.QueryString("ID"))
      lblInvoiceAmount.Text = DR("InvoiceTotal")
      DR.Close()

      Dim DS As DataSet = _
        DB.GetDataSet("sp_RetrieveUnbilledTimecardsByProject " _
        & Request.QueryString("ID"))
      If DS.Tables(0).Rows.Count = 0 Then
        lblMessage.Text = "<br><br><b>All work in this " _
          & "project has been billed.</b>"
      Else
        rptList.DataSource = DS
        rptList.DataBind()
      End If
      db.Close()
    End Sub
  End Class
End Namespace
```

Listing 10.26 project_invoice.aspx.vb (continued)

We're letting the stored procedure do most of the work to display the lower grid. It returns all the appropriate fields for display in the right formats (commas and two decimal places for currency amounts) so we don't need a lot of code to show the data. The rest of the information comes from the sp_RetrieveProjectDetails stored procedure that we used in the project view.

Along with showing the invoice, we need a way to mark all the unbilled items as billed. This is done using a pair of short files shown in Listing 10.27 (ASPX file) and Listing 10.28 (VB file). There is no visual component to the file, so the ASPX file is just the @Page directive.

```
<%@ Page Inherits="TWNW.ProjectBill" Src="project_bill.aspx.vb" %>
```

Listing 10.27   project_bill.aspx

The code behind this page is shown in Listing 10.28.

```
Imports System
Imports System.Web.UI

Namespace TWNW
  Public Class ProjectBill
    Inherits Page

    Private Sub Page_Load(ByVal sender As System.Object, _
      ByVal e As System.EventArgs) Handles MyBase.Load

    Dim DB As New AtWorkUtilities.Database()
    DB.Execute("sp_UpdateTimecardsByProject " _
      & Request.QueryString("ID"))
    Response.Redirect("project_view.aspx?id=" _
      & Request.QueryString("ID"))
  End Sub
  End Class
End Namespace
```

Listing 10.28   project_bill.aspx.vb

This is a short page since it only has one task: To run the stored procedure that you wrote to update the timecards as billed. This page is only shown to the owner of the project, but if you want to, you can add more security here in case a malicious user wanted to run the page by handcrafting a URL. For our purposes, we are working on the assumption that you trust the users on the system not to do this.

The last maintenance function required is the ability to delete projects. This action is only available if no tasks have been added to the project. The ASPX page for this is shown in Listing 10.29.

```
<%@ Page Inherits="TWNW.ProjectDelete" Src="project_delete.aspx.vb" %>
<%@ Register Tagprefix="TWNW" Tagname="Header" Src="Header.ascx" %>
<%@ Register Tagprefix="TWNW" Tagname="Footer" Src="Footer.ascx" %>
<!DOCTYPE HTML PUBLIC "-//W3C//DTD HTML 4.0 Transitional//EN">
<html>
<head>
  <title>Teamwork Network: Project Management</title>
  <link href="styles.css" rel="stylesheet" type="text/css">
</head>
<body>
<TWNW:Header id="PageHeader" runat="server" />
<p class="pageheading">Delete Project</p>
<p class="text">Are you sure you want to delete this project?</p>
<form runat="server" id="deleteForm">
<input type="hidden" runat="server" id="pkID">
<p class="text">
<a href="javascript:document.deleteForm.submit();">Yes</a>
  
<a href="javascript:history.go(-1);">No</a>
</p>
</form>
<TWNW:Footer id="PageFooter" runat="server" />
</body>
</html>
```

Listing 10.29   project_delete.aspx

As compared to previous delete pages, we've made a few minor changes to the control and form names. The hidden ID field is called pkID instead of something specific to the project, and the name of the form is deleteForm. This makes it easier to duplicate this page for other entity types. The code behind this page is shown in Listing 10.30.

```
Imports System
Imports System.Data
Imports System.Web.UI
Imports System.Web.UI.WebControls
Imports TWNWObjects

Namespace TWNW
  Public Class ProjectDelete
    Inherits System.Web.UI.Page

    Protected pkID As HTMLControls.HTMLInputHidden

    Sub Page_Load(objSender As Object, objArgs As EventArgs)
      If Not Page.IsPostBack Then
        pkID.Value = Request.QueryString("ID")
```

Listing 10.30   project_delete.aspx.vb

```
      Else
        Dim DB As New AtWorkUtilities.Database()
        Dim obj As New Project(DB, pkID.Value)
        Dim DR As DataRow = obj.GetRow()
        Dim intParent As Integer = DR("fkTeamID")
        DR = Nothing
        obj.Delete()
        obj = Nothing
        DB.Close()
        Response.Redirect("projects_view.aspx?tID=" & intParent)
      End If
    End Sub
  End Class
End Namespace
```

Listing 10.30   project_delete.aspx.vb (continued)

When we're done deleting the project, we go back to the team project viewer. In order to do this, we have to first recover the team ID from the project we're deleting. This is easy to do, since we can retrieve a DataRow from the Project object and keep the team ID in the intParent variable created here.

With that page done, it's time to move on to the pages dealing with project-associated tasks.

Creating the Task Pages

The next step is to build the pages dealing with the viewing, creation, editing, and deletion of tasks. These pages follow the same patterns as the pages for projects, but they use different fields and have some extra features. The first exposure a user has to tasks is on the project-viewing page, where he or she can select a task to view. This page shows the task information, as well as any timecards generated by members on this task. The code for this page is shown in Listing 10.31.

```
<%@ Page Inherits="TWNW.TaskView" Src="task_view.aspx.vb" %>
<%@ Register Tagprefix="TWNW" Tagname="Header" Src="Header.ascx" %>
<%@ Register Tagprefix="TWNW" Tagname="Footer" Src="Footer.ascx" %>
<!DOCTYPE HTML PUBLIC "-//W3C//DTD HTML 4.0 Transitional//EN">
<html>
<head>
     <title>Teamwork Network: View Task</title>
  <link href="styles.css" rel="stylesheet" type="text/css">
</head>

<body leftmargin=0 topmargin=0>
<TWNW:Header id="PageHeader" runat="server" />
<p class="pageheading">View Task Details</p>
```

Listing 10.31   task_view.aspx

```
<table width="600" cellspacing="0" cellpadding="4" border="1">
<tr>
  <td width="100" class="tabletext_gray" align="right">Task Name:</td>
  <td width="500" class="tabletext">
   <asp:label id="lblName" runat="server" />
  </td>
</tr>
<tr>
  <td width="100" class="tabletext_gray" align="right">Description:</td>
  <td width="500" class="tabletext">
   <asp:label id="lblDescription" runat="server" />
  </td>
</tr>
<tr>
  <td width="100" class="tabletext_gray" align="right">Due Date:</td>
  <td width="500" class="tabletext">
   <asp:label id="lblDueDate" runat="server" />
  </td>
</tr>
<tr>
  <td width="100" class="tabletext_gray" align="right">Task Budget:</td>
  <td width="500" class="tabletext">
  <asp:label id="lblBudget" runat="server" />
  </td>
</tr>
<tr>
  <td width="100" class="tabletext_gray" align="right">Hours Spent:</td>
  <td width="500" class="tabletext">
  <asp:label id="lblHourTotal" runat="server" />
  </td>
</tr>
<tr>
  <td width="100" class="tabletext_gray" align="right">Budget
Spent:</td>
  <td width="500" class="tabletext">
  <asp:label id="lblDollarTotal" runat="server" />
  </td>
</tr>
<tr>
  <td width="100" class="tabletext_gray" align="right">Actions:</td>
  <td width="500" class="tabletext">
   <asp:label id="lblActions" runat="server" />
  </td>
</tr>
</table>

<p class="subheading">Work Performed</p>

<asp:label id="lblMessage" class="text" runat="server" />
  <asp:Repeater id="rptList" runat="server">
  <HeaderTemplate>
```

Listing 10.31   task_view.aspx (continued)

```
    <table cellpadding="4" cellspacing="0" width="100%">
    <tr class="tableheading">
    <td width="20%">Date</td>
    <td width="25%">Member Name</td>
    <td width="40%">Description</td>
    <td width="5%">Billed Hours</td>
    <td width="5%">Billing Rate</td>
    <td width="5%">Billed?</td>
    </tr>
    </HeaderTemplate>
    <ItemTemplate>
    <tr class="tabletext">
    <td><%# DataBinder.Eval(Container.DataItem, _
      "CardDate") %></td>
    <td><%# DataBinder.Eval(Container.DataItem, _
      "MemberName") %></td>
    <td><%# DataBinder.Eval(Container.DataItem, _
      "WorkDescription") %></td>
    <td align=center><%# DataBinder.Eval(Container.DataItem, _
      "HourCount") %></td>
    <td align=center><%# DataBinder.Eval(Container.DataItem, _
      "Rate") %></td>
    <td align=center><%# DataBinder.Eval(Container.DataItem, _
      "BilledStatus") %></td>
    </tr>
    </ItemTemplate>
    <AlternatingItemTemplate>
    <tr class="tabletext_gray">
    <td><%# DataBinder.Eval(Container.DataItem, _
      "CardDate") %></td>
    <td><%# DataBinder.Eval(Container.DataItem, _
      "MemberName") %></td>
    <td><%# DataBinder.Eval(Container.DataItem, _
      "WorkDescription") %></td>
    <td align=center><%# DataBinder.Eval(Container.DataItem, _
      "HourCount") %></td>
    <td align=center><%# DataBinder.Eval(Container.DataItem, _
      "Rate") %></td>
    <td align=center><%# DataBinder.Eval(Container.DataItem, _
      "BilledStatus") %></td>
    </tr>
    </AlternatingItemTemplate>
    <FooterTemplate>
    </table>
    </FooterTemplate>
</asp:Repeater>
<p class="text"><asp:label id="lblReturn" runat="server" /></p>
</body>
</html>
<TWNW:Footer id="PageFooter" runat="server" />
</body>
</html>
```

Listing 10.31   task_view.aspx (continued)

This page uses a mix of label controls and the Repeater control to show both the summary information about the task and the timecards that have already been entered for this task. Most of the actions shown in the Actions box are only available to the owner of the project. The exception is the Add New Timecard action, which is available to all members of the team who can see this project. The code behind this page is shown in Listing 10.32.

```
Imports System
Imports System.Data
Imports System.Data.SqlClient
Imports System.Web
Imports System.Web.UI
Imports System.Web.UI.WebControls
Imports TWNWObjects

Namespace TWNW
  Public Class TaskView
    Inherits System.Web.UI.Page

    Protected lblMessage As Label
    Protected lblName As Label
    Protected lblDescription As Label
    Protected lblDueDate As Label
    Protected lblActions As Label
    Protected lblBudget As Label
    Protected lblDollarTotal As Label
    Protected lblHourTotal As Label
    Protected lblReturn As Label
    Protected rptList As Repeater

    Sub Page_Load(objSender As Object, objArgs As EventArgs)
      If (Request.Cookies("mID") Is Nothing) Then
        Response.Redirect("login.aspx?msg=403&rURL=" _
          & Request.ServerVariables("SCRIPT_NAME") _
          & "?" _
          & Request.ServerVariables("QUERY_STRING"))
      End If

      Dim DB As New AtWorkUtilities.Database()
      Dim objCookie As HTTPCookie
      Dim SB As New Text.StringBuilder()

      objCookie = Request.Cookies("mID")
      Dim DR As SqlDataReader = _
        DB.GetDataReader("sp_RetrieveTaskDetails " _
        & Request.QueryString("ID"))
      lblName.Text = DR("Name")
```

Listing 10.32 task_view.aspx.vb

```
        lblDescription.Text = DR("Description")
        If DateTime.Compare(DR("DueDate"), DateTime.Now) < 0 Then
          lblDueDate.Text = "<font color=""#FF0000"">" _
            & DR("DueDate").ToShortDateString() _
            & "</font>"
        Else
          lblDueDate.Text = _
            DR("DueDate").ToShortDateString()
        End If
        SB.AppendFormat("<a href=""tcard_create.aspx?tID={0}"">", _
          DR("pkTaskID"))
        SB.Append("Add New Timecard</a><br>")
        If objCookie.Value = DR("fkCreatorID") Then
          SB.AppendFormat("<a href=""task_create.aspx?ID={0}"">", _
            DR("pkTaskID"))
          SB.Append("Update Task</a><br>")
          If DR("TimecardCount") = 0 Then
            SB.AppendFormat("<a href=""task_delete.aspx?ID={0}"">", _
              DR("pkTaskID"))
            SB.Append("Delete Task</a><br>")
          End If
        End If
        lblActions.Text = SB.ToString()
        lblBudget.Text = DR("TaskBudget")
        lblDollarTotal.Text = DR("TaskTotal")
        lblHourTotal.Text = DR("TaskHours")

        lblReturn.Text = "<a href=""project_view.aspx?ID=" _
          & DR("fkProjectID") _
          & """>" _
          & "Return to Project View</a>"
        DR.Close()

        Dim DS As DataSet = _
          DB.GetDataSet("sp_RetrieveTimecardsByTask " _
          & Request.QueryString("ID") _
          & ", " & Request.Cookies("mID").Value)
        If DS.Tables(0).Rows.Count = 0 Then
          lblMessage.Text = "<b>No timecards have been recorded " _
            & "for this task.</b>"
        Else
          rptList.DataSource = DS
          rptList.DataBind()
        End If
        db.Close()
      End Sub
    End Class
End Namespace
```

Listing 10.32   task_view.aspx.vb (continued)

After retrieving all the details on a task, we fill in the various fields on the page with the information from the SqlDataReader object. Some of the information comes from the Project object, but some of it does not, so a single stored procedure is a better choice than having multiple objects plus a stored procedure to populate the page.

The project leader has the option to create a task from the project viewer or to update the task details from this page. Both requests go to the same file, which is shown in Listing 10.33.

```
<%@ Page Inherits="TWNW.TaskCreate" Src="task_create.aspx.vb" %>
<%@ Register Tagprefix="TWNW" Tagname="Header" Src="Header.ascx" %>
<%@ Register Tagprefix="TWNW" Tagname="Footer" Src="Footer.ascx" %>
<!DOCTYPE HTML PUBLIC "-//W3C//DTD HTML 4.0 Transitional//EN">
<html>
<head>
  <title>Teamwork Network: Task Management</title>
  <link href="styles.css" rel="stylesheet" type="text/css">
</head>
<body>
<TWNW:Header id="PageHeader" runat="server" />
<table width="600">
<tr>
<td valign="top" width="600">

<p><asp:label id="lblPageTitle" class="pageheading" runat="server"
/></p>
<asp:label id="lblErrorMessage" class="errortext" runat="server" />

<form runat="server">
<input type="hidden" runat="server" id="pkTaskID">
<input type="hidden" runat="server" id="fkProjectID">

<table cellspacing="5">
<tr class="tabletext">
  <td align="right">Name:</td>
  <td>
  <asp:textbox
   id="txtName"
   columns="40"
   maxlength="80"
   runat="server" />
  </td>
</tr>
<tr class="tabletext">
  <td valign="middle" align="right">
  Description:
  </td>
  <td>
  <asp:textbox
   id="txtDescription"
   rows="10"
```

Listing 10.33   task_create.aspx

```
columns="40"
   wrap="true"
   textmode="Multiline"
   runat="server" />
   </td>
</tr>
<tr class="tabletext">
   <td align="right">Due Date:</td>
   <td>
   <asp:textbox
    id="txtDueDate"
    columns="20"
    maxlength="20"
    runat="server" />
   </td>
</tr>
<tr class="tabletext">
   <td align="right">Budget:</td>
   <td>
   <asp:textbox
    id="txtBudget"
    columns="20"
    maxlength="20"
    runat="server" />
   </td>
</tr>
<tr class="tabletext">
   <td align="right">Default Hourly Rate:</td>
   <td>
   <asp:textbox
    id="txtDefaultHourlyRate"
    columns="20"
    maxlength="20"
    runat="server" />
   </td>
</tr>
<tr class="tabletext">
   <td align="right">Complete?</td>
   <td>
   <asp:checkbox
    id="chkIsCompleted"
    value="Y"
    runat="server" />
   </td>
</tr>

<tr class="tabletext">
   <td colspan=2 align=middle>
   <input type="submit"
    name="btnSubmit"
```

Listing 10.33   task_create.aspx (continued)

```
     runat="server"
     value="Save" />
   <input type="reset"
    name="btnReset"
    runat="server"
    value="Clear" />
   </td>
 </tr>
 </table>
 </form>
 </td>
 </tr>
 </table>
 <TWNW:Footer id="PageFooter" runat="server" />
 </body>
 </html>
```

Listing 10.33　task_create.aspx (continued)

This is a standard data-entry form, similar to the others we've built. For a new task, we submit the project ID that this task will be associated with and store that in a hidden-input field. For an existing task, we store the current task ID in the other hidden-input field. The Visual Basic code behind this page is shown in Listing 10.34.

```
Imports System
Imports System.Data
Imports System.Data.SqlClient
Imports System.Web
Imports System.Web.UI
Imports System.Web.UI.WebControls
Imports TWNWObjects

Namespace TWNW
  Public Class TaskCreate
   Inherits System.Web.UI.Page

    Protected pkTaskID As HTMLControls.HTMLInputHidden
    Protected fkProjectID As HTMLControls.HTMLInputHidden
    Protected txtName As TextBox
    Protected txtDescription As TextBox
    Protected txtDueDate As TextBox
    Protected txtBudget As TextBox
    Protected txtDefaultHourlyRate As TextBox
    Protected chkIsCompleted As CheckBox

    Protected lblPageTitle As Label
    Protected lblErrorMessage As Label
```

Listing 10.34　task_create.aspx.vb

```
Sub Page_Load(objSender As Object, objArgs As EventArgs)
  Dim DB As New AtWorkUtilities.Database()
  Dim obj As Task
  Dim DR As DataRow
  Dim objCookie As HTTPCookie
  objCookie = Request.Cookies("mID")

  If Not Page.IsPostBack Then
   If Request.QueryString("ID") <> "" Then
     lblPageTitle.Text = "Edit Task"
     obj = New Task(DB, Request.QueryString("ID"))
     DR = obj.GetRow()
     pkTaskID.Value = DR("pkTaskID").ToString()
     fkProjectID.Value = DR("fkProjectID").ToString()
     txtName.Text = DR("Name").ToString()
     txtDescription.Text = DR("Description").ToString()
     txtDueDate.Text = DR("DueDate").ToShortDateString()
     txtBudget.Text = DR("Budget")
     txtDefaultHourlyRate.Text = DR("DefaultHourlyRate")
     chkIsCompleted.Checked = DR("IsCompleted")
   Else
     lblPageTitle.Text = "Create New Task"
     fkProjectID.Value = Request.QueryString("pID")
   End If
  Else
   If pkTaskID.Value = "" Then
     obj = New Task(DB)
   Else
     obj = New Task(DB, pkTaskID.Value)
   End If
   DR = obj.GetRow()
   DR("Name") = txtName.Text
   DR("Description") = txtDescription.Text
   DR("fkProjectID") = fkProjectID.Value
   Try
     DR("DueDate") = DateTime.Parse(txtDueDate.Text)
   Catch ex As Exception
   ' do nothing, object handles missing data
   End Try
   Try
     DR("Budget") = txtBudget.Text
   Catch ex As Exception
   ' do nothing, object handles missing data
   End Try
   Try
     DR("DefaultHourlyRate") = txtDefaultHourlyRate.Text
   Catch ex As Exception
   ' do nothing, object handles missing data
   End Try
```

Listing 10.34   task_create.aspx.vb (continued)

```
      obj.SaveRow(DR)
      If Not obj.IsValid Then
        lblErrorMessage.Text = _
         obj.ValidationError("<b>ERROR:</b> The following " _
           & "errors were detected in your data:<br>", _
           "&bull; {0}<br>", "")
      Else
        obj.Save()
        DB.Close()
        Response.Redirect("project_view.aspx?ID=" _
          & fkProjectID.Value)
      End If
    End If
  End Sub
  End Class
End Namespace
```

Listing 10.34   task_create.aspx.vb (continued)

A new task is created by submitting a value for the project ID in the pID value of the query string. For an existing task, the ID value of the query string is used to look up and populate a Task object using the data from the database. We then take the object's data and populate the empty form with it. When we're ready to save the data, we reverse the process. Note that for the date and numeric data, we are wrapping the code with an exception block, as shown here:

```
Try
   DR("DueDate") = DateTime.Parse(txtDueDate.Text)
Catch ex As Exception
   ' do nothing, object handles missing data
End Try
```

If the user attempts to type an invalid date into the field, we attempt to parse the value. If the data is invalid, an exception on the Parse method is received. By suppressing the error in this manner, the field won't be populated, causing the object to go through its normal error-handling path. We've used this method on other pages with date or numeric data entry, and it gets the job done. You could also change the page to use validation controls provided by ASP.NET, but then you would have to integrate those errors with the errors generated by your object. With the potential for duplicate errors this presents, I prefer to keep error handling in the object to make it easier to use the objects in other applications.

The last task-maintenance feature we have to support is the ability to delete a task. We only allow tasks to be deleted when no timecards have been recorded for the particular task. The task viewer takes care of showing or hiding the link to this next page based on that criteria, but you might want to put the same logic in the page you're going to build after that. The code for the Task Deletion page is shown in Listing 10.35.

```
<%@ Page Inherits="TWNW.TaskDelete" Src="task_delete.aspx.vb" %>
<%@ Register Tagprefix="TWNW" Tagname="Header" Src="Header.ascx" %>
<%@ Register Tagprefix="TWNW" Tagname="Footer" Src="Footer.ascx" %>
<!DOCTYPE HTML PUBLIC "-//W3C//DTD HTML 4.0 Transitional//EN">
<html>
<head>
  <title>Teamwork Network: Task Management</title>
  <link href="styles.css" rel="stylesheet" type="text/css">
</head>
<body>
<TWNW:Header id="PageHeader" runat="server" />
<p class="pageheading">Delete Task</p>
<p class="text">Are you sure you want to delete this task?</p>
<form runat="server" id="deleteForm">
<input type="hidden" runat="server" id="pkID">
<p class="text">
<a href="javascript:document.deleteForm.submit();">Yes</a>
  
<a href="javascript:history.go(-1);">No</a>
</p>
</form>
<TWNW:Footer id="PageFooter" runat="server" />
</body>
</html>
```

Listing 10.35   task_delete.aspx

As you can see, making changes to the Project_delete.aspx page makes it easier to duplicate the file and create this page quickly. We only have to change the text on the page and the @Page directive to use the new file. The code behind this page also requires a few changes, but they are straightforward, as you can see in Listing 10.36.

```
Imports System
Imports System.Data
Imports System.Web.UI
Imports System.Web.UI.WebControls
Imports TWNWObjects

Namespace TWNW
  Public Class TaskDelete
    Inherits System.Web.UI.Page

    Protected pkID As HTMLControls.HTMLInputHidden

    Sub Page_Load(objSender As Object, objArgs As EventArgs)
      If Not Page.IsPostBack Then
        pkID.Value = Request.QueryString("ID")
```

Listing 10.36   task_delete.aspx.vb

```
      Else
        Dim DB As New AtWorkUtilities.Database()
        Dim obj As New Task(DB, pkID.Value)
        Dim DR As DataRow = obj.GetRow()
        Dim intParent As Integer = DR("fkProjectID")
        DR = Nothing
        obj.Delete()
        obj = Nothing
        DB.Close()
        Response.Redirect("project_view.aspx?ID=" & intParent)
      End If
    End Sub
  End Class
End Namespace
```

Listing 10.36   task_delete.aspx.vb (continued)

This uses the Task object to first look up the project ID before deleting the task. The page then navigates back to the project viewer, since the task's parent is the project.

With the task-maintenance pages completed, we move on to the last data-entry pages, which are the ones used for entering time cards.

Creating the Timecard Pages

The last, and smallest, portion of the maintenance involves the timecard-creation page. A member on a team with a project opens the project and then a task within the project. At that point, any member can add a timecard for that particular project. For this page to work, the previous page must submit a task ID. The rest of the information is entered by the user or supplied through other objects. The ASPX file is shown in Listing 10.37.

```
<%@ Page Inherits="TWNW.TimecardCreate" Src="tcard_create.aspx.vb" %>
<%@ Register Tagprefix="TWNW" Tagname="Header" Src="Header.ascx" %>
<%@ Register Tagprefix="TWNW" Tagname="Footer" Src="Footer.ascx" %>
<!DOCTYPE HTML PUBLIC "-//W3C//DTD HTML 4.0 Transitional//EN">
<html>
<head>
  <title>Teamwork Network: Timecard Management</title>
  <link href="styles.css" rel="stylesheet" type="text/css">
</head>
<body>
<TWNW:Header id="PageHeader" runat="server" />
<table width="600">
<tr>
<td valign="top" width="600">
```

Listing 10.37   tcard_create.aspx

```
<p><asp:label id="lblPageTitle" class="pageheading" runat="server"
/></p>
<asp:label id="lblErrorMessage" class="errortext" runat="server" />

<asp:label id="lblDeleteMessage" class="text" runat="server" />

<form runat="server">
<input type="hidden" runat="server" id="fkTaskID">
<input type="hidden" runat="server" id="pkTimecardID">

<table cellspacing="5">
<tr class="tabletext">
  <td align="right">Date:</td>
  <td>
  <asp:textbox
    id="txtTimecardDate"
    columns="20"
    maxlength="20"
    runat="server" />
  </td>
</tr>
<tr class="tabletext">
  <td valign="middle" align="right">
  Work Description:
  </td>
  <td>
  <asp:textbox
    id="txtWorkDescription"
    rows="10"
    columns="40"
    wrap="true"
    textmode="Multiline"
    runat="server" />
  </td>
</tr>

<tr class="tabletext">
  <td align="right">Hours Worked:</td>
  <td>
  <asp:textbox
    id="txtHourCount"
    columns="20"
    maxlength="20"
    runat="server" />
  </td>
</tr>
<tr class="tabletext">
  <td align="right">Hourly Rate:</td>
  <td>
  <asp:textbox
```

Listing 10.37   tcard_create.aspx (continued)

```
      id="txtHourlyRate"
      columns="20"
      maxlength="20"
      runat="server" />
    </td>
  </tr>

  <tr class="tabletext">
    <td colspan=2 align=middle>
    <input type="submit"
     name="btnSubmit"
     runat="server"
     value="Save" />
    <input type="reset"
     name="btnReset"
     runat="server"
     value="Clear" />
    </td>
  </tr>
  </table>
  </form>
  </td>
  </tr>
  </table>
  <TWNW:Footer id="PageFooter" runat="server" />
  </body>
  </html>
```

Listing 10.37   tcard_create.aspx (continued)

This follows the same format as our other data-entry forms, and is used for both adding a new timecard and editing an existing one, assuming that the user is either the creator of the timecard or the project leader. Another thing the user can do in edit mode is delete the timecard. This link becomes available in edit mode through code-behind logic that populates the lblDeleteMessage label with the link. Having the Delete link here saves us from using space on the task viewer for that link. In addition, the security provided by the stored procedure that only generates a link for authorized people means that if we're editing the record, we're allowed to edit the record and delete it, if necessary.

The Visual Basic code behind this page is shown in Listing 10.38.

```
Imports System
Imports System.Data
Imports System.Data.SqlClient
Imports System.Web
Imports System.Web.UI
Imports System.Web.UI.WebControls
```

Listing 10.38   tcard_create.aspx.vb

```
Imports TWNWObjects

Namespace TWNW
  Public Class TimecardCreate
    Inherits System.Web.UI.Page

    Protected fkTaskID As HTMLControls.HTMLInputHidden
    Protected pkTimecardID As HTMLControls.HTMLInputHidden
    Protected txtWorkDescription As TextBox
    Protected txtTimecardDate As TextBox
    Protected txtHourCount As TextBox
    Protected txtHourlyRate As TextBox
    Protected lblDeleteMessage As Label

    Protected lblPageTitle As Label
    Protected lblErrorMessage As Label

    Sub Page_Load(objSender As Object, objArgs As EventArgs)
      Dim DB As New AtWorkUtilities.Database()
      Dim obj As Timecard
      Dim DR As DataRow
      Dim objCookie As HTTPCookie
      objCookie = Request.Cookies("mID")

      If Not Page.IsPostBack Then
        If Request.QueryString("ID") <> "" Then
          lblPageTitle.Text = "Edit Timecard"
          obj = New Timecard(DB, Request.QueryString("ID"))
          DR = obj.GetRow()
          pkTimecardID.Value = DR("pkTimecardID").ToString()
          fkTaskID.Value = DR("fkTaskID").ToString()
          txtTimecardDate.Text = DR("TimecardDate").ToShortDateString()
          txtWorkDescription.Text = DR("WorkDescription").ToString()
          txtHourCount.Text = DR("HourCount")
          txtHourlyRate.Text = DR("HourlyRate")
          lblDeleteMessage.Text = "<p class=text>" _
            & "<a href=""tcard_delete.aspx?id=" _
            & Request.QueryString("ID") _
            & """>Delete this Timecard</a></p>"
        Else
          lblPageTitle.Text = "Create New Timecard"
          fkTaskID.Value = Request.QueryString("tID")
          txtTimecardDate.Text = DateTime.Now.ToShortDateString()
          Dim T As New Task(DB, Request.QueryString("tID"))
          Dim DR_T As DataRow = T.GetRow()
          txtHourlyRate.Text = DR_T("DefaultHourlyRate")
          DR_T = Nothing
          T = Nothing
        End If
      Else
```

Listing 10.38 tcard_create.aspx.vb (continued)

```
        If pkTimecardID.Value = "" Then
          obj = New Timecard(DB)
        Else
          obj = New Timecard(DB, pkTimecardID.Value)
        End If
        DR = obj.GetRow()
        DR("fkMemberID") = Request.Cookies("mID").Value
        DR("fkTaskID") = fkTaskID.Value
        DR("WorkDescription") = txtWorkDescription.Text
        Try
          DR("TimecardDate") = DateTime.Parse(txtTimecardDate.Text)
        Catch ex As Exception
        ' do nothing, object handles missing data
        End Try
        Try
          DR("HourCount") = txtHourCount.Text
        Catch ex As Exception
        ' do nothing, object handles missing data
        End Try
        Try
          DR("HourlyRate") = txtHourlyRate.Text
        Catch ex As Exception
        ' do nothing, object handles missing data
        End Try

        obj.SaveRow(DR)
        If Not obj.IsValid Then
          lblErrorMessage.Text = _
            obj.ValidationError("<b>ERROR:</b> The following " _
              & "errors were detected in your data:<br>", _
              "&bull; {0}<br>", "")
        Else
          obj.Save()
          DB.Close()
          Response.Redirect("task_view.aspx?ID=" _
            & fkTaskID.Value)
        End If
      End If
    End Sub
  End Class
End Namespace
```

Listing 10.38   tcard_create.aspx.vb (continued)

We follow the normal path of handling both additions and edits by looking at the query string for an ID value. If it is missing, a value named tID will be present, and we can add a new timecard. When we save the data, we look for the member's ID from their cookie and store it in the record as the member ID. This will let us authorize the user to make changes later, as long as the timecard hasn't been billed yet.

The last pages we need to build take care of deleting timecards. The ASPX file is shown in Listing 10.39.

```
<%@ Page Inherits="TWNW.TimecardDelete" Src="tcard_delete.aspx.vb" %>
<%@ Register Tagprefix="TWNW" Tagname="Header" Src="Header.ascx" %>
<%@ Register Tagprefix="TWNW" Tagname="Footer" Src="Footer.ascx" %>
<!DOCTYPE HTML PUBLIC "-//W3C//DTD HTML 4.0 Transitional//EN">
<html>
<head>
  <title>Teamwork Network: Timecard Management</title>
  <link href="styles.css" rel="stylesheet" type="text/css">
</head>
<body>
<TWNW:Header id="PageHeader" runat="server" />
<p class="pageheading">Delete Timecard</p>
<p class="text">Are you sure you want to delete this timecard?</p>
<form runat="server" id="deleteForm">
<input type="hidden" runat="server" id="pkID">
<p class="text">
<a href="javascript:document.deleteForm.submit();">Yes</a>
  
<a href="javascript:history.go(-1);">No</a>
</p>
</form>
<TWNW:Footer id="PageFooter" runat="server" />
</body>
</html>
```

Listing 10.39 tcard_delete.aspx

We fill in the ID of the timecard to be deleted, and when the user clicks the Yes link, we delete the record using the logic in the code-behind Visual Basic file shown in Listing 10.40.

```
Imports System
Imports System.Data
Imports System.Web.UI
Imports System.Web.UI.WebControls
Imports TWNWObjects

Namespace TWNW
  Public Class TimecardDelete
    Inherits System.Web.UI.Page

    Protected pkID As HTMLControls.HTMLInputHidden
```

Listing 10.40 tcard_delete.aspx.vb

```
    Sub Page_Load(objSender As Object, objArgs As EventArgs)
      If Not Page.IsPostBack Then
        pkID.Value = Request.QueryString("ID")
      Else
        Dim DB As New AtWorkUtilities.Database()
        Dim obj As New Timecard(DB, pkID.Value)
        Dim DR As DataRow = obj.GetRow()
        Dim intParent As Integer = DR("fkTaskID")
        DR = Nothing
        obj.Delete()
        obj = Nothing
        DB.Close()
        Response.Redirect("task_view.aspx?ID=" & intParent)
      End If
    End Sub
  End Class
End Namespace
```

Listing 10.40 tcard_delete.aspx.vb (continued)

After the deletion has taken place, we send the user back to the task viewer, since the timecards are only visible as part of the task viewer.

Wrap Up

There are a number of other features you could add to this application, such as enhanced and tighter security, tracking of when projects are billed, notifications via email to the manager if a task goes over budget, and so on. The idea behind this project was to show you that with a good framework and infrastructure, you can build what most people would consider an application too complex to create from scratch. As you can see, it's just a matter of good design and modular code.

The CD-ROM includes a bonus chapter in which you'll add a few last features to the Teamwork Network application. You'll build the user's personalized home page, which summarizes new information each time the user logs into the system. You'll also build a search utility that allows the user to find data in any of the application's subsystems.

Index